1990

ETHICS AND THE
PROFESSIONS

ETHICS AND THE PROFESSIONS

DAVID APPELBAUM

SARAH VERONE LAWTON

The College at New Paltz
State University of New York
New Paltz, New York

Prentice Hall
Englewood Cliffs, New Jersey 07632

Library of Congress Cataloging-in-Publication Data

Ethics and the professions / [edited by] David Appelbaum,
 Sarah Verone Lawton.
   p. cm.
  Bibliography: p.
  ISBN 0-13-291659-2
  1. Professional ethics. I. Appelbaum, David
II. Lawton, Sarah Verone.
BJ1725.E76 1990
174--dc20   89-16093
                                                    CIP

Editorial/production supervision and
  interior design: Karen Buck and E. A. Pauw
Cover design: 20/20 Services, Inc.
Manufacturing buyer: Peter Havens

 © 1990 by Prentice-Hall, Inc.
A Division of Simon & Schuster
Englewood Cliffs, New Jersey 07632

Printed in the United States of America
10 9 8 7 6 5 4 3 2 1

ISBN 0-13-291659-2

Prentice-Hall International (UK) Limited, *London*
Prentice-Hall of Australia Pty. Limited, *Sydney*
Prentice-Hall Canada Inc., *Toronto*
Prentice-Hall Hispanoamericana, S.A., *Mexico*
Prentice-Hall of India Private Limited, *New Delhi*
Prentice-Hall of Japan, Inc., *Tokyo*
Simon & Schuster Asia Pte. Ltd., *Singapore*
Editora Prentice-Hall do Brasil, Ltda., *Rio de Janeiro*

CONTENTS

138, 109

UNIT II   ETHICS AND THE HEALTH CARE PROFESSIONS   *53*

UNIT **III**   ETHICS IN BUSINESS, INDUSTRY, AND TECHNOLOGY   *169*

PREFACE

The field of ethics is in a state of change. Our needs are increasingly provided by people in professional roles. Health care, technical advice, legal counsel, business affairs, and police protection are examples of professions that serve our needs. Not surprisingly, more and more of the ethical choices we make in our lives take place in the context of the professions.

Undergraduates are now devoting more time to courses on a professional track. They make early career choices which require pre-professional training. The undergraduate years are less the occasion to take a broad sample of subjects and more a time to begin the work of education in a profession. Ethics, always relevant, is now relevant in a new way. In the classroom it is part of students' concern for the decision-making process of professional life.

The present volume grew out of these perceptions. The moral problems exercising today's health care, business, technological, and legal and criminal justice professionals are serious and exciting. The questions are fundamental to philosophy. They concern the means professionals have of justifying the choices they make in their professional lives. The questions require us to take a critical look at the moral grounds underlying professional attitudes and policies. Such reflection is not without its price. It demands that we become fluent in the philosophical analysis and inquiry which is the currency of ethics.

The book is structured to aid the reader's understanding of the relevant issues of professional ethics. Moral disagreements in professional decision making often uncover last the fundamental questions, those concerning the major principles, concepts, and theories developed by ethical thinkers. They are bedrock, impervious to further penetration. The introductory unit places at the student's disposal the basic tools of moral philosophy. Sections on the important ethical theories and concepts are supplemented with a discussion of the professions. Examples involving the professional in the midst of moral decision making further assist the reader to see the contours of the field. Discussion of the key points allows the nursing, prelaw, business, or engineering student who has little or no training in ethics to grasp the new approach.

An entire unit has been devoted to each of the following important professions: the health care sciences, business (including industry and technology), and criminal justice and law. The topics are fundamental to the moral decision making of each. They explore the range of dilemmas that have excited the most concern. The issues often are timely, the stuff of cover stories in news weeklies, but the focus remains fixed on the underlying analysis, the movement of moral thinking in exploring the depths of a question. From this standpoint, the student is less likely to assume that ethical questions should be decided by opinion polls. In order to point out related ethical problems, the units are cross referenced using the following shorthand: Health Care for Unit II; Business for Unit III; and Criminal Justice for

Unit IV. Thus, a cross reference to Unit III may read: **See Business, Chapter 13, Section 1.**

A premium has been placed on the breadth of reading selections. The choices represent current thinking on the issues, and they require no technical expertise to understand them. Written by practicing professionals, philosophers, public policy makers, and laypersons, they offer scientific, social, legal, and economic perspectives on the issues. In some cases conflicting viewpoints on a question are presented. Seeing the live controversy on issues permits the student to appreciate the ongoing nature of ethical discussion, counteracts the impression of beginning students that a single answer exists, and demonstrates the excitement that moral matters generate when centered on a pressing question.

Each chapter is introduced by a brief overview of the moral issues covered, which includes the factual information necessary for an understanding of the ethical positions. Since a major concern is to turn thought toward basic principles, we search out ways in which ethical theories help illuminate the problems. Whenever possible, relationships are shown between major ethical concepts discussed in Unit I and the ideas generated in the reading selections. No definitive applications of principles are offered, but rather illustrations are given of how basic moral thought may be applied to the hard dilemmas we face. The overviews enhance the effectiveness of the reading selections but do not eliminate the need to reflect on what other thinkers in the field propose.

Other features are included to facilitate the student's progress to greater understanding. Each of the professional units contains case studies, based on actual situations, which inject a note of realism into ethical thought. These allow the student to see how a moral dilemma arises in the midst of professional life. They demand a concrete application of moral understanding, not an abstract recital of general principles. The case studies focus decision making so as to test the assimilation of basic skills of the moral point of view.

Within each unit is a glossary of terms endemic to the profession or to ethics. Familiarity with the specialized vocabulary aids a grasp of the ideas and helps to orient the student in the field of professional ethics. To encourage further research and reading, bibliographies are appended to each chapter, and they reflect a diversity of positions on the issues. A comprehensive bibliography appears at the end of the book. The various reading lists offer substantial guidance for the student who wishes to pursue a question in greater depth.

We wish to thank the Department of Philosophy of The College at New Paltz for its support of this project and in particular the Department Chair, Eléanor H. Kuykendall, whose generous encouragement lightened our task. The Research Foundation of the State University of New York recognized the importance of the subject matter before the project itself evolved. We are indebted to the foundation for its award of a Grant for the Improvement of Undergraduate Instruction. We are grateful for the editorial support of Prentice-Hall, Inc., especially the enthusiasm of Bruce Kennan. Finally, without the ongoing tolerance and encouragement of family and friends, the project would never have seen completion.

David Appelbaum
Sarah V. Lawton
The College at New Paltz
State University of New York
New Paltz, New York

ETHICS AND THE PROFESSIONS

I

ETHICS AND THE PROFESSIONS

"What should we do, Doctor?" the nurse, Mrs. Philips, asked. The infant, born a half hour earlier, was barely breathing. Its color was blue, a sure sign of cyanosis brought on by a lack of oxygen in its blood. The team in the neonatal intensive care unit was calm. From the prenatal monitor as well as from early tests, they had known that the infant would be premature, with hydrocephalus and microcephaly (an abnormally small head). They were not surprised when the birth weight was a mere 4 pounds, 6 ounces.

Shortly after delivery by Caesarean section, the pediatrician had announced there was severe intracranial hemorrhaging. That meant a life of cerebral palsy, severe mental deficiency, and convulsions.

Mrs. Philips, looking at the tiny baby, felt personally that she wanted to give it every opportunity to live. However, the parents, who were poor, had already told the hospital their wish to discontinue all treatment. She heard the doctor answer her. "We do nothing," he said. "Let it be." He began gathering the instruments.

Mrs. Philips took a last look. Everything she held of personal value welled up in her and wanted to shout, "No!" But she remembered her professional role. She was no longer a private person but a nurse who obeyed as best she could the rules of her professional code.

The conflict Mrs. Philips faces is a moral one. She is faced with the recognition that her own beliefs about right and wrong have collided with her professional obligations. She must decide her priorities. Do her duties as a nurse override the personal value she places on the sanctity of all life? Or should her conscience reign supreme?

Although the conflict is always real, Mrs. Philips has grown accustomed to the confrontation between two different sets of moral values. Mrs. Philips is a *professional*. The situation reminds her that her professional role entails duties, responsibilities, rights, and obligations which she is not bound to outside of her role as a nurse. As part of her professional training, she accepts the subordination of personal beliefs to the ethics of the nursing code.

The life-and-death drama of the neonatal

intensive care unit sharpens our attention, but many less heightened situations of our professional lives present the same moral dilemma. The roles defined by professional careers—in allied health sciences, business, law, criminal justice, engineering, journalism, education, and politics—place new moral demands on persons who have entered the fields. We need a special awareness of such problems if we are to fulfill the duties of professional life.

Professions have existed since ancient times—for example, in India and Greece. At that time they were restricted to elite classes. The morality of a professional was like that of a secret club; it bore no public scrutiny. Today the situation is quite different. As our industrial society has grown more specialized in its demands and services, different professions have been integrated into the social life. Professionals have proliferated and diversified. Many walks of life have become professionalized, such as educators, journalists, and corrections officers. With the growth of professional life, we need to focus more attention on its ethical requirements. A situation like that of Mrs. Philips drives home how central ethical decision making is to professional roles.

We may be inclined to think that we are already well-equipped to handle ethical decisions in the professions. Or we may be impatient, feeling that private moral beliefs will serve us adequately on the hospital ward, in the judge's chambers, on the police beat, or in the research laboratory. In the heat of a moment like Mrs. Philips' or when we advise a colleague on an important choice, the question behind this text may arise: Are there rules or principles for morally justifying a professional decision?

The branch of philosophy that studies such rules is called *ethics*. One of the first formulations of ethics was made by Aristotle, a member of the medical profession of ancient Greece. *Professional ethics* is concerned with rules insofar as they call forth decisions and judgments regarding the practice, method, policy, and research of various professions. As Mrs. Philips recognized, ethical matters for professionals are so complex and removed from private interests that they require special study. At the same time, they derive from fundamental moral principles common to all ethical decisions. The entry examination in the field of professional ethics requires reflection on the basic questions of ethics: How can we tell right from wrong? What is the worth of an individual's pursuit of life, liberty, and happiness? What is good to strive after? How can we serve the interests of justice?

The first chapter of this unit provides material needed to take up the problems of ethical decision making within different professions: allied health sciences; business, industry, and technology; and law and criminal justice. Without a proper basis in ethics, we will deal with issues of paramount importance in a flimsy, superficial, and close-minded manner. Initially we need to be clear on three matters. First, we must know what a profession is and who can be regarded as a professional. Second, we have to understand the process of moral decision making, the nature of the inputs, and the kinds of obstacles that appear. Third, we must be familiar with the context of justification and the requirement of grounding moral choices in reasons.

The second chapter is devoted to a discussion of the four chief ethical theories. The value of each theory consists in how correctly and completely it accounts for the facts of moral life, judgment, and decision making—both privately and professionally. Conversely, each theory allows us to deepen our insight into the position our specific moral decision reflects. The virtues and defects of each will be discussed. In a preliminary way, we will be able to examine the application of these theories to issues arising in professional ethics.

The third chapter of this unit looks into several important concepts relevant to the study of ethics. Without the bedrock of theory, our moral decisions are liable to be swept away in the heat of the moment.

Without knowledge of basic concepts, we are apt to be unable to communicate the position we defend. Although Chapters 2 and 3 operate independently, fully engaging the moral point of view of the professions requires familiarity with both.

Finally, thought is needed to apply the principles and concepts to the vital situation of making a moral choice. Most professional decisions are arrived at in the midst of communication while we are addressing other professionals holding opposing points of view. We need to take account of competing choices while accepting the challenge of communication. Understanding how to be critical and open-minded, we can be in a position to evaluate competing claims. The fourth chapter addresses this area.

1. INITIAL CONCERNS

1. PROFESSIONS AND PROFESSIONALS

Even the most die-hard professional, be it doctor, lawyer, or police chief, is not a professional twenty-four hours a day. Each of us passes through a number of roles, knowingly or unknowingly, during the course of a week. A role is a form of life which a person adopts. Besides the role of a professional, one might also play the roles of parent, child, friend, consumer, and informed citizen. With each role comes characteristic responsibilities, rights and wrongs. No role completely limits our freedom to exercise personal choice, to do what we want and to believe what we believe. Much of the moral theory we are about to examine sets about to protect our liberties from invasive forces. Within any role there is room for free movement. On the other hand, being in a role can never justify doing wrong. For example, a parent cannot use discretionary judgment for the abuse of a child, nor can a person twist the truth to be disloyal to a friend.

In some ways a professional role is like a role in private life, such as friendship; in other ways it is different. In both cases, we acquire new rights, privileges, duties, and responsibilities. A lawyer in a professional role, for example, may be asked to favor unduly one's client and actually bring harm to the client's adversaries. Similarly, in friendship, we are morally bound to be loyal and to have a special interest in the person's well-being. If someone tries to harm our friend, we are duty-bound to defend him or her.

Roles in private life are "natural" to a person; they allow a person to satisfy his or her needs as a person. Many have existed as long as society has. One can fall into a role just as one can fall into a friendship. By contrast, professional roles are predominantly products of society. Although we can feel a calling, our choice of profession concerns career, wage earning, and other social benefits. Nor can we haphazardly enter a professional role. Every profession has a well-defined training period, extending sometimes more than ten years. We are required to take specified courses, pass an entry-level exam, and, in many cases, undergo a period of intensive on-job experience. We adopt our professional roles only after being educated to them.

What is a profession? A profession consists of a group of people organized to serve a body of specialized knowledge in the interests of society. Some cloistered religious orders are not professional because their interest is primarily in otherworldly matters. New professional groups emerge, such as corrections officers, as work and information grow more specialized. At the center of a profession is a set of skills, proficiencies, techniques, and competencies involving a line of work. For the nurse, they involve caring for the patient. For the corporate manager, they involve administering to the complex of stockholder, regulatory agency, and employee. Each profession maintains standards of excellence, oversees work performance, and trains new members. Each shares a professional vocabulary, usually not understood by the layperson. Each provides means of professional communication (in the form of journals and meetings). And, each has its professional code of ethics, which specifies the moral considerations of professional life as well as penalties and sanctions for violating them.

The question sometimes arises as to whether in a specific incident a person has acted out of a professional or a private role. The off-duty police officer at the scene of a crime, or the physician passing an auto accident on the highway, are examples. The question is urgent because of the different moral factors surrounding private and professional roles. Laws like the Good Samaritan laws (which defend doctors from malpractice suits when administering emergency aid) suggest two things. First, a professional remains a professional, no matter what suit he or she wears, if the situation requires the specialized skills. Second, we nonetheless feel that the professional is entitled to a freedom from the moral burden of his or her professional cloak. We grant a type of immunity against seeking recompense for unprofessional conduct.

2. THE PROCESS OF ETHICAL DECISION MAKING

Whether as layperson or professional, when we encounter a situation requiring a moral decision, we need to know what we ought to do. Such decision making is *moral* (rather than just prudent, pragmatic, or useful) if it involves a rule or principle acceptable to the moral community constituting our society. In the next section we will look at four systems of rules that meet the criterion.

Reaching a decision about a moral matter requires several types of inputs. Suppose a lawyer is trying to decide how to proceed with a client charged with a felony offense whom the lawyer strongly suspects is guilty. First, he must collect the *facts* of the case. Second, he must ascertain his personal *beliefs* regarding the matter. Third, he must refer to the *code of ethics* regarding his profession. Fourth, he must acknowledge the *moral concerns* of the community as a whole.

Philosophers find it helpful to distinguish *factual* inputs from *value-laden* ones. The two behave differently in logic and explanation. From only the facts, we cannot derive a conclusion about what should morally be done. Without the facts, we cannot apply our values to our deeds. To proceed toward the decision, the lawyer must first be clear on the facts. Much moral disagreement can be traced to disagreement about the facts. For instance, physicians may agree that to tell the truth to terminal cancer patients is best, but they may withhold full information because they believe the negative effects will harm the person. The focus of disagreement is empirical. Resolving it will require data on what factors affect patient recovery.

Suppose the lawyer has the facts. He then faces the tangle of value considerations. The second thing he needs to know is the *weight* of reason behind each, so that he can prioritize his value-laden inputs and determine which outweigh or override which. Much of moral decision making consists of creating order among the inputs. Knowing the rules of priority, the lawyer can set aside his private beliefs regarding prosecution of the guilty and can view the situation through the eyes of the professional.

The third thing to facilitate the decision is *conceptual clarification*. Suppose the lawyer holds that he should be loyal to a client. Understanding the meaning of loyalty owed to a client and knowing when the concerns of the moral community come first constitute an important step toward deciding. In the health care decision whether to abort an anecephalic fetus (lacking the neocortical brain), clarity is needed regarding the concept of a person; different professionals may agree on what morally should and should not be done to persons but may lack clarity about the status of fetal personhood. Similarly a police officer wielding a billy club to ward off an attacker may be unclear about what use, if any, constitutes lethal force; the officer may accept the rule that permits lethal force to be used to prevent a dangerous offense but may not know whether the billy club is a deadly weapon.

Even with the facts, priority rules for values, and conceptual clarity, the ethical decision may be elusive. The lawyer, for instance, may grasp the facts and may clearly see the obligation to be loyal to his client's interests even when being unfair to the client's adversary, but he may still lack the means of deciding whether the demand of fairness to the moral community overrides his professional duties. In the same way, health care professionals may agree that a mentally ill patient is offensive to others and that offensive behavior is grounds for commitment to an institution, but they may disagree about whether it is grounds *enough* for severely limiting an individual's freedom in this way.

The missing ingredient to ethical decision making is ethical theory. The combination of value-laden inputs, personal belief, and judgment about priorities is still insufficient to resolve all cases. The strongest appeal for including ethical theories as part of the decision is fairness. If we cannot handle all professional decisions without encountering unresolvable disagreements, we require additional input. This argument allows us to see how the ground of moral thought enters into every choice situation. It also underlines the need for careful study of the theories which have evolved from the most careful reflection of the moral community.

3. OBJECTIVITY AND JUSTIFYING ETHICAL DECISIONS

There are two distinct contexts in which we look at ethical decisions. One is when we are trying to discover what is morally acceptable to do. The nurse listening to the plea of an incurable patient suffering from pain to be allowed to die is in the throes of a difficult situation. He or she must decide in the heat of the moment. The other context is when, at a cooler hour, we reflect on justifying what should be done. Justification consists in showing that the weight of reason dictates that a course of action is morally acceptable. We are ill-advised to undertake an act that cannot be ethically justified, because the moral community regards such behavior as wrong.

Reasons in support of an ethical decision come from different levels of generality. The strongest derive directly from ethical theory. For example, if a company faces the option of making a moderate profit from a policy that is expected to cause severe environmental damage, one could appeal to utilitarian considerations. In one form, these state that an act ought to maximize the social good to humanity. Since the integrity of the environment outweighs the good of a moderate profit, applying the principle of utility supplies the decision-making factor. The weakest reasons come from intuitions or "feelings" about what is wrong or right. We may have an intuition that mandatory on-job drug testing is wrong, but the feeling stands in need of finding a middle-level rule to support it. Between intuitions and basic principles lie many rules important to the professional role, such as the lawyer's duty to be loyal to a client, or the physician's to care for the health of a patient. We will see, in Ross's theory of *prima facie* duties, how the rules look as an ensemble.

Are ethical decisions, even if justified, *objective?* In asking the question, people sometimes overlook the radical differences between factual and value-laden input. They observe that factual statements are objective when there is universal agreement about the data as well as support from scientific theory. Then they are liable to conclude that since value-laden statements lack universal agreement, no such thing as objectivity exists in ethics. Moral decisions, they say, are expressions of a person's subjective beliefs, at the very worst, no better than statements of personal taste, such as preferring vanilla over chocolate. They insist that moral decisions, being relative to a person's desires, may conflict with one another on the same issue without hope of resolution.

The denial of objectivity in ethics (called relativism) mistakenly assumes that facts and values behave the same way. It also misconstrues the nature of moral disagreement. Moral disagreement over the use of police discretion in bringing criminals to trial, for example, indicates an initial phase in the process of arriving at an objective moral point of view. The proponent of a narrow use of discretion challenges the statement of an advocate of wide use by citing counterexamples and objections. To produce more weighty reasons, the wide-use advocate must deepen and generalize his or her position. This revised statement is then open to further challenge and revision. The net result is the development of viewpoints having greater degrees of objectivity. Disagreement in ethical decision making is, therefore, an essential aspect of finding an objective basis for what ought to be done. Without it, our moral reasons would lack substance.

Acceptance of moral disagreement is the means we have of resolving conflicts in decision making. Ethical decisions are unlike factual ones in that the latter are based on indisputable data, but they are both ultimately grounded in principles. The process of statement, objection, and revision drives the basis of the decision to deeper ground. Whether final agreement about a single issue, such as whistle blowing or punishment, is possible is itself an open question. We have different ethical theories which appear to carry the conflict back to the level of ultimate principles. We lack a "unified field theory." Hence the commitment to objectivity in ethics is a moral commitment. In essence, we are agreeing to keep an open-minded communication alive within the moral community.

Sometimes one hears that ethical decisions should be settled by polls or votes. The viewpoint misunderstands the hard work of ethics. One's own reasons for deciding, say, in favor of governmental regulation of the investment industry, ought to be susceptible to challenge at every step. A consensus on a moral matter is a pragmatic waystation, not a final solution. Individuals have diverse training in finding reasons to act, being conceptually clear, and accepting the challenge of critics. By favoring an open forum, our society acknowledges the factor of moral change.

Many of the problems faced by professionals in the health care sciences and in engineering are direct results of technological innovation. The question of a patient's right or entitlement to a death in accordance with his or her wishes did not arise until the advent of our modern life-sustaining techniques. Not only do the facts change, however. Our understanding of our values grows (or declines) over time with our commitment to the moral community. For decisions to move in step with facts and understanding, we must relinquish the belief of settling a question "once and for all." The open-ended approach is especially relevant to the professional context. A single new input, like *Roe* v. *Wade* (which legalized abortion), throws an entire field of decision into question. Continuing vigilance is our only hope in safeguarding objectivity.

2. BASIC ETHICAL THEORIES

A student new to the study of ethical decision making sometimes asks, "Why do we have to begin with ethical theory?" Why not come directly to the particular moral issues? Because it arises from an impatience to "get on with it," the question is useful. Too often in professional contexts, impatience cuts short the search for adequate moral grounds for choice. We fail to take opposing viewpoints into account and settle on an ad hoc principle. The study of ethical theory opens us to considerations of depth, objectivity, completeness, and finality.

Against the claims of irrelevance that is heaped on ethical theory, we acknowledge the difficulty in applying it. However, a great challenge of application is quite different from inapplicability. The challenge sharpens the tools of moral consideration much as the challenge of applying scientific laws to observed facts sharpens the observer's eye. For example, we may see hundreds of cases of bodies displacing water without recognizing the application of the law of displacement. Thus, one should not assume that an introduction to ethical theory provides the total means of grounding ethical decision making, but the material supplied does set the challenge of inquiry and makes clear the demand that by working and reworking the concepts and principles, their application to objective decision making is facilitated. Only the reintroduction of ethical theory into each particular moral dilemma gives hope for the continued usefulness of a theoretical perspective.

1. COMPETING ETHICAL THEORIES

We have seen how the need for an ethical theory arises. As we look for ways to support the moral position embodied in a professional decision, our search touches on principles that are more and more general. We accept the fact that ordinary moral beliefs are incomplete, vague, and ambiguous. When we turn to ethical theory, why should there be several which may give us contradictory ways to justify one and the same decision?

An ethical theory attempts to identify the basic rules and principles for making moral decisions and evaluating proposals and past choices. An ethical theory thus serves to articulate the duties, responsibilities, and obligations that affect what we ought to do. The virtues of an ethical theory, as opposed to our ordinary feelings, opinions, and beliefs, lie in its being coherent and complete. A theory that fails to meet the basic standards must be rejected. In addition, we have two criteria for assessing whether a theory is valid. First, it must accurately explain and interpret our experience of the moral life. Second, it must give us guidance where we most need it, when two positions collide over what ought to be done. If a theory makes sense out of the moral life but does not serve to settle moral dilemmas, or vice versa, it cannot qualify as valid. On the other hand, if it accords with the "facts" of the moral community *and* it resolves otherwise insoluble perplexities, it stands as a basic ethical theory.

The two criteria still do not reduce the field to a single theory. The diversity of basic ethical theories underscores the role which disagreement plays in moral decisions. To attain objectivity and be sufficiently justified, a decision must hold itself open to objection. The expression of competing viewpoints is what moves the reasoning process out of the realm of a self-limiting subjectivity. Lack of consensus extends even to the moral rules which basic theory gives us. Here too our decision remains open to critical revision based on rules of a competing ethical theory. Our acknowledgment of other, equally sound basic theories prevents us from falling into a too easy, dogmatic defense of ethical choices in the professions.

Basic ethical theories can be grouped into two mutually exclusive kinds, *teleological* and *deontological.* If we take the fundamental concepts of morality to be the *right* and the *good,* a teleological theory first defines the good and goes on to define the right in terms of attaining goodness. The consequences of action become the means of determining the right thing to do. The predominant form of teleological theory is *utilitarianism.* By contrast, a deontological theory does not define the right as an exclusive function of the good. Instead, rightness and goodness are defined independently. The relative degree of independence gives rise to the three different deontological theories we will consider: those of Kant, W. D. Ross, and John Rawls. The strongest form of deontology, Kant's, determines the right act exclusive of all consequences. Other forms rely to a limited extent on the consequences

of the action in identifying what is right to do.

One teleological theory which we will not include is *ethical egoism.* The final and only good of ethical egoism is self-interest. Right action consists in accomplishing the most of what one's interests aim at, and consequences that affect other agents are seen as irrelevant. Regardless of the appeal of ethical egoism, its critics point out its deepseated bias against the communal basis of morality. Take the example of the ethical egoist who is a kleptomaniac. He prefers stealing things to almost all other activities. He recognizes that taking other people's property causes them harm and suffering, but he calculates that it brings him demonstrably more good to steal than not to. Besides, being unsympathetic, he is not affected by the pain of others. Hence, if he is reasonably certain not to be caught (which he does not want), he concludes he is right to go on stealing things.

Such a conclusion rejects a fundamental assumption of the moral life, that principles result from shared communication between equal (though differently situated) individuals. No one is entitled to a "desert island" morality. The ethical egoist has not bothered to engage in the communication that makes ethics possible. The proof is that one cannot publicly advocate ethical egoism and remain consistent. Consider again the kleptomaniac. It is to his advantage not to promote what his ethical principles are, since they work best only so long as other people are not ethical egoists. With competition from other egoists, his own goods are diminished. Hence, he ought to, on his own account, remain silent.

Because ethical egoism is not a consistent ethical theory, we do not include it as a valid form of teleology. Instead, we turn directly to the only teleological theory we will consider, utilitarianism as it appears in two forms: *act-utilitarianism* and *ruleutilitarianism.*

2. ACT-UTILITARIANISM

In our close-knit society, the action of a single person invariably affects the lives of other persons as well as the life of the agent. The fundamental moral stance is to take others into account *as well.* The ethical egoist, we saw, fails to account *as well* for other persons; others merely offer opportunities to further the egoist's self-interest. Once we abandon ethical egoism, the interrelation of one individual's goods to another's becomes clear.

Consider the drug addict who refuses to follow a course of rehabilitation. He claims he derives great pleasure from drugs and he is the only one to suffer the ill consequences of his habit. However, the effect of his drug use on his immediate family and his colleagues is negative. They experience higher anxiety and possibly financial strain. If his habit turns him to crime, the addict's victims are adversely affected. His eventual hospitalization or imprisonment entails costs which society will bear. As we take an expanded picture of his addictive behavior, including others *as well,* a complex mix of positive and negative consequences appears.

The great appeal of act-utilitarianism lies in the simplicity of its basic principle, called the *principle of utility.* It is also called by its first formulators, Jeremy Bentham (1748–1832) and John Stuart Mill (1806–1873), the *greatest happiness principle.* It says: One's action ought to produce the greatest happiness for the greatest number of people. The principle is true to the form of teleological theory. No action is in itself right or wrong. Nor do the intentions, motives, character, or expectations of the agent enter into the moral account. Only the consequences of what is to be done count insofar as the happiness of those concerned is increased or decreased. We are thus able to make moral decisions on the basis of a simple formula: We add up the positive impact of a proposed act, taking account of everyone potentially affected. From the total, we subtract the negative impact, the hardship, disadvantage, pain, and suffering we calculate will occur as a result of the action. The remainder, the action's overall *utility,* yields a convenient measure of whether the decision is morally acceptable. Act-utilitarianism says: Act always so as to maximize utility.

Act-utilitarianism places the familiar *cost-benefits analysis* at the center of morality. Whereas in determining the economic feasibility of a decision the goods are measured in dollars and cents, the act-utilitarian has no such convenient measure. What is the nature of the good for act-utilitarianism? If it is happiness, we need to know what happiness consists of, since Aristotle says a person has happiness as the aim of every action. In Bentham's classical formulation, the good or *intrinsic value* is pleasure. Making more pleasure and avoiding more pain for more people tells us the right thing to do. We rely on hedonism, the doctrine that pleasure is the sole good in life, to fill in the gap of act-utilitarianism.

Mill took issue with the narrow account of goodness. He preferred to include quality as well as quantity of pleasure in the calculation of right action. He said it is "better to be Socrates dissatisfied than a fool satisfied."[1] Mill's account is more in keeping with the realities of the moral life. It also creates difficulties. When we replace a simple view of pleasure with one more complicated, we lose the elegance of the initial principle of utility. The difficulties are compounded when modern act-utilitarians use a nonhedonistic or a plural theory of intrinsic value. In this theory, doing the right thing is producing the most of intrinsic good, however defined. Our discussion will keep to the original formulation, taking the good as happiness or pleasure.

Making a moral decision, for the act-utilitarian, means first listing all probable

---

[1]John Stuart Mill, *Utilitarianism,* chap. II, "What Utilitarianism Is."

outcomes of our action. Next, we must foresee the consequences, both short-term and long-term, of each outcome. To each consequence we then attach a calculation of intrinsic value, both positive and negative. The option having the highest number will be the right thing to do. Some unfortunate choices present us with all alternatives showing a negative number. In such cases, we are called to act so as to incur the least pain or unhappiness. In no case are we to rely on ordinary moral rules like "Do not lie," "Do no harm," "Tell the truth," and "Be loyal to friends." In the act-utilitarian view, these rules cannot replace the rigorous calculation of utility.

Many times, an act in accordance with a rule of thumb yields the same result as one that is calculated, but this fact does not validate ordinary moral rules since other times results will diverge. For instance, lying is usually wrong, but if a doctor's lie to a terminal patient produces a greater sense of well-being than the truth would, the act-utilitarian requires the physician to lie. Some act-utilitarians urge us not to be naive in calculating consequences. Long-term effects may be subtle and difficult to discern. Lying may serve one patient well but its indirect consequence may be to break down the trust patients place in their physicians. Or it may tend to make doctors more authoritarian and less sensitive to their patients as persons.

How Act-Utilitarianism Works in a Professional Context

The following examples can help us apply the principle of utility to professional decisions. They are not necessarily instances which the act-utilitarian would agree are complete and exhaustive.

A woman fourteen weeks pregnant has had an amniocentesis. The test shows that the fetus has a chromosomal defect indicative of Huntington's chorea, an incurable, degenerative condition in which a person suffers increasing pain and dies before the age of 30. Her physician and her genetic counselor urge an abortion. She and her husband, however, want to have the child though they will not be able to afford the expensive treatment. Their interests will be served by bringing the infant into existence, while the physicians' and society's will not. The prolonged treatment is calculated as a negative good which is, on the balance, less than the parents' suffering would be if the fetus were aborted. The value of an individual existence known to involve deep agony is problematic. Does the good of a short life outweigh the anticipated pain and degeneration of all human faculties? But aborting the fetus removes even the possibility of a momentary happiness, so foregoing abortion is on the whole the right thing to do.

A research engineer of a large biotechnical corporation discovers that the company is venting live recombinant DNA into the air. The act is in violation of federal regulations and is potentially dangerous to the environment. She informs her supervisor, who says all the employees in the unit will lose their jobs if the information is uncovered. Furthermore, company stock will plummet in value, throwing much valuable research and development into question. The interests of the corporation are clearly served if the engineer keeps mum. The happiness of those in her unit and possibly those in other research units likewise depend on her not whistle blowing. The engineer herself shares in the good of working at an activity she enjoys. One could also argue that stockholders would benefit if the news were not known, thereby avoiding suffering and hardship in their lives and their dependents' lives. On the other hand, the intrinsic value of environmental protection rules is at stake. Disregarding the rules would weaken the value of the legislation. The chief benefactor of EPA rules is society. Long-term damage to the environment exerts a negative impact on everyone alive and for generations to come. The weight of interest in the social value of the environment greatly outweighs any short-term unhappiness of people losing jobs or financial security. The engineer should make the information public.

The police have a gang of dangerous urban terrorists surrounded. The terrorists are armed and have fired at the police. The gang is known to have committed several acts of armed robbery in which two police officers were killed. The terrorists' townhouse is attached to a block of twenty-five other houses in a densely packed part of the city. The police SWAT team wants permission to use explosives to drive out the terrorists. Although the option is risky, they argue that otherwise there is bound to be a greater loss of human life. In deciding what is right, the overwhelming social interest is in capturing the terrorists and bringing them to trial. More questionable is the value of killing them outright, since we place great value on the rule of law. Police concerns are apparently served in minimizing loss of life, particularly police and other citizens. The well-being of the terrorists is a factor only insofar as it is preserved until trial. Furthermore, the risk of additional, potentially widespread, property damage weighs heavily against a possibly more efficient means of ending the terrorists' rampage. Use of explosives is wrong.

Assessing Act-Utilitarianism

A moral theory must be evaluated according to how well it corresponds with our experience as members of the moral community. On the whole, act-utilitarianism underperforms as an acceptable moral theory. The following objections can be made against it.

1. Act-utilitarianism gives an overly complex calculation of right action. Critics point out that to make a moral decision, one must envisage all consequences, direct and indirect, short-term and long-term. In addition, one must attach the proper weight of intrinsic value to each. How can the extent of environmental damage, as in our second example, be determined? Or the anxiety a stockholder may feel at the sudden loss of equity after whistle blowing? We seem also to lack a calculus of probability in common sense morality to invest in such decision making. Put another way, we would need to become superhuman computers in order to live the way the act-utilitarian advocates.

2. Act-utilitarianism yields a rigid, unbending morality. We normally view our moral lives as only one part of life. A sphere of action exists in which we are free to pursue what we want, like, need, are inclined to seek, or have a yen for. In this discretionary space, rigorous moral considerations have no play. If we want a new car, we need not apply any moral standard, everything else being equal. The act-utilitarian, however, insists on deploying the calculation of utility in every instance. The result is an invasion of our free space to pursue our interests as we wish. Our lives become duty-bound to the extent that no room exists for anything else.

3. Act-utilitarianism gives results that do not accord with our experience of the moral life. The act-utilitarian tells us, in certain circumstances, to do immoral acts. Take, for example, the Nazis' demand to a besieged French village to hand over ten innocent persons for execution or face total annihilation. Applying the principle of utility, we arrive at the conclusion that far less unhappiness would result if they complied with the criminal demand than if they did not. However, our ordinary moral intuitions tell us that permitting the wanton killing of innocent persons should not be accepted even under such dire conditions. If we did, we would betray a deeply held principle of the moral community. The act-utilitarian misleads in assuming that utility overrides the individual's right not to be killed. Some critics claim that act-utilitarianism contains a hidden bias against the rights of the individual. When a social value ("the greatest happiness for the most people") takes precedence over the moral life of the person, act-utilitarianism seems at odds with morality. The principle of utility ruthlessly uses whatever means are justified by its end, maximizing utility.

3. RULE-UTILITARIANISM

Rule-utilitarianism is a fairly recent revision of classical act-utilitarianism. It shares with the latter the principle of utility but applies the principle to rules of conduct rather than to specific acts. It states: one's action ought to accord with the rule that, if followed by most people, would produce in the situation more intrinsic value than any other rule. Rules of conduct, not the acts themselves, must measure up to the standard of utility in order for one to do the right thing.

The act-utilitarian applies the principle of utility *directly* to decide what ought to be done. The rule-utilitarian is sensitive to criticisms concerning the act-utilitarian's callous attitude toward commonsense moral rules. Rule-utilitarianism applies the principle of utility *indirectly*. Moral rules enjoy a precedence which is absent in act-utilitarianism.

To determine whether an act is morally acceptable, the rule-utilitarian uses a two-step operation. First, the action is placed under the moral rule that governs it. Second, the moral rule is assayed in accordance with the principle of utility. For example, suppose a lawyer publicly states untruths in defense of a client. The act-utilitarian would weigh the utility gained by lawyer and client (and perhaps client's family and associates) against that lost by a truth-telling society as a whole. Lying would be morally impermissible. The rule-utilitarian, however, would first place the lawyer's act of lying under the intermediate rule, "Lawyers ought to do everything professionally possible in advocacy of a client's case." The rule itself, when measured against the principle of utility, shows the overriding benefit of lying in maintaining the institution of advocacy which is at the heart of our legal system. Lying would be morally permissible.

The initial task of the rule-utilitarian (as opposed to the act-utilitarian) is to articulate a set of moral rules which meet the test of maximizing utility. Often, ordinary moral rules like "Keep promises," "Do not kill," "Do not steal," and "Be loyal" are chosen. The rule for promise keeping will illustrate how the rule-utilitarian justifies the choice. Suppose people in general did not keep their word and it was customary to say one thing and do another. Distrust and lack of cooperation would then grow in the climate created by broken promises. People could no longer count on joint ventures, mutual aid, cooperation, and community action—institutions that promote the basic moral relations of the moral community. The negative utility of this result demonstrates the moral acceptability of the rule to keep promises.

Similarly, if theft were the usual mode, we could not count on keeping the things and ideas that are ours. We would be naturally suspicious of others, with increasing anxiety and stress in human relations. We would also lose incentive to pursue our interests if we thought they would invariably be taken from us. The institution of private property is basic to the moral community. This reasoning shows us that on the whole the rule against stealing has greater utility than one promoting theft.

Relying on ordinary moral rules is only the initial phase of the rule-utilitarian's search for an acceptable ethical code. Realistically, the need exists to make rules more specific, more closely tailored to our experience of the moral life. The rule "do not lie" has a generality that cuts across many situations of moral choice. For example, if a psychotic killer came to our office asking where the manager was, the rule would not be helpful in determining what course of action held the maximal utility. Proponents of rule-utilitarianism often build *exceptions* into the formulation of their rules. "Do not lie unless telling the truth threatens an innocent life" is one way to rewrite the rule to be in accordance with our moral experience.

Incorporating exceptions into rules creates two further problems, however. First, the exception is rarely specific enough. The health care professional knows situations in which telling the truth is life-threatening to the patient, but the patient wants to know the truth. Second, even if we can justify the exception, a large number of rules rewritten with exceptions are liable to be unmanageable, overly complex, and inconsistent. For example, in a personal relationship, rules for loyalty and truth telling sometimes come into conflict.

How Rule-Utilitarianism Works in a Professional Context

The rule-utilitarian, like the act-utilitarian, must apply his or her reasoning to decision making in the professions. The following serve as examples.

A large corporation consults its advertising agency about a new product it is developing, which is supposed to cure baldness in men. The marketing division knows that tests show a 7 percent cure rate. The ad agency wants to run a national campaign based on the slogan, "You'll never be bald again." A rule-utilitarian would want to examine the rule against deception, together with the exception: "unless for the purposes of advertising a line of products." (An act-utilitarian would weigh the utility gained from the campaign against its costs, perhaps in terms of irate consumers.) Determining whether the revised rule ought to be adopted on the basis of its utility involves a complex reasoning. Advertising appears to be a legitimate practice in its own right. If it employs various forms of deception to accomplish its aim, they have a claim to justification. On the other hand, could the corporation market its product in another way? Or is advertising a necessary component to corporate sales? The rule-utilitarian would also have to consider the weakening effect advertising has on truth telling in the moral community. Nonetheless, rule-utilitarianism would probably find moderate justification for the exception to the rule not to deceive other people.

A black man has been convicted of murder. The state in which he is tried permits the death penalty. The jury, which can recommend sentencing, knows that 87 percent of those executed by capital punishment have been black. It wants to determine whether that fact mitigates against executing the ac-

cused man. Act-utilitarianism, but not rule-utilitarianism, would calculate the benefits of capital punishment in terms of the relief provided to the victim's family, friends, and those anguished by the brutal nature of the murder. Rule-utilitarianism would instead point out the positive deterrent effect that the rule of capital punishment has on future felonies. With regard to adding an exception based on discrimination against blacks, the rule-utilitarian might note that discrimination as a rule has negative utility. It weakens the moral relations of the community which are needed to observe the entire moral code. Nonetheless, rule-utilitarianism would have difficulty in accommodating discrimination in light of the deterrence it claims capital punishment provides. It apparently would not mitigate sentencing.

Recent discussion has called into question the rule of medical confidentiality. Confidentiality requires that all information acquired within the context of the health care relationship be kept in strictest confidence. With regard to testing for acquired immune deficiency syndrome (AIDS), the rule of confidentiality requires that no result be publicly disclosed. A professional football team plans to test its players for AIDS. Advocates of testing point out that the test serves no real end if the information is not made available to sexual partners liable to be infected with the disease. But the players' union objects to the stigma liable to result from disclosure. Confidentiality has a clear basis in rule-utilitarianism. Only when the exchange of information in a health care context is kept confidential, the rule-utilitarian points out, can the institution of medical trust be maintained. When information leaks out, trust is eroded. Can the rule-utilitarian justify rewriting the rule with the exception? One could argue that innocent third parties will not otherwise be saved from a fatal infection. Further, a reduction in near-panic levels of anxiety would allow the moral code as a whole to function more smoothly. On the other hand, breaking confidentiality would be costly in terms of the rule of trust. Nonetheless, the rule-utilitarian would likely advocate making disclosure of AIDS infection morally acceptable.

Assessing Rule-Utilitarianism

Rule-utilitarianism arose historically as a re-action to the criticisms of act-utilitarianism. Not surprisingly, it eliminates many objections leveled against the act-utilitarian. The cumbersome calculation of utility in terms of an act's total consequences is no longer necessary. The rule-utilitarian, we saw, re-lies on a set of moral rules drawn largely from ordinary moral experience. One result is that rule-utilitarianism easily meets one of the two criteria for an acceptable moral the-ory: it closely corresponds to our everyday experience of life in the moral community. Employing rules we are likely to meet in daily commerce, rule-utilitarianism cannot be accused of favoring the abstract and ar-cane in morality. Nor does it need to defend itself against accusations of rigorism, which finds moral import in the slightest whim. Rule-utilitarianism has no difficulty in al-lowing space between the rules of its code. Within the discretionary space, we are at liberty to pursue what we will—without a moralizing Big Brother watching.

On other criticisms, rule-utilitarianism does not fare as well.

1. Rule-utilitarianism contains conflicting rules of action. Critics claim that a large set of rules is needed to round out the moral code envisaged by the rule-utilitarian. Once all exceptions are written in, there are likely to be contradictory rules. We saw this possi-bility in the example concerning advertis-ing, where the rule not to use deception and the rule to advertise products came into conflict. Critics maintain that rule-utilitari-anism has no means for settling the conflicts between rules once they arise.

2. Rule-utilitarianism gives an obscure ac-count of individual rights. Act-utilitarian-ism, we saw, tends to overlook the rights of the individual in favor of social utility. The rule-utilitarian would never sanction the ex-ecution of a single innocent individual in or-der to advance the utility of others. In order to prohibit killing, say, the aged terminal pa-tient who has no family nor friends, rule-utilitarianism looks at the rewritten rule, "Do not kill except if the person is aged, has no family, and is a burden to society." The rule obviously has low utility since it would fill the lives of the elderly with stress and foreboding. According to critics of rule-utili-tarianism this is too roundabout a means of justifying the individual's rights. A person's rights appear only as correlates of rules that make certain kinds of actions wrong. Whether the rule-utilitarian can supply a more straightforward basis of personal rights remains an unresolved question.

3. Rule-utilitarianism is inconsistent. Al-though it says otherwise, rule-utilitarianism justifies as being right the same acts as does act-utilitarianism. The rule-utilitarian chooses a set of moral rules that maximize utility, and these rules work by requiring the acts in accordance with them to produce the greatest utility. In certain instances, we saw, the act-utilitarian says that the right thing to do is to allow the killing of an innocent life or to commit fraud. Rule-utilitarianism therefore justifies both a rule and its nega-tion, which is inconsistent.

4. Rule-utilitarianism gives an inadequate account of social justice. Justice, which we will discuss below, is synonymous with "fair shares." It is concerned with justly dis-tributing the goods to those who ought to share in them. Depending on the theory of value, what is good includes material things, vital services (like health care, legal counsel, and education), and intrinsic goods (like happiness, peace, and wisdom). Critics of rule-utilitarianism charge that it lacks ex-plicit rules for justly distributing shares of the goods but rather leaves the matter to chance. Accordingly, the door to discrimi-nation and unjust treatment of the disadvan-taged remains open. Rule-utilitarians deny that consequence. They say that once the set of rules that maximize utility are worked out in detail, social justice occurs. They maintain that justice is adequately grounded in the utilitarian moral code. Nonetheless,

the absence of a specific principle of justice leaves a controversial gap in rule-utilitarianism.

4. CLASSICAL DEONTOLOGY

The word "deontology" comes from the Greek stem *deont-,* which means "that which is obligatory." The central concern of a deontological theory is to identify the factor that makes particular actions right or morally obligatory. In its classical form, it was forcefully developed by the German philosopher Immanuel Kant (1724–1804).

Kant has a strong reaction to utilitarianism, both in the act- and rule- form. His main objection is that when we decide to act on the basis of consequences and their utility, we give only conditional and hypothetical assent to morality. Our motives become mixed. In part, they concern what is right to do, but they also concern a nonmoral interest based on outcomes. For Kant, only when the decision making is insulated from consequences can there be a moral decision. Moral decision making is unconditioned by what will result, or, as Kant says, is *categorical.* He tells us that reasoning "'*If,* or *because,* you will this object, you ought to act thus or thus' . . . can never give a moral—that is, a categorical—command."[2]

Kant discusses the means by which one arrives at a moral decision without referring to consequences. First, one looks at the intended act itself, for example, a physician withholding from a patient full information of the patient's condition. One then formulates a policy statement, or "maxim," of the act itself: "A doctor should, in circumstances like these, not tell the patient the whole truth." Third, one assesses the moral soundness of the maxim by means of a master rule which Kant calls the *categorical imperative.* In its first version, it states: "Act only on that maxim through which you can at the same time will that it should become a universal law."[3] One is thereby asked to imagine the maxim for the specific act to be done by all doctors. In its universalized form, the maxim will be morally acceptable or morally unacceptable. In our example, if all doctors withheld complete disclosure of information from patients in similar circumstances, the institution of medical trust would be undermined. The result would be morally unacceptable. Therefore, the act originally intended is the wrong thing to do.

Our approach to ethical decision making, following Kant's first formula for the categorical imperative, makes no appeal to the consequences of what is to be done. It is not a teleological theory. But its procedure for universalizing the act can be faulted for being abstract. No matter what it tells us, its approach seems to have little in common with our experience of the moral life. Proponents of classical deontology point to a second version which Kant gives of the categorical imperative: "Act in such a way that you treat humanity, whether in your own person or in the person of any other, never simply as a means, but always at the same time as an end."[4] The strong appeal of the second formulation lies in its main idea: respect for the person. Kant's deontology is an *ethics of respect.* An ethics of respect has immediate and direct application to decision making in the professional context.

At the heart of Kant's view lies the intrinsic *dignity* of the person. The inner value of dignity entitles each of us always to be treated, by others and by ourselves, with respect. The recognition of dignity gives us the peculiar quality of freedom which belongs to the moral life. Kant calls this important concept *autonomy;* we will discuss it in the next chapter. The entitlements of respect yield particular kinds of *duty* which we are morally bound to observe. Kant's

---

[2]Immanuel Kant, *Groundwork of the Metaphysic of Morals,* trans. H. J. Paton (London: Hutchinson University Library, 1948), p. 111.

[3]Ibid., p. 88.
[4]Ibid., p. 96.

deontology regards being duty-bound as being independent of the consequences of action and independent of the motives, intentions, objectives, feelings, and character of the agent. Deontology, then, is an ethical theory of duties and the rights which correlate to them. It accords well with our commonsense approach to decision making in the professions.

Kant makes several important distinctions among the kinds of duties derived from the idea of human dignity. Duties are (1) narrow or wide, (2) negative or positive, and (3) to oneself or to others. Division 3 specifies the person to whom we are duty-bound to do the right thing. For example, the duty of *beneficence,* to increase happiness, familiar to the utilitarian, is owed to others and not to ourselves. The duty of *moral perfection,* to increase moral understanding and awareness is owed to ourselves and not to others. Division 2 tells us whether we are duty-bound to refrain from doing something (a negative duty) or to undertake doing it (a positive duty). For example, the duty not to commit suicide is obviously a negative duty. The duty of beneficence is a positive one. Division 1 is the most difficult distinction. A narrow or perfect duty stipulates a line of action from which no justified exceptions exist. For example, the duty to refrain from killing an innocent person is narrow and perfect. A wide or imperfect duty, according to Kant, "leaves a play-room for free choice in following (observing) the law."[5] With wide duties, we have more discretionary space for deciding whether to pursue a course of action. For example, the wide or imperfect duty of gratitude allows us to choose what means, if any, we will use to repay another person for a good action on our behalf. Narrow duties forbid our making a sizable breach in respecting a person. We should not treat the person *merely* as a means to attain our interest. Wide duties rule out attitudes of disrespect where we fail to take the person's dignity seriously even though our means may not be disrespectful.

Kant's deontological theory is a carefully structured system of duties. To understand it better, we need a closer look at the four main kinds of duties: wide duties to others and to oneself, and narrow duties to others and to oneself.

Narrow duties to others make up an important cluster of our commonsense rules of right. The most obvious examples are the positive duty to keep one's word, and the negative duties not to lie and not to harm an innocent individual. According to Kant, no matter what the consequences, we should perform each of the duties. For instance, the lawyer who knows that deceptively presenting evidence will win the case for his or her client ought never to follow that line of action. Or, the physician who believes that lying about a patient's condition will reinforce the will to live should resist following the judgment. Or, the advertising executive who thinks up a brilliant campaign based on deception ought to rethink the project. In each case, the professional must recognize the authority of individuals to actualize their lives on the basis of the reasons that guide conduct. The lawyer who lies shows disrespect for persons who try to organize their life plans on the basis of being informed of the truth. Likewise, the physician, regardless of benevolent motives, fails to honor the fundamental dignity of the patient who makes decisions on the basis of the evidence. The advertising executive with a deceptive campaign shows disrespect for people whose lives are affected by the misleading information and who have been used merely as a means to the advertiser's end.

Kant's deontology also contains duties to oneself. Utilitarians, especially act-utilitarians, find problems with the category. If maximizing utility is the sole moral principle, the only action involving oneself must be self-interest, which lies beyond the pale of morality. Deontologists reject the argu-

[5]Immanuel Kant, *The Doctrine of Virtue,* trans. Mary J. Gregor (New York: Harper & Row, 1964), p. 49.

ment that duties to self reduce to self-interest. They point to the ordinary moral concern of deepening and broading one's ethical understanding as a legitimate duty to self. Moral education serves not only the general good (or utility) but also the good of oneself. Kant's second version of the categorical imperative makes clear that he intends to take duties to self seriously. "Act in such a way that you treat humanity, whether in your own person or in any other, never simply as a means, but always at the same time as an end." We owe the same measure of respect to the person in ourselves as we do to another person. If we deprecate our capacity to think, feel, and perceive as persons, we undercut our inherent dignity. The clearest example Kant gives of a perfect duty to oneself is the negative duty to refrain from suicide. Acting to end our existence, we treat ourselves merely as a means to alleviate the suffering (physical or psychological) which envelops our lives. Whether the patient who experiences incurable pain at the terminal stages of an illness is duty-bound to refrain from assisting the end of life is a difficult question. Other perfect duties to self include prohibitions against immoderate eating or drinking. Being oversated or drunk are states which temporarily damage a person's capacity to make rational, informed decisions about a life plan. We are duty-bound to avoid them out of respect for that part of ourselves which is lost to us when drunk or stupified by overeating.

The notion of wide duties is more elusive than that of narrow ones. In general, wide duties require us to adopt broad policy rules rather than ones specifying particular acts. A policy to express one's gratitude, for instance, does not tell us when nor in what form to do so. We are not necessarily doing the wrong thing by not showing gratitude. When and how we express it is up to us. On the other hand, we are not at liberty to abandon the policy of gratitude. A minimum expression is morally required. Wide or imperfect duties fall under two general classes:

obligatory policies that increase one's moral perfection, and those that advance the happiness of others. The first is a wide duty to oneself. The second is a wide duty to others. Under duty-bound polices toward self, Kant cites the duty to develop one's natural talents. Striving toward personal perfection may involve choosing to study the law rather than to go to dance school. Or it may mean taking voice lessons and not the extra course in statistics. Which aspect of our many-sided lives we decide to enhance is up to us. So is deciding how much time, effort, and expense we are willing to extend. Much leeway exists also in seeing through the policy we have adopted. We are not at liberty, however, to refrain altogether from the commitment to become more fully developed. That would be a breach of duty to self.

The final category of duties in Kant's deontology is wide duties to others. These fall under the rubric of *beneficence*. Beneficence has both a restricted and a more unrestricted meaning. In its restricted sense, it is equivalent to nonmaleficence, that is, not inflicting harm or injury on another person. The Hippocratic Code for physicians specifies the duty of nonmaleficence, but there it is a negative duty, whereas Kant's obligatory policy of beneficence is a positive one. In its more unrestricted sense, beneficence means actively removing the harm preventing a person's happiness. It also means actually promoting the individual's well-being. For Kant, we are free to choose how and to what extent we realize the commitment to further another's life plan. Financial support, affection, sharing knowledge, and spending time are all legitimate means toward discharging the duty of beneficence. In keeping with the width of the duty, we may on occasion even refuse to help. We cannot, however, abandon the general aim of promoting others' happiness without being in the wrong.

Kant's deontological theory is not helpful in prioritizing the vast array of duties. How are we to decide which duty applies first and foremost to a decision-making context? He tells us that narrow duties always override wide ones. For instance, if an engineer sincerely wants to help the people of an impoverished region (wide duty of beneficence), he is not free to lie to planning boards about the availability of resources (narrow duty not to tell lies). Similarly, if a person wants to develop her analytic skills as a lawyer (wide duty to perfect natural talents), she is not free to steal notes on crucial cases (narrow duty not to steal). The rules of priority do not go far enough, however. For instance, do we express our gratitude toward our dance instructor (wide duty to express gratitude) or accept a part in a performance which he or she also sought (wide duty to perfect our natural talents)? The proponent of Kant's deontology has to argue that without the latitude in priorities, we would be unable to advance our moral understanding.

How Kant's Deontology Works in Professional Decision Making

Despite its cumbersome look, Kantian deontology has many direct applications in the field of professional ethics. The following examples illustrate the relevance of Kant's theory to the decision making of the professional.

Company A, a small, aggressive pharmaceutical corporation, is on the verge of a breakthrough on a multipurpose vaccine against the flu. The test vaccine promises to be superior to ones currently on the market, both in breadth and in effectiveness of immunization. Company A must act quickly because a large pharmaceutical house is close behind. A researcher suggests going directly to experimentation with human subjects instead of dilly-dallying with animal experimentation. In the proposed test, subjects would not be told what they were being used for. Company A's institutional review board (IRB), however, objects. It cites Kant's duty never to use another person merely as a means to attaining an end. Not informing subjects that they are

to be inoculated with an untested flu vaccine amounts to using them merely to get experimental data. The IRB points out that if the motive were solely advancement of human knowledge, their objection would disappear. Otherwise, informing the subject and gaining his or her consent are necessary conditions to respecting the subject as a person.

Mr. Adams runs a mail-order business out of his home. Recently he suffered heavy financial losses. The well-being of his family is in question. In order to save himself from creditors, he helps initiate a chain letter. Mr. Adams knows it is fraudulent in its claims, but there is no other way out of his difficulties. The Kantian deontologists disagree. They point out that Mr. Adams confuses narrow and wide duties. Mr. Adams has a duty of beneficence which obligates him to maintain and promote the happiness of his family, but the duty of beneficence is a wide duty which gives him many options on how to fulfill his commitment. Mr. Adams also has a duty not to lie to others nor to defraud them. The duty to refrain from lying is a narrow duty. It permits no exceptions. The act of lying is never a morally acceptable way to conduct oneself beneficently. Mr. Adams is morally required to choose an alternative line of conduct.

The state legislature is facing a number of "get tough with crime" bills in an election year. The sponsors argue that unless the state shows potential felons that it means business, crime rates will continue to mushroom. One state senator takes a surprising position. She objects to the argument that is based on the alleged deterrent force of punishment. "It is empirical and unfounded," she says. But she favors stricter laws. She takes the position of the Kantian deontologist. A felon has already shown disrespect in the act of crime. The disrespect is directed both toward the victim(s) and toward the moral community which advocates the rule of law. The criminal has therefore called into question his or her claims to being a person. The state senator advocates exacting "an eye for an eye, a tooth for a tooth." She feels that punishment ought to inflict an injury on the perpetrator equal to the injury he or she has inflicted on the victim.

Assessing Kant's Deontological Theory

Compared with the simple operation of utilitarianism, Kant's theory is complex. The complexity is a two-edged sword. Positively, we saw how the diversity of deontological rules correlates quite well with our experience of the moral life. The actions we customarily regard as the wrong thing to do—lying, stealing, harming others, breaking promises, ignoring others' needs—are ruled out on the theory as morally unacceptable. The fundamental reason given also corresponds to commonsense views of ethics. The wrongness of the acts derives from disrespecting the inherent dignity of a person, either oneself or another. Negatively, the complexity raises difficulties regarding the soundness of Kant's deontology as a moral theory. What are some of the difficulties?

1. Kant's theory gives no format for creating an order among the rules of right action. We have already seen the lack of rules for prioritizing duties. Especially in decisions involving a mixture of wide and narrow duties, we are in the dark about what ought to be done. One's wide duty to become a better manager of corporate sales (duty to develop one's natural talents) and to help others (duty of beneficence) may come into sharp conflict with the narrow duty not to lie. The Kantian would point to the need to exercise one's moral understanding. He would say that only by repeatedly balancing the diverse rules of duty do we deepen our experience of the moral life. Nonetheless, the lack of guidance is a serious gap in applying the theory to our ethical decision making. To learn how to prioritize moral rules on our own, we need to know how Kant envisages it being done.

2. Kant's theory does not clarify the notion of a person. The second version of the categorical imperative requires us to make decisions always on the basis of respect for persons, and the duties following from the categorical imperative are ways of implementing that respect. Kant tells us little more about the crucial notion of a person. At times he equates it with "rational being," presumably an individual able to discriminate his or her options with clarity enough to realize a life plan. To be a person, must we act rationally in every choice-situation? Or is rationality more like a potential which sometimes is actualized and sometimes not? Certain ethical problems in professional decision making turn on the pivotal question of who is a person. For example, the health care professional faces the question of whether to abort a fetus. Is the fetus a person? Similarly, the police officer chasing a fleeing felon faces the question of whether to fire a gun, causing a potentially fatal wound. Is the felon a person? Further development of the very rich notion of a person is needed before Kant's theory is ready for application in professional decision making.

3. Kant's theory contains an element of rigorism. Rigorism, we saw, tends to take away our liberty to decide matters from free moral considerations. It puts us in a tight moral box. Critics charge, for instance, that the narrow duty to refrain from lying means that we are duty-bound without exception never to lie. We are morally required not to tell an intruding neighbor that we are busy when we are not. Our being less than frank about our host's bad cooking is likewise morally unacceptable. Similar examples surround the narrow duty not to break promises. If we tell the postman we will leave him 25 cents for a stamp tomorrow, our forgetting is a breach of duty. When everything we do is hemmed in by duty, morality has grown invasive. Something is wrong. Critics who point to this defect regard it as a serious one.

4. Kant's theory makes a hidden appeal to consequences. Recall that a deontological theory claims to make ethical decisions independent of the consequences of the act being considered. A teleological theory, such as utilitarianism, uses consequences to compute right action. Critics say that Kant's

theory does also. Consider, for example, the employee who is trying to decide whether to tell a lie. She is planning to say, "Yes, we'll be able to ship your order at a reduced rate," knowing that her supervisor is counting on the lie for an account. But only when she includes the consequences of what she is planning to say does the lie appear. Critics point out that no way exists to draw a clear line between the act itself and its consequences. They also say that Kant's theory contains a secret utilitarian calculation; its usefulness as a moral theory does not come from a deontological basis but from its hidden utilitarian agenda.

5. THE DEONTOLOGICAL THEORY OF W. D. ROSS

In an important book entitled *The Right and the Good* (1930), the English philosopher W. D. Ross developed a new deontological theory. Ross took into account the criticisms of Kant's theory and also incorporated into his theory ideas of utilitarianism, particularly act-utilitarianism. He was persuaded that the absence of clear priority rules in Kant's theory required revision since we are often faced with real moral dilemmas, and he believed that the theory should provide explicit guidance for such difficult conflict situations. Ross's theory is deontological because Ross holds that rightness is a property unto itself and not definable in terms of goodness. An act is right because it embodies the property of rightness, not because it increases happiness or utility. However, the theory is less restrictive than Kant's because it gives the consequences a role in moral decisions.

Ross's theory matches well with how we discover rules of right in our ordinary moral experience. Consider a situation in which the duty not to lie is in conflict with the duties of loyalty and beneficence. The Kantian would say that the narrow duty prohibiting lies must always take precedence over the

wide duties to be loyal and to promote the happiness of others. Is this account plausible? A lawyer who acknowledges the need to lie in order to win the client's case thinks otherwise. He or she knows any scheme that orders rules in a hard-and-fast way is inadequate. Being sensitive to the particular situation requires a flexibility which Kant's deontological theory lacks. The rigid or absolute nature of the rules needs to be modified. Accordingly, Ross introduces the idea of *prima facie* duties.

Prima facie comes from the Latin expression meaning "on first appearance." A prima facie duty, for Ross, is what, on first looking at a situation, we take our duty to be. It is, other things being equal, our duty on the condition that no overriding obligations conflict with it. If an employee promises a supervisor a particular piece of work by the end of the week, he or she has a prima facie duty to complete the work. The employee is bound by a moral reason but is not necessarily under obligation. Suppose the piece of work involves fraud or industrial espionage. To turn over the work would be to become involved in fraudulent acts or acts of spying. Then the employee's *actual duty* or *duty on the balance* differs from the prima facie duty. Moral reasons exist not to do the work, and in this situation they outweigh the reason given in the prima facie duty.

In fortunate situations, we find ourselves bound only by what "on first appearance" looks obligatory. Then the prima facie duty coincides with our actual duty and tells us the right thing to do. Frequently, our situation contains a number of prima facie duties in conflict with one another. As a member of the moral community, each of us enjoys numerous kinds of relations with other members such as parent to child, employee to employer, friend to friend, patient to doctor, colleague to colleague, and the like. According to Ross's theory, the variety of moral relationships accounts for the diversity of prima facie duties. Ross says, "Each of these relations is the foundation of a prima facie duty, which is more or less incumbent on me according to the circumstances of the case."[6] In this complex situation we are asked to reflect on the prima facie claims on our duty and come up with a "considered decision," that is, the one in which we earnestly try to apply the prima facie duties to the situation.

To resolve conflicts between different prima facie duties, our moral intuitions serve us best. Are they enough? Ross gives two rules for guiding decision in the complex situation. First, if two prima facie duties are in collision, one's duty lies with the one that is more stringent. Second, if more than two prima facie duties are in conflict, one's duty lies in the course of action having the greatest balance of prima facie rightness over prima facie wrongness.

Ross's rules of prioritizing, however, raise as many questions as they answer. We have no information as to what "stringency" is regarding prima facie duties. Also we lack means for deciding where the balance lies when we are determining the excess of rightness over wrongness. Like Kant's deontology, Ross's theory leaves unsolved the problem of ordering the different prima facie duties. The best we can do is to reflect seriously, try to apply the prioritizing rules, and recognize that no automatic method exists for coming to our actual duty. Perhaps uncertainty is part and parcel of the moral condition and cannot be totally eliminated.

One appeal of Ross's theory is the easy access we have to the many prima facie duties. The theory dispenses with the need to rely on the principle of utility with its intricate calculation of consequential value. It also disposes of a reference to the categorical imperative, with the danger of vagueness which surrounds the concept. Ross believes that we come to know prima facie duties in a simple, direct way. We intuit their truth. He says:

> I . . . am claiming that we *know* them to be truth. To me it seems as self-evident as anything could be. . . . Many readers will perhaps say that they do *not* know this to be true. If so I certainly cannot prove it to them. I can only ask them to reflect again, in the hope that they will ultimately agree that they also know it to be true."[7]

In a fashion similar to the way we *know* directly the blueness of the sky or the redness of an apple, Ross holds that we possess a moral intuition which corresponds to these examples of a nonmoral intuition.

Ross gives a systematic and complete list of the prima facie duties of his theory. The following seven enter into considerations of how to decide which is the right thing to do.

1. Duties of fidelity: keeping one's word, honoring contracts, telling the truth, avoiding use of deception, and being loyal. As one enters a profession, new duties of fidelity come into existence. Examples are the nurse who should inform a patient's family of the medical facts and who should keep the facts confidential from other persons, and the lawyer whose loyalty to the client's case should make him or her committed to try to win it.
2. Duties of reparation: repaying other persons for the wrongs one committed against them. The criminal who treated an individual fraudently should make reparation to the victim for the morally unacceptable action.
3. Duties of gratitude: repaying other persons for the intrinsic value they have given to one in a state of need. The client who is well served by his or her lawyer is duty-bound to find the means of returning the service.
4. Duties of beneficence: promoting the intrinsic values of others. The intrinsic values or goods include virtue, intelligence, and pleasure. One is duty-bound to act so that others' lives will be filled with greater moral understanding, insight, and enjoyment.

---

[6]W. D. Ross, *The Right and the Good* (Cambridge: Cambridge University Press, 1930), p. 19.

[7]Ibid., p. 37.

5. Duties of nonmaleficence: refraining from harming others in the sense of decreasing their share of intrinsic worth. Not stealing, not plagiarizing, not injuring, and not killing are examples of nonmaleficent action.
6. Duties of justice: correcting wrong distributions of pleasure or happiness. A right distribution is one that gives shares based on merit. A wrong distribution allocates shares based on market value, social worth, past achievement, or even chance.
7. Duties of self-improvement: improving oneself with respect to the intrinsic values of intelligence or virtue.

Several categories of prima facie duties are familiar from Kant's deontological theory. Kant, we saw, discusses duties of gratitude, beneficence, lying, and self-improvement. Other kinds of duty are Ross's innovations, such as the duties of reparation. In a single situation, diverse classes of duty may all find application. For instance, the nurse who informs a patient of the unavailability of a kidney transplant is duty-bound to give a truthful account of the facts (duty of fidelity), to maintain good health care (duty of beneficence) while avoiding any further harm to the patient (duty of nonmaleficence), and to ensure that selection of the organ recipient has been made fairly (duty of justice). Because she views the nurse–patient relation as one of education, she tries to use the situation as a learning experience (duty of self-improvement). Seeing so many prima facie duties having an impact on a single decision, we may appreciate the necessity of rules for determining the actual duty or duty on the balance.

How Ross's Theory Works in a Professional Context

Ross does not claim that his list of prima facie duties is complete but he believes that the advantage of his theory is its easy access to ethical decision making. The means of applying the theory to professional situations are more operational than with other theories. Obviously, some kinds of duties are, in the professional context, more important than others. The following can serve as examples of how the theory operates in the decision-making process with which the professional is familiar.

Larry has worked for the cement company for fifteen years as the foreman of second shift. One day his supervisor says that to ''help the books'' it will be necessary to put less lime in the ready-mix bags. Lime is the most expensive component of cement mixture. Larry does not believe it is fair or in the best interests of the company. He feels he is facing a moral dilemma. Ross's theory can help us structure this dilemma. Larry has a moral reason to ''water down'' the cement because of his subordinate position to the plant supervisor. He has a prima facie duty of fidelity to obey the orders of the supervisor. At the same time, another prima facie duty of fidelity is in conflict with the duty of obedience. Larry is duty-bound to the cement company to keep his word, not act fraudulently, and honor the terms of the job description under which he works. The duty of nonmaleficence also applies. Since weakening the cement mix is likely to injure others (as when a building collapses), Larry is bound by the prima facie duty of nonmaleficence. Also, Larry may feel grateful toward the cement company for what it has done for him. If so, the duty of gratitude must be weighed in resolving the dilemma. Which duty would Ross's theory hold outweighs the others? What is Larry's actual duty? Two different considerations arise. First, the duty of nonmaleficence is especially stringent on Ross's view. Like a narrow duty in Kant's theory, where the threat of potential harm exists, Larry ought to refrain from the action. Since the potential danger from weakened cement is great, Larry should disobey his supervisor. Second, the balance of rightness over wrongness seems greatest with the duty of nonmaleficence. More people stand liable to injury than with other prima facie duties. Thus, Larry has a double-barrel reason for thinking he is morally right to refuse to follow his boss's orders.

The night nurse has just given away the last bed in the intensive care unit (ICU). The new occupant is an escaped felon who has been brought in with gunshot wounds following an attempted rape. The nurse has strong feelings about giving the bed away. She herself was a rape victim. It is Saturday night, and five minutes later someone from a severe car accident is brought in. She feels conflicted. Ross's theory helps sort out the aspects of the moral dilemma. The nurse first is bound by the duty of beneficence, which says that she ought to act to promote the well-being of the patient. This prima facie duty gives her reason to allow the felon the last bed in the ICU. The duty of fidelity tells her the same thing. She has a prima facie reason to fulfill the implicit agreement between her and a patient to promote the patient's medical interests. Fidelity is owed also to the doctor who admitted the felon to the ICU. On the other hand, the nurse may feel herself bound by a duty of reparation since she is a rape victim. A stronger consideration for denying the new admission his bed lies in the duty of justice. Does the felon merit having a scarce medical resource? The stringency of the prima facie duty of justice seems strong, but is it strong enough to override the nurse's duty of nonmaleficence to not injure the patient? Part of the answer depends on how just we view the "first come, first served" allocation of beds in the ICU. If the nurse believes that merit is a better way to distribute the beds, she must conclude that she is right in withholding the bed from the felon.

A lawyer engages in plea bargaining for his client. Plea bargaining is pleading guilty for a lesser offense in order to forgo trial for one that is more severe. A number of prima facie duties come into conflict. The lawyer is under the duty of fidelity to his or her client to do what is necessary to win the case. The lawyer is also bound by the duty of fidelity to be truthful and to serve the rule of law. At the same time, he or she must act so as to prevent injury to the client (duty of maleficence). The lawyer must justify the choice of plea bargaining by an appeal to the duty of beneficence. The judicial process as a whole is served best by shortening the time a case is kept in the courts, and plea bargaining accomplishes this end. The duty of justice would seem to require fair treatment in the hands of the law.

Whether plea bargaining can be justified in terms of the prima facie duty of distributing benefits on the basis of merit is questionable. If the lawyer weighs the prima facie reasons by fidelity and beneficence most heavily, plea bargaining becomes the duty on the balance.

Assessing Ross's Deontological Theory

Ross developed his theory partly in response to criticisms of utilitarianism and Kantian deontology. Utilitarianism, we saw, oversimplifies the complex nature of our moral understanding by insisting on a single principle of morality. It also places too much moral surveillance over our most insignificant acts. Kant gives us a diverse collection of moral rules and removes the overconcern for ethically acceptable action in utilitarianism. However, he leaves justice out of his account and does not tell us how to organize our thinking when several rules apply to a given situation. Ross's theory on the other hand, leaves us with a plurality of prima facie duties, including the duty of justice. Priorities of duty, however, present difficulties. We saw some problems regarding Ross's guidelines. To choose the most stringent prima facie, or the one that maximizes the amount of rightness over wrongness, we must know more about the matters of stringency, rightness, and wrongness. Without this crucial clarification, the deontology is open to objections similar to what critics have said about Kantian theory.

Opponents to Ross's theory point out the difficulty of formulating prima facie duties. Ross claims that each of his classes of duty is known directly by our moral understanding, but the fact is that moral understanding itself is a product of education. What one learns depends in part on place, opportunity, influence, experience, and also on how seriously one undertakes one's duty for self-improvement, particularly of the moral understanding. Different individuals apparently have different moral understandings. The basic pluralism of our moral community makes agreement on prima facie reasons for moral action unlikely. Unless Ross holds an external standard of what the "best" moral understanding is, disagreement is inherent in the matter of decision making. But if the "best moral understanding" is alone responsible for enumerating the prima facie duties, Ross is wrong in saying they are obvious to everyone's intuition. Either way, we have an important gap in his account.

Critics also point out various problems with the list of prima facie duties. As it stands, it seems incomplete (Ross would accept this criticism). The prima facie duty not to commit theft, for example, does not seem to belong with duties of fidelity. A thief who steals industrial secrets has not really broken a trust with the corporation if he never worked for it. While some acts of stealing violate a prior trust, many do not. Should the duty not to steal be a separate category of prima facie duties? Other critics question the inclusion of the duty of self-improvement, which involves the questionable idea of duties to self. Still others wonder whether prima facie reasons exist for acting in the ways Ross says. For instance, if one promises to help a friend cheat on an entrance exam, is there a duty one incurs by virtue of the unsound promise? If not, not all promises involve a prima facie duty to keep one's word.

In spite of critical objections, Ross's theory provides us with a powerful tool in facing ethical decision making. A proponent might point out that expecting Ross's deontology to prioritize our duties completely is unrealistic. A gap always exists between theory and practice. Only an acute moral understanding can bridge the gap. Otherwise, computers could give us the answers to our moral dilemmas. Since they cannot, we must accept the central role moral consciousness plays in ethical choice. Perhaps the search for a complete decision-procedure reflects our unwillingness to face the inherent uncertainty of moral dilemmas.

6. THE DEONTOLOGICAL THEORY OF JOHN RAWLS

In his book *A Theory of Justice* (1971), the American philosopher John Rawls works out a new deontological theory, one that continues to attract a good deal of attention. Rawls tries to temper the strictness of classical deontology, like Kant's, without ignoring the obvious appeal of making decisions independent of the consequences. At the same time, he finds Ross's less restrictive theory lax when it comes to deciding priorities. With each version of deontology, Rawls agrees that rightness is the fundamental moral property, that it is defined independent of goodness, and that respect for persons occupies the center stage of ethical decision making.

According to Rawls' theory, earlier versions of deontology contain a large flaw. Their starting point is the moral understanding of a single individual. They then enumerate different duties that a person has in relation to others and to oneself. The moral community is a secondary consideration. Because the individual is primary, the concept of justice, we saw, lacks a full account. Rawls' intention is to invert the earlier order. Placing the moral community first, he makes *justice* the primary moral consideration. What is right for an individual to do takes a secondary position. Rawls' interest is in developing a blueprint for a just society and not for a moral human being. A person will act morally when he or she belongs to a just society.

A deontological theory that has formulated a principle of justice is in a good position. A principle of justice tells the moral community how to go about distributing fair shares of things that are in short supply, such as medical resources, legal services, quality education, and opportunity for career advancement and wage earning. The principle functions on two levels, which correspond to the differences between act-utilitarianism and rule-utilitarianism. On the first level, the principle of justice tells us the kinds of social institutions and practices we ought to have in order to promote fair distribution. Health care provision, legal structures, corporate responsibilities, and technological services all would need to be consistent with justice at this level. One could argue that the concept of a profession would have to be examined in light of the principle of justice. On the second level, the principle of justice settles disagreements between individuals. Conflicting ethical decisions would be resolved, up to a certain point, by a consideration of how justice operates.

Rawls' theory describes how the principle of justice is chosen. Rawls takes a hypothetical group of individuals in what he calls "the original position." They are representative human beings, with ordinary intelligence, capabilities, needs, desires, and socioeconomic advantages. In the original position, Rawls imagines them behind what he calls "the veil of ignorance." Although they possess abilities, needs, and the like, they do not know what they are, e.g., their social standing, income, intelligence, state of health, or degree of education. They have somehow become detached from what makes up personal identity and instead act on their essential humanity. Rawls' theory assumes that such essential human beings are interested in cooperating with one another. It also assumes that they will follow a decision-making process that uses the power of reason and that they have an inherent (if undeveloped) sense of justice. Lastly, it assumes they want the same basic things, or "primary goods," which consist in power, wealth, rights, and opportunities and which make possible the specific things individuals value.

The ideal moral community, on Rawls' account, has an agenda: to decide which rule or rules of justice should apply to the community once the veil of ignorance is lifted. The choice would determine justice on the two levels noted above. It would select the kinds of institutions people live by

and would settle moral conflicts between individuals. The conditions surrounding the ideal community's choice eliminate many possibilities for a just principle. For instance, no one would rationally select a principle of extreme inequality in order to pursue self-interest (like ethical egoism). If one did, one might end up on the short end of the stick once the veil of ignorance is lifted. One's social position then might be in the disadvantaged class which would be worsened by further inequality. Thus choice of a principle in the original position cannot be dictated by self-interest alone. One is not being reasonable in choosing a rule that might later condemn one to a greatly disadvantaged life.

The choice of the ideal community proceeds, according to Rawls, by well-reasoned debate. Since ignorance of one's social and personal facts makes a kind of equality, the spirit of the debate is cooperative. Everyone stands to gain or to lose together. Rawls argues that the original position favors one strategic approach to rational choice (as developed in game theory) known as *maximin*. The maximin principle, which was developed to handle conditions of uncertainty in economics, allows one to choose the alternative whose worse possible outcome is better than any other worse possible outcome. It is the rule of making the best of the worst. When individuals in the original position follow the maximin principle, no one would select a principle of gross inequality. If one does not know whether one would be victimized by gross inequality, it is not the best of the worse.

The original position in Rawls' deontology is a complex choice situation. Out of it, individuals select rules by which to make further moral decisions. Rawls argues extensively that two particular rules of justice would be selected by the ideal moral community.

1. Each person is to have an equal right to the most extensive total system of equal basic liberties compatible with a similar system of lib-

erty for all. 2. Social and economic inequalities are to be arranged so that they are both: (a) to the greatest benefit of the least advantaged . . . , and (b) attached to offices and positions open to all under conditions of fair equality of opportunity.[8]

On Rawls' theory, the two rules together define a just society. Each operates independently of the other. The first rule distributes liberty (an intrinsic good) to everyone in an egalitarian manner. Each person has as much basic freedom as he or she can have so long as no one is disadvantaged by that amount. Rawls also thinks of the first rule as having priority over the second. Liberty is nonnegotiable. No one can trade it away to get more of other social goods like wealth, property, reputation, or social privilege. Furthermore, people in the original position have to decide how to distribute liberty before distributing any other social good.

Once fair shares of freedom are given out, selection of the second rule begins: the distribution of the remaining social goods. Rawls argues that this distribution operates on a maximin principle, with people in the original position trying to make the best of the worst. They do this by regarding the most disadvantaged individuals as a litmus test. Whatever differences in social status and wealth result from a distribution of goods, they must benefit the most disadvantaged persons. A distribution cannot make the most disadvantaged even worse off. They must stand to benefit at least as much as any other group. Rawls' deontological theory recognizes that different individuals possess different amounts of social goods, but it says the differences are just, and can be justified, only when they work to the advantage of those at the bottom of the ladder. Justice works not by leveling social differences but by allowing opportunities for upward movement.

Rawls' theory is deontological because

[8]John Rawls, *A Theory of Justice* (Cambridge, Mass.: Harvard University Press, 1971), p. 52.

conditions of the original position rule out appeal to the consequences of decision making. The theory escapes the criticism of utilitarianism, which makes each of our acts one of moral choice. A good deal of discretionary space surrounds a person's decision. One idea of the first rule of justice is to safeguard the area of choice in order that a person be free to pursue a life plan. Too restrictive a moral code rules out this possibility. At the same time, Rawls' theory is not open to the objection directed to those of Kant and Ross, that it leaves justice out of account. Justice is deontology's primary focus. Respect for the person follows from the two rules of justice.

Although the original position is concerned with justice first and foremost, other choices are delineated in its rich moral atmosphere. The responsibility of those in the original position is to envision the just community. Their vision, according to Rawls, extends in three other directions. First, the theory recognizes "natural duties." Natural duties are acknowledged by those in the original position because such duties are independent of social and personal particularities. Among the natural duties are the duty of nonmaleficence (not to harm others), the duty of mutual aid (to help others in need), the duty of promise keeping, and the duty of just action (obeying the rules of justice). Natural duties are not chosen but nonetheless obligate us once the veil of ignorance is lifted. They fill out the gaps surrounding what the right thing is for a person to do once basic rules of the moral community are in place.

Second, Rawls' theory argues that rules other than those of justice come out of the original position. The participants' discussion is not limited to the two rules of justice. Their aim is to structure right action for the just community, and so they formulate and choose other duties. These are distinct from natural duties because they arise *from* debate and not prior to it. They include the duty of beneficence (promoting others' social goods), the duty of fidelity (keeping one's word), the duty of respect (not violating others' liberties), and the duty of fairness (not cheating others out of their fair share of social goods). These two additional categories of duty are similar to the prima facie duties of Ross's theory. Rawls can be seen as adding the groundwork of justice to the list of duties which Ross already provided for us.

Finally, Rawls believes that certain duties to oneself follow from the original position. Unlike the utilitarian, he finds validity in the idea of duty to self. One duty to self having appeal to participants in the original position is a version of *paternalism*. Paternalism allows others to act on behalf of our best interests, desires, hopes, or needs when we are unable to. Rawls argues that an individual has an interest in care-taking by another in order to have his or her full measure of freedom eventually restored. Hence, paternalism is regarded as a duty to self. We will see the importance of paternalism in different professional decision-making situations.

Rawls' deontological theory is complex and innovative in its approach. Its central ideas of fairness and the original position do not lend themselves easily to the brief exposition we have given. Nonetheless, we recognize the intent to synthesize and go beyond other formulations of deontology. When we come to evaluating Rawls' project, this fact will be helpful.

How Rawls' Deontological Theory Applies to the Professional Context

We have seen that Rawls' primary focus lies in the institutional structure of the just community. Many professions, such as health care and the justice and law enforcement systems, can be regarded as institutions. The original position would determine in part the moral rules on which the professions stand. If health is a social good, as some proponents argue, providing health care would be regulated by the second rule of justice. The availability of legal services would be

another example, since whether one has proper legal support determines one's share of other social goods, like power.

Rawls' theory also has provision for decision making *within* a professional field. Many of the specific duties of a professional coincide with Ross's list of prima facie obligations. The following cases illustrate how Rawls' theory works.

Myron applied for a promotion in the engineering firm in which he worked. He was told by the affirmative action officer that he was the most qualified for the position but that the company was searching for a minority member or a woman. Myron felt unfairly treated. He felt he was a victim of "reverse discrimination." How does Rawls' theory view the decision? The second rule of justice requires a distribution of any good to be of greatest benefit to the most disadvantaged persons. It also requires fairness in opportunity for those seeking positions. Myron's point is that his opportunity for promotion has been unfairly blocked by the affirmative action officer's condition. If we assume Myron does not belong to the most disadvantaged class, the situation becomes quite different. His company, and society as a whole, are duty-bound to rectify inequalities of the past which are responsible for the existence of severely disadvantaged people. Rawls' theory would demand positive action rather than simply refraining from acts that caused the inequalities. Otherwise the second rule of justice is not served. As a single instance, Myron may believe he has been unfairly singled out. Seen from the community's standpoint, however, the affirmative action officer's decision is the right thing to do. While society is moving toward a fairer distribution of social goods, some people, like Myron, may suffer short-term losses.

A group of public health officials is to decide how to allocate supplies of a new influenza-B vaccine. The vaccine has proven especially effective among the elderly. Some argue it should simply be placed on the market for whoever can afford it. Others favor a lottery, or a first-come-first-served basis. Still others say people in important places should be vaccinated first. What does Rawls' theory have to say? Rules of justice have tried to claim different indices of distribution, such as social value, market value, random choice, need, and merit. According to Rawls, the crucial factor is the maximin principle. The least advantaged group must receive the greatest benefit from the distribution of social good, and the poor and elderly are candidates for this group. The additional factor of greater effectiveness among the elderly is cream on the pudding. The public health officials need to find a way to distribute the vaccine among free clinics that serve geriatric patients.

Coal mining officials are deciding what position to take on pneumoconiosis (black lung disease). Present policy does not hold employers responsible for workers incurring the disease. A significant number of coal miners suffer from the debilitating disease, which is sometimes fatal. However, the officials claim that no one *has* to be a coal miner; one chooses to be. The officials feel that a compensation scheme would require the cost to be passed on to the consumer and that doing this would raise prices of many products, making American coal less competitive. It might even drive American coal into bankruptcy. Preventing the disease would cost even more. What should they do? Rawls' theory would point out two significant factors. First, the coal miners, as a group, are severely disadvantaged by the current policy. Whether all have chosen to be in the coal mines (which is unlikely) is beside the point. The question is whether they should be asked to pay disproportionately for the social good of coal. Second, driving the price of coal up, thereby favoring imported coal, may be more disadvantageous to workers and people at the bottom of the ladder than to others. Loss of jobs, increases in the welfare rolls, aggravated poverty, hunger, increased suicide rate: These results are potential outcomes of a large-scale industry going bankrupt. One needs to know more facts. Would adequate compensation for, and prevention of, black lung disease really cause bankruptcy? Or are there other factors such as the profit margin of the mining corporations? Unless a strong case is made for the mines going bankrupt, the miners have a prior moral claim for just treatment.

Assessing Rawls' Deontological Theory

Rawls' theory, we saw, takes into account critics' objections to utilitarianism and other forms of deontology. It seeks out a new direction to provide a basis for deontological theory. Specifically, it tries to remedy the oversights of earlier theories regarding rules of justice. Its success lies in its filling the gaps in utilitarianism and Kantian deontology and its giving us insights into the priority of justice. Objections that have been raised about Rawls' theory include the following.

1. The original position leaves many things unclear. We are told that individuals under the veil of ignorance know nothing of their interests, desires, plans, or purposes. They do not know whether reading a good book, watching a TV soap opera, riding a horse, or eating a candy bar brings more pleasure, yet they are asked to make a rational choice concerning the social goods of wealth, privilege, self-respect, and power. Critics claim that they lack sufficient moral knowledge about themselves to decide what Rawls has them decide and that the original position is an artificial device Rawls uses to get the answers he wants.

2. Rawls' theory is abstract and lacks relevance. The individuals in the original position are fully rational, self-interested beings. They think out moral matters under very special conditions. The rules of justice which they agree to live by have little relevance to our actual moral situations. Ordinarily, our moral understanding is quite imperfect. We are moved by feelings, moods, distractions, whims, and sudden inclinations which determine our decisions. Even when we think through an issue, depth of clarity is often lacking. What Rawls gives us is a foundation of thinking about morality in general. What we lack are the means of applying it to our fuzzy, obscure thought. We are not nearly the individuals of the original position and are not helped in ethical decision making by the examples of perfect rationality.

3. Rawls' theory offers nothing new regarding day-to-day moral decisions. We have seen how Rawls inserts most of Ross's prima facie duties in the original position. They do service for the "lower-level" ethical decisions while the two rules of justice serve the "upper-level" ones. Critics maintain that Rawls gives us no new moral ground for the moral dilemmas we need to resolve. Other critics argue that Rawls' theory falls into the same problem that utilitarianism does. Utilitarianism, we saw, allows inequalities in dealing with people if the inequalities serve social utility. Similarly, with Rawls, one could say that mandatory AIDS testing benefits everyone, even the AIDS victims, who are better off by finding out, and therefore we ought justly to force everyone to be tested. This position overrides a person's right to be respected in life decisions. Rawls' theory and utilitarianism seem to converge in permitting the violation of personal rights.

3. THE CENTRAL CONCEPTS OF ETHICS

We have examined four major ethical theories, two classical ones (utilitarianism and Kant's deontology) and two modern ones (Ross's and Rawls' deontologies). Each of these theories provides principles to deepen and ground the justification of decision making. Each is indispensable in the search for objectivity in ethical decision making. As in the nonnormative disciplines of physics and biology, the data of our experience get their final meaning and validity from theory. In ethics, as well as other normative studies, we face inherent uncertainty. To assist further the process of decision making, we will now look at some of the central concepts of ethics: autonomy, beneficence (and nonmaleficence), and paternalism; in addition, we will have a brief introduction to the concepts of rights and responsibilities in the professional setting. We can safely say that each concept receives the endorsement of all the ethical theories we discussed. In the field of professional ethics, the concepts can help broaden one's moral understanding.

1. AUTONOMY

Many decisions of ethical import in the professions presume the autonomy of the person. Autonomy has to do with the power to choose courses of action in accordance with the reasons one has for acting in that way. The idea that a person has the unique capability of giving himself or herself a rule for action comes from Kant's deontological theory. Kant compared moral choice to self-governance. Making an ethical decision amounts to legislating for oneself. Autonomy as self-determination follows directly from the second version of the categorical imperative. We ought to treat all persons, ourselves and others, as ends in themselves and not merely as means. Being an end in oneself means finding intrinsic value in one's life and one's pursuits. When our morally acceptable choices of means to our life plans are violated, we are being treated as less than persons.

We often place supreme value on an individual's autonomy. The psychiatrist who breaks confidentiality with a patient to divulge a potentially dangerous action may be blamed for disregarding the patient's rights; even though harm to another individual is threatened, violating the patient's autonomy is morally more important. The elaborate rules regulating the police officer who takes a confession of a crime also safeguard the alleged criminal's autonomy. The increasing weight of rights which consumers claim stems from the need for their autonomy in the marketplace to be protected. These examples underline the necessity for us to understand how autonomy operates in the professional field. Two questions arise: What is the meaning of autonomy of the person? What is the groundwork for autonomy in the experience of the moral community?

The Meaning of Autonomy

A person's self-governance involves a complex of moral factors, both positive and negative. We require a measure of freedom *from* certain forces as well as a freedom *to* exercise relevant powers in order to act autonomously. Autonomy must be protected from limitations and infringements on it. It must also be developed and cultivated as a human capability. The concept of autonomy is built up from a number of different levels. Some proponents think of the levels as different degrees of embodiment of the full, unrestricted concept. Others feel that autonomy exists both in a weak (restricted) and strong (unrestricted) form. The component levels of the full concept correspond to the following ideas: (1) autonomy as freedom from coercive restraint; (2) autonomy as freedom to choose; (3) autonomy as informed, reasoned choice; and (4) autonomy as choice based on the recognition of moral value. Let us turn to a discussion of the component senses of autonomy.

Autonomy as Freedom from Coercive Restraint

We think of a person as arriving at a choice about what to do in a voluntary, intentional way. Although one sometimes discovers one did what one wanted to do, we usually view choice as the reverse of having things "just happen." Questions may arise concerning how aware a person must be of his or her options, of the consequences of action, and of the effectiveness of the act in accomplishing the end. We are more certain that something has gone wrong, however, when we are restrained from the chosen act. One is no longer at liberty to act on one's choice. If we are on the way to the movies and a stranger assaults us, we are coercively prevented from doing what we want. A basic element of our freedom has been taken from us. Thomas Hobbes (1588–1679), an English philosopher, describes this aspect of autonomy, saying, "a 'freeman' is he that in those things which by his strength and wit he is able to do, is not hindered to do what he has a will to."[1]

[1]Thomas Hobbes, *Leviathan,* Part II, chap. XXI, "Of the Liberty of Subjects."

Assault is an example of direct, physical interference with our freedom of movement. Someone intends to restrain us and uses threat of harm to that end. A police officer making an arrest removes the basic degree of autonomy from the suspect. Not all coercion follows this pattern, however. The employee who discovers an illegality in the company's operations and who is threatened with loss of job is restrained in the ability to act. So are prisoners who are asked to "volunteer" for a medical research experiment and told their free time will be taken away unless they do. The threat of coercion can be implied and circumstantial. Some argue that the law may be a coercive element, such as when it makes illegal the administration of active euthanasia to patients who request it. When we take implied coercion into account, the line between forcible restraint and persuasion gets blurred. For instance, does advertising the virtues of diet pills remove a measure of freedom from the obese person who wishes to eat?

Autonomy as freedom from coercion remains clear at least in the simple case. The absence of invasion and interference is an obvious condition to acting according to one's intentions.

Autonomy as Freedom to Choose

A person may arrive, intentionally and voluntarily, at a decision to act, be free from coercion, and still not be able to act autonomously. Between the decision and the action lies a gray area, a zone in which a person may lack effective means to bring his or her choice to reality. For instance, the mother on Medicaid who wants an abortion but lives in a state that outlaws Medicaid funds for abortion lacks the means of carrying out her choice. Or the terminal patient who is too weak to carry out his decision of active euthanasia lacks the capability of seeing out his option. Or the paint pigment company which wants to dispose of waste in a nearby landfill cannot follow the chosen course of action because of EPA regulations.

Freedom from coercive restraint is the minimum negative condition for autonomy. A minimum positive condition also exists. We must have at our disposal the means of implementing our decision. Many factors take away this capability. Physical disability, legal regulation, scarcity of resources, and the lack of just or beneficent action on the part of others are a few. Removing some of the obstacles to autonomy as freedom to choose is often a responsibility of professional decision making. To put the person back in the driver's seat of choice is the goal of this degree of autonomy.

Autonomy as Informed, Reasoned Choice

Autonomy involves more than not being blocked in using effective means of choice. The first two degrees of autonomy relate only to factors external to a person. In addition, internal factors play an important role in carrying out autonomous action. An uninformed person can decide to participate in an important piece of medical research without knowing the risk factors involved. Choice is uncoerced and the person has the effective means of participating at his or her disposal, but the lack of information is crucial. The person would be acting with less than a full measure of autonomy unless he or she considered the reasons for being a human subject.

Autonomy at this level means coming to a reasoned and reasonable decision. Choice based on whimsy, blind passion, or misinformation fails to qualify as autonomous. So does choice when one's mind is distorted by alcohol, drugs, or pain. The criterion of rationality dates back to the Greek philosopher Aristotle (384–322 B.C.), who said that "choice involves a rational principle and thought."[2] Self-determination as reasoned

[2]Aristotle, *Nicomachean Ethics,* trans. David Ross (Oxford: Oxford University Press, 1925), Book III, chap. 2.

choice rules out many acts that qualify at the first two levels of autonomy. The lawyer who misinforms a client about his options in trying the case limits the client's access to information and prevents the client from coming to a rational decision. Similarly, the police officer who arrests a suspect without disclosing full information about his or her rights precludes autonomous action on the part of the suspect. The stock market trader who fails to disclose his interests in a stock to clients limits their capability for reasoned choice. The health care team which does not inform a patient of his or her condition prevent the patient from engaging in fully autonomous decisions.

Rationality since Aristotle's time is thought of as having two aspects. We need to be reasonable in our choice of the ends worth pursuing, and at the same time we need to use reason in our choice of appropriate means to the ends. The ends can be long term, like choice of career, or short term, like choice of what to say to a friend. Together, the ends and their appropriate means make up a person's life plan, the totality of things worth pursuing. Rational choice involves both aspects.

What constitutes a choice of an irrational end is open to dispute. Some argue, for instance, that choosing to end one's life is never rational. Others believe that a person can reasonably decide in favor of suicide if he or she is clear about what is happening. A profitable corporation choosing to give away its assets and go bankrupt is an example of a self-defeating, irrational action. So is the sick patient who decides never to listen to the doctor's advice. In general, choosing to pursue a goal that leads only to self-frustration illustrates the first aspect of irrationality.

Irrational choice of means represents the second aspect of rationality. The means a person uses to attain a goal must "fit" the aim. Using diet pills that weaken the body's health is an inappropriate means of controlling weight. Often the professions establish rules that specify appropriate means. The corrections officer who chooses corporal punishment in order to reprimand a prisoner uses inappropriate means; he should have relied on procedures dealing with the wrongdoing of prisoners. Likewise, the engineer who uses substandard materials chooses inappropriate means of construction since the building code specifies proper use. Sometimes choice of appropriate means to an end requires a person to postpone immediate short-term gratifications. The lawyer clerking for a justice must be willing to forgo the movies every night if he or she is to get the work done. The insomniac whose passion is good coffee needs to give up the habit in order to get a decent night's sleep.

Full rationality is an ideal. Even if we fail to meet its demands, we need to be clear on its requirements. A fully rational choice is a step in actualizing a person's life plan. It involves several factors. A person must be able to identify worthwhile ends, both long term and short term. Among the various ends, a person must then be able to prioritize and select which is most important. A person must have the capability to pick appropriate means for the list of goals. A person must be able to give up seeking short-term satisfactions when the priorities demand it. Finally, a person must be able to assess the outcome of goal seeking in order to discard inadequate means or undesirable ends. When we fall short of full rationality, we nonetheless may embody a degree of rationality in our choices. Our decisions are reasonable to the degree that they measure up to the full standard.

Autonomy at the level of informed, reasoned choice is quite unrestricted. Persons require the power to use reasons to come to decisions as well as the ability to exercise the power. Where the exercise of the power is limited, choice is not fully autonomous. Many kinds of limitations exist. One may be born with a lack of potential to reason, as is an individual with Down's syndrome. One may never have the potential sufficiently developed, because of inequalities in educational opportunity. One may have an ability to reason but not use it because of bad habits, addictions, pain, medication, or fatigue.

Autonomy as Choice Based on the Recognition of Moral Value

The highest degree of autonomy is rational self-determination "plus." It is freedom from coercion to choose on the basis of reasons "plus" the awareness that ethical reasons are most adequate in the job of determining choice. In other words, it is self-governance grounded in morality.

When a person's choice is shaped by moral concerns, a new dimension is added to self-determining. Without this addition, autonomy lacks an ethical content. An ethical egoist, we saw, always chooses so as to maximize his self-interest. His rationality may be acute and cold-blooded in attaining his ends. He is effective in choice of means and has his life plan prioritized, and so his action meets the requirements of autonomy of the third degree. However, his conduct may bring harm to others, whereas full-bodied autonomy involves respect for all persons. The egoist shows an incomplete understanding of autonomy.

This fourth and final degree of autonomy derives from Kant's deontological theory. Kant tells us, "Rational nature exists as an end in itself."[3] Autonomous action requires us to value respect for persons in our decision making, to remember that others also are self-determining beings who need a free space in order to act autonomously. To pursue our life plan at the expense of others defeats autonomy of the fourth degree. We become something less than the fully endowed person each of us potentially is. Behind Kant's idea is the notion that right action realizes the greatest degree of our humanity. Moral decisions, according to him, do not lessen what we can attain in action, but

[3]Immanuel Kant, *Groundwork of the Metaphysic of Morals,* trans. H. J. Paton (London: Hutchinson University Library, 1948), p. 96.

maximize it. His view makes right action the highest achievement of a person. Fully autonomous action may demand that we restrict seeking what we desire in order to act consistently with morality. For Kant, no sacrifice results. The gain in moral value offsets any loss.

Autonomy as self-determination "plus" rules out many actions considered autonomous at the third degree. For instance, the physician who decides it is reasonable to withhold information from a dying patient falls short of autonomous choice. He or she fails to recognize the moral value of the other person and instead treats the patient merely as a means. Or the police officer who tries to recruit a mobster to turn state's witness by lying about evidence does not act autonomously. The officer relates to the would-be witness merely as a means to bring a case to court.

Critics of autonomy as self-determination "plus" argue that the concept of autonomy should be free of moral content. For them, freedom of choice is of fundamental value. They object to adding the "plus." They argue that self-determination suffices to explain autonomy so long as we recognize the need to put limitations on self-governance. Self-determination is a very important value, but reasons exist to curb a person's rational choices in certain situations. An extreme example is the Leopold-Loeb murder case. The two young men rationally decided arbitrarily to murder someone. Their choice was consistent with the standards of self-determination but was obviously the wrong thing to do.

The understanding of autonomy using principles to limit self-determination may give us the same concept as self-determination "plus." The principles themselves are not without controversy. Furthermore, the limiting power is only prima facie, as in Ross's moral theory. The presumption is always that a person is free to do something until principled reasons strong enough to outweigh that right appear. A person has unrestricted freedom until proven bound by the limiting effect of one or another restrictive principle. The formulation makes clear that one has as much power to choose how to act that is compatible with allowing others the same measure of freedom. We will discuss five principled restrictions on a person's autonomy: the principle of paternalism, the harm principle, the offense principle, the welfare principle, and the principle of legal moralism.

The Principle of Paternalism. The principle of paternalism has two versions. The weak version states that a person's self-determination may be restricted justifiably and with reason to prevent the person from harming himself or herself. The emotionally distraught person who threatens to throw himself or herself down a flight of stairs ought to be placed under protective surveillance or even committed to an institution. Questions arise when the weak version of paternalism gets applied to habits. For instance, some argue that stiffer laws on cigarette consumption are justified in order to protect smokers from harming themselves over the long run. Critics claim that one is free to injure oneself if on the balance the course of action is preferable to avoiding the habit.

The strong version of the principle of paternalism states that a person's self-determination may be justifiably restricted in order to benefit the person. The weak principle is negative in keeping a person from self-harm. The strong principle is positive in promoting a person's good. Some justify stiffer jail terms for first offenders by the strong version. They claim that one learns about freedom and responsibility by serving time; hence, the sentence ultimately benefits a person who has broken the law.

Paternalism, in one or the other form, plays an important role in ethical decision making in the professions. Laws and public policies embody the expression of paternalism. The illegality of certain drugs and (in some locales) sexually explicit entertainment is justified by reference to this principle. A person may want to use marijuana, and not being able to use it legally places a restriction on his or her self-determination. The prohibition is justified on the basis of the harm the substance causes the user. We will examine the central concept of paternalism in a separate section.

The Harm Principle. The harm principle says that a person's self-determination may be justifiably and with reason restricted in order to prevent harm to others. The harm principle extends the scope of the weak version of paternalism into the public arena. The idea is that where one's choice is likely to bring injury to other persons, one's freedom to choose ought to be placed under moral limitation. Advocates of mandatory drug testing for commercial airlines pilots cite the harm principle. They claim testing against a pilot's will is morally justified because of the threat of potential great harm to passengers. Applying the harm principle is more obvious when the threat of harm is swift, apparent, and direct. Violent acts of assault, rape, armed robbery, and murder are justifiably precluded from choice. When a professional service is of great importance, the harm principle protects people from fraudulent actions. For instance, practicing medicine without a license is wrong because of the harm it brings.

The harm principle is not in itself controversial. Some attempts to limit personal choice on its basis, however, run the risk of dispute. Stop-and-search laws give the police a wide avenue of discretion. Individual choices may be restricted by unfair application of the laws. Similar claims have been made about vagrancy and loitering laws, laws of the "public good." Nonetheless, the appeal of the harm principle is clear. Acting so as to harm another person shows disrespect for the value of the other. Self-determination is legitimately narrowed when the choice shows a lack of respect for another's dignity.

The Offense Principle. The offense principle says that self-determination may be justifiably and with reason restricted when the act is publicly offensive. Offensive behavior makes others feel embarrassment or shame. An example is laws prohibiting nudity in public. The sight of a naked body, some argue, evokes shame in the onlookers. According to the offense principle, the right thing to do is to restrict a person's freedom to be nude in public.

The offense principle lacks the clear support which the principles of harm and paternalism have. Proponents of a ban on pornographic literature usually cite this principle. What we do not know is whether shame or discomfort in a person is a strong enough reason to restrict others' personal liberty. Critics say a person's reaction is subjective, a product of a particular environment. They argue that such reactions are not weighty enough to prohibit choices. The offense principle is sometimes used to justify civil commitment of a mentally or emotionally upset individual. Eccentric, unusual, or quirky action which offends the public is sufficient, advocates say, to deprive one of a full measure of freedom. A common objection to the offense principle is the "opening wedge" argument. It says that if public indecency is enough to take away a person's liberty, what next? Criticism of public policy? Advocating deviant social views?

The Welfare Principle. The welfare principle says that self-determination may be justifiably and with reason restricted in order to benefit others. Few people argue for a strong version of the principle, which would tyrannize personal choice in favor of social utility. A weaker version holds that one ought to give up a measure of freedom to the public good if the cost is not high. Some argue that persons ought to agree to donate their organs on the basis of the welfare principle. The cost in being free to do with one's dead body what one wishes is low, whereas the benefits to a society scarce in transplantable organs is high. Or some say corporations should be required to donate a very low percentage of their profits to the arts; the cost would be negligible while society as a whole would benefit.

The Principle of Legal Moralism. The principle of legal moralism says that a person's self-determination may be justifiably and with reason restricted in order to prevent immoral action. The view of the legal moralist sees the function of the law as enforcing morality. The immoral becomes the illegal.

Collapsing morality into law is a controversial position. Obviously the law makes many immoral acts illegal, such as rape, robbery, fraud, and different kinds of conspiracy. In a general way, laws express the moral community's position on right and wrong action. The question is whether we need to refer to the principle of legal moralism for justification. Critics point out that the harm principle, which is less objectionable, already supplies grounds to outlaw these immoral acts. We do not have to resort to a restriction on personal freedom which may be too stringent.

The principle of legal moralism is often used to justify laws against what are called "victimless crimes." Prostitution, pornography, practicing homosexuality, and gambling are examples. We have seen the offense principle work in a similar context. No person is identified as the victim of these acts, but proponents of the principle argue that they are nonetheless unjustified because they go against the common morality. Critics point out the vagueness of the position. They say that no infringement of personal freedom is warranted by the principle unless the common morality is clear on what it means.

The principle of legal moralism is cited in current debates on abortion. Those who consider abortion morally wrong urge that it be made once again illegal. Opponents recall that the same position once applied to the over-the-counter sale of contraceptives. They claim that the value of a person's freedom is great enough to require the availability of abortion as an option.

Collectively, the above principles restricting self-determination work on the third degree of autonomy—autonomy as informed, reasoned choice. Their effect is to amplify it and render it conscious of moral value. The net result is expressed in the fourth degree of autonomy, choice based on recognition of ethical worth. Not all of the five restrictions are indisputable. The harm principle carries the greatest weight of agreement behind it, the offense principle, the least. Each principle moderates an unbridled pursuit of self-interest in the direction of right action.

The Groundwork for Autonomy

We have looked at the meaning of autonomy in its different senses. Let us now turn to the second question we initially raised: What is the groundwork for autonomy in ethical theory? Both kinds of ethical theory, utilitarianism and deontology, support at the ground level an individual's autonomy. Kant's classical deontology, we have seen, makes right action contingent on respecting a person's dignity. In our choices of action, we are required to recognize the intrinsic value of a person. We face each decision as a "purely rational being." For Kant, this frame of mind informs us how to restrict ends and means of our life plan to take into account the value of the other. "Pure rationality" is self-determination "plus." It is choice tempered by moral worth. In Kant's utopian vision, we are most reasonable when we make ethics the basis of decision making.

Kant also derives autonomy from the first version of the categorical imperative. He says "the principle of autonomy is 'Never to choose except in such a way that in the same volition the maxims of your choice are also present as universal law.'"[4] This version is similar to the Golden Rule. We are asked to act so that, if everyone acted the same way, we too would have no objection. Being the recipient or the agent of the act would not change our evaluation. In both ways of justifying autonomy, Kant places limits on what one person can do with reason to another. In Kant's view, morality curbs and rechannels self-interest. The end result is a community where individuals have a greater chance of realizing their inherent potentials as persons.

Autonomy is also fundamental to utilitarian theory. Like any other value, autonomy must be justified in terms of the social utility it produces. John Stuart Mill speaks of autonomy as an almost absolute value: "The only freedom which deserves the name, is that of pursuing our own good in our own way, so long as we do not attempt to deprive others of theirs, or impede their efforts to obtain it."[5] For Mill, the pursuit of one's life plan is not an unqualified endeavor. Instead one is required to moderate it to take account of others' life plans. As Mill says, "The liberty of the individual must be thus far limited; he must not make himself a nuisance to other people."[6] The reason for limiting personal freedom is utilitarian. A community that allows a real diversity of life plans will turn out to be more stable, creative, tolerant, and intelligent. But Mill's conclusion could be factually incorrect. If a repressive community which provided no autonomy for individuals had a greater social utility, autonomy would be abandoned. Similarly, if a community of ethical egoists had greater social well-being, the argument for autonomy would be defeated. Thus the utilitarian justification differs from the Kantian one in allowing possible practices to encroach on autonomy.

[4]Kant, *Groundwork of the Metaphysic of Morals,* p. 108.
[5]John Stuart Mill, *On Liberty,* chap. 1.
[6]Ibid., chap. III, "Of Individuality, as One of the Elements of Well-being."

2. BENEFICENCE AND NONMALEFICENCE

The concepts of beneficence and nonmaleficence together make up the idea of care. In the professional context, care refers to the complex of duties by which a professional attends to the functions of his or her office and services the needs of the client. Professional care is a pervasive idea. When we blame someone for conduct unbefitting a professional, we are referring to a violation of standards of care. A frequent source of conflict between professional and private life is the concept of beneficence and nonmaleficence. The police officer, lawyer, doctor, or nurse who receives an on-call after hours faces the choice between the demands of professional care and those of personal affairs.

Beneficence comes from the Latin, meaning "doing good." Similarly, *maleficence* means "doing harm." The negative aspect of professional care consists in not doing harm; the positive aspect lies in doing good. Ancient codes of professional ethics mention both. For instance, the Hippocratic Oath for physicians says, "I will use treatment to help the sick according to my ability and judgment, but never with a view to injury and wrongdoing." To refrain from careless, malicious, thoughtless acts which cause harm to patients, and to promote their health, are the twin standards of medical care.

Of the two aspects, nonmaleficence is the clearer and less controversial. It follows from basic ethical considerations of respect for persons (deontology) or protection of individual freedom (utilitarianism). We usually agree that professionals should act in ways which avoid causing needless harm to others. The police officer who uses excessive violence making an arrest disregards the concept of nonmaleficence. So does the employer who makes working conditions difficult without increasing employee benefits. So does the lawyer who presents a client's case with grossly inadequate preparation.

Nonmaleficence does not mean avoiding harm altogether. In some cases, no single alternative may achieve a result free of injury. For instance, medical procedures may produce pain as a side effect. The sense of nonmaleficence is the avoidance of harm unless the action promises a greater good. The lawyer who plea-bargains for a client helps cause injury in the form of a sentence, but since the punishment is less than would have occurred for the greater crime, the lawyer meets the terms of nonmaleficence. Nonmaleficence may be violated even in the absence of malice. A nurse who with no ill intent administers the wrong medication to a patient, causing injury, has failed to act with nonmaleficence. The nurse's negligence resulted in avoidable damage to the patient. Providing due care in the professional role is part of the sense of nonmaleficence.

Defining matters of due care in the professions presents us with several difficulties. First we must avoid standards that try to do the impossible. Perfect judgment and impeccable reasoning are too close to perfection to have practical meaning. Our knowledge of outcomes too is less than perfect. For instance, the employer who insulated piping with asbestos in 1950 in order to create better working conditions did not know what we know now about the material. His nonmaleficent act turned out to be the wrong thing to do. Similarly, the uncertainty surrounding medical and juridical procedures reminds us that the health care and legal professions possess only partial knowledge of the field. We ought not hold these professions responsible for every injury or death occurring to their patients or clients.

Second, we customarily recognize a bare minimum of professional due care. Licensing laws, certification boards, degree programs, and accreditation of training facilities are ways in which we ensure getting the bare minimum. This baseline guarantees a certain level of care. We demand that professionals acquire a minimum level of knowledge before undertaking the responsibilities of the role. Some argue that professional education encourages communication, prudence, and caution as values. These characteristics give further evidence that a person has attained the bare minimum. The strength of the evidence is a matter of dispute. Critics point out that even after getting an acceptable education, a professional may be careless in work and show poor judgment in thought.

Finally, discussion of due care or nonmaleficence must include the notion of risk. Uncertainty of outcome casts a shadow backwards to the intention to act. A professional need not cause actual injury to a person to be blamed for maleficent action. If the act exposes the person to a degree of possible harm greater than it needs to be, the professional may be liable to claims of maleficence for failing to exercise due care. The police officer arresting an armed felon in a crowded public place may be guilty of maleficence in the line of duty. So may be the doctor who unnecessarily orders diagnostic tests which carry a high degree of risk. The factor of risk in nonmaleficence does not mean one should abandon all risk taking in professional care. Unnecessary risk is risk that places a person in greater danger of harm than he or she would have in a lower-risk procedure. Drawing the line between a reasonable and an unreasonable degree of risk is often difficult and requires technical information. The layperson may be in no position to evaluate a situation. Peer review boards and internal security panels are needed in these cases to determine maleficence.

Few critics raise objections regarding nonmaleficence as a legitimate part of professional care. Avoiding harm to others is a principle having universal acclaim among ethical theories. The second aspect of professional care, beneficence, is more controversial. Beneficence urges us to promote the welfare of other people. It requires more than respecting the free space of individual autonomy. Benficence insists that we assist others to realize their life plans. Kant, we saw, includes beneficence as a wide duty to others. He argues that respect for the absolute value of the person requires us to adopt policies advancing the goods of others. Ross also lists the duty of beneficence among his prima facie duties. Particularly with respect to improving the condition of others' intelligence, pleasure, or virtue, the duty of beneficence gives us "at first glance" a reason to act. On the other hand, the utilitarian sees obstacles to making beneficence a standard of professional care. The utilitarian believes that we are worthy of praise when we act beneficently but breach no duty when we do not. For him, beneficence is usually above and beyond the call of duty. It belongs to the category of the *meritorious* or *supererogatory.* One is worthy of praise for meritorious or supererogatory action but is not blamable for not acting.

Generally, the professions require something more than nonmaleficence in the delivery of care. Between avoiding injury and promoting welfare lies a large gray area. In using discretionary power, does a police officer do more than avoid harm in not arresting a suspect if the person remains influenced by destructive forces? The physician, we saw, recognizes beneficence as well as nonmaleficence in the standard of health care. The same is true of other health care professionals, such as nurses, clinical psychologists, therapists, and social workers. Some argue that lawyers are also duty-bound by beneficence.

Even where beneficence is part of the professional "due care," the matter of drawing the limits of duty is difficult. We do not expect our professionals to sacrifice all private interest. Nor do we expect them to be heroes or saints—though we give praise if they are. On the other hand, the corporate manager or engineer who always places a hobby ahead of getting the job done is at fault. The idea of reasonable sacrifice is an appealing way to indicate where beneficence leaves off and meritorious action begins.

Professional care—beneficence and non-maleficence—also has a social dimension. No professional is an island. Each professional's capability of providing due care is dependent on how well the profession provides access to care. The best example is in the medical profession. The individual physician's quality of health care depends on conditions of medical care in the community. Sanitation, immunization programs, food inspection, water treatment, and quarantine are recognized standards of public health. Without these measures, medical due care would be at a substantially lower level. Direct funding to the disadvantaged through Medicare opens health care to people who are otherwise unable to receive adequate medical attention. Indirect funding to medical research develops techniques and medication which further enhance health care. Public education regarding preventive medicine is yet another step. We need to broaden our view of professional due care to take these important social conditions into account.

Distributive Justice

The social dimension of professional care reminds us that beneficence and nonmaleficence are more than personal duties. The moral community has its role in providing certain aspects of care. In a general way, the social dimension of beneficence and nonmaleficence concerns the distribution of burdens and benefits, the things we as a society hold of value. It concerns the matter of *distributive justice.* Ross's deontological theory, which we saw left duties of justice explicitly out of its account, perhaps saw them in this way. Burdens and benefits such as income, taxes, welfare payments, voting, military service, education, and public office are included in the distributive problem. So is opportunity of access to professional services such as legal counsel, hospitalization, and police protection. We need to take a brief look at the question of distributive justice in order to complete our discussion of professional care.

The problem of distributive justice observes that we lack enough of certain social goods to provide everyone with enough, in accordance with what he or she needs. Some people argue that health care is an example of a scarce social good. Individuals who need health care attention are unable to get it because none is available where they are, or because they lack the resources to afford it. Some people are rich, some are poor, and some are in the right place at the right time. Distributive justice then asks: On what moral basis ought we to justify giving certain people a share of the goods? With regard to health care, how ought we to decide who receives care and who does not?

Several bases for making just distributions have been suggested. All formulas, however, conform to a bare minimum standard, called the formal principle of justice, or the *fairness* principle. This principle expresses the exceptionless portion of the concept of distributive justice. It says that similar cases ought to be treated in similar ways. A more elaborate formula of distribution must not allow similar cases to be treated dissimilarly. Doing so would disregard fairness. If two individuals in similar circumstances have similar health care needs but only one is to receive attention, then the formula is in error. By the same token, if two individuals receive different treatment, we want to know the relevant way or ways they are dissimilar.

To know more than the bare minimum of fairness is imperative to a workable principle of justice. Before a principle can be applied to situations, it must be made *substantial* or *material,* that is, it must tell us what factors of a person's situation are relevant in deciding whether two cases are similar. If we learn that one person's situation is relevantly different from another's, we are justified in treating each differently. Arguments supporting a material principle are usually drawn from ethical theory. The application of material principles gives us particular laws, practices, or public policies which are held to be just. The four material principles of justice which different theories

have offered are the basis of need, the basis of equality, the basis of social contribution, and the basis of effort. Because we must be brief here, we will consider them without carefully delineating the theoretical grounds.

The Basis of Need

The formula for the distribution of goods on the basis of need is that to those with a greater need goes the greater share. An individual's need shows us the relevant factor from which to make fair shares. Those with a greater need for health care, police protection, or corporate profit ought to have more of that social good. Although each person receives different proportions of the goods, the formula assumes that everyone has met his or her basic needs. Critics challenge the use of need as a basis by asking whether fairness is served in ignoring those who lack an outstanding need of one or another good. They also question what counts as a need. Some opponents, for instance, reject health care or education as a need. Even if we agree on "hard-core" needs like food, shelter, and clothing, what about the psychological and mental conditions for pursuing a life plan?

The Basis of Equality

The formula for distributing goods on the basis of equality is equal shares to all. Equality as a basis for justice rejects as relevant factors differences between individuals such as need, social contribution, or effort. Instead, it claims that everyone is entitled to be treated the same in all respects while sharing the goods. Equality finds its strongest appeal when a society enjoys just enough of the good to go around. Under these conditions, dividing shares on the basis of need leaves some people short. When the efforts of a few individuals produce a great surplus of goods, critics argue that equality is an unfair basis because the work of those persons ought justly to be recognized.

The Basis of Social Contribution

The formula for distributing goods on the basis of social contribution is that each person is entitled to a share proportional to his or her contribution to society. The idea makes an appeal to how justice works in a small group. If a group tends a garden together, the fair way to divide the harvest is by how much work each one puts in. Another basis seems unfair to the collective initiative. When we look at complexly structured modern societies, however, social contribution as a basis encounters problems. Farmers, assembly line workers, soldiers, professionals, entertainers, and investors all make a social contribution. Some create goods, others provide services, still others help people further their life plans. How are we to decide how much each one puts into the social garden? Critics of social contribution as a basis for assigning fair shares advance another argument. They say that society as a whole is responsible for creating most goods. To look at individuals' contributions is therefore a wrong approach.

The Basis of Effort

The formula for distributing social goods on the basis of effort is that to each is given according to his or her degree of effort. The appeal of the basis of effort is obvious with a team project. If the team wins, we feel that the greatest share of the reward belongs to the ones whose hard work made the victory possible. Similarly, if the star turns in a lackadaisical performance, we feel that he or she does not deserve as much as the ones who worked hard.

Using effort as the basis of fair shares assumes that everyone has equal opportunity to turn in his or her best performance. Lack of effort is understood to be a matter of personal decision. Critics point out that the assumption is shortsighted. Social equality is imperfect. Because of job availability, prejudice, lack of education, or peer pressure, one may want to do a good job but still be unable to. Equal access to good performance is not a reality. Critics also point out that a person's state of health, handicap, or emotional misfortune may also ruin chances of attaining a personal best.

The four material bases for distributive justice may seem abstract and difficult to apply to the problem of treating people in need of professional services beneficently and nonmaleficently. However, they provide standards of a just society in which access to professional care is guaranteed to everyone. Similarly, they give us guidelines in our day-to-day dealings with professional services which assure us that not only the rich, clever, and vocal receive their fair share.

3. PATERNALISM

The concept of paternalism comes to us from the image of a traditional, male-centered authority, like feudalism, where those in command regulated conduct of subordinates and supplied their needs. In law and public policy, paternalism is given as the justification for different ways of interfering coercively with personal freedom. In ethical decision making, paternalism is the call of professional authority to intervene in matters of a client's self-determination by appeals to the interests of the client himself or herself. We often see the claims of paternalism and autonomy on opposite sides of the fence.

The concept of paternalism derives from John Stuart Mill's book *On Liberty* (1859). It has been formulated by Gerald Dworkin as "the interference with a person's liberty of action justified by reasons referring exclusively to the welfare, good, happiness, needs, interests, or values of the person being coerced."[7] Mill's discussion of paternal-

---

[7]Gerald Dworkin, "Paternalism," *The Monist* (LaSalle, Ill.), 56, no. 1 (January 1972), 65.

ism is in the defense of personal rights at the expense of state authority. Mill argues against paternalism in the law. For instance, the law against selling oneself into slavery, which is to protect the freedom of the would-be seller against a foolish act, is not justifiable on paternalistic grounds. Laws often carry the threat of punishment for their violation, a coercive means.

In the context of professional decision making, however, we need a broader concept of paternalism. Autonomy, we saw, may be encroached upon at a number of different levels. Restriction by coercive threat of harm is only one way. Paternalistic interference occurs in many other ways. The lawyer or nurse who uses deception in communicating information to a client violates a person's autonomy. So does the physician or clinical psychologist who, for the patient's own good, makes public medical information given by a patient in confidence. So does the corporate manager who deliberately lies to employees concerning a job in order for them to have an easier time at it. The broadened concept of paternalism refers to any infringement on a person's autonomy which is justified in terms of the person's good, interests, or welfare.

Paternalism in the context of professional decision making is a powerful concept. It permits limitations of personal liberty in the name of professional authority, expertise, specialization, or superior judgment. Can it be justified? Let us look back to Mill's original insight. Speaking of morally permissible restrictions on autonomy, Mill says:

> that the sole end for which mankind are warranted, individually or collectively, in interfering with the liberty of action of any of their number is self-protection. That the only purpose for which power can be rightfully exercised over any member of a civilized community, against his will, is to prevent harm to others. He cannot rightfully be compelled to do or forbear because it will be better for him to do so, because it will make him happier,

because, in the opinion of others, to do so would be wise, or even right.[8]

Mill tells us that the only reason for infringing upon a person's autonomy is the harm principle. Only when the outcome of someone's act threatens injury to others ought we to limit the individual's action. If no other person is involved, if the consequences damage only the agent, we have no justification for interfering.

Mill rejects paternalism as a ground for restricting autonomy. He bases his argument on the principle of utility. Utility shows us that stopping a person's potentially harmful act is the right thing to do. The damage to others' well-being would outweigh any loss of freedom the individual suffers. But if one threatens harm only to oneself? Applying the principle of utility, Mill finds great value in individual self-determination. On the whole, society gains by the unrestricted exercise of personal choice. Mill says, "Mankind are greater gainers by suffering each other to live as seems good to themselves, than by compelling each other to live as seems good to the rest."[9] Minimizing paternalistic interference maximizes social utility.

Kant's deontological theory also rules out encroaching paternalistically on individual freedom. Autonomy, according to Kant, is action based on the recognition of the moral value of the person. Autonomous action always treats the other not merely as a means to an achievement but as a person worthy of dignity. Paternalism carries with it a presumption against a person's capabilities of self-governance. The paternalistic point of view claims one suffers from a weakened sense of reason, an ineffectiveness in means, or a powerlessness in body, and it argues for the necessity of taking care of one's autonomous pursuits "in the meantime." Kant's theory, however, rejects the paternalistic appeal to care-taking. It maintains that any

[8]Mill, *On Liberty,* chap. 1, "Introductory."
[9]Ibid.

breach, even if temporary, of a person's autonomy is unjustified.

Both utilitarianism and classical deontology deny the grounds for paternalistic action. With Mill's rugged individualism, ''The only freedom which deserves the name, is that of pursuing our own good in our own way, so long as we do not attempt to deprive others of theirs, or impede their efforts to obtain it.''[10] What Mill leaves out of his account are those individuals *in*capable of pursuing their life plan. Three different kinds of incapacity exist. First, individuals whose abilities have not yet developed, matured, or received training cannot govern themselves. Infants and children are examples. Second, individuals suffering permanent or nearly permanent impairment of the abilities cannot choose for themselves. Examples include the congenitally severely mentally handicapped, as well as those who lost the power of self-determination, such as the persistently vegetative patient. Third, individuals undergoing temporary loss of self-determination are not in a position to pursue their life plan. Persons under heavy sedation, in emotional crisis, under agonizing pain, or in temporary civil commitment are examples.

Professional care takes very different attitudes for each of these groups of individuals. For the young, we feel the need to have a designated proxy to make decisions with regard to legal, medical, and business matters. Our understanding is that the proxy stands in for the young person only until he or she comes of responsible age. For the chronically incapacitated, we also recognize the power of proxy consent, in the person of a relative, friend, or an agent of the state. In this case the proxy is thought to have a near-permanent status. For the temporarily incapacitated, the proxy is valid only as long as the debilitated condition exists. Afterward the person resumes full authority over his or her life choices.

Granting proxy authority to all three

classes of incapacitation shows the professional's willingness to entertain a weakened version of paternalism. Paternalistic interference is allowable in cases of permanently damaged autonomy where the threat of harm to self is real. In cases of temporary injury, paternalistic interference is allowable where the goal is to restore the full measure of autonomy to the person. Notice that neither instance of weakened paternalism affects Mill's or Kant's rejection of full-strength paternalism. Neither Mill nor Kant considers individuals whose capability for realizing a life plan is diminished. With individuals who retain total authority over self-determination, no paternalistic intervention is allowable. All their choices are up to themselves.

Provision for a weakened version of paternalism is compatible with our experience of the moral life. Paternalism also appears to be essential to decision making in the professions. Difficulties arise in trying to specify the range of incapacitation in which paternalism validly operates. Autonomy, we saw, is a complex, multilevel concept. In different ways, external coercion, misinformation, and ineffective reasoning prevent one from being autonomous. The third of these, damage (temporary or permanent) to one's rational capacity, provides us with guidelines for paternalistic intervention. Not being able to apply reasoning to practical situations is evidence that an individual requires support for autonomy. For example, a severe mental handicap sometimes leaves an individual unable to feed and wash himself or herself. Suppose that a handicapped individual decides to live alone. We have good grounds for doubting that person's survival. The connection between what the individual wants and what he or she is capable of getting is questionable. Since the life has value, a paternalistic intervention is justified. For another example, the emotionally imbalanced person on a felony charge who insists on representing himself or herself in court may be incapable for periods of time of coherent reasoning. To

[10]Ibid.

lose the case would mean a long jail term. Incarceration is a further constraint on personal autonomy. This incapacitation is an argument for a court-appointed attorney to do the legal work. This decision is paternalistic.

The weakened version of paternalism has two aspects. First, it justifies paternalistic action on the basis of prevention of self-harm on behalf of seriously incapacitated individuals whose condition is chronic. Second, it also justifies paternalistic action on the basis of potential self-harm on behalf of incapacitated individuals whose full autonomy is expected to be restored. The second aspect is called *custodial paternalism.*

Both aspects of the weakened version of paternalism present difficulties. Regarding the first, chronic emotional imbalance, as a condition, raises questions about whether the individual even qualifies as autonomous. When an individual is unable to formulate ends, determine appropriate means, and effectually utilize the means, a crucial element of rationality is missing. Lacking "zero-level" rationality, an individual appears to fall short of the threshold of self-determination. If we justify paternalism by reference to autonomy, such individuals fall through the safety net. Their autonomy is not greatly incapacitated. It is missing. In this case, a defense of the weakened version of paternalism collapses into that of strong paternalism. Strong paternalism, as we saw in Mill, tries to justify its interventions in terms of the benefits it brings to the individuals.

Second, custodial paternalism (paternalism which is justified as long as it tries to restore autonomy) also has difficulties. The problem lies in drawing the line between reason and unreason. For instance, the police sometimes incarcerate a homeless person temporarily. They defend the action by saying the person gets a shower, a free meal, and a bed and is kept from trouble. The assumption is that certain lifestyles show inherent irrationality and that anyone having the lifestyle is a candidate for custodial paternalism. In a similar vein, police advocates of custodial paternalism argue in favor of su-

icide intervention as a policy. They say (as Kant did) that an attempt to kill oneself is inherently irrational. One's autonomy is in need of a caretaker. In both examples, applying the weakened version of paternalism begs the question. Individuals may be driven to live in the streets, or to kill themselves, out of despair, desperation, disorientation, or illness. Their rational decision making may then suffer. Their lifestyle or action expresses an incapacitation. On the other hand, homelessness or suicide may be entered by deliberation, applying cold reason to the options, and making the choice. The decision may be consistent with a life plan, or with the sudden revelation of new value. In such cases, paternalistic interference is not warranted, and the professional decision ought to acquiesce to the individual's chosen action.

The custodial situation is the most frequent occasion of paternalism in the professional context. The person viewed by the professional is incapacitated by illness, injury, crime victimization, or lack of information. The information lack may result from the different knowledge that layperson and professional enjoy. Critics point out that a paternalistic attitude may be built into the professional role, and they advocate an entirely different model to build professional–patient relations. One piece of evidence in their favor is the fact that the most common form of paternalism in the professions is withholding "the whole truth" from clients. For instance, in the health care professions, patients usually do not have enough knowledge about how their bodies work to understand their condition. A health care professional may cite the patient's ignorance when passing misinformation or deceptive information on to the patient. Lack of concern for truthfulness, critics say, shows a paternalistic attitude. So does the claim made by health care professionals that patients "don't want to hear the truth," or that the truth would damage the progress of the patient.

Similar practices exist in the legal and

criminal justice professions. The technical nature of the subject matter combines with client ignorance to produce a paternalistic relationship. The lawyer does not communicate all the facts which would make it harder for the client. His or her main interest is to allay the client's fear, not to respect autonomy. As with the health care professional, we need to ask how to draw the line between not telling the whole truth and using deceptive means to communicate. In the criminal justice professions, such as with police and corrections officers, the difficulty lies in the fact of dissimilarity before the law. The offender has broken the law. The suspect is under arrest in order to be tried before the law. The professional, in both cases, must relate to someone whose autonomy has been fractured. Nonetheless, the police and corrections officers are bound by duties of truthfulness, at least with respect to the prisoner's and the suspect's legal rights. The extent of paternalism in these professions needs to be examined more closely.

4. RIGHTS AND RIGHT ACTION

Ethics fosters diversity of opinion. It offers us a pluralism of language for expressing our viewpoints concerning right action. Its richness makes it difficult to focus on issues of rightness and wrongness. Obligations, responsibilities, exceptions, duties, rights, extenuations, exclusions, and entitlements make a complicated picture. For expedience, discussion often centers on one aspect, rights. Especially with ethical decision making in the professions, we find that our concerns can be expressed adequately in the language of rights. Other key moral terms may be translatable into the rights of individuals (or agencies) entering into the situation. Where they are not so translatable, the result is still beneficial since we are left with fewer moral terms to deal with.

We are accustomed to speak and think

morality in terms of rights. Our Bill of Rights gives protections for basic freedoms. The Patient's Bill of Rights, the G.I. Bill of Rights, and the U.N. Declaration of Human Rights are other examples of organizations limiting infringements on personal liberty for different groups. The central concept of autonomy is spoken of as the right to self-determination or, as the Constitution puts it, the right to "life, liberty, and the pursuit of happiness." In the day-to-day experience of professionals, rights play an important part. The arresting officer, by the Miranda rule, must read the suspect his or her rights upon arrest. Corporate managers are familiar with employee claims about a right to unionize. Nursing professionals argue for a right to withhold agreement with a physician's orders. We hear about a woman's right to choice (regarding abortion), the fetus's right to life, a patient's right to die, the rights of visitation of prisoners, the right to adequate legal defense, and the right to enter a competitive market. We even hear about animals' rights and the rights of an ecosystem.

Critics charge that the language of rights comes too easily. Rights have proliferated. We no longer know which kinds of beings have what rights. For instance, does the fetus which dies unborn have a right to nonabusive care? Or does an endangered species have the right to continued existence, if that requires the relocation of a major water project? Critics also say that when many rights apply to a situation, we cannot come to an ethical decision about whose right is most important. Does the fetus's right outweigh the mother's right to choose a lifestyle in accordance with her desires? Does the endangered species' right override the rights of the company's stockholders favoring a dam, or the rights of the potential subscribers who want electrical power? Finally, critics argue that grounding rights in deeper principles and in moral theory is often difficult. For instance, does an unborn individual who may have in potential the same rights as a living person get them from the concept of autonomy? Does the concept apply to the yet unborn? Or, if endangered species have rights, since they are not persons, from what idea does one derive the rights?

A right, in a formal sense, gives one the power, privilege, or entitlement to do something or not to be done to in some way. A right says that one is at liberty to act, or not to be acted on, in a certain way. It is a specific recipe for freedom. The right to own property, the right to a jury trial, the right to freedom of speech, and the right to vote are good examples.

Rights come in an astonishing array. Rights are *positive* or *negative,* depending on whether one is free to do something or free from interference to choose other things. The right to die is a positive right; the right not to be harmed (nonmaleficence) is a negative one. Some argue that certain rights are *inalienable* or *absolute,* such as the right not to be a slave. Different categories of rights exist in different spheres of action. The law recognizes *legal* rights, such as the right to practice law if one has passed the examination, or not to testify on matters of medical confidentiality. Our political institutions recognize *political* rights, such as the right to fair representation in governmental affairs. Our immediate concern is with *moral* rights, guaranteed by ethical principles. Examples are the right to quality professional care, the right to the truth in one's own case, and the right to die with dignity.

To complicate matters more, having a right and exercising it rightly are two different things. Medical professionals enjoy the right not to communicate information on a patient's medical condition to people outside the immediate family. However, the nurse who keeps a patient's dangerous psychosis private may be doing the wrong thing if warning a potential victim would save a life.

Even with the difficulties in the language of rights, the widespread use of rights in ethical decision making requires us to be as clear as we can about what a right is. What

does it mean to say that we have a right to something? The meaning has three aspects.

1. *A right is correlated with a duty which other persons bear toward us with respect to the right.* The duty is either not to interfere with the freedom the right expresses or to provide something directly to us. For example, if we have the right to confidential medical records, then health care professionals are duty-bound to keep our information from falling into the hands of unauthorized persons or agencies. Or, if we have the right to have our legal rights told to us upon arrest, the arresting police officers have the duty to provide the information. In both cases, our right is violated if the professional fails to keep his or her correlative duty.

The right is positive when it is correlated with a duty to provide the bearer of the right with some good or benefit. The right is negative when its correlative duty is not to interfere with the actions of the rights holder. People who advance the right to health care mean that society is bound by the correlative duty to provide the means of health care to anyone who claims the right. The right to health care is an example of a positive right. People who object to wiretapping and who claim the right to privacy mean that society has the correlative duty not to interfere with the personal communications of its members. The right to privacy is an example of a negative right. Notice in each case that the holder of the correlative duty needs to be identified. Specifying rights in terms of correlative duties requires that we know what person, group, or agency is under obligation with respect to the rights. Where we cannot, critics presume that no such right exists. People who object to the idea of human rights such as the right to work (named in the U.N. Declaration of Human Rights) argue that no group is actually duty-bound to provide persons with work. The absence of such a group means that the right itself does not exist.

Some critics claim that specifying rights in terms of correlative duties casts too wide a net. They say the only rights are legal rights, those given by law. The law is a system of codified rules which provides means of enforcing correlative duties and providing compensation for victims of rights violation. Without the means of enforcement and redress, critics say that a right is another way of talking about a value. Proponents of this point of view reject many rights we have seen operative in the ethical decision making of professionals. The right of being told the truth, the right to adequate legal services, and the right to a pollution-free environment are examples of moral rights having questionable legal status. For someone holding that the only rights are legal ones, such moral rights are fictions.

2. *A right provides an individual with a guarantee of autonomy in the free pursuit of his or her interest.* A right defines a "free space" where one must be left at liberty to choose to do or not to do a course of action. Any intrusion by others into the free space is prohibited except for the most weighty reasons. For instance, the right one has to choose the professional one wants to use means that no person, agency, or organization has the moral authority to make the selection. Nor does one have to seek the permission of some other person, agency, or organization before making the choice. One reason for the apparent multiplication of personal rights today is the increased threat of intrusion into the free space. Our rights, as guarantees of autonomy, are articulated as each threat is identified. The moral term for speaking of the noninvasive zone belonging to each of us is the right of privacy. Our right to privacy, which has a legal basis in the Bill of Rights, becomes more defined as new protections to autonomy are added to our moral understanding. We need to bear in mind that our experience of the moral world is not a static affair but one always in the process of resolution.

3. *A right gives a person a justification for doing something as well as a reason for seeking the protection of others when exercising the right is thwarted.* In ethical decision making we look for reasons in support of a course of action. Rights provide us with reasons for doing or refraining from doing. The reasons may not be on balance the ones that tell us what to do, but they are factors in the complex weighing of reasons during ethical decision making. Violation of an individual's rights is a reason to seek the help of other persons in rectifying the situation. For example, the client who believes his or her rights to confidentiality has been violated by a lawyer is entitled to bring the facts to the attention of others. Because a right has a correlative duty on the part of a person, agency, or group, violations of rights ought to be investigated and (if necessary) redressed by the proper organization. Many professions, like physicians, lawyers, and the police, have created internal review boards to oversee violations of rights. The violation of a right is a serious moral matter, and potential rights violations occupies a good deal of ethical decision making in the professions.

4. CONFLICTS IN DECISION MAKING

We have had two main tasks in this introductory unit. First, we have tried to provide an understanding of the important ethical theories available to professional decision making today. The account of the right and wrong thing to do, as well as the matter of moral value, gives us a solid basis for justifying ethical choices. Second, we have reviewed some major moral concepts. These concepts enter into many professional deliberations about what to do about a situation. Understanding them allows us to follow the arguments used to justify a decision.

Without understanding ethical theory and the important ethical concepts, the selections which occupy the major part of the book lose much of their benefit. Confronting the moral issues of professional decision making, people invariably find themselves relying on theory and concepts. To study the issues without the background in theory and concept is like building a house without tools: It *could* be done, but it would not stand the test of opposing forces. We expect a professional decision to meet the opposition with reliability, endurance, and confidence. These virtues of a sound decision-making process derive from the grounding in theory and concept.

Another purpose exists for our discussion of ethical theory and concepts. Nothing in ethics, we saw, is immune to revision. The nature of ethical decision making requires a constant openness to new facts, moral considerations, and theoretical discoveries. The selections give us the chance to test the theories. Just as scientific theories are subject

to scrutiny in test cases, so are ethical ones. Within each profession, one or another ethical theory, principle, or concept may seem more satisfactory than others. Some may lead to contradictory conclusions which are difficult to accept. Others may remain vague and ambiguous in areas demanding careful definition of assumption. Still others may give definitions to key ideas but may rest on ideas that are troublesome or questionable. The back-and-forth checking of ethical theory against practical results may be slow and tedious. Yet it is similar to the process of arriving at a particular moral choice. Both the application of theory to practice and the making of a justified ethical decision are examples of *dialectics,* the study of how opposing viewpoints collide, interact, and get resolved.

People approaching ethics for the first time are often overwhelmed by the controversy. They take conflict as a sign that no answers exist, any position can be taken, and whoever says the most is likely to win. We saw earlier the dangers of relativism. When we take a shortsighted view, we overlook the fact that controversy is an essential phase of arriving at a viable ethical decision. Consensus ethics is not a real option. It omits the hard work of relating to opposing positions. Choice arrived at by easy consensus is likely not to work.

Well-thought-out positions emerge only through exchange. This means that the challenge of ethical decision making is communication. A person may be familiar with theories and concepts and may know how to come to a justified position on a professional matter, but unless communication is kept open with others holding different positions, moral dilemmas are not resolved. They are avoided. Open communication means working together to clarify facts and concepts. It also means digging until the deeper principles begin to appear. Controversy over deeper principles and engaging a moral theory signals us that we are putting more important reasons for choice on the table. It tells us that our initial impatience with conflict has given way to a more objective way of arriving at a decision. Formulation of reasons at this stage is crucial for justification.

People refuse to meet the challenge of communication in different ways. One is expedience. "We have to do something, anything!" is the way this person thinks. For decisions made in the heat of the moment, expedience often wins out. Another is dogmatism. The person who holds a position without giving in to strong opposing reasons and without offering a further defense of his or her own is being dogmatic. The dogmatic person says, "I am right and you can't prove me wrong." A third way to refuse the challenge of communication is to hold out for the "best" choice. The "best" choice is indisputable, unanimously agreed upon, and unrevisable. At any point in the process of decision making, the person waiting for the "best" finds an inadequacy. "Show me something better," he or she says.

In weighing reasons, we sometimes need to be satisfied with less than the "best" justification. The process remains open, so our hope may be for the "best." However, the demands of practicality require us to settle for the best *possible* reason for doing or not

doing something. Sometimes we adopt positions that are still in the development stage. We are able to show the inadequacies of opposing positions, but our reasons are exploratory. We have not yet uncovered the combination of ethical theory principle, and concept that gives us the confidence that the decision is reliably grounded. We may even be able to show possible problems in what we think is the right thing to do.

In the selections that follow, different positions are taken and defended by their authors. In some, authors tell us that they are exploring a ground and that the position lacks the weight of the "best" reason for choice. In others, authors analyze an opposing position to show the contradictory conclusions it yields. In others, examples showing contrary evidence to the author's position are given. The many different positions have one thing in common: They meet the challenge of communication in the process of arriving at an ethical decision. They share an awareness of participating in a search for resolving difficult moral conflicts. None shows the strains of dogmatism, thinking itself beyond criticism. Professional ethics—the ethics of the health care professions, law, criminal justice, business, and the technological professions—is a field in which the legitimate questions outnumber the answers. As in any field of thinking, a good question goes further than a good answer. We need to retain a sense of the process and development in the field as well as the means of evaluating and criticizing provisional results as they appear. Not much more ought to be expected of us. Careful, diligent appraisals of others' work in professional ethics shows our own thinking to be responsible and professional.

SUGGESTED FURTHER READING
FOR UNIT I

Brandt, Richard B., *Ethical Theory.* Englewood Cliffs, N.J.: Prentice-Hall, 1959.

Frankena, William K., *Ethics.* Englewood Cliffs, N.J.: Prentice-Hall, 1963.

Fried, Charles, *Right and Wrong.* Cambridge, Mass.: Harvard University Press, 1978.

Goldman, Alan, *The Moral Foundations of Professional Ethics.* Totowa, N.J.: Rowman and Littlefield, 1980.

Ladd, John, *Ethical Relativism.* Belmont, Calif.: Wadsworth Publishing Co., 1973.

Taylor, Paul W., *Principles of Ethics: An Introduction.* Encino, Calif.: Dickenson, 1975.

Wellman, Carl, *Morals and Ethics.* New York: Scott, Foresman, 1975.

White, Alan R., *Rights.* Oxford: Clarendon Press, 1984.

Williams, Bernard, *Morality: An Introduction to Ethics.* New York: Harper and Row, 1972.

UNIT II

ETHICS AND THE HEALTH CARE PROFESSIONS

Ethical dilemmas in the field of health care involve some of the most troubling and dramatic incidents of professional life. The task of applied ethics is to provide a reasoned and justifiable response to the question, "What is the right thing to do (in a particular situation)?" Health care professionals have to make literally life-and-death decisions, and often they must decide quickly, without the luxury of time for reflection. In order to develop a moral consciousness to guide their choices, they need a firm grounding in ethical principles, combined with an understanding of the nature of justifications. The material in this unit—together with Unit I—is aimed at providing the necessary groundwork.

Many problem areas in health care ethics are not new: abortion and euthanasia are examples. However, recent advances in medical technology have added new dimensions to old questions and fostered a sense of urgency in attempts to resolve them. In the case of euthanasia, for instance, techniques have been developed to prolong biological functioning in persons who are irretrievably comatose and in neonates with severe defects. Individuals who previously would have died can now be sustained at some level, sometimes for years. The question arises whether an organism with no more than artificially maintained respiration and heartbeat is truly alive. Is it right to prolong such a life? The line between life and death, once easily recognized, has become agonizingly difficult to locate.

Shifts in social patterns and attitudes also affect issues in health care ethics. For example, the changing status of women in American society has had an impact on views concerning the morality of abortion. As women gain greater independence and rights of self-determination, more importance has been placed on the right of an individual woman to choose whether or not to bear a child. Changes in women's career patterns have increased the demand for family planning, with abortion as the last-resort means to terminate unwanted pregnancies.

While some problems are long-standing ones, others have come to light as a direct result of technological innovation. Reproductive techniques like *in vitro* fertilization and long-term preservation of sperm and ova by freezing raise ethical questions that are unprecedented. Still another source of problems is the changed setting of contemporary health care. The one-on-one relation of physician and patient has given way to a complex pattern of institutional care. The diversity of professionals in the institutional setting makes it harder to fix responsibility and aggravates problems of communication and authority.

The first chapter of this unit focuses on the relations between patients and professionals. Separate sections are devoted to the issues of Paternalism, Confidentiality, Informed Consent, and Truth Telling. The underlying theme of the chapter is the nature of communication and authority in the professional–patient relationship. Traditional medical practice is grounded in paternalism and places strong emphasis on professional authority. Dissatisfaction with the traditional approach has led to greater awareness of patients' rights to know the truth and to make their own choices.

The values of autonomy and self-determination play an important role in issues of reproductive health, the subject of Chapter 6. The problem areas examined are Abortion, Selective Abortion, Genetic Screening, and Reproductive Technologies. Conflicts exist between those who support women's right to make personal reproductive choices and those who believe that fertilized ova have a right to live. New techniques for examining a fetus *in utero* raise questions about reproductive responsibility. What kind of genetic screening is appropriate? How should test results affect abortion decisions? Advanced reproductive technologies prompt questions about the morality of their use and the responsibility for resulting offspring.

In Chapter 7 we move from the "right to life" to the "right to die." These sections deal with Euthanasia and Treatment of Defective Neonates. How far does the autonomy of individuals extend in making decisions about the end of life? Do health care providers have a duty to prolong life at all costs? Where infants are concerned, who should make the decision to continue or refrain from treatment? Questions arise, as they do in the area of abortion, about the quality and value of an individual life.

Issues of autonomy, paternalism, informed consent, and proxy consent surface again in Chapter 8, concerning Treatment of Mental Illness and Rights of the Mentally Retarded. To what extent is interference with the freedom of mentally handicapped or disturbed persons justifed? Should such persons be institutionalized or subjected to medical intervention (such as lobotomy or sterilization) without their consent? Who should make decisions on their behalf? Is the concept of mental illness a myth, as some theorists argue?

Chapter 9, the final chapter in the unit, is devoted primarily to issues in the broader context of social policy concerning health care. The sections deal with The Concept of Health, Macroallocation Decisions, and Microallocation Decisions. The basic concepts of health and disease require study and clarification, because defining health has important implications for the allocation of health care funds and services. Ideas about social justice also affect allocation decisions, both at the policy level and in individual cases. How much of the nation's budget should be spent for health care? When lifesaving treatments are scarce, which candidates should receive them? In this chapter, as in the preceding ones, we attempt to show how ethical theory applies to specific problems. Using the principles of basic theory makes it possible to frame a coherent moral response to questions that otherwise might seem irresolvable.

It is important to remember that the article that follows each section should *not* be seen as the right answer to a problem. Rather, each is an example of *one* way of reasoning out the problem and justifying a decision. Other arguments and approaches can be found in the suggested reading list at the end of each section.

5. PROFESSIONAL–PATIENT RELATIONS

1. PATERNALISM

Many problems in biomedical ethics revolve around issues of professional–patient relations. Which moral rules ought to govern the conduct of health care professionals toward patients, and what rights should an individual retain upon assuming the role of a patient? The traditional paternalistic approach in medicine assumes that the professional always knows what is best for the patient. The issue of paternalism is involved in questions of confidentiality, informed consent, and truth telling, and each of these concepts is considered in a separate section.

We place a high value upon autonomy and the right of individuals to self-determination. However, patients seek out the knowledge and special skills of physicians, technicians, nurses, and the like and voluntarily surrender some of their autonomy to these experts. They place a great deal of power in the hands of physicians in particular, whose opinions and decisions generally take precedence over those of other health care professionals.

The dependency of the patient upon a physician carries a considerable weight of responsibility, and this responsibility is reflected in medical codes of ethics dating back as far as the Hippocratic Oath, which is believed to have been written in the late fourth century, B.C. Traditional medical ethics stresses the obligation of physicians to help patients and not to harm them. The tradition overlooks or places little emphasis on the right of patients to self-determination,

however. Physicians are enjoined from exploiting the vulnerability of patients in a relationship of unequal power. The problems of dependency and unequal power are also factors in assessing the obligations of corporations to employees and consumers and of attorneys to clients. **[See Business, Chapter 10, Section 1; Chapter 11, Section 1; Criminal Justice, Chapter 16, Section 2.]** Patients are willing to accept the powerful influence of physicians because of a trust in the latter's adherence to the principles of *beneficence* and *nonmaleficence* (summed up in the command, "Do good and do no harm").

In recent years people have begun to question the paternalism implicit in the dependency of patients upon physicians. It is argued that physicians ought to be viewed like consultants whose advice may be freely accepted or rejected. As medical knowledge and technology grow increasingly complex, the argument appears impractical. How can a layperson be expected to understand and make reasonable judgments about the desirability or efficacy of different courses of available treatment? Nevertheless, a belief exists that patients ought to retain a greater measure of self-determination in their relationships with health care professionals.

Respect for a patient's right to autonomy at times conflicts with the physician's professional or personal judgment regarding treatment. Physicians are tempted, because of their special knowledge, to disregard or give insufficient weight to patients' opinions. On occasion, a patient's power of judgment is (or may appear to be) weakened by a condition of injury or illness. In such situations, who ought to make proxy decisions on the patient's behalf: the physician, family members, the courts, or another party?

The patient and physician may simply disagree about what constitutes or will promote the patient's well-being. Under what circumstances are physicians morally justified in interfering with patient autonomy? Consequentialists justify paternalism by arguing that highly trained professionals can make better decisions regarding health care than laypersons. According to this view, the medical benefits resulting from expert decision making outweigh the utility of respecting a patient's right to choose. By contrast, a deontological approach assigns greater value to the respect due to individuals. In this approach, paternalism is justified only

in special situations, such as when a patient's ability to decide is temporarily impaired and limited paternalistic intervention can restore the person to an autonomous state.

In the following selection Dan W. Brock argues for the use of a contract model to delineate the nurse–patient relationship. Applying the model, Brock asserts, clarifies the duties and obligations of the nurse toward the patient and demonstrates the limitations of professional authority. Paternalism is most often discussed in the context of the physician–patient relationship. Brock's analysis is particularly useful as a critique of paternalism in health care since nurses typically exercise less authority over patients than do physicians. The author's decision to employ what might be viewed as sexist language (using only female pronouns to refer to nurses and male pronouns to refer to physicians) is explained in a footnote.

DAN W. BROCK

The Nurse–Patient Relationship

There are at least two sorts of moral considerations relevant to a full understanding of the moral relationship between the nurse and patient. First, those general moral considerations, rights and duties, that the nurse and patient would have simply as individuals and apart from their roles as nurse or patient— e.g., on most any moral theory it is prima facie wrong to kill or seriously injure another human being, and this holds for persons generally, not merely for nurses and patients. Second, there are moral considerations which arise only out of the particular relationship

that exists between a nurse and her[1] patient, just as there are in other relationships such as parent and child, public official and citizen, and so forth. A complete account of the nurse's moral situation must include both sorts of considerations, and would be far too complex and lengthy to attempt here: I shall emphasize considerations of the second sort, and even then my discussion will not be at all comprehensive. On virtually any account of the nurse–patient relationship, the nurse owes at least some care to her patient and the patient has a right to expect that care; this is not,

This paper originally appeared in a longer version as "The Nurse–Patient Relation: Some Rights and Duties," in *Nursing: Images and Ideals*, ed. Stuart F. Spicker and Sally Gadow (New York: Springer Publishing Co., 1980). © 1980 by Stuart F. Spicker. Reprinted by permission.

however, an obligation the nurse has to just anyone, but only to her patients, nor a right a person has towards just anyone, or even towards any nurse, but rather only towards his nurse. How then does each get into a relationship at all, how does he become *her* patient, and she become *his* nurse? If we pose the question in this way, I think it is clear that the common alternative accounts of the nurse–patient relationship are not all plausibly construed as even possible answers to this question, and that more generally, they address two different questions—some speak to the origin of the relationship, how it comes about, while others speak to the nature or content of the relationship. I think we gain a clearer understanding of the relationship if we separate these two issues, because the account of the origin of the relationship will affect in turn the account of its content. Consider six of the more common accounts of the relationship, of the role of the nurse vis-à-vis the patient:[2]

1. The nurse as parent surrogate.
2. The nurse as physician surrogate.
3. The nurse as healer.
4. The nurse as patient advocate or protector.
5. The nurse as health educator.
6. The nurse as contracted clinician.

I do not want to deny that nurses do not at times, and at times justifiably, fill each of the first five of these roles, though none of them are unique to her. And at least most of these first five roles refer to professional duties a nurse assumes in entering the profession of nursing. But how is it a nurse has any duty to perform in any of these roles towards a particular person (patient), and how is it that a person (patient) has any right to expect a particular nurse to perform in these roles toward him? Only the last model, the nurse as contracted clinician can explain that—we must be able to make reference to a contract, or better an agreement, between the two to explain this. This point may be obscured somewhat by the fact that what a nurse would do for a patient in any of the first five roles can be gen-

erally assumed to be beneficial for the patient, or at least intended to be beneficial. If it is for the patient's good, why must he agree before she is permitted to act? But just imagine someone coming up to you on the street and giving you an injection, even one intended to be, and in fact, beneficial to you. A natural response would be, "You have no right to do that," and underlying that response would likely be some belief that each person has a moral right to determine what is done to his body, however difficult it may be to determine the precise nature, scope, and strength of that right. Or, imagine a strange woman in a white uniform coming up to you and lecturing you about the health hazards of your smoking or failing to exercise. Well-intentioned though it might be, a natural response again might be, "What business is it of yours, what right do you have to lecture me about my health habits?" Again, the point would be that it is a person's right to act even in ways detrimental to his health if he chooses to do so and bears the consequences of doing so, a particular right usually derived from some more general and basic right to privacy, liberty, or self-determination (autonomy). Yet both these actions are, of course, of the sort frequently performed by nurses toward their patients. Likewise, any duties of a nurse to provide care to a particular person cannot come simply from duties she assumes from her role as a nurse, nor can any right of a particular patient to care from a specific nurse.

If we think of the nurse–patient relationship as arising from a contract or agreement between the nurse and her patient, then these otherwise problematic rights and duties become readily explicable. The patient contracts to have specified care provided by the nurse, in return for payment by the patient, and the patient in so doing grants permission for the nurse to perform actions (give him injections, perform tests, etc.) that she would otherwise have no right or duty to do. In agreeing to perform these duties, the nurse incurs an obligation to the patient to do so, as well as a right to be paid for doing so.

A natural objection to such an account is

that it seems to rest on a fiction, since in the great majority of cases nurses and patients never in fact make any such agreement; rather, the patient finds himself in a physician's office, or in a hospital, where the nurse as a matter of course performs certain tasks, while the nurse if she makes any such agreements at all, makes them with the physician or hospital that employs her. This reflects the fact that the provision of health care is considerably more complex and institutionalized than any simple nurse–patient account would suggest, but it does not, in my view, show the contract or agreement model to be mistaken. The patient makes his agreement generally with the physician or the hospital's representative, and that agreement is to have a complex of services performed by a variety of health care professionals. The nurse is indirectly a party to this agreement, and can become committed by it, by having contracted or agreed with the employing physician or hospital to perform a particular role, carrying out its attendant duties, in the health care context.

A related objection to this account is that at both these intervening agreement points, it is still the case that the contract or agreement often, if not generally, never takes places, certainly not where what is to be done is spelled out in any detail, and so the account still rests on a fiction. But these agreements can and do have implicit terms, terms which can be just as binding on the parties as if they had been explicitly spelled out. These implicit terms are to be found in the generally known and accepted understanding of the nature of such health care relationships, and in the warranted social expectations the parties to them have concerning who will do what in such relationships. The content of such expectations will in large part derive from the nature of the training of various health care professionals, the professional codes and legal requirements governing their conduct, as well as more general public understandings of their roles.

Why insist on a contract or agreement model of the nurse–patient relationship that requires appeal to agreements between inter-

vening parties, as well as to implicit terms that are generally not spelled out? The reason is that such an account makes clearer than does any other alternative the fundamental point that the right to determine what is done to and for the patient, and to control, within broad limits, the course of the patient's treatment and care, originates and generally remains with the patient. One important reason for insisting on this is that it is insufficiently appreciated and respected by health care professionals. Many health care professionals believe that if what they are doing is in the best interests of the patient, that is sufficient justification for doing it. That, however, is in my view a mistake of primary importance, because it does not take adequate account of the patient's right to control the course of his treatment.

An important part of at least one common understanding of the physician–patient relationship, and in turn of the patient–other-health-care-professional (including, but not limited to, the nurse) relationship, is that the health care professional will, with limited exceptions (e.g., public health problems arising from highly contagious diseases), act so as maximally to promote the interests of his or her patient. Treatment recommendations and decisions are to be made solely according to how they affect the interests of the patient, and ought not be influenced by the interests or convenience of others.[3] The confidence that the health professional will act in this way is especially important because of the extreme vulnerability and apprehension the ill patient often feels, the patient's incapacity to provide for himself the care he needs, and the patient's often very limited capacity to evaluate for himself whether a proposed course of treatment and care is in fact the best course for him. This focus on the patient's interests to the exclusion of others, however, is different from and should not be confused with, the physician or nurse being justified in acting in whatever manner they reasonably believe to be in the patient's best interest.

The right of the physician or nurse to act in the patient's interest is *created* and *limited* by the permission or consent (from the patient–nurse/physician agreement) the patient has given. To take two extremes, a patient might say to his physician or nurse, ''I want you to do whatever you think best, and don't bother me with the details,'' or he might insist that he be fully informed about all factors and alternatives concerning his treatment and that he retain the right to reject any aspect of that treatment at any stage along the way. In my view, should the patient desire, either of these arrangements can be justifiable, as well, of course, as many modified versions of them. This has the important implication that the various expectations referred to above concerning what the health professional will do, which generally give content to the nurse–patient relationship, only partially determine that relationship, and it is subject to modification determined principally by what the patient desires of the relationship, and how he in turn constructs it. This is the other difficulty, besides their failure to explain how the relationship comes into being between particular persons, of the five alternatives mentioned above to the contract or agreement model of the nurse–patient relation. One cannot speak generally about the extent to which the nurse ought to act or has a duty to act, for example, as health educator or parent surrogate, because it ought to be the patient's right to determine in large part the extent to which the nurse is to take those roles with him. What the patient wants will often only become clear in the course of treatment, but to put the point in obligation language, the nurse's obligation is in large part to accommodate herself to the patient's desires in these matters.

I have been considering the case of patients who satisfy conditions of competence, that is persons who possess the cognitive and other capacities necessary to being able to form purposes and make plans, to weigh alternative courses of action according to how they fulfill those purposes and plans, and to act on the basis of this deliberative process; such persons are able to form and act on a conception of their own good.[4] Some of the more difficult moral problems in health care

generally arise in cases where these conditions of competence are not satisfied, e.g., with infants and young children, with cases of extreme senility, and with some forms of mental illness.[5] However, I think we must first understand the nurse–patient relation in the case of the competent patient, before determining how that relationship may have to be modified when the patient is not competent. It may, then, be useful to consider what the contract or agreement model of the nurse–patient relation, with its emphasis on the patient's rights, might imply for some typical moral problems the nurse encounters with the competent patient. Common to many such problems insofar as they involve only the nurse and her patient is a conflict between what the patient wants and believes is best for him, and what the nurse believes is either in his best interests, in the interests of all persons affected, or morally acceptable. Consider the following cases:

Case 1. Patient A has requested of the nurse that she inform him fully of the nature of his condition and of the course of treatment prescribed for it. However, the treatment called for, and which the nurse believes will be most effective in his case, is such that given her knowledge of the patient, she believes that fully informing the patient will reduce his ability and willingness to cooperate in the treatment and so will significantly reduce the likely effectiveness of the treatment. What should she tell him?

Case 2. Patient B instructs his nurse that if his condition deteriorates beyond a specified point, he considers life no longer worth living and wishes all further treatment withdrawn. The nurse believes that life still has value even in such a deteriorated state, that it would be wrong for the patient to deliberately bring about his own death in this way, and in turn wrong for her to aid him in doing so. Should she follow his instructions?

Case 3. Patient C, after being fully informed of principal alternative treatments for his condition, has insisted on a course of treatment that the nurse has good reason to believe is effective in a substantially smaller proportion of cases than an alternative treatment procedure would be. She considers the additional risk in the rejected treatment, which seems to have affected the patient's choice, completely insignificant. Should she insist on the more effective treatment, for example, even by surreptitiously substituting it, if she is able to do so?

Each of these cases lacks sufficient detail to allow a full discussion of it, and in particular, each artificially ignores the presence and role of other health care practitioners, most notably the physician, who is generally prominent if not paramount in such decision making. But the cases are instructive even in this oversimplified form. Case 3 is perhaps the least difficult. It would be permissible for any interested party, and a duty of the nurse following from her roles as health educator and healer, to discuss the treatment decision with her patient, and to attempt to convince him that he has made a serious mistake in his choice of treatments. But just as the patient should be free to refuse any treatment for his condition if he is competent and so decides, he is likewise entitled to select and have the treatment that the nurse (or physician, for that matter) would not choose if it were her choice; the point simply is that it is not her choice. She has no moral (or professional) right to insist on a treatment the patient does not want, even if it is clearly the "best" treatment, and it would be still more seriously wrong to surreptitiously and deceptively substitute the treatment she prefers.

Case 2 can be somewhat more difficult because it may at least involve action in conflict with the nurse's moral views rather than a conflict over what course of action is, all things considered, medically advisable, as in Case 3. Case 2, of course, raises the controversial issue of euthanasia and the so-called right to die. This is a complex question that I have considered elsewhere, and here I only want to note that Case 2 involves only fully voluntary euthanasia, generally accepted to be the least morally controversial form of euthanasia.[6] I shall suppose here, as I think is the case, that a patient's right to control his treatment, and to refuse treatment he does not

want, includes the right to order withdrawal of treatment even when that will have the known and intended consequence of terminating his life. If we interpret the nurse's view that life under the circumstances in question would still be worth living as merely her own view about what she would do in similar circumstances, then her view is relevant only to what she would do if she were the patient and nothing more; it entails nothing about what should be done here where it is another's life and his attitude to it that is in question. She would not waive her right not to be killed in these circumstances, but the patient would and does, and it is his life and so his right that is in question. I would suggest as well that a mere difference over what it is best to do in the circumstances (apart from moral considerations) does not justify the nurse's refusal to honor the patient's expressed wishes. However, her difference with the patient may be a moral one; in particular she may hold as a basic moral principle that she has an inviolable moral duty not deliberately to kill an innocent human being. In that case, to assist in the withdrawal of treatment in order to bring about the patient's death will be on her moral view to commit a serious wrong, to participate in a serious evil. The nurse's professional obligations to provide care should not, in my view, be understood to require her to do such, just as she should not be required to assist in abortions if she holds fetuses to be protected by a duty not deliberately to take innocent human life. While there should be no requirement in general for her to participate in medical procedures that violate important moral principles that she holds, that of course in no way implies that another nurse who does not hold such duty-based views about killing should not assist in the withdrawal of treatment. (Of course, if she holds killing to be wrong because it violates a person's right not to be killed, then she will correctly reason that the patient in Case 2 has waived that right, and so no conflict between her moral views and what the patient wants will arise.)[7]

Finally, consider Case 1. The "Patient's Bill of Rights" proposed by the American Hospital

Association specifically allows that "when it is not medically advisable to give . . . information to the patient" concerning his diagnosis, treatment, and prognosis, such information need only "be made available to an appropriate person in his behalf" but need not be given to the patient himself. This would seem clearly to permit the nurse to withhold the information from the patient in Case 1. However, I believe the Patient's Bill of Rights is mistaken on this point. This is a particular instance of a general over-emphasis on and consequent over-enlargement of the area in which health professionals should be permitted to act towards patients on the basis of their own judgment of the "medical advisability" of their action toward the patient. It is perhaps natural that health professionals, trained to provide medical care for patients, and who undertake professional responsibilities to do so, should consider medical advisability a sufficient condition generally for acting contrary to a patient's wishes, and here for withholding relevant information from the patient. But once again, so long as we are dealing with patients who satisfy minimal conditions of competence to make decisions about their treatment, then unless the patient has explicitly granted the nurse the right to withhold information he seeks when she considers it medically advisable to do so, medical advisability is not sufficient justification for doing so. Our moral right to control what is done to our body, and our right in turn not to be denied relevant available information for decisions about the exercise of that right, does not end at the point where others decide, even with good reason, that it is medically advisable for us not to be free to exercise that right. In general, one element of the moral respect owed competent adults is to respect, in the sense of honor, their right to make decisions of this sort even when their doing so may not be deemed medically advisable by others, and even when those others are health professionals generally in a better position to make an informed decision. When other health professionals are in a better position to make an informed decision, a patient may have good reason to transfer his

rights to decide to them, or to allow himself to be strongly influenced by what they think best, but he is not required to do so, and so they have no such rights to decide for him what is in his best interests when he has not done so.

I want to emphasize that on my view moral rights generally, and in particular the rights of the patient relevant in the three cases above, are not absolute in the sense that they are never justifiably overridden by competing moral considerations. But such justifiable overriding requires a special justification, and that human welfare generally, or the welfare of the person whose right is at issue, will be better promoted by violation of the right is *not* such a special justification.[8] Thus, rights need not be absolute in order to have an important place in moral reasoning. And it is not necessary that a nurse never be justified, for example, in withholding information from a patient for the patient's right to control his treatment to limit importantly when she may do so. Cases involving young children and non-competent adults are important instances where specifically paternalistic interference with a person's exercise of their rights can be justified.

Perhaps the point of emphasizing the contract or agreement between the patient and the health care professional is now a bit clearer. That contract model emphasizes the basis for and way in which the right to control the directions one's care will take ought to rest with the patient. It is not, of course, that the nurse is mistaken in taking her role to be a healer, or health educator, for these are important professional services she performs, but rather that her performance in these roles ought to be significantly constrained and circumscribed by the rights of her patients to control what is done to their bodies.

I should like to end by noting that focusing on the nurse–patient relationship, as I have done here, has the effect of ignoring at least one extremely important aspect of most nurses' overall moral situation. Specifically, most nurses now work in hierarchic, institutional settings in which they are in the employ of others—hospitals, physicians, etc. Many of the most important moral uncertainties and conflicts nurses experience concerning their rights, duties, and responsibilities derive from their role in this hierarchical structure, and from questions about their consequent authority to decide and act in particular matters. The patient has a place in such issues, but the issues do not arise when only the nurse and patient are considered. To fill in the picture would require consideration of what might be called the nurse–physician/hospital relation, but that is a complex matter that cannot be pursued here.

Notes

1. I have chosen throughout this paper to use feminine pronouns to refer to nurses and masculine pronouns to refer to physicians, rather than to adopt gender-neutral pronouns. Since something on the order of 96% of nurses are women, while the great majority of physicians are men, gender-neutral usage in this context seems to mask a significant social reality and problem. My pronoun usage acknowledges the gender distribution among nurses and physicians, while in no way endorsing it.

2. I have drawn these from the very helpful paper by Sally Gadow, "Humanistic Issues at the Interface of Nursing and the Community," in *Nursing: Images and Ideals,* eds. S. Gadow and S. Spicker (New York, 1980).

3. Such a view, with specific reference to the dying patient, is advocated in, among other places, Leon Kass, "Death as an Event: A Commentary on Robert Morrison," *Science* 173 (August 20, 1971), 698–702. To what extent this account of the physician–patient relationship is defensible, or is in fact adhered to in practice by physicians, is problematic.

4. Plans of life, and their relation to a conception of one's good, are discussed in John Rawls, *A Theory of Justice* (Cambridge, 1971), ch. 7, and Charles Fried, *An Anatomy of Values* (Cambridge, 1970).

5. For philosophical accounts of the principles of paternalism relevant to treatment of the incompetent see, for example, Gerald Dworkin, "Paternalism" in *Morality and the Law,* ed. R. Wasser-

strom (Belmont, Calif., 1971) and John Hodson, "The Principle of Paternalism," *American Philosophical Quarterly* 14 (1977), 61–69. I have discussed paternalism with specific reference to the mentally ill in, "Involuntary Civil Commitment: The Moral Issues," in *Mental Illness: Law and Public Policy,* eds. Baruch Brody and H. Tristram Engelhardt, Jr. (Dordrecht, Holland, 1978).

6. I have discussed some implications of a rights-based view for euthanasia in my "Moral Rights and Permissible Killing," in *Ethical Issues Relating to Life and Death,* ed. John Ladd (New York, 1979). See also the paper by Michael Tooley, "The Termination of Life: Some Moral Isuses," in the same volume.

7. On the general distinction between duty-based and rights-based moral views, see Ronald Dworkin, *Taking Rights Seriously,* ch. 6, (Cambridge, 1977).

8. For an attempt to specify the limits of such special justifications, see R. Dworkin, *op. cit.,* ch. 7.

Suggested Further Reading

Buchanan, Allen, "Medical Paternalism," *Philosophy and Public Affairs,* 7, no. 4 (Summer 1978), 370–90.

Gadow, Sally, "Existential Advocacy: Philosophical Foundation of Nursing," in *Nursing: Images and Ideals,* ed. Stuart F. Spicker and Sally Gadow. New York: Springer Publishing Co., 1980, pp. 79–101.

Gert, Bernard, and Charles M. Culver, "The Justification of Paternalism," *Ethics,* 89, no 2 (January 1979), 199.

Smith, Sheri, "Three Models of the Nurse–Patient Relationship," in *Nursing: Images and Ideals,* ed. Stuart F. Spicker and Sally Gadow. New York: Springer Publishing Co., 1980, pp. 176–88.

Veatch, Robert M., "Models for Ethical Medicine in a Revolutionary Age," *Hastings Center Report,* 2, no. 3 (June 1972), 5–7.

Zembaty, Jane S., "A Limited Defense of Paternalism," *Proceedings of the 13th Conference on Value Inquiry: The Life Sciences and Human Values,* State University of New York College at Geneseo, pp. 145–58.

2. CONFIDENTIALITY

The rule of confidentiality in professional–patient relations has been affirmed in a wide variety of ethical codes for physicians, nurses, and other health care professionals; these include the Hippocratic Oath, the A.M.A. Code, and the World Medical Association International Code of Medical Ethics (see Appendix for examples). The principle of confidentiality is recognized by laws which exempt physicians and psychotherapists from giving testimony about patients and which provide sanctions against practitioners who divulge patient information given them in confidence.

Confidentiality is important in the practice of medicine in part because of its practical function. Physicians require private and possibly intimate information about patients in order to make correct diagnoses and prescribe proper treatment. It is argued that unless patients feel confident that such information will not be revealed to others, they are unlikely to entrust it to physicians. The professional obligation for attorneys to preserve client confidentiality is based upon a similar argument. **[See Criminal Justice, Chapter 16, Section 2.]** Additionally, a patient's trust in the practitioner is believed to play a part in successful treatment. Emphasis on the practical benefits of confidentiality reflects a consequentialist approach.

From a deontological standpoint, preserving patient confidentiality and privacy is one expression of the broader respect physicians owe to patients as autonomous individuals. The principle of confidentiality is related to the right of privacy. Privacy—personal control over information about oneself—is an important element of individual autonomy.

Ethical dilemmas arise when a health care professional is forced to choose between a duty to respect a patient's confidentiality and a conflicting obligation to other persons or institutions within the society. In some cases a breach of trust is thought necessary in the patient's best interest (a paternalistic approach), as with a patient who threatens suicide. Breaching confidentiality, it is argued, permits eventual resumption of autonomy by a person whose competence is temporarily compromised. On other occasions, the physician may be legally obligated to violate confidentiality, as in the duty to report gunshot wounds, suspected child abuse, and certain communicable diseases.

The dilemmas posed by conflicting loyalties are acute in the area of psychiatric medicine. Suppose a patient reveals a strong feeling of anger or actually threatens other persons or their property. Does a therapist have an obligation to warn law enforcement officials or the intended victim of possible harm? Such questions are more urgent in view of the special importance of trust in the psychotherapeutic relationship. In the following article, William J. Curran discusses a widely publicized case in which the California Supreme Court ruled that a group of psychotherapists were negligent in their duty to warn a woman whose life had been threatened by a patient, despite the fact that they *had* notified security personnel about the threats. Curran raises questions regarding the obligations of physicians in situations of conflicting loyalties.

WILLIAM J. CURRAN

Confidentiality and the Prediction of Dangerousness in Psychiatry: The Tarasoff Case

The California Supreme Court continues to make financial awards to patients in suits against physicians with seemingly little regard for the effect of these awards and decisions upon the practice of medicine and the availability of insurance to cover this largesse of the judiciary, and without regard for the social consequences of this "money-for-everything" attitude.

The particular case, *Tarasoff vs. Regents of the University of California*,[1] has already become infamous among mental health programs in California and among college and university student medical programs all over the country as it has taken its course through the various levels of trial and appeals courts in the Golden State.

The facts of the situation are undisputed. A student at the University of California's Berkeley campus was in psychotherapy with the student health service on an outpatient basis. He told his therapist, a psychologist, that he wanted to kill an unmarried girl who lived in Berkeley but who was then on a summer trip to Brazil. The psychologist, with the concurrence of another therapist and the assistant director of the Department of Psychiatry, reported the matter orally to the campus police and on their suggestion sent them a letter requesting detention of the student and his commitment for observation to a mental hospital. The campus police picked up the student for questioning but "satisfied" that he was "rational," released him on his "promise to stay away" from Miss Tarasoff. The police reported back to the director of psychiatry, Dr. Powelson. Dr. Powelson asked for the return of the psychologist's letter to the police and directed that all copies of the letter be de-stroyed. Nothing more was done at the health service about the matter. Two months later, shortly after Miss Tarasoff's return, the student went to her home and killed her.

The parents of Miss Tarasoff brought suit for damages against the University and against the therapists and the campus police, as employees of the University and individually. In suing Dr. Powelson, the plaintiffs sought not only general money damages for negligence in failure to warn the girl and her parents and to confine the student, but exemplary or punitive damages (which could be assessed in huge amounts as multiples of the general damages or in any amount at the determination of the jury) for malicious and oppressive abandonment of a dangerous patient.

The Superior Court dismissed all these grounds for legal action against the defendants. The Supreme Court, in a four-to-two decision, reversed the decision and found that on these facts a cause of action was stated for general damages against all the therapists involved in the case and the assistant director and the director of psychiatry and against the University as their employer for breach of the duty to warn Miss Tarasoff. The Court dismissed the claim for exemplary damages against the therapists. It also dismissed the action against the police as protected from a suit by a statutory immunity, as well as the suit against the therapists for failure to confine the student under a commitment order, again because of a statutory immunity. The Court implied that without the immunity, both these actions might have been meritorious.

It seems to me that most physicians would throw up their hands in dismay over this result

Reprinted with permission from *The New England Journal of Medicine*, 293 (August 7, 1975), 285–86.

and the massive contradictions in the assessment of who was and who was not legally responsible for this death. If I were to describe in detail the reasoning of the court, the confusion of the medical mind would be compounded a thousand times.

The Court asserted that the *Principles of Medical Ethics of the American Medical Association,* Section 9, did not bar breaching the confidentiality of this patient ''in order to protect the welfare of this individual [the patient] or the community.'' From this premise the Court jumped wholeheartedly to a positive duty to warn Miss Tarasoff. This is not what the *Principles* said. The traditional code of medical ethics allows a physician in his sound discretion to breach the confidentiality, but does not require it. It is almost impossible to draft an ethical principle to force a duty on physicians to breach confidences. Must they always warn of death threats, but have discretion on less dangerous threats? Must they warn if the patient is psychotic, but not if he is less disturbed? Does this case mean that every time a patient makes a threat against an unnamed person, the therapist must take steps to find out who it is and warn him (of anything at all, from vague threats to murder) or suffer money damages in the thousands or tens of thousands if the threat, or an aspect of the threat, is carried out?

This case was greatly confused by the array of immunities from suits created under California law. It can be strongly argued that the thrust of these immunity statutes regarding the duty to warn should also have been applied to the therapists, since the statutes were intended to encourage police and mental health personnel to release patients and not confine them on the basis of unreliable diagnoses of dangerousness. In the past it was thought that too many mental patients were confined for years and years because of their threats to other people, rarely carried out, and because of the conservatism of mental health personnel in exercising any doubt about dangerousness in favor of confinement as the safest way to prevent harm to third parties.

It seems clear that the therapists here thought that they had done all they could to protect their patient and the community by reporting the case to the police. They had exercised their discretion to warn the community and to breach the confidence of the patient, for his own sake, and that of the unknown girl. They could hardly warn her, since she was not even in the country at the time. Also, the threat to Miss Tarasoff might actually have been vaguely directed. The student could well have turned his anger and violence toward another person or toward himself. The only basic recourse was to recommend temporary observational commitment. The practice was to make this to the campus police. It was the police who acted, and they decided to release the student with a warning and a promise to stay away from the girl. How many thousands of such warnings—and releases—do police departments make every year? How many people then proceed to kill? The immunity statute was established to encourage release in these circumstances. But the statutory armor had a hole in it. The director of psychiatry was found by the Court to have a ''duty'' to warn the girl, irrespective of the police action. The Court utilized some precedents, none clearly applicable to this case, to justify its decision. It seems, however, that the real rationale was the aggravated nature of the case—a killing—in which the family was left without someone else to sue. The therapists, particularly Dr. Powelson, could have warned the girl if they had wanted to go against the police action and if they had thought the specific threat to Miss Tarasoff so serious as to warrant that action. The Court did not apply any test to ascertain the custom of psychiatrists and mental health programs actually in such situations. The Court declared the duty as a matter of law, regardless of the accepted practices of the profession. As in the *Helling* decision[2] discussed in an earlier column,[3] the Court made the physician a guarantor against harm to this party, here not even a patient, on the basis of its own concept of monetary justice.

Notes

1. 529 P. 2d 553
2. *Helling vs. Carey and Laughlin,* 519 P. 2d 981.
3. Curran W. J. Glaucoma and streptococcal pharyngitis: diagnostic practices and malpractice liability. *N Engl J Med* 291:508–509, 1974.

Suggested Further Reading

Abrams, Natalie, et al., "The Urban Emergency Department: The Issue of Professional Re-

sponsibility," *Annals of Emergency Medicine,* 11, no. 2 (February 1982), 86–90.

Gaylin, Willard, "What's an FBI Poster Doing in a Nice Journal Like That?" *The Hastings Center Report,* 2 (April 1972), 1–3.

Siegler, Mark, "Confidentiality in Medicine—A Decrepit Concept," *The New England Journal of Medicine,* 307 (1982), 1518–21.

Walters, LeRoy, "The Principles of Medical Confidentiality," *Contemporary Issues in Bioethics,* ed. Tom L. Beauchamp and LeRoy Walters. Encino, Calif.: Dickenson Publishing Co., Inc., 1978, pp. 170–73.

DECISION SCENARIO 1

Confidentiality

As a young boy, Thomas was perceived by his father, a former all-conference football player, as oversensitive and effeminate. The father repeatedly tried to direct Thomas's interests toward athletics and outdoor activities. During adolescence, the conflict was transformed into Thomas's silent rebelliousness. In high school Thomas was placed on academic probation although he was regarded as an intelligent student.

Thomas's father placed him in an all-boys' prep school in the area. After a year, his grades improved. When his father arranged to transfer him back to public school, Thomas went into a deep depression. He told his parents of his homosexual activities.

He was given tranquilizers and treated for gonorrhea. His blood test for AIDS was negative.

Thomas took a job for a large corporation which did defense contract work. Although he received security clearance, his homosexual tendencies were noted on his record.

When he was thirty, he met Tanya, fell in love, and prepared to marry. Tanya went to her family physician for the blood test required by the state. In their conversation, it came out that Thomas was her fiancé. The doctor realized that it was the same person he had several years before treated for venereal disease. He said nothing.

The marriage lasted little more than a year. Thomas told Tanya of his homoerotic preference. He also told her about the physician whom they had in common. Tanya felt betrayed and confused. She required psychiatric support for many months after the separation. She felt deep hostility toward the doctor whom, to her mind, ought to have spared her the trauma of a bad marriage.

Questions

1. Did the physician's obligation to keep confidentiality override his duty to inform Tanya of the facts of the matter?

2. Was the physician too literal in his understanding of confidentiality? Was there another way for him to deal with the two persons under his care?

3. Is keeping silent about information the way to tell the truth in this case?

4. What if Thomas's test for AIDS had come back positive? How would the case be different?

3. INFORMED CONSENT

The notion of informed consent is grounded in the principle of autonomy and the right of self-determination. Individuals have a right to control what is done to their bodies. They must freely agree to medical intervention and must be given sufficient information upon which to base their judgment. Some theorists argue that informed consent is an ethical concern in other professions such as advertising **[See Business, Chapter 11, Section 1]** and engineering **[See Business, Chapter 13, Section 1].**

The moral and legal requirement of informed consent seems at first glance to be fairly straightforward. In application, however, it proves troublesome. At least three questions need to be considered in deciding whether the requirement is met. First, how much information must be supplied in order for a patient to make a competent decision? Some physicians insist that offering patients too much complex medical data serves to confuse and frighten them. The paternalistic attitude leads to the assumption that no layperson fully understands all the information relevant to his or her treatment and that obtaining informed consent is a meaningless formality. Others argue that the fact that medical procedures and theories are complicated and unfamiliar (and frequently couched in difficult, technical language) imposes a special obligation on physicians to find a way to explain the information so that patients understand it.

The second question is whether the patient is competent to make rational decisions regarding treatment. Certain persons, such as young children, the severely mentally retarded, and those with psychiatric disturbances, lack such competence. Even otherwise rational adults are at times less-than-competent decision makers. For example, a person suffering extreme pain or fear or having an illness that causes confusion or disorientation might not be fully competent to give consent.

A third question involves the voluntary nature of consent. Pressures exist within the hospital setting as well as in other institutions that may compromise the voluntary character of patient consent. The authority of medical personnel, particularly physicians, can be intimidating, and patients may feel obliged to be ''good'' and accept the judgment of these powerful figures. In such situations, is the patient's consent truly voluntary?

Informed consent is problematic in the area of medical research and experimentation. The literature about informed consent centers on the context of experimentation. Ethical codes and guidelines exist to identify the conditions under which human experimentation is permissible. One of the foremost among these is the ''Nuremburg Code,'' written after World War II in response to the barbarous experiments conducted by German doctors on concentration camp inmates. The first and longest provision of the Nuremburg Code deals in great detail with the importance of informed consent. The use of prisoners as research subjects is strongly criticized on the basis that such persons are subject to duress and coercion and can never consent freely.

In the following article Franz J. Ingelfinger, editor of the *New England Journal of Medicine,* discusses the problem of informed consent in medical research. Ingelfinger holds that some coercion exists in almost all transactions between researchers and potential subjects. The objections raised by the author are also applicable to physician–patient relations.

FRANZ J. INGELFINGER

Informed (but Uneducated) Consent

The trouble with informed consent is that it is not educated consent. Let us assume that the experimental subject, whether a patient, a volunteer, or otherwise enlisted, is exposed to a completely honest array of factual detail. He is told of the medical uncertainty that exists and that must be resolved by research endeavors, of the time and discomfort involved, and of the tiny percentage risk of some serious consequences of the test procedure. He is also reassured of his rights and given a formal, quasilegal statement to read. No exculpatory language is used. With his written signature, the subject then caps the transaction, and whether he sees himself as a heroic martyr for the sake of mankind, or as a reluctant guinea pig dragooned for the benefit of science, or whether, perhaps, he is merely bewildered, he obviously has given his "informed consent." Because established routines have been scrupulously observed, the doctor, the lawyer, and the ethicist are content.

But the chances are remote that the subject really understands what he has consented to—in the sense that the responsible medical investigator understands the goals, nature, and hazards of his study. How can the layman comprehend the importance of his perhaps not receiving, as determined by the luck of the draw, the highly touted new treatment that his roommate will get? How can he appreciate the sensation of living for days with a multi-lumen intestinal tube passing through his mouth and pharynx? How can he interpret the information that an intravascular catheter and radiopaque dye injection have an 0.01 per cent probability of leading to a dangerous thrombosis or cardiac arrhythmia? It is moreover quite unlikely that any patient-subject can see himself accurately within the broad context of the situation, to weigh the inconve-niences and hazards that he will have to undergo against the improvements that the research project may bring to the management of his disease in general and to his own case in particular. The difficulty that the public has in understanding information that is both medical and stressful is exemplified by [a] report [in the *New England Journal of Medicine*, August 31, 1972, page 433]—only half the families given genetic counseling grasped its impact.

Nor can the information given to the experimental subject be in any sense totally complete. It would be impractical and probably unethical for the investigator to present the nearly endless list of all possible contingencies; in fact, he may not himself be aware of every untoward thing that might happen. Extensive detail, moreover, usually enhances the subject's confusion. Epstein and Lasagna showed that comprehension of medical information given to untutored subjects is inversely correlated with the elaborateness of the material presented.[1] The inconsiderate investigator, indeed, conceivably could exploit his authority and knowledge and extract "informed consent" by overwhelming the candidate-subject with information.

Ideally, the subject should give his consent freely, under no duress whatsoever. The facts are that some element of coercion is instrumental in any investigator–subject transaction. Volunteers for experiments will usually be influenced by hopes of obtaining better grades, earlier parole, more substantial egos, or just mundane cash. These pressures, however, are but fractional shadows of those enclosing the patient-subject. Incapacitated and hospitalized because of illness, frightened by strange and impersonal routines, and fearful for his health and perhaps life, he is far from

Reprinted with permission from *The New England Journal of Medicine*, 287, no. 9 (August 31, 1972), 465–66.

exercising a free power of choice when the person to whom he anchors all his hopes asks, "Say, you wouldn't mind, would you, if you joined some of the other patients on this floor and helped us to carry out some very important research we are doing?" When "informed consent" is obtained, it is not the student, the destitute bum, or the prisoner to whom, by virtue of his condition, the thumb screws of coercion are most relentlessly applied; it is the most used and useful of all experimental subjects, the patient with disease.

When a man or woman agrees to act as an experimental subject, therefore, his or her consent is marked by neither adequate understanding nor total freedom of choice. The conditions of the agreement are a far cry from those visualized as ideal. Jonas would have the subject identify with the investigative endeavor so that he and the researcher would be seeking a common cause: "Ultimately, the appeal for volunteers should seek . . . free and generous endorsement, the appropriation of the research purpose into the person's [i.e., the subject's] own scheme of ends."[2] For Ramsey, "informed consent" should represent a "covenantal bond between consenting man and consenting man [that] makes them . . . joint adventurers in medical care and progress."[3] Clearly, to achieve motivations and attitudes of this lofty type, an educated and understanding, rather than merely informed, consent is necessary.

Although it is unlikely that the goals of Jonas and of Ramsey will ever be achieved, and that human research subjects will spontaneously volunteer rather than be "conscripted,"[3] efforts to promote educated consent are in order. In view of the current emphasis on involving "the community" in such activities as regional planning, operation of clinics, and assignment of priorities, the general public and its political leaders are showing an increased awareness and understanding of medical affairs. But the orientation of this public interest in medicine is chiefly socioeconomic. Little has been done to give the public a basic understanding of medical research and its requirements not only for the

people's money but also for their participation. The public, to be sure, is being subjected to a bombardment of sensation-mongering news stories and books that feature "breakthroughs," or that reveal real or alleged exploitations—horror stories of Nazi-type experimentation on abused human minds and bodies. Muckraking is essential to expose malpractices, but unless accompanied by efforts to promote a broader appreciation of medical research and its methods, it merely compounds the difficulties for both the investigator and the subject when "informed consent" is solicited.

The procedure currently approved in the United States for enlisting human experimental subjects has one great virtue: patient-subjects are put on notice that their management is in part at least an experiment. The deceptions of the past are no longer tolerated. Beyond this accomplishment, however, the process of obtaining "informed consent," with all its regulations and conditions, is no more than elaborate ritual, a device that, when the subject is uneducated and uncomprehending, confers no more than the semblance of propriety on human experimentation. The subject's only real protection, the public as well as the medical profession must recognize, depends on the conscience and compassion of the investigator and his peers.

References

1. Epstein, L. C., Lasagna, L.: "Obtaining informed consent: form or substance." *Arch Intern Med* 123:682–688, 1969.

2. Jonas, H.: "Philosophical reflections on experimenting with human subjects." *Daedalus* 98:219–247, Spring, 1969.

3. Ramsey, P.: "The ethics of a cottage industry in an age of community and research medicine." *N Engl J Med* 284:700–706, 1971.

Suggested Further Reading

Alfidi, Ralph J., "Informed Consent: A Study of Patient Reactions," *Journal of the American*

Medical Association, 216 (May 24, 1971), 1325–29.

Beauchamp, Tom L., and James F. Childress, "The Principle of Autonomy," *Principles of Biomedical Ethics,* ed. Tom L. Beauchamp and James F. Childress. New York: Oxford University Press, 1979, p. 63.

Freedman, Benjamin, "A Moral Theory of Consent," *Hastings Center Report,* vol. 5, October 1975.

Slovenko, Ralph, "Commentary on Psychosurgery," *The Hastings Center Report,* vol. 5, October 1975.

4. TRUTH TELLING

When, if ever, is it morally acceptable to lie? The issue of truth telling in health care raises questions about the justifiability of deceiving or lying to patients. Do patients have a right to know the full truth about their condition and treatment? Does telling patients the truth actually cause harm in some situations?

From a deontological standpoint, lying to patients indicates a lack of respect for their dignity as persons and cannot be justified. Lying or withholding pertinent information from patients diminishes their autonomy and hampers their ability to make life decisions. Some writers claim that corporations have a similar duty to avoid deceiving or lying to consumers **[See Business, Chapter 11, Section 1].** If the requirement of informed consent is to be met, patients need adequate information upon which to base decisions regarding treatment. The concept of truth telling, like confidentiality and informed consent, leads us to probe the legitimacy of medical paternalism.

It has been argued that deceptive practices are justified because some patients do not want to know the truth. On this account, lying or deception does not violate patients' rights, because they are afraid to hear bad news and tacitly consent to having information withheld. The argument reflects a paternalistic attitude on the part of medical professionals. It presupposes that the professional can correctly predict a patient's response to information and that it is appropriate to lie or withhold data on the basis of such predictions.

Some physicians insist that a patient's optimistic attitude is a factor in successful treatment and that "knowing the worst" leads to depression or deterioration. Critics maintain that it is morally unacceptable for health care providers to control patient access to information. Some utilitarians hold that telling patients the truth does not harm them but in fact produces medical benefits such as better pain management and quicker recovery from surgery. It is difficult to strike a balance between the professional's desire to promote patient welfare and the obligation to respect a patient's trust and right to self-determination.

Another concern about truth telling involves the use of placebos. Patients sometimes show a favorable response to *any* medication or therapy so long as they believe that it will be effective. A physician worried about the danger of too-frequent doses of opiates (because of their depressant effect on respiration) may order injections of glucose to be given alternately with the pain-killing drugs. The effectiveness of treatment depends upon the patient's belief that all the injections contain pain-killers. To sustain that belief, medical personnel must lie or mislead the patient. Professionals may feel that if the patient stands to benefit medically from the procedure, then the deception is justified on utilitarian grounds.

Placebos are sometimes administered

when a patient is convinced that he or she requires treatment but the physician cannot find anything organically wrong. If the professional refuses to prescribe medication, the patient loses confidence in the physician. Accordingly, physicians prescribe an inert substance, such as starch or sugar pills, to placate the patient. Is this course of action in the patient's best interest as some physicians maintain? Critics argue that treating complaints with placebos is inappropriate for at least two reasons. First, it encourages dependence upon drugs to solve problems. Second, it prevents the patient from dealing with psychological problems which underlie the (presumably imaginary) ailment.

The general question involved in the preceding examples is whether it is ethically acceptable to deceive patients "for their own good." Cases exist in which a patient derives benefit from placebos or from ignorance of disturbing facts. On the other hand,

lies and deception undermine the trust which patients place in medical professionals. Ethical codes for health care providers have little to say about truth telling. However, respect for the dignity of patients as autonomous persons requires according them a measure of honesty, the same honesty a professional would demand if the situation were reversed.

In the following article Joseph S. Ellin examines moral distinctions between lying and deception. On Ellin's view, it is never permissible for physicians to lie to patients, but he holds that there is not even a prima facie duty not to deceive. The author bases the argument on his conception of the physician–patient relation as a "fiduciary relationship." Lying is unacceptable because it undermines the trust essential to the fiduciary relationship. However, Ellin contends, deceptive practices (like the use of placebos) may be used as one of the physician's tools for achieving the goals of the relationship.

JOSEPH S. ELLIN

Lying and Deception: The Solution to a Dilemma in Medical Ethics

Should doctors deceive their patients? Should they ever lie to them? Situations arise in the practice of medicine in which it appears that a medically desirable course of treatment cannot be undertaken, or cannot succeed, unless the patient is deceived; or that a patient's health or state of mind would be damaged unless some information is concealed from him, at least temporarily. Sometimes medical personnel feel justified in practicing deceit for reasons which do not directly benefit patients; for example, Veatch's case of the medical stu-

dents who are instructed to introduce themselves to hospital patients as "Doctor Smith" (instead of "Medical Student Smith") so as to overcome more quickly the anxiety they feel as they begin the transformation from layperson to physician.[1] Since in such cases most writers concede that patients ought not to be deceived unless something more important than truth is at stake, the problem is typically analyzed as determining the relative weight of the rights and interests involved: the patient's interest in the truth versus his or her interest

Reprinted with permission of the author and publisher from *Westminster Institute Review*, 1 (May 1981), 3–6.

in health and peace of mind, or perhaps the patient's right to the truth versus someone else's right to or interest in something else. When, however, the problem is posed in this way, the patient's right to the truth seems relatively unimportant, especially compared to an interest as obviously important as health, so that it seems evident that deception is justified, or even obligatory. The principle of not deceiving patients seems to have little weight when deception is thought necessary to achieve some desirable end.

The alternative, however, would seem to be to adopt the rigorist position that the duty of veracity is absolute, and this seems even less attractive. Most writers concede that the duty of veracity is prima facie only, at least as a principle of medical ethics where life and suffering are at stake; it does not appear plausible to adopt an ethic in which it is made obligatory to inflict avoidable anguish on someone already sick, especially where hope and good spirits, in addition to being desirable in themselves, may promote healing and help prolong life. One could hope to avoid this dilemma by holding that the duty of veracity, though not absolute, is to be given very great weight, and may be overridden only in the gravest cases; but this line conflicts with many of our intuitions about actual cases and will probably prove useless because ad hoc. There is a temptation to deceive, or at the very least to conceal information and blur the truth, not only to prevent anxiety and stimulate hope and good spirits, but to make possible the use of placebos, to persuade patients to abandon harmful habits, to generate confidence in the medical team and the like. The whole problem is to determine what counts as a sufficiently important end to justify an exception to the veracity principle. Hence the dilemma: either we say that veracity is an absolute duty, which is too strict; or we admit that it is prima facie only, which seems ad hoc, useless, and mushy.

I would like to suggest that the solution to this dilemma is to be found in the simple distinction between lying and deception. Writers on medical ethics do not seem to acknowledge this distinction, though it is commonly made in ordinary morality. But if we allow it, assuming also that we adopt a certain conception of the doctor–patient relationship, we can say that the duty not to lie is indeed absolute, but that there is no duty at all not to practice deception. Deception, on this view, is not even wrong prima facie, but is simply one tool the doctor may employ to achieve the ends of medicine. The conception of the doctor–patient relationship which allows us to reach this result is that of a fiduciary relationship, and the argument I wish to make is that two principles, the one prohibiting lying and the other allowing deception, may be defended through this conception.

A little reflection will make clear that in ordinary morality we do distinguish between lying and deception. Most of us would not lie, but we are much less scrupulous about deceiving. We might even make it a point of honor not to actually lie when we feel justified in planting false ideas in other people's minds. You ask me how my book is coming. I have done nothing on it in a month. I reply, "The work is very difficult." This is not a lie (the work *is* very difficult); but I have managed to convey a false impression. I prefer such evasion even to a white lie or harmless fiction ("Very well." "Slowly."). Countless examples suggest themselves. An amusing story is told of a certain St. Athanasius. His enemies coming to kill him, but mistaking him for another, asked, "Where is the traitor Athanasius?" The Saint replied, "Not far away."[2]

One reason we do not distinguish between lying and deception in the medical context is that deception is sometimes used for unacceptable ends. An example of such malignant deception is given by Marsha Millman. A doctor performs a liver biopsy (a procedure not without risk) under circumstances in which the procedure is probably not justified. He avoids telling the patient the results for some days. Finally he says, "Don't worry, the biopsy didn't show anything wrong with your liver." When the patient after much agitation is allowed to read her chart, she discovers that the report on her biopsy reads, ''No analysis, specimen insufficient for diagnosis.''[3]

When doctors deceive for self-interested motives, to cover up their bad judgment or their failures, we are apt to think the distinction between lying and deception is mere hair-splitting. Millman asserts that the doctor ''had evasively lied.'' Though strictly speaking inaccurate, this characterization is correct from the moral point of view, since because of the doctor's bad motive, the evasion may be considered morally no different from a lie. But the situation is different when the motives are benevolent. James Childress gives the interesting case of a patient who, due to constant pain caused by chronic intestinal problems, injects himself six times daily with a strong (but allegedly nonaddictive) pain-killer. When the patient is admitted to the hospital with another complaint, the staff decides to wean him from the drug by gradually diluting the dosage with saline solution. After a time, when the pain does not recur, the patient is told that he is no longer receiving the medication.[4]

Here we have a treatment plan that can work only through deception; if the patient knows he is not receiving the usual dosage, his pain will recur. Hence the staff does not have the option of simply telling him what they intend to do and then doing it over his objections. The staff's alternatives therefore are: comply with the patient's wishes and administer medication they believe to be unnecessary and harmful; promise to do what he wants and then follow their withdrawal plan anyway, i.e., lie; avoid telling him what they are doing without actually lying about it. If it were not possible to carry out the plan without lying, if for example the patient asked direction questions about his medication, the choice thus posed between abandoning the plan and lying to him would seem far more difficult than the choice between abandoning the plan and simply deceiving him. It seems preferable to carry out the plan without actually lying; so much so that we are tempted to

say that if the staff could not avoid lying, it would be better to abandon the plan, whereas employing the plan using deception is quite justifiable, given the alternative.

The distinction between lying and deception may, however, seem unjustified from what Sissela Bok has called ''the perspective of the deceived.'' As far as the deceived is concerned, deception can be just as bad as a lie. Both give rise to resentment, disappointment and suspicion. Those deceived, as Bok says, ''feel wronged; . . . They see that they were manipulated, that the deceit made them unable to make choices for themselves. . . unable to act as they would have wanted to act.''[5] The deceived has been led to have false beliefs, has been deprived of control of a situation, has been subjected to manipulation, and so suffers a sense of betrayal and wounded dignity. Like lying, deception harms many interests. We have an interest in acquiring true beliefs, in having the information needed to make wise decisions about our lives, in being treated as trustworthy and intelligent persons, in being able to trust those in whom we put our trust. The deceiver, either intentionally or inadvertently, harms these interests. To the person whose interests are harmed by deceit, it is small comfort that the deceit did not involve an actual lie.

Those who find the lying/deception distinction objectionable are probably thinking of the harm each does to the deceived. Their argument is that if it is equally harmful to deceive and to lie, then no distinction between the two should be allowed. However, such a view oversimplifies the moral situation, as analysis of deception will reveal.

Intentional deception, short of lying, involves two elements: a statement or action from which it is expected that the person who is the target of the deception will draw a false conclusion, and failure to provide information which would prevent the conclusion from being drawn. The important thing is that the false information itself is not actually presented to the person deceived: everything said and done is in a sense innocent and within the rights of the deceiver. Because of this, it is possible to take the view that intentional deception is no moral wrong at all. No less a moralist than Kant writes: "I can make believe, make a demonstration from which others will draw the conclusion I want, though they have no right to expect that my action will express my real mind. In that case, I have not lied to them . . . I may, for instance, wish people to think that I am off on a journey, and so I pack my luggage."[6] Kant evidently sees nothing wrong with this; his view seems to be that he has every right to pack his luggage if he chooses and if others draw certain conclusions (however reasonable) which turn out to be false, they have only themselves to blame. This, however, is too lenient on deceivers. If a person says or does something, knowing or believing that others are likely to draw false conclusions from it, and if the person refrains from providing them information he knows would prevent the false conclusions from being drawn, then he is at least in part responsible for the deception. But though he is partly responsible, he is not as responsible as he would be were he to present the false conclusion himself. Even when there is a lie, of course, the victim must bear some of the blame for being deceived, since he has imprudently trusted the liar and failed to confirm the statements made. But when a victim is deceived without a lie, he is more to blame, since he has not only failed to investigate a situation, but has also drawn or jumped to a conclusion which goes beyond the statements made to him. Even where the conclusion is a very natural inference from the statements or actions, the fact that it is an inference shows that the deceived participates in his own deception.

However, this is not the only reason why deception is considered less bad than lying. When I lie, I tell you something which, since it is false, ought not to be believed; this harms your interest in having true beliefs. When I deceive, however, I merely give you grounds for an inference which does not actually follow; this harms your interest in having good grounds for inferences, but does not directly harm your interest in having true beliefs.

The third reason why deception is not as bad as lying is that lying violates the social contract in a way that deception does not. In a sense, the social contract is renewed by every act of speech (more properly by every assertion), since to speak is implicitly to give an assurance that what one says is true. Every statement implies a promise or certification of its truth. A lie, which with a single act both implies a promise and violates it, thus involves a self-contradiction. It could be said that the social contract prohibits deception generally, on the rule-utilitarian ground that social life would be unduly burdened if, as in a spy novel, every apparently innocent action were a potential source of misinformation. But though deception may be a violation of the rules (lying, too, is a violation of the rules in this sense), it is not at the same time a reaffirmation of the rules, and hence is not an implicit self-contradiction. We can understand this when we see that although the social contract may prohibit deception, it cannot prohibit deceptive statements, since deceptive statements which are not lies are true, and the social contract cannot prohibit true statements. The contract does prohibit making true statements with the intent to deceive, or in circumstances such that the speaker does or should realize that the statement is likely to deceive. But an intention is not a promise, not even an implicit promise, hence there is nothing self-contradictory about deception. To the extent that the deceiver affirms the contract by his statement, he also obeys the contract, since his statement is true.

This analysis has an important consequence for the theory of professional morality I am defending here, since it enables us to see the difference between lying and deception with regard to trust. In everyday life we have the feeling that the liar is less trustworthy than the deceiver. Why is this, since they both intend to mislead? The conceptual basis of this perception is that the liar reaffirms the promise of the social contract in the very act (the lie) by which he violates that promise. The deceiver may violate the social contract but does not promise to obey it in the very act of violation. Doubtless a deceiver should not be trusted, but it seems reasonable that we would be even more wary, more on guard against a person who not only deceives, but breaks a promise in the very act of reaffirming it. The significance of this distinction for professional morality I shall explain shortly.

So far I have argued that morality draws a distinction between lying and intentional deception. Now I must address the more controversial question of what the doctor's obligations are with respect to the duty of veracity. I will argue that if we conceive the doctor–patient relationship as a fiduciary relationship, then the doctor has an absolute duty not to lie, but not even a prima facie duty not to deceive. This is different from the view of ordinary morality which condemns both lying and deception, holds both wrong prima facie only, but holds lying morally worse. My defense of the above propositions as principles of medical ethics rests partly on conceptual points, and partly on contingent psychological facts having to do with the conditions of trust. It is because trust is more important in the doctor–patient relationship, conceived as fiduciary, than in ordinary life, that there is a difference between ordinary and professional morality.

As is well-known, there are many conceptions of the doctor–patient relationship. One can think of doctors as priests, friends, engineers, business partners, or partners in health. One can think of the relationship with patients as contractual, philanthropic, collegial, even exploitive. Doubtless there is merit in each of these points of view; each represents some significant truth about some doctor–patient relationships. Such conceptions or models are useful because they illuminate ethical principles; there are connections between the model of the relationship and the ethical principles which should govern it. A doctor who thinks of himself as a body mechanic will have different views about providing information to patients than one who thinks of himself as engaged with the patient in a partnership in healing. (It is unlikely that the doctors in the previous examples thought of themselves as engaged in a partnership with their patients.) Similarly, a doctor who imagines himself to be a patient's friend takes a different view of how much time he should spend with a patient than one who believes he is merely fulfilling a contract for services.

Undoubtedly many medical personnel think of themselves as having a fiduciary relationship, or something like it, with their patients or clients. The fiduciary conception is based on the legal notion of someone, the fiduciary, who has certain responsibilities for the welfare of another, the beneficiary. It is important to recognize that a fiduciary's responsibilities are limited to the specific goals of the relationship. A lawyer, for example, has responsibility for the client's legal affairs (or some of them), an accountant for his financial affairs, etc. Every beneficiary will have many interests which are external to the responsibilities of the fiduciary. This is not to say that these other interests might not impinge on the content of that relationship, but only that since the relationship was established for certain purposes relative to the specific competencies of the professional, the professional's responsibilities stop at the edges of these purposes.

If I seek legal assistance, it is because I want my legal interests to be protected; I do not expect my lawyer to take responsibility for my emotional stability, the strength of my marriage, how I use my leisure time, etc., though of course these other interests of mine might be affected by my legal condition. Where my legal interests conflict with some of my other interests, it is up to me, not my lawyer, to make the necessary choices. Those who expect their lawyer or doctor to look after a broad range of their interests, perhaps even their total welfare, obviously do not have a fiduciary conception of the professional relationship; they think of the professional as priest, friend, or some similarly broad model.

Since a fiduciary relationship is limited by

specific defining goals, it is not a contractual relationship, although a legal contract may be the instrument that binds the relationship. A contractual relationship is more open, in that the parties may write anything they please into the contract. The responsibilities of the professional are exactly those stated in the contract, neither more nor less. In a contractual relationship, the professional's decisions will be guided by his interpretation of what the contract requires. Thus if a doctor believes he has agreed with the patient to do everything possible to restore the patient's health and preserve the patient's life, he will take one course of action. If, however, he believes he has also agreed to protect the patient's family from prolonged worry and exhaustion of resources, though these are not strictly speaking medical goals, he may well do or recommend something else.

Now in addition to one's interests in health, financial condition, etc., a person has moral interests, I have an interest not to be lied to, not to be manipulated, not to be treated with contempt. There is no theoretical reason why these moral interests could not conflict with other interests such as health. But since under the fiduciary conception a professional's responsibility is to foster only those interests which define the relationship, the professional is not obligated to foster the client's moral interests. Normally, of course, there will not be a conflict, and no doubt in certain professions, such as law, opportunity for conflict is small. But such conflicts do arise in the practice of medicine (the Childress example is a clear case). The fiduciary conception imposes no professional obligation on the doctor to be concerned with these interests. This is not to say that a doctor ought not to be concerned with such interests. But if he should be, this is either because the doctor–patient relationship ought not to be construed as fiduciary, or because under certain circumstances, the commands of ordinary morality ought to override the commands of medical ethics.

Since a patient's interest in not being deceived is a moral interest and not a health in-terest, the doctor–patient relationship, construed as fiduciary, does not even prima facie exclude deception. To argue that it does, is to construe the relationship as priestly, friendly, contractual or something else. One could hold that if general moral obligations take precedence over professional obligations, the doctor has a general moral obligation not to deceive, even if he has no such professional obligation. That general moral obligations take precedence over professional obligations is a proposition many professionals would dispute, however; lawyers for example will argue that their general moral obligation not to harm or pain innocent people is overridden by their professional obligation to do everything possible to protect their client's legal interests.[7]

It may seem to follow from this that doctors also have no obligation to avoid actual lying when, in their best judgment, a patient's health might be injured were he to learn some truth. To see why this is not the case we have to distinguish between the obligations *of* the doctor–patient relationship, and the obligations which make the relationship possible. In a fiduciary relationship, the only obligation *of* the relationship is to do whatever is necessary to further the goals by which the relationship is defined. But it might be the case that the relationship could not be established unless other obligations were respected. If this is the case, it follows that obligations which make the relationship possible override, in cases of conflict, obligations *of* the relationship, since the latter could not exist without the former (if the relationship is not established, then neither are any of its obligations). Hence, if the obligation not to lie is an obligation which makes the relationship possible, it follows that this obligation overrides even the obligation to protect health, and is thus an absolute.

The argument that lying destroys the doctor–patient relationship, conceived as fiduciary, is partly a conceptual argument, partly an argument based on judgment and experience. It is often said that the doctor–patient relationship depends heavily on trust. The patient puts himself (often literally) in the hands of his doctor. Although this could be true to an extent of any interpretation of the relationship, it is less true of some interpretations than others. Contracts, for example, do not depend on trust so much as on an understanding of mutual self-interest; a contractual relationship succeeds when each party understands that it is not in either party's best interest to violate the contract. Even the priest or friend roles do not require trust as their foundation, though they do generate trust. A priest is someone who has a special calling or vocation; his entire life is dedicated to an ideal of service. We trust him because his life witnesses his trustworthiness.[8] A friendship relation is based on personal satisfactions and mutual compatibility; these generate trust but do not rest on it. It is the fiduciary relationship which depends heavily on trust. A fiduciary must be trusted to act with the true interests of the beneficiary in view; the law recognizes this by defining trust as "a fiduciary relationship."[9] If, however, we were to allow the fiduciary to lie, the trust basis of the relationship would be undermined and the relationship itself jeopardized. A lie, it will be recalled, violates a kind of implicit assurance we give when we speak, namely, that our words will be used to state the truth. Deception through evasive or misleading statements which are nonetheless true does not violate such an assurance but accords with it. The deceiver can thus be trusted at least to speak the truth, while the liar violates the very assurance he is giving with his speech.

Although the argument that the liar undermines the basis of the fiduciary relationship by showing himself to be untrustworthy is empirical, it is not open to one kind of objection commonly brought against empirical arguments in ethics. The objection is that if the only reason to avoid a certain practice is that the practice leads to undesirable consequences, then the solution is to employ the practice anyway, but do so in such a way that the consequences are avoided. Thus Alan Goldman criticizes arguments which oppose lying or deceiving by "appeal to certain systematic disutilities that might be projected, e.g., effects upon the agent's trustworthiness

and upon the trust that other people are willing to accord him if his lies are discovered." According to Goldman, "The only conclusion that I would draw from the empirical points . . . is that doctors should perhaps be better trained in psychology in order to be able to judge the effects . . ." of the decision to lie or not.[10]

Goldman's argument is good not against those who oppose lying on the ground that it destroys trust, but only against those who hold this and *also* hold (as Goldman himself holds) that lying would be wrong even if it didn't affect trust. If lying is wrong whether it affects trust or not, then the fact that it affects trust obviously cannot be the reason why it is wrong. But as I do not claim that lying is wrong (in the professional–client relationship) if it does not affect trust, I need not deny that the tendency of lying to destroy trust might from time to time be countered by certain clever psychological tactics on the part of liars. This does not in the least show that lying does not tend to destroy trust. However, I maintain that the tendency of lying to destroy trust is considerably greater than the tendency of deception to destroy trust, and this I argue partly on the basis of the conceptual difference between lying and deception, partly on the basis of experience. Lying is more destructive to trust than deception because lying is a greater violation of the social contract. The liar by his false speech violates the very promise that he makes in speaking, the promise to speak the truth. And it is for this reason, as I think experience reveals, that we find ourselves less trusting of someone who has lied to us, than of someone who has misled us or created a false impression.

Given this threat to trust, it seems plausible to hold that lying is too dangerous ever to be allowed in a relationship founded on trust. Suppose we adopted a rule which made lying only prima facie wrong, and thus permitted lying in certain very serious cases. The patient would know that the doctor could not be trusted to tell the truth, even in response to a direct question, when the doctor deemed it unwise to do so; and therefore the patient would know that the doctor could never be believed, since even an apparently trivial matter might in fact be serious enough for the doctor to feel justified in lying about. Of course the fact that the patient would know this does not necessarily mean that the patient would not trust the doctor anyway. But a patient who has been lied to has been given very strong grounds to conclude that the doctor is not to be trusted, so that even a single justified lie is likely to undermine the patient's trust.

Let us test the prohibition of lying against a case where our intuitions seem to lead us to the opposite conclusion. Gert and Culver give the following case: "Mrs. E is in extremely critical condition after an automobile accident which has taken the life of one of her four children and severely injured another. Dr. P believes that her very tenuous hold on life might be weakened by the shock of hearing of her children's conditions, so he decides to deceive her for a short period of time."[11] According to these authors, a rational person would choose to be deceived in such circumstances, so there is nothing wrong with the doctor's decision to deceive her. As is typical of the medical ethics literature, the authors do not distinguish between lying and deception. On our principles, there is nothing even prima facie wrong with the doctor's use of evasive or misleading statements to conceal the truth. But suppose Mrs. E demands a straight answer from which evasion offers no escape. Gert and Culver seem to propose that the question to be answered is whether a rational person would want to be lied to in these circumstances, but as there does not seem to be any way to arrive at an answer to this question, their proposal does not really advance beyond our intuitions. In this case, our intuitions strongly suggest that lying would be justified in order to protect the woman's health, but on the principles advanced in this essay, lying is not permitted, since if Dr. P lies in response to Mrs. E's direct question, she will eventually discover that he cannot be trusted, and that therefore they cannot enjoy a relationship based on trust. Of course this is not to say that the doctor must tell her the truth in the blunt-

est or most painful way, but only that he must not lie. Where a harmful truth cannot be concealed, it is up to the doctor to reveal it in a way least damaging to the patient. To take a different view is to hold that the doctor–patient relationship is not a fiduciary relationship based on trust, but something else, friendship perhaps, or maybe some form of paternalism, in which the doctor has the responsibility of balancing all of the patient's interests and making decisions in light of his conception of the patient's total welfare. If, however, these conceptions of the relationship seem unattractive to us (and I have not argued that they should seem unattractive), we will have to take the view, intuitions to the contrary notwithstanding, that even in the situation just described, the doctor's duty is to tell the truth.

Notes

1. Robert Veatch, *Case Studies in Medical Ethics* (Cambridge: Harvard University Press, 1977), pp. 147f.

2. I found this example in an unpublished paper by James Rachels, "Honesty." Rachels evidently borrowed it from P. T. Geach, *The Virtues* (Cambridge: Cambridge University Press, 1977), p. 115.

3. Marcia Millman, *The Unkindest Cut* (New York: William Morrow and Co., 1977), pp. 138f.

4. James Childress, "Paternalism and Health Care," in *Medical Responsibility,* ed. Wade L. Robison and Michael S. Pritchard (New York: Humana Press, 1979), pp. 15–27.

5. Sissela Bok, *Lying* (New York: Pantheon Books, 1978), ch. 2.

6. Immanuel Kant, *Lectures on Ethics,* trans. Louis Infled (New York: Harper and Row, 1963), pp. 147–154.

7. The contention that, as a general rule, professional obligations override ordinary moral obligations is critically examined and disputed by Alan H. Goldman, *The Moral Foundations of Professional Ethics* (Totowa, N.J.: Littlefield, Adams and Co., 1980).

8. On the idea of medicine as a calling founded on "covenant" which transforms the doctor, see William F. May, "Code, Covenant, Contract or Philanthropy," *Hastings Center Report* 5, 6 (December 1975): 29–38.

9. "Trust. Noun: a fiduciary relationship; a matter of confidence." *Ballantine's Law Dictionary*, 3rd ed.

10. Goldman, *Professional Ethics*, p. 176.

11. Bernard Gert and Charles Culver, "The Justification of Paternalism" in Robison and Pritchard, *Medical Responsibility*, p. 7.

Suggested Further Reading

Appleton, William S., "The Importance of Psychiatrists' Telling Patients the Truth," *American Journal of Psychiatry*, 129, no. 6 (December 1972), 742–45.

Bok, Sissela, "Lies to the Sick and Dying," *Lying: Moral Choice in Public and Private Life*, ed. Sissela Bok. New York: Pantheon Books, 1978, pp. 220–41.

Meyer, Bernard C., "Truth and the Physician," in *Ethical Issues in Medicine*, ed. E. Fuller Torrey. Boston: Little, Brown, 1968, pp. 159–77.

Oken, Donald, "What to Tell Cancer Patients," *Journal of the American Medical Association*, 175 (1961), 1120–28.

6. ISSUES IN REPRODUCTIVE HEALTH

1. ABORTION

The sharpest conflict in the discussion of abortion arises between those who assert that a woman has an unqualified *right to choose* abortion and those who argue that, since every fetus has a *right to life,* abortion is equivalent to murder. The U.S. Supreme Court ruled in the landmark *Roe* v. *Wade* decision of 1973 that state laws restricting abortion were unconstitutional except under narrowly defined conditions. While the ruling made abortion legal, controversy about its ethical acceptability continues. Early in 1989 the Court announced that it would rule on a case involving abortion laws in the state of Missouri. The decision could result in a reversal of *Roe* v. *Wade.*

In another ruling (*Harris* v. *McRae,* 1980), the court upheld the constitutionality of the so-called Hyde Amendment, which restricted Medicaid funding of abortions to cases in which the mother's life is threatened or where the pregnancy is a result of rape or incest. Since the Medicaid program provides federal financing for the health care of the poor, the decision means that impoverished women seldom obtain abortions paid for out of public funds. Although abortion is no longer against the law, it is out of reach for many. Right-to-choose forces argue that the policy is ethically unsound on grounds of social injustice.

One way of approaching the ethical problem of abortion is to examine the moral status of the fetus. The issue of moral status (of animals, plants, and nonliving objects) has

also been raised by writers concerned with environmental protection. **[See Business, Chapter 11, Section 2.]** What moral position should be assigned to the fetus: Is it or is it not a person? Those who take a *conservative* position on abortion contend that the developing organism is a person and has the same rights we accord to any human being. If we are willing to grant full moral status to the fetus, it follows that abortion is equivalent to killing and can be justified only under very limited conditions, as when the mother's life is in danger. Proponents of this view maintain that the state, which is under obligation to protect its weaker members, should extend that protection to the unborn.

If, on the other hand, the fetus does not have the moral status of a person, then abortion is no more ethically problematic than the removal of any other piece of tissue—the tonsils, say, or the appendix. The typically *liberal* position assigns no rights to the fetus and instead stresses the right of a pregnant woman to self-determination. From this standpoint, abortion is morally similar to contraception, the preventing of a possible person.

A *moderate* position on abortion grants partial moral status to the fetus, on grounds of its potential personhood or its strong resemblance in later stages of development to a person. On this view, some abortions are justifiable while others are not. What factors are relevant to making the determination?

Some hold that the pregnant woman's reasons for seeking an abortion bear on whether or not it is justified. Others believe that the fetus's stage of development is a consideration.

Attempts have been made to draw the line at some point in the biological development of the fetus after which it possesses the moral status of a person. Such points as implantation, quickening, and viability have been suggested as appropriate places to draw the line. The Supreme Court addressed the line-drawing problem in *Roe* v. *Wade* and drew the line at viability, ruling that states may regulate or prohibit abortion after that point. However, it has proven difficult to establish the moral relevance of any particular point in a continuous process of fetal development.

Conservatives often argue that conception is the only nonarbitrary point at which the line can be drawn. They sometimes employ what is referred to as a *slippery slope*-type argument, maintaining that wherever the line is drawn, it will necessarily slide back to the point of conception. At the other extreme, some liberal ethicists have proposed criteria for personhood which would exclude newborn infants. A position of this kind suggests that the line can be drawn at some point *after* birth and leads to the moral justifiability of infanticide as well as abortion.

While drawing the line is one way of developing a moderate position, other strategies have been employed. Moderates argue that even if the fetus has full moral status (as conservatives typically contend), abortion is permissible in some cases. Others moderate the liberal position by granting the libertarian assumption that the fetus has no moral status, while denying that all abortions are acceptable. In the following article Jane English first argues that it is not possible to determine (1) whether the fetus is a person or (2) where to draw the line. Using strategies similar to those outlined above, she develops two arguments aimed at moderating both the liberal and the conservative positions.

JANE ENGLISH

Abortion and the Concept of a Person

The abortion debate rages on. Yet the two most popular positions seem to be clearly mistaken. Conservatives maintain that a human life begins at conception and that therefore abortion must be wrong because it is murder. But not all killings of humans are murders. Most notably, self-defense may justify even the killing of an innocent person.

Liberals, on the other hand, are just as mistaken in their argument that since a fetus does not become a person until birth, a woman may do whatever she pleases in and to her own body. First, you cannot do as you please with your own body if it affects other people adversely.[1] Second, if a fetus is not a person, that does not imply that you can do to it anything you wish. Animals, for example, are not persons, yet to kill or torture them for no reason at all is wrong.

At the center of the storm has been the issue of just when it is between ovulation and adulthood that a person appears on the scene. Conservatives draw the line at conception, liberals at birth. In this paper I first exam-

Reprinted from *Canadian Journal of Philosophy*, vol. V, no. 2 (October 1975) by permission of Canadian Association for Publishing in Philosophy.

ine our concept of a person and conclude that no single criterion can capture the concept of a person and no sharp line can be drawn. Next I argue that if a fetus is a person, abortion is still justifiable in many cases; and if a fetus is not a person, killing it is still wrong in many cases. To a large extent, these two solutions are in agreement. I conclude that our concept of a person cannot and need not bear the weight that the abortion controversy has thrust upon it.

I

The several factions in the abortion argument have drawn battle lines around various proposed criteria for determining what is and what is not a person. For example, Mary Anne Warren[2] lists five features (capacities for reasoning, self-awareness, complex communication, etc.) as her criteria for personhood and argues for the permissibility of abortion because a fetus falls outside this concept. Baruch Brody[3] uses brain waves. Michael Tooley[4] picks having-a-concept-of-self as his criterion and concludes that infanticide and abortion are justifiable, while the killing of adult animals is not. On the other side, Paul Ramsey[5] claims a certain gene structure is the defining characteristic. John Noonan[6] prefers conceived-of-humans and presents counterexamples to various other candidate criteria. For instance, he argues against viability as the criterion because the newborn and infirm would then be non-persons, since they cannot live without the aid of others. He rejects any criterion that calls upon the sorts of sentiments a being can evoke in adults on the grounds that this would allow us to exclude other races as non-persons if we could just view them sufficiently unsentimentally.

These approaches are typical: foes of abortion propose sufficient conditions for personhood which fetuses satisfy, while friends of abortion counter with necessary conditions for personhood which fetuses lack. But these both presuppose that the concept of a person can be captured in a strait jacket of necessary and/or sufficient conditions.[7] Rather, "per-

son" is a cluster of features, of which rationality, having a self-concept and being conceived of humans are only part.

What is typical of persons? Within our concept of a person we include, first, certain biological factors: descended from humans, having a certain genetic makeup, having a head, hands, arms, eyes, capable of locomotion, breathing, eating, sleeping. There are psychological factors: sentience, perception, having a concept of self and of one's own interests and desires, the ability to use tools, the ability to use language or symbol systems, the ability to joke, to be angry, to doubt. There are rationality factors: the ability to reason and draw conclusions, the ability to generalize and to learn from past experience, the ability to sacrifice present interests for greater gains in the future. There are social factors: the ability to work in groups and respond to peer pressures, the ability to recognize and consider as valuable the interests of others, seeing oneself as one among "other minds," the ability to sympathize, encourage, love, the ability to evoke from others the responses of sympathy, encouragement, love, the ability to work with others for mutual advantage. Then there are legal factors: being subject to the law and protected by it, having the ability to sue and enter contracts, being counted in the census, having a name and citizenship, the ability to own property, inherit, and so forth.

Now the point is not that this list is incomplete, or that you can find counterinstances to each of its points. People typically exhibit rationality, for instance, but someone who was irrational would not thereby fail to qualify as a person. On the other hand, something could exhibit the majority of these features and still fail to be a person, as an advanced robot might. There is no single core of necessary and sufficient features which we can draw upon with the assurance that they constitute what really makes a person; there are only features that are more or less typical.

This is not to say that no necessary or sufficient conditions can be given. Being alive is a necessary condition for being a person, and being a U.S. Senator is sufficient. But rather than falling inside a sufficient condition or outside a necessary one, a fetus lies in the penumbra region where our concept of a person is not so simple. For this reason I think a conclusive answer to the question whether a fetus is a person is unattainable.

Here we might note a family of simple fallacies that proceed by stating a necessary condition for personhood and showing that a fetus has that characteristic. This is a form of the fallacy of affirming the consequent. For example, some have mistakenly reasoned from the premise that a fetus is human (after all, it is a human fetus rather than, say, a canine fetus), to the conclusion that it is a human. Adding an equivocation on "being," we get the fallacious argument that since a fetus is something both living and human, it is a human being.

Nonetheless, it does seem clear that a fetus has very few of the above family of characteristics, whereas a newborn baby exhibits a much larger proportion of them—and a two-year-old has even more. Note that one traditional anti-abortion argument has centered on pointing out the many ways in which a fetus resembles a baby. They emphasize its development ("It already has ten fingers . . .") without mentioning its dissimilarities to adults (it still has gills and a tail). They also try to evoke the sort of sympathy on our part that we only feel toward other persons ("Never to laugh . . . or feel the sunshine?"). This all seems to be a relevant way to argue, since its purpose is to persuade us that a fetus satisfies so many of the important features on the list that it ought to be treated as a person. Also note that a fetus near the time of birth satisfies many more of these factors than a fetus in the early months of development. This could provide reason for making distinctions among the different stages of pregnancy, as the U.S. Supreme Court has done.[8]

Historically, the time at which a person has been said to come into existence has varied widely. Muslims date personhood from fourteen days after conception. Some medievals followed Aristotle in placing ensoulment at forty days after conception for a male fetus and eighty days for a female fetus.[9] In European common law since the Seventeenth Century, abortion was considered the killing of a person only after quickening, the time when a pregnant woman first feels the fetus move on its own. Nor is this variety of opinions surprising. Biologically, a human being develops gradually. We shouldn't expect there to be any specific time or sharp dividing point when a person appears on the scene.

For these reasons I believe our concept of a person is not sharp or decisive enough to bear the weight of a solution to the abortion controversy. To use it to solve that problem is to clarify *obscurum per obscurius*.

II

Next let us consider what follows if a fetus is a person after all. Judith Jarvis Thomson's landmark article, "A Defense of Abortion,"[10] correctly points out that some additional argumentation is needed at this point in the conservative argument to bridge the gap between the premise that a fetus is an innocent person and the conclusion that killing it is always wrong. To arrive at this conclusion, we would need the additional premise that killing an innocent person is always wrong. But killing an innocent person is sometimes permissible, most notably in self-defense. Some examples may help draw out our intuitions or ordinary judgments about self-defense.

Suppose a mad scientist, for instance, hypnotized innocent people to jump out of the bushes and attack innocent passers-by with knives. If you are so attacked, we agree you have a right to kill the attacker in self-defense, if killing him is the only way to protect your life or to save yourself from serious injury. It does not seem to matter here that the attacker is not malicious but himself an innocent pawn, for your killing of him is not done in a spirit of retribution but only in self-defense.

How severe an injury may you inflict in self-defense? In part this depends upon the severity of the injury to be avoided: you may not shoot someone merely to avoid having your clothes torn. This might lead one to the mistaken conclusion that the defense may only equal the threatened injury in severity; that to avoid death you may kill, but to avoid a black eye you may only inflict a black eye or the equivalent. Rather, our laws and customs seem to say that you may create an injury somewhat, but not enormously, greater than the injury to be avoided. To fend off an attack whose outcome would be as serious as rape, a severe beating or the loss of a finger, you may shoot; to avoid having your clothes torn, you may blacken an eye.

Aside from this, the injury you may inflict should only be the minimum necessary to deter or incapacitate the attacker. Even if you know he intends to kill you, you are not justified in shooting him if you could equally well save yourself by the simple expedient of running away. Self-defense is for the purpose of avoiding harms rather than equalizing harms.

Some cases of pregnancy present a parallel situation. Though the fetus is itself innocent, it may pose a threat to the pregnant woman's well-being, life prospects or health, mental or physical. If the pregnancy presents a slight threat to her interests, it seems self-defense cannot justify abortion. But if the threat is on a par with a serious beating or the loss of a finger, she may kill the fetus that poses such a threat, even if it is an innocent person. If a lesser harm to the fetus could have the same defensive effect, killing it would not be justified. It is unfortunate that the only way to free the woman from the pregnancy entails the death of the fetus (except in very late stages of pregnancy). Thus a self-defense model supports Thomson's point that the woman has a right only to be freed from the fetus, not a right to demand its death.[11]

The self-defense model is most helpful when we take the pregnant woman's point of view. In the pre-Thomson literature, abortion is often framed as a question for a third party; do you, a doctor, have a right to choose between the life of the woman and that of the fetus? Some have claimed that if you were a passer-by who witnessed a struggle between the innocent hypnotized attacker and his equally innocent victim, you would have no reason to kill either in defense of the other.

They have concluded that the self-defense model implies that a woman may attempt to abort herself, but that a doctor should not assist her. I think the position of the third party is somewhat more complex. We do feel some inclination to intervene on behalf of the victim rather than the attacker, other things equal. But if both parties are innocent, other factors come into consideration. You would rush to the aid of your husband whether he was attacker or attackee. If a hypnotized famous violinist were attacking a skid row bum, we would try to save the individual who is of more value to society. These considerations would tend to support abortion in some cases.

But suppose you are a frail senior citizen who wishes to avoid being knifed by one of these innocent hypnotics, so you have hired a bodyguard to accompany you. If you are attacked, it is clear we believe that the bodyguard, acting as your agent, has a right to kill the attacker to save you from a serious beating. Your rights of self-defense are transferred to your agent. I suggest that we should similarly view the doctor as the pregnant woman's agent in carrying out a defense she is physically incapable of accomplishing herself.

Thanks to modern technology, the cases are rare in which a pregnancy poses as clear a threat to a woman's bodily health as an attacker brandishing a switchblade. How does self-defense fare when more subtle, complex and long-range harms are involved?

To consider a somewhat fanciful example, suppose you are a highly trained surgeon when you are kidnapped by the hypnotic attacker. He says he does not intend to harm you but to take you back to the mad scientist who, it turns out, plans to hypnotize you to have a permanent mental block against all your knowledge of medicine. This would automatically destroy your career which would in turn have a serious adverse impact on your family, your personal relationships and your happiness. It seems to me that if the only way you can avoid this outcome is to shoot the innocent attacker, you are justified in so doing. You are defending yourself from a drastic injury to your life prospects. I think it is no exaggeration to claim that unwanted pregnancies (most obviously among teenagers) often have such adverse life-long consequences as the surgeon's loss of livelihood.

Several parallels arise between various views on abortion and the self-defense model. Let's suppose further that these hypnotized attackers only operate at night, so that it is well known that they can be avoided completely by the considerable inconvenience of never leaving your house after dark. One view is that since you could stay home at night, therefore if you go out and are selected by one of these hypnotized people, you have no right to defend yourself. This parallels the view that abstinence is the only acceptable way to avoid pregnancy. Others might hold that you ought to take along some defense such as Mace which will deter the hypnotized person without killing him, but that is this defense fails, you are obliged to submit to the resulting injury, no matter how severe it is. This parallels the view that contraception is all right but abortion is always wrong, even in cases of contraceptive failure.

A third view is that you may kill the hypnotized person only if he will actually kill you, but not if he will only injure you. This is like the position that abortion is permissible only if it is required to save the woman's life. Finally we have the view that it is all right to kill the attacker, even if only to avoid a very slight inconvenience to yourself and even if you knowingly walked down the very street where all these incidents have been taking place without taking along any Mace or protective escort. If we assume that a fetus is a person, this is the analogue of the view that abortion is always justifiable, "on demand."

The self-defense model allows us to see an important difference that exists between abortion and infanticide, even if a fetus is a person from conception. Many have argued that the only way to justify abortion without justifying infanticide would be to find some characteristic of personhood that is acquired at birth. Michael Tooley, for one, claims infanticide is justifiable because the really significant characteristics of person are acquired some time after birth. But all such approaches look to characteristics of the developing human and ignore the relation between the fetus and the woman. What if, after birth, the presence of an infant or the need to support it posed a grave threat to the woman's sanity or life prospects? She could escape this threat by the simple expedient of running away. So a solution that does not entail the death of the infant is available. Before birth, such solutions are not available because of the biological dependence of the fetus on the woman. Birth is the crucial point not because of any characteristics the fetus gains, but because after birth the woman can defend herself by a means less drastic than killing the infant. Hence self-defense can be used to justify abortion without necessarily thereby justifying infanticide.

III

On the other hand, supposing a fetus is not after all a person, would abortion always be morally permissible? Some opponents of abortion seem worried that if a fetus is not a full-fledged person, then we are justified in treating it in any way at all. However, this does not follow. Non-persons do get some consideration in our moral code, though of course they do not have the same rights as persons have (and in general they do not have moral responsibilities), and though their interests may be overridden by the interests of persons. Still, we cannot treat them in any way at all.

Treatment of animals is a case in point. It is wrong to torture dogs for fun or to kill wild birds for no reason at all. It is wrong *period,* even though dogs and birds do not have the same rights persons do. However, few people think it is wrong to use dogs as experimental animals, causing them considerable suffering in some cases, provided that the resulting research will probably bring discoveries of great benefit to people. And most of us think it all right to kill birds for food or to protect our crops. People's rights are different from the consideration we give to animals, then, for it is wrong to experiment on people, even if others might later benefit a great deal as a result of their suffering. You might volunteer to be a subject, but this would be supererogatory; you certainly have a right to refuse to be a medical guinea pig.

But how do we decide what you may or may not do to non-persons? This is a difficult problem, one for which I believe no adequate account exists. You do not want to say, for instance, that torturing dogs is all right whenever the sum of its effects on people is good—when it doesn't warp the sensibilities of the torturer so much that he mistreats people. If that were the case, it would be all right to torture dogs if you did it in private, or if the torturer lived on a desert island or died soon afterward, so that his actions had no effect on people. This is an inadequate account, because whatever moral consideration animals get, it has to be indefeasible, too. It will have to be a general proscription of certain actions, not merely a weighing of the impact on people on a case-by-case basis.

Rather, we need to distinguish two levels on which consequences of actions can be taken into account in moral reasoning. The traditional objections to Utilitarianism focus on the fact that it operates solely on the first level, taking all the consequences into account in particular cases only. Thus Utilitarianism is open to "desert island" and "lifeboat" counterexamples because these cases are rigged to make the consequences of actions severely limited.

Rawls' theory could be described as a teleological sort of theory, but with teleology operating on a higher level.[12] In choosing the principles to regulate society from the original position, his hypothetical choosers make their decision on the basis of the total consequences of various systems. Furthermore, they are constrained to choose a general set of rules which people can readily learn and apply. An ethical theory must operate by generating a set of sympathies and attitudes toward others which reinforces the functioning of that set of moral principles. Our prohibition against killing people operates by

means of certain moral sentiments including sympathy, compassion and guilt. But if these attitudes are to form a coherent set, they carry us further: we need to perform supererogatory actions, and we tend to feel similar compassion toward person-like non-persons.

It is crucial that psychological facts play a role here. Our psychological constitution makes it the case that for our ethical theory to work, it must prohibit certain treatment of non-persons which are significantly person-like. If our moral rules allowed people to treat some person-like non-persons in ways we do not want people to be treated, this would undermine the system of sympathies and attitudes that makes the ethical system work. For this reason, we would choose in the original position to make mistreatment of some sorts of animals wrong in general (not just wrong in the cases with public impact), even though animals are not themselves parties in the original position. Thus it makes sense that it is those animals whose appearance and behavior are most like those of people that get the most consideration in our moral scheme.

It is because of "coherence of attitudes," I think, that the similarity of a fetus to a baby is very significant. A fetus one week before birth is so much like a newborn baby in our psychological space that we cannot allow any cavalier treatment of the former while expecting full sympathy and nurturative support for the latter. Thus, I think that anti-abortion forces are indeed giving their strongest arguments when they point to the similarities between a fetus and a baby, and when they try to evoke our emotional attachment to and sympathy for the fetus. An early horror story from New York about nurses who were expected to alternate between caring for six-week premature infants and disposing of viable 24-week aborted fetuses is just that—a horror story. These beings are so much alike that no one can be asked to draw a distinction and treat them so very differently.

Remember, however, that in the early weeks after conception, a fetus is very much unlike a person. It is hard to develop these feelings for a set of genes which doesn't yet have a head, hands, beating heart, response to touch or the ability to move by itself. Thus it seems to me that the alleged "slippery slope" between conception and birth is not so very slippery. In the early stages of pregnancy, abortion can hardly be compared to murder for psychological reasons, but in the latest stages it is psychologically akin to murder.

Another source of similarity is the bodily continuity between fetus and adult. Bodies play a surprisingly central role in our attitudes toward persons. One has only to think of the philosophical literature on how far physical identity suffices for personal identity or Wittgenstein's remark that the best picture of the human soul is the human body. Even after death, when all agree the body is no longer a person, we still observe elaborate customs of respect for the human body; like people who torture dogs, necrophiliacs are not to be trusted with people.[13] So it is appropriate that we show respect to a fetus as the body continuous with the body of a person. This is a degree of resemblance to persons that animals cannot rival.

Michael Tooley also utilizes a parallel with animals. He claims that it is always permissible to drown newborn kittens and draws conclusions about infanticide.[14] But it is only permissible to drown kittens when their survival would cause some hardship. Perhaps it would be a burden to feed and house six more cats or to find other homes for them. The alternative of letting them starve produces even more suffering than the drowning. Since the kittens get their rights second-hand, so to speak, *via* the need for coherence in our attitudes, their interests are often overridden by the interests of full-fledged persons. But if their survival would be no inconvenience to people at all, then it is wrong to drown them, *contra* Tooley.

Tooley's conclusions about abortion are wrong for the same reason. Even if the fetus is not a person, abortion is not always permissible, because of the resemblance of a fetus to a person. I agree with Thomson that it would be wrong for a woman who is seven months pregnant to have an abortion just to avoid

having to postpone a trip to Europe. In the early months of pregnancy when the fetus hardly resembles a baby at all, then, abortion is permissible whenever it is in the interests of the pregnant woman or her family. The reasons would only need to outweigh the pain and inconvenience of the abortion itself. In the middle months, when the fetus comes to resemble a person, abortion would be justifiable only when the continuation of the pregnancy or the birth of the child would cause harm—physical, psychological, economic or social—to the woman. In the late months of pregnancy, even on our current assumption that a fetus is not a person, abortion seems to be wrong except to save a woman from significant injury or death.

The Supreme Court has recognized similar gradations in the alleged slippery slope stretching between conception and birth. To this point, the present paper has been a discussion of the moral status of abortion only, not its legal status. In view of the great physical, financial and sometimes psychological costs of abortion, perhaps the legal arrangement most compatible with the proposed moral solution would be the absence of restrictions, that is, so-called abortion "on demand."

So I conclude, first, that application of our concept of a person will not suffice to settle the abortion issue. After all, the biological development of a human being is gradual. Second, whether a fetus is a person or not, abortion is justifiable early in pregnancy to avoid modest harms and seldom justifiable late in pregnancy except to avoid significant injury or death.[15]

Notes

1. We also have paternalistic laws which keep us from harming our own bodies even when no one else is affected. Ironically, anti-abortion laws were originally designed to protect pregnant women from a dangerous but tempting procedure.

2. Mary Anne Warren, "On the Moral and Legal Status of Abortion," *Monist* 57 (1973), p. 55.

3. Baruch Brody, "Fetal Humanity and the

Theory of Essentialism," in Robert Baker and Frederick Elliston (eds.), *Philosophy and Sex* (Buffalo, N.Y., 1975).

4. Michael Tooley, "Abortion and Infanticide," *Philosophy and Public Affairs* 2 (1971).

5. Paul Ramsey, "The Morality of Abortion," in James Rachels, ed., *Moral Problems* (New York, 1971).

6. John Noonan, "Abortion and the Catholic Church: A Summary History," *Natural Law Forum* 12 (1967), pp. 125–131.

7. Wittgenstein has argued against the possibility of so capturing the concept of a game, *Philosophical Investigations* (New York, 1958), § 66–71.

8. Not because the fetus is partly a person and so has some of the rights of persons, but rather because of the rights of person-like non-persons. This I discuss in part III below.

9. Aristotle himself was concerned, however, with the different question of when the soul takes form. For historical data, see Jimmye Kimmey, "How the Abortion Laws Happened," *Ms.* 1 (April, 1973), pp. 48ff, and John Noonan, *loc. cit.*

10. J. J. Thomson, "A Defense of Abortion," *Philosophy and Public Affairs* 1 (1971).

11. Ibid., p. 52.

12. John Rawls, *A Theory of Justice* (Cambridge, Mass., 1971), § 3–4.

13. On the other hand, if they can be trusted with people, then our moral customs are mistaken. It all depends on the facts of psychology.

14. Op. cit., pp. 40, 60–61.

15. I am deeply indebted to Larry Crocker and Arthur Kuflik for their constructive comments.

Suggested Further Reading

Armstrong, Robert L., "The Right to Life," *Journal of Social Philosophy*, 8 (January 1977), 13–19.

Foot, Phillipa, "The Problem of Abortion and the Doctrine of Double Effect," *Oxford Review*, no. 5 (1967), 5–15.

Noonan, John T., "An Almost Absolute Value in History," *The Morality of Abortion: Legal and Historical Perspectives*, ed. John T. Noonan. Cambridge, Mass.: Harvard University Press, 1970, pp. 46–50.

Thomson, Judith Jarvis, "A Defense of Abortion," *Philosophy and Public Affairs*, 1, no. 1 (Fall 1971), 47–66.

Tooley, Michael, "Abortion and Infanticide," *Philosophy and Public Affairs*, 2 (Fall 1972), 37–65.

Warren, Mary Anne, "On the Moral and Legal Status of Abortion," *Journal of Social Philosophy*, 8 (January 1977), 13–19.

2. SELECTIVE ABORTION AND GENETIC SCREENING

The issue of selective abortion has emerged with the development of technologies which predict many characteristics of an unborn child. Such techniques as amniocentesis, ultrasound, and *chorionic villi* sampling make it possible to determine the sex of a fetus, along with possible abnormalities in its development. Prenatal diagnosis is frequently undertaken with the idea that if serious defects are found, the pregnancy will be terminated. The possibility that amniocentesis may be used for purposes of sex selection is disturbing to critics. Some health facilities refuse to administer prenatal tests to patients who intend to abort purely on grounds of the fetus's sex. A number of ethical questions concerning reproductive responsibility are associated with selective abortion. Similar concerns have been voiced by critics of gene-splicing technology. **[See Business, Chapter 12, Section 3.]** Do parents have an unqualified right to abort a possibly defective fetus? Do they have a right to abortion on the basis of the sex of the fetus? (One should bear in mind that certain genetic diseases—hemophilia, for example—

cannot be diagnosed prenatally but are known to affect children only of a particular sex.)

Some argue that it is unethical knowingly to bear children likely to be physically or mentally handicapped. Arguments of this nature are based on primarily utilitarian considerations. Such children place a severe burden on public resources in addition to the problems borne by their families. Other writers hold that each child born has a right to an acceptable quality of life. On this deontological view, persons who knowingly enable the birth of a defective child are violating the infant's rights.

Genetic screening also involves problems of reproductive responsibility. Screening programs fall into two categories. One type is designed to identify *carrier states* in prospective parents that would cause offspring to be born with serious defects or health problems. Some writers warn that genetic screening for carrier states involves the risk that persons identified as having "defective" genes will be traumatized by the knowledge and stigmatized by society.

The second type of genetic screening program is aimed at detecting genetic diseases in the fetus or newborn infant. When programs are voluntary and function to detect diseases for which treatment is available, they present few ethical difficulties. Problems arise if the testing is made mandatory or if the disease cannot be treated. Mandatory (adult) participation in programs of either type raises the issue of paternalism. Both genetic screening and prenatal testing for abnormalities carry a risk that the state might attempt to impose standards for who has the right to be born or to reproduce.

In the following article Leon R. Kass discusses the issue of selective abortion of fetuses determined by prenatal testing to be genetically defective. Kass contends that acceptance of the practice erodes our belief in the "radical moral equality of all human beings." As a result, those who escape detection and are born with defects will be viewed more negatively. In addition, he argues, acceptance of the practice implies acceptance of a dangerous principle, namely that "defectives should not be born."

LEON R. KASS

Perfect Babies: Prenatal Diagnosis and the Equal Right to Life

We hold these truths to be self-evident, that all men are created equal, that they are endowed by their Creator with certain unalienable Rights, that among these are Life, Liberty, and the pursuit of Happiness.

—DECLARATION OF INDEPENDENCE

All animals are equal, but some animals are more equal than others.

—GEORGE ORWELL, Animal Farm

It is especially fitting on this occasion to begin by acknowledging how privileged I feel and how pleased I am to be a participant in this symposium. I suspect that I am not alone among the assembled in considering myself fortunate to be here. For I was conceived after antibiotics yet before amniocentesis, late enough to have benefited from medicine's ability to prevent and control fatal infectious

Excerpt reprinted with permission of the author and publisher from *Ethical Issues in Human Genetics*, ed. Bruce Hilton et al. (New York: Plenum Publishing Corp., 1973). A longer version of the article appears in the author's current book, *Toward a More Natural Science: Biology and Human Affairs* (New York: The Free Press, 1985; paperback ed. 1988).

diseases, yet early enough to have escaped from medicine's ability to prevent me from living to suffer from my genetic diseases. To be sure, my genetic vices are, as far as I know them, rather modest, taken individually—myopia, asthma and other allergies, bilateral forefoot adduction, bowleggedness, loquaciousness, and pessimism, plus some four to eight as yet undiagnosed recessive lethal genes in the heterozygous condition—but, taken together, and if diagnosable prenatally, I might never have made it.

Just as I am happy to be here, so am I unhappy with what I shall have to say. Little did I realize when I first conceived the topic, "Implications of Prenatal Diagnosis for the Human Right to Life," what a painful and difficult labor it would lead to. More than once while this paper was gestating, I considered obtaining permission to abort it, on the grounds that, by prenatal diagnosis, I knew it to be defective. My lawyer told me that I was legally in the clear, but my conscience reminded me that I had made a commitment to deliver myself of this paper, flawed or not. Next time, I shall practice better contraception.

Any discussion of the ethical issues of genetic counseling and prenatal diagnosis is unavoidably haunted by a ghost called the morality of abortion. This ghost I shall not vex. More precisely, I shall not vex the reader by telling ghost stories. However, I would be neither surprised nor disappointed if my discussion of an admittedly related matter, the ethics of aborting the genetically defective, summons that hovering spirit to the reader's mind. For the morality of abortion is a matter not easily laid to rest, recent efforts to do so notwithstanding. A vote by the legislature of the State of New York can indeed legitimatize the disposal of fetuses, but not of the moral questions. But though the questions remain, there is likely to be little new that can be said about them, and certainly not by me.

Yet before leaving the general question of abortion, let me pause to drop some anchors for the discussion that follows. Despite great differences of opinion both as to what to think and how to reason about abortion, nearly everyone agrees that abortion is a moral issue.[1] What does this mean? Formally, it means that a woman seeking or refusing an abortion can expect to be asked to justify her action. And we can expect that she should be able to give reasons for her choice other than "I like it" or "I don't like it." Substantively, it means that, in the absence of good reasons for intervention, there is some presumption in favor of allowing the pregnancy to continue once it has begun. A common way of expressing this presumption is to say that "the fetus has a right to continued life."[2] In this context, disagreement concerning the moral permissibility of abortion concerns what rights (or interests or needs), and whose, override (take precedence over, or outweigh) this fetal "right." Even most of the "opponents" of abortion agree that the mother's right to live takes precedence, and that abortion to save her life is permissible, perhaps obligatory. Some believe that a woman's right to determine the number and spacing of her children takes precedence, while yet others argue that the need to curb population growth is, at least at this time, overriding.

Hopefully, this brief analysis of what it means to say that abortion is a moral issue is sufficient to establish two points. First, that the fetus is a living thing with some moral claim on us not to do it violence, and therefore, second, that justification must be given for destroying it.

Turning now from the general questions of the ethics of abortion, I wish to focus on the special ethical issues raised by the abortion of "defective" fetuses (so-called "abortion for fetal indications"). I shall consider only the cleanest cases, those cases where well-characterized genetic diseases are diagnosed with a high degree of certainty by means of amniocentesis, in order to sidestep the added moral dilemmas posed when the diagnosis is suspected or possible, but unconfirmed. However, many of the questions I shall discuss could also be raised about cases where genetic analysis gives only a statistical prediction about the genotype of the fetus, and also about cases where the defect has an infectious or chemical rather than a genetic cause (e.g., rubella, thalidomide).

My first and possibly most difficult task is to show that there is anything left to discuss once we have agreed not to discuss the morality of abortion in general. There is a sense in which abortion for genetic defect is, after abortion to save the life of the mother, perhaps the most defensible kind of abortion. Certainly, it is a serious and not a frivolous reason for abortion, defended by its proponents in sober and rational speech—unlike justification based upon the false notion that a fetus is a mere part of a woman's body, to be used and abused at her pleasure. Standing behind genetic abortion are serious and well-intentioned people, with reasonable ends in view: the prevention of genetic diseases, the elimination of suffering in families, the preservation of precious financial and medical resources, the protection of our genetic heritage. No profiteers, no sex-ploiters, no racists. No arguments about the connection of abortion with promiscuity and licentiousness, no perjured testimony about the mental health of the mother, no arguments about the seriousness of the population problem. In short, clear objective data, a worthy cause, decent men and women. If abortion, what better reason for it?

Yet if genetic abortion is but a happily wagging tail on the dog of abortion, it is simultaneously the nose of a camel protruding under a rather different tent. Precisely because the quality of the fetus is central to the decision to abort, the practice of genetic abortion has implications which go beyond those raised by abortion in general. What may be at stake here is the belief in the radical moral equality of all human beings, the belief that all human beings possess equally and independent of merit certain fundamental rights, one among which is, of course, the right to life.

To be sure, the belief that fundamental human rights belong equally to all human beings has been but an ideal, never realized, often ignored, sometimes shamelessly. Yet it has been perhaps the most powerful moral idea at work in the world for at least two centuries. It is this idea and ideal that animates most of the current political and social criticism around the globe. It is ironic that we should acquire the power to detect and eliminate the genetically unequal at a time when we have finally succeeded in removing much of the stigma and disgrace previously attached to victims of congenital illness, in providing them with improved care and support, and in preventing, by means of education, feelings of guilt on the part of their parents. One might even wonder whether the development of amniocentesis and prenatal diagnosis may represent a backlash against these same humanitarian and egalitarian tendencies in the practice of medicine, which, by helping to sustain to the age of reproduction persons with genetic disease has itself contributed to the increasing incidence of genetic disease, and with it, to increased pressures for genetic screening, genetic counseling, and genetic abortion.

No doubt our humanitarian and egalitarian principles and practices have caused us some new difficulties, but if we mean to weaken or turn our backs on them, we should do so consciously and thoughtfully. If, as I believe, the idea and practice of genetic abortion points in that direction, we should make ourselves aware of it. . . .

Genetic Abortion and the Living Defective

The practice of abortion of the genetically defective will no doubt affect our view of and our behavior toward those abnormals who escape the net of detection and abortion. A child with Down's syndrome or with hemophilia or with muscular dystrophy born at a time when most of his (potential) fellow sufferers were destroyed prenatally is liable to be looked upon by the community as one unfit to be alive, as a second-class (or even lower) human type. He may be seen as a person who need not have been, and who would not have been, if only someone had gotten to him in time.

The parents of such children are also likely to treat them differently, especially if the mother would have wished but failed to get an amniocentesis because of ignorance, poverty, or distance from the testing station, or if the prenatal diagnosis was in error. In such cases, parents are especially likely to resent the child. They may be disinclined to give it the kind of care they might have before the advent of amniocentesis and genetic abortion, rationalizing that a second-class specimen is not entitled to first-class treatment. If pressed to do so, say by physicians, the parents might refuse, and the courts may become involved. This has already begun to happen.

In Maryland, parents of a child with Down's syndrome refused permission to have the child operated on for an intestinal obstruction present at birth. The physicians and the hospital sought an injunction to require the parents to allow surgery. The judge ruled in favor of the parents, despite what I understand to be the weight of precedent to the contrary, on the grounds that the child was Mongoloid, that is, had the child been "normal," the decision would have gone the other way. Although the decision was not appealed to and hence not affirmed by a higher court, we can see through the prism of this case the possibility that the new powers of human genetics will strip the blindfold from the lady of justice and will make official the dangerous doctrine that some men are more equal than others.

The abnormal child may also feel resentful. A child with Down's syndrome or Tay-Sachs disease will probably never know or care, but what about a child with hemophilia or with Turner's syndrome? In the past decade, with medical knowledge and power over the prenatal child increasing and with parental authority over the postnatal child decreasing, we have seen the appearance of a new type of legal action, suits for wrongful life. Children have brought suit against their parents (and others) seeking to recover damages for physical and social handicaps inextricably tied to their birth (e.g., congenital deformities, congenital syphilis, illegitimacy). In some of the American cases, the courts have recognized the justice of the child's claim (that he was injured due to parental negligence), although

they have so far refused to award damages, due to policy considerations. In other countries, e.g., in Germany, judgments with compensation have gone for the plaintiffs. With the spread of amniocentesis and genetic abortion, we can only expect such cases to increase. And here it will be the soft-hearted rather than the hard-hearted judges who will establish the doctrine of second-class human beings, out of compassion for the mutants who escaped the traps set out for them.

It may be argued that I am dealing with a problem which, even if it is real, will affect very few people. It may be suggested that very few will escape the traps once we have set them properly and widely, once people are informed about amniocentesis, once the power to detect prenatally grows to its full capacity, and once our "superstitious" opposition to abortion dies out or is extirpated. But in order even to come close to this vision of success, amniocentesis will have to become part of every pregnancy—either by making it mandatory, like the test for syphilis, or by making it "routine medical practice," like the Pap smear. Leaving aside the other problems with universal amniocentesis, we could expect that the problem for the few who escape is likely to be even worse precisely because they will be few.

The point, however, should be generalized. How will we come to view and act toward the many "abnormals" that will remain among us—the retarded, the crippled, the senile, the deformed, and the true mutants—once we embark on a program to root out genetic abnormality? For it must be remembered that we shall always have abnormals—some who escape detection or whose disease is undetectable *in utero*, others as a result of new mutations, birth injuries, accidents, maltreatment, or disease—who will require our care and protection. The existence of "defectives" cannot be fully prevented, not even by totalitarian breeding and weeding programs. Is it not likely that our principle with respect to these people will change from "We try harder" to "Why accept second best?" The idea of "the unwanted because abnormal child" may become a self-fulfilling prophecy, whose consequences may be worse than those of the abnormality itself.

Genetic and Other Defectives

The mention of other abnormals points to a second danger of the practice of genetic abortion. Genetic abortion may come to be seen not so much as the prevention of genetic disease, but as the prevention of birth of defective or abnormal children—and, in a way, understandably so. For in the case of what other diseases does preventive medicine consist in the elimination of the patient-at-risk? Moreover, the very language used to discuss genetic disease leads us to the easy but wrong conclusion that the afflicted fetus or person is rather than has a disease. True, one is partly defined by his genotype, but only partly. A person is more than his disease. And yet we slide easily from the language of possession to the language of identity, from "He has hemophilia" to "He is a hemophiliac," from "She has diabetes" through "She is diabetic" to "She is a diabetic," from "The fetus has Down's syndrome" to "The fetus is a Down's." This way of speaking supports the belief that it is defective persons (or potential persons) that are being eliminated, rather than diseases.

If this is so, then it becomes simply accidental that the defect has a genetic cause. Surely, it is only because of the high regard for medicine and science, and for the accuracy of genetic diagnosis, that genotype defectives are likely to be the first to go. But once the principle, "Defectives should not be born," is established, grounds other than cytological and biochemical may very well be sought. Even ignoring racialists and others equally misguided—of course, they cannot be ignored—we should know that there are social scientists, for example, who believe that one can predict with a high degree of accuracy how a child will turn out from a careful, systematic study of the socio-economic and psycho-dynamic environment into which he is born and in which he grows up. They might

press for the prevention of socio-psychological disease, even of "criminality," by means of prenatal environmental diagnosis and abortion. I have heard rumor that a crude, unscientific form of eliminating potential "phenotypic defectives" is already being practiced in some cities, in that submission to abortion is allegedly being made a condition for the receipt of welfare payments. "Defectives should not be born" is a principle without limits. We can ill afford to have it established.

Up to this point, I have been discussing the possible implications of the practice of genetic abortion for our belief in and adherence to the idea that, at least in fundamental human matters such as life and liberty, all men are to be considered as equals, that for these matters we should ignore as irrelevant the real qualitative differences amongst men, however important these differences may be for other purposes. Those who are concerned about abortion fear that the permissible time of eliminating the unwanted will be moved forward along the time continuum, against newborns, infants, and children. Similarly, I suggest that we should be concerned lest the attack on gross genetic inequality in fetuses be advanced along the continuum of quality and into the later stages of life.

I am not engaged in predicting the future; I am not saying that amniocentesis and genetic abortion will lead down the road to Nazi Germany. Rather, I am suggesting that the principles underlying genetic abortion simultaneously justify many further steps down that road. The point was very well made by Abraham Lincoln:

> If A can prove, however conclusively, that he may, of right, enslave B—Why may not B snatch the same argument and prove equally, that he may enslave A?
>
> You say A is white, and B is black. It is color, then; the lighter having the right to enslave the darker? Take care. By this rule, you are to be slave to the first man you meet with a fairer skin than your own.
>
> You do not mean color exactly? You mean the whites are intellectually the superiors of the blacks, and, therefore have the right to enslave

them? Take care again. By this rule, you are to be slave to the first man you meet with an intellect superior to your own.

But, say you, it is a question of interest; and, if you can make it your interest, you have the right to enslave another. Very well. And if he can make it his interest, he has the right to enslave you.[3]

Perhaps I have exaggerated the dangers; perhaps we will not abandon our inexplicable preference for generous humanitarianism over consistency. But we should indeed be cautious and move slowly as we give serious consideration to the question "What price the perfect baby?"[4] . . .

Notes

1. This strikes me as by far the most important inference to be drawn from the fact that men in different times and cultures have answered the abortion question differently. Seen in this light, the differing and changing answers themselves suggest that it is a question not easily put under, at least not for very long.

2. Other ways include: one should not do violence to living or growing things; life is sacred; respect nature; fetal life has value; refrain from taking innocent life; protect and preserve life. As some have pointed out, the terms chosen are of different weight, and would require reasons of different weight to tip the balance in favor of abortion. My choice of the "rights" terminology is not meant to beg the questions of whether such rights really exist, or of where they come from. However, the notion of a "fetal right to life" presents only a little more difficulty in this regard than does the notion of a "human right to life," since the former does not depend on a claim that the human fetus

is already "human." In my sense of terms "right" and "life," we might even say that a dog or fetal dog has a "right to life," and that it would be cruel and immoral for a man to go around performing abortions even on dogs for no good reason.

3. Lincoln, A. (1854). In *The Collected Works of Abraham Lincoln*, R. P. Basler, editor. New Brunswick, New Jersey, Rutgers University Press, Vol. II, p. 222.

4. For a discussion of the possible biological rather than moral price of attempts to prevent the birth of defective children see Motulsky, A. G., G. R. Fraser, and J. Felsenstein (1971). In Symposium on Intrauterine Diagnosis, D. Bergsma, editor. *Birth Defects: Original Article Series*, Vol. 7, No. 5. Also see Neel, J. (1972). In *Early Diagnosis of Human Genetic Defects: Scientific and Ethical Considerations*, M. Harris, editor. Washington, D.C., U.S. Government Printing Office, pp. 366–380.

Suggested Further Reading

Holtzman, Neil A., "Genetic Screening: For Better or for Worse?" *Pediatrics*, 59, no. 1 (January 1977), 131–33.

Lappé, Marc, "Moral Obligations and the Fallacies of Genetic Control," *Theological Studies*, 33, no. 3 (September 1972), 411–27.

Purdy, L. M., "Genetic Diseases: Can Having Children Be Immoral?" *Genetics Now: Ethical Issues in Genetic Research*, ed. John Buckley, Jr. Washington, D.C.: University Press of America, 1978.

Tormey, Judith Farr, "Ethical Considerations of Prenatal Genetic Diagnosis," *Clinical Obstetrics and Gynecology* 19 (December 1976), 957–63.

DECISION SCENARIO 2

Selective Abortion

Sandy Harriman is a 31-year-old lawyer working for an advertising agency. She is fifteen weeks pregnant. Her husband is a tax accountant. The demands of her position have for some time placed a strain on the marital relation, since she often has to work late hours and travel overseas.

After a stressful period, Sandy experienced discomfort and nausea. Her obstetrician referred her to a genetic counselor. Sandy revealed that she had taken Lithium, a tranquilizer, and heavy doses of an antibiotic to contain a nagging throat infection. The physician recommends amniocentesis to help evaluate the condition of the fetus.

The results of the genetic evaluation, the counselor reports, indicate a risk of webbed fingers and/or cleft palate. The risk is nine or ten times that of a normal fetus and, according to the doctor, a minor defect in the field of possibilities. Furthermore, though Sandy is over 30, the genetic counselor finds nothing in her medical background, or that of her husband, to warrant mentioning other concerns.

The news disturbs Sandy, who is being considered for an important promotion in her department. She tells the physician that she will discuss the situation with her husband.

At the visit the next week, Sandy announces that even the minimal risk is more than she wants to subject the fetus to. She confides that the strain the pregnancy is causing on her job and marriage is more than she can bear. She asks for an abortion.

Questions

1. Are the reasons, stated and unstated, behind Sandy's decision strong enough to support the option of abortion?

2. What is the role of the genetic counselor in the decision-making process? Did the doctor fulfill it?

3. If Sandy's husband favors having the child and facing the consequences, what rights does he have? Do they ever outweigh the mother's right to choose?

4. If the genetic screening had shown that the fetus had Down's syndrome (mongolism, having a mental handicap, but otherwise normal), what decision-making factors would change?

5. Sandy consented to an abortion. Was the consent informed? How much information is needed to inform consent?

3. REPRODUCTIVE TECHNOLOGIES

The natural process of human reproduction involves sexual intercourse, fertilization in the fallopian tube, and implantation and gestation in the uterus. The term *reproductive technologies* applies to procedures developed to replace one or more of the steps, usually to overcome infertility. Among the techniques are artificial insemination, *in vitro* (literally, "in glass") fertilization, and egg donation. Artificial insemination is designed to achieve tubal fertilization by the artificial introduction into a fertile female of sperm obtained from her husband (AIH) or from a donor (AID). The technique is used when the husband is infertile or has a genetic disorder that endangers offspring. AID also is employed by unmarried women who wish to bear children. *In vitro* fertilization involves uniting sperm (of a husband or do-nor) with ova (of a wife or donor) in a glass laboratory dish, followed by implantation of the resulting embryo in a woman's uterus. This procedure may be successful for women whose infertility results from fallo-pian tube obstruction. Egg donation is em-ployed when a woman has infertility prob-lems caused by absent or nonfunctioning ovaries. If her uterus is functional, an ovum obtained from a donor is united with sperm from the woman's husband and the embryo is implanted in her uterus. A woman with functioning ovaries but a nonfunctional uterus can donate an egg to be fertilized *in vitro* with her husband's sperm and subse-quently implanted in another woman's uterus for gestation. The latter arrangement represents one type of so-called surrogate motherhood.

A brief look at some of the reproductive technologies in use today indicates their complexity as well as that of the moral ques-tions surrounding their use. Other tech-niques are currently under development, among which is *cloning*. This technique, if successful, produces a human being with a genetic makeup identical to that of one do-nor "parent."

Ethical concerns about reproductive technologies were highlighted by the con-troversy surrounding the "Baby M" case. In that case, a New Jersey woman contracted with a childless couple to be artificially in-seminated with the husband's sperm and bear his child. After the child's birth, the surrogate mother attempted to breach the contract and retain custody of the child. Fol-lowing a lengthy hearing, a judge ruled in favor of the genetic father and his wife, but the case was appealed to a higher court, which restored some of the surrogate's pa-rental rights. To some observers, the bitter custody battle over Baby M was a vivid dem-onstration that surrogate motherhood ar-rangements produce undue suffering and should be outlawed.

In March 1987, at the same time that testi-mony was being heard in the case of Baby M, the Vatican issued a document condemn-ing the use of many reproductive technolo-gies. The basis of the statement was the Catholic Church's doctrine that birth should result only from the sexual union of a mar-ried couple. The Vatican raised moral objec-tions to procedures resulting in the destruc-tion of fertilized ova. (For example, during *in vitro* fertilization a number of ova may be fertilized, but only one implanted.) These objections are based on the view that a fer-tilized egg has the moral status of a human being and should not be unnecessarily harmed (see the arguments under Abortion in this chapter).

While some moral questions about repro-ductive technologies stem from religious be-liefs (for instance, AID is viewed by some as a form of adultery), objections arise on other grounds. Some writers argue that sur-rogate motherhood arrangements are little more than trafficking in human lives and are ethically equivalent to the practice of slav-ery. Others view the use of surrogates as a form of economic exploitation leading to the creation of a class of female "breeders" for wealthy couples. Supporters of the prac-tice point to the humanitarian value of pro-viding infertile couples with much-desired children having genetic kinship with at least one of the parents.

Other ethical objections center around the perceived "unnaturalness" and deperso-nalizing effect of technological intervention on human reproduction. These objections are answered by an appeal to the benefits gained by couples for whom infertility is an anguishing condition. Arguments exist charging that reproductive technologies in-flict unforeseen harm on the developing em-bryo. Cloning is viewed as an ominous pos-sibility belonging to a "Brave New World," because it compromises the genetic unique-ness of individual persons. Others warn that if cloning becomes widespread, it could un-dermine the adaptability of the species by limiting the variety of human genotypes.

In the following article George J. Annas examines ethical issues arising from surrogate motherhood contracts. Annas maintains that the well-being of the child must be the primary consideration when one is making decisions about surrogate parenting. The author argues that the surrogate mother has a clear legal right to custody of the baby:

". . . if she wants to keep it, she almost certainly can." In fact, he suggests that she may even be able to sue the biological father for child support. The argument is interesting in light of the Baby M case, in which the surrogate mother was denied custody.

GEORGE J. ANNAS

Contracts to Bear a Child: Compassion or Commercialism?

Many medical students (and others) supplement their income by selling their blood and sperm. But while this practice seems to have been reasonably well accepted, society does not permit individuals to sell their vital organs or their children. These policies are unlikely to change. Where on this spectrum do contracts to bear a child fall? Are they fundamentally the sale of an ovum with a nine-month womb rental thrown in, or are they really agreements to sell a baby? While this formulation may seem a strange way to phrase the issue, it is the way courts are likely to frame it when such contracts are challenged on the grounds that they violate public policy.

In a typical surrogate-mother arrangement, a woman agrees to be artificially inseminated with the sperm of the husband of an infertile woman. She also agrees that after the child is born she will either give it up for adoption to the couple or relinquish her parental rights, leaving the biological father as the sole legal parent. The current controversy centers on whether or not the surrogate can be paid for these services. Is she being compensated for inconvenience and out-of-pocket expenses, or is she being paid for her baby?

Two personal stories have received much media attention. The first involves Patricia Dickey, an unmarried twenty-year-old woman from Maryland who had never borne a child, and who agreed to be artificially inseminated and give up the child to a Delaware couple without any compensation. She was recruited by attorney Noel Keane of Michigan, known for his television appearances in which he has said that for a $5,000 fee he will put "host mothers" in touch with childless couples. Ms. Dickey explained her motivation in an interview with the *Washington Post:* "I had a close friend who couldn't have a baby, and I know how badly she wanted one. . . . It's just something I wanted to do" (Feb. 11, 1980, p. 1). The outcome of Dickey's pregnancy—if one occurred—has not been reported.

More famous is a woman who has borne a child and relinquished her parental rights. Elizabeth Kane (a pseudonym), married and the mother of three children, reportedly agreed to bear a child for $10,000. The arrangement ·was negotiated by Dr. Richard Levin of Kentucky, who is believed to have about 100 surrogates willing to perform the same services for compensation. Levin says, "I clearly do not have any moral or ethical problems with what we are doing" (*American Medical News,* June 20, 1980, p. 13). Mrs. Kane describes her relationship to the baby by saying, "It's the father's child. I'm simply

Reprinted with permission of the author and publisher from *Hastings Center Report*, vol. 11, April 1981. © The Hastings Center.

growing it for him" (*People*, Dec. 8, 1980, p. 53).

Even this brief sketch raises fundamental questions about the two approaches. Should the surrogate be married or single; have other children or have no children? Should the couple meet the surrogate (they were in the delivery room when Mrs. Kane gave birth to a boy)? Should the child know about the arrangement when he grows up (the couple plans to tell the child when he is eighteen)? Is monetary compensation the real issue (the sperm donor has agreed to give Ms. Dickey more sperm if she wants to have another child for her own—could this cause more problems for both him and her)? What kind of counseling should be done with all parties, and what records should be kept? And isn't this a strange thing to be doing in a country that records more than a million and a half abortions a year? Why not attempt to get women who are already pregnant to give birth instead of inducing those who are not to go through the "experience"?

These questions, and many others, merit serious consideration. So far legal debate has focused primarily on just one: can surrogate parenting properly be labeled "baby selling"? Some have argued that it can be distinguished from baby selling because one of the parents (the father) is biologically related to the child, and the mother is not pregnant at the time the deal is struck and so is not under any compulsion to provide for her child. But the only two legal opinions rendered to date disagree. Both a lower court judge in Michigan and the attorney general of Kentucky view contracts to bear a child as baby selling.

Court Challenge in Michigan

In the mid-1970s most states passed statutes making it criminal to offer, give, or receive anything of value for placing a child for adoption. These statutes were aimed at curtailing a major black market in babies that had grown up in the United States, with children selling for as much as $20,000. Anticipating that Michigan's version of this statute might prohibit him from paying a surrogate for carrying a child and giving it up for adoption, attorney Keane sought a declaratory judgment. He argued that the statute was unconstitutional since it infringed upon the right to reproductive privacy of the parties involved. The court was not impressed, concluding that "the right to adopt a child based upon the payment of $5,000 is not a fundamental personal right and reasonable regulations controlling adoption proceedings that prohibit the exchange of money (other than charges and fees approved by the court) are not constitutionally infirm." The court characterized the state's interest as one "to prevent commercialism from affecting a mother's decision to execute a consent to the adoption of her child," and went on to argue that: "Mercenary considerations used to create a parent–child relationship and its impact upon the family unit strike at the very foundation of human society and are patently and necessarily injurious to the community."

The case is on appeal, but is unlikely to be reversed. The judge's decision meant that Ms. Dickey, and others like her, could not charge a fee for carrying a child. It did not, however, forbid her from carrying it as a personal favor or for her own psychological reasons.

The Kentucky Statutes

One of the prime elements of surrogate mother folklore held that contracts to bear a child were "legal" in Kentucky. On January 26, 1981, Steven Beshear, the attorney general of the Commonwealth of Kentucky, announced at a Louisville news conference that contracts to bear a child were in fact illegal and unenforceable in the state. He based his advisory opinion on Kentucky statutes and "a strong public policy against 'baby buying.'"

Specifically, Kentucky law invalidates consent for adoption or the filing of a voluntary petition for termination of parental rights prior to the fifth day after the birth of a child. The purpose of these statutes, according to the attorney general, is to give the mother time to "think it over." Thus, any agreement or contract she entered into before the fifth day after the birth would be unenforceable. Moreover, Kentucky, like Michigan, prohibits the charging of a "fee" or "remuneration for the procurement of any child for adoption purposes." The attorney general argued that even though there is no similar statute prohibiting the payment of money for the termination of parental rights, "there is the same public policy issue" regarding monetary consideration for the procurement of a child: "The Commonwealth of Kentucky does not condone the purchase and sale of children" (Op. Atty. Gen., 81–18). The attorney general has since brought an action to enjoin Dr. Levin and his corporation from making any further surrogate-mother arrangements in the state.

Who Cares?

Surrogate parenting, open or behind a wall of secrecy, is unlikely ever to involve large numbers of people. Should we care about it; or should we simply declare our disapproval and let it go at that? I don't know, but it does seem to me that the answer to that question must be found in the answer to another: what is in the best interests of the children? Certainly they are more prone to psychological problems when they learn that their biological mother not only gave them up for adoption, but never had any intention of mothering them herself. On the other hand, one might argue that the child would never have existed had it not been for the surrogate arrangement, and so whatever existence the child has is better than nothing.

A Surrogate Mother's View

"Elizabeth Kane" says she felt regret only once—during labor. "I thought to myself, 'Elizabeth, you're out of your mind. Why are you putting yourself through this?' But it was only for a moment." She also says she "felt so many emotions during the pregnancy that I wrote a book," now in the hands of an agent (*Washington Post,* Dec. 4, 1980).

One of the major problems with speculating on the potential benefits of such an arrangement to the parties involved is that we have very little data. Only anecdotal information is available on artificial insemination by donor, for example. It does not seem to harm family life. But the role of the mother is far greater biologically than that of the father, and family disruption might be proportionally higher if the mother is the one who gives up the child. The sperm donor in the Patricia Dickey case is quoted as having said:

It may sound selfish, but I want to father a child on my own behalf, leave my own legacy. And I want a healthy baby. And there just aren't any available. They're either retarded or they're minorities, black, Hispanic. . . . That may be fine for some people, but we just don't think we could handle it.

Is this man really ready for parenthood? What if the child is born with a physical or mental defect—could he handle that? Or would the child be left abandoned, wanted neither by the surrogate nor by the adoption couple? The sperm donor has made no biological commitment to the child, and cannot be expected to support it financially or psychologically if it is not what he expected and contracted for.

Perhaps the only major question in the entire surrogate mother debate that does have a clear legal answer is: Whose baby is it? On the maternal side, it is the biological mother's baby. And if she wants to keep it, she almost certainly can. Indeed, under the proper circumstances, she may even be able to keep the child and sue the sperm donor for child support. On the paternal side, it is also the biological child of the sperm donor. But in all states, children born in wedlock are presumed to be the legitimate children of the married couple. So if the surrogate is married, the child will be presumed (usually rebuttable only by proof beyond a reasonable doubt) to be the offspring of the couple and not of the sperm donor. The donor could bring a custody suit—if he could prove beyond a reasonable doubt that he was the real father—and then the court would have to decide which parent would serve the child's "best interests."

It is an interesting legal twist that in many states with laws relating to artificial insemination, the sperm donor would have no rights even to bring such a suit. For example, to protect donors the Uniform Parentage Act provides that "The donor of semen provided . . . for use in artificial insemination of a woman other than the donor's wife is treated in law as if he were not the natural father of a child thereby conceived." The old adage, "Mama's baby, papa's maybe" aptly describes the current legal reaction to a surrogate who changes her mind and decides to keep the child.

Should There Be a Law?

The Science and the Family Committee (which I chair) of the Family Law Section of the American Bar Association is currently studying the surrogate mother situation (and the broader issue of *in vitro* fertilization) in an attempt to determine what, if any, legislation is appropriate in this area. DHEW's Ethics Advisory Board's final recommendation on *in vitro* fertilization and embryo transfer was that a "uniform or model law" be developed to "clarify the legal status of children born as a result of *in vitro* fertilization and embryo transfer." This seems to make some sense—although it does seem to be premature. We need a set of agreed-on principles regarding artificial insemination by donor and surrogate mothers—both technologies currently in use—if legislation on *in vitro* fertilization and embryo transplant is to have a reasonable chance of doing more good than harm.

Suggested Further Reading

Callahan, Daniel, et al., "In Vitro Fertilization: Four Commentaries," *Hastings Center Report,* 8 (October 1978), 7–14.

Eisenberg, Leon, "The Outcome as Cause: Predestination and Human Cloning," *The Journal of Medicine and Philosophy,* 1 (December 1976), 318–31.

Kass, Leon R., "New Beginnings in Life," in *The New Genetics and the Future of Man,* ed. Michael Harrington. Grand Rapids, Mich.: Eerdmans, 1972, pp. 15–63.

McCormick, Richard A., "Reproductive Technologies: Ethical Issues," *Encyclopedia of Bioethics,* 4 (1978), 1454–64.

Walters, LeRoy, "Human In Vitro Fertilization: A Review of the Ethical Literature," *Hastings Center Report,* 9 (August 1979), 23–43.

7. ISSUES IN DEATH AND DYING

1. EUTHANASIA

If human beings have a right to autonomy and self-determination in the conduct of their lives, do they also have the right to control the circumstances of their deaths insofar as possible? If people have a "right to life," do they have a "right to die" as well, or a right to "death with dignity"? As in the issues of abortion and genetic responsibility, questions arise about who is entitled to assess the quality and value of an individual life. Should it be the state, medical professionals, the family, the individual, or some combination of these? Just as abortion raises the question of when human life begins, euthanasia calls up questions about when it ends.

The term *euthanasia* comes from Greek words meaning "good death." In our society, a good death is usually thought to be one that is painless and quick. Most people hope that dying will spare them and their loved ones prolonged suffering and the crushing expenses and loss of dignity of lengthy hospitalization. Advances in medical technology make it possible—even likely—for biological life to be sustained in persons who in earlier times would have died. A person in an irreversible coma, one who has a completely deteriorated personality, or one whose consciousness alternates between excruciating pain and drug-induced stupor has lost the capacity for meaningful or satisfying experiences of life. Many argue that such persons are "better off dead," that mercy would be on the side of

death. One might feel tempted to hasten the arrival of death for such persons, or for oneself in a similar situation. However, the ethical implications of an action to assist death are profound. Is providing an easy death for oneself the same as suicide? If we aid in the death of another—whatever the motive may be—are our actions a form of murder? Can such acts ever be justified?

Utilitarians argue that expending health care resources on persons who lack the capacity for meaningful life is unjustified. Deontological support for euthanasia arises from an ethic of respect for individual human dignity. Patients who request an end to their suffering should have their choices respected. Others, who cannot express their choices (such as those in a persistent vegetative state), should be allowed to die on grounds that distinctively human life involves certain minimum standards of quality.

Philosophers distinguish between killing and letting die, or *active* versus *passive* euthanasia. The former involves performing an act to help bring about death (for example, giving a lethal injection), whereas the latter refrains from actions prolonging life (such as administering an antibiotic). The code of ethics of the American Medical Association recognizes the distinction and officially endorses the "standard view" regarding the morality of euthanasia. The view holds that passive euthanasia is morally acceptable (under specified conditions), but that active euthanasia is never acceptable. Others construe the active versus passive distinction in a different way. They reserve the term euthanasia for acts that aid the death of a person (also called *mercy killing*); allowing someone to die does not count as euthanasia.

Further controversy revolves around the distinction between *ordinary* and *extraordinary* means of sustaining life. Some believe that it is morally justifiable to withhold or withdraw extraordinary means of life support (such as a respirator), but that to refrain from ordinary treatment is not justifiable. Attempting to apply the distinction can be problematic, given the difficulty of saying what counts as extraordinary means. Such treatments as hemodialysis or coronary bypass surgery were once rare but are now routine. If a physician fails to perform surgery to correct intestinal obstruction in a severely defective newborn who is likely to die from other causes, should the surgery be considered ordinary (since it is a routine medical procedure) or extraordinary treatment? Has the physician engaged in euthanasia by refraining from operating?

Still others argue that a moral distinction exists between withdrawing extraordinary means of life support ("pulling the plug") and withholding such treatment in the first place. They consider the former, but not the latter, active euthanasia or killing. A less controversial distinction involves the difference between *voluntary* and *involuntary* euthanasia. Involuntary euthanasia occurs when a person is incapable of giving informed consent, whereas voluntary euthanasia has been previously consented to by the person. Cases of involuntary euthanasia arise with adults who are incompetent or comatose (the well-known case of Karen Ann Quinlan is an example). Involuntary euthanasia also arises with severely defective neonates. The special problems involving defective newborns are addressed in a separate section of the chapter.

Another problem has evolved with the development of medical technologies capable of sustaining biological functions in severely damaged patients. Patients may have brains that have irreversibly ceased to function ("brain dead"), but their heartbeat and respiration can be maintained mechanically. Others may have damage to the cerebral cortex, or "higher brain," but retain enough brainstem function to sustain heartbeat and respiration. The second group is in a "persistent vegetative state." A person in either group suffers irreversible loss of consciousness and cognitive ability. Should that person be regarded as alive or dead, and what medical treatment is ethically indicated?

Some call for a redefinition of the standard of death. Traditionally death occurs with the permanent cessation of cardiopulmonary function (heartbeat and respiration). By this standard, the "brain dead" patient on a life-support system is alive. An ad hoc committee of the Harvard Medical School addressed this issue in a report published in the *Journal of the American Medical Association* in 1968. The committee outlined tests for diagnosing the condition of "brain death" or permanent nonfunctioning of the whole brain. The committee recommended that, once such a condition is identified, the person be declared dead and life-support systems be turned off. In other words, death occurs despite continuing heartbeat and respiration.

A redefinition of death has a substantial effect on our views about euthanasia. If a person is "dead" before the removal of life-support systems, the act does not constitute euthanasia in its active or passive form. However, if the "brain-dead" patient is alive, withdrawing life-support systems represents active or passive euthanasia, depending on how the terms are construed. Additionally, the way death is defined affects the practice of harvesting organs for transplantation. If a "brain-dead" patient is alive, removal of vital organs is a partial cause of death and is ethically problematic. On the other hand, if the patient is already dead (and appropriate consent has been obtained), no such problem arises.

To avoid the possibility of being kept alive by artificial means or so-called "heroic measures," some advise competent adults to make a *living will* to express their wishes should they ever become incompetent. While not legally binding in most states, the living will serves as a guideline for medical professionals as well as family members. It relieves them of the painful responsibility of making euthanasia decisions on another's behalf.

Legislation concerning euthanasia has been actively debated in several states in recent years. Most proposals have sought to establish an individual's right to be "allowed to die," without advocating voluntary or involuntary euthanasia (which is illegal in all fifty states). Critics warn that legalizing passive euthanasia could lead to legalization of active euthanasia. Some who oppose legalization of (voluntary) active euthanasia feel that it is inherently immoral. Others believe that it is morally acceptable in individual cases but oppose making it a social policy because of the dangers of abuse. They suggest that such a policy could undermine respect for the sanctity of human life and lead to the legalization of involuntary active euthanasia practiced not only on the comatose but also on persons deemed socially undesirable.

The issue of euthanasia presents severe ethical dilemmas for health care providers. Traditionally, one of the primary tenets of the medical profession is the injunction, "Do no harm." The Hippocratic Oath specifies that a physician "will neither give a deadly drug to anybody . . . nor . . . make a suggestion to this effect."[1] In the same oath, the physician promises to "keep them [the sick] from harm and injustice." The first principle affirmed by the ethical code of

the AMA states that "A physician shall be dedicated to providing competent medical service with compassion and respect for human dignity" (see Appendix). The requirements to protect patients from injustice and to care for them with compassion and respect for dignity provide the moral groundwork for euthanasia. If a patient's condition is deteriorated to the extent that life becomes meaningless or unbearable, should the professional's duty to preserve life be overriden by the demands of compassion, respect, and justice? In such a case, helping the patient to die seems not only ethically permissible but, on grounds of humane treatment, obligatory.

In the following article James Rachels examines the conventional view condoning passive euthanasia while condemning active euthanasia. He argues that active euthanasia is often more humane than passive euthanasia. This is an important consideration since compassion is the primary justification for euthanasia. Rachels also suggests three other grounds for challenging the acceptability of the conventional view and urges physicians to reconsider its moral validity.

In the second article, physician David Hellerstein argues against the excessive use of medical technologies for "very ill people whose physical existence can be prolonged almost indefinitely but whose quality of life will be intolerable." Hellerstein suggests that, in order to combat overreliance on technological solutions, medical students should be trained in listening to patient concerns and communicating with patients, especially the terminally ill and their families. Practicing physicians should also be counseled (via hospital- and medical association-sponsored conferences) in avoiding "technological overkill." The author's third proposal is to institute "technology evaluation teams" to help physicians and patients set treatment goals and evaluate uses of technology.

[1] *Ancient Medicine: Selected Papers of Ludwig Edelstein,* ed. Owsei Temkin and C. Lillian Temkin (Baltimore: Johns Hopkins University Press, 1967), p. 6.

JAMES RACHELS

Active and Passive Euthanasia

The distinction between active and passive euthanasia is thought to be crucial for medical ethics. The idea is that it is permissible, at least in some cases, to withhold treatment and allow a patient to die, but it is never permissible to take any direct action designed to kill the patient. This doctrine seems to be accepted by most doctors, and it is endorsed in a statement adopted by the House of Delegates of the American Medical Association on December 4, 1973:

> The intentional termination of the life of one human being by another—mercy killing—is contrary to that for which the medical profession stands and is contrary to the policy of the American Medical Association.
> The cessation of the employment of extraordinary means to prolong the life of the body when there is irrefutable evidence that biological death is imminent is the decision of the patient and/or his immediate family. The advice and judgment of the physician should be freely available to the patient and/or his immediate family.

However, a strong case can be made against this doctrine. In what follows I will set out some of the relevant arguments and urge doctors to reconsider their views on this matter.

To begin with a familiar type of situation, a patient who is dying of incurable cancer of the throat is in terrible pain, which can no longer be satisfactorily alleviated. He is certain to die within a few days, even if present treatment is continued, but he does not want to go on living for those days since the pain is unbearable. So he asks the doctor for an end to it, and his family joins in the request.

Suppose the doctor agrees to withhold treatment, as the conventional doctrine says he may. The justification for his doing so is that the patient is in terrible agony, and since he is going to die anyway, it would be wrong to prolong his suffering needlessly. But now notice this. If one simply withholds treatment, it may take the patient longer to die, and so he may suffer more than he would if more direct action were taken and a lethal injection given. This fact provides strong reason for thinking that, once the initial decision not to prolong his agony has been made, active euthanasia is actually preferable to passive euthanasia, rather than the reverse. To say otherwise is to endorse the option that leads to more suffering rather than less, and is contrary to the humanitarian impulse that prompts the decision not to prolong his life in the first place.

Part of my point is that the process of being "allowed to die" can be relatively slow and painful, whereas being given a lethal injection is relatively quick and painless. Let me give a different sort of example. In the United States about one in 600 babies is born with Down's syndrome. Most of these babies are otherwise healthy—that is, with only the usual pediatric care, they will proceed to an otherwise normal infancy. Some, however, are born with congenital defects such as intestinal obstructions that require operations if they are to live. Sometimes, the parents and the doctor will decide not to operate, and let the infant die. Anthony Shaw describes what happens then:

> . . . When surgery is denied [the doctor] must try to keep the infant from suffering while natural forces sap the baby's life away. As a surgeon whose natural inclination is to use the scalpel to fight off death, standing by and watching a salvageable baby die is the most emotionally exhausting experience I know. It is easy at a conference, in a theoretical discussion, to decide that such infants should be allowed to die. It is altogether different to stand by in the nur-

Reprinted with permission from *The New England Journal of Medicine*, 292, no. 2 (January 9, 1975), 78–80.

sery and watch as dehydration and infection wither a tiny being over hours and days. This is a terrible ordeal for me and the hospital staff—much more so than for the parents who never set foot in the nursery.[1]

I can understand why some people are opposed to all euthanasia and insist that such infants must be allowed to live. I think I can also understand why other people favor destroying these babies quickly and painlessly. But why should anyone favor letting "dehydration and infection wither a tiny being over hours and days"? The doctrine that says that a baby may be allowed to dehydrate and wither, but may not be given an injection that would end its life without suffering, seems so patently cruel as to require no further refutation. The strong language is not intended to offend, but only to put the point in the clearest possible way.

My second argument is that the conventional doctrine leads to decisions concerning life and death made on irrelevant grounds.

Consider again the case of the infants with Down's syndrome who need operations for congenital defects unrelated to the syndrome to live. Sometimes, there is no operation, and the baby dies, but when there is no such defect, the baby lives on. Now, an operation such as that to remove an intestinal obstruction is not prohibitively difficult. The reason why such operations are not performed in these cases is, clearly, that the child has Down's syndrome and the parents and doctor judge that because of that fact it is better for the child to die.

But notice that this situation is absurd, no matter what view one takes of the lives and potentials of such babies. If the life of such an infant is worth preserving, what does it matter if it needs a simple operation? Or, if one thinks it better that such a baby should not live on, what difference does it make that it happens to have an unobstructed intestinal tract? In either case, the matter of life and death is being decided on irrelevant grounds. It is the Down's syndrome, and not the intestines, that is the issue. The matter should be decided, if

at all, on that basis, and not be allowed to depend on the essentially irrelevant question of whether the intestinal tract is blocked.

What makes this situation possible, of course, is the idea that when there is an intestinal blockage, one can "let the baby die," but when there is no such defect there is nothing that can be done, for one must not "kill" it. The fact that this idea leads to such results as deciding life or death on irrelevant grounds is another good reason why the doctrine should be rejected.

One reason why so many people think that there is an important moral difference between active and passive euthanasia is that they think killing someone is morally worse than letting someone die. But is it? Is killing, in itself, worse than letting die? To investigate this issue, two cases may be considered that are exactly alike except that one involves killing whereas the other involves letting someone die. Then, it can be asked whether this difference makes any difference to the moral assessments. It is important that the cases be exactly alike, except for this one difference, since otherwise one cannot be confident that it is this difference and not some other that accounts for any variation in the assessments of the two cases. So, let us consider this pair of cases:

In the first, Smith stands to gain a large inheritance if anything should happen to his six-year-old cousin. One evening while the child is taking his bath, Smith sneaks into the bathroom and drowns the child, and then arranges things so that it will look like an accident.

In the second, Jones also stands to gain if anything should happen to his six-year-old cousin. Like Smith, Jones sneaks in planning to drown the child in his bath. However, just as he enters the bathroom Jones sees the child slip and hit his head, and fall face down in the water. Jones is delighted; he stands by, ready to push the child's head back under if it is necessary, but it is not necessary. With only a little thrashing about, the child drowns all by himself, "accidentally," as Jones watches and does nothing.

Now Smith killed the child, whereas Jones "merely" let the child die. That is the only difference between them. Did either man behave better, from a moral point of view? If the difference between killing and letting die were in itself a morally important matter, one should say that Jones's behavior was less reprehensible than Smith's. But does one really want to say that? I think not. In the first place, both men acted from the same motive, personal gain, and both had exactly the same end in view when they acted. It may be inferred from Smith's conduct that he is a bad man, although that judgment may be withdrawn or modified if certain further facts are learned about him—for example, that he is mentally deranged. But would not the very same thing be inferred about Jones from his conduct? And would not the same further considerations also be relevant to any modification of this judgment? Moreover, suppose Jones pleaded, in his own defense, "After all, I didn't do anything except just stand there and watch the child drown. I didn't kill him; I only let him die." Again, if letting die were in itself less bad than killing, this defense should have at least some weight. But it does not. Such a "defense" can only be regarded as a grotesque perversion of moral reasoning. Morally speaking, it is no defense at all.

Now, it may be pointed out, quite properly, that the cases of euthanasia with which doctors are concerned are not like this at all. They do not involve personal gain or the destruction of normal, healthy children. Doctors are concerned only with cases in which the patient's life is of no further use to him, or in which the patient's life has become or will soon become a terrible burden. However, the point is the same in these cases: the bare difference between killing and letting die does not, in itself, make a moral difference. If a doctor lets a patient die for humane reasons, he is in the same moral position as if he had given the patient a lethal injection for humane reasons. If his decision was wrong—if, for example, the patient's illness was in fact curable—the decision would be equally regrettable no matter which method was used to carry it out. And if the doctor's decision was the right one, the method used is not in itself important.

The AMA policy statement isolates the crucial issue very well; the crucial issue is "the intentional termination of the life of one human being by another." But after identifying this issue, and forbidding "mercy killing," the statement goes on to deny that the cessation of treatment is the intentional termination of life. This is where the mistake comes in, for what is the cessation of treatment, in these circumstances, if it is not "the intentional termination of the life of one human being by another"? Of course it is exactly that, and if it were not, there would be no point to it.

Many people will find this judgment hard to accept. One reason, I think, is that it is very easy to conflate the question of whether killing is, in itself, worse than letting die, with the very different question of whether most actual cases of killing are more reprehensible than most actual cases of letting die. Most actual cases of killing are clearly terrible (think, for example, of all the murders reported in the newspapers), and one hears of such cases every day. On the other hand, one hardly ever hears of a case of letting die, except for the actions of doctors who are motivated by humanitarian reasons. So one learns to think of killing in a much worse light than of letting die. But this does not mean that there is something about killing that makes it in itself worse than letting die, for it is not the bare difference between killing and letting die that makes the difference in these cases. Rather, the other factors—the murderer's motive of personal gain, for example, contrasted with the doctor's humanitarian motivation—account for different reactions to the different cases.

I have argued that killing is not in itself any worse than letting die; if my contention is right, it follows that active euthanasia is not any worse than passive euthanasia. What arguments can be given on the other side? The most common, I believe, is the following:

"The important difference between active and passive euthanasia is that, in passive euthanasia, the doctor does not do anything to bring about the patient's death. The doctor does nothing, and the patient dies of whatever ills already afflict him. In active euthanasia, however, the doctor does something to bring about the patient's death: he kills him. The doctor who gives the patient with cancer a lethal injection has himself caused his patient's death; whereas if he merely ceases treatment, the cancer is the cause of the death."

A number of points need to be made here. The first is that it is not exactly correct to say that in passive euthanasia the doctor does nothing, for he does do one thing that is very important: he lets the patient die. "Letting someone die" is certainly different, in some respects, from other types of action—mainly in that it is a kind of action that one may perform by way of not performing certain other actions. For example, one may let a patient die by way of not giving medication, just as one may insult someone by way of not shaking his hand. But for any purpose of moral assessment, it is a type of action nonetheless. The decision to let a patient die is subject to moral appraisal in the same way that a decision to kill him would be subject to moral appraisal: it may be assessed as wise or unwise, compassionate or sadistic, right or wrong. If a doctor deliberately let a patient die who was suffering from a routinely curable illness, the doctor would certainly be to blame for what he had done, just as he would be to blame if he had needlessly killed the patient. Charges against him would then be appropriate. If so, it would be no defense at all for him to insist that he didn't "do anything." He would have done something very serious indeed, for he let his patient die.

Fixing the cause of death may be very important from a legal point of view, for it may determine whether criminal charges are brought against the doctor. But I do not think that this notion can be used to show a moral difference between active and passive euthanasia. The reason why it is considered bad to be the cause of someone's death is that death is regarded as a great evil—and so it is. However, if it has been decided that euthanasia—even passive euthanasia—is desirable in a

given case, it has also been decided that in this instance death is no greater an evil than the patient's continued existence. And if this is true, the usual reason for not wanting to be the cause of someone's death simply does not apply.

Finally, doctors may think that all of this is only of academic interest—the sort of thing that philosophers may worry about but that has no practical bearing on their own work. After all, doctors must be concerned about the legal consequences of what they do, and active euthanasia is clearly forbidden by the law. But even so, doctors should also be concerned with the fact that the law is forcing upon them a moral doctrine that may well be indefensible, and has a considerable effect on their practices. Of course, most doctors are not now in the position of being coerced in this matter, for they do not regard themselves as merely going along with what the law requires. Rather, in statements such as the AMA policy statement that I have quoted, they are endorsing this doctrine as a central point of medical ethics. In that statement, active euthanasia is condemned not merely as illegal but as "contrary to that for which the medical profession stands," whereas passive euthanasia is approved. However, the preceding considerations suggest that there is really no moral difference between the two, considered in themselves (there may be important moral differences in some cases in their *consequences*, but, as I pointed out, these differences may make active euthanasia, and not passive euthanasia, the morally preferable option). So, whereas doctors may have to discriminate between active and passive euthanasia to satisfy the law, they should not do any more than that. In particular, they should not give the distinction any added authority and weight by writing it into official statements of medical ethics.

Note

1. Shaw A.: "Doctor, Do We Have a Choice?" *The New York Times Magazine,* January 30, 1972, p. 54.

DAVID HELLERSTEIN

Overdosing on Medical Technology

A few years ago, when I was in medical school, I spent a long Sunday afternoon squeezing bags of blood. I was on Surgery service then, and had half a mind of becoming a surgeon—I loved the cutting and sewing, the urgent rush to the operating room, and the feeling of omnipotence that came from excising disease and suturing together what was left.

This particular Sunday, an old alcoholic was brought into the emergency room, nearly dead. His name was Kalicki (all the names in this article have been changed), and his bloated belly was rigid. His body had all the stigmata of the end-stage boozer—beef-red palms, dilated webs of veins across his stomach, spidery bursts of broken blood vessels on his face and chest. There seemed to be no question of what to do. The excited voices of residents and nurses filled the emergency room, as intravenous lines were started, blood was drawn, and catheters passed into stomach and bladder. Soon old Kalicki was in the operating room. His belly was shaved and prepped, and in a few minutes the surgeon had made an incision along the line of his ribs.

Kalicki's insides were a confusion of old scars and adhesions. With each slice of the surgeon's scalpel, each movement of a blunt probe, new blood bubbled up black from within. The electric bovie, which usually stops bleeding with its cauterizing jolt, only brought forth new oozing. Kalicki's pressure began to drop; the intravenous lines were opened wide. His pressure kept falling. The blood bank was notified of the state of emergency, and soon soft plastic bags of blood began to arrive. Plastic tubing was uncoiled, new lines were started in the arms and neck, and in a few minutes what seemed like a forest of weird maroon fruit with long purple stems

hung over the table. Yet Kalicki's blood pressure stayed low.

That was when they told me to drop the retractor I had been holding and grab a bag of blood in my gloved hands. And to squeeze. I squeezed. I squeezed like hell. I must have squeezed a dozen bags until my hands went limp. Then somebody else took over, pushing hands together to force blood through the limp plastic tubing, frantically fighting to replace the deluge on the table. Of course it didn't work. Every suture put inside Kalicki's belly to stop the bleeding only brought new blood softly pumping to the surface. Finally, after 30-odd units of precious blood had traveled through Kalicki's leaky system, the chief surgeon said to stop. And everyone stood there in that stainless steel and tile room, gowned and gloved, as the pressure fell and Kalicki died. By the time somebody went to tell Kalicki's son, it was 7:30 at night; the day was gone. The son was not much surprised. Really, he said, it was for the best. The family had been expecting this for years.

That was it. Or almost it. A few weeks later, in the monthly morbidity and mortality conference, somebody brought up Kalicki's case, and mentioned a paper about the regretably high incidence of uncontrollable bleeding in end-stage cirrhosis of the liver. Our chief commented that as soon as he made the first cut, he knew he wouldn't be able to stop the bleeding. But once he'd started, what choice did he have?

Pointless Displays of Technique

The events of that afternoon have stuck with me. Even without them I doubt I'd have been a surgeon, but they did cast a pall on the whole endeavor. What had looked so heroic now seemed bullheaded and pointless, a display of technique for its own sake.

At first such displays seemed peculiar to surgery, but as I finished medical school and began my internship and residency I began to see the same sequence of events played out over and over in different settings—in internal medicine, pediatrics, neurology, and oncology. Time after time we'd be there, in situations with no hope of survival. What I was seeing, I realized finally, was not an isolated phenomenon but something pervading the contemporary practice of medicine in America.

Certainly there are some situations where the motives for continuing aggressive treatment are more or less rational. If there is a slight hope of recovery, it's always difficult to stop treatment. And in an emergency, it's often better to act first and question later. Sometimes there are educational reasons for making a vigorous push—so interns and residents can learn to deal with the failure of multiple systems. Other times there's a need to experiment with a new drug or technique. Still other times I think there's a vague fear that lawyers might be sniffing around for malpractice possibilities or that an outraged family member might turn up after the fact. And in still other situations, unethical practitioners may perform extra tests for their own financial gain. But in many terminal situations, the barrage of testing and treatment continues without any apparent reason. The machinery of the hospital, once set in motion, just continues rolling.

These are the most baffling situations. For some reason we doctors don't seem to know how *not* to treat, how not to make the first cut, how to stand back and let nature have its way. To decide not to treat the pneumococcal pneumonia in a dying patient seems like negligence—even if it may be mercy. To leave a cancer drug on the shelf seems like a crime.

To some degree, this obsession with technology reflects a bias of our culture. But to blame this situation solely on our culture would be futile. It would also be a mistake, because the problem has as much to do with the habits of the medical profession as anything else. Over the past century, medicine has grown from being a relatively passive clinical discipline with an emphasis on the observation of disease into a scientifically based profession dedicated to the collection of data, the close monitoring of organ function, and above all the aggressive treatment of disease. The medical profession embraces—indeed, endorses—technology with little critical examination. It rewards overtesting and overtreating. And worst of all, it has trained an entire generation of doctors—mine—in certain attitudes and thought patterns that are often detrimental to patient care.

My own experience was a textbook example. I received my training in a medical center that prides itself on delivering highly specialized, state-of-the-art care. But along with my excellent formal education in high-tech medicine came a number of informal lessons that often led to bad treatment.

Technology Pays

One was the lesson of our patients' lab sheets. Every day, a new computerized record of all lab tests would be put into all the patient's charts; it was a record of all tests done since the person entered the hospital. By the time someone had been in the hospital for a few weeks, this record could amount to 30 or 40 pages. The sense one got from this was that it would be a good idea to order a whole new set of tests every day—to check against the day before.

A second lesson—which I occasionally wish I had learned better—was that technology pays. Technology gets people grants, promotions, tenure. The surest way to power in a medical center is to ally oneself with technology. I can think of one resident in my psychiatry program who has learned this lesson particularly well. When he heard that our medical center was about to get an NMR scanner, an experimental diagnostic device, he learned as much as he could about the new machine and its possible relevance to psychiatry. He became instrumental in writing up protocol for research on the new machine and in supervising the research. This affiliation has given him power—the power to control access to this device—and will eventually enable him to publish a stream of research papers that can only increase his standing among other psychiatrists.

In addition, technology reimburses its followers well. The anesthesiologist makes more than the pediatrician, and the internist who performs more procedures to make a diagnosis makes more money than the internist who does only a few.

A third lesson, not explicitly stated but obviously followed in practice, was that virtually everyone should be treated. Instead of acknowledging that one patient might stand a chance of being cured while another might only have his or her terminal pain relieved, our approach was that we should try to do everything for everybody. It was extremely difficult for us to step back and ask what our overall goals should be or even more important, to find out what the patient might want.

The same lessons, apparently, are still being taught today. In the first major review since 1932 of what doctors study for their M.D. diploma, a panel of the Association of the American Medical Colleges (AAMC) found that medical students are being swamped by science and technology at the expense of basic healing skills. "Specialization and the rapid rate of advancement of knowledge and technology may tend to preempt the attention of both teachers and students from the central purpose of medicine, which is to heal the sick and relieve the suffering," was how the AAMC panel phrased it.

Aside from doctors' attitudes, another reason for the excessive use of technology has to do with its consumers—patients and their families. Technology often serves the purposes that religious ritual once did. Better than prayers or candles or offerings, technology conveys hope. For the dying patient, the lab test and the CAT scan are symbols of recovery, and the administration of drugs or futile emergency operations brings a certain degree of relief. For the family, there is also some consolation in the thought that everything that can be done is being done. "Intensive care" sounds like love, so the dying patient is surrounded by monitors and catheters and respirators.

Hiding Behind Machines

Technology is often used as a distraction as well—to avoid painful and difficult issues. During my internship, this happened with an old man dying of stomach cancer. Mr. Johnson came to my hospital floor in a terminal state. But before we'd let him die, we did an enormous workup: CAT scans of body and head, X-rays of soft and hard tissues, collections of all available body fluids. He spent days in radiology waiting for these tests. He was sure we'd cure him; he had great faith in medicine. He'd already gone through one regimen of anticancer drugs with no effect; we gave him a second, experimental regimen. When that failed, a third course was begun. The most difficult thing to recall in retrospect is his suffering, not only the pain of his disease but the long waits for tests and his extreme pain from the corrosive chemotherapy. He'd cry when the futile medication went through his IV. Only in the last day or so did he realize that it was having no effect, and then he began screaming that we were killing him. There was no way to console him.

He was wrong, of course—we weren't killing him, but we weren't doing him any favor either. We were just adding to his expense and suffering, misleading him with technology. Probably we, his doctors, were misleading ourselves too; the oncologists I was working with knew full well they couldn't save Mr. Johnson, but nobody could admit it. And that's the problem. Despite all the promise of medical technology, in the crucial moments, many of us are ashamed to admit how woefully inadequate it remains.

Technology serves still another function: that of communication. There is no language anymore for sitting by the bedside; the doctor has no time for waiting and consoling. More and more, the monitor's beep and squeal replaces the doctor's voice. The sounds of communication in the hospital are not English words but the respirator and the CAT scan. Many patients, like Mr. Johnson, are falsely reassured by these sounds, only to learn too late that they mean nothing.

Whether serving as communication, ritual, habit, or evasion, medical technology fulfills often fundamentally dishonest purposes. It is expensive, wasteful, and not infrequently inhumane to communicate through machines. And it may not even improve doctors' ability to diagnose disease, according to a recent study by physicians at Boston's Brigham and Women's Hospital. The study was conducted to determine whether the new diagnostic hardware was making autopsies obsolete as a way of helping doctors learn from their mistakes. The investigators studied the results of 100 post-mortem examinations performed at their hospital in 1960, 1970, and 1980, and they found that the percentage of diagnostic error was about the same in each of the three time periods. So much for the infallibility of technology.

Learning How to Listen

What, then, can be done to remedy this addiction to machines, this technological fix? Ironically, sheer cost is forcing policymakers on the state and federal level to act. Already, five states have devised their own hospital-reimbursement plans based, for the most part, upon fixed fees for services. The Reagan administration is proposing a similar package that would replace the traditional Medicaid reimbursement system with one that establishes, in advance, prices for 467 specific diagnoses. If a hospital spends less than the set Medicaid price, it gets to pocket the difference, creating an incentive to hold costs down. However, under this system, hospitals may end up denying patients care beyond a certain arbitrary limit. Particularly needy patients may suffer, and I don't believe this approach will make doctors more selective in their use of technology.

Any truly effective changes must come from the medical profession itself. And the place to start is at the beginning—by changing the values taught in medical school. The AAMC panel has wisely concluded that students must be taught to pay attention to treating minor problems, compiling patient histories, and using fundamental instruments such as the stethoscope. I would also suggest instruction in how to deal with terminally ill patients and their families, how to rely less on tests and more on diagnostic judgment, how to listen to patients' concerns. Such courses should be required, beginning in medical school and continuing through the clinical years of training.

Furthermore, we should attempt to change the attitudes of doctors already out of school. Many practitioners, in an effort to keep up with the bewildering pace of clinical research, regularly attend conferences and read two or three professional journals a week. Why not hold conferences, sponsored by individual hospitals or medical associations, in which the questions of technological overkill are discussed regarding specific cases? Answers to questions such as what tests are unnecessary and at what point treatment should be abandoned become increasingly important as newer technologies emerge, as we implant artificial hearts as well as kidneys, as the prospect of artificial livers becomes less fantastic. We may soon face a day when all our hospitals will be filled with very ill people whose physical existence can be prolonged almost indefinitely but whose quality of life will be intolerable.

The Team Approach

I also think it essential that we get directly into the medical arena to affect decisions as they are being made. Most hospitals have professional groups that evaluate patient care, but these "utilization review" committees are not very effective in dealing with the problem of overtreatment. They basically want to make sure that some kind of active treatment—or testing—is under way; they don't look too closely at whether it's really necessary. In fact, these committees may sometimes encourage a frenzy of overactivity among doctors who don't even know whether a particular patient should be hospitalized.

What I propose instead is the team approach—a group of medical professionals who would go on regular hospital rounds to evaluate the use of technology in patient care. Such a team could be similar to the "pain team" I know of at one hospital that evaluates the best approach to relieving the pain of terminal cancer patients. The team includes an internist, a neurologist, a psychiatrist, a social worker, and a nurse. Similarly, a "technology evaluation team" could be composed of an internist, an intensive-care specialist, a psychiatrist, a nurse, and a few patient advocates. Team members would work with doctors and patients to help them decide on reasonable treatment goals and on the best use of medical technology. Such teams could help restore medical technologies to their proper role as useful, but fallible, tools. Some doctors may perceive this kind of team as a threat to their own authority or as a potential source of embarrassment. But I think many would welcome the support in making difficult clinical decisions.

One final example. At the end of my internship, an elderly man, a Mr. Stone, came to my floor with severe heart failure. Despite high doses of all the right medications, his body filled up with excess fluid. He was almost unable to breathe; only by giving him intravenous Lasix, which increases the flow of urine, could his lungs be kept clear. I was shocked when his cardiologist, Dr. Evans, took me aside one afternoon to recommend that I stop giving Lasix. Dr. Evans said that Mr. Stone was not enjoying life anymore, that he was very unlikely to make it out of the hospital, that he, Dr. Evans, had discussed intensive care and dialysis with the Stones and they had decided

against that kind of intervention, and that Mrs. Stone was suffering because of her husband's protracted illness.

I can't see it, I said—it's just a few squirts of Lasix every day. So I continued. Mr. Stone kept getting heavier and had more trouble breathing. Mrs. Stone was sitting at his bedside every day, suffering. So one day I decided that I was being ridiculous and did what Dr. Evans suggested. Mr. Stone died. Mrs. Stone cried and thanked me and went home.

I knew I'd done the right thing yet I felt strange, because I knew that if I *wanted* to I could have kept his heart going for quite a long time. It was very unsettling, after the kind of training I'd received, to just stand aside and let nature have its way.

Suggested Further Reading

Engelhardt, H. Tristram, "Defining Death: A Philosophical Problem for Medicine and Law," *American Review of Respiratory Disease*, 112 (1975), 587–90.

Foot, Phillipa, "Euthanasia," *Philosophy and Public Affairs*, 6, no. 2 (Winter 1977), 85–112.

Imbus, Sharon, and Bruce E. Zawacki, "Autonomy for Burned Patients when Survival Is Unprecedented," *The New England Journal of Medicine*, 297, no. 6 (August 11, 1977), 309–11.

Kamisar, Yale, "Euthanasia Legislation: Some Nonreligious Objections," *Minnesota Law Review*, 42, no. 6 (1958), 969–1042.

Sullivan, Thomas D., "Active and Passive Euthanasia: An Impertinent Distinction?" *Human Life Review*, 111, no. 3 (Summer 1977), 40–46.

Williams, Glanville, "Euthanasia Legislation: A Rejoinder to the Nonreligious Objections," *Minnesota Law Review*, 43, no. 1 (November 1958), 1–12.

DECISION SCENARIO 3

Euthanasia

Woody watched his brother, R.C., become more and more incapacitated with amyotrophic lateral sclerosis (Lou Gehrig's disease). Woody and R.C. had had an extremely close relationship. For years they had worked the family farm together. When R.C. was admitted to a nursing home, Woody's pain increased even more. Woody came to visit every day.

R.C. then had a series of strokes unrelated to the disease. They left his body contorted, with his left side partially paralyzed. R.C.'s breathing was labored, and the medical team had decided to place him on a ventilator after the weekend.

The latest series of events gave Woody no rest. He went to R.C.'s wife, begging her to do something to allow R.C. to die with dignity. The wife agreed that it was important but did not want to bring the matter up with the physician. R.C. had had a good life and now she wanted to let nature take its course. Woody himself felt there was no help from the doctors at the nursing home.

With that, Woody had his mind made up. On Sunday he visited his brother one last time. "God forgive me," he said, "but I know you don't want to end up a vegetable." He pulled out a handgun and fired one shot at point-blank range into R.C.'s left temple. He laid the gun on R.C.'s chest and gave himself up to the supervising nurse.

Questions

1. Is Woody's act an example of euthanasia?

2. Did he do the morally right thing? Ought he to have considered alternative courses of action? Should he be punished by law?

3. Suppose Woody argues that he knew what his brother wanted and that he was carrying out his wishes. Does this fact make his choice of a quick and painless means of death right?

4. If the doctors had the legal right to dispense lethal drugs to induce death, Woody would have felt differently. Should the means of active euthanasia be legislated?

5. How do you compare the motives of Woody, R.C.'s wife, and the nursing home medical staff? Does the duty to respect a patient imply respecting the patient's right not to have death postponed?

2. TREATMENT OF DEFECTIVE NEONATES

The moral problems associated with treating infants born with severe defects and deformities are especially painful for health care professionals and for the infants' families. The atmosphere of joyous expectation is transformed into an occasion of sorrow and anxiety when the newborn is found to be defective. The central moral question regarding treatment of severely defective neonates is whether (and under what circumstances) they ought to be allowed to die. A related question is the level of care appropriate for such infants. Since not all defects are equally severe, morally acceptable treatment varies considerably from case to case. Should the infant be given extraordinary care, ordinary care, or no care at all and simply permitted to die? The question relates primarily to passive euthanasia, but active euthanasia may also come under consideration. If compassion is on the side of death, does acting in the infant's best interest require that he or she be mercifully killed?

Underlying these questions are two, more basic ethical issues. The first involves assigning a moral status to the newborn. This issue is related to the question of the moral status of fetuses, outlined in the section on abortion. Should the severely defective infant be regarded as a person? If the answer is yes, an obligation exists to provide the same treatment we would extend to other persons. As in the discussion of euthanasia, opinions vary widely as to what treatment should be. If the defective newborn does not have the status of personhood, then different criteria for treatment need to be developed. Some utilitarian arguments stress the social, emotional, and economic costs of saving the life of a severely defective infant. On these grounds, the infant ought not to be permitted to live, and no extraordinary steps should be taken to preserve its life. Arguments from a deontological standpoint, while recognizing the inherent value of a human life, find justification for withholding treatment by appealing to the duty to further the well-being of others. In such a case, extending life is a greater harm to the individual than allowing death. Such harm is an "injury of continued existence."

The second underlying issue concerns the fact that newborn infants are inherently incapable of making decisions for themselves. Who has the right or obligation to make choices on behalf of the newborn? Some argue that the decisions are medical in nature and ought to be made by health care professionals. Others believe that primary responsibility lies with the parents because they have the greatest interest in the welfare of their offspring. Some hospitals have ethics committees charged with the responsibility of reviewing all decisions regarding the treatment of defective newborns. Conflicts sometimes develop between family members and the medical professionals about choices of treatment, and the final decision is made by the courts. On occasion, when physicians and parents decide to allow a newborn to die without treatment, an outside party institutes legal procedures aimed at forcing them to provide additional care.

Arguments about the moral acceptability of allowing a severely defective neonate to die range from the strictly conservative position, which holds that no decision of the kind is ever permissible, to more liberal views, which develop various ethical criteria to be satisfied. Conservatives often argue that quality-of-life judgments and cost considerations are not valid reasons to withhold treatment. They assert that defective newborns are entitled to any and all care which we would provide for a normal infant, on the assumption that both have the same basic right to live.

In the following article Richard A. McCormick argues that life is a relative good and not an absolute one. It has a value, he maintains, as a condition which allows for other, "higher" goods, particularly the good of human relationships. If a life severely compromises the potential for human relationship by the struggle to survive, extraordinary efforts to preserve that life are no longer morally required. McCormick stresses the need to make decisions strictly on the basis of the infant's interest, without consideration of the emotional or financial burdens which others may incur in saving a defective newborn's life.

RICHARD A. McCORMICK

To Save or Let Die: The Dilemma of Modern Medicine

On February 24, the son of Mr. and Mrs. Robert H. T. Houle died following court-ordered emergency surgery at Maine Medical Center. The child was born February 9, horribly deformed. His entire left side was malformed; he had no left eye, was practically without a left ear, had a deformed left hand; some of his vertebrae were not fused. Furthermore, he was afflicted with a tracheal esophageal fistula and could not be fed by mouth. Air leaked into his stomach instead of going to the lungs, and fluid from the stomach pushed up into the lungs. As Dr. André Hellegers recently noted, "It takes little imagination to think there were further internal deformities" (*Obstetrical and Gynecological News*, April 1974).

As the days passed, the condition of the child deteriorated. Pneumonia set in. His reflexes became impaired and because of poor circulation, severe brain damage was suspected. The tracheal esophageal fistula, the immediate threat to his survival, can be corrected with relative ease by surgery. But in view of the associated complications and deformities, the parents refused their consent to surgery on "Baby Boy Houle." Several doctors in the Maine Medical Center felt differently and took the case to court. Maine Superior Court Judge David G. Roberts ordered the surgery to be performed. He ruled: "At the moment of live birth there does exist a human being entitled to the fullest protection of the law. The most basic right enjoyed by every human being is the right to life itself."

"Meaningful Life"

Instances like this happen frequently. In a recent issue of the *New England Journal of Medicine*, Drs. Raymond S. Duff and A. G. M. Campbell[1] reported on 299 deaths in the special-care nursery of the Yale-New Haven Hospital between 1970 and 1972. Of these, 43 (14%) were associated with discontinuance of treatment for children with multiple anomalies, trisomy, cardiopulmonary crippling, meningomyelocele, and other central nervous system defects. After careful consideration of each of these 43 infants, parents and physicians in a group decision concluded that the prognosis for "meaningful life" was extremely poor or hopeless, and therefore rejected further treatment. The abstract of the Duff–Campbell report states: "The awesome finality of these decisions, combined with a potential for error in prognosis, made the choice agonizing for families and health professionals. Nevertheless, the issue has to be faced, for not to decide is an arbitrary and potentially devastating decision of default."

In commenting on this study in the *Washington Post* (October 28, 1973), Dr. Lawrence K. Pickett, chief-of-staff at the Yale-New Haven Hospital, admitted that allowing hopelessly ill patients to die "is accepted medical practice." He continued: "This is nothing new. It's just being talked about now."

It has been talked about, it is safe to say, at least since the publicity associated with the famous "Johns Hopkins Case"[2] some three years ago. In this instance, an infant was born with Down's syndrome and duodenal atresia. The blockage is reparable by relatively easy surgery. However, after consultation with spiritual advisors, the parents refused permission for this corrective surgery, and the child died by starvation in the hospital after 15 days. To feed him by mouth in this condition would have killed him. Nearly everyone who has commented on this case has disagreed with the decision.

It must be obvious that these instances—

Reprinted with permission of the author and publisher from *The Journal of the American Medical Association*, 229 (July 8, 1974), 172–76. Copyright © 1974 American Medical Association.

and they are frequent—raise the most agonizing and delicate moral problems. The problem is best seen in the ambiguity of the term "hopelessly ill." This used to and still may refer to lives that cannot be saved, that are irretrievably in the dying process. It may also refer to lives that can be saved and sustained, but in a wretched, painful, or deformed condition. With regard to infants, the problem is, which infants, if any, should be allowed to die? On what grounds or according to what criteria, as determined by whom? Or again, is there a point at which a life that can be saved is not "meaningful life," as the medical community so often phrases the question? . . .

Thus far, the ethical discussion of these truly terrifying decisions has been less than fully satisfactory. Perhaps this is to be expected since the problems have only recently come to public attention. In a companion article to the Duff–Campbell report,[1] Dr. Anthony Shaw[3] of the Pediatric Division of the Department of Surgery, University of Virginia Medical Center, Charlottesville, speaks of solutions "based on the circumstances of each case rather than by means of a dogmatic formula approach." Are these really the only options available to us? Shaw's statement makes it appear that the ethical alternatives are narrowed to dogmatism (which imposes a formula that prescinds from circumstances) and pure concretism (which denies the possibility of usefulness of any guidelines).

Are Guidelines Possible?

Such either-or extremism is understandable. It is easy for the medical profession, in its fully justified concern with the terrible concreteness of these problems and with the issue of who makes these decisions, to trend away from any substantive guidelines. As *Time* remarked in reporting these instances: "Few, if any, doctors are willing to establish guidelines for determining which babies should receive lifesaving surgery or treatment and which should not" (*Time*, March 25, 1974). On the other hand, moral theologians, in their fully justified concern to avoid total normlessness

and arbitrariness wherein the right is "discovered," or really "created," only in and by brute decision, can easily be insensitive to the moral relevance of the raw experience, of the conflicting tensions and concerns provoked through direct cradleside contact with human events and persons.

But is there no middle course between sheer concretism and dogmatism? I believe there is. Dr. Franz J. Ingelfinger,[4] editor of the *New England Journal of Medicine,* in an editorial on the Duff–Campbell–Shaw articles, concluded, even if somewhat reluctantly: "Society, ethics, institutional attitudes and committees can provide the broad guidelines, but the onus of decision making ultimately falls on the doctor in whose care the child has been put." Similarly, Frederick Carney of Southern Methodist University, Dallas, and the Kennedy Institute . . . stated of these cases: "What is obviously needed is the development of substantive standards to inform parents and physicians who must make such decisions" (*Washington Post,* March 20, 1974).

"Broad guidelines," "substantive standards." There is the middle course, and it is the task of a community broader than the medical community. A guideline is not a slide rule that makes the decision. It is far less than that. But it is far more than the concrete decision of the parents and the physician, however seriously and conscientiously this is made. It is more like a light in a room, a light that allows the individual objects to be seen in the fullness of their context. Concretely, if there are certain infants that we agree ought to be saved in spite of illness or deformity, and if there are certain infants that we agree should be allowed to die, then there is a line to be drawn. And if there is a line to be drawn, there ought to be some criteria, even if very general, for doing this. Thus, if nearly every commentator has disagreed with the Hopkins decision, should we not be able to distill from such consensus some general wisdom that will inform and guide future decisions? I think so.

The task is not easy. Indeed, it is so harrowing that the really tempting thing is to run from it. The most sensitive, balanced, and penetrating study of the Hopkins case that I have seen is that of the University of Chicago's James Gustafson.[2] Gustafson disagreed with the decision of the Hopkins physicians to deny surgery to the mongoloid infant. In summarizing his dissent, he notes: "Why would I draw the line on a different side of mongolism than the physician did? While reasons can be given, one must recognize that there are intuitive elements, grounded in beliefs and profound feelings, that enter into particular judgments of this sort." He goes on to criticize the assessment made of the child's intelligence as too simplistic, and he proposes a much broader perspective on the meaning of suffering than seemed to have operated in the Hopkins decision. I am in full agreement with Gustafson's reflections and conclusions. But ultimately, he does not tell us where he would draw the line or why, only where he would *not*, and why.

This is very helpful already, and perhaps it is all that can be done. Dare we take the next step, the combination and analysis of such negative judgments to extract from them the positive criterion or criteria inescapably operative in them? Or more startlingly, dare we *not* if these decisions are already being made? Gustafson is certainly right in saying that we cannot always establish perfectly rational accounts and norms for our decisions. But I believe we must never cease trying, in fear and trembling to be sure. Otherwise, we have exempted these decisions in principle from the one critique and control that protects against abuse. Exemption of this sort is the root of all exploitation whether personal or political. Briefly, if we must face the frightening task of making quality-of-life judgments—and we must—then we must face the difficult task of building criteria for these judgments.

Facing Responsibility

What has brought us to this position of awesome responsibility? Very simply, the sophistication of modern medicine. Contemporary resuscitation and life-sustaining devices have brought a remarkable change in the state of the question. Our duties toward the care and preservation of life have been traditionally stated in terms of the use of ordinary and extraordinary means. For the moment and for purposes of brevity, we may say that, morally speaking, ordinary means are those whose use does not entail grave hardships to the patient. Those that would involve such hardship are extraordinary. Granted the relativity of these terms and the frequent difficulty of their application, still the distinction has had an honored place in mecical ethics and medical practice. Indeed, the distinction was recently reiterated by the House of Delegates of the American Medical Association in a policy statement. After disowning intentional killing (mercy killing), the AMA statement continues: "The cessation of the employment of extraordinary means to prolong the life of the body when there is irrefutable evidence that biological death is imminent is the decision of the patient and/or his immediate family. The advice and judgment of the physician should be freely available to the patient and/or his immediate family" (JAMA 227:728, 1974).

This distinction can take us just so far—and thus the change in the state of the question. The contemporary problem is precisely that the question no longer concerns only those for whom "biological death is imminent" in the sense of the AMA statement. Many infants who would have died a decade ago, whose "biological death was imminent," can be saved. Yesterday's failures are today's successes. Contemporary medicine with its team approaches, staged surgical techniques, monitoring capabilities, ventilatory support systems, and other methods, can keep almost anyone alive. This has tended gradually to shift the problem from the means to reverse the dying process to the quality of the life sustained and preserved. The questions, "Is this means too hazardous or difficult to use" and "Does this measure only prolong the patient's dying," while still useful and valid, now often become "Granted that we can easily save the life, what kind of life are we saving?" This is a quality-of-life judgment. And we fear it. And certainly we should. But with increased power goes increased responsibility. Since we have the power, we must face the responsibility.

A Relative Good

In the past, the Judeo-Christian tradition has attempted to walk a balanced middle path between medical vitalism (that preserves life at any cost) and medical pessimism (that kills when life seems frustrating, burdensome, "useless"). Both of these extremes root in an identical idolatry of life—an attitude that, at least by inference, views death as an unmitigated, absolute evil, and life as the absolute good. The middle course that has structured Judeo-Christian attitudes is that life is indeed a basic and precious good, but a good to be preserved precisely as the condition of other values. It is these other values and possibilities that found the duty to preserve physical life and also dictate the limits of this duty. In other words, life is a relative good, and the duty to preserve it a limited one. These limits have always been stated in terms of the *means* required to sustain life. But if the implications of this middle position are unpacked a bit, they will allow us, perhaps, to adapt to the type of quality-of-life judgment we are now called on to make without tumbling into vitalism or a utilitarian pessimism.

A beginning can be made with a statement of Pope Pius XII[5] in an allocution to physicians delivered November 24, 1957. After noting that we are normally obliged to use only ordinary means to preserve life, the Pontiff stated: "A more strict obligation would be too burdensome for most men and would render the attainment of the higher, more important good too difficult. Life, death, all temporal activities are in fact subordinated to spiritual ends." Here it would be helpful to ask two questions. First, what are these spiritual ends, this "higher, more important good"? Second, how is its attainment rendered too difficult by insisting on the use of extraordinary means to preserve life?

The first question must be answered in terms of love of God and neighbor. This sums up briefly the meaning, substance and consummation of life from a Judeo–Christian perspective. What is or can easily be missed is that these two loves are not separable. St. John wrote: "If any man says 'I love God' and hates his brother, he is a liar. For he who loves not his brother, whom he sees, how can he love God whom he does not see?" (I John 4:20–21). This means that our love of neighbor is in some very real sense our love of God. The good our love wants to do Him and to which He enables us, can be done only for the neighbor, as Karl Rahner has so forcefully argued. It is in others that God demands to be recognized and loved. If this is true, it means that, in Judeo-Christian perspective, the meaning, substance, and consummation of life is found in human *relationships*, and the qualities of justice, respect, concern, compassion, and support that surround them.

Second, how is the attainment of this "higher, more important (than life) good" rendered "too difficult" by life-supports that are gravely burdensome? One who must support his life with disproportionate effort focuses the time, attention, energy, and resources of himself and others not precisely on relationships, but on maintaining the condition of relationships. Such concentration easily becomes overconcentration and distorts one's view of and weakens one's pursuit of the very relational goods that define our growth and flourishing. The importance of relationships gets lost in the struggle for survival. The very Judeo-Christian meaning of life is seriously jeopardized when undue and unending effort must go into its maintenance. . . .

The Quality of Life

. . . Life's potentiality for other values is dependent on two factors, those external to the individual, and the very condition of the individual. The former we can and must change to maximize individual potential. That is what social justice is all about. The latter we sometimes cannot alter. It is neither inhuman nor unchristian to say that there comes a point where an individual's condition itself represents the negation of any truly human—i.e., relational—potential. When that point is reached, is not the best treatment no treatment? I believe that the *implications* of the traditional distinction between ordinary and extraordinary means point in this direction.

In this tradition, life is not a value to be preserved in and for itself. To maintain that would commit us to a form of medical vitalism that makes no human or Judeo-Christian sense. It is a value to be preserved precisely as a condition for other values, and therefore insofar as these other values remain attainable. Since these other values cluster around and are rooted in human relationships, it seems to follow that life is a value to be preserved only insofar as it contains some potentiality for human relationships. When in human judgment this potentiality is totally absent or would be, because of the condition of the individual, totally subordinated to the mere effort for survival, that life can be said to have achieved its potential.

Human Relationships

If these reflections are valid, they point in the direction of a guideline that may help in decisions about sustaining the lives of grossly deformed and deprived infants. That guideline is the potential for human relationships associated with the infant's condition. If that potential is simply nonexistent or would be utterly submerged and undeveloped in the mere struggle to survive, that life has achieved its potential. There are those who will want to continue to say that some terribly deformed infants may be allowed to die *because* no extraordinary means need be used. Fair enough. But they should realize that the term "extraordinary" has been so relativized to the condition of the patient that it is this condition that is decisive. The means are extraordinary because the infant's condition is extraordinary. And if that is so, we must face this fact head-on—and discover the substantive standard that allows us to say this of some infants, but not of others.

Here several caveats are in order. First, this guideline is not a detailed rule that preempts decisions; for relational capacity is not subject to mathematical analysis but to human judgment. However, it is the task of physicians to provide some more concrete categories or presumptive biological symptoms for this human judgment. For instance, nearly all would very likely agree that the anencephalic infant is without relational potential. On the other hand, the same cannot be said of the mongoloid infant. The task ahead is to attach relational potential to presumptive biological symptoms for the gray area between such extremes. In other words, individual decisions will remain the anguishing onus of parents in consultation with physicians.

Second, because this guideline is precisely that, mistakes will be made. Some infants will be judged in all sincerity to be devoid of any meaningful relational potential when that is actually not quite the case. This risk of error should not lead to abandonment of decisions; for that is to walk away from the human scene. Risk of error means only that we must proceed with great humility, caution, and tentativeness. Concretely, it means that if err we must at times, it is better to err on the side of life—and therefore to tilt in that direction.

Third, it must be emphasized that allowing some infants to die does not imply that "some lives are valuable, others not" or that "there is such a thing as a life not worth living." Every human being, regardless of age or condition, is of incalculable worth. The point is not, therefore, whether this or that individual has value. Of course he has, or rather *is* a value. The only point is whether this undoubted value has any potential at all, in continuing physical survival, for attaining a share, even if reduced, in the "higher, more important good." This is not a question about the inherent value of the individual. It is a question about whether this worldly existence will offer such a valued individual any hope of sharing those values for which physical life is the fundamental condition. Is not the only alternative an attitude that supports mere physical life as long as possible with every means?

Fourth, this whole matter is further complicated by the fact that this decision is being made for someone else. Should not the decision on whether life is to be supported or not be left to the individual? Obviously, wherever possible. But there is nothing inherently objectionable in the fact that parents with physicians must make this decision at some point for infants. Parents must make many crucial decisions for children. The only concern is that the decision not be shaped out of the utilitarian perspectives so deeply sunk into the consciousness of the contemporary world. In a highly technological culture, an individual is always in danger of being valued for his function, what he can do, rather than for who he is.

It remains, then, only to emphasize that these decisions must be made in terms of the child's good, this alone. But that good, as fundamentally a relational good, has many dimensions. Pius XII,[5] in speaking of the duty to preserve life, noted that this duty "derives from well-ordered charity, from submission to the Creator, from social justice, as well as from devotion towards his family." All of these considerations pertain to that "higher, more important good." If that is the case with the duty to preserve life, then the decision not to preserve life must likewise take all of these into account in determining what is for the child's good.

Any discussion of this problem would be incomplete if it did not repeatedly stress that it is the pride of the Judeo-Christian tradition that the weak and defenseless, the powerless and unwanted, those whose grasp on the goods of life is most fragile—that is, those whose potential is real but reduced—are cherished and protected as our neighbor in greatest need. Any application of a general guideline that forgets this is but a racism of the adult world profoundly at odds with the gospel, and eventually corrosive of the humanity of those who ought to be caring and supporting as long as that care and support has human meaning. It has meaning as long as there is hope that the infant will, in relative comfort, be able to experience our caring and love. For when this happens, both we and the child are sharing in that "greater, more important good."

Were not those who disagreed with the Hopkins decision saying, in effect, that for the infant, involved human relationships were still within reach and would not be totally submerged by survival? If that is the case, it is potential for relationships that is at the heart of these agonizing decisions.

References

1. Duff S., Campbell A. G. M.: "Moral and ethical dilemmas in the special-care nursery." *N Engl J Med* 289:890–894, 1973.

2. Gustafson J. M.: "Mongolism, parental desires, and the right to life." *Perspect Biol Med* 16:529–559, 1973.

3. Shaw A.: "Dilemmas of 'informed' consent in children." *N Engl J Med* 289:885–890, 1973.

4. Ingelfinger F.: "Bedside ethics for the hopeless case." *N Engl J Med* 289:914, 1973.

5. Pope Pius XII: *Acta Apostolicae Sedis* 49:1031–1032, 1957.

Suggested Further Reading

Duff, Raymond S., and A. G. M. Campbell, "Moral and Ethical Dilemmas in the Special-Care Nursery," *The New England Journal of Medicine*, 289, no. 17 (October 25, 1973), 890–94.

Shaw, Anthony, "Doctor, Do We Have a Choice?" *The New York Times Magazine*, January 30, 1972.

—— and Iris A. Shaw, "Dilemmas of 'Informed Consent' in Children," *New England Journal of Medicine*, 289, no. 17 (October 25, 1973), 885–90.

Zachary, R. B., "The Ethical and Social Aspects of Spina Bifida," *The Lancet*, 3 (August 1968), 274–76.

8. TREATMENT OF THE MENTALLY ILL AND MENTALLY RETARDED

Mental health and mental illness are familiar terms which, however, can be controversial and ambiguous. While health care professionals generally agree on a diagnosis of, say, pneumonia, they have widely differing opinions about the diagnosis of psychological symptoms. Some even question the correctness of using a medical model to describe ideas and behaviors unacceptable to the majority. Psychiatrist Thomas S. Szasz argues that there is no such thing as "mental illness." He insists that the concept of mental illness is a myth comparable to the notion of witchcraft. He maintains that persons who exhibit deviant behavior are experiencing "problems in living" and should not be characterized as diseased.[1]

A variety of key issues in the ethics of health care professions is raised by the question of caring for the mentally ill and the mentally retarded. Among these concepts are autonomy, informed consent, proxy consent, paternalism, and the right to health care. Society's right to regulate and control individual behavior (which may be distasteful but not dangerous) is problematic from an ethical standpoint. For example, at various times in history, homosexuals and sexually promiscuous women have been labeled and treated (often involuntarily) as mentally ill. Medical science identifies normal physiology with little difficulty. However, classifying behaviors and mental states as normal or abnormal is much less certain and may lead to political or social abuse. A case in

point is the Soviet Union's use of mental hospitals to confine political dissidents.

Disagreements about the morality of controlling the mentally ill arise along conceptual, empirical, and ethical grounds. For example, Szasz's objections to the current concept of mental illness represent a conceptual dispute. Others accept standard definitions of mental illness but question the assumption that mentally ill persons are necessarily dangerous or incompetent. Support for this view comes from studies showing the difficulty in predicting the dangerousness of any individual mental patient. Furthermore, as a group, mental patients are no more dangerous than other people. Still other thinkers question the moral validity of limiting the liberty of adults whose mental state may be partially distorted but who wish to make decisions about their own treatment. A recent Supreme Court ruling upheld the right of patients in psychiatric hospitals to refuse medication. The ruling recognizes the continued autonomy and right to self-determination of persons diagnosed as mentally ill.

Attempts to alter or control the behavior of the mentally ill take many forms, including psychotherapy, psychosurgery, the use of psychotropic (literally, "mind-changing") drugs, and commitment to mental institutions. Some question whether psychotherapy is behavior control, since it requires voluntary participation of the patient. Nonetheless, the aim of psychotherapy is to change a person's thinking and/or behavior. Therapists, like physicians, occupy a position of considerable power in relation to pa-

---

[1]Thomas S. Szasz, *Ideology and Insanity* (New York: Doubleday & Co., 1970).

tients. They exercise their authority to shape a patient's behavior to conform with approved views of what is normal.

Psychosurgery and the use of psychotropic drugs are methods of altering behavior by physical alteration of the brain. Mood elevators and anti-schizophrenic agents have gained widespread use in the last thirty years and have proved highly effective for some patients. Between 1955 and 1971 the population of U.S. mental hospitals decreased over 40 percent, despite increased admissions, largely as a result of treatment with psychotropic drugs.[2] These drugs can have serious, long-term side effects, and questions are currently being raised about whether they are prescribed too indiscriminately. Controversy over the use of psychosurgery is even more heated. Because its effects are irreversible, its use demands restraint and careful consideration. Some argue that because little is known about how the brain functions, psychosurgery is a morally unacceptable form of experimentation on humans. Both psychosurgery and treatment with psychotropic chemicals raise the basic moral question of whether it is acceptable to control human behavior by the deliberate use of technology.

Involuntary civil commitment to a mental institution represents a direct exercise of the state's power to control the lives of people classified as mentally ill. What ethical grounds exist for drastically limiting the liberty of adults who have broken no laws? (The ethics of incarcerating criminals is examined in the unit on criminal justice.) Justification of involuntary commitment derives from one or more of the following reasons: (1) to prevent a person from harming others; (2) to prevent a person from harming him- or herself; (3) to prevent a person from offending others; or (4) to benefit a person. How valid are these justifications? Who should determine the sufficiency of the rea-

sons in an individual case: psychiatrists, family members, the courts?

Protecting others from harm is a strong ground for commitment. Some argue, however, that behavior classified as dangerous may in fact be merely offensive, and that offensiveness is not in itself sufficient reason to deprive someone of liberty. Commitment on grounds of protecting persons from harming themselves or for their supposed benefit are instances of paternalism. Consequentialist arguments supporting involuntary commitment derive from the more general justifications for paternalism (see the first section in Chapter 5). As in other areas of health care, it is not clear that paternalistic intervention is justified. Involuntary commitment may foster an individual's autonomy in the long run by helping to restore a temporarily disturbed person to a former state of competence. Justification on this ground is based on the deontological principle of respect for individual persons. Others maintain that such coercive treatment may cause the person's condition to deteriorate further. They oppose the practice on utilitarian grounds. Their reasoning draws support from studies indicating that the longer a person stays in a mental hospital, the more likely repeated or permanent institutionalization becomes.

The mentally retarded are subject to many of the same limitations on their freedom as persons classified as mentally ill. Their treatment poses similar ethical problems. On grounds of incompetence to make their own decisions, mentally retarded persons are institutionalized, denied educational opportunity, prevented from marrying and having children, and even sterilized without their consent (and sometimes without their knowledge). Justification for such treatment derives from a paternalistic attitude which views the retarded as children who need to be protected and controlled for their own good.

Mentally retarded persons differ widely in their ability to make decisions and func-

---

[2]Ronald Munson, *Intervention and Reflection* (Belmont, Calif.: Wadsworth Publishing, 1979), p. 296.

tion independently. The most severely retarded often have physical handicaps and may require constant care to survive. Since they lack the capacity for autonomous action, few take issue with treating them in a paternalistic manner. Controversy about what constitutes morally acceptable treatment usually centers on mildly retarded persons, who comprise about 80 percent of those classified as retarded in the United States. Involuntary sterilization, in particular, has been challenged as a morally unjustified infringement on the retarded person's reproductive freedom. Proponents respond that such an infringement is justified because it enhances the individual's freedom in other areas (such as the enjoyment of heterosexual intercourse).

As with the mentally ill, disputes over ethical treatment arise on conceptual, empirical, or moral grounds. Advocates for the retarded assert that they should be referred to as "intellectually disadvantaged" and that they should have the same basic rights as any citizen. Proponents of this view reject the idea of a special classification for the retarded. Empirical arguments concern the attribution of qualities like dangerousness and incompetence to the retarded. (Denial of rights to the retarded is often justified on grounds that they pose a danger to themselves or to others.)

In the following article Joseph M. Livermore, Carl P. Malmquist, and Paul E. Meehl examine a variety of justifications for involuntary commitment of the mentally ill. They argue that most common justifications are based on false premises or ones that are too broad. While not totally rejecting involuntary commitment, the authors urge caution and restraint in the use of a "power . . . that ought rarely to be exercised."

JOSEPH M. LIVERMORE, CARL P. MALMQUIST, AND PAUL E. MEEHL

On the Justifications for Civil Commitment

Involuntary confinement is the most serious deprivation of individual liberty that a society may impose. The philosophical justifications for such a deprivation by means of the criminal process have been thoroughly explored. No such intellectual effort has been directed at providing justifications for societal use of civil commitment procedures.

When certain acts are forbidden by the criminal law, we are relatively comfortable in imprisoning those who have engaged in such acts. We say that the imprisonment of the offender will serve as an example to others and thus deter them from violating the law. If we even stop to consider the morality of depriving one man of his liberty in order to serve other social ends, we usually are able to allay anxiety by referring to the need to incarcerate to protect society from further criminal acts or the need to reform the criminal. When driven to it, at last, we admit that our willingness to permit such confinement rests on the notion that the criminal has justified it by his crime. Eligibility for social tinkering based on guilt, retributive though it may be, has so far satisfied our moral sensibilities.

Reprinted with permission of the publisher and Fred B. Rothman & Co. from *University of Pennsylvania Law Review,* 117 (November 1968), 75–96. Copyright © 1968 by the University of Pennsylvania.

It is, we believe, reasonably clear that the system could not be justified were the concept of guilt not part of our moral equipment. Would we be comfortable with a system in which any man could go to jail if by so doing he would serve an overriding social purpose? The normal aversion to punishment by example, with its affront to the principle of equality, suggests that we would not. Conversely, could we abide a rule that only those men would be punished whose imprisonment would further important social ends? Again, the thought of vastly different treatment for those equally culpable would make us uneasy.

Similarly, if we chose to justify incarceration as a means of isolating a group quite likely to engage in acts dangerous to others, we would, without the justification of guilt, have difficulty explaining why other groups, equally or more dangerous in terms of actuarial data, are left free. By combining background environmental data, we can identify categories of persons in which we can say that fifty to eighty percent will engage in criminal activities within a short period of time. If social protection is a sufficient justification for incarceration, this group should be confined as are those criminals who are likely to sin again.

The same argument applies when rehabilitative considerations are taken into account. Most, if not all of us could probably benefit from some understanding of psychological rewiring. Even on the assumption that confinement should be required only in those cases where antisocial acts may thereby be averted, it is not at all clear that criminals are the most eligible for such treatment. In addition, most people would bridle at the proposition that the state could tamper with their minds whenever it seemed actuarially sound to do so.

Fortunately, we can by reason of his guilt distinguish the criminal from others whom we are loathe to confine. He voluntarily flouted society's commands with an awareness of the consequences. Consequently, he may serve utilitarian purposes without causing his imprisoners any moral twinge.

This same sort of analysis is not available once we move beyond the arena of the criminal law. When people are confined by civil process, we cannot point to their guilt as a basis for differentiating them from others. What can we point to?

The common distinguishing factor in civil commitment is aberrance. Before we commit a person we demand either that he act or think differently than we believe he should. Whether our label be inebriate, addict, psychopath, delinquent, or mentally diseased, the core concept is deviation from norms.[1] Our frequently expressed value of individual autonomy, however, renders us unable to express those norms, however deeply they may be felt, in criminal proscriptions. We could not bring ourselves to outlaw senility, or manic behavior, or strange desires. Not only would this violate the common feeling that one is not a criminal if he is powerless to avoid the crime, but it might also reach conduct that most of us feel we have a right to engage in. When a man squanders his savings in a hypomanic episode, we may say, because of our own beliefs, that he is "crazy," but we will not say that only reasonable purchases are allowed on pain of criminal punishment. We are not yet willing to legislate directly the Calvinist ideal.

What we are not willing to legislate, however, we have been willing to practice through the commitment process. That process has been used to reach two classes of persons, those who are mentally ill and dangerous to themselves or others and those who are mentally ill and in need of care, custody or treatment. While those terms seem reasonably clear, on analysis that clarity evaporates.

One need only glance at the diagnostic manual of the American Psychiatric Association to learn what an elastic concept mental illness is. It ranges from the massive functional inhibition characteristic of one form of catatonic schizophrenia to those seemingly slight aberrancies associated with an emotionally unstable personality, but which are so close to conduct in which we all engage as to define the entire continuum involved. Obviously, the definition of mental illness is left largely to the user and is dependent upon the norms of adjustment that he employs. Usually the use of the phrase "mental illness" effectively masks the actual norms being applied. And, because of the unavoidably ambiguous generalities in which the American Psychiatric Association describes its diagnostic categories, the diagnostician has the ability to shoehorn into the mentally diseased class almost any person he wishes, for whatever reason, to put there.

All this suggests that the concept of mental illness must be limited in the field of civil commitment to a necessary rather than a sufficient condition for commitment. While the term has its uses, it is devoid of that purposive content that a touchstone in the law ought to have. Its breadth of meaning makes for such difficulty of analysis that it answers no question that the law might wish to ask.

Dangerousness to Others

The element of dangerousness to others has, at least in practice, been similarly illusive. As Professors Goldstein and Katz have observed, such a test, at a minimum, calls for a determination both of what acts are dangerous and how probable it is that such acts will occur. The first question suggests to a criminal lawyer the answer: crimes involving a serious risk of physical or psychical harm to another. Murder, arson and rape are the obvious examples. Even in criminal law, however, the notion of dangerousness can be much broader. If one believes that acts that have adverse effects on social interests are dangerous, and if one accepts as a generality that the criminal law is devoted to such acts, any crime can be considered dangerous. For example, speeding in a motor vehicle, although traditionally regarded as a minor crime, bears great risk to life and property, and thus may be viewed as a dangerous act. Dangerousness can bear an even more extensive definition as well. An act may be considered dangerous if it is offensive or disquieting to others. Thus, the man who walks the street repeating, in a loud monotone, "fuck, fuck, fuck," is going to wound many sensibilities even if he does not violate the criminal law. Other examples would be

the man, found in most cities, striding about town lecturing at the top of his lungs, or the similar character in San Francisco who spends his time shadow boxing in public. If such people are dangerous, it is not because they threaten physical harm but because we are made uncomfortable when we see aberrancies. And, of course, if dangerousness is so defined, it is at least as broad a concept as mental illness. The cases are unfortunately silent about what meaning the concept of danger bears in the commitment process.

Assuming that dangerousness can be defined, the problem of predictability still remains. For the man who can find sexual release only in setting fires, one may confidently predict that dangerous acts will occur. For the typical mentally aberrant individual, though, the matter of prediction is not susceptible of answer. However nervous a full-blown paranoiac may make us, there are no actuarial data indicating that he is more likely to commit a crime than any normal person. Should he engage in criminal activity, his paranoia would almost certainly be part of the etiology. But on a predictive basis we have, as yet, nothing substantial to rely on.

Even if such information were available, it is improbable that it would indicate that the likelihood of crime within a group of individuals with any particular psychosis would be any greater than that to be expected in a normal community cross-section. Surely the degree of probability would not be as high as that in certain classes of convicted criminals after their release from prison or that in certain classes of persons having particular sociological or psychological characteristics.

Dangerousness to Self

The concept of "dangerousness to self" raises similar problems. The initial thought suggested by the phrase is the risk of suicide. But again it can be broadened to include physical or mental harm from an inability to take care of one's self, loss of assets from foolish expenditures, or even loss of social standing or reputation from behaving peculiarly in the presence of others. Again, if read very broadly this concept becomes synonymous with that of mental illness. And, of course, reliable prediction is equally impossible.

In Need of Care, Custody, or Treatment

The notion of necessity of care or treatment provides no additional limitation beyond those imposed by the concepts already discussed. One who is diagnosably mentally ill is, almost by definition, in need of care or treatment. Surely the diagnostician reaching the first conclusion would reach the second as well. And, if a man is dangerous, then presumably he is in need of custody. The problem, of course, lies with the word "need." If it is defined strictly as, for example, "cannot live without," then a real limitation on involuntary commitment is created. In normal usage, however, it is usually equated with "desirable," and the only boundary on loss of freedom is the value structure of the expert witness.

It is difficult to identify the reasons that lie behind incarceration of the mentally ill. Three seem to be paramount:

1. It is thought desirable to restrain those people who may be dangerous;
2. It is thought desirable to banish those who are a nuisance to others;
3. It is thought humanitarian to attempt to restore to normality and productivity those who are not now normal and productive.

Each of these goals has social appeal, but each also creates analytic difficulty.

As already mentioned, in order to understand the concept of danger one must determine what acts are dangerous and how likely is it that they will occur. There is a ready inclination to believe that experts in the behavioral sciences will be able to identify those members of society who will kill, rape, or burn. The fact is, however, that such identification cannot presently be accomplished. First, our growing insistence on privacy will, in all but a few cases, deny the expert access

to the data necessary to the task of finding potential killers. Second, and of much greater importance, even if the data were available it is unlikely that a test could be devised that would be precise enough to identify only those individuals who are dangerous. Since serious criminal conduct has a low incidence in society, and since any test must be applied to a very large group of people, the necessary result is that in order to isolate those who will kill it is also necessary to incarcerate many who will not. Assume that one person out of a thousand will kill. Assume also that an exceptionally accurate test is created which differentiates with ninety-five percent effectiveness those who will kill from those who will not. If 100,000 people were tested, out of the 100 who would kill 95 would be isolated. Unfortunately, out of the 99,900 who would not kill, 4,995 people would also be isolated as potential killers.[2] In these circumstances, it is clear that we could not justify incarcerating all 5,090 people. If, in the criminal law, it is better than ten guilty men go free than that one innocent man suffer, how can we say in the civil commitment area that it is better that fifty-four harmless people be incarcerated lest one dangerous man be free?

The fact is that without any attempt at justification we have been willing to do just this to one disadvantaged class, the mentally ill. This practice must rest on the common supposition that mental illness makes a man more likely to commit a crime. While there may be some truth in this, there is much more error. Any phrase that encompasses as many diverse concepts as does the term "mental illness" is necessarily imprecise. While the fact of paranoid personality might be of significance in determining a heightened probability of killing, the fact of hebephrenic schizophrenia probably would not. Yet both fit under the umbrella of mental illness.

Even worse, we have been making assessments of potential danger on the basis of nothing as precise as the psychometric test hypothesized. Were we to ignore the fact that no definition of dangerous acts has been agreed upon, our standards of prediction have still been horribly imprecise. On the armchair assumption that paranoids are dangerous, we have tended to play safe and incarcerate them all. Assume that the incidence of killing among paranoids is five times as great as among the normal population. If we use paranoia as a basis for incarceration we would commit 199 non-killers in order to protect ourselves from one killer. It is simply impossible to justify any commitment scheme so premised. And the fact that assessments of dangerousness are often made clinically by a psychiatrist, rather than psychometrically and statistically, adds little if anything to their accuracy.

We do not mean to suggest that dangerousness is not a proper matter of legal concern. We do suggest, however, that limiting its application to the mentally ill is both factually and philosophically unjustifiable. As we have tried to demonstrate, the presence of mental illness is of limited use in determining potentially dangerous individuals. Even when it is of evidentiary value, it serves to isolate too many harmless people. What is of greatest concern, however, is that the tools of prediction are used with only an isolated class of people. We have alluded before to the fact that it is possible to identify, on the basis of sociological data, groups of people wherein it is possible to predict that fifty to eighty percent will engage in criminal or delinquent conduct. And, it is probable that more such classes could be identified if we were willing to subject the whole population to the various tests and clinical examinations that we now impose only on those asserted to be mentally ill. Since it is perfectly obvious that society would not consent to a wholesale invasion of privacy of this sort and would not act on the data if they were available, we can conceive of no satisfactory justification for this treatment of the mentally ill.

One possible argument for different treatment can be made in terms of the concept of responsibility. We demonstrate our belief in individual responsibility by refusing to incarcerate save for failure to make a responsible decision. Thus, we do not incar-

cerate a group, eighty percent of whom will engage in criminal conduct, until those eighty percent have demonstrated their lack of responsibility—and even then, the rest of the group remains free. The mentally diseased, so the argument would run, may be viewed prospectively rather than retrospectively because for them responsibility is an illusory concept. We do not promote responsibility by allowing the dangerous act to occur since, when it does, we will not treat the actor as responsible. One way of responding to this is to observe that criminal responsibility and mental illness are not synonymous, and that if incarceration is to be justified on the basis of responsibility, only those mentally ill who will probably, as a matter of prediction, commit a crime for which they will not be held responsible should be committed. A more fundamental response is to inquire whether susceptibility to criminal punishment is reasonably related to any social purpose. Granted that there is a gain in social awareness of individual responsibility by not incarcerating the responsible in advance of their crime, it does not necessarily follow that it is sufficiently great to warrant the markedly different treatment of the responsible and the irresponsible.

The other possible justification for the existing differential is that the mentally diseased are amenable to treatment. We shall explore the ramifications of this at a later point. It is sufficient now to observe that there is no reason to believe that the mentally well, but statistically dangerous, individual is any less amenable to treatment, though that treatment would undoubtedly take a different form.

Another basis probably underlying our commitment laws is the notion that it is necessary to segregate the unduly burdensome and the social nuisance. Two cases typify this situation. This first is the senile patient whose family asserts inability to provide suitable care. At this juncture, assuming that the family could put the person on the street where he would be unable to fend for himself, society must act to avoid the unpleasantness associated with public disregard of helplessness. This caretaking function cannot be avoided.

Its performance, however, is a demonstration of the psychological truth that we can bear that which is kept from our attention. Most of us profess to believe that there is an individual moral duty to take care of a senile parent, a paranoid wife, or a disturbed child. Most of us also resent the bother such care creates. By allowing society to perform this duty, masked in medical terminology, but frequently amounting in fact to what one court has described as "warehousing," we can avoid facing painful issues.

The second case is the one in which the mentally ill individual is simply a nuisance, as when he insists on sharing his paranoid delusions or hallucinations with us. For reasons that are unclear, most of us are extremely uncomfortable in the presence of an aberrant individual, whether or not we owe him any duty, and whether or not he is in fact a danger to us in any defensible use of that concept. Our comfort, in short, depends on his banishment, and yet that comfort is equally dependent on a repression of any consciousness of the reason for his banishment. It is possible, of course, to put this in utilitarian terms. Given our disquietude, is not the utility of confinement greater than the utility of liberty? Perhaps so, but the assertions either that we will act most reasonably if we repress thinking about why we are acting or, worse yet, that our legislators will bear this knowledge for us in order to preserve our psychic ease make us even more uncomfortable than the thought that we may have to look mental aberrance in the eye.

Again, we do not wish to suggest that either burden or bother is an inappropriate consideration in the commitment process. What we do want to make clear is that when it is a consideration it ought to be advertently so. Only in that way can intelligent decisions about care, custody, and treatment be made.

The final probable basis for civil commitment has both humanitarian and utilitarian overtones. When faced with an obviously aberrant person, we know, or we think we know, that he would be "happier" if he were as we are. We believe that no one would want

to be a misfit in society. From the very best of motives, then, we wish to fix him. It is difficult to deal with this feeling since it rests on the unverifiable assumption that the aberrant person, if he saw himself as we see him, would choose to be different than he is. But since he cannot be as we, and we cannot be as he, there is simply no way to judge the predicate for the assertion.

Our libertarian views usually lead us to assert that treatment cannot be forced on anyone unless the alternative is very great social harm. Thus while we will require smallpox vaccinations and the segregation of contagious tuberculars, we will not ordinarily require bed rest for the common cold, or a coronary, or even require a pregnant woman to eat in accordance with a medically approved diet. Requiring treatment whenever it seemed medically sound to do so would have utilitarian virtues. Presumably, if death or serious incapacitation could thereby be avoided society would have less worry about unsupported families, motherless children, or individuals no longer able to support themselves. Similarly, if the reasoning were pursued, we could insure that the exceptionally able, such as concert violinists, distinguished scholars, and inspiring leaders would continue to benefit society. Nonetheless, only rarely does society require such treatment. Not only does it offend common notions of bodily integrity and individual autonomy, but it also raises those issues of value judgment which, if not insoluble, are at least discomforting. For example, is the treatment and cure of the mentally ill individual of more benefit to society than the liberty of which he is deprived and the principle (lost, or tarnished) that no one should assert the right to control another's beliefs and responses absent compelling social danger?

The reason traditionally assigned for forcing treatment on the mentally ill while making it voluntary for other afflicted persons is that the mentally ill are incapable of making a rational judgment whether they need or desire such help. As with every similar statement, this depends on what kind of mental illness is present. It is likely that a pederast understands that society views him as sick, that certain kinds of psychiatric treatment may "cure" him, and that such treatment is available in certain mental institutions. It is also not unlikely that he will, in these circumstances, decide to forego treatment, at least if such treatment requires incarceration. To say that the pederast lacks insight into his condition and therefore is unable to intelligently decide whether or not to seek treatment is to hide our real judgment that he ought to be fixed, like it or not. It is true that some mentally ill people may be unable to comprehend a diagnosis and, in these instances, forced treatment may be more appropriate. But this group is a small proportion of the total committable population. Most understand what the clinician is saying though they often disagree with his view.

We have tried to show that the common justifications for the commitment process rest on premises that are either false or too broad to support present practices. This obviously raises the question of alternatives. Professor Ehrenzweig has suggested in another context that the definition of mental illness ought to be tailored to the specific social purpose to be furthered in the context in question. That is what we propose here.

Returning to the first of our considerations supporting commitment, we suggest that before a man can be committed as dangerous it must be shown that the probabilities are very great that he will commit a dangerous act. Just how great the probabilities need be will depend on two things: how serious the probable dangerous act is and how likely it is that the mental condition can be changed by treatment. A series of hypotheticals will indicate how we believe this calculus ought to be applied.

Case 1: A man with classic paranoia exhibits in clinical interview a fixed belief that his wife is attempting to poison him. He calmly states that on release he will be forced to kill her in self-defense. The experts agree that his condition is untreatable. Assume that statistical data indicate an eighty percent probability that homicide will occur. If society will accept as a general rule of commitment, whether or not mental illness is present, that an eighty percent probability of homicide is sufficient to incarcerate, then this man may be incarcerated. In order to do this, of course, we must be willing to lock up twenty people out of 100 who will not commit homicide.

Case 2: Assume the same condition with only a forty percent probability of homicide. We do not know whether, if the condition is untreatable, commitment is justified in these circumstances. If lifetime commitment is required because the probabilities are constant, we doubt that the justification would exist. Our own value structure would not allow us to permanently incarcerate sixty harmless individuals in order to prevent forty homicides. On the other hand, if incarceration for a year would reduce the probability to ten percent, then perhaps it is justified. Similarly, if treatment over the course of two or three years would substantially reduce the probability, then commitment might be thought proper.

Case 3: A man who compulsively engages in acts of indecent exposure has been diagnosed as having a sociopathic personality disturbance. The probability is eighty percent that he will again expose himself. Even if this condition is untreatable, we would be disinclined to commit. In our view, this conduct is not sufficiently serious to warrant extended confinement. For that reason, we would allow confinement only if "cure" were relatively quick and certain.

The last case probably is more properly one of nuisance than of danger. The effects of such conduct are offensive and irritating but it is unlikely that they include long-term physical or psychical harm. That does not mean, however, that society has no interest in protecting its members from such upset. Again, the question is one of alternatives. Much nuisance behavior is subject to the control of the criminal law or of less formal social restraints. In mental institutions patients learn that certain behavior or the recounting of delusions or hallucinations will be met with disapproval. Accordingly, they refrain from such behavior or conversation. There is no reason to believe that societal disapproval in the form of criminal proscriptions or of less formal sanctions will be less effective as a deterrent. And, from our standpoint, the liberty of many mentally ill individuals is worth far more than the avoidance of minor nuisances in society.

Case 4: A person afflicted with schizophrenia walks about town making wild gestures and talking incessantly. Those who view him are uncomfortable but not endangered. We doubt that commitment is appropriate even though it would promote the psychic ease of many people. Arguably we would all be happier if our favorite bogey man, whether James Hoffa, Rap Brown, Mario Savio, or some other, were incarcerated. Most of us would be outraged if any of these men were committed on such a theory. If we cannot justify such a commitment in these cases, we doubt that it is any more justifiable when social anxiety is a consequence of seeing mentally ill individuals. While it might be proper to commit if speedy cure were possible, such cures are, as a matter of fact, unavailable. Moreover, we have some difficulty distinguishing the prevention of psychic upset based on cure of the mentally ill and prevention based on neutralizing other upsetting behavior.

The next justification of commitment is more solid, though it too presents the question of the necessity of utilizing less burdensome alternatives. This is the rationale of care for the person who is unable to care for himself and who has no one else to provide care for him. As we suggested earlier, such care must be provided if we are unwilling to allow people to die in the streets.

Case 5: An elderly woman with cerebro-vascular disease and accompanying cerebral impairment has the tendency to leave her home, to become lost, and then to wander helplessly about until someone aids her. At other times she is perfectly able to go shopping or visit friends. She has no relatives who will care for her in the sense that they will prevent her from wandering or will find her when she has become lost. In some ways, this is another case of a public nuisance and it may well be that it is impossible to find a justification for incarcerat-

ing this woman. On the other hand, to allow this woman to die from exposure on one of her forays is as disquieting as the loss of her freedom. Since her condition is untreatable, provision of treatment offers no justification for confinement. It might be justifiable to exercise some supervision over her, but surely that justification will not support total incarceration. In these circumstances, we believe that if the state wishes to intervene it must do so in some way that does not result in a total loss of freedom. The desire to help ought not to take the form of simple jailing.

Case 6: A schizophrenic woman is causing such an upset in her family that her husband petitions for commitment. It is clear that the presence of this woman in the family is having an adverse effect on the children. Her husband is simply unwilling to allow the situation to continue. The alternatives here are all unpleasant to contemplate. If the husband gets a divorce and custody, he may accomplish his end. But the social opprobrium attaching to that solution makes it unlikely. The question, then, is whether the state should provide a socially acceptable alternative. If that alternative is her loss of freedom, we find it hard to justify. Assuming that the condition is untreatable, that the woman is not dangerous, and that her real sin is her capacity to disrupt, it is almost incomprehensible that she should be subject to a substantial period of incarceration. Yet that is what it has meant. Presumably, in order to isolate the woman from her family, it is necessary to transport her to a location where she will no longer bother her family. Then, if she is able to support herself she could have complete freedom. If she is not able, the state will have to provide care. That care, of course, need not involve a total deprivation of freedom.

The final justification for commitment—the need to treat—is in many ways the most difficult to deal with. As we have said before, society has not traditionally required treatment of treatable diseases even though most people would agree that it was "crazy" for the diseased person not to seek treatment. The problem has been complicated by the fact that religious beliefs against certain forms of treatment often are present and by the fact that most cases of stubborn refusal to accept treatment never come into public view. There is, however, a competing analogy that suggests that mandatory treatment may sometimes be appropriate.

Without going into unnecessary detail, we think it can be said that one of the reasons society requires compulsory education is that it believes a certain minimum amount of socialization is necessary for everyone lest they be an economic burden or a personal nuisance. That principle can also be used to support mandatory psychiatric rewiring if the individual to be refurbished is in fact a burden or nuisance and can be fixed. The difficulty, of course, lies in the extent to which the principle can be carried. To take a mild example outside the field of mental disease, assume an unemployable individual who is unable to support his large and growing family. Could society incarcerate him until he had satisfactorily acquired an employable skill? In the context of mental disease, then, can society demand that an individual obtain an employable psyche?

Case 7: An individual has been suffering from paranoid schizophrenia for several years without remission and has lost his job because of his behavior. He is divorced, but he is able to support himself from prior savings. He is not dangerous, and if he is committed it is unlikely that he will be cured since the recovery rates from such long-term schizophrenia are very low. In addition, the availability of treatment in a state mental institution is problematic. We doubt that he can justifiably be committed. If treatment is an adequate basis for confinement, it surely ceases to be so either when the illness is untreatable or when treatment is in fact not given or given in grossly insufficient amounts. No other basis for commitment being present, it is unjustifiable.

Case 8: A distinguished law school professor, known for a series of brilliant articles, is suffering from an involutional depression. His scholarship has dried up, and, while he is still able to teach, the spark is gone and his classes have become extremely depressing. There is a chance, though probably not more than twenty-five percent, that he will commit suicide. He has been told that he would recover his old élan if he were subjected to a series of electroshock treatments but this he has refused to do. In fact, in years past when he was teaching a course in law and psychology, he stated that if he ever became depressed he wanted it known that before the onset of depression he explicitly rejected such treatment. Should he be compelled to undergo treatment? The arguments of social utility would suggest that he should. Yet we are unable to dislodge the notion that potential added productivity is not a license for tampering.

Case 9: A woman suffers from a severe psychotic depression resulting in an ability to do little more than weep. Again shock treatment is recommended with a reasonable prospect of a rapid recovery. The woman rejects the suggestion saying that nothing can make her a worthy member of society. She is, she claims, beyond help or salvation. It is possible to distinguish this from the preceding case on the ground that her delusional thought processes prevent her from recognizing the desirability of treatment. But any distinction based on a proposed patient's insight into her condition will probably be administered on the assumption that any time desirable treatment is refused, insight is necessarily lacking. And that, of course, would destroy the distinction.

These cases suggest that the power to compel treatment is one that rarely ought to be exercised. We are unable to construct a rationale that will not as well justify remolding too many people to match predominant ideas of the shape of the ideal psyche. We recognize, of course, that we are exhibiting a parade of horrors. In this instance, however, we believe such reference justified. The ease with which one can be classified as less than mentally healthy, and the difficulty in distinguishing degrees of sickness, make us doubt the ability of anyone to judge when the line between minimum socialization and aesthetically pleasing acculturation has been passed. Regardless of our views, however, it seems clear that if society chooses to continue to exercise the power to compel treatment, it ought to do so with constant awareness of the threat to autonomy thus posed.

Different considerations are present when commitment is not based on the need to treat. If one is committed as dangerous, or as a nuisance, or as unable to care for oneself, and treatment can cure this condition, then it is easier to strike the balance between deprivation of liberty and the right to refuse treatment in favor of compulsory treatment. If told that this is the price of freedom, the patient may accede; if he prefers confinement to treatment, perhaps the state ought not to override his wishes. But at least in this situation the question is ethically a close one.

The difficulty with present commitment procedures is that they tend to justify all commitments in terms that are appropriate only to some, and to prescribe forms of treatment that are necessary in only some cases. Thus, while danger stemming from mental illness may be a proper basis for commitment, it does not follow that all mentally ill are dangerous, or that the standards of danger should be markedly less rigid in cases of mental illness. Similarly, because mentally ill people may be a nuisance and some means of preventing such nuisance must be found, it does not follow that nuisance commitments ought to involve the same restraints as commitments based upon potential danger. Finally, because treatment is humanitarian when applied to those confined for danger, nuisance, or care, does not in itself suggest that treatment can be applied whenever administrators believe it proper or humane to do so.

We recognize that many people will not agree with the manner in which we have drawn the balance in individual cases. We hope that few will disagree that the balance must be drawn. We suggest, therefore, that in each case of proposed commitment, the following questions be asked:

I. What social purpose will be served by commitment?
   A. If protection from potential danger, what dangerous acts are threatened? How likely are they to occur? How long will the individual have to be confined before time or treatment will eliminate or reduce the danger so that he may be released?
   B. If protection from nuisance, how onerous is the nuisance in fact? Ought that to justify loss of freedom? If it should, how long will confinement last before time or treatment will eliminate or reduce the risk of nuisance so that release may occur?
   C. If the need for care, is care in fact necessary? If so, how long will confinement last before time or treatment will eliminate the need for care so that release may occur?
II. Can the social interest be served by means less restrictive than total confinement?
III. Whatever standard is applied, is it one that can comfortably be applied to all members of society, mentally ill or healthy?
IV. If confinement is justified only because it is believed that it will be of short term for treatment, is the illness in fact treatable? If it is, will appropriate treatment in fact be given?

If these questions are asked—and we view it as the duty of the attorney for the potential patient to insure that they are—then more intelligent commitment practices may follow.

Notes

1. The concept "abnormal" or "aberrant" is sorely in need of more thorough logical analysis than it has, to our knowledge, as yet received. It seems fairly clear that several components—perhaps even utterly distinct kinds of meaning—can be discerned in the current usage of medicine and social science. The most objective meaning is the purely statistical one, in which "abnormal" designates deviation from the (statistical) "norm" of a specified biological or social population of organisms. Whether an individual specimen, or bit of behavior, is abnormal in this sense is readily ascertained by adequate sampling methods plus a more or less arbitrary choice of cutting score (e.g., found in less than 1 in 100 cases). But for legal purposes this purely statistical criterion does not suffice, because the *kind* and *direction* of statistical deviation from population norms, as well as the *amount* of deviation which threatens a protected social interest sufficiently to justify legal coercion, are questions not answerable by statistics alone. Thus, anyone who has an IQ of 180, or possesses absolute pitch, or is color-blind, is statistically abnormal but hardly rendered thereby a candidate for incarceration, mandatory treatment, or deprivation of the usual rights and powers of a "normal" individual.

A second component in the concept of normality relies upon our (usually inchoate or implicit) notions of biological health, of a kind of proper functioning of the organism conceived as a teleological system of organs and capacities. From a biological viewpoint, it is not inconsistent to assert that a sizable proportion—conceivably a majority—of persons in a given population are abnormal or aberrant. Thus, if an epidemiologist found that 60% of the persons in a society were afflicted with plague or avitaminosis, he would (quite correctly) reject an argument that "Since most of them have it, they are okay, i.e., not pathological and not in need of treatment." It is admittedly easier to defend this non-statistical, biological-fitness approach in the domain of physical disease, but its application in the domain of behavior is fraught with difficulties. See W. Schofield, *Psychotherapy: The Purchase of Friendship* 12 (1964). Yet even here there is surely something to be said for it in extreme cases, as, for example, the statistically "normal" frigidity of middle-class Victorian women, which any modern sexologist would confidently consider a biological maladaptation in need of repair, induced by "unhealthy" social learnings. A third component invokes some sort of subjective norm, such as an aesthetic, religious, ethical, or political ideal or rule. Finally, whether an a priori concept of "optimal psychological adjustment" should be considered as yet a fourth meaning of normality, or instead subsumed under one or more of the preceding, is a difficult question. In any event, it is important to keep alert to hidden fallacies in legal and policy arguments that rely upon the notion of abnormality or aberration, such as subtle transitions from one of these criteria to another. It is especially tempting to the psychiatrist or clinical psychologist, given his usual clinical orientation, to slip unconsciously from the idea of "sickness," where treatment of a so-called "patient" is the model, to an application that justifies at most a statistical or ideological or psychological-adjustment usage of the word "norm." Probably the most pernicious error is committed by those who classify as "sick" behavior that is aberrant in *neither* a statistical sense *nor* in terms of any defensible biological or medical criterion, but solely on the basis of the clinician's personal ideology of mental health and interpersonal relationships. Examples might be the current psychiatric stereotype of what a good mother or a healthy family must be like, or the rejection as "perverse" of forms of sexual behavior that are not biologically harmful, are found in many infra-human mammals and in diverse human cultures, and have a high statistical frequency in our own society. See generally F. Beach, *Sexual Behavior in Animals and Men* (1950); H. Ellis, *Studies in the Psychology of Sex* (1936); C. Ford and F. Beach, *Patterns of Sexual Behavior* (1951); A. Kinsey, W. Pomeroy and C. Martin, *Sexual Behavior in the Human Male* (1948); A. Kinsey, W. Pomery, C. Martin and P. Gebhard, *Sexual Behavior in the Human Female* (1953); W. Masters and V. Johnson, *Human Sexual Response* (1966); H. Ellis, "What is "Normal" Sexual Behavior," 28 *Sexology* 364 (1962); S. Freud, "Three Essays on the Theory of Sexuality," in 7 *Complete Psychological Works* 123 (J. Strachey ed. 1962).

2. See Meehl and Rosen, "Antecedent Probability and the Efficiency of Psychometric Signs, Patterns, or Cutting Scores," 52 *Psychological Bull.* 194 (1955); Rosen, "Detection of Suicidal Patients: An Example of Some Limitations in the Prediction of Infrequent Events," 18 *J. Consulting Psychology* 397 (1954).

Suggested Further Reading

Boorse, Christopher, "What a Theory of Mental Health Should Be," *Journal for the Theory of Social Behavior*, 6 (April 1976), 61–84.

Hasker, William, "The Critique of 'Mental Illness': Conceptual and/or Ethical Crisis?" *Journal of Psychology and Theology*, 5 (Spring 1977), 110–24.

Kramer, John R., "The Right Not to Be Mentally Retarded," in *The Mentally Retarded Citizen and the Law*, ed. Michael Kindred, et al. New York: The Free Press, 1976, pp. 31–59.

Macklin, Ruth, "Mental Health and Mental Illness: Some Problems of Definition and Concept Formulation," *Philosophy of Science*, 39 (September 1972), 341–65.

Petchesky, Rosalind Pollack, "Reproductive Freedom and the Mentally Retarded," *Hastings Center Report*, 9 (October 1979), 37–39.

Rosenthal, D. L., "On Being Sane in Insane Places," *Science*, 179 (January 19, 1973), 250–58.

Wald, Patricia M., "Basic Personal and Civil Rights," in *The Mentally Retarded Citizen and the Law*, ed. Michael Kindred, et al. New York: The Free Press, 1976.

Will, George F., "Sterilization and the Retarded," *Washington Post*, December 3, 1978, p. c7.

DECISION SCENARIO 4

Sterilization and the Retarded

Judy is a 16-year-old adolescent with an IQ in the mid-forties. She has lived with her mother, Mrs. Dubois, a widow for the last decade. Mrs. Dubois works part-time for a custodial agency. She is devoted to Judy and provides the necessities for life in their one-bedroom apartment.

Judy has just been transferred to a school specializing in teen-aged mental handicaps. Initially the move was a big success. Then Mrs. Dubois grew concerned about the possibility of sexual activity involving her daughter. The least of what she needs is to care for an infant. "My daughter will never be able to be responsible enough to have a family," she says.

Accordingly, Mrs. Dubois asks the state hospital to sterilize Judy by means of a tubal ligation. The procedure is considered to be without risk. It is irreversible. Mrs. Dubois argues that sterilization is in her daughter's best interests since the pregnancy would be a traumatizing experience. Neither she nor Judy would be able to care for a child. She confides her long-standing fear of what will become of Judy after Mrs. Dubois dies. She also expresses doubts about the viability of contraceptions for someone in her daughter's situation.

Questions

1. Is Mrs. Dubois morally right in her argument?

2. Do the mentally disadvantaged have the same right to reproduce as those who are not disadvantaged? Under what conditions, if any, can the state override a person's reproductive right?

3. If a reversible sterilization procedure were an alternative, would Mrs. Dubois be morally justified in seeking it for Judy? Who should act as the advocate of Judy's rights?

4. What difference in the decision would it make if Judy's retardation were genetically inherited and if her offspring were likely to have the same condition?

9. JUSTICE OF HEALTH CARE DELIVERY

1. THE CONCEPT OF HEALTH

Ideas about justice in the delivery of health care are affected by the way we define the concept of health. (Similarly, ideas about criminal justice are affected by the way we define crime **[See Criminal Justice, Chapter 14, Section 1].**) Should the notion of health be limited to considerations of physical functioning or should it have a broader scope? The World Health Organization (WHO), in the preamble to its constitution of 1946, defines health as "a state of complete physical, mental, and social well-being and not merely the absence of disease or infirmity."[1] A further entitlement that "the enjoyment of the highest attainable standard of health is one of the fundamental rights of every human being" is described. If a society accepts the expansive WHO definition, an enormous amount of its resources must be allocated to providing health care. Is attempting to meet this ideal of health a desirable and practical goal?

Many criticize the WHO definition, particularly for its inclusion of a social dimension of health. They argue that describing social problems (such as unemployment or crime) as forms of ill health is not only contrary to common sense but is also counterproductive to combatting the problems. Medical professionals, they maintain, have neither the expertise nor the authority to

resolve social problems. **[See Business, Chapter 11, Section 4.]** The argument is based on primarily utilitarian considerations. Other ethicists object to the use of a medical model for describing psychological problems (this argument is discussed in the chapter on mental health). If they are correct, the concept of health ought to be restricted to the physical domain.

Another area of concern in defining the concept of health (and the concept of disease) centers on whether the concepts are inherently value-laden. A value-laden concept is one that is not merely descriptive but implies approval or disapproval. For example, concepts such as courage or cruelty, while having a descriptive function, necessarily include a positive or negative evaluation. If health and disease are value-laden concepts, to identify a certain state as healthy is to say that it is desirable or appropriate to seek. By the same token, to call a condition unhealthy or diseased implies that it is undesirable or improper. The dispute is not an academic matter with no practical significance. If the concept of health is not strictly scientific or value-free but varies with social values, this fact will have considerable impact on the way certain conditions are regarded and acted upon. For example, if fatness is considered an attractive or enviable condition, obesity is not unhealthy, and health care resources would not be allocated to helping people control their weight.

[1]*The First Ten Years of the World Health Organization* (Geneva: WHO, 1958).

135

In the following article Daniel Callahan analyzes the WHO definition of health and describes possible abuses which result from attempting to implement it. Callahan is especially critical of including social well-being as a necessary component of health and recommends limiting the definition to "a state of physical well-being."

DANIEL CALLAHAN

The WHO Definition of Health

There is not much that can be called fun and games in medicine, perhaps because unlike other sports it is the only one in which everyone, participant and spectator, eventually gets killed playing. In the meantime, one of the grandest games is that version of king-of-the-hill where the aim of all players is to upset the World Health Organization (WHO) definition of "health." That definition, in case anyone could possibly forget it, is "Health is a state of complete physical, mental, and social well-being and not merely the absence of disease or infirmity." Fair game, indeed. Yet somehow, defying all comers, the WHO definition endures, though literally every other aspirant to the crown has managed to knock it off the hill at least once. One possible reason for its presence is that it provides such an irresistible straw man; few there are who can resist attacking it in the opening paragraphs of papers designed to move on to more profound reflections.

But there is another possible reason which deserves some exploration, however unsettling the implications. It may just be that the WHO definition has more than a grain of truth in it, of a kind which is as profoundly frustrating as it is enticingly attractive. At the very least it is a definition which implies that there is some intrinsic relationship between the good of the body and the good of the self. The attractiveness of this relationship is obvious: it thwarts any movement toward a dualism of self and body, a dualism which in any event immediately breaks down when one drops a brick on one's toe; and it impels the analyst to work toward a conception of health which in the end is resistant to clear and distinct categories, closer to the felt experience. All that, naturally, is very frustrating. It seems simply impossible to devise a concept of health which is rich enough to be nutritious and yet not so rich as to be indigestible.

One common objection to the WHO definition is, in effect, an assault upon any and all attempts to specify the meaning of very general concepts. Who can possibly define words as vague as "health," a venture as foolish as trying to define "peace," "justice," "happiness," and other systematically ambiguous notions? To this objection the "pragmatic" clinicians (as they often call themselves) add that, anyway, it is utterly unnecessary to know what "health" means in order to treat a patient running a high temperature. Not only that, it is also a harmful distraction to clutter medical judgment with philosophical puzzles.

Unfortunately for this line of argument, it is impossible to talk or think at all without employing general concepts; without them, cognition and language are impossible. More damagingly, it is rarely difficult to discover, with a bit of probing, that even the most "pragmatic" judgment (whatever *that* is) presupposes some general values and orientations, all of which can be translated into def-

Reprinted with permission of the author and publisher from *Hastings Center Studies*, 1, no. 3 (1973), 77–87.

initions of terms as general as "health" and "happiness." A failure to discern the operative underlying values, the conceptions of reality upon which they are based, and the definitions they entail, sets the stage for unexamined conduct and, beyond that, positive harm both to patients and to medicine in general.

But if these objections to any and all attempts to specify the meaning of "health" are common enough, the most specific complaint about the WHO definition is that its very generality, and particularly its association of health and general well-being as a positive ideal, has given rise to a variety of evils. Among them are the cultural tendency to define all social problems, from war to crime in the streets, as "health" problems; the blurring of lines of responsibility between and among the professions, and between the medical profession and the political order; the implicit denial of human freedom which results when failures to achieve social well-being are defined as forms of "sickness," somehow to be treated by medical means; and the general debasement of language which ensues upon the casual habit of labeling everyone from Adolf Hitler to student radicals to the brat next door as "sick." In short, the problem with the WHO definition is not that it represents an attempt to propose a general definition, but that it is simply a bad one.

That is a valid line of objection, provided one can spell out in some detail just how the definition can or does entail some harmful consequences. Two lines of attack are possible against putatively hazardous social definitions of significant general concepts. One is by pointing out that the definition does not encompass all that a concept has commonly been taken to mean, either historically or at present, that it is a partial definition only. The task then is to come up with a fuller definition, one less subject to misuse. But there is still another way of objecting to socially significant definitions, and that is by pointing out some baneful effects of definitions generally accepted as adequate. Many of the objections to the WHO definition fall in the latter category,

building upon the important insight that definitions of crucially important terms with a wide public use have ethical, social, and political implications; defining general terms is not an abstract exercise but a way of shaping the world metaphysically and structuring the world politically.

Wittgenstein's aphorism, "Don't look for the meaning, look for the use," is pertinent here. The ethical problem in defining the concept of "health" is to determine what the implications are of the various uses to which a concept of "health" can be put. We might well agree that there are some uses of "health" which will produce socially harmful results. To carry Wittgenstein a step further, "Don't look for the uses, look for the abuses." We might, then, examine some of the real or possible abuses to which the WHO definition leads, recognizing all the while that what we may term an "abuse" will itself rest upon some perceived *positive* good or value. . . .

Health and Happiness

Let us examine some of the principle objections to the WHO definition in more detail. One of them is that, by including the notion of "social well-being" under its rubric, it turns the enduring problem of human happiness into one more medical problem, to be dealt with by scientific means. That is surely an objectionable feature, if only because there exists no evidence whatever that medicine has anything more than a partial grasp of the sources of human misery. Despite Dr. Chisholm's optimism, medicine has not even found ways of dealing with more than a fraction of the whole range of physical diseases; campaigns, after all, are still being mounted against cancer and heart disease. Nor is there any special reason to think that future forays against those and other common diseases will bear rapid fruits. People will continue to die of disease for a long time to come, probably forever.

But perhaps, then, in the psychological and psychiatric sciences some progress has been made against what Dr. Chisholm called the "psychological ills," which lead to wars, hostility, and aggression? To be sure, there are many interesting psychological theories to be found about these "ills," and a few techniques which can, with some individuals, reduce or eliminate antisocial behavior. But so far as I can see, despite the mental health movement and the rise of the psychological sciences, war and human hostility are as much with us as ever. Quite apart from philosophical objections to the WHO definition, there was no empirical basis for the unbounded optimism which lay behind it at the time of its inception, and little has happened since to lend its limitless aspiration any firm support.

Common sense alone makes evident the fact that the absence of "disease or infirmity" by no means guarantees "social well-being." In one sense, those who drafted the WHO definition seem well aware of that. Isn't the whole point of their definition to show the inadequacy of negative definitions? But in another sense, it may be doubted that they really did grasp that point. For the third principle enunciated in the WHO Constitution says that "the health of all peoples is fundamental to the attainment of peace and security. . . ." Why is it fundamental, at least to peace? The worst wars of the twentieth century have been waged by countries with very high standards of health, by nations with superior life-expectancies for individuals and with comparatively low infant mortality rates. The greatest present threats to world peace come in great part (though not entirely) from developed countries, those which have combatted disease and illness most effectively. There seems to be no historical correlation whatever between health and peace, and that is true even if one includes "mental health."

How are human beings to achieve happiness? That is the final and fundamental question. Obviously, illness, whether mental or physical, makes happiness less possible in most cases. But that is only because they are only one symptom of a more basic restriction, that of human finitude, which sees infinite human desires constantly thwarted by the limita-

tions of reality. "Complete" well-being might, conceivably, be attainable, but under one condition only: that people ceased expecting much from life. That does not seem about to happen. On the contrary, medical and psychological progress have been more than outstripped by rising demands and expectations. What is so odd about that, if it is indeed true that human desires are infinite? Whatever the answer to the question of human happiness, there is no particular reason to believe that medicine can do anything more than make a modest, finite contribution.

Another objection to the WHO definition is that, by implication, it makes the medical profession the gate-keeper for happiness and social well-being. Or if not exactly the gate-keeper (since political and economic support will be needed from sources other than medical), then the final magic-healer of human misery. Pushed far enough, the whole idea is absurd, and it is not necessary to believe that the organizers of the WHO would, if pressed, have been willing to go quite that far. But even if one pushes the pretension a little way, considerable fantasy results. The mental health movement is the best example, casting the psychological professional in the role of high priest.

At its humble best, that movement can do considerable good; people do suffer from psychological disabilities and there are some effective ways of helping them. But it would be sheer folly to believe that all, or even the most important, social evils stem from bad mental health: political injustice, economic scarcity, food shortages, unfavorable physical environments, have a far greater historical claim as sources of a failure to achieve "social well-being." To retort that all or most of these troubles can, nonetheless, be seen finally as symptoms of bad mental health is, at best, self-serving and, at worst, just plain foolish.

A significant part of the objection that the WHO definition places, at least by implication, too much power and authority in the hands of the medical profession need not be based on a fear of that power as such. There is no reason to think that the world would be any worse off if health professionals made all decisions than if any other group did, and no reason to think it would be any better off. That is not a very important point. More significant is that cultural development which, in its skepticism about "traditional" ways of solving social problems, would seek a technological and specifically a medical solution for human ills of all kinds. There is at least a hint in early WHO discussions that, since politicians and diplomats have failed in maintaining world peace, a more expert group should take over, armed with the scientific skills necessary to set things right; it is science which is best able to vanquish that old Enlightenment bogeyman, "superstition." More concretely, such an ideology has the practical effect of blurring the lines of appropriate authority and responsibility. If all problems—political, economic and social—reduce to matters of "health," then there cease to be any ways to determine who should be responsible for what.

The Tyranny of Health

The problem of responsibility has at least two faces. One is that of a tendency to turn all problems of "social well-being" over to the medical professional, most pronounced in the instance of the incarceration of a large group of criminals in mental institutions rather than prisons. The abuses, both medical and legal, of that practice are, fortunately, now beginning to receive the attention they deserve, even if little corrective action has yet been taken. (Counterbalancing that development, however, are others, where some are seeking more "effective" ways of bringing science to bear on criminal behavior.)

The other face of the problem of responsibility is that of the way in which those who are sick, or purportedly sick, are to be evaluated in terms of their freedom and responsibility. Siegler and Osmond [*Hastings Center Studies*, vol. 1, no. 3, 1973, pp. 41–58] discuss the "sick role," a leading feature of which is the ascription of blamelessness, of non-responsibility, to those who contract illness. There is no reason to object to this kind of

ascription in many instances—one can hardly blame someone for contracting kidney disease—but, obviously enough, matters get out of hand when all physical, mental, and communal disorders are put under the heading of "sickness," and all sufferers (all of us, in the end) placed in the blameless "sick role." Not only are the concepts of "sickness" and "illness" drained of all content, it also becomes impossible to ascribe any freedom or responsibility to those caught up in the throes of sickness. The whole world is sick, and no one is responsible any longer for anything. That is determinism gone mad, a rather odd outcome of a development which began with attempts to bring unbenighted "reason" and free self-determination to bear for the release of the helpless captives of superstition and ignorance.

The final and most telling objection to the WHO definition has less to do with the definition itself than with one of its natural historical consequences. Thomas Szasz has been the most eloquent (and most single-minded) critic of that sleight-of-hand which has seen the concept of health moved from the medical to the moral arena. What can no longer be done in the name of "morality" can now be done in the name of "health": human beings labeled, incarcerated, and dismissed for their failure to toe the line of "normalcy" and "sanity."

At first glance, this analysis of the present situation might seem to be totally at odds with the tendency to put everyone in the blame-free "sick role." Actually, there is a fine, probably indistinguishable, line separating these two positions. For as soon as one treats all human disorders—war, crime, social unrest—as forms of illness, then one turns health into a normative concept, that which human beings must and ought to have if they are to live in peace with themselves and others. Health is no longer an optional matter, but the golden key to the relief of human misery. We *must* be well or we will all perish. "Health" can and must be imposed; there can be no room for the luxury of freedom when so much is at stake. Of course the matter is rarely put so bluntly, but it is to Szasz's great credit that he has discerned what actually happens when "health" is allowed to gain the cultural clout which morality once had. (That he carries the whole business too far in his embracing of the most extreme moral individualism is another story, which cannot be dealt with here.) Something is seriously amiss when the "right" to have healthy children is turned into a further right for children not to be born defective, and from there into an obligation not to bring unhealthy children into the world as a way of respecting the right of those children to health! Nor is everything altogether lucid when abortion decisions are made a matter of "medical judgment" (see *Roe* vs. *Wade*); when decisions to provide psychoactive drugs for the relief of the ordinary stress of living are defined as no less "medical judgment"; when patients are not allowed to die with dignity because of medical indications that they can, come what may, be kept alive; when prisoners, without their consent, are subjected to aversive conditioning to improve their mental health.

Abuses of Language

In running through the litany of criticisms which have been directed at the WHO definition of "health," and what seem to have been some of its long-term implications and consequences, I might well be accused of beating a dead horse. My only defense is to assert, first, that the spirit of the WHO definition is by no means dead either in medicine or society. In fact, because of the usual cultural lag which requires many years for new ideas to gain wide social currency, it is only now coming into its own on a broad scale. (Everyone now talks about everybody and everything, from Watergate to Billy Graham to trash in the streets, as "sick.") Second, I believe that we are now in the midst of a nascent (if not actual) crisis about how "health" ought properly to be understood, with much dependent upon what conception of health emerges in the near future.

If the ideology which underlies the WHO

definition has proved to contain many muddled and hazardous ingredients, it is not at all evident what should take its place. The virtue of the WHO definition is that it tried to place health in the broadest human context. Yet the assumption behind the main criticisms of the WHO definition seem perfectly valid. Those assumptions can be characterized as follows: (1) health is only a part of life, and the achievement of health only a part of the achievement of happiness; (2) medicine's role, however important, is limited; it can neither solve nor even cope with the great majority of social, political, and cultural problems; (3) human freedom and responsibility must be recognized, and any tendency to place all deviant, devilish, or displeasing human beings into the blameless sick-role must be resisted; (4) while it is good for human beings to be healthy, medicine is not morality; except in very limited contexts (plagues and epidemics) "medical judgment" should not be allowed to become moral judgment; to be healthy is not to be righteous; (5) it is important to keep clear and distinct the different roles of different professions, with a clearly circumscribed role for medicine, limited to those domains of life where the contribution of medicine is appropriate. Medicine can save some lives; it cannot save the life of society.

These assumptions, and the criticisms of the WHO definition which spring from them, have some important implications for the use of the words "health," "illness," "sick," and the like. It will be counted an abuse of language if the word "sick" is applied to all individual and communal problems, if all unacceptable conduct is spoken of in the language of medical pathologies, if moral issues and moral judgments are translated into the language of "health," if the lines of authority, responsibility, and expertise are so blurred that the health profession is allowed to pre-empt the rights and responsibilities of others by redefining them in its own professional language.

Abuses of that kind have no possibility of being curbed in the absence of a definition of health which does not contain some intrinsic elements of limitation—that is, unless there is a definition which, when abused, is self-evidently *seen* as abused by those who know what health means. Unfortunately, it is in the nature of general definitions that they do not circumscribe their own meaning (or even explain it) and contain no built-in safeguards against misuse, e.g., our "peace with honor" in Southeast Asia—"peace," "honor"? Moreover, for a certain class of concepts—peace, honor, happiness, for example—it is difficult to keep them free in ordinary usage from a normative content. In our own usage, it would make no sense to talk of them in a way which implied they are not desirable or are merely neutral: by well-ingrained social custom (resting no doubt on some basic features of human nature) health, peace, and happiness are both desired and desirable—good. For those and other reasons, it is perfectly plausible to say the cultural task of defining terms, and settling on appropriate and inappropriate usages, is far more than a matter of getting our dictionary entries right. It is nothing less than a way of deciding what should be valued, how life should be understood, and what principles should guide individual and social conduct.

Health is not just a term to be defined. Intuitively, if we have lived at all, it is something we seek and value. We may not set the highest value on health—other goods may be valued as well—but it would strike me as incomprehensible should someone say that health was a matter of utter indifference to him; we would well doubt either his sanity or his maturity. The cultural problem, then, may be put this way. The acceptable range of uses of the term "health" should, at the minimum, capture the normative element in the concept as traditionally understood while, at the maximum, incorporate the insight (stemming from criticisms of the WHO definition) that the term "health" is abused if it becomes synonymous with virtue, social tranquility, and ultimate happiness. Since there are no instruction manuals available on how one would go about reaching a goal of that sort, I will offer no advice on the subject. I have the horrible

suspicion, as a matter of fact, that people either have a decent intuitive sense on such matters (reflected in the way they use language) or they do not; and if they do not, little can be done to instruct them. One is left with the pious hope that, somehow, over a long period of time, things will change.

In Defense of WHO

Now that simply might be the end of the story, assuming some agreement can be reached that the WHO definition of "health" is plainly bad, full of snares, delusions, and false norms. But I am left uncomfortable with such a flat, simple conclusion. The nagging point about the definition is that, in badly put ways, it was probably on to something. It certainly recognized, however inchoately, that it is difficult to talk meaningfully of health solely in terms of "the absence of disease or infirmity." As a purely logical point, one must ask about what positive state of affairs disease and infirmity are an absence of—absent from what? One is left with the tautological proposition that health is the absence of non-health, a less than illuminating revelation. Could it not be said, though, that at least intuitively everyone knows what health is by means of the experiential contrast posed by states of illness and disease; that is, even if I cannot define health in any positive sense, I can surely know when I am sick (pain, high fever, etc.) and compare that condition with my previous states which contained no such conditions? Thus one could, in some recognizable sense, speak of illness as a deviation from a norm, even if it is not possible to specify that norm with any clarity.

But there are some problems with this approach, for all of its commonsense appeal. Sociologically, it is well known that what may be accounted sickness in one culture may not be so interpreted in another; one culture's (person's) deviation from the norm may not necessarily be another culture's (person's) deviation. In this as in other matters, common-sense intuition may be nothing but a reflection of different cultural and personal evaluations. In addition, there can be and usually are serious disputes about how great a deviation from the (unspecified) norm is necessary before the terms "sickness" and "illness" become appropriate. Am I to be put in the sick role because of my nagging case of itching athlete's foot, or must my toes start dropping off before I can so qualify? All general concepts have their borderline cases, and normally they need pose no real problems for the applicability of the concepts for the run of instances. But where "health" and "illness" are concerned, the number of borderline cases can be enormous, affected by age, attitudinal and cultural factors! Worse still, the fact that people can be afflicted by disease (even fatally afflicted) well before the manifestation of any overt symptoms is enough to discredit the adequacy of intuitions based on how one happens to feel at any given moment.

A number of these problems might be resolved by distinguishing between health as a norm and as an ideal. As a norm, it could be possible to speak in terms of deviation from some statistical standards, particularly if these standards were couched not only in terms of organic function but also in terms of behavioral functioning. Thus someone would be called "healthy" if his heart, lungs, kidneys (etc.) functioned at a certain level of efficiency and efficacy, if he was not suffering physical pain, and if his body was free of those pathological conditions which even if undetected or undetectable could impair organic function and eventually cause pain. There could still be dispute about what should count as a "pathological" condition, but at least it would be possible to draw up a large checklist of items subject to "scientific measurement"; then, having gone through that checklist in a physical exam, and passing all the tests, one could be pronounced "healthy." Neat, clean, simple.

All of this might be possible in a static culture, which ours is not. The problem is that any notion of a statistical norm will be superintended by some kind of ideal. Why, in the first place, should anyone care at all how his organs are functioning, much less how well they do so? There must be some reason for that, a reason which goes beyond theoretical interest in statistical distributions. Could it possibly be because certain departures from the norm carry with them unpleasant states, which few are likely to call "good": pain, discrimination, unhappiness? I would guess so. In the second place, why should society have any interest whatever in the way the organs of its citizens function? There must also be some reason for that, very possibly the insight that the organ functioning of individuals has some aggregate social implications. In our culture at least (and in every other culture I have ever heard of) it is simply impossible, finally, to draw any sharp distinction between conceptions of the human good and what are accounted significant and negatively evaluated deviations from statistical norms.

That is the whole point of saying, in defense of the WHO definition of health, that it discerned the intimate connection between the good of the body and the good of the self, not only the individual self but the social community of selves. No individual and no society would (save for speculative, scientific reasons only) have any interest whatever in the condition of human organs and bodies were it not for the obvious fact that those conditions can have an enormous impact on the whole of human life. People do, it has been noticed, die; and they die because something has gone wrong with their bodies. This can be annoying, especially if one would, at the moment of death, prefer to be busy doing other things. Consider two commonplace occurrences. The first I have alluded to already: dropping a heavy brick on one's foot. So far as I know, there is no culture where the pain which that event occasions is considered a good in itself. Why is that? Because (I presume) the pain which results can not only make it difficult or impossible to walk for a time but also because the pain, if intense enough, makes it impossible to think about anything else (or think at all) or to relate to anything or anyone other than the pain. For a time, I am "not myself" and that simply because my body is making excessive demands on my attention that nothing is possible to me except to howl. I cannot, in sum, dissociate my "body" from my "self" in that situation; my self is my body and my body is my pain.

The other occurrence is no less commonplace. It is the assertion the old often make to the young, however great the psychological, economic, or other miseries of the latter: "at least you've got your health." They are saying in so many words that, if one is healthy, then there is some room for hope, some possibility of human recovery; and even more they are saying that, without good health, nothing is possible, however favorable the other conditions of life may be. Again, it is impossible to dissociate good of body and good of self. Put more formally, if health is not a sufficient condition for happiness, it is a necessary condition. At that very fundamental level, then, any sharp distinction between the good of bodies and the good of persons dissolves.

Are we not forced, therefore, to say that, if the complete absence of health (i.e., death) means the complete absence of self, then any diminishment of health must represent, correspondingly, a diminishment of self? That does not follow, for unless a disease or infirmity is severe, it may represent only a minor annoyance, diminishing our selfhood not a whit. And while it will not do to be overly sentimental about such things, it is probably the case that disease or infirmity can, in some cases, increase one's sense of selfhood (which is no reason to urge disease upon people for its possibly psychological benefits). The frequent reports of those who have recovered from a serious illness that it made them appreciate life in a far more intense way than they previously had are not to be dismissed (though one wishes an easier way could be found).

Modest Conclusions

Two conclusions may be drawn. The first is that some minimal level of health is necessary if there is to be any possibility of human happiness. Only in exceptional circumstances can the good of self be long maintained in the absence of the good of the body. The second conclusion, however, is that one can be healthy without being in a state of "complete physical, mental, and social well-being." That conclusion can be justified in two ways: (a) because some degree of disease and infirmity is perfectly compatible with mental and social well-being; and (b) because it is doubtful that there ever was, or ever could be, more than a transient state of "complete physical, mental, and social well-being," for individuals or societies; that's just not the way life is or could be. Its attractiveness as an ideal is vitiated by its practical impossibility of realization. Worse than that, it positively misleads, for health becomes a goal of such all-consuming importance that it simply begs to be thwarted in its realization. The demands which the word "complete" entail set the stage for the worst false consciousness of all: the demand that life deliver perfection. Practically speaking, this demand has led, in the field of health, to a constant escalation of expectation and requirement, never ending, never satisfied.

What, then, would be a good definition of "health"? I was afraid someone was going to ask me that question. I suggest we settle on the following: "Health is a state of physical well-being." That state need not be "complete," but it must be at least adequate, i.e., without significant impairment of function. It also need not encompass "mental" well-being; one can be healthy yet anxious, well yet depressed. And it surely ought not to encompass "social well-being," except insofar as that well-being will be impaired by the presence of large-scale, serious physical infirmities. Of course my definition is vague, but it would take some very fancy semantic footwork for it to be socially misused; that brat next door could not be called "sick" except when he is running a fever. This definition would not, though, preclude all social use of the language of "pathology" for other than physical disease. The image of a physically well body is a powerful one and, used carefully, it can be suggestive of the kind of wholeness and adequacy of function one might hope to see in other areas of life.

Suggested Further Reading

Boorse, Christopher, "On the Distinction Between Disease and Illness," *Philosophy and Public Affairs,* 5 (Fall 1975), 49–68.

Engelhardt, H. Tristram, Jr., "The Disease of Masturbation: Values and the Concept of Disease," *Bulletin of the History of Medicine,* Summer 1974, pp. 234–48.

———, "Health and Disease: Philosophical Per-

spectives," *Encyclopedia of Bioethics,* 2 (1978), 599–606.

Hastings Center Studies, 1, no. 3 (1973). Entire issue devoted to "The Concept of Health."

Journal of Medicine and Philosophy, 1, September 1976. Entire issue devoted to "Concepts of Health and Diseases."

Temkin, Owsei, "Health and Disease," *Dictionary of the History of Ideas,* vol. II, pp. 395–407.

2. MACROALLOCATION DECISIONS

How much of society's total resources ought to be devoted to health care? How should this amount be divided among various types of care? Should more emphasis be placed (and more dollars spent) on preventive programs, biomedical research, treatment of disease and injury? Federal, state, and local agencies and governments face many policy decisions of this nature, usually termed *macroallocation decisions.* Allocation problems arise and conflicts must be resolved because demands for health care outstrip available resources.

Some of the moral issues in macroallocation spring from conflicting beliefs about what constitutes justice in the distribution and delivery of health care. What should be the basic aims of society in this regard? Do people have a "right to health care"? Does society have an obligation to assist them in meeting their medical needs? What is the scope of the obligation? As we saw in the previous section, the answers to these questions depend in part upon how we define health. They further depend upon how we define the concept of justice.

Two basic moral values are often at issue in contemporary discussions of social justice: the ideal of liberty and the ideal of equality. Some theorists assert the primacy of liberty as a moral ideal. According to this view, the function of government is to prevent interference with the life, liberty, and property rights of individuals. On this basis people would have no particular right to health care, and society would have no obligation to provide it. Insisting upon such a right requires unjustified interference with the liberty of health care providers to sell their labor in a free market. By contrast, those who emphasize the value of equality uphold the need for measures that promote the welfare of individuals equally. On this view, all human beings have an equal right to have their basic needs met, regardless of their economic status. If they cannot provide themselves with adequate food, housing, health care, and so forth, then society has a duty to help them.

Still other thinkers attempt to strike a balance between the ideals of liberty and equality. They advocate policies that provide for the basic needs of poorer members of society with the least possible interference with individual liberty. Our system of distributing legal services seemingly reflects such a policy. While every defendant has a right to be represented by counsel, court-appointed public defenders are notoriously overworked. Critics charge that the system is unfair and results in unequal representation for the poor. **[See Criminal Justice, Chapter 16, Section 2.]**

The health care system in the United

States is similarly based on the moderate concept of social justice. It is a primarily *private medical care* system with some of the costs being paid out of public funds. The majority of physicians and dentists are in private practice, and most hospitals are owned either by nonprofit or for-profit corporations. While there is no legally recognized right to health care, government-financed insurance programs such as Medicare and Medicaid provide for the elderly and for those whose income falls below a certain level. This system contrasts with *public medical care* systems, like that of Great Britain, which are primarily owned and operated by the central government.

Other macroallocation questions concern the proper way to apportion the total health care budget. Should health care policies be oriented more toward prevention or treatment? How much should be spent for biomedical research? Some of the most expensive technological advances in medicine benefit a relatively small number of patients. It has been argued that public funds are better spent on services—such as prenatal care centers or community clinics—that benefit a large number of people. Another question concerns the extent of individual responsibility for maintaining good health. For example, research shows a link between cigarette smoking and heart and lung diseases. Consumption of alcohol and drugs, obesity,

lack of exercise, not wearing seat belts, and other lifestyle factors have also been shown to contribute to health risk. Should persons who choose to engage in high-risk behaviors be required to pay a larger share of taxes for health care?

Recent concern over the problem of Acquired Immune Deficiency Syndrome (AIDS) has given rise to controversy about several macroallocation questions. Some maintain that public education is the key to controlling the disease. Others urge more government funding for research into the cause and treatment of AIDS. Still others call for mandatory testing programs to identify those who have been exposed to the AIDS virus. Intravenous drug users and male homosexuals currently have the highest risk of contracting the disease, and some writers charge that public disapproval of homosexuality and drug use has resulted in inadequate government support for AIDS research and treatment.

In the following article Samuel Gorovitz analyzes the concepts of equity and efficiency as values for guiding health care policy decisions. He discusses problems which arise when the goals of equity and efficiency conflict. Gorovitz also enumerates a variety of government functions in providing health care and suggests principles for distributing services.

SAMUEL GOROVITZ

Equity, Efficiency, and the Distribution of Health Care

We spend a stunning amount on health care. That amount is soaring, and there seems no end in sight. Yet a significant portion of the American public suffers from poor health, and

a different, but overlapping segment of the American public receives poor health care, or none. The vast sums that are spent on high-technology medicine not only benefit just a

Reprinted with permission of the author and publisher from *Philosophic Exchange*, 2 (Summer 1979), 3–12.

small number of patients, but do so in ways that raise new and troubling moral dilemmas. Nearly everyone agrees that our total system of health care delivery—including the distribution of costs and benefits—is not in excellent health, in spite of our large investment in it. There is a fair amount of agreement about the symptoms, a scant amount about the diagnosis, and next to none about the treatment. Complicating our attempts to set the matter right is the fact that we want our expenditures to be used efficiently, and we believe in, or at least say we believe in, equity as a value to be reflected in the functioning of all our social arrangements. But we are not very clear about what efficiency and equity are. And we have barely begun to consider the relationship between these two notions in the specific context of our concerns about containing the costs of health care.

I will look first, and separately, at the notions of efficiency and of equity, then at the relationship between them, and finally, briefly, at a few of the issues that arise as we apply these notions to the context of health care. . . .

When we speak of efficiency, we tend to do so in a way that reflects the usage of that notion in physics. There, efficiency is a calculable ratio—the ratio of work input to work output—which approaches the value one as a limiting and unachievable ideal. Every machine has an efficiency, every efficiency is a number, and any two efficiencies can therefore be compared. But when we leave the realm of physics, we leave its precision behind. Our talk of efficiency in other contexts suffers from the tempting but false assumption that it is still a precise notion, quite serviceable for making quantitative decisions. And it doesn't help to dress the old notion of efficiency up in the fancy new clothes of cost-benefit or cost-effectiveness language.

Consider this illustration. Two automobile engines are mounted on a bench. Engine A, which can propel a two-ton car for twenty-five miles on a gallon of gasoline, hums smoothly on the bench. Engine B, in contrast, can propel a two-ton car only for fifteen miles

on one gallon of the same gasoline at the same speed. It sits on the bench, clattering and sputtering, whistling and clanging. Which is the more efficient engine? So long as it is propelling cars that is at issue, of course Engine A is more efficient. But if I tell you that I am a movie producer at work on the sound track of a film about antique automobiles and that what I am after is the most automotive engine clatter I can get per gallon, then it is obviously Engine B that is more efficient.

The point should be clear enough. Implicit in any use of the notion of efficiency is an assumption about what the desired outcome is. In classical physics, it is well defined. In ordinary discourse about cars, it is contextually implied. In the example of the two engines, it was hidden at first, and perhaps surprising when revealed.

When we talk about efficiency in health care, what exactly are the values and the output products in terms of which—and only in terms of which—we can make sense of claims about efficiency? We have not answered this question in any adequate way. But until we can reach some clarity about what the output objectives of medical care are to be, we cannot usefully make more than impressionistic judgments about efficiency.

Lest it be thought that the answer is clear enough, except to the fussing of the philosopher, let me illustrate:

1. If an investment by a hospital in one of those infamous CAT scanners saves 30 additional lives a year, is it an efficient investment as compared with endowing a community diagnostic program that could improve the health of hundreds of people?
2. Is a multi-million dollar public immunization program an efficient investment of health care dollars if it protects most of the population at risk against an epidemic of unknown likelihood?

These questions are not clear yet hard to answer. Rather, the questions themselves are unclear. They utilize a notion of efficiency which is not well defined or well understood.

Regarding the first example: we often spend a great deal to save the life of an identified person. We are less likely to invest in the statistical saving of lives—to incur expenses that will save the lives of persons unspecified. Sometimes, however, we invest heavily to that end—for instance, in the establishment of a shock-trauma unit or in a hospital's acquisition of a hyperbaric chamber. Yet we do not make all the investments that would surely save lives, in part because we are not sure how important to us it is to save all the lives it is medically possible to save. But unless we know how much a life is worth to us, how can we judge the efficiency of an investment that saves the life? Further, it is impossible to compare such an investment with one that provides non-vital medical care without understanding what value we place on good health. It is not obvious, anyway, that we clearly favor saving a few lives over substantially improving the well-being of a large number of people.

Regarding the second example: the problem is not just one of empirical uncertainty about the epidemic and its severity. It is partly an uncertainty about how important it is to relieve anxiety and about what the prevention of symptoms is worth.

These questions, of course, are not for philosophy to answer alone. They are problems of social decision, the answers to which must be fashioned by all those whose risk and whose resources are involved. Further, the question of what to take as the appropriate objective in terms of which to evaluate efficiency is itself a question of value on which considerations of equity can have bearing.

It is time, then, to turn to equity—what common usage and the dictionary both take as equivalent to justice, fairness, doing the right thing. There are various competing views of what constitutes equity. One prominent view is that equity is or requires equality. What might that mean in the context of the distribution of health care? There are at least these choices:

(1) *Equality in the dollar expenditure on each individual.* This interpretation makes little sense. Some lucky people just don't need health care; they thrive until they die, and there isn't anything to spend their health care dollars on. Perhaps we could approximate to equal expenditure by adopting a plan invented, I think, by Dan Callahan, whereby each person is allowed some fixed amount—say $100,000—over his lifetime, with a refund of any unused portion to go to his estate.

(2) *Equality in the state of health of each individual.* The problem here is that this sort of equality is impossible no matter what we spend or how. Some people enjoy robust health, some are sickly or worse all their lives, and we have only limited leverage on the natural distribution of physiological characteristics.

(3) *Equality in the maximum to which each individual is benefited.* This would mean that each person has equal access to medical care up to some limit, to be drawn on as needed, with no pretense of equalizing actual expenditures. We may find this becoming a position to be taken seriously, though the question of what sorts of limits should be set is just beginning to rear its vexsome head.

(4) *Equality in the treatment of like cases.* Under this interpretation, a national health service, for example, could have a program in renal dialysis, treating as needed all medically qualified cases. At the same time, it could refuse to treat cases of hemophilia at all—arguing that such an exclusion was necessary on grounds of economy, and going on to claim that the health care was wholly equitable, thoroughly equal, in the sense that each person had equal claim on such treatments as were made available. Both the patient with kidney failure and the hemophyliac would have equal access to dialysis as needed according to this plan.

So if we interpret equity as equality in some sense or other, we immediately face problems of interpretation. Each interpretation, moreover, is problematic. It is not clear, nor unchallenged, that any sort of egalitarian interpretation of equity is tenable. First, there is the problem of scarcity. There will always be medical treatments or supplies in short supply—at least the ones that have just been developed. How are we to achieve equality here, except by a lottery that provides not equal treatment, but an equal *chance* of getting treatment? Second, there is the problem of entitlement. Consider the research scientist who has devoted his life to the search for a vaccine that is effective against a disease that has slaughtered his ancestors for generations. Now he has the vaccine, but initially in short supply. Are we to deny his claim on a dose for himself or his child because that would violate our commitment to equal access? Many would argue that he has an entitlement that sets him apart from the rest; that to deny it would itself be to abandon our commitment to equity.

So equity, like efficiency—although for different reasons—is an elusive notion. We rely on them both in the rhetoric that surrounds the defense of policy, and we rely on our intuitions about them in the setting and advocacy of policy. But when it comes to a specific case of defending a policy under careful scrutiny, these notions slip away from precise clarification. What, then, is to be said for them?

One way to interpret the notion of efficiency—a way that seems to correspond well with the way we actually use it—is as a measure of the extent to which an action produces good—where good is itself defined as the satisfaction of human needs and desires. That action, program or policy then is the most efficient which, at a given level of expenditure, is the one among all available alternatives that maximizes good. Comparative judgments are then possible to the degree to which we have a clear conception of what is good, and also a clear account of what consequences will flow from the various acts we contemplate.

This is classical utilitarianism, and moral philosophy for the last century, like economics and Anglo-American legislative policy over the same century, has been dominated by the influence of utilitarian theory. The objections to it are numerous and powerful, but its appeal is nonetheless unsurpassed as an account of what we ought to do, individually and collectively, and why. This appeal rests ultimately in the simple fact that we do care about the satisfaction of human wants and needs—about the production of good—and we therefore want our efforts and our resources to produce as much of it as possible. This want translates into our concern with efficiency.

Equity is a more obviously moral notion. It means justice, fairness in our dealings with one another. But how are we to understand what is just? Here, again, there is a historical tradition of thought to guide us. From the ancient Pythagorean rules of conduct and the ten commandments, through the austere moral strictures of Immanuel Kant, to an extensive body of antiutilitarian moral theory, we have nurtured and sustained a sense that some kinds of actions are right and other kinds are wrong, regardless of the consequences they lead to or the ends they serve, simply because of the kinds of acts they are. Thus we condemn the framing of an innocent man, no matter how great the social benefits of the conviction might be, just as we condemn torture, slavery, and other moral abominations without regard to the role they may play in the larger pursuit of noble ends. Or, at least, all of us do except the most intransigent of the hard-core utilitarians. And we do so not because such actions strike us as inefficient in the production of good, but because they violate our sense of justice.

Providing an account of that sense of justice is no small task. But it does seem that Mill's view that justice is derivative from considerations of utility, of efficiency in the production of good results, is in decline. Recent moral philosophy has shown reluctance to consider justice as a derivative concept. Rather, it has come to be largely viewed as a dimension of morality that is separate from and independent of utility, and which can therefore be in conflict with it.

Efficiency as a value thus reflects our concern with the maximum production of good, and equity as a value reflects our concern with doing what is just or fair, regardless of its efficiency. In an ideal world, these values would never be in conflict, but in fact the conflict is notorious. We may want both equity and efficiency, but at least sometimes one may be purchased only at the cost of the other.

To see the conflict between equity and efficiency etched sharply, consider a hypothetical example. Real cases, if they are interesting, involve complexity of the sort that can obscure a simple point; I use an artificial example, just as the physicist does when he speaks of the frictionless plane. Imagine that we are all on a desert island, struggling to survive. Most of us cluster into a village, but a few set out for remote parts of the island where the fishing is perhaps better. There is little rain, so drinking water is a constant problem; there is just marginally enough to keep us alive. Suddenly, a rescue mission flies overhead. Using remote sensing technology, they assess our situation. They depart, then return with a large crate which they parachute to the island. We open the crate and find a tank truck filled with pure water and a message that the water is for all the people on the island. How shall we distribute the water?

There are 100 people on the island: 1000 gallons in the tank. Specify whatever distribution you think is equitable. You can favor ten gallons per person, or more for those who work more, or most for those in positions of authority—it doesn't matter which distribution you favor as most equitable. For you now discover that the tank truck has a steam engine. In order to move it around at all you have to use water. And the conflict between efficiency and equity—however you construe equity—becomes plain. Assuming that each gallon of water is as valuable to each person as any other gallon—that is, there is no diminishing marginal utility of water in the range of quantities at issue—then the most efficient thing to do is not use the engine at all. Let water go to those who come for it—to the able-bodied who live nearby. The weak, the ill, the aged, the distant will get none, but since there is linearity in the good produced by incremental allocations of water, their deprivation is of no consequence, for we produce more good this way than by spending some of the water on operating the delivery truck. It would be hard

to argue that justice is served, however, especially given that the water was sent to all the people on the island.

So equity costs something. In some situations the most efficient action and the most equitable action are not the same. Some balance must then be struck between the two competing values. For one who places justice above all, considerations of efficiency may legitimately come into play, but only after justice is fully served. This position would be exemplified by the egalitarian who insisted on an equal distribution of water to all island inhabitants, even if most of the water were used by delivering it. But he could still be seriously concerned with mapping the best route, in order to conserve water, and thus to distribute it most efficiently within the constraints of equity. He would be the mirror image of the complete utilitarian who advocated making the decision solely on the grounds of efficiency and therefore leaving the truck in place. For many people, myself among them, some middle ground is best—some approximation to complete equity, tempered by an unwillingness to let efficiency fall too low.

I have not shown, of course, that equity and efficiency are always in conflict—only that they are competing values in some situations. It is a separate question whether the kinds of situations that arise in regard to the distribution of health care are of the sort in which equity and efficiency are in conflict. But the answer is apparent; one example should suffice to show that the conflict is present.

Assume that considerations of equity—of justice or fairness in the treatment of persons—require that each individual be free to choose the geographical location in which he or she will seek work. Assume further that considerations of equity require that in an affluent industrialized nation like ours a minimally decent level of health care should be available to all citizens, including those in poor, rural communities. Finally, assume that our concern with containing the costs of health care places limits on the amount of financial incentive we can provide to induce physicians to practice in otherwise undesirable locations. Then the conflict is evident: we can resolve the problem only by some sacrifice in the freedom of the physician, the health care of the poor, or the pocketbook of the public. And any such sacrifice will be to some extent a concession with respect either to equity or efficiency.

Having argued that equity and efficiency, however we interpret them, are different and competing values, I want to turn next to some further questions of health care distribution and cost containment.

Since health is not the only thing we care about—nor should it be—we want to have substantial resources available for other expenditures. It may, therefore, seem obvious that we ought to decide how much to spend on health care, and also how it should be spent. It would be a mistake, however, to think that any such determination takes place in any systematic or comprehensive way. Rather, what we spend on health care is the total of the expenditures in diverse sectors ranging from the individual buying a bottle of useless cold pills or a much needed bandage to the government building a useless new 21 million dollar Navy hospital in New Orleans or purchasing essential medical care for a large class of people in need. There simply is no coherent, organized or regulated arrangement regarding how much is spent, what it is spent on, or how care is distributed. Nor is there much effective coordination among the various sectors of health care activity. Therefore there is no overall determination of a total level of expenditure—indeed, we know only approximately what the total expenditure is. And there is no systematic control over the ways in which the funds are spent. Any approach to health care distribution or cost containment must therefore be piecemeal, addressing individual aspects of the health care landscape one locale at a time.

If we are speaking of a single individual or family, it is relatively easy to say how to keep costs down: live prudently, carry a good medical insurance program, and be an alert, informed, active and critical consumer of health care services. Then, most probably, the costs of health care will be reasonably well contained. But that by itself will not relieve the rising costs associated with high-technology medicine nor will it keep insurance costs from rising beyond the reach of increasingly many people. For the problem is not fundamentally one of individual choice and action; it is one of a cumulative financial effect that can only be addressed, however piecemeal, by collective response—that is, as a matter of public policy.

Governmental expenditure on health care is approximately 75 billion dollars a year, and the government role is exceedingly diverse. The government functions:

1. *As direct provider of care.* Example: the Veterans Administration's system of nearly 200 hospitals, for which the 1978 fiscal year budget appropriation for medical care is over 4.7 billion dollars.
2. *As provider of medical insurance.* Example: the Medicare and Medicaid programs, through which the government is the largest provider of medical insurance in the country.
3. *As the operator of support systems for health care research and delivery.* Example: the National Center for Disease Control in Atlanta.
4. *As a medical educator.* Example: the Uniformed Services University of the Health Sciences.
5. *As a supporter of medical education.* Example: capitation grants to medical, nursing, and allied health professional schools.
6. *As a sponsor and operator of medical research programs.* Example: the National Institutes of Health.
7. *As a regulator of persons, substances, and institutions.* Example: rulings by the Food and Drug Administration. And finally,
8. *As an indirect influence on health care.* Example: OSHA regulations, automobile safety standards, EPA rulings, and the like.

Each of these functions is itself diverse, and each thus provides a complex context of expenditure wherein questions of efficiency and of equity can be raised. Further, the government's regulatory and legislative powers will play a crucial role in any collective response to the problems associated with cost containment. So the government is the central figure in the story.

Any consideration of containing costs must deal with problems of distribution and supply, among others. Basically, there are just two possibilities for containing costs: one can limit or reduce service, or one can limit or reduce the cost for the average instance of service. One way to reduce or limit service is to distribute it only to a limited portion of those cases where a need is present.

The reduction of service is also possible, however, through the redefinition of need. We can increase or diminish the claims for health care services by broadening or narrowing the definitions of illness, without thereby affecting anyone medically. If our clinics are too crowded, we can thin the crowds by a decision that although people with dandruff, obesity, bizarre noses, and lackadaisical libido may have problems, they are not necessarily sick, and do not qualify to make claims on the health care facilities. The closer we move toward publicly funded health care or health care insurance, the more critical it will become to clarify what is to count as illness for purposes of claiming entitlement to health care resources.

Now consider the notion of limiting costs by leaving some needs unmet. Recall specifically those inevitably cited patients with kidney failure. In the early days of renal dialysis, we had a classic problem of allocating limited vital resources. There were not enough machines to go around. That problem is now essentially past, but a similar situation exists with respect to live organ transplants. Many more patients are medically qualified to receive transplanted kidneys than can be accommodated given the present rate of supply. How shall we respond to this situation?

Various principles of distribution come to mind. Consider:

1. *To each according to his means.* This is a free market policy. Kidneys go to those who can afford them, with the price determined by market phenomena.

2. *To each according to his social utility.* This is roughly the approach adopted in the original dialysis selection in Seattle, where an assessment was made of the social utility of the applicants. It is the utilitarian approach, the one that seeks to maximize efficiency.

3. *To each according to his entitlement or status.* A policy like this might favor veterans, landowners, members of the party in power, or other groups or individuals making special claims.

4. *To each according to his luck.* This is the policy of the strict egalitarian: count every medically qualified individual as an equal, and draw lots to determine who will get the kidneys.

5. *To each according to his need.* To implement this policy, of course, requires an increase in the supply of the resource the scarcity of which presents the problem in the first place.

The choice among these distributional policies will be difficult because our values do not all point to a single choice. In particular, we are sympathetic both to considerations of social utility and to the desirability of meeting everyone's need where we have the ability to meet anyone's. So there is a pressure to increase service to meet demand, thereby to eliminate some of the conflict we feel, and that yields pressure to increase the supply of transplantable kidneys while keeping a lid on the costs. Is there any possibility of doing that?

ABC news reported in the autumn of 1978 that recent legislation in France makes a person's organs available at death for transplantation unless the individual has exercised a prior option of objection. Should we adopt a similar policy? The government could go a step beyond France, requiring organ donation without option of prior objection. Or it could go two steps beyond, drafting people into a national organ bank battalion. These people might be selected if they are in good health, late in life and of low social utility. They would then be required to donate one kidney, with the rest of their organs to be taken at death. The French policy is moderate in the context of what is possible. Still, it is seen as overly coercive by many critics. Milder measures include a proposal made recently by an officer of the American Kidney Foundation, who suggested that each individual agree or decline at the time of registration with the Social Security Administration. But Sidney Wolfe, of the Health Research Group, responded that any such association with a government agency that provides vital support services could be implicitly coercive. Still milder measures are available, however. The government could decide to support the present system of total voluntarism with a campaign aimed at persuading large numbers of people to become donors. Or the government could leave the matter wholly to the workings of the private sector.

For an illuminating comparison, consider briefly a different problem. We provide military manpower in various ways at various times depending not only on our national security needs but also on our moral priorities. The draft, favored in wartime, is the most efficient way to provide the manpower, especially combined with selective deferment. The government conscripts soldiers, paying what it decides to pay—thereby containing payroll costs, and exempting those whose greater social utility lies elsewhere—thereby maximizing social efficiency. The principle is: *from each according to his usefulness.* But this policy is criticized on grounds of equity. It sends the poor and underprivileged off to battle, favoring further the already favored, while the benefit of national defense—that is, the security of the nation—is equally enjoyed by all. Moved by conscience to provide military manpower more equitably, we change to a lottery. Now the principle is: *from each according to his luck in an equal risk lottery.* But this policy has critics, for it obliterates the freedom of the unlucky draftee, as well as reducing efficiency by drafting some who would be more usefully placed elsewhere. So out of respect for personal liberty, we move to a volunteer service: *from each according to his choice.* Freedom is honored, but the costs soar because the incentive to join is not great for most people in a reasonably sound economy. And now we hear lamentation from the Pentagon: we have liberty, but the price is getting beyond our

reach, and the efficiency is low. So once again we may move to another system, striking a different balance among the competing values of efficiency, equality and liberty.

A parallel situation exists in regard to kidney supply and distribution. The various plans clearly exhibit different degrees of respect for different values. A plausible utilitarian case can be made for the very coercive plans to increase supply, and as we move through the shadings of coercion from a draft or universal requirement, to coercion of varying degrees, to persuasion, education, and voluntarism, the level of efficiency seems to drop. At the same time, the level of equity in the treatment of persons seems to rise, especially if we take equity to require respect for personal autonomy and the bodily integrity of individual persons. But now a curious bind seems to emerge. For if the most equitable policy for distribution requires meeting the needs of all patients who require transplants, that policy also seems to require, as a practical matter, a highly efficient policy for obtaining transplantable kidneys. Yet the policies that seem most efficient in this regard seem least equitable from the point of view of potential donors. Thus we see equity not only in opposition to efficiency, but to equity itself.

We need to sustain a systematic inquiry into the considerations of equity and efficiency in health care, and as part of that process we need a more sophisticated understanding of how to assess the value of the outcomes that health care provides. This is particularly important as our concern with cost containment heightens, for although the crisis in health care costs is not primarily a government spending crisis, only the government is in any position to get real leverage on the currents of supply and distribution of health care goods and services. And when we look to government to solve large scale social problems, we should remember that we are looking to a ponderous and unpredictable force, mighty in itself, yet subject to the shifting drifts of political sentiment. We are well advised to understand what we are asking it to do.

My own view is that we have a tendency to weigh efficiency too heavily in its conflict with equity, in part—but only in part—because of the difficulty of measuring the value of considerations of equity. Perhaps the basic mistake is to assume that the kind of assessment needed can be *measurement* at all, as opposed to the informed and sensitive judgment that lies at the heart of leadership and statesmanship.

One final example: imagine a large family next door. They treat all their children well except the youngest. That one is neglected, disdained—an outcast. We would, I think, judge that family harshly, accepting as a mark of its degree of decency the way it treats the one whom it treats least well. John Rawls, in *A Theory of Justice,* argues that equity requires us to use a similar criterion in judging social institutions. The keystone of his theory is respect for liberty conjoined with concern for the least advantaged among us. Those who suffer from debilitating illness or handicap are, in an important sense, the least advantaged among us, and we neglect them at our own moral risk. There is no way to assign a dollar value to such considerations, and they may in tragic circumstances even be defeasible on grounds of excessive cost. Nonetheless they have a force that should not be underestimated. It may be useful to keep Rawls' criterion in mind as a prima facie constraint on our pursuit of efficiency. That constraint would prevent us from assessing health care policies in a purely utilitarian way or in a way that excludes the interests of any segment of the population. It would not by itself determine what policies we should set, but by narrowing the range of choices it would play some role in the process. That larger process of setting public policies for health care that are equitable and affordable will be more complex even than the systems of supply and distribution, and it would be futile to expect any stable resolution of policy to be achieved Rather, there must be a process of assessment and reassessment in the public and political forums—an ongoing exchange of which the perspectives of philosophy are an essential part.

Acknowledgment

I am grateful to Norman Weissman, Ruth Macklin, and Norman Daniels for criticisms of an earlier draft of this essay. They are, of course, wholly innocent in respect to its remaining faults. I am also grateful to the Hastings Center, under whose auspices this work was done with the support of a grant from the National Center for Health Services Research, for permission to provide this essay to the Philosophic Exchange.

Suggested Further Reading

Beauchamp, Dan E., "Public Health as Social Justice," *Inquiry,* 13 (March 1976), 3–14.

Erenreich, Barbara, and John Erenreich, "Health Care and Social Control," *Social Policy,* 5 (May–June 1974), 26–40.

Guttman, Amy, "For and Against Equal Access to Health Care," *Millbank Memorial Fund Quarterly/Health and Society,* 59 (Fall 1981), 542–60.

Sade, Robert M., "Medical Care as a Right: A Refutation," *New England Journal of Medicine,* 285 (1971), 1288–92.

Telfer, Elizabeth, "Justice, Welfare, and Health Care," *Journal of Medical Ethics,* 2 (September 1976), 107–11.

3. MICROALLOCATION DECISIONS

Decisions about the ethical distribution of scarce lifesaving medical resources are called *microallocation decisions.* Unlike macroallocation, which involves policy decisions on a broad scale, microallocation is concerned with the treatment of individual patients in specific situations. If not all patients who need a treatment can be provided with it, who should be given the opportunity to live and who will be denied that opportunity? Who should make the decisions, and what criteria ought to guide them?

In the 1960s public attention was focused on the ethical issues of microallocation because of the scarcity of artificial kidney machines. With the machines, patients suffering from kidney failure could have their blood "washed" (*hemodialysis*) at regular intervals and remain alive; without the treatment they would die. Hemodialysis equipment was expensive, however, and in short supply. Hospitals formed committees to develop ethical criteria for choosing among the competing candidates. In 1972 a macroallocation decision by Congress provided Medicare funding of kidney dialysis and kidney transplants for nearly all those who needed them. While the decision eliminated most of the problems of allocating one particular resource, the issue of microallocation continues to present ethical difficulties.

The issue aroused controversy in 1985 in the case of "Baby Jesse," a California infant born with a defective heart. Initially, hospital officials refused to place Baby Jesse on a list of prospective patients for heart transplantation, because they maintained that his unmarried parents could not provide him with adequate postoperative care. Only after the infant's grandparents were made his legal guardians did the hospital agree to include him in the transplant program. The hospital thus used social status as a criterion

for assessing the likelihood of successful treatment (and the right, therefore, to receive the scarce treatment). Some ethicists believe that social factors should not be a consideration in microallocation decisions. Others argue that consideration of social factors is justified.

Some criteria proposed for microallocation decisions are based on utilitarian considerations. This approach takes into account the social consequences of choosing one candidate over another. Some argue that the principle of utility requires giving priority to those likely to make a greater social contribution. Other utilitarians believe that distributing scarce resources on the basis of "social worth" judgments will eventually produce more harm than benefit; hence they support different selection procedures, such as a random or "first-come, first-served" approach.

Approaching microallocation from a Kantian perspective of respect for persons leads some writers to maintain that if every patient cannot be treated, then none should be. Others attempt to moderate this extreme position by arguing for random selection procedures or by developing criteria which recognize and protect the fundamental interests of each candidate.

In the following selection James F. Childress proposes a two-stage selection process for distributing scarce lifesaving resources. In the first stage, medical criteria are used to establish a pool of applicants "who have some reasonable chance of responding to the treatment." The second stage uses random or chance selection procedures. Childress rejects utilitarian arguments for selection criteria based on estimations of a patient's social value. He maintains that the use of randomness or chance is more in keeping with respect for human dignity, fairness, and trust.

JAMES F. CHILDRESS

Who Shall Live When Not All Can Live?

Who shall live when not all can live? Although this question has been urgently forced upon us by the dramatic use of artificial internal organs and organ transplantations, it is hardly new. George Bernard Shaw dealt with it in "The Doctor's Dilemma":

> *Sir Patrick.* Well, Mr. Savior of Lives: which is it to be? that honest decent man Blenkinsop, or that rotten blackguard of an artist, eh?
> *Ridgeon.* It's not an easy case to judge, is it? Blenkinsop's an honest decent man; but is he any use? Dubedat's a rotten blackguard; but he's a genuine source of pretty and pleasant and good things.
> *Sir Patrick.* What will he be a source of for that poor innocent wife of his, when she finds him out?
> *Ridgeon.* That's true. Her life will be a hell.
> *Sir Patrick.* And tell me this. Suppose you had this choice put before you: either to go through life and find all the pictures bad but all the men and women good, or go through life and find all the pictures good and all the men and women rotten. Which would you choose?[1]

A significant example of the distribution of scarce medical resources is seen in the use of penicillin shortly after its discovery. Military officers had to determine which soldiers would be treated—those with venereal disease or those wounded in combat.[2] In many respects such decisions have become routine in medical circles. Day after day physicians and others make judgments and decisions "about allocations of medical care to various segments of our population, to various types of hospitalized patients, and to specific individuals,"[3] for example, whether mental illness or cancer will receive the higher proportion of available funds. Nevertheless, the dramatic forms of "Scarce Life-Saving Medical Resources" (hereafter abbreviated as SLMR) such as hemodialysis and kidney and heart transplants have compelled us to examine the moral questions that have been concealed in many routine decisions. I do not attempt in this paper to show how a resolution of SLMR cases can help us in the more routine ones which do not involve a conflict of life with life. Rather I develop an argument for a particular method of determining who shall live when not all can live. No conclusions are implied about criteria and procedures for determining who shall receive medical resources that are not directly related to the preservation of life (e.g., corneal transplants) or about standards for allocating money and time for studying and treating certain diseases.

Just as current SLMR decisions are not totally discontinuous with other medical decisions, so we must ask whether some other cases might, at least by analogy, help us develop the needed criteria and procedures. Some have looked at the principles at work in our responses to abortion, euthanasia, and artificial insemination.[4] Usually they have concluded that these cases do not cast light on the selection of patients for artificial and transplanted organs. The reason is evident: in abortion, euthanasia, and artificial insemination, there is no conflict of life with life for limited but indispensable resources (with the possible exception of therapeutic abortion). In current SLMR decisions, such a conflict is inescapable, and it makes them so morally perplexing and fascinating. If analogous cases are to be found, I think that we shall locate them in moral conflict situations.

Reprinted with permission of the publisher from *Soundings, An Interdisciplinary Journal,* 53, no. 4 (Winter 1970), 339–355. Note: footnotes have been renumbered.

Analogous Conflict Situations

An especially interesting and pertinent one is *U.S. v. Holmes.*[5] In 1841 an American ship, the *William Brown,* which was near Newfoundland on a trip from Liverpool to Philadelphia, struck an iceberg. The crew and half the passengers were able to escape in the two available vessels. One of these, a longboat, carrying too many passengers and leaking seriously, began to founder in the turbulent sea after about twenty-four hours. In a desperate attempt to keep it from sinking, the crew threw overboard fourteen men. Two sisters of one of the men either jumped overboard to join their brother in death or instructed the crew to throw them over. The criteria for determining who should live were "not to part man and wife, and not to throw over any women." Several hours later the others were rescued. Returning to Philadelphia, most of the crew disappeared, but one, Holmes, who had acted upon orders from the mate, was indicted, tried, and convicted on the charge of "unlawful homicide."

We are interested in this case from a moral rather than a legal standpoint, and there are several possible responses to and judgments about it. Without attempting to be exhaustive I shall sketch a few of these. The judge contended that lots should have been cast, for in such conflict situations, there is no other procedure "so consonant both to humanity and to justice." Counsel for Holmes, on the other hand, maintained that the "sailors adopted the only principle of selection which was possible in an emergency like theirs—a principle more humane than lots."

Another version of selection might extend and systematize the maxims of the sailors in the direction of "utility"; those are saved who will contribute to the greatest good for the greatest number. Yet another possible option is defended by Edmond Cahn in *The Moral Decision.* He argues that in this case we encounter the "morals of the last day." By this phrase he indicates that an apocalyptic crisis renders totally irrelevant the normal differences between individuals. He continues:

In a strait of this extremity, all men are reduced—or raised, as one may choose to denominate it—to members of the genus, mere congeners and nothing else. Truly and literally, all were "in the same boat," and thus none could be saved separately from the others. I am driven to conclude that otherwise—that is, if none sacrifice themselves of free will to spare the others—they must all wait and die together. For where all have become congeners, pure and simple, no one can save himself by killing another.[6]

Cahn's answer to the question "who shall live when not all can live" is "none" unless the voluntary sacrifice by some persons permits it.

Few would deny the importance of Cahn's approach although many, including this writer, would suggest that it is relevant mainly as an affirmation of an elevated and, indeed, heroic or saintly morality which one hopes would find expression in the voluntary actions of many persons trapped in "borderline" situations involving a conflict of life with life. It is a maximal demand which some moral principles impose on the individual in the recognition that self-preservation is not a good which is to be defended at all costs. The absence of this saintly or heroic morality should not mean, however, that everyone perishes. Without making survival an absolute value and without justifying all means to achieve it, we can maintain that simply letting everyone die is irresponsible. This charge can be supported from several different standpoints, including society at large as well as the individuals involved. Among a group of self-interested individuals, none of whom volunteers to relinquish his life, there may be better and worse ways of determining who shall survive. One task of social ethics, whether religious or philosophical, is to propose relatively just institutional arrangements within which self-interested and biased men can live. The question then becomes: which set of arrangements—which criteria and procedures of selection—is most satisfactory in view of the human condition (man's limited altruism and inclination to seek his own good) and the conflicting values that are to be realized?

There are several significant differences between the *Holmes* and SLMR cases, a major one being that the former involves *direct* killing of another person, while the latter involves only *permitting* a person to die when it is not possible to save all. Furthermore, in extreme situations such as Holmes, the restraints of civilization have been stripped away and something approximating a state of nature prevails, in which life is "solitary, poor, nasty, brutish and short." The state of nature does not mean that moral standards are irrelevant and that might should prevail, but it does suggest that much of the matrix which normally supports morality has been removed. Also, the necessary but unfortunate decisions about who shall live and die are made by men who are existentially and personally involved in the outcome. Their survival too is at stake. Even though the institutional role of sailors seems to require greater sacrificial actions, there is obviously no assurance that they will adequately assess the number of sailors required to man the vessel or that they will impartially and objectively weigh the common good at stake. As the judge insisted in his defense of casting lots in the *Holmes* case: "In no other than this [casting lots] or some like way are those having equal rights put upon an equal footing, and in no other way is it possible to guard against partiality and oppression, violence, and conflict." This difference should not be exaggerated since self-interest, professional pride, and the like obviously affect the outcome of many medical decisions. Nor do the remaining differences cancel *Holmes'* instructiveness.

Criteria of Selection for SLMR

Which set of arrangements should be adopted for SLMR? Two questions are involved: Which standards and criteria should be used? and, Who should make the decision? The first question is basic, since the debate about implementation, e.g., whether by a law committee or physician, makes little progress until the criteria are determined.

We need two sets of criteria which will be applied at two different stages in the selection of recipients of SLMR. First, medical criteria should be used to exclude those who are not "medically acceptable." Second, from this group of "medically acceptable" applicants, the final selection can be made. Occasionally in current American medical practice, the first stage is omitted, but such an omission is unwarranted. Ethical and social responsibility would seem to require distributing these SLMR only to those who have some reasonable prospect of responding to the treatment. Furthermore, in transplants such medical tests as tissue and blood typing are necessary, although they are hardly fully developed.

"Medical acceptability" is not as easily determined as many non-physicians assume since there is considerable debate in medical circles about the relevant factors (e.g., age and complicating diseases). Although ethicists can contribute little or nothing to this debate, two proposals may be in order. First, "medical acceptability" should be used only to determine the group from which the final selection will be made, and the attempt to establish fine degrees of prospective response to treatment should be avoided. Medical criteria, then, would exclude some applicants but would not serve as a basis of comparison between those who pass the first stage. For example, if two applicants for dialysis were medically acceptable, the physicians would *not* choose the one with the *better* medical prospects. Final selection would be made on other grounds. Second, psychological and environmental factors should be kept to an absolute minimum and should be considered only when they are without doubt critically related to medical acceptability (e.g., the inability to cope with the requirements of dialysis which might lead to suicide).

The most significant moral questions emerge when we turn to the final selection. Once the pool of medically acceptable applicants has been defined and still the number is larger than the resources, what other criteria should be used? How should the final selection be made? First, I shall examine some of the difficulties that stem from efforts to make the final selection in terms of social value; these difficulties raise serious doubts about the feasibility and justifiability of the utilitarian approach. Then I shall consider the possible justification for random selection or chance.

Occasionally criteria of social worth focus on past contributions but most often they are primarily future-oriented. The patient's potential and probable contribution to the society is stressed, although this obviously cannot be abstracted from his present web of relationships (e.g., dependents) and occupational activities (e.g., nuclear physicist). Indeed, the magnitude of his contribution to society (as an abstraction) is measured in terms of these social roles, relations, and functions. Enough has already been said to suggest the tremendous range of factors that affect social value or worth.[7] Here we encounter the first major difficulty of this approach: How do we determine the relevant criteria of social value?

How does one quantify and compare the needs of the spirit (e.g., education, art, religion), political life, economic activity, technological development? Joseph Fletcher suggests that "some day we may learn how to 'quantify' or 'mathematicate' to 'computerize' the value problem in selection, in the same careful and thorough way that diagnosis has been."[8] I am not convinced that we can ever quantify values, or that we should attempt to do so. But even if the various social and human needs, in principle, could be quantified, how do we determine how much weight we will give to each one? Which will have priority in case of conflict? Or even more basically, in the light of which values and principles do we recognize social "needs"?

One possible way of determining the values which should be emphasized in selection has been proposed by Leo Shatin.[9] He insists that our medical decisions about allocating resources are already based on an unconscious scale of values (usually dominated by material worth). Since there is really no way of escaping this, we should be self-conscious and critical about it. How should we proceed? He recommends that we discover the values that most people in our society hold and then use them as criteria for distributing SLMR. These values can be discovered by attitude or opinion surveys. Presumably if 51 percent in this testing period put a greater premium on military needs than technological developments, military men would have a greater claim on our SLMR than experimental researchers. But valuations of what is significant change, and the student revolutionary who was denied SLMR in 1970 might be celebrated in 1990 as the greatest American hero since George Washington.

Shatin presumably is seeking criteria that could be applied nationally, but at the present, regional and local as well as individual prejudices tincture the criteria of social value that are used in selection. Nowhere is this more evident than in the deliberations and decisions of the anonymous selection committee of the Seattle Artificial Kidney Center where such factors as church membership and Scout leadership have been deemed significant for determining who shall live.[10] As two critics conclude after examining these criteria and procedures, they rule out "creative nonconformists, who rub the bourgeoisie the wrong way but who historically have contributed so much to the making of America. The Pacific Northwest is no place for a Henry David Thoreau with bad kidneys."[11]

Closely connected to this first problem of determining social values is a second one. Not only is it difficult if not impossible to reach agreement on social values, but it is also rarely easy to predict what our needs will be in a few years and what the consequences of present actions will be. Furthermore it is difficult to predict which persons will fulfill their potential function in society. Admissions committees in colleges and universities experience the frustrations of predicting realization of potential. For these reasons, as someone has indicated, God might be a utilitarian, but we cannot be. We simply lack the capacity to predict very accurately the consequences which we then must evaluate. Our incapacity is never more evident than when we think in societal terms.

Other difficulties make us even less confident that such an approach to SLMR is advisable. Many critics raise the spectre of abuse, but this should not be overemphasized. The fundamental difficulty appears on another level: the utilitarian approach would in effect reduce the person to his social role, relations, and functions. Ultimately it dulls and perhaps even eliminates the sense of the person's transcendence, his dignity as a person which cannot be reduced to his past or future contribution to society. It is not at all clear that we are willing to live with these implications of utilitarian selection. Wilhelm Kolff, who invented the artificial kidney, has asked: "Do we really subscribe to the principle that social standing should determine selection? Do we allow patients to be treated with dialysis only when they are married, go to church, have children, have a job, a good income and give to the Community Chest?"[12]

The German theologian Helmut Thielicke contends that any search for "objective criteria" for selection is already a capitulation to the utilitarian point of view which violates man's dignity.[13] The solution is not to let all die, but to recognize that SLMR cases are "borderline situations" which inevitably involve guilt. The agent, however, can have courage and freedom (which, for Thielicke, come from justification by faith) and can

> go ahead anyway and seek for criteria for deciding the question of life or death in the matter of the artificial kidney. Since these criteria are . . . questionable, necessarily alien to the meaning of human existence, the decision to which they lead can be little more than that arrived at by casting lots.[14]

The resulting criteria, he suggests, will probably be very similar to those already employed in American medical practice.

He is most concerned to preserve a certain *attitude* or *disposition* in SLMR—the sense of guilt which arises when man's dignity is violated. With this sense of guilt, the agent remains "sound and healthy where it really counts."[15] Thielicke uses man's dignity only as a judgmental, critical, and negative standard. It only tells us how all selection criteria and procedures (and even the refusal to act) implicate us in the ambiguity of the human condition and its metaphysical guilt. This approach is consistent with his view of the task of theological ethics: "to teach us how to understand and endure—not "solve"—the borderline situation."[16] But ethics, I would contend, can help us discern the factors and norms in whose light relative, discriminate judgments can be made. Even if all actions in SLMR should involve guilt, some may preserve human dignity to a greater extent than others. Thielicke recognizes that a decision based on any criteria is "little more than that arrived at by casting lots." But perhaps selection by chance would come the closest to embodying the moral and nonmoral values that we are trying to maintain (including a sense of man's dignity).

The Values of Random Selection

My proposal is that we use some form of randomness or chance (either natural, such as "first come, first served," or artificial, such as a lottery) to determine who shall be saved. Many reject randomness as a surrender to non-rationality when responsible and rational judgments can and must be made. Edmond Cahn criticizes "Holmes' judge" who recommended the casting of lots because, as Cahn puts it, "the crisis involves stakes too high for gambling and responsibilities too deep for destiny."[17] Similarly, other critics see randomness as a surrender to "non-human" forces which necessarily vitiates human values (e.g., it is important to have persons rather than impersonal forces determining who shall live). Sometimes they are identified with the outcome of the process (e.g., the features such as creativity and fullness of being which make human life what it is are to be considered and respected in the decision). Regarding the former, it must be admitted that the use of chance seems cold and impersonal. But presumably the defenders of utilitarian criteria in SLMR want to make their application as objective and impersonal as possible so that subjective bias does not determine who shall live.

Such criticism, however, ignores the moral and nonmoral values which might be supported by selection by randomness or chance. A more important criticism is that the procedure that I develop draws the relevant moral context too narrowly. That context, so the argument might run, includes the society and its future and not merely the individual with his illness and claim upon SLMR. But my contention is that the values and principles at work in the narrower context may well take precedence over those operative in the broader context both because of their weight and significance and because of the weaknesses of selection in terms of social worth. As Paul Freund rightly insists, "The more nearly total is the estimate to be made of an individual, and the more nearly the consequence determines life and death, the more unfit the judgment becomes for human reckoning. . . . Randomness as a moral principle deserves serious study."[18] Serious study would, I think, point toward its implementation in certain conflict situations, primarily because it preserves a significant degree of *personal dignity by providing equality* of opportunity. Thus it cannot be dismissed as a "non-rational" and "non-human" procedure without an inquiry into the reasons, including human values, which might justify it. Paul Ramsey stresses this point about the *Holmes* case:

> Instead of fixing our attention upon "gambling" as the solution—with all the frivolous and often corrupt associations the word raises in our minds—we should think rather of equality of opportunity as the ethical substance of the relations of those individuals to one another that might have been guarded and expressed by casting lots.[19]

The individual's personal and transcendent dignity, which on the utilitarian approach would be submerged in his social role and function, can be protected and witnessed to by a recognition of his equal right to be saved. Such a right is best preserved by procedures which establish equality of opportunity. Thus selection by chance more closely approximates the requirements established by human dignity than does utilitarian calculation. It is not infallibly just, but it is preferable to the alternatives of letting all die or saving only those who have the greatest social responsibilities and potential contribution.

This argument can be extended by examining values other than individual dignity and equality of opportunity. Another basic value in the medical sphere is the relationship of trust between physician and patient. Which selection criteria are most in accord with this relationship of trust? Which will maintain, extend, and deepen it? My contention is that selection by randomness or chance is preferable from this standpoint too.

Trust, which is inextricably bound to respect for human dignity, is an attitude of expectation about another. It is not simply the expectation that another will act toward him in certain ways—which will respect him as a person. As Charles Fried writes:

> Although trust has to do with reliance on a disposition of another person, it is reliance on a disposition of a special sort: the disposition to act morally, to deal fairly with others, to live up to One's undertakings, and so on. Thus to trust another is first of all to expect him to accept the principle of morality in his dealings with you, to respect your status as a person, your personality.[20]

This trust cannot be preserved in life-and-death situations when a person expects decisions about him to be made in terms of his social worth, for such decisions violate his status as a person. An applicant rejected on grounds of inadequacy in social value or virtue would have reason for feeling that his "trust" had been betrayed. Indeed, the sense that one is being viewed not as an end in himself but as a means in medical progress or the achievement of a greater social good is incompatible with attitudes and relationships of trust. We recognize this in the billboard which was erected after the first heart transplants:

"Drive Carefully. Christiaan Barnard Is Watching You." The relationship of trust between the physician and patient is not only an instrumental value in the sense of being an important factor in the patient's treatment. It is also to be endorsed because of its intrinsic worth as a relationship.

Thus the related values of individual dignity and trust are best maintained in selection by chance. But other factors also buttress the argument for this approach. Which criteria and procedures would men agree upon? We have to suppose a hypothetical situation in which several men are going to determine for themselves and their families the criteria and procedures by which they would want to be admitted to and excluded from SLMR if the need arose.[21] We need to assume two restrictions and then ask which set of criteria and procedures would be chosen as the most rational and, indeed, the fairest. The restrictions are these: (1) That men are *self-interested*. They are interested in their own welfare (and that of members of their families), and this, of course, includes survival. Basically, they are not motivated by altruism. (2) Furthermore, they are ignorant of their own talents, abilities, potential, and probable contribution to the social good. They do not know how they would fare in a competitive situation, e.g., the competition for SLMR in terms of social contribution. Under these conditions which institution would be chosen—letting all die, utilitarian selection, or the use of chance? Which would seem the most rational? the fairest? By which set of criteria would they want to be included in or excluded from the list of those who will be saved? The rational choice in this setting (assuming self-interest and ignorance of one's competitive success) would be random selection or chance since this alone provides equality of opportunity. A possible response is that one would prefer to take a "risk" and therefore choose the utilitarian approach. But I think not, especially since I added that the participants in this hypothetical situation are choosing for their children as well as for themselves; random selection or chance could be more easily justified to the children. It would

make more sense for men who are self-interested but uncertain about their relative contribution to society to elect a set of criteria which would build in equality of opportunity. They would consider selection by chance as relatively just and fair.

An important psychological point supplements earlier arguments for using chance or random selection. The psychological stress and strain among those who are rejected would be greater if the rejection is based on insufficient social worth than if it is based on chance. Obviously stress and strain cannot be eliminated in these borderline situations, but they would almost certainly be increased by the opprobrium of being judged relatively "unfit" by society's agents using society's values. Nicholas Rescher makes this point very effectively:

> ...a recourse to chance would doubtless make matters easier for the rejected patient and those who have a specific interest in him. It would surely be quite hard for them to accept his exclusion by relatively mechanical application of objective criteria in whose implementation subjective judgment is involved. But the circumstances of life have conditioned us to accept the workings of chance and to tolerate the element of luck (good or bad): human life is an inherently contingent process. Nobody, after all, has an absolute right to ELT [Exotic Lifesaving Therapy]—but most of us would feel that we have "every bit as much right" to it as anyone else in significantly similar circumstances.[22]

Although it is seldom recognized as such, selection by chance is already in operation in practically every dialysis unit. I am not aware of any unit which removed some of its patients from kidney machines in order to make room for later applicants who are better qualified in terms of social worth. Furthermore, very few people would recommend it. Indeed, few would even consider removing a person from a kidney machine on the grounds that a person better qualified *medically* had just applied. In a discussion of the treatment of chronic renal failure by dialysis at the University of Virginia Hospital Renal Unit from

November 15, 1965 to November 15, 1966, Dr. Harry Abram writes: "Thirteen patients sought treatment but were not considered because the program had reached its limit of nine patients."[23] Thus, in practice and theory, natural chance is accepted at least within certain limits.

My proposal is that we extend this principle (first come, first served) to determine who among the medically acceptable patients shall live or that we utilize artificial chance such as a lottery or randomness. "First come, first served" would be more feasible than a lottery since the applicants make their claims over a period of time rather than as a group at one time. This procedure would be in accord with at least one principle in our present practices and with our sense of individual dignity, trust, and fairness. Its significance in relation to these values can be underlined by asking how the decision can be justified to the rejected applicant. Of course, one easy way of avoiding this task is to maintain the traditional cloak of secrecy, which works to a great extent because patients are often not aware that they are being considered for SLMR in addition to the usual treatment. But whether public justification is instituted or not is not the significant question; it is rather what reasons for rejection would be most acceptable to the unsuccessful applicant. My contention is that rejection can be accepted more readily if equality of opportunity, fairness, and trust are preserved, and that they are best preserved by selection by randomness or chance.

This proposal has yet another advantage since it would eliminate the need for a committee to examine applicants in terms of their social value. This onerous responsibility can be avoided.

Finally, there is a possible indirect consequence of widespread use of random selection which is interesting to ponder, although I do *not* adduce it as a good reason for adopting random selection. It can be argued, as Professor Mason Willrich of the University of Virginia Law School has suggested, that SLMR cases would practically disappear if these scarce resources were distributed randomly

rather than on social worth grounds. Scarcity would no longer be a problem because the holders of economic and political power would make certain that they would not be excluded by a random selection procedure; hence they would help to redirect public priorities or establish private funding so that lifesaving medical treatment would be widely and perhaps universally available.

In the framework that I have delineated, are the decrees of chance to be taken without exception? If we recognize exceptions, would we not open Pandora's box again just after we had succeeded in getting it closed? The direction of my argument has been against any exceptions, and I would defend this as the proper way to go. But let me indicate one possible way of admitting exceptions while at the same time circumscribing them so narrowly that they would be very rare indeed.

An obvious advantage of the utilitarian approach is that occasionally circumstances arise which make it necessary to say that one man is practically indispensable for a society in view of a particular set of problems it faces (e.g., the President when the nation is waging a war for survival). Certainly the argument to this point has stressed that the burden of proof would fall on those who think that the social danger in this instance is so great that they simply cannot abide by the outcome of a lottery or a first come, first served policy. Also, the reason must be negative rather than positive; that is, we depart from chance in this instance not because we want to take advantage of this person's potential contribution to the improvement of our society, but because his immediate loss would possibly (even probably) be disastrous (again, the President in a grave national emergency). Finally, social value (in the negative sense) should be used as a standard of exception in dialysis, for example, only if it would provide a reason strong enough to warrant removing another person from a kidney machine if all machines were taken. Assuming this strong reluctance to remove anyone once the commitment has been made to him, we would be willing to put this patient ahead of another applicant for a vacant machine only if we would be willing (in circumstances in which all machines are being used) to vacate a machine by removing someone from it. These restrictions would make an exception almost impossible.

While I do not recommend this procedure of recognizing exceptions, I think that one can defend it while accepting my general thesis about selection by randomness or chance. If it is used, a lay committee (perhaps advisory, perhaps even stronger) would be called upon to deal with the alleged exceptions since the doctors or others would in effect be appealing the outcome of chance (either natural or artificial). This lay committee would determine whether this patient was so indispensable at this time and place that he had to be saved even by sacrificing the values preserved by random selection. It would make it quite clear that exception is warranted, if at all, only as the "lesser of two evils." Such a defense would be recognized only rarely, if ever, primarily because chance and randomness preserve so many important moral and nonmoral values in SLMR cases.

Notes

1. George Bernard Shaw, *The Doctor's Dilemma* (New York, 1941), pp. 132–133.

2. Henry K. Beecher, "Scarce Resources and Medical Advancement," *Daedalus* (Spring 1969), pp. 279–280.

3. Leo Shatin, "Medical Care and the Social Worth of a Man," *American Journal of Orthopsychiatry,* 36 (1967), 97.

4. Harry S. Abram and Walter Wadlington, "Selection of Patients for Artificial and Transplanted Organs," *Annals of Internal Medicine,* 69 (September 1968), 615–620.5.

5. *United States* v. *Holmes* Fed Cas 360 (C.C.E.D. Pa 1842). All references are to the text of the trial as reprinted in Philip E. Davis, ed. *Moral Duty and Legal Responsibility: A Philosophical-Legal Casebook* (New York, 1966), pp. 102–118.

6. Edmund Cahn, *The Moral Decision* (Bloomington, Ind., 1955) p. 71.

7. I am excluding from consideration the question of the ability to pay because most of the people involved have to secure funds from other sources, public or private, anyway.

8. Joseph Fletcher, "Donor Nephrectomies and Moral Responsibility," *Journal of the American Medical Women's Association,* 23 (Dec. 1968), p. 1090.

9. Leo Shatin, op. cit., pp. 96–101.

10. For a discussion of the Seattle selection committee, see Shana Alexander, "They Decide Who Lives, Who Dies," *Life,* 53 (Nov. 9, 1962), 102. For an examination of general selection practices in dialysis see "Scarce Medical Resources," *Columbia Law Review* 69:620 (1969) and Harry S. Abram and Walter Wadlington, op. cit.

11. David Sanders and Jesse Dukeminier, Jr., "Medical Advance and Legal Lag: Hemodialysis and Kidney Transplantation," *UCLA Law Review* 15:367 (1968), 378.

12. "Letters and Comments," *Annals of Internal Medicine,* 61 (Aug. 1964), 360. Dr. G. E. Schreiner contends that "if you really believe in the right of society to make decisions on medical availability on these criteria you should be logical and say that when a man stops going to church or is divorced or loses his job, he ought to be removed from the programme and somebody else who fulfills these criteria substituted. Obviously no one faces up to this logical consequence." (G. E. W. Wolstenholme and Maeve O'Connor, ed. *Ethics in Medical Progress: With Special Reference to Transplantation,* A Ciba Foundation Symposium [Boston, 1966], p. 127.)

13. Helmut Thielicke, "The Doctor as Judge of Who Shall Live and Who Shall Die," *Who Shall Live?* ed. Kenneth Vaux (Philadelphia, 1970), p. 172.

14. Ibid., pp. 173–174.

15. Ibid., p. 173.

16. Thielicke, *Theological Ethics,* Vol. I, *Foundations* (Philadelphia, 1966), p. 602.

17. Cahn, op. cit., p. 71.

18. Paul Freund, "Introduction," *Daedalus* (Spring 1969), xiii.

19. Paul Ramsey, *Nine Modern Moralists* (Englewood Cliffs, N.J., 1961), p. 245.

20. Charles Fried, "Privacy," in *Law, Reason, and Justice,* ed. Graham Hughes (New York, 1969), p. 52.

21. My argument is greatly dependent on John Rawls's version of justice as fairness, which is a reinterpretation of social contract theory. Rawls, however, would probably not apply his ideas to "borderline situations." See "Distributive Justice: Some Addenda," Natural Law Forum, 13 (1968), 53. For Rawls's general theory, see "Justice as Fairness," Philosophy, Politics and Society (Second

Series), ed. by Peter Laslett and W. G. Runciman (Oxford, 1962), pp. 132–157 and his other essays on aspects of this topic.

22. [Nicholas Rescher, "The Allocation of Exotic Medical Lifesaving Therapy," *Ethics* 79 (1969): 173–180.]

23. Harry S. Abram, M.D., "The Psychiatrist, the Treatment of Chronic Renal Failure, and the Prolongation of Life: II" *American Journal of Psychiatry* 126:157–167 (1969), 158.

Suggested Further Reading

Basson, Marc D., "Choosing Among Candidates for Scarce Medical Resources," *Journal of Medicine and Philosophy*, 4 (September 1979).

Fein, Rashi, "On Achieving Access and Equity in Health Care," *Milbank Memorial Fund Quarterly/Health and Society*, 50 (October 1972), 157–90.

Kilmer, John F., "A Moral Allocation of Scarce Lifesaving Medical Resources," *The Journal of Religious Ethics*, 9, no. 2 (Fall 1981), 245–85.

Rescher, Nicholas P., "The Allocation of Exotic Medical Lifesaving Therapy," *Ethics*, 79, no. 3 (April 1969), 173–86.

DECISION SCENARIO 5

Allocation of Scarce Medical Resources

John and his friend Mary, both 20 and in good health, had mistakenly eaten a poisonous mushroom after a foraging expedition. They went to the emergency room, where Dr. Lee discovered acute gastrointestinal inflammation, nausea, and vertigo. After speaking with the regional Poison Control Center, he placed them in the last two beds of the small hospital's intensive care unit (ICU).

Professor Harrington, a micologist at the local college, confirmed the fact that John and Mary ate a species of *Amanita*, known for its lethal properties. He explained that the patient initially feels better but that the toxin works its deadly effects on the liver and kidney function. Just as the patient feels well again, these functions collapse in a catastrophic fashion. Dr. Lee placed both of them on intravenous penicillin and cortisone, and monitored their vital signs continuously. The ICU nursing staff objected to having two young people, in apparent good health, occupy beds on an already overcrowded floor.

Just at the time of the expected crisis, two elderly emphysema patients arrived at the hospital. Physicians determined that their condition might require artificial respiration, available only in the ICU. Both had had long histories of hospitalization for the illness, wherein it proved difficult to wean each from the respirator.

Dr. Lee tries to treat the two new patients without resorting to the ICU. At the same time, he checks John and Mary, who feel fine and are engaged in a lively conversation. When he returns to the emphysema patients, both are increasingly lethargic. It is obvious to Dr. Lee that they are in respiratory failure and will probably die before the night is out unless attached to a respirator. The ICU nursing staff is vociferously pressing for removing John and Mary immediately. When Dr. Lee looks at the kidney monitor, there is a small, possibly insignificant, decrease in function.

Questions

1. Should Dr. Lee give away John and Mary's beds in the ICU?

2. How much of a consideration ought the two emphysema patients' hospital history be? What is the difference in the medical and the moral factors in deciding who should have the ICU beds?

3. Is "first-come, first-served" a valid rule of jus-tice when it comes to the utilization of scarce medical resources? Are there better rules?

4. What is the moral basis for a prioritizing of life when not everyone can be saved?

5. Dr. Lee was much less familiar with the medical facts of mushroom toxins than with those of emphysema. Should this make a difference in his decision?

GLOSSARY FOR UNIT II

HEALTH CARE

active euthanasia. An act of commission or omission which intends to bring about the death of a person whose wish is to be relieved of incurable suffering or the hopelessness of illness.

amniocentesis. The technique of analyzing a sample of amniotic fluid (which surrounds the developing fetus) to discover aspects of and defects in the chromosomal makeup of the fetus.

brain death. As defined by the President's Commission, whole brain death regards "the cessation of the vital functions of the entire brain—and not merely portions thereof," such as the cognitive functions—as the basis of a person's death.

consent. A person's voluntary agreement to undergo a procedure, treatment, or process; it involves the aspects of (1) absence of coercion, (2) freedom of information, and (3) competency.

dangerousness. The prediction of high risk in the consequences of one's action, to self or others, which may allow an infringement of one's right to privacy.

Down's syndrome. Also called *mongolism,* a chromosomal defect detectable by amniocentesis and characterized by certain physical features, a lower IQ, and a decreased life expectancy.

experimentation. Undertaking a procedure or treatment whose primary intent is to further research, and which, if performed with human subjects, may or may not promote health (therapeutic or nontherapeutic experimentation, respectively).

genetic engineering. The use of methods of chromosomal recombination to produce life forms having certain desired characteristics.

infanticide. The killing of infants, which, according to some thinkers, is not different morally from abortion.

Nuremberg Code. A code developed at the Nuremberg War Tribunals to specify criteria for morally acceptable experimentation with human subjects.

privacy. A fundamental right which a person holds to have his or her dignity respected by others and access to information about his or her person limited strictly by informed consent.

quality of life. A measure of a patient's ability to function as a person who communicates with others, has consciousness, responds to the environment, and is cognitively intact.

risk disclosure. Making information available to a patient or potential subject of an experiment which allows him or her to form a judgment about whether to consent to the anticipated action or treatment.

Roe **v.** *Wade.* The United States Supreme Court decision (1973) which held it unconstitutional for a state to have laws prohibiting the abortion of a previable fetus.

sanctity of life. The religious view which

166

holds that life in all forms is an object of reverence and therefore ought not to be harmed or destroyed.

selective abortion. The aborting of a fetus shown by prenatal testing to have a significant abnormality or defect.

treatability. The medical judgment that an injury or illness will respond to procedures intended to restore health.

voluntary commitment. A patient's willing consent to be confined to a mental institution for the purpose of treatment or for fear of the dangerousness of his or her condition.

ETHICS IN BUSINESS, INDUSTRY, AND TECHNOLOGY

Ethics in business is a subject that often meets with skepticism. People claim that ordinary moral standards are irrelevant in the business world. On this view, businesspeople have a special obligation to pursue corporate profits, and that obligation legitimizes actions otherwise unacceptable. Similar claims are made for other professionals. Lawyers, for example, are said to have a special obligation of client advocacy and physicians a special obligation to protect patients' health. In each case, professionalism is invoked to provide a form of moral license superseding the usual standards for ethical behavior.

Does acting in a professional role exempt one from ordinary moral rules? The question recurs throughout the field of professional ethics. Businesspeople seem particularly prone to claim professional exemption from ethical standards. Assessing that claim requires us to weigh several competing values and interests. Suppose, for example, that a corporation proposes to build a factory which will provided needed jobs and products but will also pollute neighboring water-

ways. The company's interest lies in its projected profits. Creation of new jobs serves the interests of workers, their families, and the surrounding community. Consumers benefit from the availability of new products. At the same time, society has an interest in protecting the environment. Even a brief examination of the project reveals the diversity of interests at stake and makes it difficult to accept the notion of decision-making based solely on profit considerations. Businesspeople have substantial obligations to employers and shareholders, but they also have duties as members of a wider moral community. To disregard the latter requires strong justification. We will consider some proposed justifications in this unit.

The unit is divided into four chapters. Chapter 10 focuses on ethical issues arising within corporations. Sections include Hiring, Firing, and Pay Practices, Quality of Life for Employees, and Employee Obligations. What moral rules ought to govern the relations between employers and employees? What are the nature and scope of each party's responsibilities in the relationship? Is whistleblowing justified and, if so, under what circumstances? Is affirmative action an appropriate way to ensure fair employment opportunity?

In Chapter 11 we examine moral issues arising from the relations between business organizations and external constituencies. The section on Buyers' Rights and Sellers' Obligations concerns business's dealings with consumers. What obligations does a corporation owe to its customers? What sort of advertising and marketing practices are acceptable? What is the best means to ensure product safety? The second section discusses Environmental Responsibilities of Business. Should corporations share the costs of repairing ecological damage? How can the benefits of a clean environment be measured against the costs? Section 3 concerns International Responsibility. Critics charge that multinational corporations unfairly exploit Third World countries. Business spokespersons reply that expanding markets and developing resources abroad are justified and benefit developing nations as well as corporations.

In the fourth section of Chapter 11 we examine the Social Responsibility of Business. Conflicts exist between those who view business as having a strictly economic function and others who advocate broader social responsibility for corporations. The conflict can be seen as an extension of the argument raised at the start of this introduction. If business's role is purely economic, it would have no obligation to further or protect any outside interests. By the same token, if a businessperson's paramount obligation is to serve the corporation, he or she is warranted in ignoring the normal rules of ethical conduct. Without a commitment to moral purposes beyond the requirements of economic gain, business ethics has no substantive meaning.

Many moral concerns of the 1980s are the result of technological development. The extraordinary changes in areas such as information technology, nuclear and space technology, medical technology and bioengi-

neering, and agricultural and industrial techniques have troubling ethical dimensions. Critics warn that technological innovation is not synonymous with progress. They question the direction of technological development and call for greater social controls. Proponents, on the other hand, insist that anxiety and pessimism are unwarranted. They point to the many benefits of technology in extending and enhancing human life. The controversy reflects the ambivalence felt by many people: while they enjoy technology's comforts and pleasures, they remain uneasy about the problems it creates.

Unit II outlined some of the moral problems connected with health care technology. Chapter 12 of this unit focuses on ethical dilemmas in three other areas of technology. Information Technology—the so-called "computer revolution"—is the subject of the first section. Some ethical problems associated with computers, such as computer crime and the displacement of workers by automation, are not peculiar to the new technology and require no special analysis. Stealing data from a computer is morally equivalent to other forms of theft. Similarly, loss of jobs due to improved machinery is a long-standing issue in employer–employee relations.

Special problems in information technology include the question of accountability for computer errors and the loss of personal privacy due to computerized record-keeping. Who should be liable for harm resulting from computer errors: the user or the program designer? Does large-scale record-keeping by organizations using computers threaten individual privacy? If so, what controls are needed? Another area of concern is the effect of computer technology on the distribution of power. Some theorists believe that the use of computers favors decentralization of power. Others insist that government use will lead to further centralization.

Ethical issues in Military and Space Technology, the subject of section 2, arise on two levels. The first involves questions of national policy. The second concerns individual participation in the defense industry. What is the best way to ensure peace and reduce the threat of nuclear catastrophe? How can professionals justify their involvement in weapons work?

In the third section we consider Gene-Splicing Technology or bioengineering, a subject of recent intense controversy. In 1987 the U.S. Patent Office ruled that higher life forms, including mammals, could be patented. This ruling prompted a new round of debate about recombinant DNA technology. Particular concern is expressed about the possibility of genetically altering human beings. Critics argue that gene-splicing technology is dangerous and should be banned. Proponents insist that risks are overestimated and that research discoveries promise many benefits.

Chapter 13 outlines the ethical issues of The Technologist's Role. The first section deals with moral responsibilities of professionals whose work is experimental. The need to obtain informed consent is acknowledged in medical research and the health care professions. Theorists suggest that engineers and other technologists should also recognize the experimental character of their work and secure informed consent from persons affected by it. It is further argued that a professional obligation exists to protect the health and safety of those affected by technological projects and products.

The final section, Which Technology Is Appropriate?, examines the outgrowth of widespread concern about the dangers and problems of rapid technological development. Among its central values are self-sufficiency, decentralization, nonalienating work, cultural diversity, and individual freedom. Critics argue that organizing principles like decentralization and self-sufficiency are impractical or undesirable in many instances. They suggest that the goals of Appropriate Technology require further analysis and clarification. Despite these criticisms, the movement represents an ethical response to technological concerns that deserves consideration.

10. ISSUES IN INTERNAL CORPORATE RELATIONS

1. HIRING, FIRING, AND PAY PRACTICES

The relations between a corporation and the people it employs give rise to several ethical concerns. Does a corporation have moral responsibilities toward its workers? If so, what are the nature and scope of those responsibilities? What are the moral aspects of corporate actions regarding hiring, payment, promotion, disciplining, and firing of employees?

The traditional model of employer–employee relations stressed the company's obligation to pay a fair wage and the worker's duty to be obedient, loyal, and efficient. An employee's rights were generally limited to those specified in the work contract. Most of the rights involved wages, hours, pension benefits, job description, and similar matters. If an employee was dissatisfied with the terms of the contract or with the company's treatment, he or she could resign. By the same token, an employer could fire a worker for any reason, or for no specified reason. Such a model implies that both parties to a work contract have equal freedom to accept or reject its terms. However, since it is often easier for employers to find workers than for a worker to find a job, some argue that the balance of power is tipped in favor of the corporation, with employees retaining little control over the conditions of their working life.

In the areas of hiring, firing, discipline, promotion, and payment practices, ethical questions center on fair treatment of workers. Policies are generally thought to be fair if they apply equally to all individuals with similar qualifications and are based strictly on job performance and job-related qualifications. Corporations today are subject to a variety of government regulations concerning minimum wages, maximum hours, safety conditions, and discriminatory hiring, firing, and promotion policies. Despite these safeguards, many still challenge the fairness of corporate policies and actions toward employees.

What constitutes a fair wage, and how should pay scales be established? Are some forms of labor intrinsically more valuable to society and thus deserving of greater compensation? Do workers have a right to due process and the demonstration of just cause in the areas of discipline and firing? Does a corporation have an obligation to mitigate the harmful effects a worker may suffer from being laid off or fired? The answers depend on how one views the social responsibility of corporations. Some theorists believe that the primary responsibility of business is to operate efficiently so as to maximize profits. Others insist that business must serve wider social and public functions. The conflict over social responsibility is common to many areas of business ethics.

It has been suggested that employees should be given more extensive and explicit rights, comparable to the civil rights guaranteed by the Constitution to protect citizens from abuses of governmental power. Proponents of this view maintain that the power of many large corporations is so great that employees require formal legal protection of their rights. Opponents argue that establishing such rights for employees unnecessarily restricts the freedom of private enterprise, lowers efficiency, and raises production costs, resulting in higher prices to consumers. They maintain that no widespread demand by workers or by labor unions exists for more extensive rights in the workplace.

One of the most controversial issues of recent years is the establishment of laws and government programs to ensure fair treatment for women and minority group members in employment. The Civil Rights Act of 1964 prohibited discrimination on the basis of race, color, religion, sex, or national origin and established the Equal Employment Opportunity Commission to enforce compliance with the law. In the early 1970s the federal government went a step further in the effort to promote equal employment opportunities and instituted an *affirmative action* program. Advocates of affirmative action insist that mere "passive nondiscrimination" by business is insufficient to correct past and present injustices. Affirmative action requires businesses to take positive measures to promote the hiring of persons from groups suffering from past discrimination. Measures include wider advertising of employment opportunities and searches for job candidates from disadvantaged or underemployed groups. An additional mechanism for ending job discrimination is the *preferential hiring* of women and minorities. This involves selecting a candidate from a disadvantaged group over another candidate with similar (or in some instances, better) qualifications. Affirmative action and preferential hiring are sometimes thought to be synonymous, but that is not the case.

Those who support preferential hiring programs often appeal to principles of *com-pensatory justice*. On this view, preferential treatment for women and minorities is justified because they have been and continue to be victims of discrimination and are thus entitled to compensation. Opponents of preferential treatment claim that the programs are themselves discriminatory and that they compound the problems of past injustices by adding further injustice. They argue that corporations, in an effort to comply with affirmative action guidelines, sometimes practice "*reverse discrimination*" against qualified job candidates such as white males. Critics further argue that policies that involve discrimination of any kind (whether reverse or otherwise) cannot in the long run advance the goal of a fair society in which none are discriminated against.

In the first article that follows, Judith Jarvis Thomson argues that compensatory justice requires the adoption of preferential hiring policies which favor those who have been denied a fair opportunity for work. Thomson acknowledges that the policies may discriminate against young white males and deprive them of equal consideration, even if they have not personally violated the rights of minority group members. Nonetheless, she argues, since young white males as a group have benefited either directly or indirectly from previous unjust practices, it is not inappropriate for them to bear the burden of compensation.

In the second article Lisa H. Newton argues that if discriminating against blacks or women in employment is wrong, then it is also wrong to discriminate in their favor with preferential hiring programs. The author maintains that both practices undermine the principle of equality for all citizens under the law. Newton also challenges the claim that reverse discrimination is justified as a way of compensating victims of discrimination. She argues that legal restitution can be made only to persons whose legal rights have been violated and that "restitution for a disadvantaged group whose grievance is that there was no law to protect them simply is not [possible]." The reader will note that while Thomson stresses the positive aspects of practices she terms "preferential hiring," Newton uses the term "reverse discrimination" to emphasize the negative character of similar practices.

JUDITH JARVIS THOMSON

Preferential Hiring

Many people are inclined to think preferential hiring an obvious injustice.[1] I should have said "feel" rather than "think": it seems to me the matter has not been carefully thought out, and that what is in question, really, is a gut reaction.

I am going to deal with only a very limited range of preferential hirings: that is, I am concerned with cases in which several candidates present themselves for a job, in which the hiring officer finds, on examination, that all are equally qualified to hold that job, and he then straightway declares for the black, or for the woman, because he or she *is* a black man or woman. And I shall talk only of hiring decisions in the universities, partly because I am most familiar with them, partly because it is in the universities that the most vocal and articulate opposition to preferential hiring is now heard—not surprisingly, perhaps, since no one is more vocal and articulate than a university professor who feels deprived of his rights.

I suspect that some people may say, Oh well, in *that* kind of case it's all right, what we object to is preferring the less qualified to the better qualified. Or again, What we object to is refusing even to consider the qualifications of white males. I shall say nothing at all about these things. I think that the argument I shall give for saying that preferential hiring is not unjust in the cases I do concentrate on can also be appealed to to justify it outside that range of cases. But I won't draw any conclu-

sions about cases outside it. Many people do have that gut reaction I mentioned against preferential hiring in *any* degree or form; and it seems to me worthwhile bringing out that there is good reason to think they are wrong to have it. Nothing I say will be in the slightest degree novel or original. It will, I hope, be enough to set the relevant issues out clearly.

I

But first, something should be said about qualifications.

I said I would consider only cases in which the several candidates who present themselves for the job are equally qualified to hold it; and there plainly are difficulties in the way of saying precisely how this is to be established, and even what is to be established. Strictly academic qualifications seem at a first glance to be relatively straightforward: the hiring officer must see if the candidates have done equally well in courses (both courses they took, and any they taught), and if they are recommended equally strongly by their teachers, and if the work they submit for consideration is equally good. There is no denying that even these things are less easy to establish than first appears: for example, you may have a suspicion that Professor Smith is given to exaggeration, and that his "great student" is in fact less strong than Professor Jones's "good student"—but do you *know* that this is so? But there is a more serious diffi-

Judith Jarvis Thomson, "Preferential Hiring," *Philosophy and Public Affairs 2*, no. 4 (Summer 1973), 364–384. Copyright © 1973 by Princeton University Press. Reprinted by permission of Princeton University Press.

culty still: as blacks and women have been saying, strictly academic indicators may themselves be skewed by prejudice. My impression is that women, white and black, may possibly suffer more from this than black males. A black male who is discouraged or down-graded for being black is discouraged or down-graded out of dislike, repulsion, a desire to avoid contact; and I suspect that there are very few teachers nowadays who allow themselves to feel such things, or, if they do feel them, to act on them. A woman who is discouraged or down-graded for being a woman is not discouraged or down-graded out of dislike, but out of a conviction she is not serious.

II

Suppose two candidates for a civil service job have equally good test scores, but that there is only one job available. We could decide between them by coin-tossing. But in fact we do allow for declaring for A straightway, where A is a veteran, and B is not.[2] It may be that B is a nonveteran through no fault of his own: perhaps he was refused induction for flat feet, or a heart murmur. That is, those things in virtue of which B is a nonveteran may be things which it was no more in his power to control or change than it is in anyone's power to control or change the color of his skin. Yet the fact is that B is not a veteran and A is. On the assumption that the veteran has served his country,[3] the country owes him something. And it seems plain that giving him preference is a not unjust way in which part of that debt of gratitude can be paid.

And now, finally, we should turn to those debts which are incurred by one who wrongs another. It is here we find what seems to me the most powerful argument for the conclusion that the preferential hiring of blacks and women is not unjust.

I obviously cannot claim any novelty for this argument: it's a very familiar one. Indeed, not merely is it familiar, but so are a battery of objections to it. It may be granted that if we have wronged A, we owe him something: we

should make amends, we should compensate him for the wrong done him. It may even be granted that if we have wronged A, we must make amends, that justice requires it, and that a failure to make amends is not merely callousness, but injustice. But (a) are the young blacks and women who are amongst the current applicants for university jobs amongst the blacks and women who were wronged? To turn to particular cases, it might happen that the black applicant is middle class, son of professionals, and has had the very best in private schooling; or that the woman applicant is plainly the product of feminist upbringing and encouragement. Is it proper, much less required, that the black or woman be given preference over a white male who grew up in poverty, and has to make his own way and earn his encouragements? Again, (b), did we, the current members of the community, wrong any blacks or women? Lots of people once did; but then isn't it for them to do the compensating? That is, if they're still alive. For presumably nobody now alive owned any slaves, and perhaps nobody now alive voted against women's suffrage. And (c) what if the white male applicant for the job has never in any degree wronged any blacks or women? If so, *he* doesn't owe any debts to them, so why should *he* make amends to them?

These objections seem to me quite wrong-headed.

Obviously the situation for blacks and women is better than it was a hundred and fifty, fifty, twenty-five years ago. But it is absurd to suppose that the young blacks and women now of an age to apply for jobs have not been wronged. Large-scale, blatant, overt wrongs have presumably disappeared; but it is only within the last twenty-five years (perhaps the last ten years in the case of women) that it has become at all widely agreed in this country that blacks and women must be recognized as having, not merely this or that particular right normally recognized as belonging to white males, but all of the rights and respect which go with full membership in the community. Even young blacks and women have lived through down-grading for being black or female: they have not merely not been given that very equal chance at the benefits generated by what the community owns which is so firmly insisted on for white males, they have not until lately even been felt to have a right to it.

And even those who were not themselves down-graded for being black or female have suffered the consequences of the down-grading of other blacks and women: lack of self-confidence, and lack of self-respect. For where a community accepts that a person's being black, or being a woman, are right and proper grounds for denying that person full membership in the community, it can hardly be supposed that any but the most extraordinarily independent black or woman will escape self-doubt. All but the most extraordinarily independent of them have had to work harder—if only against self-doubt—than all but the most deprived white males, in the competition for a place amongst the best qualified.

If any black or woman has been unjustly deprived of what he or she has a right to, then of course justice does call for making amends. But what of the blacks and women who haven't actually been deprived of what they have a right to, but only made to suffer the consequences of injustice to other blacks and women? *Perhaps* justice doesn't require making amends to them as well; but common decency certainly does. To fail, at the very least, to make what counts as public apology to all, and to take positive steps to show that it is sincerely meant, is, if not injustice, then anyway a fault at least as serious as ingratitude.

Opting for a policy of preferential hiring may of course mean that some black or woman is preferred to some white male who as a matter of fact has had a harder life than the black or woman. But so may opting for a policy of veterans' preference mean that a healthy, unscarred, middle class veteran is preferred to a poor, struggling, scarred, non-veteran. Indeed, opting for a policy of settling who gets the job by having all equally qualified candidates draw straws may also mean

that in a given case the candidate with the hardest life loses out. Opting for any policy other than hard-life preference may have this result.

I have no objection to anyone's arguing that it is precisely hard-life preference that we ought to opt for. If all, or anyway all of the equally qualified, have a right to an equal chance, then the argument would have to draw attention to something sufficiently powerful to override that right. But perhaps this could be done along the lines I followed in the case of blacks and women: perhaps it could be successfully argued that we have wronged those who have had hard lives, and therefore owe it to them to make amends. And then we should have in more extreme form a difficulty already present: how are these preferences to be ranked? shall we place the hard-lifers ahead of blacks? both ahead of women? and what about veterans? I leave these questions aside. My concern has been only to show that the white male applicant's right to an equal chance does not make it unjust to opt for a policy under which blacks and women are given preference. That a white male with a specially hard history may lose out under this policy cannot possibly be any objection to it, in the absence of a showing that hard-life preference is not unjust, and, more important, takes priority over preference for blacks and women.

Lastly, it should be stressed that to opt for such a policy is not to make the young white male applicants themselves make amends for any wrongs done to blacks and women. Under such a policy, no one is asked to give up a job which is already his; the job for which the white male competes isn't his, but is the community's, and it is the hiring officer who gives it to the black or woman in the community's name. Of course the white male is asked to give up his equal chance to the job. But that is not something he pays to the black or woman by way of making amends; it is something the community takes away from him in order that *it* may make amends.

Still, the community does impose a burden

on him: it is able to make amends for its wrongs only by taking something away from him, something which, after all, we are supposing he has a right to. And why should *he* pay the cost of the community's amends-making?

If there were some appropriate way in which the community could make amends to its blacks and women, some way which did not require depriving anyone of anything he has a right to, then that would be the best course of action for it to take. Or if there were anyway some way in which the costs could be shared by everyone, and not imposed entirely on the young white male job applicants, then that would be, if not best, then anyway better than opting for a policy of preferential hiring. But in fact the nature of the wrongs done is such as to make jobs the best and most suitable form of compensation. What blacks and women were denied was full membership in the community; and nothing can more appropriately make amends for that wrong than precisely what will make them feel they now finally have it. And that means jobs. Financial compensation (the cost of which could be shared equally) slips through the fingers; having a job, and discovering you do it well, yield—perhaps better than anything else—that very self-respect which blacks and women have had to do without.

But of course choosing this way of making amends means that the costs are imposed on the young white male applicants who are turned away. And so it should be noticed that it is not entirely inappropriate that those applicants should pay the costs. No doubt few, if any, have themselves, individually, done any wrongs to blacks and women. But they have profited from the wrongs the community did. Many may actually have been direct beneficiaries of policies which excluded or downgraded blacks and women—perhaps in school admissions, perhaps in access to financial aid, perhaps elsewhere; and even those who did not directly benefit in this way had, at any rate, the advantage in the competition which comes of confidence in one's full member-

ship, and of one's rights being recognized as a matter of course.

Of course it isn't only the young white male applicant for a university job who has benefited from the exclusion of blacks and women: the older white male, now comfortably tenured, also benefited, and many defenders of preferential hiring feel that he should be asked to share the costs. Well, presumably we can't demand that he give up his job, or share it. But it seems to me in place to expect the occupants of comfortable professional chairs to contribute in some way, to make some form of return to the young white male who bears the cost, and is turned away. It will have been plain that I find the outcry now heard against preferential hiring in the universities objectionable; it would also be objectionable that those of us who are now securely situated should placidly defend it, with no more than a sigh of regret for the young white male who pays for it.

III

One final word: "discrimination." I am inclined to think we so use it that if anyone is convicted of discriminating against blacks, women, white males, or what have you, then he is thereby convicted of acting unjustly. If so, and if I am right in thinking that preferential hiring in the restricted range of cases we have been looking at is *not* unjust, then we have two options: (a) we can simply reply that to opt for a policy of preferential hiring in those cases is not to opt for a policy of discriminating against white males, or (b) we can hope to get usage changed—e.g., by trying to get people to allow that there is discriminating against and discriminating against, and that some is unjust, but some is not.

Best of all, however, would be for that phrase to be avoided altogether. It's at best a blunt tool: there are all sorts of nice moral discriminations [*sic*] which one is unable to make while occupied with it. And that bluntness itself fits it to do harm: black and women are hardly likely to see through to what precisely is owed them while they are being accused of welcoming what is unjust.

Notes

1. This essay is an expanded version of a talk given at the Conference on the Liberation of Female Persons, held at North Carolina State University at Raleigh, on March 26–28, 1973, under a grant from the S & H Foundation. I am indebted to James Thomson and the members of the Society for Ethical and Legal Philosophy for criticism of an earlier draft.

2. To the best of my knowledge, the analogy between veterans' preference and the preferential hiring of blacks has been mentioned in print only by Edward T. Chase, in a Letter to the Editor, *Commentary*, February 1973.

3. Many people would reject this assumption, or perhaps accept it only selectively, for veterans of this or that particular war. I ignore this. What interests me is what follows if we make the assumption—as, of course, many other people do, more, it seems, than do not.

LISA H. NEWTON

Reverse Discrimination as Unjustified

I have heard it argued that "simple justice" requires that we favor women and blacks in employment and educational opportunities, since women and blacks were "unjustly" excluded from such opportunities for so many years in the not so distant past. It is a strange argument, an example of a possible implication of a true proposition advanced to dispute the proposition itself, like an octopus absentmindedly slicing off his head with a stray tentacle. A fatal confusion underlies this argument, a confusion fundamentally relevant to our understanding of the notion of the rule of law.

Two senses of justice and equality are involved in this confusion. The root notion of justice, progenitor of the other, is the one that Aristotle (*Nichomachean Ethics* 5.6; *Politics* 1.2; 3.1) assumes to be the foundation and proper virtue of the political association. It is the condition which free men establish among themselves when they "share a common life in order that their association bring them self-sufficiency"—the regulation of their relationships by law, and the establishment, by law, of equality before the law. Rule of law is the name and pattern of this justice; its equality stands against the inequalities—of wealth, talent, etc.—otherwise obtaining among its participants, who by virtue of that equality are called "citizens." It is an achievement—complete, or, more frequently, partial—of certain people in certain concrete situations. It is fragile and easily disrupted by powerful individuals who discover that the blind equality of rule of law is inconvenient for their interests. Despite its obvious instability, Aristotle assumed that the establishment of justice in this sense, the creation of citizenship, was a permanent possibility for men and that the resultant association of citizens was the natural home of the species. At levels below the political association, this rule-governed equality is easily found; it is exemplified by any group of children agreeing together to play a game. At the level of the political asso-

From *Ethics*, 83:4, (July 1973), 308–312. Reprinted by permission of The University of Chicago Press. A version of this paper was read at a meeting of the Society for Women in Philosophy in Amherst, Massachusetts, November 5, 1972.

ciation, the attainment of this justice is more difficult, simply because the stakes are so much higher for each participant. The equality of citizenship is not something that happens of its own accord, and without the expenditure of a fair amount of effort it will collapse into the rule of a powerful few over an apathetic many. But at least it has been achieved, at some times in some places; it is always worth trying to achieve, and eminently worth trying to maintain, wherever and to whatever degree it has been brought into being.

Aristotle's parochialism is notorious; he really did not imagine that persons other than Greeks could associate freely in justice, and the only form of association he had in mind was the Greek *polis*. With the decline of the *polis* and the shift in the center of political thought, his notion of justice underwent a change. To be exact, it ceased to represent a political type and became a moral ideal: the ideal of equality as we know it. This ideal demands that all men be included in citizenship—that one Law govern all equally, that all men regard all other men as fellow citizens, with the same guarantees, rights, and protections. Briefly, it demands that the circle of citizenship achieved by any group be extended to include the entire human race. Properly understood, its effect on our associations can be excellent: it congratulates us on our achievement of rule of law as a process of government but refuses to let us remain complacent until we have expanded the associations to include others within the ambit of the rules, as often and as far as possible. While one man is a slave, none of us may feel truly free. We are constantly prodded by this ideal to look for possible unjustifiable discrimination, for inequalities not absolutely required for the functioning of the society and advantageous to all. And after twenty centuries of pressure, not at all constant, from this ideal, it might be said that some progress has been made. To take the cases in point for this problem, we are now prepared to assert, as Aristotle would never have been, the equality of sexes and of persons of different colors. The

ambit of American citizenship, once restricted to white males of property, has been extended to include all adult free men, then all adult males including ex-slaves, then all women, The process of acquisition of full citizenship was for these groups a sporadic trail of half-measures, even now not complete; the steps on the road to full equality are marked by legislation and judicial decisions which are only recently concluded and still often not enforced. But the fact that we can now discuss the possibility of favoring such groups in hiring shows that over the area that concerns us, at least, full equality is presupposed as a basis for discussion. To that extent, they are full citizens, fully protected by the law of the land.

It is important for my argument that the moral ideal of equality be recognized as logically distinct from the condition (or virtue) of justice in the political sense. Justice in this sense exists *among* a citizenry, irrespective of the number of the populace included in that citizenry. Further, the moral ideal is parasitic upon the political virtue, for "equality" is unspecified—it means nothing until we are told in what respect that equality is to be realized. In a political context, "equality" is specified as "equal rights"—equal access to the public realm, public goods and offices, equal treatment under the law—in brief, the equality of citizenship. If citizenship is not a possibility, political equality is unintelligible. The ideal emerges as a generalization of the real condition and refers back to that condition for its content.

Now, if justice (Aristotle's justice in the political sense) is equal treatment under law for all citizens, what is injustice? Clearly, injustice is the violation of that equality, discriminating for or against a group of citizens, favoring them with special immunities and privileges or depriving them of those guaranteed to the others. When the southern employer refuses to hire blacks in white-collar jobs, when Wall Street will only hire women as secretaries with new titles, when Mississippi high schools routinely flunk all black boys above ninth grade, we have examples of injustice, and we work to restore the equality of the public realm by ensuring that equal opportunity will be provided in such cases in the future. But of course, when the employers and the schools *favor* women and blacks, the same injustice is done. Just as the previous discrimination did, this reverse discrimination violates the public equality which defines citizenship and destroys the rule of law for the areas in which these favors are granted. To the extent that we adopt a program of discrimination, reverse or otherwise, justice in the political sense is destroyed, and none of us, specifically affected or not, is a citizen, a bearer of rights—we are all petitioners for favors. And to the same extent, the ideal of equality is undermined, for it has content only where justice obtains, and by destroying justice we render the ideal meaningless. It is, then, an ironic paradox, if not a contradiction in terms, to assert that the ideal of equality justifies the violation of justice; it is as if one should argue, with William Buckley, that an ideal of humanity can justify the destruction of the human race.

Logically, the conclusion is simple enough: all discrimination is wrong prima facie because it violates justice, and that goes for reverse discrimination too. No violation of justice among the citizens may be justified (may overcome the prima facie objection) by appeal to the ideal of equality, for that ideal is logically dependent upon the notion of justice. Reverse discrimination, then, which attempts no other justification than an appeal to equality, is wrong. But let us try to make the conclusion more plausible by suggesting some of the implications of the suggested practice of reverse discrimination in employment and education. My argument will be that the problems raised there are insoluble, not only in practice but in principle.

We may argue, if we like, about what "discrimination" consists of. Do I discriminate against blacks if I admit none to my school when none of the black applicants are qualified by the tests I always give? How far must I go to root out cultural bias from my application forms and tests before I can say that I have not discriminated against those of different cultures? Can I assume that women are not strong enough to be roughnecks on my

oil rigs, or must I test them individually? But this controversy, the most popular and well-argued aspect of the issue, is not as fatal as two others which cannot be avoided: if we are regarding the blacks as a "minority" victimized by discrimination, what is a "minority"? And for any group—blacks, women, whatever—that has been discriminated against, what amount of reverse discrimination wipes out the initial discrimination? Let us grant as true that women and blacks were discriminated against, even where laws forbade such discrimination, and grant for the sake or argument that a history of discrimination must be wiped out by reverse discrimination. What follows?

First, are there other groups which have been discriminated against? For they should have the same right of restitution. What about American Indians, Chicanos, Appalachian Mountain whites, Puerto Ricans, Jews, Cajuns, and Orientals? And if these are to be included, the principle according to which we specify a "minority" is simply the criterion of "ethnic (sub) group," and we're stuck with every hyphenated American in the lower-middle class clamoring for special privileges for *his* group—and with equal justification. For be it noted, when we run down the Harvard roster, we find not only a scarcity of blacks (in comparison with the proportion in the population) but an even more striking scarcity of those second-, third-, and fourth-generation ethnics who make up the loudest voice of Middle America. Shouldn't they demand *their* share? And eventually, the WASPs will have to form their own lobby, for they too are a minority. The point is simply this: there is no "majority" in America who will not mind giving up just a bit of their rights to make room for a favored minority. There are only other minorities, each of which is discriminated against by the favoring. The initial injustice is then repeated dozens of times, and if each minority is granted the same right of restitution as the others, as entire area of rule governance is dissolved into a pushing and shoving match between self-interested groups. Each works to catch the public eye and political popularity by whatever means of advertising and power politics lend themselves to the effort, to capitalize as much as possible on temporary popularity until the restless mob picks another group to feel sorry for. Hardly an edifying spectacle, and in the long run no one can benefit: the pie is no larger—it's just that instead of setting up and enforcing rules for getting a piece, we've turned the contest into a free-for-all, requiring much more effort for no larger a reward. It would be in the interests of all the participants to reestablish an objective rule to govern the process, carefully enforced and the same for all.

Second, supposing that we do manage to agree in general that women and blacks (and all the others) have some right of restitution, some right to a privileged place in the structure of opportunities for a while; how will we know when that while is up? How much privilege is enough? When will the guilt be gone, the price paid, the balance restored? What recompense is right for centuries of exclusion? What criterion tells us when we are done? Our experience with the Civil Rights movement shows us that agreement on these terms cannot be presupposed: a process that appears to some to be going at a mad gallop into a black takeover appears to the rest of us to be at a standstill. Should a practice of reverse discrimination be adopted, we may safely predict that just as some of us begin to see ''a satisfactory start toward righting the balance,'' others of us will see that we ''have already gone too far in the other direction'' and will suggest that the discrimination ought to be reversed again. And such disagreement is inevitable, for the point is that we could not *possibly* have any criteria for evaluating the kind of recompense we have in mind. The context presumed by any discussion of restitution is the context of rule of law: law sets the rights of men and simultaneously sets the method for remedying the violation of those rights. You may exact suffering from others and/or damage payments for yourself if and only if the others have violated your rights; the suffering you have endured is not sufficient reason for them to suffer. And remedial rights exist only where there is law: primary human rights are useful guides to legislation but can-

not stand as reasons for awarding remedies for injuries sustained. But then, the context presupposed by any discussion of restitution is the context of preexistent full citizenship. No remedial rights could exist for the excluded; neither in law nor in logic does there exist a right to *sue* for a standing to sue.

From these two considerations, then, the difficulties with reverse discrimination become evident. Restitution for a disadvantaged group whose rights under the law have been violated is possible by legal means, but restitution for a disadvantaged group whose grievance is that there was no law to protect them simply is not. First, outside of the area of justice defined by the law, no sense can be made of ''the group's rights,'' for no law recognizes that group or the individuals in it, qua members, as bearers of rights (hence *any* group can constitute itself as a disadvantaged minority in some sense and demand similar restitution). Second, outside of the area of protection of law, no sense can be made of the violation of rights (hence the amount of the recompense cannot be decided by any objective criterion). For both reasons, the practice of reverse discrimination undermines the foundation of the very ideal in whose name it is advocated; it destroys justice, law, equality, and citizenship itself, and replaces them with power struggles and popularity contests.

Suggested Further Reading

Beauchamp, Tom L., ''The Justification of Reverse Discrimination in Hiring,'' in *Social Justice and Preferential Treatment*, ed. Blackstone and Heslep. Athens, Ga.: University of Georgia Press, 1977.

Blackstone, William T., ''Reverse Discrimination and Compensatory Justice,'' *Social Theory Practice*, vol. 3, no. 3, Spring 1975.

Dworkin, Ronald, ''The Rights of Allan Bakke,'' *The New York Review of Books*, 1977. Reprinted in *Contemporary Issues in Business Ethics*, ed. Joseph R. DesJardins and John J. McCall. Belmont, Cal.: Wadsworth Publishing, 1985, pp. 407–13.

DECISION SCENARIO 1

Comparable Pay

On October 14, 1986, the professors of the State University walked out on strike. The strike was unusual in that it was over the issue of equal pay for comparable work. The teachers' union agreed that women and men were entitled to receive equal pay when they held the same job, but it claimed that positions traditionally held by women paid less than those held by men.

The union was under pressure. The strike was also illegal: State workers could not, by state law, go out on strike.

The strike could be traced back to a study done in 1980 by the University Committee on the Status of Women. This committee had been formed in response to a charge by the Chancellor "to establish whether the university is in compliance with Title VI statutes," the section of the expanded Civil Rights Act dealing with the matter of comparable pay.

The committee studied the problem. It decided to use a "pairing" method to present data. Each female professor would be paired with a male counterpart who occupied a comparable position and who had similar credentials, experience, and ability. The study took two semesters to complete. Its conclusion was clear: Women in the university were not receiving comparable pay.

The results of the study were attacked by critics as misleading. They said that a more sophisticated statistical method was needed to discover the trend of disparities, and they stated that the committee's work was not valid.

Trustees of the university agreed, saying

that "the dollar value of jobs is what an employer must pay to attract and keep qualified personnel." The State Assembly also agreed. They said that taxpayer dollars should be used most efficiently and that to pay wages above the going rate was unfair to the citizens of the state.

The teachers' union had support from its national affiliate. Union leaders there pointed out the need to "fundamentally alter the marketplace because it is inherently discriminatory." They said that the study of the Committee on the Status of Women was significant because its results clearly indicated pay inequalities of the kind the committee was charged to reveal.

The university claimed it had met its obligations. When it refused to meet union demands for pay equality, the teachers' union voted to strike—even if striking was illegal.

Questions

1. Was the teachers' union correct in claiming unjust discrimination as the basis of its strike? What kind of injustice was this?

2. The university claimed that women were last hired and therefore on the job a shorter amount of time. It argued that salary disparities derived from that fact. Evaluate this argument.

3. Would the university have been justified in firing striking professors, or penalizing them in other ways?

4. Some union members objected to joining the strike. Were they morally justified in not striking?

5. Are affirmative action programs justified in terms of ethical theory?

2. QUALITY OF LIFE FOR EMPLOYEES

In addition to hiring, firing, and pay practices, other aspects of the relations between a corporation and its employees prompt ethical concern. What is the moral significance of issues such as worker health, safety, and working conditions? What is the extent of corporate responsibility for the well-being of workers? Since health is a necessary precondition for the enjoyment of most other values, protecting workers' health becomes a value of primary importance. This is especially true because exposure to occupational hazards is almost always involuntary. Although workers may enjoy the freedom to choose a particular job, it would be unfair to say that they choose job-related risks to their health or safety. Some risks are obvious, others may be subtle or hidden. As technology changes the nature of many industries, workers are exposed to new hazards (such as contact with carcinogens or other toxic substances) whose ill effects become apparent only after many years have passed.

The Occupational Safety and Health Act of 1970 was intended "to ensure so far as possible every working man and woman safe and healthful working conditions." However, implementation of the act, by the Occupational Safety and Health Administration (OSHA), has been uneven and has prompted criticism both by advocates of workers' rights (who seek greater protection for employees) and by industry representatives (who challenge the fairness of some OSHA regulations and tactics). Reagan Administration policies concerning OSHA have had the effect of reducing the agency's protective influence. For example, in 1981 the administration announced that OSHA would concentrate its efforts on certain industries known to be hazardous. The policy undermined the agency's effectiveness in at least two ways. First, it left workers in untargeted industries outside OSHA's protection, and second, it essentially removed the threat of unannounced inspections, which

had been one of OSHA's most potent weapons.

Although industry spokespersons complain that rigorous health and safety standards unnecessarily hamper the ability of corporations to compete in the marketplace, industrial accidents and work-related health problems carry a high cost to the whole society. Despite employer-paid worker compensation benefits, much of the expense of health care and compensation for lost earning power for disabled workers is borne by public resources. It seems fair, therefore, that industries responsible for harming workers' health should pay a higher share of the cost of preventing such injuries.

In addition to worker health and safety, there are other areas of ethical concern in the workplace. An example is the issue of workers' right to privacy. Certain practices such as psychological testing, polygraph testing, and testing for drug use have been challenged as invasions of employee privacy. The use of hidden cameras and bugging or monitoring devices has also been characterized as an invasion of privacy, and this practice may adversely affect employee morale as well.

Many companies attempt to influence employees' conduct outside the workplace, in areas such as civic and political activity, donations to charity, or sexual preferences and practices. Are such pressures an invasion of workers' privacy? What rights should a person retain upon assuming the role of an employee? Some argue that employees have a right to free expression of personal preferences and that corporations should not interfere with behavior not directly related to job performance. Others maintain that an employee is a company representative in the community as well as at work. On this view, companies have a legitimate interest both in curtailing actions that reflect adversely on an employer and, conversely, in promoting behavior that enhances an employer's reputation. Questions about privacy and free expression voice concern for workers' rights to autonomy and self-determination. They echo problems regarding the autonomy of clients with respect to health care and legal professionals. **[See Health Care, Chapter 5, Section 1 and Criminal Justice, Chapter 16, Section 2.]**

Another issue in employer–employee relations is workers' satisfaction in their jobs. Do employers have an obligation to provide work that is meaningful and satisfying? Studies show that worker satisfaction is a strong motivator for good job performance. In the long run a company's best interest is served by furthering satisfaction. On the other hand, efficiency of operation requires allocating tasks without regard for individual satisfaction. Assembly line work is a frequently cited example. Corporations must decide whether to place a higher value on employee satisfaction or on efficiency. A similar dilemma arises in other contexts. For example, some jobs require that employees travel extensively, absenting themselves from spouses and children. Should employers take into account the harmful effects of travel requirements on family life? Should job transfers be considered from the standpoint of detrimental impact on workers and their families? Shift changes also affect worker health, productivity, and morale. Should employers plan shift changes to conform with natural body cycles, permitting workers to sleep adequately?

In the following essay George G. Brenkert discusses the use of polygraph testing in screening prospective employees. He argues that the tests may violate privacy "even when the employer seeks the answers to legitimate questions." Brenkert maintains that the value of privacy overrides claims of employer interest advanced to justify polygraph testing.

GEORGE G. BRENKERT

Privacy, Polygraphs, and Work

The rights of prospective employees have been the subject of considerable dispute, both past and present. In recent years, this dispute has focused on the use of polygraphs to verify the claims which prospective employees make on employment application forms. With employee theft supposedly amounting to approximately ten billion dollars a year, with numerous businesses suffering sizeable losses and even being forced into bankruptcy by employee theft, significant and increasing numbers of employers have turned to the use of polygraphs.[1] Their right to protect their property is in danger, they insist, and the use of the polygraph to detect and weed out the untrustworthy prospective employee is a painless, quick, economical, and legitimate way to defend this right. Critics, however, have questioned both the reliability and validity of polygraphs, as well as objected to the use of polygraphs as demeaning, affronts to human dignity, violations of self-incrimination prohibitions, expressions of employers' mistrust, and violations of privacy.[2] Though there has been a great deal of discussion of the reliability and the validity of polygraphs, there has been precious little discussion of the central moral issues at stake. Usually terms such as "dignity," "privacy," and "property rights" are simply bandied about with the hope that some favorable response will be evoked. The present paper seeks to redress this situation by discussing one important aspect of the above dispute—the supposed violation of personal privacy. Indeed, the violation of "a right to privacy" often appears to be the central moral objection to the use of polygraphs. However, the nature and basis of this claim have not yet been clearly established.[3] If they could be, there would be a serious reason to oppose the use of polygraphs on prospective employees.

I

There are three questions which must be faced in the determination of this issue. First, is the nature of the information which polygraphing seeks to verify, information which can be said to violate, or involve the violation of, a person's privacy? Second, does the use of the polygraph itself as the means to corroborate the responses of the job applicant violate the applicant's privacy? Third, even if—for either of the two preceding reasons—the polygraph does violate a person's privacy, might this violation still be justified by the appeal to more weighty reasons, e.g., the defense of property rights?

It might be maintained that only the last two questions are meaningful since "there is no such thing as violating a man's right to privacy by simply knowing something about him"[4]; rather, a violation of one's right to privacy may occur because "we have a right that certain steps shall not be taken to find out facts, and because we have a right that certain uses shall not be made of facts."[5] Thus, it is said that to torture, to extort information by threat, to spy, etc. are all illegitimate ways to obtain information. If one obtains information in these ways one violates various rights of a person—and thereby also one's right to privacy.

If this view is correct, then an employer who knows, or comes to know, certain facts about a prospective employee would not as such violate the prospective employee's right to privacy. Only the use of certain means (e.g., spying or perhaps the polygraph) or the use of these facts in certain ways would violate this privacy. Thus, there could be no violation of rights of privacy by knowing certain

information (the first question), only in the manner of obtaining it and the use of it (the second and third questions).

This view is, I believe, implausible when the (private) information concerned is intentionally sought, as it is in the case of polygraphs. In this case, it would seem, there are certain things which people (in their various roles as employers, government officials, physicians, etc.) and institutions (governments and businesses, etc.) ought not to know about individuals, however they might come to know these facts. Indeed, since they ought not to know such facts, those individuals who are the ultimate object of this knowledge may legitimately object to a violation of their rights and demand that steps should be taken to make sure that others do not come to know this information. For example, it would be wrong, however they went about it, for government officials to make it their business to know the details of the sexual practices of each particular citizen. It would be wrong, it has been claimed, for a physician to know by what means a patient intends to pay for the health care administered.[6] Finally, the following case suggests that there is information which an employer ought not to know about an employee. A warehouse manager had an employee who had confessed to a theft on the job take a polygraph test in order to determine whether others had helped him steal some of the missing goods. The employee answered "no" to each person he was asked about—and the polygraph bore him out, except in the case of one person. Each time he was asked about this person the employee would deny that he had helped him, but each time the polygraph reported a reaction indicative of lying. At last they asked him why each time they raised this person's name there was such a great physiological response. After some hesitation, the thief "took a deep breath and explained that one day a few weeks before, he had walked into the company bathroom and found the fellow in a stall masturbating." The employer's reaction suggests that such information he considered to be information he ought not to know—however he found it out:

I fired the thief, but I never said a word to the other guy. He was a good worker, and that's what counts. But I'll have to tell you this: Every time I saw him for months after that, I'd think about what the thief had told me, and I'd say to myself, "God, I don't have any right to know that."[7]

It is not implausible then that there are various kinds of information which people and institutions ought not to know about individuals.[8] Surely to torture a person to get information or to extort information by threat is to violate a person's right not to be threatened or tortured as well as his right to privacy. But one may do the latter without resorting to such exotic means. One might simply ask the person about the matter which is rightfully private. Some people are weak, gullible, easily persuaded, desirous of pleasing, overly trusting, etc., etc. They might not even know that they need not disclose certain information to this person or that institution. Thus, to hold that our right to privacy of information is violated only when other rights are violated (e.g., rights not to be threatened, or tortured) is to hold an overly positive and optimistic view of the actual condition of the people.

Is it possible then to characterize the nature of privacy such that one might know what kinds of information are rightfully private? If an employer had or sought access to that information he would be said to violate the person's right to privacy. Quite often one suspects that people take the view that information about a person is private in the above sense, if that person does not want it known by others.[9] Thus, the determination of which information is protected by a right to privacy is subjectively, individually, based—it is whatever an individual does not want to be known.

There are, however, good reasons to reject this view. Though we may intelligibly talk about the privacy a person seeks and equate this with a state of affairs he wants or seeks in which he does not share himself and/or information about himself with others, we are not thereby talking about that person's right to privacy. A person might not want passers-by to know that he is bald; he may not want his doctor to know exactly which aches and pains he has; he may not want his neighbors to know about the toxic chemicals he is burying on his land. It does not follow, however, that passers-by, one's doctor, and neighbors violate a person's right to privacy in acquiring such information. It is indeed true that control of information about oneself is important in the formation of the kinds of relationships one wants to have with other people.[10] But it does not follow from this that, just because one wants—or does not want—to have a certain relationship with another person or institution, a certain piece of information which one does not want revealed to that person or institution is therefore private—that others in acquiring it would violate one's right to privacy. In this sense, privacy is not like property which is itself merely a cluster of rights. We may, on the contrary, speak intelligibly of the privacy a person seeks apart from any right to privacy to which a person may be entitled.

On the other hand, one may want some things to be public, to be exposed to the view of all, but this may also be unjustified. The person who exposes his sexual organs at midday on a busy downtown street or makes a practice of revealing his most intimate thoughts and feelings to unconcerned strangers may be condemned not simply for the offense he causes others but also for his refusal to treat such matters as private rather than public. Perhaps the latter sounds strange. But one should recall that it was not simply the violation of the rights of others which shocked and disturbed non-members of the late 60's and early 70's youth revolt, but the apparent lack of any sense by those who partook of that revolt that, with regard to themselves, they ought to treat certain matters as private rather than public.[11] When they were not condemned for not treating certain (personal) matters as private, excuses and explanations were found for their behavior. They were said to be ethically immature or morally blind.[12] My purpose, however, is not to discuss this or any other particular instance in which privacy has been rejected, but to indicate that both an obligation to privacy and a right to privacy constitute the social institution surrounding privacy.

Accordingly, privacy must be seen as part of a complex social practice within which we must distinguish (a) privacy itself, (b), privacy as a value, (c) the right to privacy, and (d) the obligation to privacy which this social institution imposes upon individuals. Consequently, we cannot simply identify "A does not want X to be known" with "Knowledge of X violates A's right to privacy," although the former may be identical with "X is private to A." Similarly, "A wants (or does not care if) X (is) to be made public" is not to be equated with "Knowledge or exposure of X does not violate A's (obligation to) privacy." "X is private to A," "Knowledge or exposure of X violates A's right to privacy," and "Knowledge or exposure of X ought to be kept private by A" are not, therefore, the same, even though on occasion and by extension we may so treat them. To distinguish these notions I will speak of X being "simply private," X being "rightfully private," and X being "obligatorily private."

Upon what basis then, if it is not simply a personal determination, do we maintain that certain information is rightfully private, that the knowledge of it by others constitutes a violation of one's right to privacy? There are two points to make here. First, there is no piece of information about a person which is by itself rightfully private. Information about one's financial concerns may be rightfully private vis-a-vis a stranger or a neighbor, but not vis-a-vis one's banker. The nature of one's sex life may be rightfully private with regard to most people, including future employers, but not to one's psychiatrist, sex therapist, or mate. Accordingly, the right to privacy involves a three-place relation. To say that something is rightfully private is to say that A may withhold from or not share something, X, with Z. Thus to know whether some information, X, about a person or institution, A, is, or ought to be, treated as rightfully private, we must ask about the relationship in which A

stands to Z, another person or institution. Because the threefold nature of this relation is not recognized, the view which we have argued is implausible, viz., that "none of us has a right over any fact to the effect that that fact shall not be known by others,"[13] is confused with the view which is plausible, viz., that there is no piece of information about people or institutions which is in itself private. It does not follow from this latter truth that the knowing of a piece of information by some particular person or institution may not be a violation of one's right to privacy—it may or may not be depending upon who or what knows it.

Second, then, to speak of the right to privacy is to speak of the right which individuals, groups, or institutions have that access to and information about themselves is limited in certain ways by the relationships in which they exist to others. In general, the information and access to which a person or institution is entitled with regard to another person and/or institution is that information and access which will enable the former to fulfill, perform, or execute the role the person or institution plays in the particular relationship. All other access and information about the latter is beyond the pale. Thus one cannot be a friend of another unless one knows more about another and has a special access to that person. Similarly, one cannot be a person's lawyer, physician, or barber unless one is entitled to other kinds of knowledge and access. It follows that to speak of one's right to privacy is not simply to speak of one's ability to control information and access to him, since one may be unable to control such access or information acquisition and still be said to have a right to such. Similarly, to speak of one's privacy is not to speak of a claim one makes, since one may not claim or demand that others limit their access to oneself and still have a right that they do so.[14] Such a situation might occur when one is dominated or oppressed by others such that one does not insist on—or claim—the rights one is entitled to. On the other hand, one might also, in certain situations, decide not to invoke one's right to privacy and thus allow others access to oneself which the present relationship might not otherwise permit. It is in this sense that individuals can determine for themselves which others and when others have access to them and to information about them.

II

In order to determine what information might be legitimately private to an individual who seeks employment we must consider the nature of the employer/(prospective) employee relationship. The nature of this relationship depends upon the customs, conventions and rules of the society. These, of course, are in flux at any time—and particularly so in the present case. They may also need revision. Further, the nature of this relationship will depend upon its particular instances—e.g., that of the employer of five workers or of five thousand workers, the kind of work involved, etc. In essence, however, we have a complex relationship in which an employer theoretically contracts with a person(s) to perform certain services from which the employer expects to derive a certain gain for himself. In the course of the employee's performance of these services, the employer entrusts him with certain goods, money, etc.; in return for such services he delivers to the employee a certain remuneration and (perhaps) benefits. The goals of the employer and the employee are not at all, on this account, necessarily the same. The employee expects his remuneration (and benefits) even if the services, though adequately performed, do not result in the end the employer expected. Analogously, the employer expects to derive a certain gain for the services the employee has performed even if the employee is not (fully) satisfied with his work or remuneration. On the other hand, if the employer is significantly unable to achieve the ends sought through the contract with the employee, the latter may not receive his full remuneration (should the employer go bankrupt) and may even lose his job. There is, in short, a complicated mixture of trust and antagonism, connectedness and disparity of ends in the relation between employer and employee.

Given this (brief) characterization of the relationship between employer and employee, the information to which the employer qua employer is entitled about the (prospective) employee is that information which regards his possible acceptable performance of the services for which he might be hired. Without such information the employer could not fulfill the role which present society sanctions. There are two aspects of the information to which the employer is entitled given the employer/employee relationship. On the one hand, this information will relate to and vary in accordance with the services for which the person is to be hired. But in any case, it will be limited by those services and what they require. In short, one aspect of the information to which the employer is entitled is "job relevant" information. Admittedly the criterion of job relevancy is rather vague. Certainly there are few aspects of a person which might not affect his job performance—aspects including his sex life, etc. How then does the "job relevancy" criterion limit the questions asked or the information sought? It does so by limiting the information sought to that which is directly connected with the job description. If a typist is sought, it is job relevant to know whether or not a person can type—typing tests are legitimate. If a store manager is sought, it is relevant to know about his abilities to manage employees, stock, etc. That is, the description of the job is what determines the relevancy of the information to be sought. It is what gives the employer a right to know certain things about the person seeking employment. Accordingly, if a piece of information is not "job relevant" then the employer is not entitled qua employer to know it. Consequently, since sexual practices, political beliefs, associational activities, etc. are not part of the description of most jobs, that is, since they do not directly affect one's job performance, they are not legitimate information for an employer to know in the determination of the hiring of a job applicant.[15]

However, there is a second aspect to this matter. A person must be able not simply to perform a certain activity, or provide a service, but he must also be able to do it in an acceptable manner—i.e., in a manner which is approximately as efficient as others, in an honest manner, and in a manner compatible with others who seek to provide the services for which they were hired. Thus, not simply one's abilities to do a certain job are relevant, but also aspects of one's social and moral character are pertinent. A number of qualifications are needed for the purport of this claim to be clear. First, that a person must be able to work in an acceptable manner is not intended to legitimize the consideration of the prejudices of other employees. It is not legitimate to give weight in moral deliberations to the immoral and/or morally irrelevant beliefs which people hold concerning the characteristics of others. That one's present employees can work at a certain (perhaps exceptional) rate is a legitimate consideration in hiring other workers. That one's present employees have prejudices against certain religions, sexes, races, political views, etc. is not a morally legitimate consideration. Second, it is not, or should not be, the motives, beliefs, or attitudes underlying the job-relevant character traits, e.g., honest, efficient, which are pertinent, but rather the fact that a person does or does not perform according to these desirable character traits. This is not to say, it should be noted, that a person's beliefs and attitudes about the job itself, e.g., how it is best to be done, what one knows or believes about the job, etc., are irrelevant. Rather it is those beliefs, attitudes and motives underlying one's desired character traits which are not relevant. The contract of the employer with the employee is for the latter to perform acceptably certain services—it is not for the employee to have certain underlying beliefs, motives, or attitudes. If I want to buy something from someone, this commercial relation does not entitle me to probe the attitudes, motives, and

beliefs of the person beyond his own statements, record of past actions, and the observations of others. Even the used car salesman would correctly object that his right to privacy was being violated if he was required to submit to Rorschach tests, an attitude survey test, truth serums, and/or the polygraph in order to determine his real beliefs about selling cars. Accordingly, why the person acts the way in which he acts ought not to be the concern of the employer. Whether a person is a good working colleague simply because he is congenial, because his ego needs the approval of others, or because he has an oppressive superego is, in this instance, morally irrelevant. What is relevant is whether this person has, by his past actions, given some indication that he may work in a manner compatible with others.

Consequently, a great deal of the information which has been sought in preemployment screening through the use of polygraph tests has violated the privacy of individuals. Instances in which the sex lives, for example, of applicants have been probed are not difficult to find. However, privacy violations have occurred not simply in such generally atypical instances but also in standard situations. To illustrate the range of questions asked prospective employees and the violations of privacy which have occurred, we need merely consider a list of some questions which one of the more prominent polygraph firms includes in its current tests:

Have you ever taken any of the following without the advice of a doctor? If Yes, please check: Barbiturates, Speed, LSD, Tranquilizers, Amphetamines, Marijuana, Others.

In the past five years about how many times, if any, have you bet on horse races at the race track?

Do you think that policemen are honest?

Do you ever think about committing a robbery?

Have you been refused credit or a loan in the past five years?

Have you ever consulted a doctor about a mental condition?

Do you think that it is okay to get around the law if you don't actually break it?

Do you enjoy stories of successful crimes and swindles?[16]

Such questions, it follows from the above argument, are for any standard employment violations of one's right to privacy. An employer might ask if a person regularly takes certain narcotic drugs, if he is considering him for a job which requires handling narcotics. An employer might ask if a person has been convicted of a larceny, etc. But whether the person enjoys stories about successful larcenists, whether a person has ever taken any prescription drugs without the advice of a doctor, or whether a person bets on the horses should be considered violations of one's rightful privacy.

The upshot of the argument in the first two sections is, then, that some information can be considered rightfully private to an individual. Such information is rightfully private or not depending on the relationship in which a person stands to another person or institution. In the case of the employer/employee relationship, I have argued that information is rightfully private which does not relate to the acceptable performance of the activities as characterized in the job description. This excludes a good many questions which are presently asked in polygraph tests, but does not, by any means, exclude all such questions. There still remain many questions which an employer might conceivably wish to have verified by the use of the polygraph. Accordingly, I turn in the next section to the question whether the verification of the answers to legitimate questions by the use of the polygraph may be considered a violation of a person's right to privacy. If it is, then the violation obviously does not stem from the questions themselves but from the procedure, the polygraph test, whereby the answers to those questions are verified.

III

A first reason to believe that use of the polygraph occasions a violation of one's right to privacy is that, even though the questions to be answered are job relevant, some of them will occasion positive, lying reactions which are not necessarily related to any past misdeeds. Rather, the lying reaction indicated by the polygraph may be triggered because of unconscious conflicts, fears, and hostilities a person has. It may be occasioned by conscious anxieties over other past activities and observations. Thus, the lying reaction indicated by the polygraph need not positively identify actual lying or the commission of illegal activities. The point, however, is not to question the validity of the polygraph. Rather, the point is that the validity of the polygraph can only be maintained by seeking to clarify whether or not such reactions really indicate lying and the commission of past misdeeds. But this can be done only by the polygraphist further probing into the person's background and inner thoughts. However, inasmuch as the questions can no longer be restrained in this situation by job-relevancy considerations, but must explore other areas to which an employer is not necessarily entitled knowledge, to do this will violate a person's right to privacy.

It has been suggested by some polygraphists that if a person has "Something Else" on his mind other than the direct answer to the questions asked, a "something else" which might lead the polygraph to indicate a deceptive answer, the person might, if he so feels inclined,

> tell the examiner about this "outside troubling matter" . . . but as a special precaution obtain the examiner's promise that the disclosure of this information is secret and . . . request that the matter be held in strict confidence. The examiner will comply with your wishes. The examiner does not wish to enter into your personal problems since they tend to complicate the polygraph examination.[17]

What this suggests, however, is that a person go ahead, under the threat of the polygraph indicating that one is lying, and tell the polygraphist matters that are rightfully private. This is supposedly acceptable since one "requests'' that it be held in strict confidence. But it surely does not follow that a violation of one's right to privacy does not occur simply because the recipient promises not to pass the information on. If, under some threat, I tell another person something which he has no right to know about me, but I then get his promise that he will treat the information confidentially and that it will not be misused in any way, my right to privacy has still been violated.[18] Accordingly, whether the polygraphist attempts to prevent job applicants from producing misleading deceptive reactions by allowing them to reveal what else is on their minds or probes deceptive reactions once they have occurred to ascertain whether they might not be produced by job-irrelevant considerations, he violates the right to privacy of the job applicant.

A second reason why the polygraph must be said to violate a job applicant's right to privacy relates to the monitoring of a person's physiological responses to the questions posed to him. By measuring these responses, the polygraph can supposedly reveal one's mental processes. Now even though the questions posed are legitimate questions, surely a violation of one's right to privacy occurs. Just because I have something which you are entitled to see or know, it does not follow that you can use any means to fulfill that entitlement and not violate my privacy. Consider the instance of two good friends, one of whom has had some dental work done which puts him in a situation such that he can tune in the thoughts and feelings of his friend. Certain facts about, and emotional responses of, his friend—aspects which his friend (we will assume) would usually want to share with him—simply now stream into his head. Even though the friendship relation generally entitles its members to know personal information about the other person, the friend with the dental work is not entitled to such information in this direct and immediate way. This manner of gaining this information simply eliminates any private reserves of the person; it wholly opens his consciousness to the consciousness of another. Surely this would be a violation of his

friend's right to privacy, and his friend would rightfully ask that such dental work be modified. Even friends do not have a right to learn in this manner of each other's inner thoughts and feelings.

Such fancy dental work may, correctly, be said to be rather different from polygraphs. Still the point is that though one is entitled to some information about another, one is not entitled to use any means to get it. But why should the monitoring by an employer or his agent of one's physiological responses to legitimate questions be an invasion of privacy—especially if one has agreed to take the test? There are several reasons.

First, the claim that one freely agrees or consents to take the test is surely, in many cases, disingenuous.[19] Certainly a job applicant who takes the polygraph test is not physically forced or coerced into taking the exam. However, it is quite apparent that if he did not take the test and cooperate during the test, his application for employment would either not be considered at all or would be considered to have a significant negative aspect to it. This is surely but a more subtle form of coercion. And if this be the case, then one cannot say that the person has willingly allowed his reactions to the questions to be monitored. He has consented to do so, but he has consented under coercion. Had he a truly free choice, he would not have done so.

Now the whole point of the polygraph test is, of course, not simply to monitor physiological reactions but to use these responses as clues, indications, or revelations of one's mental processes and acts. The polygraph seeks to make manifest to others one's thoughts and ideas. However, unless we freely consent, we are entitled to the privacy of our thoughts, that is, we have a prima facie right not to have our thoughts exposed by others, even when the information sought is legitimate. Consider such analogous cases as a husband reading his wife's diary, a person going through a friend's desk drawers, a stranger reading personal papers on one's desk, an F.B.I. agent going through one's files. In each of these cases, a person attempts to determine the nature of someone else's thoughts by the use of clues and indications which those thoughts left behind. And, in each of these cases, though we may suppose that the person seeks to confirm answers to legitimate questions, we may also say that, if the affected person's uncoerced consent is not forthcoming, his or her right to privacy is violated. Morally, however, there is no difference between ascertaining the nature of one's thoughts by the use of a polygraph, or reading notes left in a drawer, going through one's diary, etc. Hence, unless there are overriding considerations to consent to such revelations of one's thoughts, the use of the polygraph is a violation of one's right to privacy.[20]

Second, it should be noted that even if a person voluntarily agreed to the polygraph test, it need not follow that there is not a violation of his privacy. It was argued in Section I that there are certain aspects of oneself which are obligatorily private, that is, which one ought to keep private. Accordingly, it may be wrong for one voluntarily to reveal various aspects of oneself to others, even though in so doing one would be responding to legitimate demands. For example, consider a person being interviewed by a health officer who is legitimately seeking information from the person about venereal diseases. Suppose that the person does not simply admit to having such a disease but also—instead of providing a corroborative statement from a physician—reveals the diseased organs. Further, suppose that the health officer is not shocked or offended in any way. The person has been asked legitimate questions, he has acted voluntarily, but still he has violated his own privacy. This is not the kind of access to oneself one ought to afford a bureaucrat. Now it may well be that, analogously, one ought not to allow employers access to one's physiological reactions to legitimate questions, for the reason that such access also violates one's obligatory privacy. To act in this way sets a bad precedent, it signifies that those with power and authority may disregard the privacy of an individual in order to achieve aims of their own. Thus, even if a job applicant readily agreed to

reveal certain aspects of himself in a polygraph test, it would not follow without more argument that he was not violating his own privacy.

Finally, if we value privacy not simply as a barrier to the intrusion of others but also as the way by which we define ourselves as separate, autonomous persons, individuals with an integrity which lies at least in part in the ability to make decisions, to give or withhold information and access, then the polygraph strikes at this fundamental value.[21] The polygraph operates by turning part of us over which we have little or no control against the rest of us. If a person were an accomplished yogi, the polygraph would supposedly be useless—since that person's physiological reactions would be fully under his control. The polygraph works because most of us do not have that control. Thus, the polygraph is used to probe people's reactions which they would otherwise protect, not expose to others. It uses part of us to reveal the rest of us. It takes the "shadows" consciousness throws off within us and reproduces them for other people. As such, the use of the polygraph undercuts the decision-making aspect of a person. It circumvents the person. The person says such and such, but his uncontrolled reactions may say something different. He does not know—even when honest—what his reactions might say. Thus it undercuts and demeans that way by which we define ourselves as autonomous persons—in short, it violates our privacy. Suppose one said something to another—but his Siamese and undetached twin, who was given to absolute truth and who correctly knew every thought, past action, and feeling of the person said, "No, he does not really believe that." I think the person would rightfully complain that his twin had better remain silent. Just so, I have a right to complain when my feelings are turned on me. This subtle form of self-incrimination is a form of invading one's privacy. An employer is entitled to know certain facts about one's background, but this relationship does not entitle him—or his agents—to probe one's emotional responses, feelings, and thoughts.

Thus, it follows that even if the only questions asked in a polygraph test are legitimate ones, the use of the polygraph for the screening of job applicants still violates one's privacy. In this case, the violation of privacy stems from the procedure itself, and not the questions. Accordingly, one can see the lameness of the defense of polygraphing which maintains that if a person has nothing to hide, he should not object to the polygraph tests. Such a defense is mistaken at least on two counts. First, just because someone believes something to be private does not mean that he believes that what is private is wrong, something to be ashamed about or to be hidden. Second, the polygraph test has been shown to violate a person's privacy, whether one person has really something to hide or not—whether he is dishonest or not. Consequently, if the question is simply whether polygraphing of prospective employees violates their privacy the answer must be affirmative.

IV

There remains one possible defense of the use of polygraphs for screening prospective employees. This is to admit that such tests violate the applicant's privacy but to maintain that other considerations outweigh this fact. Specifically, in light of the great amount of merchandise and money stolen, the right of the employers to defend their property outweighs the privacy of the applicant. This defense is specious, I believe, and the following arguments seek to show why.

First, surely it would be better if people who steal or are dishonest were not placed in positions of trust. And if the polygraphs were used in only these cases, one might well maintain that the use of the polygraph, though it violates one's privacy, is legitimate and justified. However, the polygraph cannot be so used, obviously, only in these cases—it must be used more broadly on both honest and dishonest applicants. Further, if a polygraph has a 90% validity then out of 1,000 interviewees, a full 100 would be misidentified.[22] Now if

10% of the interviewees are thieves, then 10 out of the 100 will steal, but 90 would not; in addition 90 out of the 900 would be thieves, and supposedly correctly identified. This means that 90 thieves would be correctly identified, 10 thieves would be missed, and 90 honest people would be said not to have cleared the test. Thus, for every thief "caught," one honest person would also be "caught"—the former would be correctly identified as one who would steal, while the latter could not be cleared of the suspicion that he too would steal. The point, then, is that this means of defending property rights is one that excludes not simply thieves but honest people as well— and potentially in equal numbers. Such a procedure certainly appears to constitute not simply a violation of privacy rights, but also, and more gravely, an injustice to those honest people stigmatized as not beyond suspicion and hobbled in their competition with others to get employment. If then using polygraph tests to defend property rights is not simply like preventing a thief from breaking into the safe, but more like keeping a thief from the safe plus binding the leg of an innocent bystander in his competition with others to gain employment, then one may legitimately doubt that this procedure to protect property rights is indeed defensible.[23]

Second, it has been claimed that just as the use of blood tests on suspected drunken drivers and the use of baggage searches at the airport are legitimate, so too is the polygraphing of prospective employees. Both of the former kinds of searches may also be said to violate a person's privacy; still they are taken to be justified whether the appeal is to the general good they produce or to the protection of the rights of other drivers or passengers and airline employees. However, neither the blood test nor the baggage search is really analogous to the use of the polygraph on job applicants. Blood tests are only administered to those drivers who have given police officers reason to believe that they (the drivers) are driving while under the influence of alcohol. The polygraph, however, is not applied only to those suspected of past thefts; it is applied to others as well. Further, the connection between driving while drunk and car accidents is quite direct; it immediately endangers both the safety and lives of others. The connection between polygraph tests of a diverse group of applicants (some honest and some dishonest) and future theft is not nearly so direct nor do the thefts endanger the lives of others. Baggage searches are a different matter. They are similar to polygraphing in that they are required of everyone. They are dissimilar in that they are made because of fears concerning the safety of other people. Further, surely there is a dissimilarity between officials searching one's baggage for lethal objects which one is presently trying to sneak on board, and employers searching one's mind for the true nature of one's past behavior which may or may not lead to future criminal intentions. Finally, there are signs at airports warning people, before they are searched, against carrying weapons on airplanes; such weapons could at that time be declared and sent, without prejudice, with the regular baggage. There is no similar aspect to polygraph tests. Thus, the analogies suggested do not hold. Indeed, they suggest that we allow for a violation of privacy only in very different circumstances than those surrounding the polygraphing of job applicants.

Third, the corporate defense of polygraphs seems one-sided in the sense that employers would not really desire the universalization of their demands. Suppose that the businesses in a certain industry are trying to get a new government contract. The government, however, has had difficulties with other corporations breaking the rules of other contracts. As a result it has lost large sums of money. In order to prevent this in the present case it says that it is going to set up devices to monitor the reactions of board members and top managers when a questionnaire is sent to them which they must answer. Any business, of course, need not agree to this procedure but if it does then it will be noted in their file regarding this and future government contracts. The questionnaire will include questions about the corporations' past fulfillment of contracts, competency to fulfill the present contract, loopholes used in past contracts, collusion with other companies, etc. The reactions of the managers and board members, as they respond to these questions, will be monitored and a decision on the worthiness of that corporation to receive the contract will be made in part on this basis.

There can be little doubt, I think, that the management and directors of the affected corporations would object to the proposal even though the right of the government to defend itself from the violations of its contracts and serious financial losses is at stake. It would be said to be an unjustified violation of the privacy of the decision-making process in a business; an illegitimate encroachment of the government on free enterprise. But surely if this is the legitimate response for the corporate job applicant, the same kind of response would be legitimate in the case of the individual job applicant.

Finally, it is simply false that there are not other measures which could be taken which could not help resolve the problem of theft. The fact that eighty percent of industry does not use the polygraph is itself suggestive that business does not find itself absolutely forced into the use of polygraphs. It might be objected that that does not indicate that certain industries might need polygraphs more than others—e.g., banks and drug companies more than auto plants and shipyards. But even granting this point, there are other measures which businesses can use to avoid the problem of theft. Stricter inventory controls, different kinds of cash registers, educational programs, hot lines, incentives, etc. could all be used. The question is whether the employer, management, can be imaginative and innovative enough to move in these directions.

In conclusion, it has been argued that the use of the polygraph to screen job applicants does indeed violate a prospective employee's privacy. First, it is plausible that the privacy of (prospective) employees may be violated by the employer acquiring certain kinds of information about them. Second, using a polygraph an employer may violate an employee's privacy even when the employer seeks the answers to legitimate questions. Third, other moral considerations employers have raised do not appear to outweigh the employee's right to privacy. Accordingly, on balance, a violation of the privacy of a job applicant occurs in the use of the polygraph. This constitutes a serious reason to oppose the use of the polygraph for such purposes.[24]

Notes

1. Cf. Harlow Unger, "Lie Detectors: Business Needs Them to Avoid Costly Employee Rip- Offs," *Canadian Business*, Vol. 51 (April, 1978), p. 30. Other estimates may be found in "Outlaw Lie-Detector Tests?" *U.S. News & World Report,* Vol. 84, No. 4 (January 1978), p. 45, and Victor Lipman, "New Hiring Tool: Truth Tests," *Parade* (October 7, 1979), p. 19.

2. Both the AFL-CIO and the ACLU have raised these objections to the use of the polygraph for screening job applicants; cf. *AFL-CIO Executive Council Statements and Reports: 1956–1975* (Westport, Conn.: Greenwood Press, 1977), p. 1422. See also ACLU Policy #248.

3. See, for example, Alan F. Westin, *Privacy and Freedom* (New York: Atheneum, 1967), p. 238.

4. Judith Jarvis Thomson, "The Right to Privacy," *Philosophy and Public Affairs*, Vol. IV (Summer, 1975), p. 307.

5. Ibid.

6. Cf. "A Model Patient's Bill of Rights," from George J. Annas, *The Rights of Hospital Patients* (New York: Avon Books, 1975), p. 233.

7. Frye Gaillard, "Polygraphs and Privacy," *The Progressive*, Vol. 38 (September, 1974), p. 46.

8. Cf. James Rachels' comment on the importance of the privacy of medical records in "Why Privacy Is Important," *Philosophy and Public Affairs*, Vol. IV (Summer, 1975), p. 324.

9. Alan Westin's definition of privacy suggests this view; cf. Alan F. Westin, *Privacy and Freedom*, p. 7. Also, Rachels' account of privacy suggests this view at times; cf. "Why Privacy Is Important," *Philosophy and Public Affairs*, pp. 326, 329.

10. Rachels emphasizes this point in his article; cf. "Why Privacy Is Important."

11. John W. Chapman discusses the "deadly danger" which "the moral psychology of the young" poses for privacy in his essay "Personality and Privacy." I take it that one of the major theses of his article is that, morally considered, the young ought to treat certain aspects of themselves and their relations to others as private. Cf. John W. Chapman, "Personality and Privacy," in *Privacy*, eds. J. Roland Pennock and John W. Chapman (New York: Atherton Press, 1971).

12. Ibid., pp. 239, 240.

13. Judith Jarvis Thomson, "The Right to Privacy," p. 307.

14. Alan Westin characterizes privacy in terms of the "claim" which people make; cf. *Privacy and Freedom*, p. 7.

15. This would have to be qualified for security jobs and the like.

16. John E. Reid and Associates, *Reid Report* (Chicago: By the author, 1978), passim.

17. John E. Reid and Associates, *The Polygraph Examination* (Chicago: By the author, n.d.), p. 7.

18. It should be further pointed out that the polygraphist/job-applicant relation is not legally or morally a privileged relation. What one tells one's physician one can expect to be treated confidentially. There is no similar expectation that one may entertain in the present case. At most one may hope that as another human being he will keep his promise. On the other hand, the polygraphist is an agent of the employer and responsible to him. There is and can be then no guarantee that the promise of the polygraphist will be kept.

19. The reasons why people do not submit to the polygraph are many and various. Some might have something to hide; others may be scared of the questions, supposing that some of them will not be legitimate; some may feel that they are being treated like criminals; others may fear the jaundiced response of the employer to the applicant's honest answers to legitimate questions; finally some may even object to the polygraph on moral grounds, e.g., it violates one's right to privacy.

20. See Section IV below.

21. Cf. Jeffrey H. Reiman, "Privacy, Intimacy, and Personhood," *Philosophy and Public Affairs*, Vol. VI (Fall, 1976).

22. Estimates of the validity of the polygraph range widely. Professor David Lykken has been reported as maintaining that the most prevalent polygraph test is correct only two-thirds of the time (cf.

Bennett H. Beach, ''Blood, Sweat and Fears,'' *Time*, September 8, 1980, p. 44). A similar figure of seventy percent is reported by Richard S. Sternbach et al., ''Don't Trust the Lie Detector,'' *Harvard Business Review*, Vol. XL (Nov.–Dec., 1962), p. 130. Operators of polygraphs, however, report figures as high as 95% accuracy; cf. Sternbach, p. 129.

23. This argument is suggested by a similar argument in David T. Lykken, ''Guilty-Knowledge Test: The Right Way to Use a Lie Detector,'' *Psychology Today* (March 1975), p. 60.

24. I wish to thank the following for their helpful comments on earlier versions of the present paper: Tom Donaldson, Norman Gillespie, Ken Goodpaster, Betsy Postow, William Tolhurst, and the editors of the *Business & Professional Ethics Journal*.

Suggested Further Reading

Ashford, N.A., ''Worker Health and Safety: An Area of Conflicts,'' *Monthly Labor Review*, vol. 98, September 1975.

Bluestone, Irving, ''Worker Participation in Decision Making,'' *The Humanist*, September–October 1973, pp. 50–61.

Ewing, David W., ''Privacy vs. Intrusion: Darkness at Noon?'' In David W. Ewing, *Freedom Inside the Organization: Bringing Civil Liberties to the Workplace*. New York: E.P. Dutton, 1977.

Fein, Mitchell, ''The Myth of Job Enrichment,'' *The Humanist*, September–October 1973, pp. 71–77.

DECISION SCENARIO 2

The Polygraph Test

The Oldhurst Camera Stores had a new general manager. His first objective was to ''tighten up operations'' at the company's fifteen branches. The committee he commissioned to assess Oldhurst's basic situation came back with several startling findings. One was that in-house shoplifting equaled about 12 percent of the annual profit.

As a first step, the new manager instituted lie detector tests in preemployment examinations required of prospective employees. When the turnabout in shoplifted inventory did not happen, monthly lie detector tests were required of all current employees below the managerial level.

One employee said, ''After being on the lie detector, you feel you did something dirty.''

Another employee hired the ACLU when she was asked questions such as: Are you a member of the Communist Party? Do you have health problems you have not informed your employer about? Do you have unusual sexual habits? Do you have a police record? She felt her privacy was being invaded.

The Oldhurst manager backed off. He still required the lie detector test, but he gave the agency running the polygraph a standard list of questions to be used. The questions included: Do you use drugs on the job? Do you regularly drink alcohol? Have you ever stolen merchandise from this or any other company? Have you ever had contact with AIDS? Have you ever written a bad check?

As a consequence of the lie detector tests, the in-house shoplifting problem dramatically decreased. At the end of the first six months, shoplifting stood at 20 percent of its former level.

Oldhurst felt justified in its choice of new management. It was presently considering a proposal for mandatory drug-testing for employees. When criticized by one civil libertarian, the new manager said, "If they don't like our testing programs, they can get a job somewhere else."

Questions

1. Were the questions asked in the first lie detector test justified? The second test? Explain in terms of ethical theory.

2. What kinds of moral protections do you feel were violated by the Oldhurst tests?

3. In March 1986 Congress passed legislation outlawing use of the polygraph except in unusual circumstances. Was this law fair to business?

4. The new manager justified his action in terms of the results. Was this a good justification?

5. Are mandatory drug-testing programs morally right?

3. EMPLOYEE OBLIGATIONS

The first two sections of this chapter dealt with the responsibilities of corporations toward their employees. Employees have correlative obligations creating additional ethical concerns. The traditional view of employer–employee relations stresses loyalty, obedience, and efficiency as the duties of an employee. Moral problems develop when a conflict arises between the interests of the employer and those of other parties. The term *conflict of interest* applies to situations in which an employee has a substantial personal (often financial) interest in an employer's business transactions. The employee's interest or hope of personal gain may cloud the independent judgment he or she is expected to exercise on the employer's behalf. Conflicts between the interest of an employer and those of other parties are central to several moral dilemmas of employees.

Proprietary data refers to secret or classified information belonging to a business organization. An employee's knowledge of sensitive data makes the corporation vulnerable. Suppose the worker wishes to change jobs and work for another company which could benefit from such knowledge. A conflict then exists between the worker's personal interest and the corporate interests of competing organizations. Should the employee's primary loyalty be to him- or her-

self, to the original employer, or to the new employer? The problem can also be described in terms of conflicting rights. While employees have a right to choose their employer, corporations have a right to protect trade secrets. Which right should take precedence?

Sometimes employees have access to nonpublic information which affects prices on the stock market. If employees use the information to profit in the market (or to help a third party to profit), they are said to engage in *insider trading*. Insider trading is a complex legal and ethical problem. Inside traders claim that their actions do not injure anyone and are therefore ethically permissible. Others disagree, arguing that indirect injury results to shareholders or traders who might also have profited from the information. A further problem lies in deciding exactly who is an "insider." The inside trader may be a temporary or occasional employee such as an accountant, lawyer, or contractor. In one such case, a printer gleaned information from financial documents handled by his shop and used the knowledge to trade on the stock market. The Supreme Court ruled in 1980 that the printer was not an insider and that Security and Exchange Commission (SEC) rules against insider trading did not apply. The SEC has objected to the Court's narrowing the definition of what constitutes an insider. Some SEC officials view insider trading as white-collar crime and welcome recent Congressional efforts to enlarge the scope of the definition. They hold that proper functioning of the market requires that it be perceived as honest and offering equal investment opportunities to all. On this account, insider trading is wrong because it jeopardizes that perception. Conflicts of interests and rights are less sharply defined in insider trading cases than in those involving proprietary data. A question remains whether an employee's loyalty should be directed to personal interests, to those of an employer, or to a wider community of traders and stockholders. Using confidential information for private gain may be ethically irresponsible even if no laws are violated.

An issue of particular difficulty involving employee responsibility is *whistleblowing.* The problem centers on the confidentiality of information acquired by employees. In this respect it resembles cases of insider trading and proprietary data. If an employee knows of company activities that are illegal or harmful to third parties, does the obligation of loyalty to one's employer outweigh the obligation to inform the public? Some argue that the latter duty represents a "higher morality" and is a form of ethical protest. This view recalls arguments in support of civil disobedience which claim that a higher morality overrides citizens' duty to obey the laws of the state. Since whistle-

blowing generally carries a strong risk of retaliation by the employer, some argue that it is justified only when the action has a reasonable chance of success. Workers who blow the whistle and lose their jobs may be protecting the public while harming themselves or their families. Another criterion for justifying whistleblowing focuses on the whistleblower's motive. On this analysis, it is crucial that the whistleblower act out of a desire to expose unnecessary harms or violations of human rights. No personal gain or interest must be involved. In addition, some hold that an employee is obligated to seek all available internal remedies and channels of protest before making public disclosure.

While proponents see whistleblowing in the public interest as a noble or courageous act, critics argue that it is a violation of the duty of loyalty to an employer. On this view, the burden of proof rests with the employee to demonstrate that such disloyalty is justified. In the following article Ronald Duska challenges the traditional belief that employees owe loyalty to their employer. Duska argues that "companies are not the kind of things which are proper objects of loyalty." Hence he concludes, whistleblowing involves no disloyalty and need not be justified from that standpoint. The author suggests that employees need to weigh the risk of harm to themselves from company retaliation against the obligation to prevent harm to others.

RONALD DUSKA

Whistleblowing and Employee Loyalty

Three Mile Island. In early 1983, almost four years after the near meltdown at Unit 2, two officials in the Site Operations Office of General Public Utilities reported a reckless company ef-

fort to clean up the contaminated reactor. Under threat of physical retaliation from superiors, the GPU insiders released evidence alleging that the company had rushed the TMI cleanup

Reprinted by permission of the author from *Contemporary Issues in Business Ethics*, ed. Joseph R. DesJardins and John J. McCall (Belmont, Calif.: Wadsworth Publishing Co., 1985). Copyright © 1983 by Ronald Duska.

without testing key maintenance systems. Since then, the Three Mile Island mop-up has been stalled pending a review of GPU's management.[1]

The releasing of evidence of the rushed cleanup at Three Mile Island is an example of whistleblowing. Norman Bowie defines whistleblowing as "the act by an employee of informing the public on the immoral or illegal behavior of an employer or supervisor."[2] Ever since Daniel Ellsberg's release of the Pentagon Papers, the question of whether an employee should blow the whistle on his company or organization has become a hotly contested issue. Was Ellsberg right? Is it right to report the shady or suspect practices of the organization one works for? Is one a stool pigeon or a dedicated citizen? Does a person have an obligation to the public which overrides his obligation to his employer or does he simply betray a loyalty and become a traitor if he reports his company?

There are proponents on both sides of the issue—those who praise whistleblowers as civic heroes and those who condemn them as "finks." Glen and Shearer who wrote about the whistleblowers at Three Mile Island say, "Without the *courageous* breed of assorted company insiders known as whistleblowers—workers who often risk their livelihoods to disclose information about construction and design flaws—the Nuclear Regulatory Commission itself would be nearly as idle as Three Mile Island . . . That whistleblowers deserve both gratitude and protection is beyond disagreement."[3]

Still, while Glen and Shearer praise whistleblowers, others vociferously condemn them. For example, in a now-infamous quote, James Roche, the former president of General Motors said:

Some critics are now busy eroding another support of free enterprise—the loyalty of a management team, with its unifying values and cooperative work. Some of the enemies of business now encourage an employee to be *disloyal* to the enterprise. They want to create suspicion and disharmony, and pry into the proprietary interests of the business. However this is labeled—industrial espionage, whistle blowing, or professional responsibility—it is another tactic for spreading disunity and creating conflict.[4]

From Roche's point of view, whistleblowing is not only not "courageous" and deserving of "gratitude and protection" as Glen and Shearer would have it, it is corrosive and not even permissible.

Discussions of whistleblowing generally revolve around four topics: (1) attempts to define whistleblowing more precisely; (2) debates about whether and when whistleblowing is permissible; (3) debates about whether and when one has an obligation to blow the whistle; and (4) appropriate mechanisms for institutionalizing whistleblowing.

In this paper I want to focus on the second problem, because I find it somewhat disconcerting that there is a problem at all. When I first looked into the ethics of whistleblowing it seemed to me that whistleblowing was a good thing, and yet I found in the literature claim after claim that it was in need of defense, that there was something wrong with it, namely that it was an act of disloyalty.

If whistleblowing was a disloyal act, it deserved disapproval, and ultimately any action of whistleblowing needed justification. This disturbed me. It was as if the act of a good Samaritan was being condemned as an act of interference, as if the prevention of a suicide needed to be justified. My moral position in favor of whistleblowing was being challenged. The tables were turned and the burden of proof had shifted. My position was the one in question. Suddenly instead of the company being the bad guy and the whistleblower the good guy, which is what I thought, the whistleblower was the bad guy. Why? Because he was disloyal. What I discovered was that in most of the literature it was taken as axiomatic that whistleblowing was an act of disloyalty. My moral intuitions told me that axiom was mistaken. Nevertheless, since it is accepted by a large segment of the ethical community it deserves investigation.

In his book *Business Ethics*, Norman Bowie,

who presents what I think is one of the finest presentations of the ethics of whistleblowing, claims that "whistleblowing . . . violate[s] a prima facie duty of loyalty to one's employer." According to Bowie, there is a duty of loyalty which prohibits one from reporting his employer or company. Bowie, of course, recognizes that this is only a prima facie duty, i.e., one that can be overridden by a higher duty to the public good. Nevertheless, the axiom that whistleblowing is disloyal is Bowie's starting point.

Bowie is not alone. Sissela Bok, another fine ethicist, sees whistleblowing as an instance of disloyalty.

> The whistleblower hopes to stop the game; but since he is neither referee nor coach, and since he blows the whistle on his own team, his act is seen as a *violation of loyalty* [italics mine]. In holding his position, he has assumed certain obligations to his colleagues and clients. He may even have subscribed to a loyalty oath or a promise of confidentiality. . . . Loyalty to colleagues and to clients comes to be pitted against loyalty to the public interest, to those who may be injured unless the revelation is made.[5]

Bowie and Bok end up defending whistleblowing in certain contexts, so I don't necessarily disagree with their conclusions. However, I fail to see how one has an obligation of loyalty to one's company, so I disagree with their perception of the problem, and their starting point. The difference in perception is important because those who think employees have an obligation of loyalty to a company fail to take into account a relevant moral difference between persons and corporations and between corporations and other kinds of groups where loyalty is appropriate. I want to argue that one does not have an obligation of loyalty to a company, even a prima facie one, because companies are not the kind of things which are proper objects of loyalty. I then want to show that to make them objects of loyalty gives them a moral status they do not deserve and in raising their status, one lowers the status of the individuals who work for the companies.

But why aren't corporations the kind of things which can be objects of loyalty? . . .

Loyalty is ordinarily construed as a state of being constant and faithful in a relation implying trust or confidence, as a wife to husband, friend to friend, parent to child, lord to vassal, etc. According to John Ladd "it is not founded on just *any* casual relationship, but on a specific kind of relationship or tie. The ties that bind the persons together provide the basis of loyalty."[6] But all sorts of ties bind people together to make groups. I am a member of a group of fans if I go to a ball game. I am a member of a group if I merely walk down the street. I am in a sense tied to them, but don't owe them loyalty. I don't owe loyalty to just anyone I encounter. Rather I owe loyalty to persons with whom I have special relationships. I owe it to my children, my spouse, my parents, my friends and certain groups, those groups which are formed for the mutual enrichment of the members. It is important to recognize that in any relationship which demands loyalty the relationship works both ways and involves mutual enrichment. Loyalty is incompatible with self-interest, because it is something that necessarily requires we go beyond self-interest. My loyalty to my friend, for example, requires I put aside my interests some of the time. It is because of this reciprocal requirement which demands surrendering self-interest that a corporation is not a proper object of loyalty.

A business or corporation does two things in the free enterprise system. It produces a good or service and makes a profit. The making of a profit, however, is the primary function of a business as a business. For if the production of the good or service was not profitable the business would be out of business. Since non-profitable goods or services are discontinued, the providing of a service or the making of a product is not done for its own sake, but from a business perspective is a means to an end, the making of profit. People bound together in a business are not bound together for mutual fulfillment and support, but to divide labor so the business makes a profit. Since profit is paramount, if you do not produce in a company or if there are cheaper laborers around, a company feels justified in firing you for the sake of better production. Throughout history companies in a pinch feel no obligation of loyalty. Compare that to a family. While we can jokingly refer to a family as "somewhere they have to take you in no matter what," you cannot refer to a company in that way. "You can't buy loyalty" is true. Loyalty depends on ties that demand self-sacrifice with no expectation of reward, e.g., the ties of loyalty that bind a family together. Business functions on the basis of enlightened self-interest. I am devoted to a company not because it is like a parent to me. It is not, and attempts of some companies to create "one big happy family" ought to be looked on with suspicion. I am not "devoted" to it at all, or should not be. I *work* for it because it pays me. I am not in a family to get paid, but I am in a company to get paid.

Since loyalty is a kind of devotion, one can confuse devotion to one's job (or the ends of one's work) with devotion to a company.

I may have a job I find fulfilling, but that is accidental to my relation to the company. For example, I might go to work for a company as a carpenter and love the job and get satisfaction out of doing good work. But if the company can increase profit by cutting back to an adequate but inferior type of material or procedure, it can make it impossible for me to take pride in my work as a carpenter while making it possible for me to make more money. The company does not exist to subsidize my quality work as a carpenter. As a carpenter my goal may be good houses, but as an employee my goal is to contribute to making a profit. "That's just business!"

This fact that profit determines the quality of work allowed leads to a phenomenon called the commercialization of work. The primary end of an act of building is to make something, and to build well is to make it well. A carpenter is defined by the end of his work, but if the quality interferes with profit, the business side of the venture supersedes the artisan side. Thus profit forces a craftsman to suspect his devotion to his work and commercializes his venture. The more professions subject themselves to the forces of the market-place, the more they get commercialized; e.g., research for the sake of a more profitable product rather than for the sake of knowledge jeopardizes the integrity of academic research facilities.

The cold hard truth is that the goal of profit is what gives birth to a company and forms that particular group. Money is what ties the group together. But in such a commercialized venture, with such a goal there is no loyalty, or at least none need be expected. An employer will release an employee and an employee will walk away from an employer when it is profitable to do so. That's business. It is perfectly permissible. Contrast that with the ties between a lord and his vassal. A lord could not in good conscience wash his hands of his vassal, nor could a vassal in good conscience abandon his lord. What bound them was mutual enrichment, not profit.

Loyalty to a corporation, then, is not required. But even more it is probably misguided. There is nothing as pathetic as the story of the loyal employee who, having given above and beyond the call of duty, is let go in the restructuring of the company. He feels betrayed because he mistakenly viewed the company as an object of his loyalty. To get rid of such foolish romanticism and to come to grips with this hard but accurate assessment should ultimately benefit everyone.

One need hardly be an enemy of business to be suspicious of a demand of loyalty to something whose primary reason for existence is the making of profit. It is simply the case that I have no duty of loyalty to the business or organization. Rather I have a duty to return responsible work for fair wages. The commercialization of work dissolves the type of relationship that requires loyalty. It sets up merely contractual relationships. One sells one's labor but not one's self to a company or an institution.

To think we owe a company or corporation loyalty requires us to think of that company as a person or as a group with a goal of human enrichment. If we think of it in this way we can be loyal. But this is just the wrong way to think. A company is not a person. A company is an instrument, and an instrument with a specific purpose, the making of profit. To treat an instrument as an end in itself, like a person, may not be as bad as treating an end as an instrument, but it does give the instrument a moral status it does not deserve, and by elevating the instrument we lower the end. All things, instruments and ends, become alike.

To treat a company as a person is analogous to treating a machine as a person or treating a system as a person. The system, company, or instrument get as much respect and care as the persons for whom they were invented. If we remember that the primary purpose of business is to make profit, it can be seen clearly as merely an instrument. If so, it needs to be used and regulated accordingly, and I owe it no more loyalty than I owe a word processor.

Of course if everyone would view business as a commercial instrument, things might become more difficult for the smooth functioning of the organization, since businesses could not count on the "loyalty" of their employees. Business itself is well served, at least in the short run, if it can keep the notion of a duty to loyalty alive. It does this by comparing itself to a paradigm case of an organization one shows loyalty to, the team.

Remember that Roche refers to the "management team" and Bok sees the name "whistleblowing" coming from the instance of a referee blowing a whistle in the presence of a foul. What is perceived as bad about whistleblowing in business from this perspective is that one blows the whistle on one's own team, thereby violating team loyalty. If the company can get its employees to view it as a team they belong to, it is easier to demand loyalty. The rules governing teamwork and team loyalty will apply. One reason the appeal to a team and team loyalty works so well in business is that businesses are in competition with one another. If an executive could get his employees to be loyal, a loyalty without thought to himself or his fellow man, but to the will of the company, the manager would have the ideal kind of corporation from an organizational standpoint. As Paul R. Lawrence, the organizational theorist says, "Ideally, we would want one sentiment to be dominant in all employees from top to bottom, namely a complete loyalty to the organizational purpose."[7] Effective motivation turns business practices into a game and instills teamwork.

But businesses differ from teams in very important respects, which makes the analogy between business and a team dangerous. Loyalty to a team is loyalty within the context of a sport, a competition. Teamwork and team loyalty require that in the circumscribed activity of the game I cooperate with my fellow players, so that pulling all together, we can win. The object of (most) sports is victory. But the winning in sports is a social convention, divorced from the usual goings on of society. Such a winning is most times a harmless, morally neutral diversion.

But the fact that this victory in sports, within the rules enforced by a referee (whistleblower), is a socially developed convention taking place within a larger social context makes it quite different from competition in business, which, rather than being defined by a context, permeates the whole of society in its influence. Competition leads not only to winners but to losers. One can lose at sport with precious few serious consequences. The consequences of losing at business are much more serious. Further, the losers in sport are there voluntarily, while the losers in business can be those who are not in the game voluntarily (we are all forced to participate) but are still affected by business decisions. People cannot choose to participate in business, since it permeates everyone's life.

The team model fits very well with the model of the free-market system because there competition is said to be the name of the game. Rival companies compete and their object is to win. To call a foul on one's own teammate is to jeopardize one's chances of winning and is viewed as disloyalty.

But isn't it time to stop viewing the corporate machinations as games? These games are not controlled and are not over after a specific time. The activities of business affect the lives of everyone, not just the game players. The analogy of the corporation to a team and the consequent appeal to team loyalty, although understandable, is seriously misleading at least in the moral sphere, where competition is not the prevailing virtue.

If my analysis is correct, the issue of the permissibility of whistleblowing is not a real issue, since there is no obligation of loyalty to a company. Whistleblowing is not only permissible but expected when a company is harming society. The issue is not one of disloyalty to the company, but the question of whether the whistleblower has an obligation to society if blowing the whistle will bring him retaliation. I will not argue that issue, but merely suggest the lines I would pursue.

I tend to be a minimalist in ethics, and depend heavily on a distinction between obligations and acts of supererogation. We have, it seems to me, an obligation to avoid harming anyone, but not an obligation to do good. Doing good is above the call of duty. In-between we may under certain conditions have an obligation to prevent harm. If whistleblowing can prevent harm, then it is required under certain conditions.

Simon, Powers and Gunnemann set forth four conditions:[8] need, proximity, capability, and last resort. Applying these, we get the following.

1. There must be a clear harm to society that can be avoided by whistleblowing. We don't blow the whistle over everything.
2. It is the "proximity" to the whistleblower that puts him in the position to report his company in the first place.
3. "Capability" means that he needs to have some chance of success. No one has an obligation to jeopardize himself to perform futile gestures. The whistleblower needs to have access to the press, be believable, etc.
4. "Last resort" means just that. If there are others more capable of reporting and more proximate, and if they will report, then one does not have the responsibility.

Before concluding, there is one aspect of the loyalty issue that ought to be disposed of. My position could be challenged in the case of organizations who are employers in non-profit areas, such as the government, educational institutions, etc. In this case my commercialization argument is irrelevant. However, I would maintain that any activity which merits the blowing of the whistle in the case of non-profit and service organizations is probably counter to the purpose of the institution in the first place. Thus, if there were loyalty required, in that case, whoever justifiably blew the whistle would be blowing it on a colleague who perverted the end or purpose of the organization. The loyalty to the group would remain intact. Ellsberg's whistleblowing on the government is a way of keeping the government faithful to its obligations. But that is another issue.

Notes

1. Maxwell Glen and Cody Shearer, "Going After the Whistle-blowers," *The Philadelphia Inquirer*, Tuesday, Aug. 2, 1983, Op-ed Page, p. 11a.

2. Norman Bowie, *Business Ethics* (Englewood Cliffs, N.J.: Prentice-Hall, 1982), p. 140. For Bowie, this is just a preliminary definition. His fuller definition reads, "A whistle blower is an employee or officer of any institution, profit or non-profit, private or public, who believes either that he/she has been ordered to perform some act or he/she has obtained knowledge that the institution is engaged in activities which (a) are believed to cause unnecessary harm to third parties, (b) are in violation of human rights or (c) run counter to the defined purpose of the institution and who inform the public of this fact." Bowie then lists six conditions under which the act is justified. pp. 142–143.

3. Glen and Shearer, ibid.

4. James M. Roche, "The Competitive System, to Work, to Preserve, and to Protect," *Vital Speeches of the Day* (May 1971), 445. This is quoted in Bowie, p. 141 and also in Kenneth D. Walters, "Your Employee's Right to Blow the Whistle," *Harvard Business Review*, 53, no. 4.

5. Sissela Bok, "Whistleblowing and Professional Responsibilities," *New York University Education Quarterly*, Vol. II, 4 (1980), p. 3.

6. John Ladd, "Loyalty," *The Encyclopedia of Philosophy*, Vol. 5, p. 97.

7. Paul R. Lawrence, *The Changing of Organizational Behavior Patterns: A Case Study of Decentralization* (Boston: Division of Research, Harvard Business School, 1958), p. 208, as quoted in Kenneth D. Walters, op. cit.

8. John G. Simon, Charles W. Powers, and Jon

P. Gunnemann, *The Ethical Investor: Universities and Corporate Responsibility* (New Haven: Yale University Press, 1972).

Suggested Further Reading

Bok, Sissela, "Whistleblowing and Professional Responsibilities," *New York University Education Quarterly*, vol. II, 4 (1980).

DeGeorge, Richard T., "Ethical Responsibilities of Engineers in Large Organizations," *Business and Professional Ethics Journal*, vol. I, no. 1, Fall 1981.

James, Gene G., "In Defense of Whistle Blowing," in *Business Ethics: Readings and Cases in Corporate Morality*, ed. W. Michael Hoffman and Jennifer Mills Moore. New York: McGraw Hill, 1984, pp. 249–60.

11. ISSUES IN EXTERNAL CORPORATE RELATIONS

1. BUYERS' RIGHTS AND SELLERS' OBLIGATIONS

What are the obligations of business organizations in relation to their customers? Many ethical concerns center around two general obligations: (1) the obligation to provide consumers with adequate, clear, accurate information about products or services; and (2) the obligation to supply products safe to use. At one time the majority of Americans lived on small farms and supplied themselves with most goods and services they needed. That kind of independence and self-sufficiency is no longer possible for most people. In a technological society, characterized by urbanization and specialization, consumers must rely upon business to supply their needs. Some argue that business is subject to a greater measure of moral responsibility because of the dependency of consumers. This argument is related to claims concerning the responsibility owed by health care and legal professionals to dependent clients. [See Health Care, Chapter 5, Section 1 and Criminal Justice, Chapter 16, Section 2.]

According to a traditional description of capitalist economies, relations between buyers and sellers are governed by the actions of the free market. Proponents of capitalism maintain that unregulated free enterprise maximizes efficiency and provides quality products at fair prices. When business is free to pursue the greatest possible profits, its success depends entirely on consumer demand. Unsatisfactory or overpriced products do not sell, and a business

that offers them will fail. On this account, the system itself protects the interests of sellers and consumers alike.

The legitimacy of the traditional view derives from two assumptions. One is that buyers are free to choose what they purchase. The second is that buyers have accurate and adequate information upon which to base purchasing decisions. The decision to make a purchase can be compared to a decision to permit medical treatment. In each case, a genuinely free choice involves truthful disclosure by the seller (or physician) and informed consent from the customer (or patient).

Critics of American business charge that customers cannot make free choices because advertising and marketing practices deliberately mislead buyers and manipulate consumer demand. If the accusation is true, the interests of the consumer are not protected by the free enterprise system as proponents claim.

What is the extent of business's obligation to provide customers with product information? Truth telling and informed consent are two issues raised by questions about the morality of advertising practices. [See Health Care, Chapter 5, Sections 3 and 4.] If advertisers knowingly suppress relevant information or if they make exaggerated, ambiguous, or deceptive claims, the consumer's right of informed consent is compromised. One complaint about advertising is that it is designed to appeal to consumers' emotions or emotional needs. Ads often feature psychological nuances which suggest that owning a particular product will enhance the user's sex appeal, power, status, security, or well-being. Other advertisements play upon consumers' fears of loneliness, weakness, poverty, or ill health. Critics argue that the ads are unfair as well as deceptive: unfair because customers' emotions are manipulated at an unconscious level, and deceptive because advertisers know in advance that their products cannot fulfill the promises implied in advertisements. Such ads indirectly violate the obligation to tell customers the truth.

A purchase represents an implied contract between buyer and seller in which they agree to exchange some commodity at a specified price. Critics describe a deceptive advertiser as having entered into the contract with no intention of fulfilling its terms. Such an action violates the demands of *commutative justice*, which governs relations between parties in an exchange of goods. Whereas distributive justice concerns relations between a community and its members, commutative justice involves relations between equals. If one party to a contract fails to fulfill his or her part of the agreement, the equality of the relationship is disrupted.

Another complaint about advertising is that it violates customers' freedom by creating in them needs which they would not otherwise feel. On this view, business manufactures consumer demands just as it manufactures products to satisfy them. Critics charge that the practice unfairly influences people to desire and purchase things that they do not genuinely need. Thus customers are treated as means to the end of profit making, a violation of the Kantian ethic.

Product safety is an important moral issue arising from the relation between business and consumers. What is the extent of a company's obligation to provide safe products? If customers have adequate, accurate information, theoretically they can assess the potential safety hazards of products and make a free choice of risks. Products deemed too unsafe are driven off the market and consumer safety interests protected. As with advertising, however, it is not clear whether customers are in a position to make genuinely free choices where safety is concerned. Consumers often lack the expertise to evaluate the riskiness of technologically sophisticated goods and must rely instead on manufacturers to ensure that products are safe to use.

Businesses, on the other hand, base safety considerations primarily on cost factors and may fail to provide consumers with explicit information about potential hazards. The Ford Pinto case is a notorious example. Ford apparently made a deliberate decision to continue production of a vehicle that the company knew was unsafe. The decision was based in part upon a *cost-benefit analysis* which compared the projected costs and benefits to society of correcting the hazardous fuel tank design. The study estimated that 180 burn deaths, 180 serious burn injuries, and 2,100 burned vehicles could be prevented if the design were improved. The resulting benefit was estimated at $49.5 million, based on National Highway Traffic Safety Administration (NHTSA) calculations, which assessed the social costs of a burn death at $200,725, a burn injury at $67,000, and a burned vehicle at $700. The cost of improving the fuel tank was estimated at $11 per vehicle for 12.5 million vehicles, a total of $137.5 million. Since on this analysis costs outweighed benefits by nearly three to one, the improvement was deemed too expensive, and Ford persisted with its original design for six model years.

Many critics question the morality of using cost-benefit analyses in decisions relating to safety. They argue that it is wrong to place a dollar-and-cents value on human suffering. However, the justice system itself employs formulas similar to the ones used in Ford's analysis. Under the laws of civil liability, courts assign monetary values to human life and suffering in order to assess damages.

Ford argued in defense of the Pinto that the vehicle was comparable in safety with similar models made by other producers and that it met all existing federal, state, and local fuel system standards. Nonetheless, the corporation was asked to pay millions of dollars in settlements for accidents related to the placement of the Pinto fuel tank. This result suggests that manufacturers have obligations regarding product safety which go beyond government standards. (The article by Richard T. DeGeorge in Chapter 13 of this unit examines the ethical obligations of Ford engineers in the Pinto case.)

If a customer is injured by a defective product, who should assume liability? Theories about product liability range from the *caveat emptor* (buyer beware) approach, which forces injured consumers to bear the financial burden of their injuries, to the policy of *strict liability*, under which manufacturers are liable when a customer is injured by a defective product, even if the defect is not the result of the producer's negligence. Before the early 1960s American consumers generally were able to recover damages only when they could demonstrate that the manufacturer had been negligent. The liberalized, strict liability laws now in use place much of the economic burden of product-related injuries upon manufacturers. The theory behind the law is that businesses will emphasize product safety in order to avoid the high cost of liability suits.

In the first article that follows, George G. Brenkert argues that strict products liability is a moral obligation implied by the rationale of the free enterprise system. One aspect of a free market is that individuals have an equal opportunity to participate in bargaining and competition. On Brenkert's view, a consumer who is injured by an unsafe or defective product is placed at a competitive disadvantage in the market. Compensatory justice demands that the disadvantaged individual be compensated by the person (or corporation) responsible for the harm.

Another method to ensure product safety

uses government regulation. Government policies and legislation have long played a part in regulating business activity. Until about twenty-five years ago, most government regulatory programs were designed to oversee market conditions and control competition. The actions of agencies such as the Interstate Commerce Commission, the Civil Aeronautics Board, and the Federal Communications Commission generally met with little opposition from the business community.

The early 1960s saw the blossoming of a new kind of regulatory activity. Typical of the newer agencies are the Equal Employment Opportunity Commission, the Environmental Protection Agency, the Consumer Product Safety Commission, and the Occupational Safety and Health Administration. The groups' primary objectives are preventing harm and ensuring responsible behavior by business organizations.

The newer form of government intervention in business, referred to as *social regulation*, has produced important benefits. Examples include a significant decline in air pollution, dramatic reduction in the number of accidental deaths in the workplace, and a large increase in the information available to consumers about product safety. However, the cost of regulation is high, since it includes federal expenditures for regulatory employees, increased prices for regulated products, and business expenses incurred in complying with regulations.

Business spokespersons challenge the cost effectiveness of social regulation. They argue that regulatory agencies disregard industry needs. They characterize government as inept, naive, and overbearing in its efforts to regulate business. They contend that the cost of meeting regulation standards adds to inflation, slows economic growth, and reduces productivity. Another complaint is that regulation represents an unjustified paternalistic restriction of the consumer's right to exercise free choice.

Proponents of social regulation claim that business estimates of costs are exaggerated and fail to take into account many real savings produced by the regulations (for example, reduced medical expenses resulting from pollution control). In addition, they contend that cost estimates ignore important benefits which are difficult to quantify.

In the second article below, Murray Weidenbaum argues that consumer product regulation is not the most economical or efficient way to achieve safety goals. The au-

thor maintains that regulation produces undesirable effects for consumers as well as business. The argument is primarily based on utilitarian concerns, although Weidenbaum also charges that regulation limits the free choices of consumers who "have unequal tastes for safety." The latter assertion involves the issue of individual autonomy and appeals to deontological principles.

GEORGE G. BRENKERT

Strict Products Liability
and Compensatory Justice

I

Strict products liability is the doctrine that the seller of a product has legal responsibilities to compensate the user of that product for injuries suffered due to a defective aspect of the product, even though the seller has not been negligent in permitting that defect to occur.[1] Thus, even though a manufacturer, for example, has reasonably applied the existing techniques of manufacture and has anticipated and cared for non-intended uses of the product, he may still be held liable for injuries a product user suffers if it can be shown that the product was defective when it left the manufacturer's hands.[2] To say that there is a crisis today concerning this doctrine would be to utter a commonplace observation which few in the business community would deny. The development of the doctrine of strict products liability, they say, financially threatens many businesses.[3] Further, strict products liability is said to be a morally questionable doctrine since the manufacturer or seller has not been

negligent in the occurrence of the injury-causing defect in the product. On the other hand, victims of defective products complain that they deserve full compensation for injuries sustained in using a defective product whether or not the seller is at fault. Medical expenses and time lost from one's job are costs no individual should have to bear by himself. It is only fair that the seller share such burdens.

In general, discussions of this crisis focus on the limits to which a business ought to be held responsible to compensate the injured product user. Much less frequently do discussions of strict products liability consider the underlying question of whether the doctrine of strict products liability is rationally justifiable. But unless this question is answered it would seem premature to seek to determine the limits to which businesses ought to be held liable in such cases. In the following paper I discuss this underlying philosophical question and argue that there is a rational justification for strict products liability which links it to the very nature of the free enterprise system.

II

It should be noted at the outset that strict products liability is not absolute liability. To hold a manufacturer legally (and morally) responsible for any and all injuries which product users might sustain would be morally perverse. First, it would deny the product user's own responsibility to take care in his actions and to suffer the consequences when he does not. As such, it would constitute an extreme form of moral and legal paternalism. Second, if the product is not defective, there is no significant moral connection between anything that the manufacturer has done or not done and the user's injuries other than the production and sale of the product to its user. But this provides no basis to hold the manufacturer responsible for the user's injuries. If, because of my own carelessness, I cut myself with my pocket knife, the fact that I just bought my knife from Blade Manufacturing Company provides no moral reason to hold Blade Manufacturing responsible for my injury. Finally, though the manufacturer's product might be said to have harmed the person,[4] it is wholly implausible, when the product is not defective and the manufacturer not negligent, to say that the manufacturer has harmed the user. Thus, again there would seem to be no moral basis upon which to maintain that the manufacturer has any liability to the product user. Strict products liability, on the other hand, is the view that the manufacturer can be held liable when the product can be shown to be defective even though the manufacturer himself is not negligent.[5]

There are two justifications of strict products liability which are predominant in the literature. Both justifications are, I believe, untenable. They are:

a. To hold producers strictly liable for defective products will cut down on the number of accidents and injuries which occur, by forcing manufacturers to make their products safer.[6]
b. The manufacturer is best able to distribute to others the costs of injuries which users of his defective products suffer.[7]

There are several reasons why the first justification is unacceptable. First, it has been plausibly argued that almost everything that can be attained through the use of strict liability to force manufacturers to make their products safer can also be attained in other ways through the law.[8] Hence, to hold manufacturers strictly liable will not necessarily help reduce the number of accidents. The incentive to produce safer producers already exists without invoking the doctrine of strict products liability.

Second, at least some of the accidents which have been brought under strict liability have been due to features of the products which the manufacturers could not have foreseen or controlled. At the time the product was designed and manufactured, the technological knowledge required to discover the hazard and take steps to minimize its effects was not available. It is doubtful that, in such cases, the imposition of strict liability upon the manufacturer could reduce accidents.[9] Thus, again, this justification for strict products liability fails.[10]

Third, the fact that the imposition of legal restraints and/or penalties would have a certain positive effect, viz., the reduction of accidents, does not show that the imposition of those penalties would be just. It has been pointed out before that the rate of crime might be cut significantly if the law would imprison the wives and children of men who break the law. Regardless of how correct that claim may be, to use these means in order to achieve a significant reduction in the rate of crime would be unjust. Thus, the fact, if fact it be, that strict liability would cut down on the amount of dangerous and/or defective products placed on the market, and thus reduce the amount of accidents and injuries, does not thereby justify the imposition of strict liability on manufacturers.

Finally, the above justification is essentially a utilitarian appeal which emphasizes the welfare of the product users. It is not obvious, however, that those who use this justification have ever undertaken the utilitarian analysis which would show that greater protection of the product user's safety would further the welfare of product users. If emphasis on product user safety would cut down on the number and variety of products produced, the imposition of strict liability might not, in fact, enhance product user welfare but rather lower it. Furthermore, if the safety of product users is the predominant concern, massive public and private education safety campaigns might just as well lower the level of accidents and injuries as strict products liability.

The second justification given for strict products liability is also utilitarian in nature. Among the considerations given in favor of this justification are the following:

a. "An individual harmed by his/her use of a defective product is often unable to bear the loss individually";
b. "Distribution of losses among all users of a product would minimize both individual and aggregate loss";
c. "The situation of producers and marketers in the marketplace enable them conveniently to distribute losses among all users of a product by raising prices sufficiently to compensate those harmed (which is what in fact occurs where strict liability is in force)."[11]

This justification is also defective.

First, the word "best" in the phrase "best able to distribute to others the cost" is usually understood in a non-moral sense; it is used to signify that the manufacturer can most efficiently pass on the costs of injuries to others. Once this use of "best" is recognised, then surely the question may correctly be asked: Why ought these costs be passed on to other consumers and/or users of the same product or line of products? Even if the imposition of strict liability did maximize utility, it might be the case that it was still unjust to use the producer as the distributor of losses.[12] Indeed, it has been objected that to pass along the costs of such accidents to other consumers of products of a manufacturer is unjust to them.[13] The above justification is silent to these legitimate questions.

Second, it may not be, as a matter of fact, that manufacturers are always in the best (i.e.,

most efficient and economical) position to pass costs on to customers. This might be possible in monopoly areas, but even there there are limitations. Further, some products are subject to an "elastic demand" and as such the manufacturer could not pass along the costs.[14] Finally, the present justification could justify far more than is plausible. If the reason for holding the manufacturer liable is that the manufacturer is the "best" administrator of costs, then one might plausibly argue that the manufacturer should pay for injuries suffered not simply when he is not negligent but also when the product is not defective. That is, theoretically this argument could be extended from cases of strict liability to absolute liability. Whether this argument could plausibly be made would depend upon contingent facts concerning the nature and frequency of injuries people suffer using products, the financial strength of businesses, and the kinds and levels of products liability insurance available to them. The argument would not depend on any morally significant elements in the producer/product user relation. Such an implication, I believe, undercuts the purported moral nature of this justification. It reveals it for what it is: an economic, not a moral justification.

Accordingly, neither of the major, current justifications for the imposition of strict liability appears to be acceptable. If this is the case, is strict products liability a groundless doctrine, willfully and unjustly imposed on manufacturers?

III

This question can be asked in two different ways. On the one hand, it can be asked within the assumptions of the free enterprise system. On the other hand, it could be raised such that the fundamental assumptions of that socio-economic system are also open to revision and change. In the following, I will discuss the question *within* the general assumptions of the free enterprise system. Since these are the assumptions which are broadly made in legal and business circles it is interesting to determine what answer might be given within these constraints. Indeed, I suggest, it is only within these general assumptions that strict products liability can be justified.

To begin with, it is crucial to remember that what we have to consider is the relation between an entity doing business and an individual.[15] The strict liability attributed to business would not be attributed to an individual who happened to sell some particular product he had made to his neighbor or a stranger. If Peter sold an article which he had made to Paul, and Paul hurt himself because the article had a defect which occurred through no negligence of Peter's, we would not normally hold Peter morally responsible to pay for Paul's injuries. Peter did not claim, we may assume, that the product was absolutely risk free. Had he kept it himself, he too might have been injured by it. Paul, on the other hand, bought it. He was not pressured, forced, or coerced to do so. Peter mounted no advertising campaign. Though Paul might not have been injured if the product had been made differently, he supposedly bought it with open eyes. Peter did not seek to deceive Paul about its qualities. The product, both its good and bad qualities, became his through his purchase of it. In short, we assume that both Peter and Paul are morally autonomous individuals capable of knowing their own interests, that such individuals can legitimately exchange their ownership of various products, that the world is not free of risks, and that not all injuries one suffers in such a world can be blamed on others. To demand that Peter protect Paul from such dangers and/or compensate him for injuries resulting from such dangers, is to demand that Peter significantly reduce the risks of the product he offers to Paul. He would have to protect Paul from encountering those risks himself. However, this smacks of paternalism and undercuts our basic moral assumptions about such relations. Hence, in such a case, Peter is not morally responsible for Paul's injuries or, due to this transaction, obligated to aid him. Perhaps Peter owes Paul aid because Paul is an injured neighbor or person. Perhaps simply for reasons of charity Peter ought to aid Paul. But

Peter has no moral obligation, stemming from the sale itself, to provide aid.

It is different in the case of businesses. They have been held to be legally and morally obliged to pay the victim for his injuries. Why? What is the difference? The difference has to do with the fact that when Paul is hurt by a defective product from corporation X, he is hurt by something produced in a socio-economic system purportedly embodying free enterprise. To say this is to say, among other things, that (a) each business and/or corporation produces articles or services which they sell for profit; (b) each member of this system competes with other members of the system in trying to do as well as he can for himself not simply in each exchange but through each exchange for his other values and desires; (c) competition is to be "open and free, without deception or fraud"; (d) exchanges are to be voluntary and undertaken when each party believes he can thereby benefit. One party provides the means for another party's ends if the other party will provide the first party the means to his ends[16]; (e) the acquisition and disposition of ownership rights, i.e., of private property, is permitted in such exchanges; (f) no market or series of markets constitutes the whole of a society; (g) law, morality, and government play a role in setting acceptable limits to the nature and kinds of exchange in which people may engage.[17]

What is it about such a system which would justify claims of strict products liability against businesses? Calabresi has suggested that the free enterprise system is essentially a system of strict liability.[18] Thus, the very nature of the free enterprise system justifies such liability claims. His argument has two parts. First, he claims that "bearing risks is both the function of, and justification for, private enterprise in a free enterprise society."[19] "Free enterprise is prized, in classical economics, precisely because it fosters the creation of entrepreneurs who will take such uninsurable risks, who will, in other words, gamble on uncertainty and demonstrate their utility by surviving—by winning more than others."[20] Accordingly, the nature of private enterprise requires that individual businesses assume the burden of risk in the production and distribution of its products. However, even if it be granted that this characterisation of who must bear the risks "in deciding what goods are worth producing and what new entrants into an industry are worth having" is correct, it would not follow that individual businesses ought to bear the burden of risk in cases of accidents. Calabresi himself recognises this. Thus, he maintains, in the second part of his argument, that there is a close analogy which lets us move from the regular risk bearing businesses must accept in the marketplace to the bearing of risks in accidents: "although . . . (the above characterisation) has concerned *regular* entrepreneurial-product risks, not accident risks, the analogy is extremely close."[21] He proceeds, however, to draw the analogy in the following brief sentence: "As with product-accident risks, our society starts out by allocating ordinary product-production risks in ways which try to maximize the chances that incentives will be placed on those most suited to 'manage' these risks."[22] In short, he simply asserts that the imposition of strict products liability on business will be the most effective means of reducing such risks. But such a view does not really require, as we have seen in the previous section, any assumptions about the nature of the free enterprise system. It could be held independently of such assumptions. Further, this view is simply a form of the first justificatory argument we discussed and rejected in the previous section. We can hardly accept it here under the guise of being attached to the nature of free enterprise.

Nevertheless, Calabresi's initial intuitions about a connection between the assumptions of the free enterprise system and the justification of strict products liability are correct. However, they must be developed in the following, rather different, manner. In the free enterprise system, each person and/or business is obligated to follow the rules and understandings which define this socio-economic system. Following the rules is expected to channel competition among individual persons and businesses so that the results are socially positive. In providing the means to fulfill the ends of others, the means to one's own ends also get fulfilled. Though this does not happen in every case, it is supposed that, in general, this happens. Those who fail in their competition with others may be the object of charity, but not of other duties. Those who succeed, *qua* members of this socio-economic system, do not have moral duties to aid those who fail. Analogously, the team which loses the game may receive our sympathy but the winning team is not obligated to help it so that it may win the next game, or even play better the next game. Those who violate the rules, however, may be punished or penalized, whether or not the violation was intentional and whether or not it redounds to the benefit of the violator. Thus, a team may be assessed a penalty for something a team member unintentionally did to a member of the other team but which, by violating the rules, nevertheless injured the other team's chances of competition in the game.

This point may be emphasized by another instance involving a game but one which brings us closer to strict products liability. Imagine that you are playing table tennis with another person in his newly constructed table tennis room. You are both avid table tennis players and the game means a lot to both of you. Suppose that after play has begun, you are suddenly and quite obviously blinded by the light over the table—the light shade has a hole in it which, when it turned in your direction, sent a shaft of light unexpectedly into your eyes. You lose a crucial point as a result. Surely it would be unfair of your opponent to seek to maintain his point because he was faultless—i.e., he had not intended to blind you when he installed that light shade. You would correctly object that he had gained the point unfairly, that you should not have to give up the point lost, and that the light shade should be modified so that the game could continue on a fair basis. It is only fair that the point be played over.

Businesses and their customers in a free enterprise system are also engaged in competition with each other.[23] The competition here, however, is multifaceted as each tries to gain the best agreement he can from the other with regard to the buying and selling of raw materials, products, services, and labour. Such agreements, however, must be voluntary. The competition which leads to them cannot involve coercion. In addition, such competition must be fair and ultimately result in the benefit of the entire society through the operation of the proverbial "invisible hand." Crucial to the notion of fairness of competition is not simply the demands that the competition itself be open, free, and honest, but also that each person in a society be given an equal opportunity to participate in the system in order to fulfill his own particular ends. Friedman formulates this notion in the following manner: "the priority given to equality of opportunity in the hierarchy of values . . . is manifested particularly in economic policy. The catchwords were free enterprise, competition, laissez-faire. Everyone was free to go into any business, follow any occupation, buy any property, subject only to the agreement of the other parties to the transaction. Each was to have the opportunity to reap the benefits if he succeeded, to suffer the costs if he failed. There were to be no arbitrary obstacles. Performance, not birth, religion, or nationality, was the touchstone."[24]

What is obvious in Friedman's comments is that he is thinking primarily of a person as a producer. Equality of opportunity requires that one not be prevented by arbitrary obstacles from participating (by engaging in a productive role of some kind or other) in the system of free enterprise, competition, etc. in order to fulfill one's own ends ("reap the benefits"). Accordingly, monopolies are restricted, discriminatory hiring policies have been condemned, and price collusion is forbidden. However, each person participates in the system of free enterprise *both* as a worker/producer *and* as a consumer. The two roles interact; if the person could not consume he would not be able to work, and if there were no consumers there would be no work to be done. Even if a particular individual is only

(what is ordinarily considered) a consumer, he too plays a theoretically significant role in the competitive free enterprise system. The fairness of the system depends upon the access to information, which is available to him, about goods and services on the market, the lack of coercion imposed on him to buy goods, as well as the lack of arbitrary restrictions imposed by the market and/or government on his behavior. In short, equality of opportunity is a doctrine with two sides which applies both to producers and to consumers. If, then, a person as a consumer or a producer is injured by a defective product, which is one way in which his activities might be arbitrarily restricted by the action of (one of the members of) the market system, surely his free and voluntary participation in the system of free enterprise will be seriously affected. Specifically, his equal opportunity to participate in the system in order to fulfill his own ends will be diminished.

It is here that strict products liability enters the picture. In cases of strict liability the manufacturer does not intend that a certain aspect of his product injures a person. Nevertheless, the person is injured. As a result, his activity both as a consumer and as a producer is disadvantaged. He cannot continue to play the role he might wish either as a producer or consumer. As such he is denied that equality of opportunity which is basic to the economic system in question just as surely as he would be if he were excluded from employment by various unintended consequences of the economic system which nevertheless had certain racially or sexually prejudicial implications. Accordingly, it is fair that the manufacturer compensate the person for his losses before proceeding with business as usual. That is, the user of a manufacturer's product may justifiably demand compensation from the manufacturer when a product of his which can be shown to be defective has injured him and harmed his chances of participation in the system of free enterprise.

Hence, strict liability finds a basis in the notion of equality of opportunity which plays a central role in the notion of a free enterprise system. This is why a business which does *not* have to pay for the injuries which an individual suffers in the use of a defective article made by that business is felt to be unfair to its customers. Its situation is analogous to a player's unintentional violation of a game rule which is intended to foster equality of competitive opportunity. A soccer player, for example, may unintentionally trip an opposing player. He did not mean to do it; perhaps he himself had stumbled and consequently tripped the other player. Still, he is to be penalized. If the referee looked the other way, the tripped player would rightfully object that he had been treated unfairly. Similarly, the manufacturer of a product may be held strictly liable for a product of his which injures a person who uses that product. Even though he be faultless, it is a causal consequence of his activities that renders the user of his product less capable of equal participation in the socio-economic system so as to fulfill his (the user's) own ends. The manufacturer too should be penalised by way of compensating the victim. Thus, the basis upon which manufacturers are held strictly liable is compensatory justice.

In a society which refuses to resort to paternalism or to central direction of the economy and which turns, instead, to competition in order to allocate scarce positions and resources, compensatory justice requires that the competition be fair and losers be protected.[25] Specifically no one who loses should be left so destitute that he cannot reenter the competition. Further, those who suffer injuries traceable to the defective results of the activities of others which restrict their participation in the competitive system should also be compensated. As such, compensatory justice does not presuppose negligence or evil intentions on the part of those to whom the injuries might ultimately be causally traced. It is not perplexed or incapacitated by the relative innocence of all parties involved. Rather it is concerned with correcting the disadvantaged situation an individual experiences due to accidents or failures which occur in the normal working of that competitive system. It is on

this basis that other compensatory programs which alleviate the disabilities of various minority groups are founded. It is also on compensatory justice that strict products liability finds its foundation.

An implication of the preceding argument is that business is not morally obliged to pay, as such, for the physical injury a person suffers. Rather, it must pay for the loss of equal competitive opportunity—even though it usually is the case that it is because of a (physical) injury that there is a loss of such equal opportunity. This, however, corresponds to actual legal cases in which the injury which prevents a person from going about his/her daily activities may be emotional or mental as well as physical. If it were the case that a person were neither mentally nor physically harmed, but still rendered less capable of competitively participating due to a defective aspect of a product, then there would still be grounds for holding the company liable. For example, suppose I purchased and used a cosmetic product guaranteed to last a month. When used by most people it is odorless. On me, however, it has a terrible smell. I can stand the smell, but my co-workers, and most other people, find it intolerable. My employer sends me home from work until it wears off. The product has not physically or mentally harmed me. Still, on the above argument, I would have reason to hold the manufacturer liable. Any cosmetic product with this result is defective. As a consequence my opportunity to participate in the socio-economic system so as to fulfill my own ends is disadvantaged. I should be compensated.

IV

There is another way of arguing to the same conclusion about the basis of strict products liability. To speak of business or the free enterprise system, it was noted above, is to speak of the voluntary exchanges between producer and customer which take place when each party believes he has an opportunity to benefit. Now surely customers and producers may miscalculate their benefits and something which they voluntarily agreed to buy or sell turns out actually to be something which is not to their benefit. In this situation, I have noted, the successful person does not have any moral responsibilities to the unsuccessful person—at least as a member of this economic system. If, however, one person does not benefit due to fraud on the part of another person, the system is, in principle, undermined. If such fraud were universalised, the system would collapse. Accordingly, the person committing the fraud does have a responsibility to make reparations to the one mistreated.

Now consider, once again, the instance of a person who is harmed by a product, which he bought or used, and which can reasonably be said to be defective. Has the nature of the free enterprise system, as above characterised, also been undermined or corrupted in this instance? They have exchanged the product but it has not been to their mutual benefit; the manufacturer may have benefited, but the customer has suffered due to the defectiveness of the manufacturer's product. Further, if such exchanges were universalised, the system would also be undone. Suppose that whenever people bought products from manufacturers the products turned out to be defective and the customers were always injured, even though the manufacturers could not be held negligent. Though one party to such exchanges might benefit, the other party always suffered. If the rationale of this economic system—the reason why it was adopted and is defended—was that in the end both parties share the equal opportunity to gain, surely this economic system with the above consequences would collapse. Consequently, as in the case of fraud, an economic system of free enterprise would require that injuries which result from defective products be compensated. The question is: who is to pay for the compensation?

There are three possibilities. The injured party could pay for his own injuries. However, this is implausible since what is called for is compensation and not merely payment for injuries. If the injured party had simply injured himself, if he had been negligent or

careless, then it is plausible that he should pay for his own injuries. No compensation is at stake here. But in the present case the injury stems from the actions of a particular manufacturer who, albeit unwittingly, placed the defective product on the market and stands to gain through its sale. The rationale of the free enterprise system would be undermined, we have seen, if such actions were universalized, for then the product user's equal opportunity to benefit from the system would be effectively denied. Accordingly, since the rationale and motivation for an individual to be part of this socio-economic system is his opportunity to gain from participation in it, justice requires that the injured product user receive compensation for his injuries. Since the individual can hardly compensate himself, he must receive compensation from some other source.

Second, some third party, e.g. the government, could compensate the injured person. This is not wholly implausible if one is prepared to modify the structure of the free enterprise system. And, indeed, in the long run this may be the most plausible course of action. However, if one accepts the structure of the free enterprise system, this alternative must be rejected because it permits the interference of government into individual affairs.[26] Thus, third, we are left with the manufacturer. Suppose a manufacturer's product, even though the manufacturer wasn't negligent, always turned out to be defective and injured those using his products. Though we might sympathize with his plight, he would either have to stop manufacturing altogether (no one would buy such products) or else compensate the victims for their losses (some people might buy and use his products under these conditions). If he forced people to buy and use his products he would corrupt the free enterprise system. If he did not compensate the injured users, they would not buy and he would not be able to sell his products. Hence, he could partake of the free enterprise system, i.e., sell his products, only if he compensated his user/ victims. Accordingly, the sale of this hypothetical line of defective products would only be voluntarily accepted as just or fair only if compensation were paid the user/victims of such products by the manufacturer. The same conclusion follows even if we must consider a single defective product. The manufacturer put the defective product on the market. It is because of his actions that others who seek the opportunity to participate on an equal basis in this system in order to benefit therefrom are unable to do so. Thus, it is as a result, even though unintended, of his actions that the system's character and integrity are, in principle, undermined. Accordingly, when a person is injured in his attempt to participate in this system, he is owed compensation by the manufacturer. The seller of the defective article must not jeopardize the equal opportunity of the product user to benefit from the system. The seller need not guarantee that the buyer/user will benefit from the purchase of the product—he may miscalculate or be careless in the use of a nondefective product. But supposing that he is not careless or has not miscalculated, then his opportunity to benefit from the system is illegitimately harmed if he is injured in its use because of the product's defectiveness. He deserves compensation.

Accordingly, it follows from the argument in this and the preceding section that, opposed to what some have claimed, strict products liability is not only compatible with the system of free enterprise but were it not attributed to the manufacturer the system would be itself morally defective! And the justification, we have seen, of requiring manufacturers to pay compensation in cases in which individuals are injured by defective products is that the demands of compensatory justice are fulfilled.[27]

Notes

1. This characterisation of strict products liability is adapted from Weinstein et al., *Products Liability and the Reasonably Safe Product*, ch. 1. I understand "the seller" to include the manufacturer, the retailer, as well as distributors and wholesalers. For convenience sake, I will generally refer simply to the manufacturer.

2. Cf. John W. Wade, "On Product 'Design Defects' and Their Actionability," 33 *Vanderbilt Law Review* 553 (1980). Weinstein et al., *Products Liability and the Reasonably Safe Product*, pp. 8, 28–32. Reed Dickerson, "Products Liability: How Good Does a Product Have to Be?" 42 *Indiana Law Journal* 308–316 (1967). Section 402A of the Restatement (Second) of Torts characterises the seller's situation in this fashion: "the seller has exercised all possible care in the preparation and sale of his product."

3. Cf. John C. Perham, "The Dilemma in Product Liability," *Dun's Review*, 109 (1977), pp. 48–50, 76. W. Page Keeton, "Products Liability—Design Hazards and the Meaning of Defect," 10 *Cumberland Law Review* 293–316 (1979). Alvin S. Weinstein et al., *Products Liability and the Reasonably Safe Product* (New York: John Wiley & Sons, 1978), ch. 1.

4. More properly, of course, the person's use of the manufacturer's product harmed the product user.

5. Clearly one of the central questions confronting the notion of strict liability is what is to count as "defective." With few exceptions, it is held that a product is defective if and only if it is unreasonably dangerous. There have been several different standards proposed as measures of the defectiveness or unreasonably dangerous nature of a product. However, in terms of logical priorities, it really does not matter what the particular standard for defectiveness is unless we know whether we may justifiably hold manufacturers strictly liable for defective products. It is for this reason that I concentrate in this paper on the justifiability of strict products liability.

6. Michel A. Coccio, John W. Dondanville, Thomas R. Nelson, *Products Liability: Trends and Implications* (AMA, 1970), p. 13. Keeton, "The Meaning of Defect in Products Liability Law—A Review of Basic Principles," p. 580. William L. Prosser, "The Assault Upon the Citadel (Strict Liability to the Consumer)," p. 1119.

7. Coccio, Dondanville, Nelson, *Products Liability: Trends and Implications*, p. 13. Keeton, "The Meaning of Defect in Products Liability Law—A Review of Basic Principles," pp. 580–581. Owen, "Rethinking the Policies of Strict Products Liability," p. 686. William L. Prosser, "The Assault Upon the Citadel (Strict Liability to the Consumer)," p. 1120.

8. Marcus L. Plant, "Strict Liability of Manufacturers for Injuries Caused by Defects in Products—

An Opposing View,'' 24 *Tennessee Law Review* 945 (1957). William L. Prosser, ''The Assault Upon the Citadel (Strict Liability to the Consumer),'' pp. 1114, 1115, 1119.

9. Keeton, ''The Meaning of Defect in Products Liability—A Review of Basic Principles,'' pp. 594–95. Weinstein et al., *Products Liability and the Reasonably Safe Product*, p. 55.

10. It might be objected that such accidents ought not to fall under strict products liability and hence do not constitute a counterexample to the above justification. This objection is answered in Sections III and IV.

11. These three considerations are formulated by Michael D. Smith, ''The Morality of Strict Liability in Tort,'' *Business and Professional Ethics Newsletter*, 3 (1979), p. 4. Smith himself, however, was drawing upon Guido Calabresi, ''Some Thoughts on Risk Distribution and the Law of Torts,'' 70 *Yale Law Journal* 499–553 (1961).

12. Michael D. Smith, ''The Morality of Strict Liability in Tort,'' p. 4. Cf. George P. Fletcher, ''Fairness and Utility in Tort Theory,'' 85 *Harvard Law Review* 537–573 (1972).

13. Rev. Francis E. Lucey, S. J., ''Liability Without Fault and the Natural Law,'' 24 *Tennessee Law Review* 952–962 (1957). Perham, ''The Dilemma in Product Liability,'' pp. 48–49.

14. Marcus L. Plant, ''Strict Liability of Manufacturers for Injuries Caused by Defects in Products—An Opposing View,'' pp. 946–947. By ''elastic demand'' is meant ''a slight increase in price will cause a sharp reduction in demand or will turn consumers to a substitute product'' (pp. 946–47).

15. Cf. William L. Prosser, ''The Assault Upon the Citadel,'' 69 *Yale Law Journal* 1140–1141 (1960). Wade, ''On Product 'Design Defects' and Their Actionability,'' p. 569. Coccio, Dondanville, Nelson, *Products Liability: Trends and Implications*, p. 19.

16. F. A. Hayek emphasizes this point in ''The Moral Element in Free Enterprise,'' in *Studies in Philosophy, Politics, and Economics* (New York: Simon and Schuster, 1967), p. 229.

17. Several of these characteristics have been drawn from Milton Friedman and Rose Friedman, *Free to Choose* (New York: Avon Books, 1980).

18. Calabresi, ''Product Liability: Curse or Bulwark of Free Enterprise,'' p. 325.

19. Ibid., p. 321.

20. Ibid.

21. Ibid., p. 324.

22. Ibid.

23. Cf. H. B. Acton, *The Morals of Markets* (London: Longman Group Limited, 1971), pp. 1–7, 33–37. Milton Friedman and Rose Friedman, *Free to Choose*.

24. Milton Friedman and Rose Friedman, *Free to Choose*, pp. 123–124.

25. I have heavily drawn, in this paragraph, on the fine article by Bernard Boxhill, ''The Morality of Reparation,'' reprinted in *Reverse Discrimination*, ed. Barry R. Gross (Buffalo, New York: Prometheus Books, 1977), pp. 270–278.

26. Cf. Calabresi, ''Product Liability: Curse or Bulwark of Free Enterprise,'' pp. 315–319.

27. I would like to thank the following for providing helpful comments on earlier versions of this paper: Betsy Postow, Jerry Phillips, Bruce Fisher, John Hardwig, and Sheldon Cohen.

MURRAY WEIDENBAUM

Consumer Product Regulation

The actions of numerous federal agencies relate to consumer products. Of these, the Consumer Product Safety Commission has the most direct and explicit responsibility. The Consumer Product Safety Act of 1972 created an independent regulatory agency ''to protect the public against unreasonable risks of injury associated with consumer products.''[1] A five-

Murray L. Weidenbaum, *Business, Government, and the Public*, © 1977, pp. 24–31. Excerpt reprinted by permission of Prentice-Hall, Inc., Englewood Cliffs, New Jersey.

member Consumer Product Safety Commission sets safety standards for consumer products, bans products presenting undue risk of injury, and in general polices the entire consumer product marketing process from manufacture to final sale.

In creating the Commission, Congress adopted a "no-fault" view of accidental product injuries, involving a complex interaction between the consumer, the product, and the environment. Rather than stressing punitive action against the producers and distributors of unsafe products, the emphasis in the statute is on setting new product standards. Under this approach, products would be redesigned to accommodate to possible consumer misuse and ignorance of proper operation of the product.[2]

Specific functions of the Commission include aiding consumers in the evaluation of product safety, developing uniform product safety standards, gathering medical data and conducting research on product-related injuries, and coordinating federal, state, and local product safety laws and enforcement. Consumers are assured the right to participate in the Commission's activities, as "any interested person . . . may petition the Commission to commence a proceeding for the issuance, amendment, or revocation of a consumer product safety rule."[3] Safety standards cover product performance, contents, composition, design, construction, finish, packaging, and labeling.

A provision of the Consumer Product Safety Act that became operative in November 1975 gave both business and consumers more power to force the CPSC to accelerate its standard-making process. Under Section 10(e), any private party can bring suit against the Commission if it denies a rule-making petition or if it fails to act on a petition within 120 days. No other federal agency is bound by such a deadline on its decision-making.[4]

Powers of the Commission extend to requiring manufacturers of products found to be hazardous to take corrective actions. These actions include refunds, recalls, public warnings, and reimbursements to consumers for expenses of the recall process. Any product representing an unreasonable risk of personal injury or death may, by court order, be seized and condemned. Under the Consumer Product Safety Act of 1972, the Commission's jurisdiction extends to more than 10,000 products. In addition to banning offending products and requiring expensive recalls and debates, it can charge offending executives with violations that are subject to jail sentences.[5]

The Impact on Consumers— Benefits and Costs

Important benefits to the public can be expected from an agency designed to make consumers more aware of product hazards and to require the removal from the market of products likely to cause serious injuries. Simultaneously, it must be noted that such actions also can generate large costs, which will be borne ultimately by the consumer. The consumer's total welfare is therefore maximized by seeking out the most economical and efficient ways of achieving safety objectives. Thus, banning products can be seen as one of a variety of alternatives. These can range from relabeling a product (so that the consumer becomes aware of a previously hidden hazard) to recalling and modifying an existing line of products.

The Stanford Research Institute has estimated that the mandatory safety standards developed by Consumers Union for the Commission would add $250 million to the price tag for power lawn mowers and put 25 companies out of the business. The Institute estimated that the proposed standards could raise the price of a $100 gasoline-powered rotary mower to as much as $186. Push mowers would increase in price between 30 and 74 percent. The cost of more expensive riding mowers would go up at a slower rate, between 19 and 30 percent. The largest price rises, in the range of 35 to 86 percent, would occur on manual-start push rotary motors.[6]

At times, higher consumer product prices result from the Commission's actions and are brought about by their forcing expensive complexity on the manufacturers of consumer products. Poor, and even middle income, families may thus be priced out of many markets for consumer products. A case in point is the four million electric frying pans for which the Commission has ordered formal hearings to determine if they are hazardous. What is puzzling, however, is that, out of the four million pans, not a single injury has been reported by the Commission.[7]

Professor Max Brunk of Cornell University gets to the heart of the matter: "Consumerism is aimed at the consumer . . . look what it does to the consumer who pays the cost and loses the benefits that a prohibited product or service could have provided."[8] Following this line of reasoning, business can better adjust to these controls than can the consumer, because it can pass on the added costs that result.

Brunk notes that it is interesting to observe that consumer advocates sometimes have as much difficulty convincing the consumer of his or her need for protection as in convincing a regulatory body to provide the protection.[9] The truth-in-lending law is a cogent example. The compulsory requirement to show true interest costs has not slowed down the growth of consumer debt or the rise in interest rates. Since the passage of the act, the ratio of consumer debt to consumer income has reached an all-time high, and interest rates, for many reasons, have risen sharply. The average credit purchaser still seems to be more interested in the absolute amount of the monthly payment than in the rate of interest that is included in it. Similarly, despite the justification for unit pricing as a means of helping low income families to stretch their dollars further, available surveys show that it is the high income, well-educated customers who are most aware of this information.[10]

In the area of product safety, it should be recognized that consumers have unequal tastes for safety as well as other characteristics of product performance. Particularly where the safety hazard is minor (the occasional blister on a finger), policy makers need to realize

that very large cost increases may merely deprive many consumers of the use of many products. As elsewhere, there is the need to recognize trade-offs between safety and other criteria important to consumers.

For example, a power tool selling for $20 may not have the capability of being in use for more than an hour; the $500 piece of equipment may be safely used for a much longer period. Although the instructions on each tool may be very clear in this respect, some consumers may willingly buy the cheaper model and knowingly take the chance of burning it out. A policy of complete product safety would ban the cheaper item, thereby effectively depriving the low income consumer of buying a power tool.[11]

A vast majority of Americans is concerned over product safety, and this concern has risen steadily since 1971. However, 87 percent of the adult Americans participating in a Harris survey blame consumers themselves for injury from products. Many believe that "most products are safe, but a lot of people do not read the directions or misuse products, so it is unfair to put all the safety blame on manufacturers." In the same survey a distinct opposition was shown to bans on products. Of the consumers surveyed, 73 percent believed that product safety objectives should be accomplished through publicity on product risks and dangers and by health warnings such as those required on cigarettes and drugs.[12]

The Effect on Business

The recordkeeping requirements imposed by the Consumer Product Safety Commission's early actions are substantial. In its first major proposed rule in August 1973, it called on every manufacturer, distributor, or retailer—upon learning that a product it sold "creates a substantial risk of injury"—to inform and provide the Commission with a wide array of information including:

1. The number of products that present a hazard or potential hazard.

2. The number of units of each product involved.
3. The number of units of each product in the hands of consumers.
4. Specific dates when the faulty units were manufactured and distributed.
5. An accounting of when and where such products (and the number of units of each) were distributed.
6. The model and serial numbers affected.
7. A list of names and addresses of every distributor, retailer, and producer, if known.
8. A description of the effort made to notify consumers of the defect.
9. Details of corrective tests, quality controls, and engineering changes made or contemplated.[13]

The reporting requirement is not completed until the company submits a final report indicating that the "potential" product hazard has been corrected. Thus, the Commission shifts to the company the responsibility and costs of determining and remedying potential product defects with the possibility of criminal sanctions should the Commission disagree with the company's decisions. Product safety reporting by companies is a necessary input to the Commission's evaluation of potentially dangerous products. The reporting requirements are substantial and, therefore, costly. It is not, however, a question of whether or not companies should report information on product injuries, but of how much detail is needed for decision-making.

An example of prudent action on the part of the Commission was its handling of the alleged hazards involving spray adhesives. In August 1973, the Commission quickly banned these products when informed of findings by a University of Oklahoma scientist suggesting a causal relationship between the adhesives and chromosome breaks leading to birth defects.[14] The following January, however, the Commission announced that the ban was being lifted after in-depth research and independent evaluation reversed the conclusion of the initial study. In this case not only was the Commission quick to impose a ban on a product that it thought might be potentially hazardous, but it also acted expeditiously in conducting confirmatory studies and lifted the ban once evidence negated the original study.

The Commission has turned down the most extreme demands of consumer advocates. It rejected the petition of Ralph Nader's Health Research Group, which warned of the "imminent hazard to the public health" represented by lead-wick candles. The petition asserted that small children might chew or swallow the candles, taking lead into their systems, and candlelit suppers would result in "meals literally bathed in lead." In a letter to the Nader group, Commissioner Laurence M. Kushner stated that the petition "was drawn either with abysmal ignorance of elementary physical science, colossal intent to deceive the public, or both. The calculations, in the petition, of possible concentrations of lead in air which might result from burning such candles, were based on assumptions that are physically impossible. . . ."[15]

The Power of Government Regulation

In the words of Chairman Arnold Elkind of the National Commission on Product Safety, whose recommendations led to the creation of the Consumer Product Safety Commission:

> It's true that the CPSC may be the most powerful independent regulatory agency ever created . . . but it has to be. It has to have a wide choice of weapons to cope with the diverse range of situations it confronts.[16]

The Commission does have an impressive array of powers and at times uses them in a fashion that could seem arbitrary, at least to some people. For example, in promulgating its ban lists, the CPSC appears to have taken the position, perhaps unwittingly, that a company can be guilty until proved innocent. This surprising stand, which contradicts the basic notion of fairness in legal matters, seems implicit in the following statement in an issue of the CPSC's Banned Products List:

Articles not meeting the requirements of the regulation are to be considered as banned even though they have not yet been reviewed, confirmed as banned, and added to the Banned Products List by the Consumer Product Safety Commission.[17]

Taken literally, the Commission's statement means that the responsibility for treating a product as being banned can fall entirely on the company involved, and in circumstances where the Commission is not even aware of the product's existence, much less of its supposedly hazardous characteristic.

The case of Marlin Toy Products of Horicon, Wisconsin, illustrates the dangers that can arise in the excessive use of CPSC's great powers. Due to an "editorial error," the Commission put Marlin's major products on its new ban list in 1973. When the error was called to its attention, CPSC refused to issue a prompt retraction. As a result, Marlin was forced out of the toy business.

Although the Congress has assigned it responsibility for product safety, the Commission members have tried to extend this task to newspapers and magazines. In a session with reporters, the chairman and other members of the Commission stated their belief that publishers should attempt to verify the safety of the products advertised in their publications. Richard O. Simpson, CPSC chairman, was quoted as saying that newspapers and magazines who carry advertisements should consider hiring specialists to look over products or should farm out the task to outside consultants.[18] Thus, producers and distributors would have to satisfy not only the federally chartered Consumer Product Safety Commission but also the private safety commissioners appointed by each individual private publication.

Despite having substantial resources at its disposal and after several years of operation, the Commission has been chastized for its slowness in carrying out its principal function—the writing of safety standards for products. As of late 1975, no standards had been completed. In September 1975, the first standards—for swimming pool slides—were proposed.

In addition to difficulties in developing standards, the Commission has encountered problems in determining the boundaries of its own jurisdiction. This was displayed by its involvement in the handgun controversy. In response to a request to ban handgun ammunition as a hazardous substance, the Commission was required by statute to ask for public comments. It received more than 130,000 cards and letters, all on an issue that four of the five commissioners believed they had no business investigating.[19]

The stepped-up pace of regulation by the CPSC is resulting in "reverse distribution"— product recalls—becoming an important part of the marketing function of many companies. In addition to motor vehicles, increasing numbers of manufacturers of television sets, bicycles, ovens, and other nonautomotive products are being involved in recall situations. Product recalls in these cases are frequently justified and may well withstand the test of cost-benefit analysis.

This relatively new activity, however, is requiring a major expansion in recordkeeping so that owners of the recalled product can be promptly notified. The Consumer Product Safety Commission ultimately may require manufacturers to keep records of all product complaints and to turn them over to the Commission if it so requests. This information thus could form the basis for additional product recalls. It is, therefore, likely that more of the complaint letters from consumers will be kept in company files—and perhaps acted on.

A particularly costly aspect of the newer product safety regulations is that they often contain retroactive clauses. Should a company discover a product defect several years after it begins selling a product, and if the defect requires a recall, the firm may find that the recall costs exceed the company's net worth.[20]

The cost of recalls varies with the number of products sold, the amount of time and effort required to track down the purchasers, and the percentage of products that require repair, replacement, or refund. It cost General Motors $3.5 million for postage alone to notify by certified mail, as required by law, the 6.5 million owners of cars with questionable engine mounts. The cost to Panasonic to recall and repair 280,000 television sets, as ordered by the CPSC because of possible harmful radiation emission, may total $11.2 million—the equal of the company's profits in the United States for the past several years.

Expectations, either for private or public activities, should not be set too high. Considering the importance of the problems confronting the CPSC and the difficulties involved in solving them, perhaps the sympathetic, thoughtful comments of Paul Weaver may provide an appropriate ending note for this section:

> In the end there is no such thing as a perfect safety regulation; in most cases, in fact, even a fairly good one is hard to find. Thus there's nothing surprising or dishonorable about the failure of the Commission to issue perfect regulations in wholesale lots.
>
> But the environment within which they work—the law, the expectations of Congress, the conflicting pressures from consumerists and industry, the nature of government, the climate of public opinion, the methods and ambitions of the staff, and above all the monumental complexity of the task—makes good judgment difficult. The scarcest ingredient in this marvelously intricate and rational system is the homely virtue of common sense.[21]

Notes

1. Consumer Product Safety Act, Public Law 92–573.

2. Paul H. Weaver, "The Hazards of Trying to Make Consumer Products Safer," *Fortune*, July 1975, pp. 133–34.

3. Consumer Product Safety Act, Public Law 92–573.

4. "Spurring New Action on Product Safety," *Business Week*, November 10, 1975, p. 60.

5. Consumer Product Safety Act, Public Law 92–573.

6. *Reprints of Selected News Items* (Menlo Park, Cal.: Stanford Research Institute, 1975), p. 8.

7. "Some Fry Pans and Chain Saws May Be Unsafe," *St. Louis Post-Dispatch*, January 15, 1974, p. 8A.

8. Max E. Brunk, "Consumerism and Marketing," in *Issues in Business and Society*, ed. George Steiner (New York: Random House, 1972), p. 462.

9. Ibid., p. 463.

10. Ibid., p. 465.

11. J. Fred Weston, "Economic Aspects of Consumer Product Safety," in *Issues in Business and Society*, ed. George Steiner (New York: Random House, 1972), p. 499.

12. Louis Harris, "Concern over Product Safety," *Washington Post*, June 1, 1975, p. F-2.

13. *Federal Register*, August 3, 1973, vol. 38, no. 149.

14. *CPSC Bans Three Spray Adhesives—Asks Manufacturers of Others to Halt Production* (Washington, D.C.: U.S. Consumer Product Safety Commission, August 20, 1973).

15. "Please Don't Eat the Candles," *Wall Street Journal*, January 16, 1974, p. 12.

16. William H. Miller, "Consumer Product Safety Commission," *Industry Week*, October 29, 1973, p. 41.

17. U.S. Consumer Product Safety Commission, *Banned Products*, October 1, 1973, p. 1.

18. "Consumer Agency Is Critical of Ads," *New York Times*, February 13, 1974, p. 47.

19. Burt Schoor, "Consumer Product Safety Commission Finds Deep Hazards In Just Getting Itself Rolling," *Wall Street Journal*, May 6, 1975.

20. E. Patrick McGuire, "The High Cost of Recalls," *New York Times*, March 30, 1975, p. E-1.

21. Weaver, "Trying to Make Consumer Products Safer," p. 140.

Suggested Further Reading

Arrington, Robert L., "Advertising and Behavior Control," *Journal of Business Ethics*, 1, no. 1 (February 1982), 3–12.

Bandow, D., "Restraining the Regulators," *The Libertarian Review*, Summer 1980.

Hightower, Jim, "Food Monopoly: Who's Who in the Thanksgiving Business," *The Texas Observer*, November 17, 1978.

Howard, Niles, and Susan Antilla, "What Price Safety? The 'Zero-Risk' Debate," *Dun's Review*, September 1979, pp. 47–57.

Kelman, Steven, "Regulation and Paternalism," *Public Policy*, vol. 29, no. 2, Spring 1981.

Levitt, Theodore, "The Morality(?) of Advertising," *Harvard Business Review*, July–August 1970, pp. 84–92.

Lilly, William, III, and James C. Miller III, "The New Social Regulation," *Public Interest*, 45 (Spring 1977), 5–51.

Steiner, George A., "New Patterns in Government Regulation of Business," *MSU Business Topics*, Autumn 1978.

DECISION SCENARIO 3

Marketing Hand Lotions

The Food and Drug Administration (FDA) discovered that a chemical used in hand lotions, M-oxypropyl-3-nitrobutylene, produced malignant tumors in laboratory animals. It immediately ordered all products using "Moxy," as it was called, to have a warning label. The label was to read:

> **Warning**: contains substance known to cause cancer in laboratory animals.

Hand lotions sales played a significant role in the marketplace, topping some $1.6 million a year. Moxy was an important ingredient which facilitated the permeability of the substance. When products lacked it, consumers in test situations complained of a greasy feeling.

Most major cosmetic and pharmaceutical houses reacted to the FDA announcement. Moxy had been used for over twenty years without complaints about side effects. The industry argued that someone would have to use over a gallon of lotion a day in order to duplicate the results that the FDA claimed. However, when the FDA stuck to its research, the houses agreed to comply—up to a point. They would carry the new label if the product used Moxy, or they would use a new formulation; however, they would not recall products already on the shelf which had Moxy without a label. Sometimes a couple of years passed before hand lotions were reinventoried.

The Orange Blossom Company was a small, family-owned corporation which sold a few kinds of lotions to local, unfranchised health food shops. Its brand of hand lotion contained Moxy. Its sales department determined that carrying the new label would have a significant negative effect on overall corporate sales. To remove Orange Blossom Hand Lotion from their list altogether would likely produce a negative cash flow.

Orange Blossom decided to do two things. It would remarket its old formula to its developing Canadian market; the FDA regulation did not apply to foreign sales. Also it would reformulate Orange Blossom Hand Lotion using P-desoxy-4-butylene.

PD4B also raised questions at the FDA. Early testing using strains of bacteria showed possible mutations. The FDA wrote a letter to the Orange Blossom president, suggesting that the new product be kept off the market until tests with laboratory animals were completed. The FDA can require warning labels only after animal testing. The process would take over three years.

Orange Blossom decided not to comply with the FDA. It argued that PD4B is not known to be unsafe to humans. It also said that without its hand lotion line, it would have to file for bankruptcy.

Questions

1. Was it sufficient, from a moral point of view, for hand lotions to carry a warning label if they contained Moxy?

2. Did the FDA do the right thing with the data it had on animal testing?

3. Was the hand lotion industry morally right in its response to the FDA regulation?

4. Explain the moral conflict of the Orange Blossom Company. Did it resolve it in a morally acceptable manner?

5. On what ethical basis does a company like the Orange Blossom Company inherit its obligation to inform consumers of risks associated with its product?

2. ENVIRONMENTAL RESPONSIBILITIES OF BUSINESS

In the past, business tended to view the environment as a "free good." The resources of the environment—air, water, land, animals, plants, and minerals—were available for use in whatever manner business saw fit. For example, mills and factories discharged waste materials into waterways or into the air without regard to the effects on the environment.

Because levels of population and industry were relatively low in proportion to the land area, it was easy to disregard the burdens placed on the *ecosystem* (the total interrelated community of living and nonliving entities). Now, contamination and depletion of natural resources have reached levels that cannot be ignored.

In recent years a growing ecological consciousness has developed, causing major struggles between environmentalists and the business community. Some ecologists argue that caring for the natural environment is a moral obligation and that polluting or degrading the environment is unjust because it violates the right of natural objects and nonhuman living things to be respected. Others believe that environmental quality should be maintained because human beings have a right to a clean, livable environment; this approach focuses upon protecting the safety and health interests of currently living humans. Still another argument stresses the responsibility to preserve the environment as a legacy for future generations.

Questions arise concerning the extent of businesses' responsibility for environmental protection. What methods would best ensure responsible practices? Governments attempt to control the uses of the environment and to force businesses to share costs of repairing ecological damage. Businesspeople see environmental protection measures as a threat to their interests. They insist that strict environmental regulation is not in the public interest because it results in decreased economic growth and increased unemployment. On this account, the high costs of pollution control and resource conservation hamper businesses' ability to operate profitably and lead to plant closings, layoffs, community instability, and economic hardships.

An equitable solution to what some believe is now an environmental crisis requires careful balancing of competing rights and interests over a wide range of values. Do animals, plants, and nonliving natural objects have moral status that would make it wrong to exploit or damage them? If so, should they be granted legal standing as a way of establishing their right to protection? (The issue of moral status if often raised in arguments concerning abortion **[See Health Care, Chapter 6, Section 1]**.) In the first article that follows, Christopher Stone calls for an expansion of the concept of legal rights to include nonhuman beings and natural objects. He argues that such beings and objects should have designated legal guardians to manage and protect their interests and he compares the proposal to guardianships for legally incompetent persons.

Another approach to environmental problems focuses on the notion of *externality* (or "spillover"). Economists use the term to refer to the divergence between public social costs and private industrial costs. For example, an industry that pollutes waterways may impose added costs on the public in the form of lost recreational use, higher prices for fish, or reduced drinking water quality (which causes health problems or requires community investment in water-treatment facilities). The industry benefits unfairly because external expenses are not figured into production costs. Some theorists propose forcing business to "internalize" the costs of pollution rather than allowing the burden to fall on the public. They argue that if industries have to take previously external costs into account, they will have an economic incentive to conserve environmental resources and minimize damage. Proponents maintain that this approach satisfies requirements of both compensatory and retributive justice. *Compensatory justice* requires that injured parties be compensated by those who injure them. If industries pay for pollution control, neighboring communities benefit and thereby gain compensation for losses they have suffered due to pollution. *Retributive justice* requires that the burden of rectifying an injury falls upon those who benefit from and are responsible for it. The stockholders and customers of a firm that pollutes benefit from the resultant artificially low production costs, but internalization of the costs of pollution restores the imbalance.

Cost-benefit analyses are sometimes used to evaluate proposed pollution control measures. Cost-benefit analysis represents a utilitarian approach to dealing with environmental problems. If, for example, one company's pollution causes $2,000 worth of damage and a device to eliminate the pollution would cost the firm $100, a clear utilitarian benefit exists from installing the device. However, if the figures were reversed, the investment would no longer be cost effective. Problems with using the approach lie in the difficulty of measuring the benefits of pollution control accurately. The benefits of ending a form of pollution derive in part from the risks which the pollution causes. How can risks be estimated and evaluated? For instance, what is the risk to public health from burning coal to produce electricity, and how does the danger compare with the risk of operating nuclear power plants?

The potential pollution effects and attendant risks involved in emerging technologies are difficult to predict. The problem of measurement is an important technical obstacle to cost-benefit analysis. In addition, cost-benefit analyses include factors not easy to quantify. For example, what monetary value should be placed on human life or health or the lives of other species? Is there a way to calculate the social and esthetic value of a clean environment?

In view of the problems in the utilitarian approach, some writers advocate absolute bans on pollution and on certain technologies which carry the risk of irreversible consequences. Reversing the effects of pollution, however, requires a more fundamental change in social attitudes. While it is easy to condemn corporations for contaminating the environment, finding long-range solutions demands a recognition that we all play a part in the problem. In the second article that follows, David R. Frew examines the disparity between individual values and organizational behavior. The author observes that individuals who deplore pollution still knowingly participate in organizations that cause it. Frew calls for an increased sense of responsibility "for the outcome of our participation in social organizations."

CHRISTOPHER D. STONE

Should Trees Have Standing?—
Toward Legal Rights for Natural Objects

Throughout legal history, each successive extension of rights to some new entity has been, theretofore, a bit unthinkable. We are inclined to suppose the rightlessness of rightless "things" to be a decree of Nature, not a legal convention acting in support of some status quo. It is thus that we defer considering the choices involved in all their moral, social, and economic dimensions. And so the United States Supreme Court could straight-facedly tell us in *Dred Scott* that Blacks had been denied the rights of citizenship "as a subordinate and inferior class of beings, who had been subjugated by the dominant race. . . ."[1] In the nineteenth century, the highest court in California explained that Chinese had not the right to testify against white men in criminal matters because they were "a race of people whom nature has marked as inferior, and who are incapable of progress or intellectual development beyond a certain point . . . between whom and ourselves nature has placed an impassable difference."[2] The popular conception of the Jew in the 13th century contributed to a law which treated them as "men *ferae naturae*, protected by a quasi-forest law. Like the roe and the deer, they form an order apart."[3] Recall, too, that it was not so long ago that the foetus was "like the roe and the deer." In an early suit attempting to establish a wrongful death action on behalf of a negligently killed foetus (now widely accepted practice), Holmes, then on the Massachusetts Supreme Court, seems to have thought it simply inconceivable "that a man might owe a civil duty and incur a conditional prospective liability in tort to one not yet in being."[4] The first woman in Wisconsin who thought she might have a right to practice law was told that she did not, in the following terms:

The law of nature destines and qualifies the female sex for the bearing and nurture of the children of our race and for the custody of the homes of the world. . . . [A]ll life-long callings of women, inconsistent with these radical and sacred duties of their sex, as is the profession of the law, are departures from the order of nature; and when voluntary, treason against it. . . . The peculiar qualities of womanhood, its gentle graces, its quick sensibility, its tender susceptibility, its purity, its delicacy, its emotional impulses, its subordination of hard reason to sympathetic feeling, are surely not qualifications for forensic strife. Nature has tempered woman as little for the juridical conflicts of the court room, as for the physical conflicts of the battle field. . . .[5]

The fact is, that each time there is a movement to confer rights onto some new "entity," the proposal is bound to sound odd or frightening or laughable. This is partly because until the rightless thing receives its rights, we cannot see it as anything but a *thing* for the use of "us"—those who are holding rights at the time. In this vein, what is striking about the Wisconsin case above is that the court, for all its talk about women, so clearly was never able to see women as they are (and might become). All it could see was the popular "idealized" version of *an object it needed*. Such is the way the slave South looked upon the Black. There is something of a seamless web involved: there will be resistance to giving the thing "rights" until it can be seen and valued for itself; yet, it is hard to see it and value it for itself until we can bring ourselves to give it "rights"—which is almost inevitably going to sound inconceivable to a large group of people.

The reason for this little discourse on the

Excerpt reprinted by permission from the *Southern California Law Review*, 45 (1972), 453–60, 463–64, 480–81, 486–87.

unthinkable, the reader must know by now, if only from the title of the paper. I am quite seriously proposing that we give legal rights to forests, oceans, rivers and other so-called "natural objects" in the environment—indeed, to the natural environment as a whole.

As strange as such a notion may sound, it is neither fanciful or devoid of operational content. In fact, I do not think it would be a misdescription of recent developments in the law to say that we are already on the verge of assigning some such rights, although we have not faced up to what we are doing in those particular terms. We should do so now, and begin to explore the implications such a notion would hold.

Toward Rights for the Environment

Now, to say that the natural environment should have rights is not to say anything as silly as that no one should be allowed to cut down a tree. We say human beings have rights, but—at least as of the time of this writing—they can be executed. Corporations have rights, but they cannot plead the fifth amendment; *In re Gault* gave 15-year-olds certain rights in juvenile proceedings, but it did not give them the right to vote. Thus, to say that the environment should have rights is not to say that it should have every right we can imagine, or even the same body of rights as human beings have. Nor is it to say that everything in the environment should have the same rights as every other thing in the environment.

But for a thing to be a *holder of legal rights*, something more is needed than that some authoritative body will review the actions and processes of those who threaten it. As I shall use the term, "holder of legal rights," each of three additional criteria must be satisfied. All three, one will observe, go towards making a thing *count* jurally—to have a legally recognized worth and dignity in its own right, and not merely to serve as a means to benefit "us" (whoever the contemporary group of rights-holders may be). They are, first, that the thing can institute legal actions *at its behest*; sec-

ond, that in determining the granting of legal relief, the court must take *injury to it* into account; and, third, that relief must run to the *benefit of it*.

The Rightlessness of Natural Objects at Common Law

Consider, for example, the common law's posture toward the pollution of a stream. True, courts have always been able, in some circumstances, to issue orders that will stop the pollution. . . . But the stream itself is fundamentally rightless, with implications that deserve careful reconsideration.

The first sense in which the stream is not a rights-holder has to do with standing. The stream itself has none. So far as the common law is concerned, there is in general no way to challenge the polluter's actions save at the behest of a lower riparian—another human being—able to show an invasion of *his* rights. This conception of the riparian as the holder of the right to bring suit has more than theoretical interest. The lower riparians may simply not care about the pollution. They themselves may be polluting, and not wish to stir up legal waters. They may be economically dependent on their polluting neighbor. And, of course, when they discount the value of winning by the costs of bringing suit and the chances of success, the action may not seem worth undertaking. . . .

The second sense in which the common law denies "rights" to natural objects has to do with the way in which the merits are decided in those cases in which someone is competent and willing to establish standing. At its more primitive levels, the system protected the "rights" of the property owning human with minimal weighing of any values: "*Cujus est solum, ejus est usque ad coelum et ad infernos.*" Today we have come more and more to make balances—but only such as will adjust the economic best interests of identifiable humans.

. . . None of the natural objects, whether held in common or situated on private land, has any of the three criteria of a rights-holder.

They have no standing in their own right; their unique damages do not count in determining outcome; and they are not the beneficiaries of awards. In such fashion, these objects have traditionally been regarded by the common law, and even by all but the most recent legislation, as objects for man to conquer and master and use—in such a way as the law once looked upon "man's" relationships to African Negroes. Even where special measures have been taken to conserve them, as by seasons on game and limits on timber cutting, the dominant motive has been to conserve them *for us*—for the greatest good of the greatest number of human beings. Conservationists, so far as I am aware, are generally reluctant to maintain otherwise. As the name implies, they want to conserve and guarantee *our* consumption and *our* enjoyment of these other living things. In their own right, natural objects have counted for little, in law as in popular movements. . . .

As I mentioned at the outset, however, the rightlessness of the natural environment can and should change; it already shows some signs of doing so.

Toward Having Standing in Its Own Right

It is not inevitable, nor is it wise, that natural objects should have no rights to seek redress in their own behalf. It is no answer to say that streams and forests cannot have standing because streams and forests cannot speak. Corporations cannot speak either; nor can states, estates, infants, incompetents, municipalities or universities. Lawyers speak for them, as they customarily do for the ordinary citizen with legal problems. One ought, I think, to handle the legal problems of natural objects as one does the problems of legal incompetents—human beings who have become vegetable. If a human being shows signs of becoming senile and has affairs that he is de jure incompetent to manage, those concerned with his well-being make such a showing to the court, and someone is designated by the court with the authority to manage the incompetent's affairs. The guardian (or "conserva-

tor" or "committee"—the terminology varies) then represents the incompetent in his legal affairs. Courts make similar appointments when a corporation has become "incompetent"—they appoint a trustee in bankruptcy or reorganization to oversee its affairs and speak for it in court when that becomes necessary.

On a parity of reasoning, we should have a system in which, when a friend of a natural object perceives it to be endangered, he can apply to a court for the creation of a guardianship. . . .

. . . One reason for making the environment itself the beneficiary of a judgment is to prevent it from being "sold out" in a negotiation among private litigants who agree not to enforce rights that have been established among themselves. Protection from this will be advanced by making the natural object a party to an injunctive settlement. Even more importantly, we should make it a beneficiary of money awards. . . .

The idea of assessing damages as best we can and placing them in a trust fund is far more realistic than a hope that a total "freeze" can be put on the environmental status quo. Nature is a continuous theatre in which things and species (eventually man) are destined to enter and exit. In the meantime, co-existence of man and his environment means that *each* is going to have to compromise for the better of both. Some pollution of streams, for example, will probably be inevitable for some time. Instead of setting an unrealizable goal of enjoining absolutely the discharge of all such pollutants, the trust fund concept would (a) help assure that pollution would occur only in those instances where the social need for the pollutant's product (via his present method of production) was so high as to enable the polluter to cover *all* homocentric costs, plus some estimated costs to the environment *per se*, and (b) would be a corpus for preserving monies, if necessary, while the technology developed to a point where repairing the damaged portion of the environment was feasible. Such a fund might even finance the requisite research and development.

I do not doubt that other senses in which the environment might have rights will come to mind, and, as I explain more fully below, would be more apt to come to mind if only we should speak in terms of their having rights, albeit vaguely at first. "Rights" might well lie in unanticipated areas. It would seem, for example, that Chief Justice Warren was only stating the obvious when he observed in *Reynolds* v. *Sims* that "legislators represent people, not trees or acres." Yet, could not a case be made for a system of apportionment which *did* take into account the wildlife of an area? It strikes me as a poor idea that Alaska should have no more congressmen than Rhode Island primarily *because there are in Alaska all those trees and acres, those waterfalls and forests*. I am not saying anything as silly as that we ought to overrule *Baker* v. *Carr* and retreat from one man–one vote to a system of one man-or-tree–one vote. Nor am I even taking the position that we ought to count each acre, as we once counted each slave, as three-fifths of a man. But I am suggesting that there is nothing unthinkable about, and there might on balance even be a prevailing case to be made for, an electoral apportionment that made some systematic effort to allow for the representative "rights" of non-human life. And if a case can be made for that, which I offer here mainly for purpose of illustration, I suspect that a society that grew concerned enough about the environment to make it a holder of rights would be able to find quite a number of "rights" to have waiting for it when it got to court.

Notes

1. *Dred Scott* v. *Sandford*, 60 U.S. (19 How.) 396, 404–5 (1856).
2. *People* v. *Hall*, 4 Cal. 399, 405 (1854).
3. Schechter, "The Rightlessness of Medieval English Jewry," 45 *Jewish Q. Rev.*, 121, 135 1954) quoting from M. Bateson, *Medieval England*, 139 (1904).
4. *Dietrich* v. *Inhabitants of Northampton*, 138 Mass. 14, 16 (1884).
5. *In re* Goddell, 39 Wisc. 232, 245 (1875).

DAVID R. FREW

Pollution: Can People Be Innocent While Their Systems Are Guilty?

Two very diverse events recently led to the formulation of a thesis which is presented in this paper; that thesis involves the synergistic property of organizational behavior. First, an essay by Charles Hampden-Turner entitled, "Synergy as the Optimization of Differentiation and Integration by the Human Personality (1)," very effectively dealt with the idea of synergy as an important aspect of both the physical and social systems of life. Secondly, research activity as an organization theorist occasioned a visit to a rather large corporation which is a major polluter of both air and water in its community.[1] A relationship, which became apparent almost immediately, served to explain the pollution in terms of the synergy. The purpose of this paper, then, is to evolve and discuss the basic relationship between these two concepts—organizational behavior and environmental pollution.

Reprinted by permission of the author and publisher from *Academy of Management Review*, March 1973.

Synergy

In its purest definition, synergism[2] is energy which exists in unexplainable proportion to entropy,[3] the movement of all organisms toward death. More specifically, it is that property by which an arrangement or system of component parts takes on an identity which is essentially different from the aggregate of the parts of the system.[4] An example of this process is the human body, which is a combination of water and a number of rather complex carbon molecules. If a strange being from another planet were studying the earth's water, for example, he might view a human being as simply an unusual arrangement of H_2O. But clearly, the particular arrangement, that is to say the person himself, takes on an identity which transcends his "parts list." Another and perhaps more visible example is a transistor radio. In its unassembled form the instrument consists of transistors, capacitors, resistors, diodes, wire, and a number of other parts. But the particular combination of those parts which is called a radio suddenly exhibits behavior which is unlike the behavior which might be expected of a typical electrical part. It plays music!

The Components of Human Behavior

Returning to the practical matter at hand, the task is to understand the actions of particular business firms. Essential to that problem, however, is an introduction to the notion of human behavior.

Most living organisms exhibit behavior of one sort or another, and many sciences have organized themselves around the study of this behavior. For example, zoologists study animal behavior, and botanists study the behavior of plants. The study of human behavior, however, is particularly fascinating and challenging to science because unlike most of his cohabitor organisms in the known world, man's behavior takes place on a number of nesting levels.

First there is individual behavior, the component which mankind has in common with other organisms and which has concerned psychologists for many years. Each of us is a behavior generating device which responds to all kinds of stimuli by behaving in various ways. At a second level there is group behavior. People have persistently demonstrated a tendency to congregate into groups for the pursuit of goals which would appear to be unattainable on the basis of individual efforts alone (5, p. 5). There is some controversy surrounding the notion that this aspect of human behavior is particular only to humans. Some say that other primates also exhibit group behavior (3, p. 250), but for the moment, that shall remain an open question, since it is the third and final component, organizational behavior, which is most critical to the present discussion.

Organizations

There is very little controversy surrounding the observation that man appears to be the only species that ties together individuals and groups into the logically structured multi-goal seeking systems which have come to be called organizations. It is a fact that these systems have become, at least for western man, the core of life. Almost all of us work, play, worship, and recreate under the auspices of one or more formal organizations. From the attention which has been focused upon this 20th century phenomenon a new behavioral science has emerged calling itself Organization Theory[5] and addressing itself to the profound problems of behavior; both inter- and intraorganizational.

One Organization in Perspective

As a caseworking theorist, the author recently was exposed to a number of persons who were working at various levels in the hierarchy of a company which is popularly considered to be a substantial polluter. From interviews with these persons, an extremely simple but at the same time profound realization emerged. Although each interviewee recognized his organization's role as a polluter, none either was acting in a way which would be interpreted (at least in a direct sense) as causing the pollution, nor was any individual in a position to end or to significantly change the process.

In a lengthy discussion with the president of the corporation, it became apparent that the man who occupied the role of president was just as concerned about the pollution as the people who were standing outside of the front gate with vindictive signs. He indicated his love for "nature" and discussed at some length his particular hobbies, which included forestry, bird watching and a number of other kinds of activities which appeared to be, at least at the surface level, incongruous with the behavior of his organization. Further interview sessions with executives, middle managers, and finally rank and file workers of the same organization confirmed this finding. Members of the organization consistently were in opposition to the pollution which their company was generating, but at the same time they were content to continue their day to day existence as contributors to the very problem which they opposed. One respondent commented that it was only a matter of time until the plant in question utterly despoiled its entire surrounding area and that it was a "real crime" since the area was at one time a beautiful natural resource. When questioned further about his personal response to the situation, he stated that he was powerless to stop the process but that he had purchased a second home (out of the immediate surrounding area) and was planning to move as the effects of the plant became ecologically overwhelming.

The Dilemma
of Organizational Synergy

Seeing these relatively intelligent and thoughtful persons acting in such an ecologically schizophrenic manner was a particularly frightening revelation. How can an organiza-

tion behave in a way that is so different from the desires and the ends of its aggregate membership?

Perhaps the answer to this dilemma revolves about the concept of synergy. Just as the behavior of a transistor radio is essentially different from the behavior of any individual component, the behavior of a human organization may be essentially different from the behavior of its component parts, the members of the organization.

It may be concluded, then, that organizational synergy is a product of systemic or structured relationships which are implied by the concept of organization itself. Further, this synergism, by the nature of synergistic behavior, would appear not to be closely related to the kinds of behavior which are expected of the components of the organizations—individuals and/or groups. The implied danger is that while we seem to expect that interorganizational behavior will essentially appear as, and affect society as, a multiplication or aggregate of individual behavior, the property of organizational synergy would suggest that this is not true. Using individual or group behavior, the actions of organizations have and will continue to be unpredictable.

The Implications

Given a number of random behavior generating devices, in the form of organizations within society, one might well expect to encounter some social problems in terms of behavioral manifestations. This is particularly true considering the extent to which our resources are controlled by contemporary organizations.

Thus, it might be expected, due to the random nature of inter-organizational behavior (random in the sense of human values), that some of the resulting activities of organizations would be of negative social value. Pollution is a prime example of this kind of behavior. While organizations may consist of altruistic, nature loving ecologists, the systems themselves continue to pollute.

A Prescription

We live in an organized society and in an organized world. But as yet we have not begun to evaluate the problem of organizational behavior which is in opposition to human values from an ecological viewpoint. If we are to create a new world; one which will provide an improved life style for all, it would seem that we must cease our naive practice of assuming that our organizations, by definition, must help us. To the contrary, the empirical evidence indicates the ever-present danger of organizations behaving in ways which violate basic social justice. The synergistic property of organizational behavior would appear to make this fact not just logical, but perfectly predictable.

To meet and solve this challenge we must seek increasing knowledge of organized activity and the behavior which follows. We must try to explain, by way of behavioral sciences, the previously unexpected behavior of these organizations which we have generated. We can no longer plead innocent, as individuals, to the responsibility for the behavior of our social systems. Rather, a new consciousness is called for: an understanding and acceptance of responsibility for the outcome of our participation in social organizations. It is only with this kind of a systemic morality that we will be able to work for ecological balance by utilizing both internal and external organizational pressures.

Notes

1. For obvious reasons the name of the particular firm shall remain anonymous; however, the role of that firm as polluter is almost without question. It has been and continues to be a source of controversy in its community news media and among residents. Even the people who worked for the firm recognized their own pollution problem.

2. For another definition of the term see Katz and Kahn, p. 33 (ref. 2).

3. Katz and Kahn also deal with the entropy concept. See pp. 19, 21, 23, 28 (ref. 2).

4. Much of the credit for arriving at this definition must be given to Charles Hampden-Turner's essay (ref. 1).

5. A comprehensive introduction to the field is contained in the first chapter of *Organizational Psychology* by Edgar Schein (ref. 4).

References

1. Hampden-Turner, Charles. "Synergy as the Optimization of Differentiation and Integration by the Human Personality," in J. W. Lorsch and Paul R. Lawrence (Eds.), *Studies in Organizational Design* (Homewood, Ill.: Irwin, 1970), pp. 187–196.

2. Katz, D., and R. L. Kahn. *The Social Psychology of Organizations* (New York: Wiley, 1966).

3. Pfeiffer, John. *The Emergence of Man* (New York: Harper & Row, 1969).

4. Schein, Edgar. *Organizational Psychology* (Englewood Cliffs, N.J.: Prentice-Hall, 1964).

5. Shepherd, Clovis. *Small Groups* (San Francisco: Chandler, 1964).

Suggested Further Reading

Beckerman, Wilfred, "The Case for Economic Growth," *Public Utilities Fortnightly*, September 26, 1972.

Blackstone, William T., "Ethics and Ecology." Reprinted in *Ethical Theory and Business*, ed. Tom L. Beauchamp and Norman E. Bowie. Englewood Cliffs, N.J.: Prentice-Hall, 1979, pp. 550–57.

Boulding, Kenneth E., "Fun and Games with the Gross National Product: The Role of Misleading Indicators in Social Policy," *The Environmental Crisis*, ed. Harold W. Helfrich, Jr. New Haven, Conn.: Yale University Press, 1970, pp. 157–70.

Hardin, Garret, "The Tragedy of the Commons," *Science* 162 (December 1968), 1243–1248.

Singer, Peter, "All Animals Are Equal," *Philosophic Exchange*, vol. 1, no. 5, Summer 1974.

DECISION SCENARIO 4

Responsibilities to the Environment

The Polychrome Pigment factory was a well-known sight to all river-goers at Poughkeepsie. The building was turn-of-the-century brick, whose sloping roofs had earned it a historical designation. The product of the Polychrome factory was more questionable.

Polychrome used the Poughkeepsie site to manufacture pigments for its lead-based paints. The company had grown and diversified from its early days as a maker of house paints. Aerodynamics and forest products were now its profitable units. The pigment factory still eked out a profit, however, and when it didn't, it was a useful tax write-off.

The factory had been constructed long before regulations protecting the environment came into being. Waste was dumped into the Hudson River. The waste contained lead, which sank to the bottom of the river bed, where it was incorporated into the ecosystem. Bottom scavengers such as striped bass were found to have abnormally high lead deposits in their bodies. In addition, a few downriver communities used river water for irrigation, and even for drinking.

In July 1984 the Environmental Protection Agency mandated waste treatment for the Poughkeepsie Polychrome plant. It announced that it intended to enforce federal regulations requiring an 80 percent reduction in waste lead content. It said that unless lead waste efflux was reduced, the fishing industry faced a $75 million a year loss, since striped bass would be taken off the market. In addition, it cited a marked increase in lead poisoning in communities downriver from Poughkeepsie.

The Polychrome Company estimated that updating their waste treatment plant would cost about $50 million. Disposing of it another way would cost $8 to $10 million a year. The old factory was a beauty, but it wasn't worthwhile to the company.

The factory employed about 330 people and played a significant role in the local economy. In accordance with EPA policy, a hearing was called for Poughkeepsie residents to air their views. Their choice was either to face a negative blow to local industry or to risk closing down the fishing industry whose impact was unclear. Emotion ran high on both sides. Young mothers voiced their fear of lead poisoning their babies. The president of the city council spoke of the need for a stable tax base. The EPA defended its position of giving local communities the final say in determining what level of environmental risk was acceptable.

Questions

1. How much moral weight should be given to pollution control in corporate decisions such as the one the Polychrome Company faced?

2. How much risk to the environment is too much to be morally acceptable?

3. How do you justify obligations the corporation has to the environment in terms of ethical theory?

4. What ought the citizens of Poughkeepsie to do about the Polychrome situation?

5. Are the ethics of the EPA correct in allowing local views to be the decisive factor?

3. INTERNATIONAL RESPONSIBILITY

Perceived abuses in international business practices have drawn increasing criticism in recent years. Critics charge that businesses exploit the economies, resources, and people of foreign countries in ways that would not be acceptable at home. For example, the Nestlé Corporation's aggressive marketing of powdered infant formula in developing countries was condemned as being exploitative, immoral, and irresponsible. Babies who were fed the formula, rather than being breastfed, often developed severe diarrhea or malnutrition because the formula was improperly prepared, overdiluted, or mixed with contaminated water. The company was accused (along with other producers) of complicity in the death of Third World infants whose mothers had been pressured by advertising to use the formula, and a major international boycott was instituted against Nestlé. In May 1981 the World Health Organization adopted a "Code of Marketing Breastmilk Substitutes" which called for government bans on advertising that discourages breastfeeding. The United States cast the sole dissenting vote among 119 members of the organization.

In another case, critics allege that multinational agri-business practices supply luxury goods for export to developed nations at the expense of subsistence farmers in poor countries. The critics argue that the so-called "green revolution"—touted as an aid to agriculture in underdeveloped nations—in reality benefits companies and consumers in developed countries while damaging the environments and economic systems of Third World farmers. In response to these claims, corporations argue that their primary obligation is to maximize profits and that expanding markets or developing resources in other nations is in conformity with that obligation. They maintain also that developing countries benefit from the introduction of sophisticated technologies and products which have been perfected elsewhere.

Dumping is another international business practice that raises ethical questions. It is not uncommon for products banned on the U.S. market because of safety or health hazards to be exported and sold ("dumped") overseas. One might think that government regulatory agencies would attempt to prevent the practice, but often they tolerate or even support it. The case of the Dalkon Shield intrauterine contraceptive device is one example. When the device was shown to cause pelvic inflammation, blood poisoning, tubal pregnancies, uterine perforation, and possibly even death, the domestic market for the product diminished sharply. Despite the known hazards, an office of the U.S. Agency for International Development arranged to purchase a large number of the devices at a discount for use in population-control programs in Third World countries. The agency maintained that the countries' high rates of maternal death in childbirth justified the distribution of virtually any contraceptives.

Export of banned or dangerous products is regulated by a State Department system that requires notifying foreign governments whenever a product has been banned, deregulated, suspended, or cancelled by an American agency. Beyond notification, however, there is little or no further involvement on the part of the U.S. government. Supporters of this policy justify it on grounds that it protects the right of other nations to establish their own standards. They maintain that it would be paternalistic for the United States to interfere with foreign governments' decisions regarding public health and safety.

The issue of paternalism gives rise to an additional ethical question about international business practice. Should corporations attempt to exercise moral influence over policies or conditions in foreign countries? For example, some theorists have argued that it is wrong for American companies to participate in the economy of South Africa, where the black majority is severely oppressed by the government's apartheid policies. They maintain that U.S. business should in effect boycott South Africa to express disapproval of apartheid and that companies, by remaining, lend moral and economic support to an unethical system. Others argue that continued involvement by U.S. companies is more likely to improve the position of blacks in South Africa. These proponents believe that U.S. multinationals are a force for beneficial change in South Africa and that withdrawal would result in a faltering economy in which blacks would suffer more than others. In either case the question remains whether it is appropriate for corporations to try to influence the moral climate of nations in which they operate.

In the essay that follows, Louis Turner examines some of the harmful effects which can result from extensive investment by multinational companies in the Third World. Among the hazards Turner describes is the problem of dependency. To illustrate the dangers of dependency, the author asks readers to imagine what the consequences might have been for the United States if it had been similarly dependent on the technology and corporations of Great Britain at the time of the American Revolution.

LOUIS TURNER

There's No Love Lost Between Multinational Companies and the Third World

Managers of multinational corporations excel at such tasks as transferring products, technology, and advanced management thinking to all quarters of the globe. In doing so, they tend to assume that the problems of New Delhi, Lagos, or Rio de Janeiro can be solved by hardware and concepts developed in Frankfurt or Detroit. Critics deny this. They argue that the impact of such corporations in the Third World is, in fact, harmful in that they exacerbate the tensions found within such societies and help create the kind of tragically polarized societies which we can see throughout Latin America. What is good for General Motors is probably, in the long run, not so good for Gabon and Guatemala.

To take a simple example: The Swiss company, Nestlé, introduced powdered milk as a baby food into West Africa as an alternative to breast feeding. Emulating Western fashion, local mothers adopted bottle feeding wholeheartedly. The result was increased infant mortality: To combat their extreme poverty, mothers were diluting the milk to the point that a bottle had virtually no nutrition.

In earlier times, few managers worried about such niceties. The bulk of corporations in the Third World were looking for minerals or tropical produce which they would ship back to the industrialized world as fast as possible. Rather than contribute to the wider development of the societies in which they found themselves, they created "enclaves," virtual states-within-states, in which their rule was law. Due to their influence, some countries with diversified agricultural economies became dependent on single crops; the Central American "banana republics" and the rubber economies of Malaya and Liberia are examples. Even if such countries were formally independent, they were in fact shackled by their nearly total dependence on the benevolence of companies such as Firestone and United Fruit. Political leaders and local entrepreneurs either flourished or were overthrown at the whim of these companies, thus stifling the development of local economic and political initiative. On occasions, the companies even tried to redraw political boundaries, as when the Belgian mining company, Union Minière, helped finance the attempted breakaway of Katanga soon after the ex-Belgian Congo (now Zaire) attained independence.

Today, despite the abortive coup attempts of ITT in Chile, the situation is less stark. As Third World economies have grown, they have become more diversified, reducing their dependence on single companies and forcing managements to become more circumspect in their outward behavior. In the aftermath of the Independence Era, governments have been growing in self-confidence and experience, and they are now willing to attack corporations which get out of line. Obviously the example of OPEC (Organization of Petroleum Exporting Countries) have been extremely important, as it has shown how relatively powerless the oil giants actually are. Since the oil producers began their onslaught, the bauxite producers have started to follow suit, with significant actions also coming from the governments of Malaysia (rubber) and Morocco (phosphates). However, despite this Third World militancy, the multinationals remain formidable adversaries.

Squeezing Out Local Entrepreneurs

For one thing, the multinationals are still very large by Third World standards. They possess the technical and marketing skills that countries trying to industrialize desperately need. The result is often a dependence on foreign companies to a degree embarrassing to see. Take the case of Unilever's subsidiary in Nigeria, the United Africa Co. (UAC), which originally entered that country to produce palm oil needed for the manufacture of margarine. By natural expansion it diversified into shipping and a general import-export trade aimed at the Nigerian market. As the country grew, so did the UAC, establishing itself in all the new markets created by Nigeria's fledgling industrialization. By the mid-1960s, it was four times the size of the next largest company, and one could almost claim that the industrialization of Nigeria was the industrialization of UAC. From its start as an agricultural and trading company, it moved into textiles, sugar, beer, cement, cigarettes, building contracting, radio assembly, plastic products, bicycle and truck assembly, etc. In any sector which mattered, the company was involved.

UAC is generally credited with having used its power responsibly; but, in microcosm, its history reflects what has been happening throughout the Third World. In the case of Latin America, foreign industrialists were squeezing local competitors out of all key industries as early as the nineteenth century. Every time there was a slump, it would be the undercapitalized local businessmen who would go to the wall, leaving the multinationals to emerge ever more dominant. Only during the two world wars, when European and American companies had other things on their minds, did local entrepreneurs have a chance to flourish—but this was not enough. Today, it is virtually meaningless to talk of Third World entrepreneurship in the sense in which Carnegie or Rockefeller were entrepreneurs. What we find instead is Third World planners and businessmen passively accepting technologies which have been developed by the multinationals, perhaps modifying them slightly for local needs, but certainly not trying to produce innovations which might challenge the foreigners' sway. This approach has probably contributed to the long-term political stagnation found in many Third World countries. Furthermore, it is culturally dangerous in that it assumes that products produced by the multinationals are suitable for Third World needs. In many cases, this is blatantly untrue.

The vast majority of multinationals are just not interested in the Third World except as a convenient residual market in which extra profits can be made once a product has proved itself in the American and European arenas. I once tested this belief by reading a couple of hundred company reports, looking for examples of involvement with the Third World which the companies might want to emphasize. It was a depressing experience. The majority of companies gave Third World activities no coverage at all, instead stressing things like the companies' contribution to the American space program. Otherwise, apart from CPC (the Corn Products Corp.), which had its chairman pictured knee-deep in a paddy field, the reports boasted of products like refrigerator fronts of Formica-based laminate (American Cyanamid in Argentina), car radios (Bosch in Brazil), or the lighting, traffic lights, and illustrated fountains along eighteen miles of road in the oil-rich Trucial States (Philips). Nothing about searches for nutritionally enriched forms of tropical fruits and vegetables; virtually nothing about the search for cures for tropical diseases; nothing about the search for labor-intensive industries which might well mop up the vast armies of the unemployed found everywhere in the poor countries. Instead, the companies listed trivial products which can contribute nothing to the long-term development of the Third World, but which are symptomatic of the overall corrupting effect which the multinationals tend to have on Third World elites.

Corrupting the Elite

These elites should be concerned with the majority of their countrymen who are still in the countryside working outside the market economy (if working at all—only some 2 percent of Nigeria's 63 million population is earn-

ing a wage or salary). They ought to be thinking of ways to cope with spiraling urban unemployment (some estimates suggest that 20 percent of the world's potential work force is without a job). Above all, they ought to be preaching austerity, since the task of pulling the world's poorest 40 percent above their current near-starvation level is one which will take decades, if not centuries.

The multinationals have very little constructive to offer. What they are good at is identifying and filling gaps in the markets of industrialized consumer societies; but, as Galbraith has pointed out, private enterprise does not lead automatically to the satisfaction of wider social needs. A dynamic auto industry, for instance, does not guarantee a good educational or health system; in the Third World, such an industry may even harm the interests of the bottom 40 percent of the population, since the elites will divert precious resources to building the roads and importing the gasoline which a flourishing auto industry demands. Thus the inequality of such societies increases, precisely the danger which the World Bank is starting to warn against. It contends that social inequality is growing noticeably within the Third World, even within rapidly growing economies like Brazil's. And it is starting to argue that the classic measurement of growth, GNP, is (by itself) a misleading indicator of development, that slower growing countries which put more stress on reducing social inequalities may well produce stabler societies in the long run.

The multinationals, whether they know it or not, are firmly on the side of inequality, forming a deadly alliance with corruptible Third World elites. The latter have been brought up to believe that one should envy the slick consumer society of the West, and they see the multinationals as the organizations which will deliver the goods. The elites want record players, refrigerators, cars, television, telephones, etc., and the multinationals are only too happy to deliver them. There are some managers who are aware that none of this is helping the starving and unemployed at the bottom of the pile. Sometimes they make token protests, but the elites prevail, since national pride tells them that their country is not modern unless it has things like an airport, an airline, a car industry, and a Hilton hotel. They can be extremely insistent on getting them. For instance, a Fiat manager once told me of the efforts they made in the late 1960s to persuade various national governments that truck plants were far better investments than car plants for countries at a low level of development. The technologies involved in assembling trucks are simpler, less import-intensive and more labor-intensive, and produce products which are of direct use in activities like farming and civil engineering. Their arguments were to no avail; the government officials insisted on having a car plant.

While the multinationals are not all to blame, clearly they are a vital part of the process which corrupts the elites. Hollywood films, television programs, and advertising are all instrumental in creating a certain image of Western society. The expatriate managers of multinational subsidiaries are a flesh and blood demonstration of this way of life. Highly paid (by local standards), they provide a model to the indigenous managers (who are increasingly replacing them) and to local officials. Their replacement can cause problems. In Africa, for instance, local replacements have been expecting not only similar levels of pay to those of the expatriate managers, but even some of the latters' "perks," like the free trip to Europe every eighteen months. From the start, local managers have expectations which can be satisfied only at the expense of the less powerful in their societies. In East Africa they have coined the name *Wa-Benzi* for the African elite which rides about in Mercedes-Benzes while the peasants and unemployed starve.

Another insidious effect arises from tourism, an industry in which multinationals are playing an increasing role. Tourists are flying more and more to exotic (i.e., poor) Third World destinations like the Pacific Islands, the Caribbean, and North and East Africa. Although many tourist resorts are "golden ghettos," located away from the centers of population, the social harm done by this industry is extraordinarily difficult to avoid. The local population learns to despise and cheat tourists, whose wealth appears limitless and who normally have no clear idea how much anything costs. Prostitution springs up, as seen in the Boys' towns, like Tijuana, along the U.S.–Mexican border. Even more grotesque are government attempts to build an image of friendliness toward tourists, launching "Be-Nice" campaigns and going so far as to have school children taught that tourists are friends who must be smiled at and treated well. Such campaigns are necessary in the sense that expressions of hostility may keep tourists from returning. But there is something intensely degrading about nations like Jamaica, Barbados, and the Bahamas launching such programs, particularly when they are part of a culture steeped deeply in the slave trade, with all its connotations of black servitude.

Real Development Does Not Pay

Despite everything, we should not be too harsh on the multinationals, since they are merely symbols for the general capitalist system, of which most of us are just as much a part. Asking them to contribute positively to the development of the Third World is to ask them to perform a task for which they were not designed. They are motivated by money, and yet we critics are asking them to develop goods for part of the world which is still predominantly outside the market economy. A bank, the Barclay's, lost $4.2 million in the early 1960s when its managers in West Africa were instructed to lend much more adventurously in rural areas. They managed to pull in small savings, but the amounts were so small, and so expensive to collect, that normal banking practices seemed almost irrelevant. Undoubtedly there was an overall social gain for Nigeria in the attempts to attract rural savings into productive investments, but a profit-oriented institution was obviously not the right vehicle for extending the experiment. Likewise, tractor manufacturers are searching for a mini-tractor which can compete effectively with the traditional ox and plough. Ford, for instance, spent at least six years trying to develop a simple, one-speed, seven-horse-power, rope-started model which could be easily assembled by local dealers, but after field-testing in Jamaica, Mexico, and Peru, and market-testing in Jamaica, they finally concluded that the returns were not going to be enough to justify their utilizing a dispropor-tionately high number of their executives on this product.

One is tempted to argue that there is little that the multinationals can do in key fields like population control, tropical diseases, and tropical agriculture—just the areas which would do most for that bottom 40 percent of the Third World. This is simply because on the scale on which most multinationals work, there just is not sufficient money to be made, and the risks are horrendous. So a pharma-ceutical company will always choose to inves-tigate a possible cure for arthritis, rather than a simple, self-administered, long-action con-traceptive using materials indigenous, say, to India. A cure for arthritis would be an instant gold mine; a long-action contraceptive for In-dia would run the risk that the company might have to sell to the Indian government at a loss, or might have its patents ignored. Either way, the product aimed at the Third World is just not an acceptable risk.

The multinationals play safe. They develop products for the U.S. and Europe and are pleasantly surprised if they find Third World markets as well. Obviously, the formula some-times works well for the poor. The discovery of DDT, for instance, did, with all its side ef-fects, eradicate malaria. On balance, though, the multinationals are happiest doing business with urbanized, westernized elites—the sol-diers who will buy their weapons, the manag-ers who will buy their consumer goods. It would be nice if all the people of the Third World were as rich as those of Rio de Janeiro and Sao Paulo; unfortunately, they are not. Multinationals have a lot to contribute to these cities, but virtually nothing for the peas-ants living in grinding poverty in Brazil's northeast.

The Evils of "Dependencia"

Finally, if we are looking at the cultural impact of multinationals, we must examine argu-ments stemming from Latin America about "Dependencia"—the contention that many of the ills of that continent can be blamed on the polarization of societies by overdependence on foreign markets, technology and culture. If this is indeed true of Latin America, what chance have the less developed continents of Africa and Asia?

This argument is difficult to substantiate conclusively, but it is not dissimilar to the charges raised by Ralph Nader and Mark Green about the effect of corporate domina-tion of U.S. communities. They have written that when a community's economy is con-trolled by national or multinational conglom-erates, the overall well-being of the commu-nity is threatened. Civic leadership suffers since corporate officials do not identify with communities which are merely one step on the career ladder. The independent middle classes are eliminated and income becomes less equitably distributed. Local society be-comes more polarized. They cite the words of C. Wright Mills: "Big business tends to de-press, while small business tends to raise the level of civic welfare."

On the international level, one can make a similar argument. Multinationals certainly pre-fer to do business with authoritarian regimes, which can guarantee a "secure" investment climate. They are happier investing in Brazil or Spain than in radical states like Allende's Chile or Nyerere's Tanzania. Nor do they show much sympathy toward democracies like Italy and India, where underlying social tensions interfere with the smooth running of the economy. Governments encourage multi-nationals to invest by repressing potential troublemakers. Taiwan, Singapore, and Ma-laysia vie with each other by guaranteeing for-eign investors freedom from trade union activ-ities.

On a deeper level, reliance on multina-tionals saps a nation's vitality. Multinationals do not encourage indigenous research and development, almost always choosing to locate these facilities in North America or Europe. Local businessmen become mere intermediaries, adapting foreign technologies (if at all) to local conditions. Where countries are industrializing, multinationals move in to snuff out local competition before it has any chance of getting established.

The American Lesson

The degree of dominance exercised, however benevolently, by companies like UAC in Nigeria is a phenomenon which no Western commentator is entitled to gloss over. It is totally unlike anything in the history of the United States or Europe. To begin to comprehend it, imagine the United States as a Third World country winning its independence from a technically sophisticated Great Britain whose per capita GNP was ten times as great as that of ours, and which possessed companies fully capable of operating in the American market. The first result would have been that the incredible flowering of American entrepreneurial talent in the nineteenth century would have been nipped in the bud. Cyrus McCormick, Francis Cabot Lowell, Cornelius Vanderbilt, John D. Rockefeller, and J.P. Morgan would, at best, have ended up as talented managers for some British conglomerate. After all, who would need to design an American reaper when perfectly adequate British designs already existed and could be imported or assembled under license? Public ire in the late nineteenth century would not have focused on "the trusts," but would have vented itself against a handful of British giants, one of which might well have owned not just the oil industry, but the key American railroads and transatlantic shipping lines as well. Congress would have been in the pay of the British, and independent presidents would have invited bombardment by the British navy or coups from the British intelligence service.

This is a fair picture of what multinational investment has meant to many Third World countries. Clearly, the American political tradition would have been totally different had it sprung from such a background. For one thing, political divisions would have been far deeper than they are. Labor disputes and left-wing politics would be tinged with greater intensity, for there would be a xenophobic element to all controversies. Radical critics would face a much less powerful middle class, since the entrepreneurial element of U.S. society would be much smaller. Above all, the unifying belief in the American dream would not exist. How could there be a filling of hope and optimism in a society where material "success" means working for some giant foreign company? The forces of the left would thus be relatively strong, forcing foreign corporate interests into relatively extreme defensive action. The likelihood of coups, armed repression, and terrorist tactics would be high.

So, we come to the harsh conclusion that multinational investment in the Third World has long-term harmful social and cultural effects. The multinational managers who complain about political chaos in Latin America are deluding themselves, since they are an integral part of the problem. This is not to claim that the majority of such managers are not perfectly well-meaning citizens; nor is it to deny that many of the products of their companies are of vital importance in the Third World. But we would do well to look more sympathetically at alternative approaches to development, while agreeing sadly with the words of George Bernard Shaw:

> Capitalism is not an orgy of human villainy, but a utopia that has dazzled and misled very amiable and public spirited men. The upholders of capitalism are dreamers and visionaries who, instead of doing good with evil intentions like Mephistopheles, do evil with the best of intentions.

Suggested Further Reading

Brown, Lester R., and Erik P. Eckhol, "The Empty Breadbasket," *Ceres*, March–April 1974, p. 59.

Clement, Doug, "Infant Formula Malnutrition:

Threat to the Third World," *The Christian Century*, March 1, 1978, p. 209.

Galbraith, John Kenneth, "The Defense of the Multi-National Company," *Harvard Business Review,* 56, no. 2 (March–April 1978), 83–93.

Jagjit, B., R. D. Ramsey, and R. Wright, "Six Challenges to Global Corporations," *Collegiate Forum*, Spring, 1982.

O'Neill, Onora, "Lifeboat Earth," *Philosophy and Public Affairs*, IV, no. 3 (Spring 1975), 288.

4. THE SOCIAL RESPONSIBILITY OF BUSINESS

Many people view the enterprise of investigating business ethics with skepticism. When discussions arise about morality in business, one commonly voiced opinion is that ethics is irrelevant to business. What is the reasoning behind the view that ordinary moral standards do not apply in a business context? Some believe that corporate managers have special obligations which legitimize behavior that would normally be unacceptable. A similar argument is advanced to justify questionable behavior by attorneys. **[See Criminal Justice, Chapter 16, Section 2.]** On this view, the primary obligation of a businessperson is to increase the profits of the corporation he or she represents.

The notion of special corporate responsibilities is in turn based on a commitment to the ideology of a free market economy. On this analysis, a business is private property which functions to produce profits for the proprietors, and as entrepreneurs pursue profit, their combined efforts will result in social well-being. Implicit in this view is the assumption that the welfare of the community is identical with the combined welfare of individual members. Not everyone is equally successful in the capitalist system, and some end up with much more than others, but the inequality is not viewed as a problem. In an economic system based on self-interest, the unequal reward to individuals is a product of their unequal contributions to the economy. According to this view, economic justice results because those who have made a greater contribution are thought to deserve a larger reward. In addition, the productive innovations developed by entrepreneurs pursuing self-interest create more wealth in which everyone shares to some degree.

In the article that follows, Milton Friedman argues that businesspeople are obligated to carry out the desires of proprietors who employ them. As a rule, the owners' objective is increased profits. Friedman, a forceful exponent of the values of the free market system, insists that corporate employees are bound to perform a specific *economic* function. Managers, he maintains, have no obligation to help alleviate social problems such as pollution or discrimination. Rather, the moral decisions of managers should be guided by their primary duty to further the interests of shareholders. The author insists that businesspeople have neither the expertise nor the authority to exercise "social responsibility" in making business decisions. This argument recalls a similar claim concerning health care professionals. **[See Health Care, Chapter 9, Section 1.]** The only ethical constraints upon business activity which Friedman endorses are the avoidance of coercion and fraud. On his view, government regulation should be confined to maintaining free competition and preventing deception.

Many ethicists challenge the belief that business has no responsibility to society beyond avoiding coercion and deception. Some question the underlying principle of distributive justice in capitalism. Distributive justice is satisfied when each person deserves what he or she receives. In a capitalist system rewards are distributed primarily on the basis of contributions to the economy. However, conditions outside the control of individuals may prevent them from making the contributions which would bring economic rewards. Because of the inequality of opportunity and reward under capitalism, some critics call for a radical restructuring of the economic system. *Socialists* advocate social rather than private ownership of the means of production. A socialist system distributes rewards on the basis of need rather than economic contribution. Proponents of socialism regard need as the most important principle of distributive justice.

Other critics reject Friedman's narrow view of corporate social responsibility but do not demand fundamental changes in the economy. They hold that business as a social institution has other functions besides the specifically economic function of profit making. Some businesspeople fear that demands for increased social responsibility will lead to increases in government regulation and control. Others argue that if business takes the initiative in addressing social responsibility issues, government intervention can be avoided.

Advocates of increased social responsibility on the part of business encounter a problem which stems from the nature of corporations. A corporation is not a person; rather, it comprises a group of individuals who make decisions and carry out policy collectively. Some theorists claim that only persons are capable of moral responsibility. Thus, they insist, it is inappropriate to view corporations as moral agents and to judge them by ethical standards pertaining to individuals. Friedman locates ethical responsibility in the "invisible hand" of the free market system. Others stress the role of government in enforcing business morality. Still others believe that responsibility for ethical behavior should be assigned to corporate managers.

MILTON FRIEDMAN

The Social Responsibility of Business Is to Increase Its Profits

When I hear businessmen speak eloquently about the "social responsibilities of business in a free-enterprise system," I am reminded of the wonderful line about the Frenchman who discovered at the age of 70 that he had been speaking prose all his life. The businessmen believe that they are defending free enterprise when they declaim that business is not concerned "merely" with profit but also with promoting desirable "social" ends; that business has a "social conscience" and takes seriously its responsibilities for providing employment, eliminating discrimination, avoiding pollution and whatever else may be the catchwords of the contemporary crop of reformers. In fact they are—or would be if they or anyone else took them seriously—preaching pure and unadulterated socialism. Businessmen who talk this way are unwitting puppets of the intellectual forces that have been undermining the basis of a free society these past decades.

The discussions of the "social responsibilities of business" are notable for their analytical looseness and lack of rigor. What does it mean to say that "business" has responsibilities? Only people can have responsibilities. A corporation is an artificial person and in this sense may have artificial responsibilities, but "business" as a whole cannot be said to have responsibilities, even in this vague sense. The first step toward clarity in examining the doctrine of the social responsibility of business is to ask precisely what it implies for whom.

Presumably, the individuals who are to be responsible are businessmen, which means individual proprietors or corporate executives. Most of the discussion of social responsibility is directed at corporations, so in what follows I shall mostly neglect the individual proprietors and speak of corporate executives.

In a free-enterprise, private-property system, a corporate executive is an employee of the owners of the business. He has direct responsibility to his employers. That responsibility is to conduct the business in accordance with their desires, which generally will be to make as much money as possible while conforming to the basic rules of the society, both those embodied in law and those embodied in ethical custom. Of course, in some cases his employers may have a different objective. A group of persons might establish a corporation for an eleemosynary purpose—for example, a hospital or a school. The manager of such a corporation will not have money profit as his objectives but the rendering of certain services.

In either case, the key point is that, in his capacity as a corporate executive, the manager is the agent of the individuals who own the corporation or establish the eleemosynary institution, and his primary responsibility is to them.

Needless to say, this does not mean that it is easy to judge how well he is performing his task. But at least the criterion of performance is straightforward, and the persons among whom a voluntary contractual arrangement exists are clearly defined.

Of course, the corporate executive is also a person in his own right. As a person, he may have many other responsibilities that he recognizes or assumes voluntarily—to his family, his conscience, his feelings of charity, his church, his clubs, his city, his country. He may feel impelled by these responsibilities to devote part of his income to causes he regards as worthy, to refuse to work for particular corporations, even to leave his job, for example, to join his country's armed forces. If we wish, we may refer to some of these responsibilities as "social responsibilities." But in these respects he is acting as a principal, not an agent; he is spending his own money or time or energy, not the money of his employers or the time or energy he has contracted to devote to their purposes. If these are "social responsibilities," they are the social responsibilities of individuals, not of business.

What does it mean to say that the corporate executive has a "social responsibility" in his capacity as businessman? If this statement is not pure rhetoric, it must mean that he is to act in some way that is not in the interest of his employers. For example, that he is to refrain from increasing the price of the product in order to contribute to the social objective of preventing inflation, even though a price increase would be in the best interests of the corporation. Or that he is to make expenditures on reducing pollution beyond the amount that is in the best interests of the corporation or that is required by law in order to contribute to the social objective of improving the environment. Or that, at the expense of corporate profits, he is to hire "hardcore" unemployed instead of better qualified available workmen to contribute to the social objective of reducing poverty.

In each of these cases, the corporate executive would be spending someone else's money for a general social interest. Insofar as his actions in accord with his "social responsibility" reduce returns to stockholders, he is spending their money. Insofar as his actions raise the price to customers, he is spending the customers' money. Insofar as his actions lower the wages of some employees, he is spending their money.

The stockholders or the customers or the employees could separately spend their own money on the particular action if they wished to do so. The executive is exercising a distinct "social responsibility," rather than serving as an agent of the stockholders or the customers or the employees, only if he spends the money in a different way than they would have spent it.

But if he does this, he is in effect imposing taxes, on the one hand, and deciding how the tax proceeds shall be spent, on the other.

This process raises political questions on two levels: principle and consequences. On the level of political principle, the imposition of taxes and the expenditure of tax proceeds are governmental functions. We have established elaborate constitutional, parliamentary and judicial provisions to control these functions, to assure that taxes are imposed so far as possible in accordance with the preferences and desires of the public—after all, "taxation without representation" was one of the battle cries of the American Revolution. We have a system of checks and balances to separate the legislative function of imposing taxes and enacting expenditures from the executive function of collecting taxes and administering expenditure programs and from the judicial function of mediating disputes and interpreting the law.

Here the businessman—self-selected or appointed directly or indirectly by stockholders—is to be simultaneously legislator, executive and jurist. He is to decide whom to tax by how much and for what purpose, and he is to spend the proceeds—all this guided only by general exhortations from on high to restrain inflation, improve the environment, fight poverty and so on and on.

The whole justification for permitting the corporate executive to be selected by the stockholders is that the executive is an agent serving the interests of his principal. This justification disappears when the corporate executive imposes taxes and spends the proceeds for "social" purposes. He becomes in effect a public employee, a civil servant, even though he remains in name an employee of a private enterprise. On grounds of political principle, it is intolerable that such civil servants—insofar as their actions in the name of social re-

sponsibility are real and not just window-dressing—should be selected as they are now. If they are to be civil servants, then they must be elected through a political process. If they are to impose taxes and make expenditures to foster "social" objectives, then political machinery must be set up to make the assessment of taxes and to determine through a political process the objectives to be served.

This is the basic reason why the doctrine of "social responsibility" involves the acceptance of the socialist view that political mechanisms, not market mechanisms, are the appropriate way to determine the allocation of scarce resources to alternative uses.

On the grounds of consequences, can the corporate executive in fact discharge his alleged "social responsibilities"? On the other hand, suppose he could get away with spending the stockholders' or customers' or employees' money. How is he to know how to spend it? He is told that he must contribute to fighting inflation. How is he to know what action of his will contribute to that end? He is presumably an expert in running his company—in producing a product or selling it or financing it. But nothing about his selection makes him an expert on inflation. Will his holding down the price of his product reduce inflationary pressure? Or, by leaving more spending power in the hands of his customers, simply divert it elsewhere? Or, by forcing him to produce less because of the lower price, will it simply contribute to shortages? Even if he could answer these questions, how much cost is he justified in imposing on his stockholders, customers and employees for this social purpose? What is his appropriate share and what is the appropriate share of others?

And, whether he wants to or not, can he get away with spending his stockholders', customers' or employees' money? Will not the stockholders fire him? (Either the present ones or those who take over when his actions in the name of social responsibility have reduced the corporation's profits and the price of its stock.) His customers and his employees can desert him for other producers and employers less scrupulous in exercising their social responsibilities.

This facet of "social responsibility" doctrine is brought into sharp relief when the doctrine is used to justify wage restraint by trade unions. The conflict of interest is naked and clear when union officials are asked to subordinate the interest of their members to some more general purpose. If the union officials try to enforce wage restraint, the consequence is likely to be wildcat strikes, rank-and-file revolts and the emergence of strong competitors for their jobs. We thus have the ironic phenomenon that union leaders—at least in the U.S.—have objected to Government interference with the market far more consistently and courageously than have business leaders.

The difficulty of exercising "social responsibility" illustrates, of course, the great virtue of private competitive enterprise—it forces people to be responsible for their own actions and makes it difficult for them to "exploit" other people for either selfish or unselfish purposes. They can do good—but only at their own expense.

Many a reader who has followed the argument this far may be tempted to remonstrate that it is all well and good to speak of Government's having the responsibility to impose taxes and determine expenditures for such "social" purposes as controlling pollution or training the hardcore unemployed, but that the problems are too urgent to wait on the slow course of political processes, that the exercise of social responsibility by businessmen is a quicker and surer way to solve pressing current problems.

Aside from the question of fact—I share Adam Smith's skepticism about the benefits that can be expected from "those who affected to trade for the public good"—this argument must be rejected on grounds of principle. What it amounts to is an assertion that those who favor the taxes and expenditures in question have failed to persuade a majority of their fellow citizens to be of like mind and that they are seeking to attain by undemocratic

procedures what they cannot attain by democratic procedures. In a free society, it is hard for "evil" people to do "evil," especially since one man's good is another's evil.

I have, for simplicity, concentrated on the special case of the corporate executive, except only for the brief digression on trade unions. But precisely the same argument applies to the newer phenomenon of calling upon stockholders to require corporations to exercise social responsibility (the recent G.M. crusade for example). In most of these cases, what is in effect involved is some stockholders trying to get other stockholders (or customers or employees) to contribute against their will to "social" causes favored by the activists. Insofar as they succeed, they are again imposing taxes and spending the proceeds.

The situation of the individual proprietor is somewhat different. If he acts to reduce the returns of his enterprise in order to exercise his "social responsibility," he is spending his own money, not someone else's. If he wishes to spend his money on such purposes, that is his right, and I cannot see that there is any objection to his doing so. In the process, he, too, may impose costs on employees and customers. However, because he is far less likely than a large corporation or union to have monopolistic power, any such side effects will tend to be minor.

Of course, in practice the doctrine of social responsibility is frequently a cloak for actions that are justified on other grounds rather than a reason for those actions.

To illustrate, it may well be in the long-run interest of a corporation that is a major employer in a small community to devote resources to providing amenities to that community or to improving its government. That may make it easier to attract desirable employees, it may reduce the wage bill or lessen losses from pilferage and sabotage or have other worthwhile effects. Or it may be that, given the laws about the deductibility of corporate charitable contributions, the stockholders can contribute more to charities they favor by having the corporation make the gift than by doing it themselves, since they can in that way contribute an amount that would otherwise have been paid as corporate taxes.

In each of these—and many similar—cases, there is a strong temptation to rationalize these actions as an exercise of "social responsibility." In the present climate of opinion, with its widespread aversion to "capitalism," "profits," the "soulless corporation" and so on, this is one way for a corporation to generate goodwill as a by-product of expenditures that are entirely justified in its own self-interest.

It would be inconsistent of me to call on corporate executives to refrain from this hypocritical window-dressing because it harms the foundations of a free society. That would be to call on them to exercise a "social responsibility"! If our institutions, and the attitudes of the public make it in their self-interest to cloak their actions in this way, I cannot summon much indignation to denounce them. At the same time, I can express admiration for those individual proprietors or owners of closely held corporations or stockholders of more broadly held corporations who disdain such tactics as approaching fraud.

Whether blameworthy or not, the use of the cloak of social responsibility, and the nonsense spoken in its name by influential and prestigious businessmen, does clearly harm the foundations of a free society. I have been impressed time and again by the schizophrenic character of many businessmen. They are capable of being extremely far-sighted and clear-headed in matters that are internal to their businesses. They are incredibly short-sighted and muddle-headed in matters that are outside their businesses but affect the possible survival of business in general. This short-sightedness is strikingly exemplified in the calls from many businessmen for wage and price guidelines or controls or income policies. There is nothing that could do more in a brief period to destroy a market system and replace it by a centrally controlled system than effective governmental control of prices and wages.

The short-sightedness is also exemplified in speeches by businessmen on social responsibility. This may gain them kudos in the short run. But it helps to strengthen the already too prevalent view that the pursuit of profits is wicked and immoral and must be curbed and controlled by external forces. Once this view is adopted, the external forces that curb the market will not be the social consciences, however highly developed, of the pontificating executives; it will be the iron fist of Government bureaucrats. Here, as with price and wage controls, businessmen seem to me to reveal a suicidal impulse.

The political principle that underlies the market mechanism is unanimity. In an ideal free market resting on private property, no individual can coerce any other, all cooperation is voluntary, all parties to such cooperation benefit or they need not participate. There are no values, no "social" responsibilities in any sense other than the shared values and responsibilities of individuals. Society is a collection of individuals and of the various groups they voluntarily form.

The political principle that underlies the political mechanisms is conformity. The individual must serve a more general social interest—whether that be determined by a church or a dictator or a majority. The individual may have a vote and say in what is to be done, but if he is overruled, he must conform. It is appropriate for some to require others to contribute to a general social purpose whether they wish to or not.

Unfortunately, unanimity is not always feasible. There are some respects in which conformity appears unavoidable, so I do not see how one can avoid the use of the political mechanism altogether.

But the doctrine of "social responsibility" taken seriously would extend the scope of the political mechanism to every human activity. It does not differ in philosophy from the most explicitly collectivist doctrine. It differs only by professing to believe that collectivist ends can be attained without collectivist means. That is why, in my book *Capitalism and Freedom*, I have called it a "fundamentally subversive doctrine" in a free society, and have said that in such a society, "there is one and only one social responsibility of business—to use its resources and engage in activities designed to increase its profits so long as it stays within the rules of the game, which is to say, engages in open and free competition without deception or fraud."

Suggested Further Reading

French, Peter A., "Corporate Moral Agency," in *Business Ethics: Readings and Cases in Corporate Morality*, ed. W. Michael Hoffman and

Jennifer Mills Moore. New York: McGraw-Hill, 1984, pp. 163–71.

Goodpaster, Kenneth E., and John B. Matthews, Jr., "Can a Corporation Have a Conscience?" *Harvard Business Review*, January–February 1982.

Ladd, John, "Morality and the Idea of Rationality in Formal Organizations," *Monist*, vol. 54, 1970.

Levitt, Theodore, "The Dangers of Corporate Social Responsibility," *Harvard Business Review*, September–October 1958, pp. 41–50.

DECISION SCENARIO 5

Lying for Business Reasons

Carl was near the end of his first month on the job and was feeling his uncertainty start to lift. When he had signed up for the Ritz Furniture Company sales program, he hadn't been sure this was what he wanted to do. He could have gone into the Army or to technical school for his diploma. Now he was almost glad about his choice.

The Ritz Furniture Company had just started its sales training program. Its sales managers had convinced the company president that the old way no longer worked. The old way was to hire established sales personnel and give them Ritz routes; they already knew the business and had only to learn new names. The new way was to take young people and show them how things worked from the word "Go." This way they got in on the ground floor and knew no other way.

Sam Jones was of the old way. Carl was assigned to Sam the day he arrived at the Rochester office. At first, Carl was intimidated by the way Sam did things. He felt that Sam's approach differed greatly from what he had learned in training school. Sam was good-natured, though, and they got along—at least until the last day of Carl's month on probation.

They were in Ivory's Department Store and Carl was completing a very large sale. He was excited. As Ivory's manager was signing the contract, he asked, "The usual shipping arrangement?" Sam Jones cut in. "Of course," he said.

Carl was confused. In the car he asked Sam what that meant. "Oh, nothing," Sam said. "You see, what we do for important customers like Ivory's is to compute triple shipping charges. That way, when the order goes through they end up with a hefty discount."

"But that's lying!" Carl objected. "We can't do that."

Sam chuckled. "It's either that or no business," he said. "You choose."

Questions

1. Was Carl being naive in expecting truthful business dealings?

2. What is a duty of veracity? How is it justified in terms of ethical theory?

3. If lying and fraudulent relations are the norm, what becomes, morally speaking, of the practices of keeping promises and telling the truth?

4. Are there sound moral arguments against the position that claims in business "Anything goes"?

5. If the cost of making a moral decision is quite high, as it may be in Carl's case, is one justified in choosing against what is morally right to do?

12. ISSUES IN TECHNOLOGY MANAGEMENT

1. INFORMATION TECHNOLOGY

Information technology has emerged with the increasingly sophisticated electronic computers developed over the past forty years. It includes the reprogrammable automated machinery made viable by such computers. Among the ethical issues associated with information technology are the problems of computer crime and the displacement of workers due to automation. Much discussion has centered on computer "hackers" breaking into confidential files for sport or, more ominously, embezzlement, stock market manipulation, and espionage practiced by computer criminals. While such unlawful uses of computers are troubling, close examination shows that the ethical problems are not peculiar to computer technology. Stealing confidential data from a computer file is ethically no different from stealing information from a locked desk or filing cabinet. It thus poses no unusual moral problems and involves no new moral rules. However, since laws have been slow to recognize the severity of computer crimes, many believe punishments have been unfairly lenient.

Controversy exists over layoffs and worker dissatisfaction caused by the introduction of microprocessors and robots in the workplace. Automation by computers eliminates some jobs and downgrades others to simple, unskilled routine. Although the dislocation of workers is a serious problem, it is not unique to information technology. Worker displacement due to improved

technology has generated controversy and opposition as far back as the early 1800s, when Luddites smashed the textile machines threatening to put them out of work. Likewise, employers' obligations to workers are familiar and much-debated topics, not new issues created by the development of computers.

What then are the special ethical problems connected with computers and associated technology? Thinkers suggest there is a special problem of accountability for errors when computer programs are used. Some errors are caused by actual malfunctions in the program; others result from poor systems design or ignorance on the part of the purchaser about what the system will do. Who should be held accountable for the errors?

A frequently cited illustration of the problem concerns the use of computers in health care. Computer programs are employed to assess patient data and provide diagnoses. Suppose a software company devises such a program and sells it to a hospital. A physician at the hospital uses the system and, on the basis of a mistaken diagnosis, prescribes treatment that seriously harms a patient. Who should be blamed for the injury: the doctor, the hospital, or the software vendor?

Some people argue that computer programs should be viewed as products (albeit intangible) and that software vendors would thus be liable for harm caused by errors or malfunctions in the same way as any manu-facturer of a product would be. Even if the error did not result from negligence on the part of the vendor (or designer), the vendor could be held legally responsible under the terms of strict liability **[See Section 1 of Chapter 11 in this unit].** This argument appears justified in the case of so-called "canned" programs that are mass marketed. However, some programs are specifically designed to fit the special requirements of the purchaser; software of this kind resembles a service more than a product. A third kind of program is one that starts out as a canned package but is then modified by the designer to fit unique needs specified by the customer. In the case of custom-designed programs, vendor liability seems to depend upon proof of negligence in providing a service. Thus, if a hospital orders a specially designed diagnostic program that proves defective, the hospital could be liable for a patient's injury unless it could demonstrate negligence by the program vendor. Determining liability for this third type of software hinges upon whether the error was due to a flaw in the original design or one in the specially modified portions.

The preceding analysis leaves the question of blame still unresolved. In particular, the physician's responsibility remains unclear, and further investigation of the accountability problem is needed as different professional groups find that computers are determining professional judgment. Using the product-versus-service analogy for software provides only a starting point for more intensive analysis.

Another ethical issue raised by information technology concerns threats to individual privacy. Computers provide the capacity to gather, store, and communicate information at a level never before possible. We are witnessing an enormous increase in the amount of information compiled about any one person and in the number of individuals monitored. In addition, the ease and speed of exchanging information have been dramatically enhanced. Gathering, storage, and exchange of information about anyone takes place without the knowledge or consent of the subject.

Privacy, or control over information about oneself, is recognized as an important component of autonomy. With the advent of computerized record-keeping, the privacy and hence the autonomy of individuals is threatened. Those who compile and use computerized records are primarily large bureaucratic corporations and government agencies, whereas those about whom records are kept are mainly individuals. The struggle over computers and privacy is thus a conflict between powerful organizations and relatively powerless individuals. Because of the imbalance, strong legislation has been suggested to protect individuals from privacy problems raised by computers.

A number of laws have been enacted to deal with computerized record-keeping. For example, credit agencies are required by the Fair Credit Reporting Act to send copies of their records to individuals upon request. However, the burden of discovering what records exist lies with the individual. Organizations have the right to establish a file on an individual without notifying him or her and without obtaining consent. In addition, individuals have no control over what types of information are recorded, although they may legally contest the accuracy in the unlikely event that they succeed in uncovering a file.

Record-keeping organizations argue that information is needed in order for them to make correct decisions. They further insist that gaining permission from each individual to set up a file or to exchange the information in it imposes too great a financial burden. In view of the threat to personal privacy implied by computer records, the economic argument seems weak.

In the absence of stronger legislation, computer professionals help to minimize abuses of privacy by treating all computer records confidentially. While employees have little control over corporate actions, they have a responsibility to respect the principle of privacy and to limit unnecessary collection and exchange of data wherever possible. The ideal of confidentiality is recognized in Canon 5 of the Association for Computing Machinery Code of Professional Conduct (see Appendix). The Disciplinary Rule intended to enforce Canon 5 is, however, disappointingly weak: the rule recommends that the professional "express his professional opinion to his employer or clients regarding any adverse consequences to the public which might result from work proposed to him" (DR 5.2.1).

Another concern about the increasing use of computers centers on their effects on the distribution of power. Critics argue that computers lead to the centralization of power. They reason that as government agencies gain the ability to keep more and more detailed records on individual citizens, government power to control citizens correspondingly increases. Proponents of this view hold that if computers did not exist, the increasing size of government bureaucracies would force decentralization. Computers allow existing systems to persist by enabling them to handle massive record-keeping demands.

Opponents of the view believe that the use of computers favors decentralization. They point out that computers in the hands of individual citizens can help them gain access to information and communicate with government agencies. Some suggest that computer technology makes possible "instant voting" by the whole electorate. Such an arrangement would enable the direct participation of each citizen in political decisions, as opposed to the representative system now used in the United States. Whether or not direct democracy would be a desirable system is uncertain and controversial.

Arguments claim that computers may be used in different ways to facilitate either centralization or decentralization of power.

The way in which they *are* used will likely depend upon the social and political forces operating in a culture and not upon the presence or absence of computers per se. While computer technology is morally neutral in this instance, neutrality should not be presumed in the area of threats to personal privacy.

The above issues concern the effects of information technology in various applications. A different issue arises from the special character of the technology. Computer programs are entirely new entities, and their legal status is problematic. Should programs be considered the private property of their creators? Should programs be owned, and if so, should ownership be regulated?

Programs presently fall under one of three types of property rights. Programs may be copyrighted as "literary works," they may be protected under trade secrecy laws, or they may be granted a patent. Each form of protection has limited usefulness, and programs vary in their ability to qualify for a particular form. Software companies argue that strong protection is needed to provide the incentive to create new programs. Some suggest that existing forms of protection are inadequate and that new legislation should be devised to deal with the unique problems arising with computer programs.

In the following essay James H. Moor examines the question of defining computer ethics. He maintains that computer ethics is a discipline with broad practical significance. Moor suggests certain parallels between the Industrial Revolution and the Computer Revolution. He argues that as computers gain wider application, they will have a transforming effect on a variety of social institutions and human activities and, as a result, values associated with the activities and institutions will face challenges and reassessment.

JAMES H. MOOR

What Is Computer Ethics?

A Proposed Definition

Computers are special technology and they raise some special ethical issues. In this essay I will discuss what makes computers different from other technology and how this difference makes a difference in ethical considerations. In particular, I want to characterize computer ethics and show why this emerging field is both intellectually interesting and enormously important.

On my view, *computer ethics* is the analysis of the nature and social impact of computer technology and the corresponding formulation and justification of policies for the ethical use of such technology. I use the phrase "computer technology" because I take the subject matter of the field broadly to include computers and associated technology. For instance, I include concerns about software as well as hardware and concerns about networks connecting computers as well as computers themselves.

A typical problem in computer ethics arises because there is a policy vacuum about how computer technology should be used. Computers provide us with new capabilities and these in turn give us new choices for action. Often, either no policies for conduct in these situations exist or existing policies seem inadequate. A central task of computer ethics is to determine what we should do in such cases, i.e., to formulate policies to guide our actions. Of course, some ethical situations confront us as individuals and some as a society. Computer ethics includes consideration of both personal and social policies for the ethical use of computer technology.

Now it may seem that all that needs to be done is the mechanical application of an ethical theory to generate the appropriate policy. But this is usually not possible. A difficulty is

that along with a policy vacuum there is often a conceptual vacuum. Although a problem in computer ethics may seem clear initially, a little reflection reveals a conceptual muddle. What is needed in such cases is an analysis which provides a coherent conceptual framework within which to formulate a policy for action. Indeed, much of the important work in computer ethics is devoted to proposing conceptual frameworks for understanding ethical problems involving computer technology.

An example may help to clarify the kind of conceptual work that is required. Let's suppose we are trying to formulate a policy for protecting computer programs. Initially, the idea may seem clear enough. We are looking for a policy for protecting a kind of intellectual property. But then a number of questions which do not have obvious answers emerge. What is a computer program? Is it really intellectual property which can be owned or is it more like an idea, an algorithm, which is not owned by anybody? If a computer program is intellectual property, is it an *expression* of an idea that is owned (traditionally protectable by copyright) or is it a *process* that is owned (traditionally protectable by patent)? Is a machine-readable program a copy of a human-readable program? Clearly, we need a conceptualization of the nature of a computer program in order to answer these kinds of questions. Moreover, these questions must be answered in order to formulate a useful policy for protecting computer programs. Notice that the conceptualization we pick will not only affect how a policy will be applied but to a certain extent what the facts are. For instance, in this case the conceptualization will determine when programs count as instances of the same program.

Even within a coherent conceptual frame-

Reprinted with permission of the author and publisher from *Metaphilosophy*, 16, no. 4 (October 1985), 266–75.

work, the formulation of a policy for using computer technology can be difficult. As we consider different policies we discover something about what we value and what we don't. Because computer technology provides us with new possibilities for acting, new values emerge. For example, creating software has value in our culture which it didn't have a few decades ago. And old values have to be reconsidered. For instance, assuming software is intellectual property, why should intellectual property be protected? In general, the consideration of alternative policies forces us to discover and make explicit what our value preferences are.

The mark of a basic problem in computer ethics is one in which computer technology is *essentially* involved and there is an uncertainty about what to do and even about how to understand the situation. Hence, not all ethical situations involving computers are central to computer ethics. If a burglar steals available office equipment including computers, then the burglar has done something legally and ethically wrong. But this is really an issue for general law and ethics. Computers are only *accidentally* involved in this situation, and there is no policy or conceptual vacuum to fill. The situation and the applicable policy are clear.

In one sense I am arguing for the special status of computer ethics as a field of study. Applied ethics is not simply ethics applied. But, I also wish to stress the underlying importance of general ethics and science to computer ethics. Ethical theory provides categories and procedures for determining what is ethically relevant. For example, what kinds of things are good? What are our basic rights? What is an impartial point of view? These considerations are essential in comparing and justifying policies for ethical conduct. Similarly, scientific information is crucial in ethical evaluations. It is amazing how many times ethical disputes turn not on disagreements about values but on disagreements about facts.

On my view, computer ethics is a dynamic and complex field of study which considers the relationships among facts, conceptualizations, policies and values with regard to constantly changing computer technology. Computer ethics is not a fixed set of rules which one shellacs and hangs on the wall. Nor is computer ethics the rote application of ethical principles to a value-free technology. Computer ethics requires us to think anew about the nature of computer technology and our values. Although computer ethics is a field between science and ethics and depends on them, it is also a discipline in its own right which provides both conceptualizations for understanding and policies for using computer technology.

Though I have indicated some of the intellectually interesting features of computer ethics, I have not said much about the problems of the field or about its practical importance. The only example I have used so far is the issue of protecting computer programs which may seem to be a very narrow concern. In fact, I believe the domain of computer ethics is quite large and extends to issues which affect all of us. Now I want to turn to a consideration of these issues and argue for the practical importance of computer ethics. I will proceed not by giving a list of problems but rather by analyzing the conditions and forces which generate ethical issues about computer technology. In particular, I want to analyze what is special about computers, what social impact computers will have, and what is operationally suspect about computing technology. I hope to show something of the nature of computer ethics by doing some computer ethics.

The Revolutionary Machine

What is special about computers? It is often said that a Computer Revolution is taking place, but what is it about computers that makes them revolutionary? One difficulty in assessing the revolutionary nature of computers is that the word "revolutionary" has been devalued. Even minor technological improvements are heralded as revolutionary. A manufacturer of a new dripless pouring spout may well promote it as revolutionary. If minor technological improvements are revolutionary, then undoubtedly everchanging computer technology is revolutionary. The interesting issue, of course, is whether there is some nontrivial sense in which computers are revolutionary. What makes computer technology importantly different from other technology? Is there any real basis for comparing the Computer Revolution with the Industrial Revolution?

If we look around for features that make computers revolutionary, several features suggest themselves. For example, in our society computers are affordable and abundant. It is not much of an exaggeration to say that currently in our society every major business, factory, school, bank, and hospital is rushing to utilize computer technology. Millions of personal computers are being sold for home use. Moreover, computers are integral parts of products which don't look much like computers such as watches and automobiles. Computers are abundant and inexpensive, but so are pencils. Mere abundance and affordability don't seem suffficient to justify any claim to technological revolution.

One might claim the newness of computers makes them revolutionary. Such a thesis requires qualification. Electronic digital computers have been around for forty years. In fact, if the abacus counts as a computer, then computer technology is among the oldest technologies. A better way to state this claim is that recent engineering advances in computers make them revolutionary. Obviously, computers have been immensely improved over the last forty years. Along with dramatic increases in computer speed and memory there have been dramatic decreases in computer size. Computer manufacturers are quick to point out that desk top computers today exceed the engineering specifications of computers which filled rooms only a few decades ago. There has been also a determined effort by companies to make computer hardware and computer software easier to use. Computers may not be completely user friendly but at least they are much less unfriendly. However, as important as these features are, they don't seem to get to the heart of the Computer Revolution. Small, fast, powerful and easy-to-use electric can openers are great improvements over earlier can openers, but they aren't in the relevant sense revolutionary.

Of course, it is important that computers are abundant, less expensive, smaller, faster, and more powerful and friendly. But, these features serve as enabling conditions for the spread of the Computer Revolution. The essence of the Computer Revolution is found in the nature of a computer itself. What is revolutionary about computers is *logical malleability*. Computers are logically malleable in that they can be shaped and molded to do any activity that can be characterized in terms of inputs, outputs, and connecting logical operations. Logical operations are the precisely defined steps which take a computer from one state to the next. The logic of computers can be massaged and shaped in endless ways through changes in hardware and software. Just as the power of a steam engine was a raw resource of the Industrial Revolution so the logic of a computer is a raw resource of the Computer Revolution. Because logic applies everywhere, the potential applications of computer technology appear limitless. The computer is the nearest thing we have to a universal tool. Indeed, the limits of computers are largely the limits of our own creativity. The driving question of the Computer Revolution is "How can we mold the logic of computers to better serve our purposes?"

I think logical malleability explains the already widespread application of computers and hints at the enormous impact computers are destined to have. Understanding the logical malleability of computers is essential to understanding the power of the developing technological revolution. Understanding logical malleability is also important in setting policies for the use of computers. Other ways of conceiving computers serve less well as a basis for formulating and justifying policies for action.

Consider an alternative and popular conception of computers in which computers are understood as number crunchers, i.e., essentially as numerical devices. On this conception computers are nothing but big calculators. It might be maintained on this view that mathematical and scientific applications should take precedence over nonnumerical applications such as word processing. My position, on the contrary, is that computers are logically malleable. The arithmetic interpretation is certainly a correct one, but it is only one among many interpretations. Logical malleability has both a syntactic and a semantic dimension. Syntactically, the logic of computers is malleable in terms of the number and variety of possible states and operations. Semantically, the logic of computers is malleable in that the states of the computer can be taken to represent anything. Computers manipulate symbols but they don't care what the symbols represent. Thus, there is no ontological basis for giving preference to numerical applications over nonnumerical applications.

The fact that computers can be described in mathematical language, even at a very low level, doesn't make them essentially numerical. For example, machine language is conveniently and traditionally expressed in 0's and 1's. But the 0's and 1's simply designate different physical states. We could label these states as "on" and "off" or "yin" and "yang" and apply binary logic. Obviously, at some levels it is useful to use mathematical notation to describe computer operations, and it is reasonable to use it. The mistake is to reify the mathematical notation as the essence of a computer and then use this conception to make judgments about the appropriate use of computers.

In general, our conceptions of computer technology will affect our policies for using it. I believe the importance of properly conceiving the nature and impact of computer technology will increase as the Computer Revolution unfolds.

Anatomy of the Computer Revolution

Because the Computer Revolution is in progress, it is difficult to get a perspective on its development. By looking at the Industrial Revolution I believe we can get some insight into the nature of a technological revolution. Roughly, the Industrial Revolution in England occurred in two major stages. The first stage was the technological introduction stage which took place during the last half of the Eighteenth Century. During this stage inventions and processes were introduced, tested, and improved. There was an industrialization of limited segments of the economy, particularly in agriculture and textiles. The second stage was the technological permeation stage which took place during the Nineteenth Century. As factory work increased and the populations of cities swelled, not only did well known social evils emerge, but equally significantly corresponding changes in human activities and institutions, ranging from labor unions to health services, occurred. The forces of industrialization dramatically transformed the society.

My conjecture is that the Computer Revolution will follow a similar two stage development. The first stage, the introduction stage, has been occurring during the last forty years. Electronic computers have been created and refined. We are gradually entering the second stage, the permeation stage, in which computer technology will become an integral part of institutions throughout our society. I think that in the coming decades many human activities and social institutions will be transformed by computer technology and that this transforming effect of computerization will raise a wide range of issues for computer ethics.

What I mean by "transformed" is that the basic nature or purpose of an activity or institution is changed. This is marked by the kinds of questions that are asked. During the introduction stage computers are understood as tools for doing standard jobs. A typical question for this stage is "How well does a computer do such and such an activity?" Later, during the permeation stage, computers become an integral part of the activity. A typical question for this stage is "What is the nature and value of such and such an activity?" In our society there is already some evidence of the transforming effect of computerization as marked by the kind of questions being asked.

For example, for years computers have been used to count votes. Now the election process is becoming highly computerized. Computers can be used to count votes and to make projections about the outcome. Television networks use computers both to determine quickly who is winning and to display the results in a technologically impressive manner. During the last presidential election in the United States the television networks projected the results not only before the polls in California were closed but also before the polls in New York were closed. In fact, voting was still going on in over half the states when the winner was announced. The question is no longer "How efficiently do computers count votes in a fair election?" but "What is a fair election?" Is it appropriate that some people know the outcome before they vote? The problem is that computers not only tabulate the votes for each candidate but likely influence the number and distribution of these votes. For better or worse, our electoral process is being transformed.

As computers permeate more and more of our society, I think we will see more and more of the transforming effect of computers on our basic institutions and practices. Nobody can know for sure how our computerized society will look fifty years from now, but it is reasonable to think that various aspects of our daily work will be transformed. Computers have been used for years by businesses to expedite routine work, such as calculating payrolls; but as personal computers become widespread and allow executives to work at home, and as robots do more and more factory work, the emerging question will be not merely "How well do computers help us work?" but "What is the nature of this work?"

Traditional work may no longer be defined as something that normally happens at a specific time or a specific place. Work for us may become less doing a job than instructing a computer to do a job. As the concept of work begins to change, the values associated with the old concept will have to be reexamined.

Executives who work at a computer terminal at home will lose some spontaneous interaction with colleagues. Factory workers who direct robots by pressing buttons may take less pride in a finished product. And similar effects can be expected in other types of work. Commercial pilots who watch computers fly their planes may find their jobs to be different from what they expected.

A further example of the transforming effect of computer technology is found in financial institutions. As the transfer and storage of funds becomes increasingly computerized the question will be not merely "How well do computers count money?" but "What is money?" For instance, in a cashless society in which debits are made to one's account electronically at the point of sale, has money disappeared in favor of computer records or have electronic impulses become money? What opportunities and values are lost or gained when money becomes intangible?

Still another likely area for the transforming effect of computers is education. Currently, educational packages for computers are rather limited. Now it is quite proper to ask "How well do computers educate?" But as teachers and students exchange more and more information indirectly via computer networks and as computers take over more routine instructional activities, the question will inevitably switch to "What is education?" The values associated with the traditional way of educating will be challenged. How much human contact is necessary or desirable for learning? What is education when computers do the teaching?

The point of this futuristic discussion is to suggest the likely impact of computer technology. Though I don't know what the details will be, I believe the kind of transformation I am suggesting is likely to occur. This is all I need to support my argument for the practical importance of computer ethics. In brief, the argument is as follows: The revolutionary feature of computers is their logical malleability. Logical malleability assures the enormous application of computer technology. This will bring about the Computer Revolution. During the Computer Revolution many of our human activities and social institutions will be transformed. These transformations will leave us with policy and conceptual vacuums about how to use computer technology. Such policy and conceptual vacuums are the marks of basic problems within computer ethics. Therefore, computer ethics is a field of substantial practical importance.

I find this argument for the practical value of computer ethics convincing. I think it shows that computer ethics is likely to have increasing application in our society. This argument does rest on a vision of the Computer Revolution which not everyone may share. Therefore, I will turn to another argument for the practical importance of computer ethics which doesn't depend upon any particular view of the Computer Revolution. This argument rests on the invisibility factor and suggests a number of ethical issues confronting computer ethics now.

The Invisibility Factor

There is an important fact about computers. Most of the time and under most conditions computer operations are invisible. One may be quite knowlegeable about the inputs and outputs of a computer and only dimly aware of the internal processing. This invisibility factor often generates policy vacuums about how to use computer technology. Here I will mention three kinds of invisibility which can have ethical significance.

The most obvious kind of invisibility which has ethical significance is invisible abuse. *Invisible abuse* is the intentional use of the invisible operations of a computer to engage in unethical conduct. A classic example of this is the case of a programmer who realized he could steal excess interest from a bank. When interest on a bank account is calculated, there is often a fraction of a cent left over after rounding off. This programmer instructed a computer to deposit these fractions of a cent to his own account. Although this is an ordinary case of stealing, it is relevant to computer

ethics in that computer technology is essentially involved and there is a question about what policy to institute in order to best detect and prevent such abuse. Without access to the program used for stealing the interest or to a sophisticated accounting program such an activity may easily go unnoticed.

Another possibility for invisible abuse is the invasion of the property and privacy of others. A computer can be programmed to contact another computer over phone lines and surreptitiously remove or alter confidential information. Sometimes an inexpensive computer and a telephone hookup is all it takes. A group of teenagers, who named themselves the "414s" after the Milwaukee telephone exchange, used their home computers to invade a New York hospital, a California bank, and a government nuclear weapons laboratory. These break-ins were done as pranks, but obviously such invasions can be done with malice and be difficult or impossible to detect.

A particularly insidious example of invisible abuse is the use of computers for surveillance. For instance, a company's central computer can monitor the work done on computer terminals far better and more discreetly than the most dedicated sweatshop manager. Also, computers can be programmed to monitor phone calls and electronic mail without giving any evidence of tampering. A Texas oil company, for example, was baffled why it was always outbid on leasing rights for Alaskan territory until it dscovered another bidder was tapping its data transmission lines near its Alaskan computer terminal.

A second variety of the invisibility factor, which is more subtle and conceptually interesting than the first, is the presence of invisible programming values. *Invisible programming values* are those values which are embedded in a computer program.

Writing a computer program is like building a house. No matter how detailed the specifications may be, a builder must make numerous decisions about matters not specified in order to construct the house. Different houses are compatible with a given set of specifications. Similarly, a request for a computer program is made at a level of abstraction usually far removed from the details of the actual programming language. In order to implement a program which satisfies the specifications, a programmer makes some value judgments about what is important and what is not. These values become embedded in the final product and may be invisible to someone who runs the program.

Consider, for example, computerized airline reservations. Many different programs could be written to produce a reservation service. American Airlines once promoted such a service called "SABRE." This program had a bias for American Airlines flights built in so that sometimes an American Airlines flight was suggested by the computer even if it was not the best flight available. Indeed, Braniff Airlines, which went into bankruptcy for awhile, sued American Airlines on the grounds that this kind of bias in the reservation service contributed to its financial difficulties.

Although the general use of a biased reservation service is ethically suspicious, a programmer of such a service may or may not be engaged in invisible abuse. There may be a difference between how a programmer intends a program to be used and how it is actually used. Moreover, even if one sets out to create a program for a completely unbiased reservation service, some value judgments are latent in the program because some choices have to be made about how the program operates. Are airlines listed in alphabetical order? Is more than one listed at a time? Are flights just before the time requested listed? For what period after the time requested are flights listed? Some answers, at least implicitly, have to be given to these questions when the program is written. Whatever answers are chosen will build certain values into the program.

Sometimes invisible programming values are so invisible that even the programmers are unaware of them. Programs may have bugs or may be based on implicit assumptions which don't become obvious until there is a crisis. For example, the operators of the ill-fated Three Mile Island nuclear power plant were trained on a computer which was programmed to simulate possible malfunctions including malfunctions which were dependent on other malfunctions. But, as the Kemeny Commission which investigated the disaster discovered, the simulator was not programmed to generate simultaneous, independent malfunctions. In the actual failure at Three Mile Island the operators were faced with exactly this situation—simultaneous, independent malfunctions. The inadequacy of the computer simulation was the result of a programming decision, as unconscious or implicit as that decision may have been. Shortly after the disaster the computer was reprogrammed to simulate situations like the one that did occur at Three Mile Island.

A third variety of the invisibility factor, which is perhaps the most disturbing, is *invisible complex calculation*. Computers today are capable of enormous calculations beyond human comprehension. Even if a program is understood, it does not follow that the calculations based on that program are understood. Computers today perform and certainly supercomputers in the future will perform calculations which are too complex for human inspection and understanding.

An interesting example of such complex calculation occurred in 1976 when a computer worked on the four color conjecture. The four color problem, a puzzle mathematicians have worked on for over a century, is to show that a map can be colored with at most four colors so that no adjacent areas have the same color. Mathematicians at the University of Illinois broke the problem down into thousands of cases and programmed computers to consider them. After more than a thousand hours of computer time on various computers, the four color conjecture was proved correct. What is interesting about this mathematical proof, compared to traditional proofs, is that it is largely invisible. The general structure of the proof is known and found in the program and any particular part of the computer's activity can be examined, but practically speaking the calculations are too enormous for humans to examine them all.

The issue is how much we should trust a computer's invisible calculations. This becomes a significant ethical issue as the consequences grow in importance. For instance, computers are used by the military in making decisions about launching nuclear weapons. On the one hand, computers are fallible and there may not be time to confirm their assessment of the situation. On the other hand, making decisions about launching nuclear weapons without using computers may be even more fallible and more dangerous. What should be our policy about trusting invisible calculations?

A partial solution to the invisibility problem may lie with computers themselves. One of the strengths of computers is the ability to locate hidden information and display it. Computers can make the invisible visible. Information which is lost in a sea of data can be clearly revealed with the proper computer analysis. But that's the catch. We don't always know when, where, and how to direct the computer's attention.

The invisibility factor presents us with a dilemma. We are happy in one sense that the operations of a computer are invisible. We don't want to inspect every computerized transaction or program every step for ourselves or watch every computer calculation. In terms of efficiency the invisibility factor is a blessing. But it is just this invisibility that makes us vulnerable. We are open to invisible abuse or invisible programming of inappropriate values or invisible miscalculation. The challenge for computer ethics is to formulate policies which will help us deal with this dilemma. We must decide when to trust computers and when not to trust them. This is another reason why computer ethics is so important.

Suggested Further Reading

Kling, Rob, "Computers and Social Power," *Computers and Society,* 5 (1973), 6–11.

Metaphilosophy, vol. 16, no. 4, October 1985, Terrell Ward Bynum, ed. Entire issue devoted to "Computers and Ethics."

Moor, James, "Are There Decisions Computers Should Never Make?" *Nature and System,* 1 (1979), 217–29.

Parker, Donn B., "Rules of Ethics in Information Processing," *Communications of the ACM,* 11 (1968), 198–201.

Prince, Jim, "Negligence: Liability for Defective Software," *Oklahoma Law Review,* 33 (1980), 848–55.

Talingdan, Arsenio, "Implications of Computer Use in Politics," *Technology and Society,* 2 (September 1980), 8–11.

Valbona, C., J. Johnson, and S. Beggs, "Moral and Legal Implications of Physician Responsibility in a Computerized Health System," *Man and Computer,* 1974, pp. 347–53.

DECISION SCENARIO 6

The Exit Poll

The midterm Congressional elections of 1986 were to supply an important national referendum on the incumbent Republican policies. They also contained races crucial to party integrity and the political careers of the candidates. The television networks planned extensive coverage.

In the New York studio which served as Election 86 Headquarters, technicians and analysts were watching data on the Ninth Congressional district of Missouri. Missouri was traditionally a "swing" state in national elections, and the Ninth had been selected by computer as the state's barometer. William

Jakker, the incumbent, who was a two-term Republican Representative, was again running on an arch-conservative platform. His opponent, Otis Grearson, was a liberal Democrat with some populist backing. He was the underdog.

Earlier on the news, the anchorman had said, "Grearson's campaign has languished in the last weeks. His slim chances of a victory depend on two factors: registration of black voters and a small electorate turnout. A high percentage vote means that the district's Republicans will have their way."

The polls stayed open until 9:00 P.M. in the state, which meant ten o'clock New York time. Since only part of the vote was done by machine, it would be well into the morning hours before the official tally came out.

At 6:50, Election 86 did a focus on District 9. The commentator highlighted Jakker's anti-abortion stand, his negative views on affirmative action, and his questions about busing minority schoolchildren into white districts. At the same time, Grearson's relative inexperience was discussed, as well as his demand for farm support and local job programs. The newscast prompted a call from Jakker's campaign manager, who decried it as biased and "jackassed liberal."

At 7:20, more than two and one-half hours before the polls closed in Missouri, Election 86 ran a computer projection of the election results. Using two dozen informants stationed at specific voting districts across the region, it relied on exit polls. The informant would ask the voter to say whether he or she had selected Jakker or Grearson. Not everyone was willing to say. On the basis of the available sampling, the computer was programmed to extrapolate the results for the whole district.

At 7:23 (5:23, Missouri time) citizens of District 9 heard that there had been a major upset. Grearson was the projected winner. Workers coming off the shift in the factories, farmers coming in from their fields, office workers on the way home: many people heard the news and decided not to vote.

Not until the early hours of the morning, when the actual count was sealed by the state inspectors of votes, did the impact of Election 86 coverage become apparent. Because of the modest turnout, Grearson was elected by a small margin. The camp of the underdog was jubilant!

Questions

1. To what extent does the method of computer projection constitute deception?

2. How do you determine the extent to which the responsibility rests with the computer professional?

3. Did Election 86's use of computer technology undermine the autonomy of voters in Missouri's District 9? If so, in what way?

4. Opponents to the exit poll argue that it represents an invasion of personal privacy, motivated by the new computer technology, and hence it should be banned on moral grounds. What is your position?

2. MILITARY AND SPACE TECHNOLOGY

The arms buildup and efforts to control it are frequent subjects of our nightly news reports. While diplomats and heads of state negotiate treaties to slow the arms race and reduce stockpiles of weapons, the work of developing and supplying the military arsenal continues. Weapons are big business.

Martin and Schinzinger estimated the worldwide annual expenditure for weapons and related equipment at $125 billion in 1983.[1] A very large number of scientists, techni-

---

[1]Mike W. Martin and Ronald Schinzinger, *Ethics in Engineering* (New York: McGraw-Hill, 1983), p. 263.

cians, and engineers are employed in space technology and weapons-related industries. The space industry has been included in this chapter because it is closely linked with the military and because most space projects have a potential for military use.

Just as ethical problems in health care allocation arise on two different levels **[see Health Care, Chapter 9, Sections 2 and 3]**, problems involving military and space technology occur in the context of national and international policy as well as that of the individual conscience. What is the best means—ethically and practically—for nations to promote peace and reduce the threat of nuclear annihilation? And what are the moral implications of weapons work for individual employees?

The express purpose of a weapon is to cause pain, destruction, and death. For this reason, weapons have an ethical dimension not shared by other products. The argument that technology is neutral seems weakest when applied to devices and systems for injuring and killing. While one may argue that a handgun serves other-than-harmful functions—target shooting, for example—it is hard to find similar vindications for such weapons as napalm and anti-personnel bombs. It is also difficult to imagine that ethically sensitive professionals could work at designing or manufacturing weapons without experiencing some qualms or reservations.

What arguments are used to justify working in the defense industry (never referred to as the "offense industry")? Supporters cite patriotic reasons. They believe that the United States has a morally superior political system and must maintain military strength to support it. This reasoning is related to the theory of just war discussed below. Others argue that their participation or abstention has no effect on whether or not the work is carried out, that "If I don't do it, someone else will." The rationale is a tempting one for employees who have little control over corporate policy. At the same time, excusing individuals from responsibility for the out-

come of their work may lead to a moral detachment like the one behind the Holocaust. It has been argued, for example, that the number of workers who actively supported the Nazis' "final solution" was small compared with the number who just went along and followed orders.

In *The Existential Pleasures of Engineering,* Samuel C. Florman argues that the most important professional satisfaction for engineers is "a strong sense of *helping,* of directing efforts toward easing the lot of one's fellows."[2] If Florman is correct, the motivation for choosing an engineering career has a distinct ethical component, a desire to prevent harm and promote good. Such moral concern seems inconsistent with the kind of detachment described above. Some professionals involved in weapons work believe that they have a positive influence on developments in the field. They argue, for example, that their special knowledge can be applied to helping reduce the risks of nuclear accidents.

Certain moral issues connected with the defense industry arise out of the secret nature of the work and the magnitude of many contracts. Because of their size, projects are difficult to oversee and are plagued with cost overruns and waste. The secrecy imposed for reasons of national security compounds the problem of monitoring project efficiency and rooting out unscrupulous contractors. Inefficiency and poor quality control can have disastrous consequences, as in the case of the 1986 Challenger shuttle explosion. Even when there is no catastrophic outcome, however, the money wasted is public money that could be used for other purposes. This group of issues involves both the macro-context of national policy and the micro-context of individual responsibility. Awarding contracts and overseeing their fulfillment is the job of the federal government, but industry professionals

[2]Samuel C. Florman, *The Existential Pleasures of Engineering* (New York: St. Martin's, 1976), p. 145.

contribute by their conscientious attention to the quality and efficiency of their work.

Nuclear weapons are more ethically troublesome than conventional ones. The extraordinary destructive capacity of nuclear weapons has led some critics to conclude that it is morally objectionable for any nation to build or maintain them. Proponents hold that the United States must be prepared to protect itself against adversaries who have nuclear armaments. They argue that maintaining nuclear capability is the only way to deter attacks by other nations and that our national security depends upon nuclear deterrence. On this view, peace can be maintained only by the threat of war.

The *doctrine of just war* states that while war is always evil, it is justified when protecting innocent persons from harm is made necessary. In the following article Robert P. Churchill examines the moral justification of nuclear deterrence in terms of the just-war doctrine. The author argues that nuclear deterrence is immoral because it "requires that we treat human life as a mere object of policy and a means rather than an end." It thus conflicts with the Kantian ethic. Churchill proposes a policy of nonviolent civilian resistance as an alternative means of deterring aggression and defending the innocent.

ROBERT P. CHURCHILL

Nuclear Arms as a Philosophical and Moral Issue

Philosophical reflection about the problems of nuclear armament and deterrence give rise to three kinds of questions: (1) logical and conceptual questions about nuclear strategy; (2) questions about the effects of nuclear technology on the meaning of humanity and our visions of life and death; and (3) moral or ethical questions about justifications for the use or threatened use of nuclear weapons.

An important role for philosophical analysis lies in scrutiny and criticism of the main concepts involved in deterrence and the assumptions underlying the arms race. What is the logic of the classical *para bellum* doctrine, which offers the paradox that the best way to ensure peace is to prepare for war? What is the meaning of "defense" and "security" in the nuclear age? What does "strategy" really mean when any use of nuclear power renders one liable to a massive counterattack? There

is presently much disagreement among strategists preparing war scenarios over the proper criteria for rational decision making under uncertainty. Some defense analysts employ models of rationality imported from economics and game theory to describe the risks and options facing world leaders. A crucial task for the logician is to examine the wisdom of extending game theoretical criteria of rationality, such as the concept of utility maximization, to the situations of deterrence strategy.[1]

A second and different category of questions concerns the meaning of human life under the cloud of nuclearism. Secretary of War Henry Stimson declared, at the dawn of the nuclear era on 31 May 1945, that the making of the atomic bomb "should not be considered simply in terms of military weapons, but as a new relationship of man to the universe."[2] What is this relationship? And what is

Robert P. Churchill, "Nuclear Arms as a Philosophical and Moral Issue," *Annals of the American Academy of Political and Social Science*, 469 (September 1983), 46–57. Copyright© 1983 by the AAPSS. Reprinted by permission of Sage Publications, Inc.

man's responsibility to the biosphere that sustains him and without which future generations will be impossible?[3] What is the phenomenon of psychic numbing that makes so many of us unable to contemplate sudden annihilation, and this strange double life that comes with the realization that all we have ever known or loved could be extinguished in a moment?[4] How has it come about that homicide has been bureaucratized and terror so easily domesticated in our lives?[5] These are among the philosophical questions to be asked about a world suddenly threatened with nuclear holocaust.

However, the issues that continue to receive most philosophical attention concern the morality or immorality of deterrence policies and the question whether the just-war doctrine can justify a national defense based on threats of massive retaliation. John Bennett forcefully stated the problem when he called on us to explain how we can live with our consciences knowing that our leaders are prepared to kill millions of children in another nation if worse comes to worse.[6]

Moral Questions

If we maintain deterrence, must we live with a troubled conscience? This article will attempt an answer, and will discuss the moral case for and against nuclear deterrence—in particular, the morality of the deterrence proposals that presently guide our defense strategies, and the justifiability of these policies given reasonable beliefs that because of the uncertainties and dangers of the world, it is necessary to prepare a defense against aggression. Thus for the purposes of this discussion I presume that (1) some form of deterrence is necessary as a national defense, and (2) however we solve our defense problems, we must do so unilaterally, without expecting cooperation from the USSR, or any other adversary, on a nuclear freeze or multilateral disarmament. Of course these assumptions may be false; in fact I hope they will soon prove to be so. But it is certainly not now known that they are false, and starting with a worse-case analy-

sis allows me to frame the issue as sharply as possible. Given quite reasonable beliefs in the need for self-defense against an adversary with nuclear arms, what is the moral justification for threatening to use our nuclear weapons to deter him from aggression?[7]

In evaluating answers to this question, I presuppose familiarity with the basics of deterrence theory. In addition the inquiry will be limited to cases in which the problem of aggression is most extreme, and therefore justifications most plausible. Thus while American strategists have often contemplated possible uses for nuclear arms in a "diplomacy of violence,"[8] I am concerned only with nuclear weapons as deterrents to direct attack upon the United States or its allies. For this purpose, strategic nuclear weapons exist as a second-strike capability that ensures U.S. ability to inflict unacceptable suffering upon the USSR even after sustaining an all-out nuclear attack. It is the threat of this retaliatory second strike, combined with the adversary's perceptions of the credibility of threats to use it, that produces the deterrent effect. As the political scientist Michael Walzer has said, "deterrence works by calling up dramatic images of human pain."[9] The object of the offense is not the adversary's armed forces so much as his mind.

Doctrine of Just War

What moral justification, if any, can there be for a policy of deterrence that rests the risk of mutual annihilation upon each superpower's perception of the other's intentions? Some theologians and ethicists do believe that such second-strike deterrence policies are not only morally permissible but morally obligatory. Their arguments are drawn from venerable tradition of reflection and moral suasion. The doctrine of just war concerns warranted uses of force or violence as a necessary means to secure a just cause: if it is necessary for a nation's leaders to threaten annihilation in order to protect innocent civilians from unjust attack, then it is morally obligatory that this threat be made.

Many contributions have been made to the doctrine of just war, but its classic formulation is generally attributed to St. Augustine.[10] St. Augustine reasoned that war is always an evil in the sense of being a human calamity, and violence in its nature is always evil. However, war viewed as a necessary measure, undertaken as the only means of defending the innocent from unjust attack, is not sinful. Under severe necessity, the lesser evil of violent resistance to injustice is the morally preferable act, tragic but not wicked.

How much does the doctrine of just war justify? It starts with the assumption that the rightness of the resistance depends upon the cause for which the war is fought. It also presupposes that the violence threatened or employed is required as the only recourse. The doctrine will therefore justify only wars waged in self-defense or for the protection of the innocent. Moreover, the cause must be backward-looking, war waged only because of something intolerably unjust done by the adversary. This means that the doctrine will not justify war waged on the basis of forward-looking consequential or utilitarian grounds, even if this were a preventive or preemptive strike on a belligerent planning an attack. Thus the doctrine justifies nuclear deterrence only insofar as threats to retaliate are necessary to prevent unjust assault.[11]

Is the threat to retaliate really necessary? The familiar but dreadful truth is that we cannot be guaranteed that a nation capable of making a nuclear threat will not use it to its—perceived—advantage. In fact the effects of an adversary's use of a nuclear advantage would be so devastating that it is an intolerable risk, however small the probability of actual use. Consequently any nation confronted by a nuclear adversary, whatever the ideologies or adversary relationship involved, and capable of developing its own nuclear armaments, will find the reasons for seeking—relative—safety in a balance of terror compelling. Against an enemy willing to use the bomb, or perceived to be willing, self-defense is impossible by any means short of threatened retaliation. It therefore makes sense to say that the only compensating step is the awful threat to respond in kind.[12]

Thus despite the monstrosity of the threat, deterrence averts a graver danger and thereby meets the test of necessity for just war. Much evidence also shows that despite the danger of instability, deterrence works. The Soviets believe in deterrence, and as David Holloway's research shows,[13] there is no evidence to suggest the Soviets believe either that they can win a nuclear war, or that victory in a global war would be anything other than catastrophic.

Jus Ad Bellum *and* Jus In Bello

Despite the air of morality given to nuclear deterrence by the doctrine of just war, there are strong reasons for believing that retaliatory threats may not be justified after all. Even if war or preparations for war are justified as measures of restraint, the instruments of enforcement are so faulty that further constraints upon the waging of war must be imposed. The most important of these are restraints on the means of pursuing the just cause. In effect the doctrine insists upon the distinction between *jus ad bellum,* the morality of going to war, and *jus in bello,* moral choice in the selection of the tactics and instruments of warfare. Among the principles of *jus in bello,* three are directly relevant to nuclear deterrence: (1) the immunity of noncombatants from direct attack; (2) the use of the least amount of force necessary to restrain or neutralize the aggressor effectively; and (3) the rule of proportionality, which asserts that there must be due proportionality between the end to be accomplished by a military action and the unavoidable harm inflicted in its pursuit.

It is in connection with the principles of *jus in bello* that charges of the immorality of nuclear deterrence arise. Threatening civilian populations completely disregards the distinction between combatants and noncombatants. Deterrence requires that millions be threatened as a means to influence the decisions of a few leaders. Thus deterrence requires that we treat human life as a mere object of policy and a means rather than an end. The theologian Paul Ramsey draws the analogy of deterring reckless automobile drivers by tying babies to the front bumpers of their cars. He points out that this would be no way to regulate traffic even if it succeeds in regulating it perfectly, for "such a system makes innocent human lives the *direct object* of attack and uses them as a mere means for restraining the drivers of automobiles."[14]

In response to Ramsey's argument by analogy, Michael Walzer maintains that the moral wrong of actions that harm the innocent is not a reason also to condemn actions that only threaten to risk harming.[15] Ramsey's innocent babies are not only exposed to terrible risks but also forced to endure a terrifying experience that is an actual harm. But nuclear deterrence, according to Walzer, imposes threats that do not restrain us or deprive us of our rights:

> We are hostages who lead normal lives. It is in the nature of the new technology that we can be threatened without being held captive. This is why deterrence, while in principle so frightening, is so easy to live with. It cannot be condemned for anything it does to its hostages . . . it involves no direct or physical violation of their rights.[16]

Yet even if nuclear deterrence does not violate the rights of its hostages, it is nevertheless immoral. It commits a nation to a course of retaliation, since if a nation bluffs its adversary may learn this through espionage. But if deterrence does fail, and the opponent launches an attack, there would be no rational or moral reason to carry out the threatened retaliation. Indeed the leaders of the stricken nation would have conclusive moral reasons not to retaliate. Retaliation would punish the leaders who committed this unprecedented crime and would prevent them from dominating the postwar world; but it would accomplish no deterrent effect while massacring millions of innocent civilians in the attacking nation, and in other nations, would set back postwar re-

covery for the world immeasurably, and might even render the earth unfit for human survival.

Immoral Threats

The immorality of nuclear deterrence lies in the threat itself, not in its present or even likely consequences. Paul Ramsey also recognizes this point: "Whatever is wrong to do is wrong to threaten, if the latter means 'means to do'. . . . If counter-population warfare is murder, then counter-population deterrence threats are murderous."[17]

Since it would be wrong to retaliate, and through moral intuition we know it to be wrong, then it cannot be right for us to intend to do it. Indeed moral systems depend upon some version of the so-called wrongful intentions principle: to intend to do what one knows to be wrong is itself wrong.[18] The necessity of this principle is obvious from reflection about our moral experience and is not denied by any major system of morality.[19]

Yet it might be objected that U.S. leaders intend not to annihilate Soviet citizens but to preserve peace. Thus by threatening to kill, they intend not to kill. This objection contains elements both of error and of truth. When these are sorted out, the intention to retaliate is still immoral, although certainly not as wicked as a direct and unconditional intention to kill.

In objecting that it is not immoral to intend retaliation, one may be confusing "intending an action" with "desiring the outcome of that action." Ordinarily an agent will form the intention to do something because he desires doing it either as an end in itself, or as a means to other ends.[20] In the case of nuclear deterrence, however, the intention to retaliate is entirely distinct from any desire to carry it out. In fact the intenion to retaliate is entirely consistent with a strong desire not to apply the sanction. Thus while the object of our leaders' deterrence intention is an evil act, it does not follow that in adopting that intention, or even desiring to adopt it, they desire to do evil, either as an end or as a means.

While the absence of a desire to kill is important, it is not sufficient to exculpate our national leaders for the intention to retaliate. What counts in establishing the immorality of their intentions are the preparations they make to retaliate, the signals they send to the adversary, and courses of action that may leave their hands tied and make retaliation almost automatic. These plans and actions underscore their willingness, in order to deter aggression, to accept the risk that in the end they will apply the sanctions and allow the world to be consumed.

The objection that it is not immoral to intend massive retaliation may also be based on the claim that the U.S. intention is entirely conditional upon the behavior of the adversary. We are intending not to attack, but to launch a strike only if the opponent attacks. Such conditional intentions seem strange because they are by nature self-extinguishing: the purpose of forming the intention to retaliate is to prevent the very circumstances in which the intended act would be performed.[21] Nevertheless the wrong intentions principle applies to conditional just as to unconditional intentions. When a terrorist hijacks an airplane at gunpoint and threatens the lives of his hostages, the immorality of his threat is not canceled by its being conditional upon the behavior of the officials he seeks to coerce. The same is true of nuclear deterrence. In addition to the leaders who decide to launch a first strike, millions who have no part in the decision will die or suffer. Thus one does not significantly change the immorality of the threat to kill innocent persons by making it conditional upon the actions of national leaders.[22]

A Moral Dilemma

Where we have persuasive moral reasons both for and against the same action, we have a moral dilemma. We must either accept our obligations to defend the innocent, in which case we threaten retaliation, or we do not threaten retaliation, in which case we abandon hope of effectively protecting the innocent. Thus it is both morally wrong for our government to commit us to a policy of massive retaliation involving immoral threats, and at the same time morally wrong not to do so. Walzer seems entirely correct when he says that "nuclear weapons explode the theory of just war."[23]

This moral dilemma surrounding nuclear deterrence policy is intolerable. But by what means can we escape from it? We could show that the dilemma does not really exist by denying one of its horns. We might marshal new arguments to show that there are moral reasons we had overlooked but which justify threats of nuclear retaliation. A second possibility is to show that there is a nuclear deterrence strategy that evades moral censure. Ramsey has asserted that just war can support a counterforce deterrence strategy.[24] His argument is especially important because since 1973 counterforce strategy has become the officially preferred nuclear strategy in the United States.[25]

Counterforce Deterrence

Ramsey argues that it is possible to prevent nuclear attack without threatening to strike population centers in response. Strategic nuclear weapons can be targeted against nuclear installations, conventional military bases, and isolated economic objectives. This strategy could have the same deterrent effect as the conventional countervalue strategy, because although only military objectives would be targeted, a consequence of retaliation would inevitably be the unacceptable loss of millions of collateral civilian deaths.

However, the civilians likely to die would be the incidental victims of legitimate military counterstrikes. Herein lies the alleged moral superiority of counterforce strategy. These civilians are not hostages whom we have formed the—conditional—intention to kill. These collateral damages would be justified as an unavoidable consequence of a justifiable response; hence it is also justifiable to intend—conditionally—such a response.

Nevertheless there are serious difficulties

with Ramsey's argument. First, could a retaliatory counterforce strategy really deter a first strike? Deterrence works only if the defender threatens unacceptable harm, and in recent years there has been much speculation that with evacuation, hardened industrial sites, and civil defense, the Soviets might escape with as little as 10 million casualties—judged to be an "acceptable loss" by some defense consultants.[26] Thus the danger of collateral damage is likely to deter only if the threatened damage would be very great indeed, disproportionate to the value of the military site targeted. The proportionality rule bars use of the doctrine of just war to justify any number of civilian casualties on the grounds that although these casualties were unavoidable, we did not intend to kill them since we did not really aim at them.

Ramsey's response is to maintain that in nuclear deterrence, proportionality is to be measured against the value not of a particular military target, but of world peace itself.[27] But how are we to reckon proportionality between the—certain—loss of human life and any—uncertain—increase in world peace? World peace is obviously an end we value very highly, but does this mean that, according to Ramsey's logic, the more highly we value peace, the more lives we may threaten so long as any actual deaths would be only collateral? If this is what Ramsey means, then the word "collateral" has lost most of its meaning and "proportionality" has been defined so broadly as to void the rules of just war.[28]

In any event, Ramsey's proposal does not overcome the problem of immoral threats. Since we know that counterforce strategy will deter aggression only if the threat to the civilian population is very great, and since we intend these threats to deter, it follows that we have formed the conditional intention to bring about their deaths after all. Like other deterrent theorists, Ramsey wants to prevent nuclear attack by threatening to kill very large numbers of innocent people, but unlike other deterrent theorists, he expects to kill these people without aiming at them. However, we

might as well aim at them, if we know that a direct and necessary consequence of our attacking military targets would be their death.[29]

Renouncing Retaliation

Counterforce deterrence provides no real solution to our moral dilemma, but there may be a second means of escape. This would involve denying the alternatives presumed in formulating the dilemma. It had been assumed, not without reason, that we must either accept our obligations to defend the innocent, in which case we threaten retaliation, or we do not threaten retaliation, in which case we abandon hope of effectively defending the innocent. But is it not possible to meet our obligations of self-defense and protection of the innocent without threatening nuclear retaliation? An affirmative answer has been offered: we develop a technological capacity for self-defense that does not require threats of massive retaliation against the adversary.

On the evening of 23 March 1983 this proposal was dramatically presented to the American people by President Reagan. The president asked, "What if free people could live secure in the knowledge that their security did not rest upon the threat of instant U.S. retaliation to deter a Soviet attack, that we could intercept and destroy strategic ballistic missiles before they reached our own soil or that of our allies?"[30] The inference he knew we would draw is that such a system of self-defense would remove the moral opprobrium surrounding present deterrence policies. Such a system, if it could work, might also inaugurate a new era in strategic nuclear deterrence, a technological solution to the problem of vulnerability created by nuclear technology in the first place.

Could such a purely defensive strategy work, and would it really eliminate the need to make immoral threats? The development of new antimissile weapons would be destabilizing and might dangerously increase the risk of a preemptive Soviet strike. In the game of deterrence, the adversary's perceptions of our intentions are what ultimately count. And the Soviets are not likely to trust our claims that the new devices are purely defensive. Soviet leaders would correctly reason that since such weapons could knock out Soviet missiles sent in a second strike, it might increase U.S. capacity to prevail in a nuclear war. At present, the Soviet deterrent to a U.S. first strike is massive retaliation, and Reagan's proposed antimissile defense would effectively eliminate that deterrent threat. Consequently the Soviet's increased vulnerability would cause them to fear the possible sense of adventurism that knowledge of this edge might give our leaders.

An antimissile defense system would also consign the United States to the spiraling costs of a runaway antiarms arms race. The history of the arms race since 1945 suggests that the new defensive systems would be quickly matched by technological breakthroughs designed to overwhelm or outmaneuver them.[31]

More important still is the following consideration. Suppose the Soviets continue to arm; then in the event of an attack, we could never be sure our antimissile system would completely neutralize their offensive weapons. Even a very low rate of failure during an all-out attack would result in horrendous losses, perhaps even annihilation. Thus it is clear that the threat of a retaliatory second strike must remain as the unexpressed but final recourse if the United States is to deter aggression with nuclear arms. The point is that Reagan and our national security managers know we would need to hold onto our second-strike forces as an insurance policy, and that is why the president's proposal seems so deceitful. By attempting to push the immoral threat of retaliation away from the light of debate and analysis, our leaders' hope will overlook its hideous reality. The Soviets also know we would keep a second-strike insurance, and that is why these so-called defensive antiballistic weapons would be perceived by them as offensive.

Moral Failure of Nuclear Deterrence

Nuclear deterrence as practiced by the superpowers fails the test of morality; its appearance of moral respectability arises from close association with perceptions of dire emergency. A stopgap effort at conflict containment or postponement, it does not resolve international conflicts by removing their cause, nor does it bring about changes that lessen the danger of clashes. By exchanging immoral threats, the superpower players merely push the real problems into the background, taking the position that no solution at all is preferable to the risk of escalating a conflict that could lead to a nuclear exchange. In fact nuclear deterrence may well be self-defeating over the long run. Although real security no longer exists, our national security managers relentlessly seek to instill a sense of security in us by pursuing actions that objectively increase the danger: they build more and deadlier weapons.[32]

Furthermore, since nuclear deterrence requires credible threats that weapons may be used, its success diminishes its own credibility, and efforts to reassert its credibility threaten to bring about its failure. The runaway arms race is due only in part to worst-case analyses on both sides and current methods of weapons procurement;[33] it is also a product of the constant need to underwrite deterrence with the image of Armageddon. Since perceptions of our preparation for self-protection and of our willingness to retaliate are directly correlated, nuclear deterrence will require greater efforts to ensure the survivability of our nuclear forces. What better way to communicate the seriousness of our intent than to commit a staggering proportion of the federal budget to the development of new weapons? President Reagan argued that defense budget cuts "will send a signal of decline, of lessened will, to friends and adversaries alike."[34]

Both President Reagan's proposal and Paul Ramsey's approach attempt to overcome the immorality of nuclear deterrence by making changes in strategic uses of nuclear weapons. Is there a common error in the assumption that deterrence is equivalent to military, and especially nuclear, defense capability? Neither deterrence nor self-defense is necessarily equivalent to threatening military might, and it may be this fact that a solution to the problem of self-defense must recognize.

Nonviolent National Defense

Deterrence connotes retaliation but this association is not logically part of the concept. As Thomas Schelling has indicated, deterrence occurs whenever a potential enemy is persuaded to abandon a certain course of activity because he sees that it is in his own self-interest to do so.[35] Thus deterrence is essentially a process of persuasion, and the method that persuades most clearly deters most effectively.

Nobody understands this fact more emphatically than the advocates of nonviolent national defense or civilian resistance. Here is offered an approach to defense that escapes the moral dilemma. It takes seriously the obligation to defend the innocent, and its advocates claim that it would deter aggression; moreover it would overcome occupation and oppression if deterrence were to fail.[36]

Civilian resistance focuses upon the defense of a nation's basic social institutions, culture, and ideological beliefs by training the civilian population in organized nonviolent resistance and noncompliance. In addition to protecting human lives, a national defense must successfully protect a way of life: the institutions, rights, and principles that form the stable framework for life and provide a group with an organized expression of conscious preferences and commitments.[37] Civilian resistance therefore seeks to deter aggression by making it clear to any potential invader that he could not control and dominate the political and social life of the nation he seeks to invade. He would see that military occupation would not by itself give him political control and would not be experienced by the population as defeat; rather it would mean an extension of the contest of will and ideology.

Gene Sharp, a leading advocate of civilian resistance, asks us to reflect about the conditions that are most likely to create a nuclear attack.[38] Who fears and expects a nuclear attack the most today, and who expects one the least? It is precisely the nuclear powers who fear a nuclear attack the most, and this fear of attack, or of defeat in a major conventional war, may itself be the overriding temptation for a superpower to launch a first strike. Civilian resistance, which unlike nuclear forces can be used only for defensive purposes, would remove that danger and thereby reduce the chances of annihilation. In addition, while there remain some circumstances under which a nuclear attack might seem rational, given present deterrence policies, there appear to be no circumstances under which a nuclear attack on an unarmed nation would appear rational. It will surely be objected that civilian resistance could not save a nation from a maniacal opponent. However, since no one can predict what a maniac would do, there is no more reason to suppose that he would respond rationally to nuclear threats than that he would pointlessly devastate an unarmed and unthreatening country.

Walzer has objected that while nuclear deterrence depends upon inspiring fear in the adversary, in nonviolent defense the adversary would experience no fear, but at best only guilt, shame, and remorse. "The success of the defense [would be] entirely dependent upon the moral convictions and sensibilities of the enemy soldiers."[39] But this presumption appears mistaken. First, it has frequently been noted that inhibitions of a political, social, and cultural nature are normally more decisive than fear in holding back the hand on the trigger.[40] Second, there is no reason to suppose that nonviolent deterrence must depend more than nuclear deterrence upon the moral sensibilities of the adversary. All deterrence policies must depend upon the adversary's calculations that the costs of aggression would outweigh the benefits, and this would be true no less for nonviolent defense than for nuclear deterrence.

The case for nonviolent defense has not been completed, but serious and intelligent criticism has also hardly begun. Civilian resistance has not received the attention it deserves. It may turn out that a nonviolent national defense would be impossible, or if possible, less acceptable morally than nuclear deterrence. But nonviolent defense is not foolish on its face, nor is it merely pacifism or unilateral disarmament under a different guise.[41] Its apparent moral superiority to nuclear deterrence obligates us to give it our careful attention. Indeed if threats of nuclear retaliation are morally permissible, then they are permissible only because deterrence is absolutely necessary, and nuclear threats are the only means of effecting this deterrence. Thus even those who argue for the moral superiority of nuclear deterrence, if they are earnest and sincere, must attempt to demonstrate the moral inadequacy of civilian resistance.

Notes

1. See Philip Green, *Deadly Logic* (Columbus: Ohio University Press, 1966); and Robert P. Wolff, "Maximization of Expected Utility as a Criterion of Rationality in Military Strategy and Foreign Policy," *Social Theory and Practice*, 1:99–111 (Spring 1970).

2. Quoted by Robert Jay Lifton and Richard Falk, *Indefensible Weapons* (New York: Basic Books, 1983), p. 66.

3. See Jonathan Schell, *The Fate of the Earth* (New York: Avon Books, 1982), pp. 99–178.

4. Lifton and Falk, *Indefensible Weapons*, pp. 3–127.

5. Henry T. Nash, "The Bureaucratization of Homicide," in *Protest and Survive*, ed. F. P. Thompson and Dan Smith (New York: Monthly Review Press, 1981), pp. 149–60.

6. "Moral Urgencies in the Nuclear Context," in *Nuclear Weapons and the Conflict of Conscience*, ed. John C. Bennett (New York: Charles Scribner's Sons, 1962), p. 109.

7. This discussion also presupposes that moral principles are relevant to issues of war and national defense. Anyone who doubts this should see Richard A. Wasserstrom, "On the Morality of War: A Preliminary Inquiry," in *War and Morality*, ed. R. A. Wasserstrom (Belmont, CA: Wadsworth Pub., 1970), pp. 78–101: and Michael Walzer, *Just and Unjust Wars* (New York: Basic Books, 1977), pp. 3–20.

8. Thomas C. Schelling, "The Diplomacy of Violence," in *Peace and War*, ed. Charles Beitz and Theodore Herman (San Francisco: W. H. Freeman and Co., 1973), pp. 74–90.

9. See *Just and Unjust Wars* p. 269.

10. See selections from his *The City of God*, in *War and Christian Ethics*, ed. Arthur F. Holmes

(Grand Rapids: Baker Book House. 1975), pp. 61–87, and Ralph Potter, "The Moral Logic of War," in *Peace and War*, ed. Beitz and Herman, pp. 7–16. Modern versions of the doctrine have a variety of theoretical bases. Barrie Paskins and Michael Dockrill, *The Ethics of War* (Minneapolis: University of Minnesota Press, 1979) pp. 191–245, derive the doctrine from Kantian ethical principles, although they deny its justification of nuclear deterence. In *Just and Unjust Wars*, Walzer develops a version of the doctrine that is independent of any particular theological or ethical position.

11. See David Wells, "How Much Can the Just War Justify?" *Journal of Philosophy*, 66:819–29 (Dec. 1969).

12. Walzer, *Just and Unjust Wars*, pp. 272–73.

13. *The Soviet Union and the Arms Race* (New Haven, CT: Yale University Press, 1983).

14. Paul Ramsey, *The Just War* (New York: Charles Scribner's Sons, 1968), p. 171.

15. *Just and Unjust Wars*, pp. 270–71.

16. Ibid. But perhaps nuclear weapons can be condemned for their psychological effects on hostages. For a discussion of the psychological evidence, see Lifton and Falk, *Indefensible Weapons*, pp. 48–52, 54, 68, 77.

17. "A Political Ethics Context for Strategic Thinking," in *Strategic Thinking and Its Moral Implications*, ed. Morton A. Kaplan (Chicago: University of Chicago Center for Policy Studies, 1973), pp. 134–35.

18. Gregory S. Kavka, "Some Paradoxes of Deterrence," *Journal of Philosophy*, 75:285–89 (June 1978).

19. Ibid.

20. Kavka, "Paradoxes of Deterrence," p. 291.

21. Kavka, "Paradoxes of Deterrence," p. 290.

22. But see Kavka's objection to this argument, ibid., p. 289.

23. *Just and Unjust Wars*, p. 282.

24. *The Just War*, pp. 285–366.

25. James Fallows, *National Defense* (New York: Vintage Books, 1981), pp. 141–45.

26. See the testimony before the Senate Foreign Relations Committee or Retired General Daniel O. Graham, former director of the Defense Intelligence Agency, as quoted in Fallows, *National Defense*, pp. 145–46.

27. *The Just War*, p. 303.

28. Walzer, *Just and Unjust Wars*, p. 280.

29. I certainly agree that threatening to kill 10–20 million civilians by counterforce retaliation is

not as immoral as threatening to kill 60–100 million by countervalue retaliation, other things being equal. But this reduction in the immorality of the threat can be achieved in a more straightforward way simply by cutting back on our overkill capacity, so that retaliation would be less massive.

30. *Washington Post*, 24 Mar. 1983, p. A12.

31. For a discussion of the arms race and the futuristic weapons defenses envisioned by some analysts, see Ground Zero, *Nuclear War: What's In it for You?* (New York: Pocket Books, 1982), pp. 72–82, 199–211.

32. Lifton and Falk, *Indefensible Weapons*, p. 25.

33. Mary Kaldor, "Disarmament: The Armament Process in Reverse," in *Protest and Survive*, ed. Thompson and Smith, pp. 134–82.

34. *Washington Post*, 24 May, 1983, p. A1.

35. *The Strategy of Conflict* (Cambridge, MA: Harvard University Press, 1960), pp. 6ff.

36. Anders Boserup and Andrew Mack, *War without Weapons* (New York: Schocken Books, 1975); B. H. Liddell Hart; *Defence of the West* (New York: Morrow, 1950): idem, *Deterrent or Defence* (New York: Praeger, 1960); H. J. N. Horsburgh, *Non-Violence and Aggression* (London: Oxford University Press, 1968); Adam Roberts, ed., *Civilian Resistance as a National Defence* (Baltimore: Penguin Books, 1969); and Gene Sharp, *The Politics of Non-violent Action* (Boston: Porter-Sargent, 1973).

37. Horsburgh, *Non-Violence and Aggression*, p. 106.

38. "National Defense without Armaments," in *Peace and War*, ed. Beitz and Herman, p. 360.

39. *Just and Unjust Wars*, p. 334.

40. Boserup and Mack, *War without Weapons*, p. 176; Green, *Deadly Logic*, p. 201.

41. Unlike many proposals for unilateral disarmament, nonviolent defense responds to the need for deterrence; and unlike traditional versions of pacifism or passive resistance, it advocates nonviolent force and coercion. On the concept of nonviolent coercion, see Judith Stiehm, *Non-violent Power* (Lexington, MA: D. C. Heath, 1972).

Suggested Further Reading

Hehir, J. Bryan, "The Relationship of Moral and Strategic Arguments in the Defense Debate," *Research in Philosophy and Technology*, 3, ed. Paul T. Durbin. Greenwich, Conn.: JAI Press, 1980, pp. 367–83.

Perry, Tekla S., "Five Ethical Dilemmas," *IEEE Spectrum*, 18, no. 6 (June 1981), 53–60.

Wiener, Norbert, "A Scientist Rebels," *Atlantic Monthly*, 179 (January 1947), 46.

Wiesner, Jerome B., and Herbert F. York, "The Test Ban," *Scientific American*, 211 (1964), 27–35.

DECISION SCENARIO 7

The C-5A

The C-5A was never built to fly. In the mid-1960s the Lockheed Corporation submitted the winning bid for a contract offered by a superheated Defense Department during the heyday of the Vietnam War. The C-5A was to be a giant cargo plane, designed to transport personnel and materials to a distant Southeast Asian battlefront. It was supposed to supersede an aging fleet of cargo planes, relics of the Second World War.

Critics initially took issue with Lockheed's capability to produce the C-5A. Lockheed had been plagued by management problems. Its poor record for quality control made Air Force and Navy test pilots leery of flying in products rolling off the Lockheed assembly line. There was even the rumor that the contract award was a prearranged gesture to bail Lockheed out of another bankruptcy.

So it came as no surprise that the C-5A was

seriously behind schedule. Nor was it a surprise that cost overruns were hampering the project. Still, no one reckoned the magnitude of the overruns.

Late in 1968 Senator William Proxmire's Sub-committee on Economy in Government took up the investigation of the C-5A situation. The star witness was Ernest Fitzgerald, then deputy for management systems under the Assistant Secretary of the Air Force. Against the strong advice of his superiors, he confirmed Proxmire's data that the overrun exceeded $2 billion.

Fitzgerald described Lockheed's work force as swollen with underutilized engineers and high-salaried sales personnel. He pointed out that defense contractors operated at efficiencies far below commercial standards. He pointed to the lack of incentive for large suppliers to comply with cost-cutting measures.

For his reward, Fitzgerald was demoted, given trivial assignments, and summarily removed from his position. Only after a decade of court battles was he reinstated to his former position.

Questions

1. The Code of Ethics for the U. S. Government Service says that employees should expose "corruption wherever discovered." Was Fitzgerald's an act of duty or of heroism?

2. Ought we require a weapons system to be cost effective?

3. If personnel of technological expertise had been given control of the C-5A project, the moral difficulties never would have happened. What are the moral difficulties? Is this position correct?

4. The argument from deterrence states that no social good has value if all social goods are lost in conquest. Is this argument sufficient to justify massive defense appropriations over funding of other social programs?

5. Proponents of the present level of defense spending say that abuses are inevitable but are no reason to reorder technological priorities. Do you agree?

3. GENE-SPLICING TECHNOLOGY

The technology of *gene splicing,* or recombinant DNA, involves the joining of pieces of genetic material from cells of one species with those of another species to produce entirely new life forms. While humans have been selectively breeding and hybridizing various species of plants and animals for centuries, the revolutionary discovery of manipulation at the genetic level raises environmental, economic, and unprecedented ethical questions. Jeremy Rifkin, a public policy activist involved in biotechnology issues, describes the extraordinary significance of the new technology:

The more powerful the technology is at expropriating and controlling the forces of nature, the more exacting the price we are forced to pay in terms of disruption and de-struction wreaked on the ecosystems that sustain life. . . . Genetic engineering represents the ultimate tool. It extends humanity's reach over the forces of nature as no other technology in history, perhaps with the one exception of the nuclear bomb. . . . With genetic technology we assume control over the hereditary blueprints of life itself. Can any reasonable person believe for a moment that such unprecedented power is without risk?[3]

Genetic engineering began in 1973 when Stanley N. Cohen of Stanford University and Herbert W. Boyer of the University of California at San Francisco sliced a fragment of DNA from one bacterium and inserted it

[3]Jeremy Rifkin, *Declaration of a Heretic* (Boston: Routledge & Kegan Paul, 1985), p. 44.

into another. In the year following the experiment, concern was expressed in the scientific community about potential dangers of the new technique. The National Institutes of Health (NIH) established a committee to monitor research and consider possible rules to govern it. An international group of 139 scientists met in February 1975 to draw up guidelines to minimize the risk of genetically altered microbes accidentally escaping from research laboratories, and the NIH adopted the guidelines in 1976.

The commercial potential of gene-splicing technology prompted the establishment of a number of bioengineering corporations and quickened the pace of research by pharmaceutical and chemical companies, among others. The Supreme Court ruled in 1980 that an oil-eating microbe could be patented. On April 16, 1987, the U.S. Patent and Trademark Office extended patent protection to higher life forms, including mammals. That decision renewed the controversy over genetic engineering and aroused criticism from several quarters.

Initial concern centered on the dangers of inadvertently releasing altered microbes and on potential ecological damage from deliberate open-air testing of such microbes. The ethical basis of opposition to the technology was concern about risks to human health and safety and to the environment. So far no damage resulting from genetic engineering research has been reported. Following the announcement of the 1987 Patent Office ruling, critics began to voice new and more complex questions about the ethics of biotechnology.

Farmers' organizations warn that the patenting of animals represents a threat to small farms. Large corporate farms would gain an unfair advantage if fewer animal breeds were available and if they required expensive royalty payments. Animal rights activists question the morality of violating natural species boundaries and creating "transgenic animals." They argue that it is ethically wrong to manipulate animals genetically because they may suffer and become weak or more vulnerable to disease. Dr. Michael Fox, scientific director of the Humane Society of the United States, calls treating animals as "simple assemblies of genes" to be manipulated by humans "very frightening" and says, "It's our feeling that the inherent nature of an animal needs to be respected."[4] However, Dr. Fox supports genetic engineering of microorganisms and plants.

Other critics express fear that the new techniques may eventually be used to engineer human beings. Many genetic diseases can already be detected, and research is aimed at curing them by the removal or addition of genes. What limits, if any, should be placed on genetic intervention in humans? Bioengineering raises the possibility that prospective parents will be able in the future to select "desirable" or "undesirable" traits for their offspring. If humans can be "improved" by altering genes to eliminate, say, diabetes or sickle cell anemia, what other characteristics might we also choose to enhance or reject: size, skin color, intelligence, strength? And who ought to make the decisions? **[See Health Care, Chapter 6, Section 2.]**

Because of concerns like these, some critics argue that recombinant DNA technology should be discontinued altogether. Jeremy Rifkin argues:

> If certain types of scientific activity undermine the ethical principles and canons of civilization, we have an obligation to ourselves and to future generations to be willing to say no.[5]

Many scientists and ethicists insist, on the other hand, that little danger exists in genetic research and that discoveries promise substantial benefits. Among the developments predicted are cures for genetic disorders as well as improved food crops, such as plants that can manufacture their own insecticides or fertilizers. Techniques that use

[4]*New York Times*, June 9, 1987, p. C8.
[5]Rifkin, *Declaration*, p. 54.

gene-altered microbes to produce large quantities of valuable pharmaceuticals like human growth hormone and insulin have already been developed and the products marketed. Supporters of the research argue that concern about manipulating genes is misplaced and that the new technology is not ethically different from accepted breeding techniques. They point out that predicted harm from escaped bacteria or open-air testing has failed to materialize. They hold that animal interests differ from human rights and that animal research to benefit humans is morally justified.

In the following article Robert L. Sinsheimer raises three questions about gene-splicing technology: Is it safe? Is it wise? Is it moral? The author concludes that while we can probably maintain safety in the short term, there is no guarantee of long-term safety. Regarding the questions of the wisdom and morality of the technology, Sinsheimer offers no concrete answers but suggests possible areas of concern. He holds that research should "continue to be available for public scrutiny" and proposes the development of a group of professionals who have both scientific expertise and training in humanistic traditions. The group would help bridge the gulf between scientists and laypersons and help to "protect the larger view."

ROBERT L. SINSHEIMER

Genetic Engineering: Life as a Plaything

In a process almost as old as the earth, a huge panoply of organisms has evolved. The process has been one of chance and selection, and the star player has been the gene. For 3 billion years, natural changes in the number, structure, and organization of genes have determined the course of evolution.

We have now come to the end of that familiar pathway. Genetics—the science of heredity—has unlocked the code book of life, and the long-hidden strategies of evolution are revealing themselves. We now possess the ability to manipulate genes, and we can direct the future course of evolution. We can reassemble old genes and devise new ones. We can plan, and with computer simulation ultimately anticipate, the future forms and paths of life. Mutation and natural selection will continue, of course. But henceforth, the old ways of evolution will be dwarfed by the role of purposeful human intelligence. In the hands of the genetic engineer, life forms could become extraordinary Tinkertoys and life itself just another design problem.

Genetic engineering is a whole new technology. To view it as merely another technological development may make sense for those who invest in its commercial exploitation. But such a view is myopic for anyone concerned with the future of humanity. I want to consider three major areas of concern that will surely arise from this new technology. The first is the transformation of the science of biology itself. The development of molecular genetics is a transition as profound for biology as the development of quantum theory was for physics and chemistry. Until recently, biology was essentially an analytical science, in which researchers undertook the dissection of Nature as observed. Genetic engineering now

Reprinted with permission from *Technology Review,* copyright 1983. April 1983, pp. 14, 15, 20.

furnishes us with the ability to design and invent living organisms as well as to observe and analyze their function. If we consider the significance of synthesis to the science of chemistry, we can perhaps envision the importance of this development for the science of biology.

A New Biology

The new techniques open the door to a detailed understanding of the form and organization of genetic structures in higher organisms, of the control of gene expression, and of the processes of cellular differentiation. Out of such knowledge will come a new biology that gives us the means to intervene in life processes at the most basic possible level.

The impact of this new biology on the practical and technical arts—the second area of development—will be profound. With this technology, human ingenuity could design agricultural crops that thrive in arid zones or brackish waters, that provide better human nutrition, that resist disease and pests. Human-designed crops, adapted to the needs of efficient agricultural technology, could leap ahead of their natural parasites and predators.

In chemistry, microorganisms could be programmed to carry out the complex organic synthesis of new pharmaceuticals, pesticides, and chemical catalysts. Other organisms could be programmed to degrade chemical compounds and reduce environmental pollution. In animal husbandry, the prospects seem equally bright for designing disease-resistant, fast-growing, nutritious animal forms. In medicine, we envision the synthesis of antibiotics, hormones, vaccines, and other complex pharmaceuticals. But these achievements, almost certainly feasible, will pale before the potential latent in the deeper understanding of biology.

Control over gene expression will provide a whole new array of therapies for genetic disorders. And that introduces the third domain of consequence and the most profound. With the decline of infectious diseases, genetic disorders are now increasingly the source of ill health. Diabetes, cystic fibrosis, sickle-cell anemia, and Tay-Sachs disease all stem from well-recognized genetic defects. The possibilities of human gene therapy—replacing the "bad" gene with the "good"—are extraordinary.

The Darker Side

It is not hard to sense the excitement, the challenge, the promise in all these ventures. But is there a catch? Is there a darker side to this vision as we have come to see in other new technologies? Some of us believe there may be—that life is not just another design problem, that life is different from nonlife. Just as nature stumbled upon life some 3 billion years ago and unwittingly began the whole pageant of evolution, so too the new creators may find that living organisms have a destiny of their own. They may find that genetic engineering has consequences far beyond those of conventional engineering.

As we become increasingly confident that this technology can, in fact, be achieved, there are a few major questions to be asked: Is it safe, is it wise, is it moral?

First, is it safe? If we can keep the developments open to public scrutiny, then I believe in the short term it probably is. We can monitor the hazards of any new product we introduce into the biosphere and can probably cope with any immediate, untoward consequence.

For the long term, however, I am considerably less sure. Life has evolved on this planet into a delicately balanced, intricate, self-sustaining network. Maintaining this network involves many interactions and equilibria that we understand only dimly. I would suggest that we must take great care, as we replace the creatures and vegetation of earth with human-designed forms, as we reshape the animate world to conform to human will, that we not forget our origins and inadvertently collapse the ecological system in which we have found our niche.

Through intensive study, we have learned of the different pathogens that prey on humans, animals, and major crops. But we have a very limited understanding of the evolutionary factors that led to their existence. We have limited knowledge about the reservoir of potential pathogens—organisms that could be converted by one or two or five mutations from harmless bugs into serious menaces. And thus we cannot really predict whether our genetic tinkering might unwittingly lead to novel and unexpected hazards.

More broadly, is it wise for us to assume responsibility for the structure and cohesion of the animate world? Do we want to engineer the planet so that its function requires the continuous input of human intelligence? Do we want to convert Earth into a giant Skylab?

Life as Our Plaything

What happens to the reverence for life when life is our creation, our plaything? Will we have species with planned obsolescence? Will we have genetic olympics for homing pigeons or racing dogs? Will we have a zoo of reconstructed vanished species—dinosaurs or sabre-toothed tigers—or as-yet unimagined species? Genetic engineering will inevitably change our sense of kinship with all our fellow creatures.

Will the extinction of species mean much when we can create new ones at will? Until now, we have all been the children of nature, the progeny of evolution. But from now on the flora and fauna of Earth will increasingly be our creations, our designs, and thus our responsibility. What will happen to our nature in such a world?

The most profound consequence of this technology is its application to humankind. The impetus to employ genetic engineering on the human race will come, I believe, out of our humanitarian tradition. Genetic engineering will be seen as just another branch of surgery, albeit at the most delicate level. Since we now know that many sources of human misery are genetic in origin, the urge to rem-

edy these defects and even eliminate their transmission to succeeding generations will be irresistible. Thus, these changes will become part of the human genetic inheritance—for better or worse.

Having acquired the technology to provide genetic therapy, will we then be able to draw a line and restrict human genetic experimentation? How will we define a "defect"? And how will we argue against genetic "improvement"? Or should we? Will we even stop to consider the morality of what's being done?

The extent to which our more specifically human qualities—our emotions and intellects, our compassion and conscience—are genetically determined is not yet known. But geneticists cannot escape the dark suspicion that more is written in our genes than we like to think.

What will happen if we tamper with our physical or mental traits, given the complexity of human development and behavior? Such banal qualities as height or weight can surely affect one's identity, and good health has its own concomitants. How many of our greatest artistic works have been produced by the afflicted or the neurotic?

I suspect human genetic engineering is repugnant to many people because they think its purpose is to impose an identity upon a descendant, to replace the sport of Nature with models of human fancy.

In some sense, education is an attempt to impose an identity. An educational system demands adherence to values of attention, concentration, delayed gratification, and so on. Mere literacy, while enlarging freedom by opening new worlds of knowledge, destroys the freedom of innocence. Yet clearly we have long decided that the virtues of literacy outweigh any drawbacks. University literacy is regarded as good and mandated in most societies. Might there be similar genetic characteristics that we would come to regard as a universal good?

Cloning can be seen as an exreme effort to impose a particular identity—upon a descendant. But all human genetic engineering will move us toward that extreme.

Genetic Lottery

Genetic engineering is the ultimate technology, for it makes plastic the very user and creator of that technology. This new tool makes conceivable a vast number of alternative evolutionary paths. We may even be able to adapt humankind to varied technological regimes.

Will we try, for instance, to breed—or mutate—people fit to work in special environments? Miniature people to travel in space or live on our overpopulated Earth? Will we create people resistant to carcinogens, radiation, and pesticides to work in chemical factories, nuclear plants, and farms? Or, alternatively, will we breed people who are better able to tolerate cytotoxic drugs should they contract cancer? What intellectual abilities, psychological strengths and life-spans would we choose?

I hope it is clear that the whole character of human life is at issue. To use a simile: Life has been a game, like cards, where each of us seeks to make the best of the hands (or genes) dealt to us. Shall it become a game like football, a collective strategy in which people play assigned roles in a coordinated plan? Or might it become more like a card game with a rigged deck, with more aces and fewer treys. If so, who designates the aces?

How will people react when they realize that their very genes are the product of a social decision? Will they rebel against such predestination? Will they become sullen and passive? Or will our descendants be proud they were each "planned," not the product of a genetic lottery but the recipient of the best inheritance our culture could devise at the time? How will they then react should a better model become available during their teens?

To what extent should we consciously leave a place for the element of chance in human affairs?

I suspect there is no turning back from the use of this awesome knowledge. Given the nature of our society, which embraces and applies any new technology, it appears that there is no means, short of unwanted catastrophe, to prevent the development of genetic engineering. It will proceed. But this time, perhaps we can seek to anticipate and guide its consequences.

Taking the Larger View

I believe the university is the place to address and analyze the social consequences of technological innovation. Yet even in academia, pressures for immediate results distract researchers from the quest for deeper understanding. Indeed, a salient characteristic of our increasingly secular society is its emphasis on the short-term payoff. We must try to avoid this myopia in developing this new technology. We must seek to protect the larger view.

Among other things, we must insist that university research continue to be available for public scrutiny in the open scientific literature, that it not be secreted as proprietary information and industrial know-how. We must also insist that private funding directed toward patentable and profitable inventions does not grossly exceed public funding directed toward the general increase of knowledge, including an understanding of possible hazards.

I would suggest that what we sorely need now is a new group of trained professionals to mediate between scientists and engineers on the one hand and citizenry on the other. Such professionals should be practicing scientists more broadly educated in our humanistic traditions. They would be trained to understand the potential implicit in this new technology, able to balance the ethos of environmentalists with the concerns of those who cherish civil liberty, able to perceive the imperatives of a technological society and still bear in mind that technology exists to serve. They would remember that the human species is very diverse, that it encompasses both a Mahatma Gandhi and an Adolf Hitler.

Ecclesiastes tells us that "he that increaseth knowledge increaseth sorrow." The modern version might be "he that increaseth knowledge increaseth power." Western society has become, in a sense, an extraordinary machine for converting knowledge into power.

Human beings, of course, are sprung from the same DNA and built of the same molecules as all other living things. But if we begin to regard ourselves as just another crop to be engineered, just another breed to be perfected, we will lose our awe of humanity and undermine all sense of human dignity.

Suggested Further Reading

Glover, Jonathan, "Some Conclusions," in *What Sort of People Should There Be?* by Jonathan Glover. New York: Penguin, 1984, pp. 178–87.

Jackson, David A., and Stephen P. Stick, eds., *The Recombinant DNA Debate.* Englewood Cliffs, N.J.: Prentice-Hall, 1979.

Macklin, Ruth, "On the Ethics of *Not* Doing Scientific Research," *Hastings Center Report,* 7 (December 1977), 11–13.

DECISION SCENARIO 8

Gene Making

"The idea is tremendous!" Louis Martin said enthusiastically. "A bacterium that eats oil."

"Yes," Katherine Fazio agreed. "Imagine being able to clean up oil spills without resorting to chemical toxins. It would help everyone."

They were in a laboratory of Biogene, Incorporated. "Here's my plan," Louis began. "This virus contains a segment of DNA we introduced into it. When it attacks a bacterium, it replicates itself by injecting the DNA into the host cell. The cell becomes a factory for synthesizing the DNA we want."

"If we're right."

"You still have doubts?" Louis's confidence was unshaken. "Once we have enough of the redesigned DNA, I'll show you."

"And if we're wrong? What about the danger that some DNA segments might produce bacteria resistant to antibiotics? What then?" Katherine asked.

"Don't play devil's advocate at this point, Katherine," Louis said. "We've been over the data time and again. That sort of thing happens only in science fiction."

"Really?"

"It's never happened yet. Whenever we release altered bacteria into the environment, they are attenuated and safe. Have faith in science!"

"I guess," Katherine replied. "But the risks seem there. Is what we're doing worth the risks?"

"Of course it is. It's very important to exploit this new technology. It's a way of making the world a better place to live in. New agricultural crops, new vaccines, new ways to produce drugs. There's no reason to repeat all that again."

"I suppose it's in everybody's interests," Katherine replied.

Questions

1. How do you compute the potential dangers and benefits of Louis's and Katherine's research?

2. Is it only "science fiction" that some cataclysmic mishap will result from genetic research?

3. How should the exploitation of genetic research be regulated? What say should be given to the layperson? To the professional?

4. How do you evaluate the argument of critics who say that we ought not to tamper with nature at the genetic level?

5. Does the deontologist have a reply to Louis's utilitarian argument in favor of proceeding with research? Would the utilitarian agree with him?

13. ISSUES IN TECHNOLOGY DEVELOPMENT

1. THE TECHNOLOGIST'S ROLE

Experimentation plays a significant role in the areas of technology discussed in the previous chapter. Basic scientific research requires experimentation to test hypotheses and confirm data acquired by observation. Technology—the practical application of scientific knowledge—also requires experiments. Designing products from a microscopically altered gene to a vast space station calls for testing at every stage. Some tests are done in laboratories under strictly controlled conditions. These may be followed by tests involving computer simulation of designs and processes. Eventually, however, the experiments move into the real world where they affect human beings.

We are familiar with the idea that medical research involving human subjects places ethical constraints upon the researcher. In particular, obtaining informed consent of the subject is a necessary moral and legal precondition to experimentation. **[See Health Care, Chapter 5, Section 3.]** Some ethicists argue that other professionals—engineers, for example—are subject to similar constraints because of the risky and unpredictable effects of their work. Mike W. Martin and Roland Schinzinger have written extensively about the concept of engineering as social experimentation. In *Ethics in Engineering* they write:

Engineering is an inherently risky activity, usually conducted with only partial knowledge of the underlying scientific laws about

nature and society and often producing uncertain results and side effects. It lends itself to being viewed as an experiment on a societal scale involving human subjects. While it differs from standard experiments using control groups, it nevertheless imposes the same moral requirements on engineers that are imposed on researchers in other experimental areas involving human subjects.[1]

Obtaining informed consent from subjects is an important obligation for biomedical researchers. Is there a similar obligation for engineers and other professionals in technology? Some say yes, although consent may be expressed indirectly. For example, consumers, like research subjects, should be able to make a free choice. The right to choose is based on their individual autonomy and right to self-determination. In each case, the subjects' freedom to choose depends upon their having sufficient accurate information upon which to base a decision. (See the first section in Chapter 11 of this unit.) Ethical relations between buyers and sellers require truthfulness and respect, especially on the part of sellers, since buyers depend upon the seller for information and are vulnerable to exploitation. A buyer's consent—in the form of a purchase—cannot be termed informed if it is based on inaccurate or incomplete information about a product and the risks it may entail.

[1]Mike W. Martin and Roland Schinzinger, *Ethics in Engineering* (New York: McGraw-Hill, 1983), p. 92.

By the same token, some proponents argue that an engineering project such as a dam or an oil-drilling platform should be undertaken only with the approval of individuals who will be affected by it. While legal requirements may differ in various localities, obtaining informed consent remains a moral obligation for corporations and individual consulting engineers.

Respect for the autonomy of consumers and other affected persons demands that they be given information and offered a free choice. In addition, it is argued that engineers and technologists have an obligation to ensure the safety and welfare of individuals affected by their work. Many ethical questions about technology involve side effects, both social and physical. For instance, building a dam to produce hydroelectric power has one primary desired effect: cheap energy. A secondary desired effect may be flood control. Side effects may include displacement of people living above the dam site who may lose their livelihood or suffer other social problems; loss of productive land to flooding; adverse ecological changes, such as the multiplication of insect and amoebic pests and the destruction of wildlife. Technologists need to be sensitive to the diverse consequences of their work. Particular attention should be paid to matters of public safety. According to Martin and Schinzinger, promoting safety is a primary ethical obligation for engineers:

> In one way or another, safety is involved in most of the thorny issues connected with engineering ethics. . . . In fact, it is perhaps only a slight exaggeration to say that whereas medical ethics centers on the role of promoting health within the bounds of patient autonomy, and legal ethics centers on advocacy of clients' rights within the bounds set by law, engineering ethics takes as its primary focus the promotion of useful technological products within the bounds of safety considerations that protect the people affected by those products.[2]

[2]Ibid., p. 141.

Because of their expertise, technology professionals are uniquely qualified to predict problems that may arise and to warn of possible risks and undesirable side effects. It may be difficult for professionals who are also employees to maintain a sense of moral accountability for the consequences of their work. There is a temptation to shift responsibility to those with greater authority, such as corporate managers or government overseers. At the same time, one element of professionalism is accountability in an area of special knowledge. Assuming the role of a professional confers privileges and compensations but also involves taking ethical responsibility for the outcome of one's work, especially when the work has an experimental character.

If, as we have suggested, engineers and other technology professionals have an obligation to ensure public safety, how can the obligation be met? One way is by testing prototypes for safety during the early design stages of a project. Not all designs, however, can be tested beforehand; in partcular, massive structures like dams and power plants must be built right the first time. In some cases, computer simulations can be used to predict systems failures and uncover design flaws. Another limitation of prototype testing is that production pressures can lead to shoddy or inadequate testing. Unless independent testing services are used, organizations may be tempted to take shortcuts or falsify test data in order to speed production.

Production pressure is one example of dilemmas faced by conscientious professionals who are also employees. Should the employee's primary obligation be to the employer or to the public interest? (See Section 3 of Chapter 10 in this unit.) According to one definition, freedom from coercion by an employer is a necessary characteristic of a professional engineer. In an article titled "The Professional Status of the American Engineer," Robert L. Whitelaw links engineering professionalism with independence from employers in this manner: ". . . so long as the individual is looked upon as an employee rather than a free artisan, to that extent there is no professional status."[3]

At the opposite extreme from Whitelaw's position are those who hold that professional engineers must regard their employers' interests as paramount. On this vew, the engineer's first obligation is to meet the expectations of clients and employers. Ethical constraints should be provided by laws and government regulation, not by the engineer's conscience. This description of the engineer's role recalls one model of the lawyer's role, according to which attorneys must provide zealous advocacy without considering their personal moral standards. **[See Criminal Justice, Chapter 16, Section 2.]**

A moderate view of the engineer's role takes into account obligations both to employers and to the public. Neither obligation receives automatic priority, but each should be weighed on a case-by-case basis. Where the interests conflict sharply and where threats to public safety are serious and substantial, whistle blowing may be justified or even obligatory.

In the following essay Richard T. De-George examines the ethical responsibilities of Ford Motor Company engineers in the well-known Pinto case. (See Section 1 of Chapter 11 in this unit.) DeGeorge argues that the engineers fulfilled their moral obligations in the situation. He holds that the decision not to modify the design to improve fuel-tank safety was properly an executive one and that "an engineer cannot be expected to second-guess managerial decisions." DeGeorge recognizes engineers' professional obligation to pay special attention to public safety and condones whistle blowing under certain conditions, but he does not believe such conditions existed in the Pinto case. He argues for changes in organizational structure to help eliminate moral dilemmas of this kind for engineering employees.

---

[3]Robert L. Whitelaw, "The Professional Status of the American Engineer: A Bill of Rights," *Professional Engineer*, 45 (August 1975), 37–38.

RICHARD T. DeGEORGE

Ethical Responsibilities of Engineers in Large Organizations

The myth that ethics has no place in engineering has been attacked, and at least in some corners of the engineering profession has been put to rest.[1] Another myth, however, is emerging to take its place—the myth of the engineer as moral hero. A litany of engineering saints is slowly taking form. The saints of the field are whistle blowers, especially those who have sacrificed all for their moral convictions. The zeal of some preachers, however, has gone too far, piling moral responsibility upon moral responsibility on the shoulders of the engineer. This emphasis, I believe, is misplaced. Though engineers are members of a profession that holds public safety paramount,[2] we cannot reasonably expect engineers to be willing to sacrifice their jobs each day for principle and to have a whistle ever

---

Reprinted with permission of the author from *Business and Professional Ethics Journal*, vol. 1, no. 1, Fall 1981.

by their sides ready to blow if their firm strays from what they perceive to be the morally right course of action. If this is too much to ask, however, what then is the actual ethical responsibility of engineers in a large organization?

I shall approach this question through a discussion of what has become known as the Pinto case, i.e., the trial that took place in Winamac, Indiana, and that was decided by a jury on March 16, 1980.

In August 1978 near Goshen, Indiana, three girls died of burns in a 1973 Pinto that was rammed in traffic by a van. The rear-end collapsed "like an accordion,"[3] and the gas tank erupted in flames. It was not the first such accident with the Pinto. The Pinto was introduced in 1971 and its gas tank housing was not changed until the 1977 model. Between 1971 and 1978 about fifty suits were brought against Ford in connection with rear-end accidents in the Pinto.

What made the Winamac case different from the fifty others was the fact that the State prosecutor charged Ford with three (originally four, but one was dropped) counts of reckless homicide, a *criminal* offense, under a 1977 Indiana law that made it possible to bring such criminal charges against a corporation. The penalty, if found guilty, was a maximum fine of $10,000 for each count, for a total of $30,000. The case was closely watched, since it was the first time in recent history that a corporation was charged with this criminal offense. Ford spent almost a million dollars in its defense.

With the advantage of hindsight I believe the case raised the right issue at the wrong time.

The prosecution had to show that Ford was reckless in placing the gas tank where and how it did. In order to show this the prosecution had to prove that Ford consciously disregarded harm it might cause and the disregard, according to the statutory definition of "reckless," had to involve "substantial deviation from acceptable standards of conduct."[4]

The prosecution produced seven witnesses who testified that the Pinto was moving at speeds judged to be between 15 and 35 mph when it was hit. Harly Copp, once a high ranking Ford engineer, claimed that the Pinto did not have a balanced design and that for cost reasons the gas tank could withstand only a 20 mph impact without leaking and exploding. The prosecutor, Michael Cosentino, tried to introduce evidence that Ford knew the defects of the gas tank, that its executives knew that a $6.65 part would have made the car considerably safer, and that they decided against the change in order to increase their profits.

Federal safety standards for gas tanks were not introduced until 1977. Once introduced, the National Highway Traffic Safety Administration (NHTSA) claimed a safety defect existed in the gas tanks of Pintos produced from 1971 to 1976. It ordered that Ford recall 1.9 million Pintos. Ford contested the order. Then, without ever admitting that the fuel tank was unsafe, it "voluntarily" ordered a recall. It claimed the recall was not for safety but for "reputational" reasons.[5] Agreeing to a recall in June, its first proposed modifications failed the safety standards tests, and it added a second protective shield to meet safety standards. It did not send out recall notices until August 22. The accident in question took place August 10. The prosecutor claimed that Ford knew its fuel tank was dangerous as early as 1971 and that it did not make any changes until the 1977 model. It also knew in June of 1978 that its fuel tank did not meet federal safety standards; yet it did nothing to warn owners of this fact. Hence, the prosecution contended Ford was guilty of reckless homicide.

The defense was led by James F. Neal who had achieved national prominence in the Watergate hearings. He produced testimony from two witnesses who were crucial to the case. They were hospital attendants who had spoken with the driver of the Pinto at the hospital before she died. They claimed she had stated that she had just had her car filled with gas. She had been in a hurry and had left the gas station without replacing the cap on her gas tank. It fell off the top of her car as she drove down the highway. She noticed this and stopped to turn around to pick it up. While stopped, her car was hit by the van. The testimony indicated that the car was stopped. If the car was hit by a van going 50 mph, then the rupture of the gas tank was to be expected. If the cap was off the fuel tank, leakage would be more than otherwise. No small vehicle was made to withstand such impact. Hence, Ford claimed, there was no recklessness involved. Neal went on to produce films of tests that indicated that the amount of damage the Pinto suffered meant that the impact must have been caused by the van's going at least 50 mph. He further argued that the Pinto gas tank was at least as safe as the gas tanks on the 1973 American Motors Gremlin, the Chevrolet Vega, the Dodge Colt, and the Toyota Corolla, all of which suffered comparable damage when hit from the rear at 50 mph. Since no federal safety standards were in effect in 1973, Ford was not reckless if its safety standards were comparable to those of similar cars made by competitors; that standard represented the state of the art at that time, and it would be inappropriate to apply 1977 standards to a 1973 car.[6]

The jury deliberated for four days and finally came up with a verdict of not guilty. When the verdict was announced at a meeting of the Ford Board of Directors then taking place, the members broke out in a cheer.[7]

These are the facts of the case. I do not wish to second-guess the jury. Based on my reading of the case, I think they arrived at a proper decision, given the evidence. Nor do I wish to comment adversely on the judge's ruling that prevented the prosecution from introducing about 40% of his case because the evidence referred to 1971 and 1972 models of the Pinto and not the 1973 model.[8]

The issue of Ford's being guilty of acting recklessly can, I think, be made plausible, as I shall indicate shortly. But the successful strategy argued by the defense in this case hinged on the Pinto in question being hit by a van at 50 mph. At that speed, the defense successfully argued, the gas tank of any subcompact would rupture. Hence that accident did not

show that the Pinto was less safe than other subcompacts or that Ford acted recklessly. To show that would require an accident that took place at no more than 20 mph.

The contents of the Ford documents that Prosecutor Cosentino was not allowed to present in court were published in the *Chicago Tribune* on October 13, 1979. If they are accurate, they tend to show grounds for the charge of recklessness.

Ford had produced a safe gas tank mounted over the rear axle in its 1969 Capri in Europe. It tested that tank in the Capri. In its over-the-axle position, it withstood impacts of up to 30 mph. Mounted behind the axle, it was punctured by projecting bolts when hit from the rear at 20 mph. A $6.65 part would help make the tank safer. In its 1971 Pinto, Ford chose to place the gas tank behind the rear axle without the extra part. A Ford memo indicates that in this position the Pinto has more trunk space, and that production costs would be less than in the over-the-axle position. These considerations won out.[9]

The Pinto was first tested it seems in 1971, after the 1971 model was produced, for rear-end crash tolerance. It was found that the tank ruptured when hit from the rear at 20 mph. This should have been no surprise, since the Capri tank in that position had ruptured at 20 mph. A memo recommends that rather than making any changes Ford should wait until 1976 when the government was expected to introduce fuel tank standards. By delaying making any change, Ford could save $20.9 million, since the change would average about $10 per car.[10]

In the Winamac case Ford claimed correctly that there were no federal safety standards in 1973. But it defended itself against recklessness by claiming its car was comparable to other subcompacts at that time. All the defense showed, however, was that all the subcompacts were unsafe when hit at 50 mph. Since the other subcompacts were not forced to recall their cars in 1978, there is prima facie evidence that Ford's Pinto gas tank mounting was substandard. The Ford documents tend to show Ford knew the danger it was inflicting on Ford owners; yet it did nothing, for profit reasons. How short-sighted those reasons were is demonstrated by the fact that the Pinto thus far in litigation and recalls alone has cost Ford $50 million. Some forty suits are still to be settled. And these figures do not take into account the loss of sales due to bad publicity.

Given these facts, what are we to say about the Ford engineers? Where were they when all this was going on, and what is their responsibility for the Pinto? The answer, I suggest, is that they were where they were supposed to be, doing what they were supposed to be doing. They were performing tests, designing the Pinto, making reports. But do they have no moral responsibility for the products they design? What after all is the moral responsibility of engineers in a large corporation? By way of reply, let me emphasize that no engineer can morally do what is immoral. If commanded to do what he should not morally do, he must resist and refuse. But in the Ford Pinto situation no engineer was told to produce a gas tank that would explode and kill people. The engineers were not instructed to make an unsafe car. They were morally responsible for knowing the state of the art, including that connected with placing and mounting gas tanks. We can assume that the Ford engineers were cognizant of the state of the art in producing the model they did. When tests were made in 1970 and 1971, and a memo was written stating that a $6.65 modification could make the gas tank safer,[11] that was an engineering assessment. Whichever engineer proposed the modification and initiated the memo acted ethically in doing so. The next step, the administrative decision not to make the modification was, with hindsight, a poor one in almost every way. It ended up costing Ford a great deal more not to put in the part than it would have cost to put it in. Ford still claims today that its gas tank was as safe as the accepted standards of the industry at that time.[12] It must say so, otherwise the suits pending against it will skyrocket. That it was not as safe seems borne out by the fact that only the Pinto of all the subcompacts failed to pass the 30 mph rear impact NHTSA test.

But the question of wrongdoing or of malicious intent or of recklessness is not so easily solved. Suppose the ordinary person were told when buying a Pinto that if he paid an extra $6.65 he could increase the safety of the vehicle so that it could withstand a 30 mph rear-end impact rather than a 20 mph impact, and that the odds of suffering a rear-end impact of between 20 and 30 mph was 1 in 250,000. Would we call him or her reckless if he or she declined to pay the extra $6.65? I am not sure how to answer that question. Was it reckless of Ford to wish to save the $6.65 per car and increase the risk for the consumer? Here I am inclined to be clearer in my own mind. If I choose to take a risk to save $6.65, it is my risk and my $6.65. But if Ford saves the $6.65 and I take the risk, then I clearly lose. Does Ford have the right to do that without informing me, if the going standard of safety of subcompacts is safety in a rear-end collision up to 30 mph? I think not. I admit, however, that the case is not clear-cut, even if we add that during 1976 and 1977 Pintos suffered 13 fiery fatal rear-end collisions, more than double that of other U.S. comparable cars. The VW Rabbit and Toyota Corolla suffered none.[13]

Yet, if we are to morally fault anyone for the decision not to add the part, we would censure not the Ford engineers but the Ford executives, because it was not an engineering but an executive decision.

My reason for taking this view is that an engineer cannot be expected and cannot have the responsibility to second-guess managerial decisions. He is responsible for bringing the facts to the attention of those who need them to make decisions. But the input of engineers is only one of many factors that go to make up managerial decisions. During the trial, the defense called as a witness Francis Olsen, the assistant chief engineer in charge of design at Ford, who testified that he bought a 1973 Pinto for his eighteen-year-old daughter, kept it a year, and then traded it in for a 1974 Pinto which he kept two years.[14] His testimony and his actions were presented as an indication that the Ford engineers had confidence in the Pinto's safety. At least this one had enough confidence in it to give it to his daughter. Some engineers at Ford may have felt that the car could have been safer. But this is true of almost every automobile. Engineers in large firms have an ethical responsibility to do their jobs as best they can, to report their observations about safety and improvement of safety to management. But they do not have the obligation to insist that their perceptions or their standards be accepted. They are not paid to do that, they are not expected to do that, and they have no moral or ethical obligation to do that.

In addition to doing their jobs, engineers can plausibly be said to have an obligation of loyalty to their employers, and firms have a right to a certain amount of confidentiality concerning their internal operations. At the same time engineers are required by their professional ethical codes to hold the safety of the public paramount. Where these obligations conflict, the need for and justification of whistle blowing arises.[15] If we admit the obligations on both sides, I would suggest as a rule of thumb that engineers and other workers in a large corporation are morally *permitted* to go public with information about the safety of a product if the following conditions are met:

1. if the harm that will be done by the product to the public is serious and considerable;

2. if they make their concerns known to their superiors; and

3. if, getting no satisfaction from their immediate superiors, they exhaust the channels available within the corporation, including going to the board of directors.

If they still get no action, I believe they are morally *permitted* to make public their views; but they are not morally *obliged* to do so. Harly Copp, a former Ford executive and engineer, in fact did criticize the Pinto from the start and testified for the prosecution against Ford at the Winamac trial.[16] He left the company and voiced his criticism. The criticism was taken up by Ralph Nader and others. In the long run it led to the Winamac trial and probably helped in a number of other suits filed against Ford. Though I admire Mr. Copp for his actions, assuming they were done from

moral motives, I do not think such action was morally required, nor do I think the other engineers at Ford were morally deficient in not doing likewise.

For an engineer to have a moral *obligation* to bring his case for safety to the public, I think two other conditions have to be fulfilled, in addition to the three mentioned above.[17]

4. He must have documented evidence that would convince a reasonable, impartial observer that his view of the situation is correct and the company policy wrong.

Such evidence is obviously very difficult to obtain and produce. Such evidence, however, takes an engineer's concern out of the realm of the subjective and precludes that concern from being simply one person's opinion based on a limited point of view. Unless such evidence is available, there is little likelihood that the concerned engineer's view will win the day simply by public exposure. If the testimony of Francis Olsen is accurate, then even among the engineers at Ford there was disagreement about the safety of the Pinto.

5. There must be strong evidence that making the information public will in fact prevent the threatened serious harm.

This means both that before going public the engineer should know what source (government, newspaper, columnist, TV reporter) will make use of his evidence and how it will be handled. He should also have good reason to believe that it will result in the kind of change or result that he believes is morally appropriate. None of this was the case in the Pinto situation. After much public discussion, five model years, and failure to pass national safety standards tests, Ford plausibly defends its original claim that the gas tank was acceptably safe. If there is little likelihood of his success, there is no moral obligation for the engineer to go public. For the harm he or she personally incurs is not offset by the good such action achieves.[18]

My first substantive conclusion is that Ford engineers had no moral *obligation* to do more than they did in this case.

My second claim is that though engineers in large organizations should have a say in setting safety standards and producing cost-benefit analyses, they need not have the last word. My reasons are two. First, while the degree of risk, e.g., in a car, is an engineering problem, the acceptability of risk is not. Second, an engineering cost-benefit analysis does not include all the factors appropriate in making a policy decision, either on the corporate or the social level. Safety is one factor in an engineering design. Yet clearly it is only one factor. A Mercedes-Benz 280 is presumably safer than a Ford Pinto. But the difference in price is considerable. To make a Pinto as safe as a Mercedes it would probably have to cost a comparable amount. In making cars as in making many other objects some balance has to be reached between safety and cost. The final decision on where to draw the balance is not only an engineering decision. It is also a managerial decision, and probably even more appropriately a social decision.

The difficulty of setting standards raises two pertinent issues. The first concerns federal safety standards. The second concerns cost-benefit analyses. The state of the art of engineering technology determines a floor below which no manufacturer would ethically go. Whether the Pinto fell below that floor, we have already seen, is a controverted question. If the cost of achieving greater safety is considerable—and I do not think $6.65 is considerable—there is a built-in temptation for a producer to skimp more than he should and more than he might like. The best way to remove that temptation is for there to be a national set of standards. Engineers can determine what the state of the art is, what is possible, and what the cost of producing safety is. A panel of informed people, not necessarily engineers, should decide what is acceptable risk and hence what acceptable minimum standards are. Both the minimum standards and the standards attained by a given car should be a matter of record that goes with each car. A safer car may well cost more. But unless a customer knows how much safety he is buying for his money, he may not know which car he wants to buy. This information, I believe, is information a car buyer is entitled to have.

In 1978, after the publicity that Ford received with the Pinto and the controversy surrounding it, the sales of Pintos fell dramatically. This was an indication that consumers preferred a safer car for comparable money, and they went to the competition. The state of Oregon took all its Pintos out of its fleet and sold them off. To the surprise of one dealer involved in selling turned-in Pintos, they went for between $1000 and $1800.[19] The conclusion we correctly draw is that there was a market for a car with a dubious safety record even though the price was much lower than for safer cars and lower than Ford's manufacturing price.

The second issue is the way cost-benefit analyses are produced and used. I have already mentioned one cost-benefit analysis used by Ford, namely, the projection that by not adding a part and by placing the gas tank in the rear the company could save $20.9 million. The projection, I noted, was grossly mistaken for it did not consider litigation, recalls, and bad publicity which have already cost Ford over $50 million. A second type of cost-benefit analysis sometimes estimates the number and costs of suits that will have to be paid, adds to it fines, and deducts that total amount from the total saved by a particular practice. If the figure is positive, it is more profitable not to make a safety change than to make it.

A third type of cost-benefit analysis, which Ford and other auto companies produce, estimates the cost and benefits of specific changes in their automobiles. One study, for instance, deals with the cost-benefit analysis relating to fuel leakage associated with static rollover. The unit cost of the part is $11. If that is included in 12.5 million cars, the total is $137 million. That part will prevent 180 burn deaths, 180 serious burn injuries and 2100 burned vehicles. Assigning a cost of $200,000 per death, $67,000 per major injury, and $700 per vehicle, the benefit is $49.5 million. The cost-benefit ratio is slightly over 3–1.[20]

If this analysis is compared with a similar cost-benefit analysis for a rear-end collision, it is possible to see how much safety is achieved per dollar spent. This use is legitimate and helpful. But the procedure is open to very serious criticism if used not in a comparative but in an absolute manner.

The analysis ignores many factors, such as the human suffering of the victim and of his or her family. It equates human life to $200,000, which is based on average lost future wages. Any figure here is questionable, except for comparative purposes, in which case as long as the same figure is used it does not change the infomation as to relative benefit per dollar. The ratio, however, has no *absolute* meaning, and no decision can properly be based on the fact that the resulting ratio of cost to benefit in the above example is 3 to 1. Even more important, how can this figure or ratio be compared with the cost of styling? Should the $11 per unit to reduce death and injury from rollover be weighed against a comparable $11 in rear-end collision or $11 in changed styling? Who decides how much more to put into safety and how much more to put into styling? What is the rationale for the decision?

In the past consumers have not been given an opportunity to vote on the matter. The automobile industry has decided what will sell and what will not, and has decided how much to put on safety. American car dealers have not typically put much emphasis on safety features in selling their cars. The assumption that American drivers are more interested in styling than safety is a decision that has been made for them, not by them. Engineers can and do play an important role in making cost-benefit analyses. They are better equipped than anyone else to figure risks and cost. But they are not better equipped to figure the acceptability of risk, or the amount that people should be willing to pay to eliminate such risk. Neither, however, are the managers of automobile corporations. The amount of acceptable risk is a public decision that can and should be made by representatives of the public or by the public itself.

Since cost-benefit analyses of the types I have mentioned are typical of those used in the auto industry, and since they are inadequate ways of judging the safety a car should have, given the state of the art, it is clear that the automobile companies should not have the last word or the exclusive word in how much safety to provide. There must be national standards set and enforced. The National Highway Traffic Safety Administration was established in 1966 to set standards. Thus far only two major standards have been established and implemented: the 1972 side impact standard and the 1977 gasoline tank safety standard. Rather than dictate standards, however, in which process it is subject to lobbying, it can mandate minimum standards and also require auto manufacturers to inform the public about the safety quotient of each car, just as it now requires each car to specify the miles per gallon it is capable of achieving. Such an approach would put the onus for basic safety on the manufacturers, but it would also make additional safety a feature of consumer interest and competition.

Engineers in large corporations have an important role to play. That role, however, is not usually to set policy or to decide on the acceptability of risk. Their knowledge and expertise are important both to the companies for which they work and to the public. But they are not morally responsible for policies and decisions beyond their competence and control. Does this view, however, let engineers off the moral hook too easily?

To return briefly to the Pinto story once more, Ford wanted a subcompact to fend off the competition of Japanese imports. The order came down to produce a car of 2,000 pounds or less that would cost $2000 or less in time for the 1971 model. This allowed only 25 months instead of the usual 43 months for design and production of a new car.[21] The engineers were squeezed from the start. Perhaps this is why they did not test the gas tank for rear-end collision impact until the car was produced.

Should the engineers have refused the order to produce the car in 25 months? Should they have resigned, or leaked the story to the newspapers? Should they have refused to speed up their usual routine? Should they have complained to their professional society that they were being asked to do the impossible—if it were to be done right? I am not in a position to say what they should have done. But with the advantage of hindsight, I suggest we should ask not only what they should have done. We should especially ask what changes can be made to prevent engineers from being squeezed in this way in the future.

Engineering ethics should not take as its goal the producing of moral heroes. Rather it should consider what forces operate to encourage engineers to act as they feel they should not; what structural or other features of a large corporation squeeze them until their consciences hurt? Those features should then be examined, evaluated, and changes proposed and made. Lobbying by engineering organizations would be appropriate, and legislation should be passed if necessary. In general I tend to favor voluntary means where possible. But where that is utopian, then legislation is a necessary alternative.

The need for whistle blowing in a firm indicates that a change is necessary. How can we preclude the necessity for blowing the whistle?

The Winamac Pinto case suggests some external and internal modifications. It was the first case to be tried under a 1977 Indiana law making it possible to try corporations as well as individuals for the criminal offenses of reckless homicide. In bringing the charges against Ford, Prosecutor Michael Cosentino acted courageously, even if it turned out to have been a poor case for such a precedent-setting trial. But the law concerning reckless homicide, for instance, which was the charge in question, had not been rewritten with the corporation in mind. The penalty, since corporations cannot go to jail, was the maximum fine of $10,000 per count—hardly a significant amount when contrasted with the 1977 income of Ford International which was $11.1 billion in revenues and $750 million in profits. What Mr. Cosentino did *not* do was file charges against individuals in the Ford Company who were responsible for the decisions he claimed were reckless. Had highly placed officials been charged, the message would have gotten through to management across

the country that individuals cannot hide behind corporate shields in their decisions if they are indeed reckless, put too low a price on life and human suffering, and sacrifice it too cheaply for profits.

A bill was recently proposed in Congress requiring managers to disclose the existence of life-threatening defects to the appropriate Federal agency.[22] Failure to do so and attempts to conceal defects could result in fines of $50,000 or imprisonment for a minimum of two years, or both. The fine in corporate terms is negligible. But imprisonment for members of management is not.

Some argue that increased litigation for product liability is the way to get results in safety. Heavy damages yield quicker changes than criminal proceedings. Ford agreed to the Pinto recall shortly after a California jury awarded damages of $127.8 million after a youth was burned over 95% of his body. Later the sum was reduced, on appeal, to $6.3 million.[23] But criminal proceedings make the litigation easier, which is why Ford spent $1,000,000 in its defense to avoid paying $30,000 in fines.[24] The possibility of going to jail for one's actions, however, should have a salutary effect. If someone, the president of a company in default of anyone else, were to be charged in criminal suit, presidents would soon know whom they can and should hold responsible below them. One of the difficulties in a large corporation is knowing who is responsible for particular decisions. If the president were held responsible, outside pressure would build to reorganize the corporation so that responsibility was assigned and assumed.

If a corporation wishes to be moral or if society or engineers wish to apply pressure for organizational changes such that the corporation acts morally and responds to the moral conscience of engineers and others within the organization, then changes must be made. Unless those at the top set a moral tone, unless they insist on moral conduct, unless they punish immoral conduct and reward moral conduct, the corporation will function without considering the morality of questions and of corporate actions. It may by accident rather than by intent avoid immoral actions, though in the long run this is unlikely.

Ford's management was interested only in meeting federal standards and having these as low as possible. Individual federal standards should be both developed and enforced. Federal fines for violations should not be token but comparable to damages paid in civil suits and should be paid to all those suffering damage from violations.[25]

Independent engineers or engineering societies—if the latter are not co-opted by auto manufacturers—can play a significant role in supplying information on the state of the art and the level of technical feasibility available. They can also develop the safety index I suggested earlier, which would represent the relative and comparative safety of an automobile. Competition has worked successfully in many areas. Why not in the area of safety? Engineers who work for auto manufacturers will then have to make and report the results of standard tests such as the ability to withstand rear-end impact. If such information is required data for a safety index to be affixed to the windshield of each new car, engineers will not be squeezed by management in the area of safety.

The means by which engineers with ethical concerns can get a fair hearing without endangering their jobs or blowing the whistle must be made part of a corporation's organizational structure. An outside board member with primary responsibility for investigating and responding to such ethical concerns might be legally required. When this is joined with the legislation pending in Congress which I mentioned, the dynamics for ethics in the organization will be significantly improved. Another way of achieving a similar end is by providing an inspector general for all corporations with an annual net income of over $1 billion. An independent committee of an engineering association might be formed to investigate charges made by engineers concerning the safety of a product on which they are working;[26] a company that did not allow an appropriate investigation of employee charges would become subject to cover-up proceedings. Those in the engineering industry can suggest and work to implement other ideas. I have elsewhere outlined a set of ten such changes for the ethical corporation.[27]

In addition to asking how an engineer should respond to moral quandaries and dilemmas, and rather than asking how to educate or train engineers to be moral heroes, those in engineering ethics should ask how large organizations can be changed so that they do not squeeze engineers in moral dilemmas, place them in the position of facing moral quandaries, and make them feel that they must blow the whistle.

The time has come to go beyond sensitizing students to moral issues and solving and resolving the old, standard cases. The next and very important questions to be asked as we discuss each case is how organizational structures can be changed so that no engineer will ever again have to face *that* case.

Many of the issues of engineering ethics within a corporate setting concern the ethics of organizational structure, questions of public policy, and so questions that frequently are amenable to solution only on a scale larger than the individual—on the scale of organization and law. The ethical responsibilities of the engineer in a large organization have as much to do with the organization as with the engineer. They can be most fruitfully approached by considering from a moral point of view not only the individual engineer but the framework within which he or she works. We not only need moral people. Even more importantly we need moral structures and organizations. Only by paying more attention to these can we adequately resolve the questions of the ethical responsibility of engineers in large organizations.

Notes

1. The body of literature on engineering ethics is now substantive and impressive. See *A Selected Annotated Bibliography of Professional Ethics and Social Responsibility in Engineering,* compiled by Robert F. Ladenson, James Choromokos, Ernest

d'Anjou, Martin Pimsler, and Howard Rosen (Chicago: Center for the Study of Ethics in the Professions, Illinois Institute of Technology, 1980). A useful two-volume collection of readings and cases is also available: Robert J. Baum and Albert Flores, *Ethical Problems in Engineering,* 2nd edition (Troy, N.Y.: Rensselaer Polytechnic Institute, Center for the Study of the Human Dimensions of Science and Technology, 1980). See also Robert J. Baum's *Ethics and Engineering Curricula* (Hastings-on-Hudson, N.Y.: Hastings Center, 1980).

2. See, for example, the first canon of the 1974 Engineers Council for Professional Development Code, the first canon of the National Council of Engineering Examiners Code, and the draft (by A. Oldenquist and E. Slowter) of a "Code of Ethics for the Engineering Profession" (all reprinted in Baum and Flores, *Ethical Problems in Engineering).*

3. Details of the incident presented in this paper are based on testimony at the trial. Accounts of the trial as well as background reports were carried by both the *New York Times* and the *Chicago Tribune.*

4. *New York Times,* February 17, 1980, IV, p. 9.

5. *New York Times,* February 21, 1980, p. A6. *Fortune,* September 11, 1978, p. 42.

6. *New York Times,* March 14, 1980, p. 1.

7. *Time,* March 24, 1980, p. 24.

8. *New York Times,* January 16, 1980, p. 16; February 7, 1980, p. 16.

9. *Chicago Tribune,* October 13, 1979, p. 1, and Section 2, p. 12.

10. *Chicago Tribune,* October 13, 1979, p. 1; *New York Times,* October 14, 1979, p. 26.

11. *New York Times,* February 4, 1980, p. 12.

12. *New York Times,* June 10, 1978, p. 1; *Chicago Tribune,* October 13, 1979, p. 1, and Section 2, p. 12. The continuous claim has been that the Pinto poses "No serious hazards."

13. *New York Times,* October 26, 1978, p. 103.

14. *New York Times,* February 20, 1980, p. A16.

15. For a discussion of the conflict, see, Sissela Bok, "Whistleblowing and Professional Responsibility," *New York University Educational Quarterly,* pp. 2–10. For detailed case studies see, Ralph Nader, Peter J. Petkas, and Kate Blackwell, *Whistle Blowing* (New York: Grossman Publishers, 1972); Charles Peters and Taylor Branch, *Blowing the Whistle: Dissent in the Public Interest* (New York: Praeger Publishers, 1972); and Robert M. Anderson, Robert Perrucci, Dan E. Schendel and Leon E. Trachtman, *Divided Loyalties: Whistle-Blowing at*

BART (West Lafayette, Indiana: Purdue University, 1980).

16. *New York Times,* February 4, 1980, p. 12.

17. The position I present here is developed more fully in my book *Business Ethics* (New York: Macmillan, forthcoming in fall 1981). It differs somewhat from the dominant view expressed in the existing literature in that I consider whistle blowing an extreme measure that is morally obligatory only if the stringent conditions set forth are satisfied. Cf. Kenneth D. Walters, "Your Employees' Right to Blow the Whistle," *Harvard Business Review,* July–August 1975.

18. On the dangers incurred by whistle blowers, see Gene James, "Whistle-Blowing: Its Nature and Justification," *Philosophy in Context,* 10 (1980), pp. 99–117, which examines the legal context of whistle blowing; Peter Raven-Hansen, "Dos and Don'ts for Whistleblowers: Planning for Trouble," *Technology Review,* May 1980, pp. 34–44, which suggests how to blow the whistle; Helen Dudar, "The Price of Blowing the Whistle," *The New York Times Magazine,* 30 October, 1977, which examines the results for whistle blowers; David W. Ewing, "Canning Directions," *Harpers,* August 1979, pp. 17–22, which indicates "how the government rids itself of troublemakers" and how legislation protecting whistleblowers can be circumvented; and Report by the U.S. General Accounting Office, "The Office of the Special Counsel Can Improve Its Management of Whistleblower Cases," December 30, 1980 (FPCD–81–10).

19. *New York Times,* April 21, 1978, IV, p. 1, 18.

20. See Mark Dowie, "Pinto Madness," *Mother Jones,* September/October 1977, pp. 24–28.

21. *Chicago Tribune,* October 13, 1979, Section 2, p. 12.

22. *New York Times,* March 16, 1980, IV, p. 20.

23. *New York Times,* February 8, 1978, p. 8.

24. *New York Times,* February 17, 1980, IV, p. 9; January 6, 1980, p. 24; *Time,* March 24, 1980, p. 24.

25. *The Wall Street Journal,* August 7, 1980, p. 7, reported that the Ford Motor Company "agreed to pay a total of $22,500 to the families of three Indiana teen-age girls killed in the crash of a Ford Pinto nearly two years ago. . . . A Ford spokesman said the settlement was made without any admission of liability. He speculated that the relatively small settlement may have been influenced by certain Indiana laws which severely restrict the

amount of damages victims or their families can recover in civil cases alleging wrongful death."

26. A number of engineers have been arguing for a more active role by engineering societies in backing up individual engineers in their attempts to act responsibly. See, Edwin Layton, *Revolt of the Engineers* (Cleveland: Case Western Reserve, 1971); Stephen H. Unger, "Engineering Societies and the Responsible Engineer," *Annals of the New York Academy of Sciences,* 196 (1973), pp. 433–37 reprinted in Baum and Flores, *Ethical Problems in Engineering,* pp. 56–59; and Robert Perrucci and Joel Gerstl, *Profession Without Community: Engineers in American Society* (New York: Random House, 1969).

27. Richard T. DeGeorge, "Responding to the Mandate for Social Responsibility," *Guidelines for Business When Societal Demands Conflict* (Washington, D.C.: Council for Better Business Bureaus, 1978), pp. 60–80.

Suggested Further Reading

Boland, R. J., "Organizational Control, Organizational Power, and Professional Responsibility," *Business and Professional Ethics Journal,* 2, no. 1 (Fall 1982), 15–27.

Harris, Robert C., Christopher Hohenemser, and Robert W. Kates, "The Burden of Technological Hazards," *Energy Risk Management,* ed.

G. T. Goodman and W. D. Rowe. (New York: Academic, 1979).

Kipnis, Kenneth, "Engineers Who Kill: Professional Ethics and the Paramountcy of Public Safety," *Business and Professional Ethics Journal,* 1, no. 1 (1981), 77–91.

Lockhart, T. W., "Safety Engineering and the Value of Life," *Technology and Society* (IEEE), 9 (March 1981), 3–5.

Sagan, L. A., "Human Cost of Nuclear Power," *Science,* 177, (August 11, 1972), 487–93.

Schiefelbein, Susan, "Is Nuclear Power a License to Kill?" *Saturday Review,* June 24, 1978.

Schinzinger, Roland, and Mike W. Martin, "The Experimental Nature of Engineering and Its Implications for the Style of Engineering Practice," *1980 Frontiers in Education Conference Proceedings (Houston),* American Society for Engineering Education, Washington, D.C., and The Institute of Electrical and Electronics Engineers, New York, 1980, pp. 204–7.

Simrall, Harry C., "The Civic Responsibility of the Professional Engineer," *The American Engineer,* May 1963, pp. 39–40.

Unger, Stephen H., "How to Be Ethical and Survive," *IEEE Spectrum,* 16, no. 11 (December 1979), 56–57.

Weinberg, Alvin M., "The Many Dimensions of Scientific Responsibility," *Bulletin of The Atomic Scientist,* November 1976, pp. 21–25.

DECISION SCENARIO 9

Three Mile Island

On March 28, 1979, people of the Susquehanna Basin slept peacefully. At four in the morning a series of events at the Three Mile Island nuclear power plant awakened the valley. During the night a maintenance crew had been dealing with a minor problem in the demineralizer unit and inadvertently they caused a water backup in the coolant piping. Through a series of valves and relays, the heat

in the reactor rose. The fail-safe system automatically lowered the control rods into the reactor core.

The pressure valve removing superheated water was closed by the control crew—or at least the control panel showed it was. Nonetheless, the reactor equipment functioned smoothly—with one notable exception. Valves regulating the auxiliary feed water had been left closed by a maintenance crew two days earlier. There was almost no heat being removed from the reactor.

The two problems, the lack of intake water and the open pressure valve (which the control team had no knowledge of), created a dangerous situation. The tops of the control rods began to crumble. Steam combining with the control rod material produced hydrogen, which was released into the containment structure. When the new shift arrived around 6:00 A.M., the radiation levels had begun to rise.

When a phone call was put through to the Nuclear Regulatory Commission's (NRC) regional office, only an answering machine responded. Operators also called Babcock and Wilcox, who had built the reactor.

Meanwhile, contaminated water splashed on the floor of an adjacent building, forcing evacuation of all but essential personnel.

When the high-pressure injection pumps were finally turned on again, the core was covered with water. Nearly fourteen hours after the episode began, the Three Mile Island reactor was brought under control.

Questions

1. What are the special safety obligations of engineers and technicians? How would a rule utilitarian justify them?

2. What are the different categories of risk involved in the Three Mile Island nuclear plant? How do you determine whether the benefits outweigh the risks associated with operating the plant?

3. How strong is the obligation to undertake emergency planning before a crisis occurs? How should the obligation be enforced?

4. Apparently, certain engineers in Babcock and Wilcox suspected defects in the design of the nuclear reactor that was installed at Three Mile Island. Memos internally circulated make this fact clear. Since no one blew the whistle, were they wrong in the way they handled the situation? Is anyone ever under obligation to blow the whistle?

2. WHICH TECHNOLOGY IS APPROPRIATE?

Concern about the problems arising in many areas of technology led to the growth of a movement sometimes labeled *appropriate technology* or *alternative technology* (AT). The movement comprised a diverse array of individuals and groups with equally diverse goals and strategies for accomplishing them, but certain recurring concepts and values link the members of the movement. First, all proponents of alternative technology are critical of the dominant technologies and their impact on society. Second, different elements are united by a common interest in certain ideals. Some members may be concerned primarily with developing nations while others focus on problems in developed countries; both groups, however, view a desirable society as one committed to the values of decentralization, self-sufficiency,

nonalienating work, cultural diversity, and individual freedom. On the whole, these values reflect a concern for the deontological principle of respect for the dignity of individual persons.

Another important AT concept is that technologies should be "nonviolent" or "soft," that is, that they should attempt to avoid social disruption and damage to ecosystems wherever possible. Appropriate technology advocates favor the use of renewable, diversified energy sources and flexible systems of distribution matched to the cultural traditions and needs of a particular society. They believe machinery should be designed in such a way that work becomes satisfying and creative rather than repetitive and meaningless. Underlying these ideas is the principle that "people matter" and that the goal of technology should be to satisfy basic human needs rather than merely to produce wealth and material goods.

Critics of the movement argue that all technology is "violent" and that all development involves major cultural changes. For example, policies such as popular education and equal rights for women seem like desirable, liberating reforms in some cultures, and yet they conflict with traditional values in other societies. Should such changes be viewed as social progress or cultural disruption? Another criticism of the AT movement focuses on its commitment to decentralization and self-sufficiency. AT proponents maintain that these organizing principles lead to reduced environmental stress and smaller, more socially satisfying communities. Critics insist that many production processes—mining of large mineral deposits, for example—are unsuited to miniaturi-zation and decentralization. They also argue that smaller communities are not necessarily more democratic or more satisfying human environments than urban areas.

While the alternative technology movement faces complex, possibly insurmountable difficulties in translating its ideals into viable structures, its focus on human needs rather than material achievement deserves attention. The movement's goals represent an ethically sensitive approach to technology, one in keeping with the Kantian principle of always treating persons as ends and never as mere means.

In the following essay Langdon Winner examines the historical background of the alternative technology movement. Winner, like most movement theorists, argues that "technologies are never neutral." Thus, choosing among different technologies actually means choosing "the kind of society in which we shall live."

LANGDON WINNER

The Political Philosophy of Alternative Technology

One of the surprising developments in 20th-century thought is that the subject of technology has finally come alive. Long considered an area virtually devoid of philosophical importance, the realm of technical activity—its ontology, ethics, history, and politics—now attracts the attention of an increasing number of phenomenological, Marxist, analytical and religious philosophers. Given the fact that the structures and processes of scientific technology are universally acknowledged as primary aspects of modern life, it is odd that it took so long for critical theories of technics to take shape. Even now it is true that if a person were to visit any library and compare the shelf of books on motion picture criticism with the best speculative writing on technology, he or she would have to conclude that the books on movies were much more numerous, thoughtful and suggestive than the works on the philosophy of technology.

One reason why it has taken so long for thinking about technology to come into its own is that for a very long time almost everyone's ideas on the subject have been governed by a powerful, thoroughly stultifying orthodoxy. That orthodoxy, which began with Francis Bacon's "Great Instauration" and matured as a central theme in the religion of "progress" of the Enlightenment and the In-

Reprinted with permission from *Technology in Society*, Vol. 1, Copyright 1979 by Pergamon Journals, Ltd.

dustrial Revolution, still informs much of our understanding of what technology is, what it does, and what it means. It is, in fact, a philosophy of sorts, but one which seldom has been subject to the light of critical scrutiny. Among the standard tenets of the technical orthodoxy in our time are the following:

- That men know best what they themselves have made.
- That the things men make are under their firm control.
- That technologies are neutral: they are simply tools that can be used one way or another; the benefit or harm they bring depends on how men use them.
- That what technicians or engineers do is simply a matter of problem solving; the world of human situations is something like a field of problems awaiting refined solutions.
- That technical solutions tend to be those which require the fabrication and maintenance of complex, large-scale, high-energy, highly resource-demanding systems; to continue building and perfecting such systems is itself a definition of "progress."
- That technologies are best judged according to an easily recognizable criterion of efficiency: input compared to output in quantifiable measures of the resources employed in a given operation.

Despite the superficiality of its premises, the technological orthodoxy has retained considerable power over our conceptions of what the modern world is about. This comes as no accident. The wonderful developments in industrial and scientific technics of the past two centuries have enabled individuals and social classes of all sorts to identify with technological progress as a way of life. Indeed, so great was the boon brought about by the combination of new discoveries, inventions and products that only the workings of technology were thought worthy of consideration. Questions of meaning could be indefinitely postponed.

I

Of course, from the very beginning, there have been difficulties in maintaining the faith

in steady, unblemished progress and technical neutrality. At the time of an expansion in material productivity unprecedented in human history, the early stages of the Industrual Revolution, conditions for the great mass of people in England grew noticeably worse. On that gnawing paradox much of 19th-century political thought found its starting point. In our own time equally annoying cracks have begun to appear in the edifice of progress. At the very point at which the mating of science and technology makes possible human accomplishments previously unimaginable—rapid geographical mobility, worldwide communications, the conquest of diseases, staggering levels of material productivity, and the possibility of release from the burdens of toil—obvious signs of social and environmental ills have cast a shadow on the most ambitious applications of technical virtuosity. There is no need here to rehearse the litany of maladies which cause concern. Suffice it to say that developments which in my own childhood were seen as the most glorious signs of the improvement of society—new and larger highways, growing acres of housing tracts, rapidly increasing energy use, the use of food additives in convenience foods, etc.—are now widely viewed as vexing problems. Thus, in present considerations of the nuclear energy question and recombinant DNA—the tendency is to reject older formulations of the notions of progress or technical neutrality and to ask: Where are developments in these fields taking us? Are these directions that our best purposes would lead us to choose? But so dogmatic has been our adherence to the technological orthodoxy that even at this date those who raise even the most obvious questions are suspected of malice and bad faith. These are matters the modern age had long ago promised itself it would not have to think about.

Beyond the well-publicized specific issue areas of our time—pollution, energy, computers, genetic engineering, and the like—philosophers in Europe and the Americas have begun to address a range of general themes bearing on the character of the technological enterprise itself. Inquiries into the relationship of human beings and nature in the Western

tradition, the qualities of instrumental rationality, the paradoxes involved in the quest for
control, and a host of moral and political
questions about the meaning of technological
phenomena have begun to fill the vacuum of
thought about such things which had grown
so conspicuous over the past century. In
another place I have tried to contribute to
these conversations by dissecting many of the
central premises of the technological orthodoxy.[1] By paying attention to a variety of reports that "technology is out of control" I
have tried to indicate what is defective in our
conceptions of tools and uses, problem solving, technical mastery, and notions of that
sort.

Rather than summarize these criticisms
again, however, I want to try to move beyond
them. If the philosophy of technology is finally
coming into its own, what projects ought it to
tackle? My suggestion would be that there is
available to us a perspective which has already begun to overthrow the technological
orthodoxy and set the philosophy (and possibly even the practice) of technology moving
in a new direction.

The basic insight upon which the perspective rests is the simple but hard-won acknowledgment that technologies are not neutral. In
the modern age a wide variety of refined techniques, apparatus and sociotechnical systems
provide the basic patterns for everyday human activity. During the past two hundred
years, most of the institutions of Western society have been either consciously or unconsciously reconstructed to accommodate the
operating conditions of new technologies in
industrial production, mechanical transporta-
tion, electronic communication, modern warfare, modern architecture, medicine, and
household convenience. When one adds up
the combined effects of those innovations,
what one has is something like a picture of the
constitution of modern life. To say this is not
to endorse a doctrine of technological determinism. For the question of what it is that
gives those technologies their shape remains
an open question. And it is true that there are
areas of human existence which even now remain untouched.

What one can say with assurance is that
once built and in operation, modern technologies are ways of life. Thus, it is misleading to
say of the automobile that it simply replaced
the horse or the mule. What it actually replaced was (among other things) the church.
To see this, ask yourself what Americans are
likely to be doing on their Sundays in 1979 as
compared to their Sundays in 1909.

II

Technologies are never neutral. They are
forms of life. In this sense they are also political insofar as they legislate and govern the
fundamental patterns which much of modern
life assumes. Indeed, in our ordinary understanding we make an uncritical distinction between "technology" on the one hand and
"society" on the other. In some ways that distinction is still useful. But in other ways it is
not. Is a factory a technological institution or
a social one? Is a mass transit system a social
or technological phenomenon in the main? Is
televison a system of apparatus or a mode of
social relationships?

Over the past two centuries one technological "improvement" after another has been
added to the constitution of society with little
attention to how it would affect the lives of
people in the broader sense. It seemed
enough to ask only the question: Will the
thing be efficient, effective or profitable in a
particular area? One can imagine what might
have happened if, in the late 18th and early
19th centuries the democratic revolution and
the Enlightenment had joined in the attempt
to bring technological development under
conscious social control. One can imagine the
founding of truly democratic institutions in
which the people could have assembled to
discuss (among other things) the social and
technical forms which the Industrial Revolution would take. In this fashion political freedom might have helped shape technological
progress by influencing the design of innovations which were about to enter the world.
One can imagine philosophical and political
debates over such questions as: What are the
implications of different designs of factory sys-

tems for our freedom? What does it mean to say that a device or system is efficient or that it serves human needs? What is the best size for a particular sociotechnical enterprise? Of course, those discussions never took place.

An important reason why this was so is that the democratic institutions which might have facilitated public deliberation on a broad scale were not included in the constitutions of nation states of the 18th and 19th centuries. What were produced instead were certain guarantees of civil liberties and the citizens' rights to participate in recurring religious rituals called elections (in which one drops a piece of paper into a box and thereby affirms one's imagined ties with the mystical body politic). The American Founding Fathers, for example, were generally agreed that government was too important a matter to be left to the people.

But even if there had been organs of direct democratic participation, it is not likely that the crucial considerations about the shape of technology in the industrial age would have been a subject for public discussion. A tacit consensus had been reached that, in the technology-building connected with economic enterprise, there were no matters for public debate or control other than those of minimizing obvious threats to health and safety and seeing to it that economic enterprises and their technological accomplishments flourished in good speed. Economic freedom (so-called), rather than political freedom, was the norm which guided innovation.

Thus, in the Industrial Revolution, a question which seems most important to ask today—what kinds of technology might best serve human needs?—was a matter for almost no one's explicit concern. Machines and systems were being built. Whatever else they did or made, they did make money. Technological patterns were largely determined by labor-saving and cost-cutting linked to calculations about making profit. The development of the American railway system is a case in point. Today we can ask why the railroads are so badly organized, so badly run, so seemingly irrational as a system to serve present transpor-

tation needs. The answer, in brief, is that the railroads were not designed according to a reasonable humane assessment of the needs of people to travel or to move freight. No, they were devised to extract profits. And when those who financed the railroads discovered that trucks and automobiles on highways were better suited for this purpose, they were more than willing to let the railroads degenerate into museum pieces.

For better or worse, capitalism was the economic system within which the Industrial Revolution took place. Of course, at the time of the Industrial Revolution, capitalism was not the only perspective from which the promise of scientific and technological development could be seen. Socialism—the view that the means of production ought to be owned and controlled by the community as a whole—introduced a much different notion of what the possibilities were.

One of the first socialists to examine the prospects for an emancipated industrial order was the early 19th-century British manufacturer Robert Owen. Owen was impressed by the capacity of the new machines to produce wealth and appalled by the spectacle of poverty everywhere about him. He announced, in effect, "If we're going to have an industrial revolution, if we're going to renovate our basic social institutions to accord with the new technology and the new wealth, let's ponder the forms that this reconstituted world will take." In Owen's thinking and in a series of ambitious attempts to build new communities, New Lanark, New Harmony, and Villages of Cooperation, Owen tried to adapt industrial development to accord with his ideas for a humane and harmonious social order. His writing and the communities he founded show careful attention to such matters as the size (number of persons) a productive organization ought to have, conditions of technical and economic self-sufficiency, and the appropriate mix of agriculture and manufacturing. He was fascinated with the range of possible forms which new innovations might take: the design of buildings, the ordering of the work process, and the kinds of machinery employed. For Owen, social innovation and technical invention were one and the same process. Unlike most other manufacturers of his time (interested only in cost-cutting, efficiency, and holding wages down), Owen insisted that industrial innovation be tailored to a comprehensive vision of a new world and guided by criteria offered by an enlightened moral philosophy.[2]

Of course, the path that Owen blazed was not the one that socialism ultimately took. In the eyes of the most influential of socialist thinkers, Karl Marx, the work of reformers like Owen simply missed the point. What was required, Marx argued, was a scientific analysis of the development of capital. That analysis would show, he believed, that the rapid growth of the industrial machine would outstrip the capacity of capitalism to control the mechanisms it had set in motion.

Marx shared the belief of capitalist entrepreneurs and liberal political economists that an unfettered development of the forces of production was not only good but also inevitable. The problem was to put the system under a different ownership. His vision pointed to the day in which a revolution would accomplish exactly that. The proletariat would take over all political and economic institutions of industrial society and reshape them to produce a fully human, socialist order. Until that day, what was needed was a rigorous, scientific study of capitalism and the organization of a working class movement. Not at all necessary, according to Marx and Engels, was idle specualtion about the appropriate design of economic and technological life. Thus, they denounced the plans and institutional devices proposed by Owen, Fourier and Proudhon as mere dreaming which only served to deflect the working class from its historical mission.[3]

Following Marx's lead, the socialist tradition has renounced "utopian" thinking. With rare exceptions, such as William Morris and the Guild Socialists, it has not thought deeply about the forms that political, economic and technical life ought to have in an emancipated society. That, it seems to me, has been an ex-

tremely debilitating tendency. Over many decades it has, in effect, neutralized the socialist imagination. Socialist thinkers have produced increasingly refined, devastating critiques of advanced capitalism. But they have not kept alive an idea of what the institutional alternatives to capitalism might be. On its political side, this has meant that, with the exception of a residual interest in workers' control, the socialist tradition has not bothred to investigate seriously the meaning that democracy might have in the modern age; that is, it has not thought very deeply about the concrete forms of direct democracy. In its technological aspect, this has meant that by and large socialists have been prepared to accept the forms of capitalist technology unquestioningly. Thus, what might have been by this time a rich, sophisticated discussion in the political philosophy of technology from a socialist viewpoint is only just now getting underway.

It seems obvious that any critical theory of modern society must include not only a critique of existing configurations of power, but also a vital notion of how things might be different. In our time many Marxists still insist on a one-sided dialectic which is fixated on the specter of the power of advanced capitalism and which sees speculation about alternative technologies or alternative institutions as a kind of betrayal. But, clearly, any fruitful attempt to think about modern society must include both criticism of existing institutions and an imagining of how things could be differently arranged, differently structured. The American left of the 1960s trumpeted the need for "basic structural change." But it never began the difficult work of specifying what those structures would look like.

III

It is that capacity of critical imagination which, it seems to me, is being reborn in our time. In dozens of localities in the United States, Europe and the Third World, one sees inchoate ideas about and projects in what is called "alternative," "appropriate" or "intermediate" technology. While the precise dimensions of this work change from project to project, the basic concerns of all these groups have a common thread. They seek to devise technologies which offer genuine alternatives to the large-scale, complex, centralized, high-energy life forms which dominate the modern age.

At the New Alchemy Institute in Falmouth, Massachusetts, for example, a group of biologists and their associates have formed a research community to investigate ecologically and socially harmonious systems for producing food and energy. The New Alchemists make their scientific and technical findings freely available to groups and individuals interested in seeking more ecologically sensible ways of life. The province of Prince Edward Island, Canada, the first government unit in the world to renounce nuclear power, recently contracted with the New Alchemists to begin building their "arks," windmills and aquacultural systems as a way of finding a hopeful technological future for the island. The first of the arks—a self-contained, solar-heated, living unit, greenhouse and fish farm—has been completed. In every detail of its operating principles and structural design, the building exemplifies a qualitatively different understanding of the relationship of science, philosophy and engineering than that which has prevailed in the West over the past several generations.

There are now dozens of organizations around the globe engaged in various aspects of the theory and practice of alternative technology—the Brace Institute in Montreal, the Intermediate Technology Development Group in London, the Faralones Institute in California, and De Kleine Aarde in the Netherlands, among others. From one point of view, this flurry of activity arises as a response to one or the other of the "crises" that have appeared on the agenda of our times: the environmental crisis, energy crisis, world food crisis, and population crisis. Some research groups have focused upon the special technological needs of less developed countries. Others have defined their work with references to difficulties now facing the devel-

oped, perhaps overdeveloped, nations of the world. Seen in this way, the important issue becomes: Do these projects in solar energy, wind power, aquaculture, and "appropriate" small-scale machinery offer workable remedies for a world faced with severe shortages? That, it seems to me, is an open question. What is important to recognize now, however, is that the significance of alternative technology is not limited to whether or not it does, for example, help solve the energy crisis. At stake in this kind of thinking, research and development is the possibility of a fundamental reevaluation of the place and meaning of technology in human activity.

From the perspective I have been sketching here, one can see that alternative technologists have revived a project which had been abandoned with the eclipse of 19th-century utopianism: the work of proposing a clear and systematic notion of the good life that can be translated into principles and criteria of institutional design. In essence, of course, that enterprise is one of the oldest in the tradition of Western thought. It begins with Plato's attempt in *The Republic* to discover the Form of the Good and to devise social and political institutions which express that Form. What was interesting about 19th-century utopians and anarchists is also a starting point for the alternative technologists of our time. They recognize that any serious attempt to propose institutions appropriate to an emancipated society in the modern age must pay careful attention to those institutions normally called "technologies."

This is not the place to launch a full-scale discussion of the promise and problems of alternative technology. But I do want to suggest some issues which seem to arise naturally as this kind of work proceeds.

During its gradual emergence as a minor social movement of the 1970s, alternative technology has exhibited an annoying tendency toward hardware fetishism—the obsession with the nuts and bolts of solar collectors, methane digestors, and other energy-renewable gadgetry to the exclusion of everything else. For many, the guiding idea seems to be roughly that of "build a better mousetrap and the world will beat a path to environmental and social well-being." But the underlying assumptions upon which this faith is founded are usually left unarticulated, uncriticized. The current enthusiasm about the notion that technology should be "appropriate" is a case in point. The term "appropriate" suggests a realm of customary understanding in which judgments about right and wrong are made as a matter of course. "Coat and tie will be appropriate" reads the invitation and we immediately understand something about the nature of the event and what is expected of us. It is precisely that sense of subtle customary distinctions and evaluations that 20th-century understandings of technology lack. Our adherence to the terms of the technological orthodoxy have brought us to see everything in terms of progress, growth, narrowly conceived efficiencies, and the myth of technical neutrality. The ordinary language of care in matters of how and why one employs tools and techniques has fallen into disuse with the decline of the craft tradition. Hence, our efforts to talk about what is appropriate in a given situation of technological application reveal a profound disorientation—a separation from the very terms of (what was once) common sense.

An obvious first task, therefore, is simply that of becoming clear about what the idea of an "alternative" or "appropriate" technology could possibly mean. It makes no sense to devise ingenious new forms of hardware unless one is able to articulate general evaluative notions through which the range of available technological means might once again be reasonably judged. In its most ambitious moments the attempt will involve setting the whole question of choice in the context of a theoretical understanding of what an emancipated modern society would look like. A more modest, but equally helpful, kind of clarification, especially in the short run, would be to reexamine the ordinary language of how things in the sphere of technical activity are done right and how they are done wrong. The work of grand theory should be accompanied by an attempt to reclaim meaningful "rules of thumb."

IV

If, as I have suggested, the work of alternative technology renews the basic intent of 19th-century utopian experiments, the context in which such an activity proceeds has obviously changed. In the time of Owen and Fourier, the question of what an industrial society would look like was still undecided. Owen's proposals for "Villages of Cooperation" and Fourier's plans for *phalansteres* had, at least in principle, some chance of influencing the social forms that the modern age would take. By contrast, the alternative technologists and new community builders of our time face a world of material accomplishments and social adaptations of astounding completeness. Even to begin raising the central issues that concern the relationship of social and political philosophy to technological design means that one must challenge existing structures and "the way things work." Thus, after one has settled (or as one is settling) the matter of first principles of evaluation with regard to technological forms of life, an obvious next question arises: are there reasonable structural alternatives to the vast, centralized, complex energy- and resource-exhausting systems that dominate the modern age? Among the themes that appear fruitful to pursue here are the following:

- The issue of technical scale and economic concentration.
- The level of complexity or simplicity best suited to technical operations of various kinds.
- Issues centering on the notion of the division of labor and its alleged necessity.
- The question of social and technical hierarchy as it relates to the design of technological systems.
- The notions of self-sufficiency and interdependence as regards the lives of individuals and communities.

Each of these themes stands in need of a great deal of elaboration and clarification.

Rather than being narrowly limited issues, each of them provides clusters of problems worthy of extensive conceptual analysis and empirical study. In its very nature, thinking about alternative technology seeks to investigate conditions far removed from those commonly found in modern technological societies. Thus, it tries to understand the practical significance of small-scale as opposed to large-scale systems, simple ways of doing things as opposed to complex ones, and so forth. Some may feel that this focus tends to bias the outcome of the inquiry in advance, that it settles questions of the best form for technological activity by assuming an answer. I would argue, however, that this approach provides an effective way to open up important issues that modern philosophy and science had set aside as closed. The elaborate ideological system of orthodox "economics" does provide ways of treating the questions that arise within each of the themes I have listed. But the categories and lessons of "economies" are so rigid and so thoughtless, insofar as they might help us understand the possibilities for building an emancipated society, that none of them—arguments about "economies of scale" or any other—need be taken as articles of true belief.

By this point the reader will understand why it seems to me that the ultimate promise of alternative technology has little to do with the new hardware that it may happen to develop. Indeed, if the success of the field is to be measured solely in terms of new inventions to solve the energy crisis, then it will have done little that is significantly new. To see technologies as forms of life is not to see them as solutions to problems in need of a "tech fix." A sign that alternative technology has reached a meaningful point of sophistication would be its ability to move logically from a set of critical, evaluative principles toward specific criteria of technological design. One must be able to employ the best insights of social and political philosophy to say: *The technical means we adopt here should have the following characteristics and conse-quences. They should not have the following characteristics and consequences.* Amory Lovins' specification of the features of what he calls "soft" technology is an example. Soft technologies, he explains, "rely on renewable energy flows that are always there whether we use them or not, such as sun and wind and vegetation: on energy income, not on depletable energy capital."[4]

Well-founded design criteria of this sort provide ways of saying "yes" to some technological institutions and "no" to others. On this basis it becomes possible to begin scientific and technical investigations guided along hopeful new paths. One is free to pursue scientific knowledge not limited by the preconceptions of the technological orthodoxy. One is able to invent devices and perfect technical skills which accord with thoughtful, humane notions of social and environmental ends. Ultimately, there is no reason why the various vocations of science and engineering could not be removed from their present position—virtual subservience to the social system and ideology of advanced capitalism—and established on more fruitful foundations.

A good illustration of the kind of activity that I have in mind comes from a research proposal written recently by the New Alchemy Institute. Working from their philosophy of humanist, decentralist environmentalism, the New Alchemists have been able to specify their criteria for scientific research and technological design. In a proposal entitled "Design and Engineering of a Windmill-Powered Food Freezer," they offer the following problem to any science or engineering student willing to take it up. "Background: Refrigeration and food freezing are some of the more difficult processes to perform without fossil fuels. A family- or community-sized freezing center, well-insulated, could operate on intermittent power from the wind with a direct windmill-compressor link. End Goal: To discover theoretically the thermodynamic feasibility of a windmill-powered freezing cycle; to design and engineer a prototype windmill/freezer suitable for a family or community."

V

Proposals of this kind express a serious attempt to bring the creativity of the inventor, the best available scientific knowledge, ingenious kinds of hardware, and considerations of social and political philosophy together in a single enterprise. It is that combination of elements which now give alternative technology its promise as one justifiable way of bridging the crevasse between the "two cultures" and engaging in meaningful interdisciplinary work.

I am told that such work would not be of any particular interest to first-rate technical minds since it would, in all likelihood, seldom deal with problems on the "frontiers of knowledge" or the most refined developments in the "state of the art." If true, that fact would be an interesting commentary on the present commitments of our scientific and technical communities. Indeed, what is needed here is a different kind of sophistication from that now commonly held in esteem. I would be the first to admit that, in spelling out the terms of that new sophistication, the resources of a political theorist will be neither rich nor detailed enough. An alternative technology which failed to attract engineers, scientists, and skilled craftsmen would be doomed from the outset. The story is told of the 19th-century utopian thinker, Charles Fourier, that he advertised for a philanthropist to finance his ambitious schemes and waited in a particular restaurant at lunchtime for many years hoping that such a person would show up. But none ever came. Perhaps the invitation alternative technology now offers will meet with a more enthusiastic response.

In point of fact, choices about major alterations in the structural foundations of technological society are before us all the time. Much of the material and social setting in which we now live depends upon the amazing bonanza given to our culture by the availability of fossil fuels during the past century. As the age of cheap petroleum draws to a close, our soceity must somehow reinstitu-tionalize its ways of obtaining and using energy. In the past any major shift in the variety or amount of energy a people employed was accompanied by and, in fact, was indistinguishable from, a social revolution. Is it not clear today that a society based on energy conservation and decentralized technologies using renewable resources would, in all likelihood, look very much different from a society based upon the massive deployment of nuclear reactors?

VI

In less dramatic, but equally powerful, ways, a new array of computerized "services"—electronic funds transfer and the like—are quietly reinstitutionalizing the patterns of everyday life. Those with a professional interest in the technical details know "how things work" in such systems. And those who hope to use the system to make a profit understand how that is done. But the rest of us will doubtless have an experience something like, "Oh, they have EFT at the supermarket now" and let it go at that. Thus, alterations of sweeping scope and significance take place with little public discussion of their workings or their meaning. Technological somnambulism becomes technological determinism.

Choices about supposedly neutral technologies—if "choices" they ever merit being called—are actually choices about the kind of society in which we shall live. Over the next several decades our common life will take on new forms powerfully influenced by the adoption of devices, techniques, and systems of various kinds and qualities. As it refines its ability to speculate and to make reasoned judgments, to demonstrate the relationship between ideas and design, the political philosophy of technology may help clarify what many of the important alternatives are.

Notes

1. Langdon Winner, *Autonomous Technology: Technics Out-of-Control as a Theme in Political Thought* (Cambridge, Mass.: MIT Press, 1977).

2. See Robert Owen, *A New View of Society* and *A Report to the Country of Lanark,* edited and with introduction by V. A. C. Gatrell (Baltimore: Penguin, 1970) and J. F. C. Harrison, *Robert Owen and the Owenites in Britain and Amerca: The Quest for the New Moral World* (London: Routledge, Kegan Paul, 1969).

3. Karl Marx and Friedrich Engels, *Manifesto of the Communist Party,* in *Collected Works,* vol. 6 (New York: International Publishers, 1976), pp. 514–517. See also Friedrich Engels, "Socialism: Utopian and Scientific," in Lewis Feuer, ed., *Marx and Engels: Basic Writings on Politics and Philosophy* (New York: Anchor, 1959), pp. 68–111.

4. Amory B. Lovins, "Energy Strategy: The Road Not Taken?" *Foreign Affairs,* vol. 55, no. 1 (October 1976), pp. 77–78. Lovins gives four additional criteria which he uses to distinguish "soft" technologies from other energy technologies.

Suggested Further Reading

Florman, Samuel C., "Small Is Dubious," in *Blaming Technology: The Irrational Search for Scapegoats.* New York: St. Martin's Press, 1981, pp. 80–96.

Lovins, Amory B., "Energy Strategy: The Road Not Taken?" *Foreign Affairs,* vol. 55, no. 1 (October 1976).

McDermott, John, "Technology: The Opiate of the Intellectuals," *New York Review of Books,* July 31, 1969.

Schumacher, E. F., "Buddhist Economics," in *Small Is Beautiful: Economics as If People Mattered.* New York: Harper & Row, 1973, pp. 50–58.

Todd, John, "A Modest Proposal," in *The Book of the New Alchemists,* ed. Nancy Jack Todd. New York: E. P. Dutton, 1977.

GLOSSARY FOR UNIT III

BUSINESS

affirmative action. A program designed to achieve a more representative distribution of minorities and women within an institutional structure by affording preferential treatment to women and minorities in hiring practices.

caveat emptor. From the Latin, literally, "Let the buyer beware!" implying that the purchaser assumes full liability in an exchange of goods or services.

commutative justice. A form of justice which governs relations between roughly equal parties involved in an exchange of goods.

compensatory justice. A form of justice which concerns restoring to a person what the person lost when he or she was the victim of wrongdoing.

conflict of interest. The situation created when the self-interest of employees in positions of trust leads them to act professionally in ways not in the best interests of the corporate body.

cost-benefits analysis (CBA). The utilitarian calculation of the difference between favorable consequences (benefits) and unfavorable consequences (cost) of a proposed line of action.

distributive justice. A form of justice wherein each person deserves what he or she receives.

ecosystem. The organic tissue of relationships between life forms in an environment in which interdependence and reciprocal maintenance ensure survival of the whole.

externality. A measure, in economics, of the difference between social and private costs when a cost factor such as industrial pollution is not included in productivity expenditures.

insider trading. Financial trading based on information about a person's business firm which the trader has obtained in the course of employment and which has not been disclosed to the public.

OSHA. The Occupational Safety and Health Administration, created by Congress in 1970, "to assure as far as possible every working man and woman in the nation safe and healthful working conditions."

preferential hiring. A policy, used in affirmative action programs, intended to rectify racial, minority, or gender imbalances resulting from past discriminatory practices.

proprietary data. Nonpublic information, owned by a company, concerning its technologies, activities, policies, strategies, or records which affects the company's ability to compete successfully in the industry.

reverse discrimination. The claim that affirmative action and preferential hiring are themselves acts of racial or sexual discrimination by making nonrelevant characteristics (minority membership or gender) the basis of employment practices.

SEC. The Securities Exchange Commission, a federal body which regulates the buying and selling of stocks, bonds, and other financial vehicles.

strict liability. The rule that the manufacturer must pay the costs of any injury sustained through defects in the product regardless of whether the manufacturer exercised due care in production and distribution.

whistle blowing. The act of an employee who knows the company is engaged in unethical activity, who tries unsuccessfully to have the company end such activity, and who resorts to disclosing the information to the public.

TECHNOLOGY

appropriate technology. The idea that technology is a means, never an end in itself, and which stresses the importance of external costs such as industrial pollution and environmental risk in selecting a technology proper to an undertaking.

bioengineering. Altering genes by direct chemical change of the DNA in order to produce a mutation of a known species or a new species altogether.

computer break-in. The unauthorized entry into the data bank or software of a computer whose information is thought to be protected.

decentralization. Displacement of a central authority or control of a political, social, or economic organization into several smaller administrative structures which then interlock in some fashion.

deterrence. Turning aside or discouraging aggressive action by means of fear of retaliation or reprisal.

"greenhouse effect." The result of increased levels of atmospheric carbon dioxide arising from industrial pollution, which prevents radiation of energy into space and increases the temperature of the earth.

information control. Regulation of access to information regarding an individual or an organization, particularly when the information is complex and computer based.

just-war doctrine. The doctrine that wars can be waged in the interests of justice when fought for a just cause, when motives are good, when the call comes from a higher authority, and when the use of force is based on necessity.

nuclear capability. The computation of the attack force of a nation's arsenal of nuclear weapons.

"people matter." A slogan which suggests that the use to which technology is put must always serve the interests of personal autonomy.

recombinant DNA. An alteration in the nucleotide sequence in DNA, produced in genetic laboratories, which results in changes of the characteristics of the organisms whose identity is determined by DNA.

software liability. Assignment of responsibility in a course of action to the computer software involved in processing the information to direct the action.

Three Mile Island. The nuclear reactor belonging to Metropolitan Edison, located near York, Pennsylvania, which experienced a melt-down in March 1979.

transgenic animals. The term applied to newly created animal life forms resulting from genetic manipulations of DNA.

weapon. An instrument of offensive or defensive combat.

U N I T
IV

ETHICS IN CRIMINAL JUSTICE AND LAW

Ethics in criminal justice concerns the moral dimensions of society's response to unlawful behavior. In the introduction to their text, *Ethics, Public Policy, and Criminal Justice,* Frederick Elliston and Norman Bowie observe that philosophers have largely neglected the field of criminal justice.

> The fact that few philosophers are (convicted) criminals may explain why few philosophers worry about crime and criminals. . . . With the exception of getting a few parking tickets, philosophers are seldom caught in the arms of the law, and do not think about getting shot by the police or raped in prison.[1]

Despite limited philosophical inquiry on the subject, ethical problems in criminal justice affect a growing number of professionals. Among them are police and probation officers, corrections officers and prison ad-

[1]Frederick Elliston and Norman Bowie, eds. *Ethics, Public Police, and Criminal Justice* (Cambridge, Mass.: Oelgeschlager, Gunn & Hain, 1982), p. xii.

ministrators, lawyers, judges, and legislators. In this unit we examine topics of ethical concern for professionals whose work involves law making, law enforcement, and administration of punishment to lawbreakers.

Chapter 14 focuses on Crime and the Goals of Criminal Justice. The first section concerns the problem of determining which acts ought to be made crimes. How does society justify limiting individual freedom in this manner? According to the harm principle, a criminal act is one that results in harm to persons who do not commit or consent to the act. On this account, "victimless crimes" and conspiracies are not prohibited. Should immoral behavior be criminalized even if it does not cause direct harm?

The second section examines goals of criminal justice systems. Utilitarians stress the goal of deterrence, whereas deontologists believe retribution is the most important aim. Retribution is deserved punishment for acts that cause harm by violating victims' rights. Other goals of criminal justice are rehabilitation and incapacitation. The cost of operating a criminal justice system is high. When the state allocates public funds to deal with crime, which goals should be emphasized?

Chapter 15 is devoted to ethical Issues in Law Enforcement. Because the task of policing is broad and complex, agencies exercise discretion in enforcing the law. Is it fair for police to investigate some crimes and overlook others? Utilitarians argue that police are justified in discretionary enforcement when they concentrate on violators whose arrest will prevent additional crimes. Retributivists reason that discretion is justified when police concentrate on more harmful crimes. However, this analysis does not supply criteria for deciding which harms are greater. Some ethicists believe that police discretion is unjustified and avoidable.

The means police employ in enforcing the law give rise to ethical questions. Do beneficial ends justify unethical means? The use of lethal force is especially troublesome. Another questionable practice is the use of deceit or trickery by police officers. Because protection of the innocent is an important value in the American criminal justice system, many restraints are placed on police methods for obtaining evidence. Critics maintain that the restraints undermine police effectiveness. Is protecting innocent persons more important than ensuring that the guilty are apprehended?

Chapter 16 examines Issues in Criminal Prosecution. The "Ideal Criminal" from the standpoint of prosecution is a rational adult who deliberately breaks the law for personal gain. Not all offenders meet these criteria, however. Should all criminals receive the same treatment under the law? Should courts recognize excuses (like the "insanity defense"), mitigations, and justifications for some crimes?

Lawyers play a significant role in criminal prosecution. The second section of Chapter 16 considers professional obligations of attorneys. The adversary system practiced in American courts requires defense lawyers to provide clients with "zealous advocacy." That obligation can lead to the use of legal tactics that critics find morally unacceptable. Full advocacy is grounded in the ideal of protecting innocent persons wrongly accused. Under the adversary system, attorneys employ ethically questionable methods to fulfill professional responsibilities. Should the system be modified? Public access to legal services is another concern. Is there a way to improve distribution of legal services so that all defendants are fairly represented?

In the final chapter we discuss the Ethics of Punishment. Is the concept of punishment justified? Some theorists compare lawbreakers to persons suffering an illness and argue that treatment is more appropriate than punishment. Others believe that crime is an outcome of unjust social conditions; they maintain that public resources should be spent to correct injustice rather than to arrest, try, and punish offenders. If the idea of punishment is accepted, what forms are justified? The predominant form of punishment in the United States is imprisonment. This was believed to be more humane than penalties such as forced labor, corporal punishment, and death. Revelations of brutal conditions in many prisons have prompted a rethinking of this view. Must punishment be humane? Should punishment be aimed at deterring crime or redressing harms? Which punishment best achieves a chosen goal?

The second section of the chapter examines questions about justice in the administration of punishment. Plea bargaining and judicial discretion in sentencing are practices that prompt ethical concern. How much discretion should judges be permitted? Is plea bargaining justified? Proponents maintain that the practices provide needed flexibility. Opponents charge that they result in less appropriate punishments for offenders. Capital punishment is a subject of heated controversy. Is it wrong for the state deliberately to take a human life, or are some crimes so atrocious that the death penalty is justified? The debate, like others in criminal justice, requires us to weigh diverse values and supply the reasons that justify a moral decision.

14. CRIME AND THE GOALS OF CRIMINAL JUSTICE

1. CRIMINALIZATION

What is crime? The simple answer is that a crime is an act that is against the law. But many ethical questions complicate the determination of which acts (or failures to act) ought to be defined as crimes and prohibited by the state. Criminalization represents an effort by the state selectively to regulate individual behavior. On what grounds can the regulation be justified? Who ought to make such decisions, and what criteria should be used? The issue of criminalization raises problems related to those concerning the proper scope of the concept of health. **[See Health Care, Chapter 9, Section 1.]**

One common way of determining criminality is the *harm principle,* which says that the state ought to prohibit acts when and only when they result in harm to persons who have not performed those acts and do not consent to them. That principle makes it easy to justify making acts such as murder crimes. However, in other situations it proves inadequate. So-called *"victimless crimes,"* for example, are not prohibited. Further, certain acts that cause harm are not usually treated as crimes in our society. For instance, opening a business in direct competition with a previously established one produces harm without being a crime.

Another difficulty with the harm principle as the basis for defining crime arises with conspiracies to commit criminal acts. A failed murder attempt is a punishable offense even when no harm results to the intended victim. Likewise, conspiring to murder someone is a crime even if the conspiracy is never carried out. However, such acts do not qualify as crimes if a harmful result is the sole criterion for assessing criminality.

Ideas about criminality often reflect beliefs about the appropriateness of using government power to control behavior. For instance, those who believe that the state primarily serves the interests of a ruling class or economic elite consider many legal definitions of crime unfair or unjustified. On this view, one might ask whether racism, economic inequality, or degradation of the environment ought not to be treated as more serious "crimes" than acts such as burglary or theft. On the other hand, those who hold that the state does not represent special interest groups but rather reflects a consensus of the governed are more likely to view legislated definitions of crime as just and fair.

The same act may be deemed a crime in some situations and not in others. For example, killing another person may or may not be defined as murder, depending upon who does the killing, who is killed, and what circumstances surround the event. Shooting someone who breaks into your home is different from randomly shooting a passerby on the sidewalk.

One area of criminalization that is especially problematic involves "victimless crimes." Suicide, marijuana smoking, sodomy, and not wearing a seat belt are all examples of victimless crimes. Some believe that acts that harm only the perpetrator (or other adults who voluntarily consent to them) ought not to be unlawful. Others argue that social harm still results even if the acts do not directly violate the rights of other persons.

In the following article A. R. Louch discusses the question of whether it is appropriate for the law to enforce morality. Louch's article is one response to an extended philosophical debate between Lord Patrick Devlin and Professor H. L. A. Hart of Oxford University. Beginning in 1958, Lord Devlin presented a series of lectures and essays arguing the legitimacy of making im-

moral conduct criminal even when no direct harm results to others. Professor Hart criticized Devlin's position primarily on the basis of principles developed in John Stuart Mill's renowned essay *On Liberty*. In that essay, published in 1859, Mill asserted that "the only purpose for which power can be rightfully exercised over any member of a civilized community, against his will, is to prevent harm to others." The specific focus of Louch's article (and the Devlin–Hart controversy) is legislation regarding sexual conduct, but similar debate is prompted by other types of laws, such as prohibitions against gambling, suicide, and drug use.

A. R. LOUCH

Sins and Crimes

A law, say, prohibits homosexual conduct or punishes the prostitute for plying her trade. According to some it is a bad law, according to others a necessary one. Those who argue that it is a bad law do so on a variety of grounds—that it is sheer folly to try to change human nature by law, that such legislation can only be effective at the price of the right to privacy, that the punishment of acts arising from compelling desires is cruel and excessive, that the law has no business meddling in what people do to others with their consent. Those who argue that it is a necessary law do so on one ground, that the act in question is immoral, and that what is wrong must be punished, lest the law itself fall into disrepute by failing to carry out a consistent campaign against wrong-doing.

The issue might seem to be a simple one. There is a standard form of sexual expression, intercourse with a person to whom one is

married. The question is as to whether the law should prohibit, ignore or condone other forms of sexual practice. The legal moralist, like James Stephen in the nineteenth century and Lord Devlin in our own, holds that unorthodox sexual conduct is manifestly wrong, and therefore must be an appropriate object for criminal legislation. Presumably then, his opponent, the libertarian, denies that unorthodox sexual acts are wrong, and so concludes that they are not appropriate objects for criminal legislation.

That, at least, comes close to Mill's attitude toward so-called moral offences, and he is surely the standard libertarian. For him, the mark of the immoral is also the mark of the criminal, for he seeks to devise a theory both of morals and of legislation that rests on facts, which he finds in the occurrence of intentionally inflicted injuries. Loss of life or limb, wounds or scars, empty safes and proofs

A. R. Louch, "Sins and Crimes," *Philosophy*, vol. 43 (1968). Reprinted with the permission of the author and Cambridge University Press.

of bankruptcy are undeniable occasions of harm, and their occurrence is susceptible of proof. Contrast such instances with feelings of embarrassment or indignation, annoyance or irritation, insult or shock and the point of Mill's criterion is made. These latter cases involve always an element of judgment, depending on differences of taste, legitimate differences in what people regard as important to them. They are inadequate bases for legislation since they leave too much to judgment; for Mill they are also inadequate grounds for determining what is moral and immoral, since morality too is to rest on a basis of unchallengeable facts. Thus consenting homosexuality, prostitution, and promiscuity escape the category of sin as well as that of crime. These acts are marked by consent and lack the signs of injury. Men and women knowingly and willingly engage in them and whether they are the worse for it is not something producible as a piece of evidence verifying a proposition or supporting an accusation in a court of law. Thus Mill's brand of libertarianism exempts consenting sexual conduct from legislative restraint because it fails the test of immorality, and not because he holds a thesis barring the influence of morality upon the law. Indeed, the paradigm case of an immoral act for Mill is the case also of a criminal act—deliberately doing something that causes palpable harm.

This view of Mill's, or my interpretation of it, is a useful way of applying pressure to other conceptions of the relation between crimes and sins, laws and morals. For example, the legal moralist could be asked to defend his view that sexual acts of various kinds are substantially immoral even though lacking the elements of coercion or deceit and palpable injury. He could thus be forced to produce, or to try to produce, an explication of morality instead of resorting to charges of immorality. More of this later. But it is especially useful as a way of accounting for the urge to raise up absolute legal barriers against legislation of certain kinds (e.g. moral legislation), an urge exhibited by many who fancy themselves good libertarians. Professor Hart is a good instance. He admits the charge of gross immo-

rality levelled against the homosexual or the promiscuous, but wants nonetheless to exclude such acts from the reach of law. Now there is something compelling about the move from the charge of gross immorality to punishment. The legal moralist seems to be on strong ground in claiming that murder is punishable because wrong, and therefore that anything that is wrong is punishable. If it is admitted that the homosexual is engaged in grossly immoral acts, it is reasonable to suppose that the law could punish him for them. To block this move, while admitting the immorality, Hart requires a principle of great power. He has to show that certain legal principles have a force that transcends the claim of sin.

It is to the credit of Hart and the many libertarians who take a line similar to his that they do such an effective job of presenting these restraining principles as absolutes. They point to two obstacles to legislative interference with private consenting acts that appear well-nigh insurmountable. The first has to do with the police work necessary to produce evidence that sexual vice has occurred. Since these crimes occur privately and with consent, methods of detection must almost certainly violate a man's privacy, by spying or resorting to trickery or fraud—e.g. by having an officer pose as a prostitute's client. Moreover, legislation against sexual vice is usually so vague that what counts as criminal wrongdoing is left to the judgment of the police officer. This may be due in part to the reticence of lawmakers to specify these crimes more exactly, since they are traditionally regarded as crimes not fit to be named. But even if the unmentionable should be mentioned it is not likely that legal specification serves the purpose intended. 'No one can see every way in which the wickedness of man may disrupt the order of society,' warns Lord Simonds, arguing in the *Shaw* case for discretionary power to law enforcers. But this is a warning to those who act as well as to those who enforce, for no one can see, either, what may appear criminally wicked to judges and policemen. There is simply something intrinsically vague and uncertain in laws directed against vice, and a danger that a man may be quite unaware that his actions are vicious in the eyes of the law.

Thus the whole attempt to use criminal law to supervise private, consenting acts jeopardises a man's right to privacy, deprives him of the possibility of knowing the precise nature of the charge against him, subjects him to *ex post facto* legislation, and licenses the police in the use of utterly nefarious investigative practices. Enough of a barrier, one might suppose, to provide an absolute limit to the scope of legislation.

If the main thrust of the libertarian argument is against vague legislation, the claim that morality is out of reach of the law is a much more modest thesis than it might otherwise appear to be. For what is at issue is whether law-enforcers should have the responsibility for determining whether an act is criminal, or whether this should always and without exception be determined by statute. This objection to the role of morals in law should not trouble the libertarian legislator, who would only be concerned to specify his immoral targets more exactly. The difference between the legal moralist and the libertarian would come down to their relative willingness or unwillingness to grant the police such discretionary powers. This, of course, is by no means a simple problem. Laws against traffic in obscenity are among the most vexing issues of this type, for obscenity is an area in which many people think some legislation is necessary, though they would agree that no guidelines can possibly be spelled out in statute determining what counts as an obscene publication or performance. Thus such legislation is only possible if the police are granted discretionary power. The complete libertarian would, in such circumstances, give up the law; the complete legal moralist would not be troubled by police judgment. Most of us would probably fall in some indeterminate and unsatisfying position in between.

In any event, it is not clear that the main thrust of the libertarian argument is, or can be, directed wholly at vague laws. Moral

offences can be perfectly clearly spelled out. Homosexuality, prostitution, fornication, adultery, fellatio, cunnilingus, bestiality—the vocabulary is both rich and definite, and laws exist on many a statute book prohibiting each and every one of these practices, and more besides. It is these quite definite acts that Hart wishes to exempt from legislative restraint, while admitting that they are substantially immoral. Hart and Devlin appear to be at loggerheads just because of their agreement that the act whose legal status they dispute is immoral. Hart says: right to undisturbed performance of private consenting acts is more important than the immorality of the act. Devlin says: 'When the help of the law is invoked by an injured citizen, privacy must be irrelevant' (p. 19). Is there any way a rational choice could be made between these claims, except to assert dogmatically either the absolute right to individual freedom or the absolute duty to punish immorality?

II

It is perhaps best to begin with the rhetoric by which Devlin manages to convince Hart that a good many private, consenting acts are vicious, even though he does not persuade him that all vicious acts should be punished.

In a way, of course, Devlin's remark, quoted above, is a piece of equivocation, borrowing the strong sense of injury from Mill and using it in the much weaker context in which injury is not shown, but alleged. It also overlooks the fact that in private consenting acts the injured citizen invoking the law's aid is not the person towards whom the act is directed and with whom it is performed. Devlin's injured citizen is the morally zealous bystander, offended at what other people do together to their mutual satisfaction. Devlin's remark makes it appear that the libertarian is denying the law's right to arrest a man for harming another in the privacy of his home. But the accent is not on privacy, but on consent, and on the absence of palpable marks of injury. Moreover, that the actions are done discreetly may seem to answer the complaint of the injured bystander. No one was setting out to offend *him*. He must have gone a bit out of his own way to suffer outrage, or even worse, his complaints must be based on his own too vivid imagination. To allow this man's complaints to require invasion of privacy is to expose the law to just those pressures Mill most feared, the intemperate and hypersensitive outcries of moral zealots. It is this fear especially that leads Mill to seek a narrow definition of crime that would deny to moral fanatics the extra force of police power in pursuing their designs against minority beliefs and practices. But Devlin, and the typical legal moralist, seem prepared to bow to the vociferous, misinterpreting it as the numerous, voice.

Still, the complaint of the moral zealot is not the whole story. Devlin is simply convinced that sexual aberrations are monstrous sins. By painting them in the most lurid colours he is able to put the maximum pressure on legal principles designed to restrain the law from punishing men for such acts. No wonder that his papers often contain passages that seem more appropriate to the ordinary man and the member of parliament than to the jurist. For in place of showing injury he must excite in his readers the emotions of fear and revulsion by harping on the corrupting power of sexual vice, as if succumbing to such temptations makes it impossible for a man to be honest, dependable, or brave. The technique is no doubt a rhetorical success, but it rests on a factual claim that is nowhere supported by evidence and probably cannot be. For this reason it may be ignored.

Devlin himself is not too pleased with his vivid pictures of sexual corruption, and turns to other means of establishing the immorality of homosexuality and licentiousness. Chief among these is the argument that sexual passion clouds judgment, and that a man at its mercy is not in a position to foresee the harm he may cause or the misery he must endure, once having succumbed to temptation. The law must protect him because he cannot be expected to protect himself.

There are analogies, of course, that nourish this paternalistic conviction. The law protects men (though it shouldn't, according to Mill) against possible sources of harm, where they are not in a position to make a judgment as to potential injury. Laws regarding the manufacture and sale of food and drugs, for example, rest on the twin suppositions that men are vulnerable, through ignorance that must characterise all but specialists, to various sources of impurity, and that these impurities cause demonstrable harm or constitute demonstrable deceit. The legal moralist must show that both these criteria are met in the sexual case, by drawing (perhaps) a convincing picture of men enticing women or boys by wile and deceit into practices that only ruin them. The law must protect the vulnerable against such scoundrels.

Unfortunately, it is not that easy to show demonstrable harm, and this is the fact that Mill harped on in the first place. The legal moralist, in fact, generally appeals to miseries that seem to be rather regular consequences of most human actions. If, on the other hand, he supports his case by appeal to the testimony of victims, he has to be rather selective, for the results of succumbing to temptation surely run all the way from misery and regret to joy and the discovery of happiness.

The moralistic argument is persuasive so long as it is clouded judgment that is stressed. This makes it appear as if law is required to prevent the meeting of opportunity and craving, for a mind disturbed by passion is incapable of judgment. Still, the other requisite of protective legislation is missing. It is not shown that injury is generally suffered as a result of failure of judgment. Other cases, like drug addiction, smoking or drinking to excess, serve the paternalist better just because the injurious consequences appear to be more nearly demonstrable. But in these cases it is difficult to show that clouded judgment prevents men from knowing the potential harm in advance. Indeed, as the fact of injury becomes increasingly uncontestable, the claim that men are incapable of making judgments as to injurious consequences becomes increasingly implausible. The paternalist is thus likely to overstate the danger or underestimate the capacity to judge. The first error saddles us with an excessive burden of legislation, the second opens the door to a situation in which the law so restricts choice that men have no alternative but to be upright.

III

Now these arguments of the legal moralist appear so easy to counter as to leave us no option but to endorse the libertarian position. This, however, is because the legal moralist fails to establish immorality, not because the libertarian has established privacy and consent as absolute restraints upon the law. To do this the libertarian would have to test these principles against a more readily admitted or established evil.

Consider the case of *consenting violence*. If a man hires me to kill him, am I guilty of murder in carrying out his instructions? If two men agree to settle their differences by a duel, and one falls, is the other guilty of murder? Of course, attitudes toward killing with consent differ from culture to culture. On the whole modern western law frowns upon it, and this is a tradition to which both legal moralists and libertarians subscribe. According to Anglo-American legal tradition, at least, violence as *such* is criminal; consent has nothing to do with it.

Some crimes, of course, require lack of consent for their performance. Stealing with consent in unintelligible; it is a bizarre form of giving. And this, perhaps, lends credence to the view that lack of consent is part of the definition of a criminal act. But the meaning of killing does not depend on lack of consent. A particular society may condone dueling, or rituals involving willing victims of human sacrifice, and in such a society where only the unwilling count as murdered, lack of consent may well be the sole criterion for crime. In a society prohibiting duelling or other voluntary acts of maiming and killing (even tattooing) it is clear that physical injury suffices to class an act as criminal.

It is, I suppose, our attitude toward vio-lence—that it is wrong and inconsistent with our conception of a decent life—that leads us to override the fact of consent in prohibiting duelling, human sacrifice or Russian roulette. Violence threatens society by encouraging attitudes inimical to peace and security. These observations, it may be noted in passing, incorporate morality into the law. But what is of interest here is that these observations are exactly the sort that men like Devlin offer with regard to the sexual case. These acts, too, threaten society with disaster. Sexual preoccupations, and also those involving drugs, alcohol or gambling, turn men away from the duties and activities that keep society going. Furthermore, sexual interests outside the bonds of matrimony threaten the order of the family on which society is based. Thus it might be claimed that society has every right to protect itself against such potential threats, even if this means legislating in a way that overrides consent or guarantees of privacy.

And yet it is not homosexual, promiscuous or orgiastic desires in themselves that appear to shake society to its foundations. It is the thought that everyone will follow the minority down these garden paths. When men like Devlin see these practices as evidence of moral decay they are imagining what a social or moral order might be like in which everyone were homosexual, or where most men constantly pursued the ladies, abandoned themselves to the card table, or withdrew into alcoholic dreams or psychedelic fantasies. So long as these are minority pursuits society can assimilate them, and the law need not concern itself. The sexual desires of men are, perhaps, uniform enough and the natural tendency of men to bow to social disapproval strong enough, to keep potentially disruptive sexual variations in a manageable minority. When such natural governors are in operation, privacy and consent have their day. The danger caused to society by the undue sexual preoccupations of a minority must seem much less serious than an extension of police power or inroads upon privacy. The danger exists when these preoccupations are no longer those of a relatively stable minority, but show signs of increase, and so of becoming a way of life. This, Devlin rightly argues, cannot be. Such practices must continue to be the pastimes of the few if society is to continue to exist.

But then the moralist finds himself in the following dilemma. If, in the main, social practice reflects social ideals, laws enforcing these ideals are unnecessary; if it does not, legal means of ensuring performance consonant with these ideals are impractical, for they are no longer the effective ideals of the community. This suggests that the proposed analogue between violent acts and sexual acts is inexact. Violence and deceit might well be regarded as incompatible with *any* form of social organisation, sexual aberrations only with a *certain* set of mores. The moralist has been perturbed by changes he sees in the attitudes of the sexes toward one another and toward sexual cravings generally. These changes may threaten society with collapse—who knows? But they may only amount to that kind of change, at first hard to live with, especially for those who have grown up in different traditions, that signify not the end of society but only its transformation. A choice between these large-scale hypotheses seems quite beyond reach of judgment. And so, once again, the principles of privacy and consent flourish, not because they are absolutes but because the arguments or the evidence that might persuade us to override them are simply not convincing.

Hart himself, though admitting to the gross immorality and thus, by implication, the social threat, of departures from sexual custom, betrays his scepticism of that very claim. For in an argument that appears fundamental to his thesis, he claims that to punish sexual offences is to punish men for their desires, and that this is persecutory in effect. It is natural to wonder why preventing men from or punishing them for their sexual appetites should be regarded as cruel punishment when it never crosses the libertarian's mind that restraints upon the murder or thief are also restraints upon his desires. It is no answer to appeal to strength of desire alone, for it must be as legitimate to suppose that murderers and thieves

are compelled by desires beyond their control as it is to excuse sexual offenders on this ground. No, the answer seems rather to be found in the fact that sexual desires are looked upon at the start as somehow legitimate, a thing that no one will accord to acts of violence or deceit. This is not to applaud all sexual desires, of course, but only to admit that sexual desire has a legitimate role in human life, unlike lusts for blood or vengeance. Sexual passions are directed at times toward unusual objects or satisfied by unusual methods, and this strains the average man's capacity to let them pass without concern. But they are pleasurable pursuits to all concerned, and it is thus difficult to view them with the jaundiced eye that one casts upon violent actions.[1] This betrays, perhaps, a utilitarian bias, though it is important to notice the form it takes here. I am not arguing that pleasure is the good, or always good, nor any other form of that philospher's dismemberment of the social views of Bentham. But I am arguing, with Mill, that pain, deliberately caused, is paradigmatic of what is bad, embodying, if you will, the definition of an immoral action, and serving at the same time as a criterion for a criminal offence. On this score there is ample reason to take the claim of gross immorality against sexual acts somewhat lightly. By the same token the right to privacy and the disbarring condition of consent loom large as ways of protecting sexual pastimes from legal interference, the stature of these legal principles having been exaggerated by the puny claim of immorality against which they are placed.

In order to make the charge of gross immorality in sexual conduct stick, one must be convinced, as Devlin appears to be, that any form of sexual practice outside the bonds of matrimony (and no doubt many within it) threatens society to its foundations. Believing this, Devlin quite rightly rejects privacy and consent as boundaries to the law's reach. To argue with Devlin is thus, inevitably, to argue morally. There are no convenient legal expedients to which to retreat. The case of abortion illustrates this. It is sometimes argued that laws against abortion bring an illegitimate third party into the agreements between doctors and their patients. But this argument has force only so long as what the Catholic assumes is denied or ignored, that abortion is a case of taking life, and in fact a murderous case of it. Sooner or later this vexing question must be disposed of, if doctor–patient privacy is to be an issue at all.

By the same token the question, is non-orthodox sexual conduct vicious? must sooner or later be faced, even though it involves deciding whether society as such is threatened, or only a particular and transitory form of social organisation and belief. It is easy to pay tribute to the difficulty of these questions by calling them sociological, making it appear that answering them is someone else's responsibility. The anthropologist, indeed, may provide instruction here, by describing the variety of sexual practices and attitudes from culture to culture. This may suggest the view that society is compatible with any form of sexual attitude. But the anthropologist also describes a wide variety of economic and social conditions within which sexual mores take shape. It may be that certain forms of sexual freedom are compatible with a relatively simple economic structure, but not with the complex urban industrial civilisation in which we happen to live. That society, we firmly believe, has witnessed the atrophy of all institutions capable of providing moral education and training for adult life save the immediate family. Noting this, Devlin might argue that sexual licence is indeed incompatible with society as we find it, whether or not totally different social forms can admit quite different sexual mores. Moreover, it is not within our power to abandon industry and flee the cities, Rousseau-like, so that we might allow the complete expression of human desires.

This is the power of Devlin's argument. The evil of deviant or excessive sexual practices is demonstrated in the threats they harbour to the very existence of society. Its weakness is simply that that threat is not proven. By the same token, the strength of the libertarian's argument is not in his appeal to immutable le-

gal principles but quite simply in his challenge to the moral claim of his opponents. Indeed, in all these terribly solemn discussions of moral vice and legal principles it is forgotten to what extent attitudes toward sex allow for comic treatment, quite unlike murder, torture or the sadistic hinterland of the sexual. It is hard to maintain the view that departures from sexual orthodoxy threaten society while laughing at them at the theatre, in books, or at cocktail parties. The exaggerated moral claim simply does not ring true. For one thing the overwhelming temptations of sexual desire still appear to lead the vast majority of generation after generation into the depressingly normal outlets of marriage and family rearing. For another the results of departures from this normal pattern do not show unequivocal injury. For this reason, more than out of respect for inviolable legal principles, the case for the punishment of any consenting sexual acts, discreetly performed, must fail. And yet, of course, this conclusion leaves wide open the possibility that in some other case consent or privacy may not be adequate barriers to legislation.

IV

In any case the law–morals dichotomy will not help, for the libertarian view depends, if I am right, on taking a moral position counter to that advanced by the legal moralist. It may be worth speculating, in conclusion, on some of the reasons why this debate has come to be cast in the form of a law–morals dispute.

One reason has pretty clearly to do with the way in which morality comes to be identified with a rather particular brand of moral sentiment or a particular object of moral concern. At the crudest level morality is simply identified with sex, and prohibitions upon it, and thus the question as to whether morality is a proper sphere for law is the question whether sexual practices should be restrained by law. Not much more sophisticated is the tendency to abdicate morality to the morally ferocious, identifying it with the feelings of outrage, disgust or revulsion that some people feel toward the pleasures of others. Mill's insistence on the fact of inquiry is perhaps the best antidote to this peculiar, yet common, aberration.

On a more subtle level, much of the argument becomes entangled in the problem of punishment. Many people think that jails and work farms ought to be thought of as methods of rehabilitating or at worst ways of deterring men from their criminal habits, and thus suppose that they have divested themselves of old-fashioned 'moralistic' views of retribution. But this move, like that by which morality comes to be identified with the sexual or the intolerant, contains a covert assimilation of the concept of morality to the retributive attitude. And then of course a man who declares himself to be against morality in the law only means that he does not want law-breakers to be treated with vengeance. But the view he puts in its place, that law-breakers should be prevented from doing so again, or that they should be given therapy, clearly rests on the supposition that something is wrong that ought to be rectified or prevented. It is not clear to me why this is not a view as moral as that of the retributionist, nor how any legal action is possible at all unless it is animated by some conceptions of what is better or worse and what ought to be done and prevented.

A further subtlety has much to do with the Mill–Stephen and Hart–Devlin debates, where practices are at issue that some regard as good and desirable and others bad and revolting. The question is then as to whether those outraged should speak through law for society as a whole. The libertarian has the bad habit of abdicating morality to his opponent with the result that morality comes to be covertly identified with essentially contested (and vociferously expressed) opinions. No doubt the libertarian is right in rejecting the pressures of moral zealots on the law; but this is not because he has himself eschewed a moral view of the law. Murder is a crime because it is wrong, and wrong because of palpable injury. If consenting homosexuality is not a crime it is because it fails to exhibit the injuries that show murder or rape or theft to

be both sins and crimes. To argue otherwise is to suppose that wrong-doing does not suffice to make an act criminal, forcing the libertarian to argue either that murder is criminal because of some nonmoral quality, or that consent and privacy are together absolute barriers to the law. The second of these alternatives is highly dubious, the first, involving as it does the consequence that malicious injury is not morally wrong, little short of bizarre.

There are other and even more general ways in which the distinction between law and morals has been taken to have relevance to the question of sexual legislation. For example, as we have seen, much legislation of this sort depends for its enforcement on granting the police wide latitude in judging that an offence has been committed. The libertarian sometimes expresses his objection to this discretionary power by saying that law-enforcers should not make moral judgments. Perhaps this is extended to judges as well, in the hope that law-enforcers can be prevented from making law. This is no doubt a perfectly plausible if not always realisable hope, but it at most excludes morality from law *enforcement*. How law-*makers* are to decide what measures to support or oppose without recourse to ideas of what is good or bad is not recorded.

Nonetheless, most libertarians do seem to want a criterion for law-making that has the character of statute, thus eliminating moral judgment from the process of legislation. There are advantages in this. Just as the policeman can, in his work, appeal to something incontrovertible, the statute, so the legislator ought to be able to appeal to something equally incontrovertible, like natural law, or scientific facts, or basic norms. At this headwater of legal philosophy, the rejection of moral influence on the law, is the insistence that all justification must have the force that statutes have for the policeman. I think myself that the separation of law and morals is vitiated in this context by the incoherence of the demand. What appears to be wanted is that justification *within* the law (e.g. appeal to statute) shall apply also to justification *of* the law.

Barring this, the legal positivist wishes to supplant appeal to principles with appeal to facts. Either alternative is self-defeating. Both ignore the necessity, in a novel situation, of making some judgment as to what sort of thing is regarded as good or bad, and thus worthy, by legal means, of facilitating or preventing. It is hard to see how the separation of law and morals at this level is anything more than a resolution to avoid thinking about law as an activity of human decision and judgment. But this is to avoid thinking about it as law.

So Hart, and many libertarians, in supposing that legislative restraint of sexual conduct should not be a matter of moral decision, appear to argue that the decision ought to rest on an appeal to statute. But the question all along is, should there be such statutes? And that question appears to depend on whether we are prepared to regard consenting sexual acts sinful enough to count as crimes.

Note

1. Perhaps this leaves de Sade out of account. The result of that will be that I will be accused of not having *really* understood, or failed to plumb

the depths, and so on. I should be inclined myself to think of sadism, whether in an obvious sexual form or not, as having primarily a violent, not a sexual character, at least for legal purposes. Thus legislation against it need not answer to the charge that the rights of private and legitimate desires are violated or consent ignored.

Suggested Further Reading

Dworkin, Gerald, "Paternalism," in *Morality and the Law*, ed. Richard A. Wasserstrom. Belmont, Calif.: Wadsworth, 1971, pp. 107–26.

Kadish, S., "The Crisis of Overcriminalization," *Annals*, 374 (1967), 157.

Schwendinger, H., and J. Schwendinger, "Social Class and the Definitions of Crime," *Crime and Social Justice*, 7 (Spring–Summer 1977), 4–13.

Skolnick, Jerome H., "Coercion to Virtue: The Enforcement of Morals," *Southern California Law Review*, 41 (1968), 588–641.

Women Endorsing Decriminalization, "Prostitution: A Non-Victim Crime?" *Issues in Criminology*, 8, (Fall 1973), 137–62.

2. THE GOALS OF CRIMINAL JUSTICE

In considering whether and for what reasons certain acts ought to be defined as crimes, it is useful to examine two important goals of criminal justice: *deterrence* of crime (making lawbreaking unpreferable), and *retribution* (meting out deserved punishment to lawbreakers). Conflicts between deterrence and retribution sometimes occur.

From a utilitarian perspective the chief goal of criminal justice is deterrence. There are two types of deterrence: specific (or special) and general. *Specific deterrences* prevent those who have already committed crimes from further criminal behavior. *Gen-

eral deterrence* is the prevention of potential acts of crime by the threat of punishment. The utilitarian analysis rests upon the assumption that a criminal justice system operates positively to prevent people from committing crimes. Critics of this view argue that this assumption is unproven since criminal behavior continues despite the interventions of criminal justice. On the other hand, proponents claim that without a criminal justice system, rates of crime would be substantially higher.

Utilitarians weigh the undesirable consequences of criminalization against the benefits it produces. Among the undesirable consequences are the cost to society of maintaining a criminal justice system, and its limitations on the freely chosen preferences of individuals. The expense of operating a criminal justice system is undesirable in that resources spent cannot be used for other socially beneficial programs such as education or health care. Thus utilitarians hold that apprehending and punishing lawbreakers is not an intrinsic good but is good only insofar as it deters socially harmful behavior. If the costs of making a particular action a crime are greater than the gains secured, then it should not be criminalized. Prohibition is an example of this type of reasoning. Although excessive use of alcohol causes demonstrable social harm, the costs of outlawing its production and sale were, in practice, extremely high. In addition, many people continued to desire the product and to use it. Critics argued that the expense of Prohibition and the interference with individual liberty outweighed the benefits of avoiding alcohol abuse. The law was eventually repealed.

A deontological approach to criminal justice stresses the goal of retribution. Whereas deterrence is primarily oriented toward future consequences, retribution is concerned with appropriate response to past events. Retributive justice involves the idea that deserved and appropriate punishment of criminals is an intrinsic good. It is just, on this view, for those guilty of harming others to suffer punishment equivalent to the harm they caused, regardless of any deterrent effect which may result. Deontologists believe that the regulation of behavior effected by criminalization is justified because society has an obligation to protect people's rights. Crimes are acts that caused harm by violating rights. Consider the example given in the previous section of opening a competing business which harms the owner of an existing one by taking away customers and income. A deontologist claims that while harm results, no rights have been violated because freedom from competition is not a right. Hence the act should not be a crime.

Deontological responses to the notion of victimless crime vary depending upon whether one believes that rights can be waived. Aiding a suicide attempt, for instance, is a crime if one believes that the right to life cannot be relinquished even voluntarily. Others believe that if the "victim" consents to the harm, no rights are violated and the act is not a crime.

In addition to deterrence and retribution, related purposes of criminal justice are *incapacitation* (confining criminals in order to protect law-abiding citizens) and *rehabilitation* (reeducating criminals for reintegration into society). The goals of retribution and rehabilitation are discernable in the different names used for penal institutions: some are called "penitentiaries," others "correctional facilities" or "reformatories." Critics of deontology argue that retribution without rehabilitation is mere vengeance and cannot be justified in a humane society. Others maintain that rehabilitation and retribution are incompatible aims both in theory and in practice.

In the following article Rosemarie Tong examines the objective of incapacitation, often thought of as a by-product of imprisonment to punish or rehabilitate. The author argues that incapacitation on grounds of dangerousness is sometimes used to justify preventive detention of persons not criminally liable. An example is the commitment of insanity acquittees to mental institutions. The practice, Tong maintains, represents a disturbing expansion of the criminal justice system into areas best handled by civil authorities.

ROSEMARIE TONG

Incapacitation and the Scope of the Criminal Law

Introduction

There are approximately as many philosophies of sentencing as there are dissatisfied policemen, lawyers, judges, offenders, and citizens in this country. Comments one criminologist, "In an age of retributivists without the lash, of deterrers who would not hang the innocent to prevent crime, and of rehabilitators who are not enamored with life imprisonment for incorrigible apple thieves, penal philosophy may have made itself irrelevant to the concerns of sentencing agencies."[1] Lacking a clear and consistent theoretical understanding of the aims of criminal punishment, it is no wonder that judges are casting about for adequate justifications to support their ideologically based impositions of sentence.[2] The result seems to be a uniform disparity in sentencing. Consequently, critics of the status quo are attempting one of two things: either to infuse rhyme and reason into the reigning philosophy of sentencing by establishing a priority among all five of the traditional penal purposes (retribution, general deterrence, special deterrence, rehabilitation, and incapacitation); or to embrace some sentencing aims to the exclusion of others. In either event a major reformulation of criminal law theory seems in the offing.

An advocate of the former, more conservative approach is Judge Marvin E. Frankel. Although Judge Frankel recognizes that the usual litany of penal purposes is debatable and that some aims of sentencing may be illegitimate, it seems that "for the time being" he would be satisfied were judges required to "state which among the allowed purposes were the supposed basis for each particular sentence." Judge Frankel makes no real attempt to discard any of the traditional purposes of the criminal sanction, although he carefully points out the dangers of relying too heavily on rehabilitation and/or incapacitation as guides for the imposition of sentence.[3] In contrast, such thinkers as Norval Morris, Andrew von Hirsch, and Hyman Gross reject, to a greater or lesser extent, a "multi-valued" approach to sentencing, applying particular pressure to the rehabilitative and incapacitory ideals.[4]

That rehabilitation has not weathered the test of time well seems certain. For several reasons, fewer and fewer theorists now think that it is particularly humane to fit punishment to the criminal—to treat, train, educate or reform the convicted offender so that he or she can become a better person or citizen. In the first place, and rather ironically, the rehabilitative ideal is criticized by some because it is not rehabilitative enough and by others because it is too rehabilitative. In some penal institutions inmates are simply warehoused. They are neither trained nor educated; at the most their treatment consists in *milieu* therapy, a euphamism for spending time with other prisoners in unsanitary and unsavory conditions.[5] In other penal compounds, however, "rehabilitation" is pursued with a vengeance. There the use of such aversive stimuli as electric shocks to the arms, feet, or groin and drugs that produce fifteen minutes to one hour of uncontrollable vomiting has been rationalized as necessary and humane "therapy."[6,7] But whether the problem is too much or too little rehabilitation, the results are equally devastating. Secondly, the rehabilitative ideal is attacked because it is not an *ideal,* because it is not the task of the criminal law to tamper with the *persons* of convicts by resocializing or reintegrating them into a society of which they may want no part. No person—

Reprinted with permission from *Ethics, Public Policy, and Criminal Justice*, ed. Frederick Elliston and Norman Bowie (Cambridge, Mass.: Oelgeschlager, Gunn & Hain, Inc., 1982), pp. 289–304.

incarcerated or not—should have to choose between freedom and personal identity or integrity. When Eldridge Cleaver refused to "behave" in exchange for an easy parole, at fault were those who tempted him with freedom, rather than he who refused to pay with his soul.[8] Finally, the rehabilitative ideal is challenged because, even when correctly conceived and administered, it is probably ineffective. There is growing empirical evidence that even the best of the reformative programs do not work. According to Charles Silberman, for example, the present array of correctional treatments seems to have little if any appreciable effect—positive or negative—on the rates of recidivism of convicted offenders, and old age rather than any sophisticated therapy may be the best cure for criminal passions.[9]

But even though rehabilitation has been debunked as one of the greatest myths of twentieth-century penology, there is a curious reluctance to discredit its darker side, incapacitation.[10] By incapacitation is meant one of two things. Understood as "confinement," "incapacitation" simply means that at least while a person is confined in prison he or she is unable to commit any crime outside the prison limits. In this sense of the term, incapacitation is the by-product of any prison sentence and is largely unobjectionable. Sometimes, however, incapacitation is used to denote that practice whereby convicted defendants are restrained longer than they would otherwise be restrained on account of their perceived or real dangerousness. In this sense of the term, incapacitation is a form of preventive detention and as such is quite problematic. Nonetheless, many legal theorists wonder whether there may not be a need for incapacitation in both of its senses. Ernest van den Haag claims that:

> . . . once having punished offenders for their offenses, we may incapacitate them when we have reason to believe that they will unlawfully harm others if released and that the harm and the likelihood of it are great enough to outweigh the harm the preventive restriction on their freedom does to them.[11]

His thoughts are expressed in somewhat more restrained fashion in the Model Penal Code, in statements of the American Bar Association, and in the Model Sentencing Act, which suggests that incapacitation is not only a proper penal aim, but the paradigm penal aim:

> The purpose of penal codes and sentencing is public protection. Sentences should not be based upon revenge and retribution. The policy of this act is that dangerous offenders shall be identified, segregated and correctively treated in custody for long terms as needed, and that other offenders may be committed for a limited period.[12]

In sum, the freedom of supposedly dangerous criminal offenders is secondary to the public's protection from the possible harm such offenders might inflict.

But despite the superficial appeal of this line of reasoning, it is riddled with a major conceptual difficulty. There are at least two kinds of dangerous persons: those who *cannot* help being dangerous—people who suffer from incapacities of body or mind that cause them on occasion to behave criminally and that make them dangerous if left at large; and those who *will not* help being dangerous—people who regard the law as an enemy to be avoided and whose regular habit is to operate outside the bounds of the law.[13] When a spokesman for the criminal justice system speaks about sentencing dangerous persons, it is not always clear to which of these two types of dangerous persons he is referring. Indeed, conflation seems to reign. Statements such as the following are all too typical: "There are certain types of individuals in every society who are vicious nonconforming types. They must be controlled and the primary concern here is not some concept of justice to them, but the right of the normal people in society to be protected from the abnormal and the irrational."[14] To be sure, the public does have an interest in being protected both from vicious, nonconforming types and from abnormal, irrational types. But do both of these "types" fall within the purview of the criminal law's sentencing powers? Perhaps, but only if the difference between those who can't help being dangerous and those who won't turns out to be a difference in degree rather than kind. Perhaps not, if the difference between those who can't help being dangerous and those who won't is qualitative rather than quantitative; and if, as we have been led to believe, the civil authorities do indeed have a task—namely, the protection of society from *non-responsible* dangerous persons. What I suspect, however, is that due to an increasing lack of public confidence in the civil authorities, the criminal authorities have been gradually expanding their own powers. Currently the criminal courts are not only processing some dangerous persons the civil law should be processing, they are also sentencing these persons to longer terms of confinement than necessary. As I see it, this trend is worrisome. By focusing on a relatively uncontested, but thoretically unwarranted policy of criminal law—the automatic mandatory and/or discretional commitment of insanity acquittees to mental institutions—I intend to show how, under the rubric of "incapacitation," a system of criminal justice can slowly degenerate into a tool of political repression.

Incapacitation and Those Who Cannot Help Being Dangerous

Supposedly it is the task of legal proceedings directed to civil commitment, and not the business of the criminal law, to remove people who cannot help being dangerous from public circulation. Or so runs the rhetoric. It does not take a very astute observer, however, to realize that the criminal law has not been minding its own business. Not only has the criminal law been loath to release insanity acquittees and to redescribe alcoholics and drug addicts as "sick,"[15] it has been quick to sponsor indeterminate confinement and treatment programs, enabling it to have some if not total

control over the fate of sexual psychopaths[16] and defective delinquents.[17] Significantly, the criminal law has not really defended its encroachment upon the civil law's territory except to indicate that it seeks to control only those non-liable, dangerous persons who have been fed into its machinery; and that it does a better job protecting society from "madmen" than soft-hearted, muddle-headed civil authorities. But if these are the grounds upon which the criminal law stakes its expansionist policies, one would expect it to keep within its clutches *all* as well as *only* dangerous, nonliable offenders. Not unexpectedly, however, the criminal law has two nets: one that is so coarse-grained that it allows some very dangerous, nonliable persons to filter through and one so fine-grained that it keeps within its confines even the least dangerous of nonliable persons. It would seem, therefore, that the so-called problems of under-inclusion and over-inclusion impede the penal sanction's incapacitative efforts.

To date, the problem of *over-inclusion* has been the one most discussed. Critics argue that our present ability to predict future behavior is so inaccurate that any system of incapacitation will mistakenly deprive many persons of their liberty who would probably not harm anyone if released. To see that this is the case, one only has to note the growing body of minor sex deviants (flashers, exhibitionists, peeping Toms) whom the criminal courts say must be hospitalized until "cured," though without treatment, at considerable financial cost to the taxpayer, and at great personal price to the confined persons. The limitation of this criticism is that those who make it would not necessarily mind confining such persons if there were relatively greater certainty that the individuals so affected would actually commit a significant crime if released. Many, if not most, of those who criticize incapacitation on these grounds urge, therefore, the expenditure of more time and money toward improving our ability to predict future behavior.[18] They do not question the criminal law's initial or continued involvement in the processing of those who cannot help being dangerous.

But because this involvement is precisely what should be challenged. I prefer to focus on the less-discussed problem of *under-inclusion*. Here I am referring not so much to those dangerous *individuals* who manage to filter through the criminal law's net, but to those *classes* of dangerous, nonliable harm doers who seem impervious to state intervention. Why, for example, does the criminal law feel quite comfortable about intervening in the lives of insanity acquittees but not in the lives of automatism acquittees who are similarly dangerous and nonliable? Could it be that at some level the penal sanction doubts the wisdom and theoretical legitimacy of its expansionist policies and seeks to restrain its own hand before it has taken over tasks it was never meant to perform? Seemingly so, and it is by carefully examining, among other practices, the criminal law's differential disposition of insanity and automatism acquittees, that one sees just how confused a course the criminal law is steering with respect to those who cannot help being dangerous. One sees also how needed a change in direction is.

The Disposition
of Insanity Acquittees

If the incapacitation of insanity acquittees were the result of ordinary civil commitment proceedings controlled by civil authorities, objections to it would be few.[19] But when such incapacitation is, as it is in several jurisdictions, the automatic outcome or rote result of a criminal court's proceedings, serious questions emerge. Automatic mandatory commitment is a policy based on the false assumption that because a defendant was dangerous at time x, he is still dangerous at time x plus i. But "insanity" is a legal, not a medical term; consequently, the determination of insanity is a legal-moral decision about a defendant's culpability at the time he or she perpetrated crime x and not a medical determination of his or her current mental health. Although mental illness is a necessary condi-

tion for insanity, past insanity does not *ex hypothesis* signal present mental illness.[20] Realizing this, some jurisdictions have opted for discretional commitment models based on a jury's or judge's determination of continuing mental illness. Although such commitments represent a conceptual advance over mandatory commitments, they are defective on two other accounts, one having to do with functions, the other with fairness. In the first place, discretional commitments are based on a confusion of functions. It is the proper role of judges or jurists to determine insanity; it is not their role to determine the existence or nonexistence of mental illness. To the extent that the expert witness (the forensic psychiatrist) should refrain from making a moral-legal judgment about a defendant's blameworthiness, the judge or jurist should not be permitted to make what is essentially a medical-clinical determination.[21] The assessment of mental illness *per se* simply falls outside the scope of the trier of fact's special competency. Secondly, discretional commitments are frequently exercises in subjectivity. Whereas some triers of fact see evidence of mental illness in a nervous twitch, others fail to see it altogether. As a result there may be some grounds for complaint among those acquittees who are detained, whenever they are unable to perceive any relevant difference between themselves and other acquittees who have not been detained.

These difficulties notwithstanding, automatic mandatory as well as discretional commitments continue to command widespread public support for several reasons that can be ranked in order of increasing cogency. The weakest arguments for these policies are those based on empirical claims that the specter of commitment discourages false pleas of insanity and encourages correct determinations of insanity on the part of judges and juries who might otherwise twist the facts, find an insane defendant guilty, and send him to a secure prison.[22] Equally unconvincing are those arguments based on a tired, currently ill-received theme—namely, that since commitment is intended as treatment and not as punishment, there need not be undue concern about an insanity acquittee's rights.[23] In contrast, the strongest arguments for these incapacitative policies, especially for automatic mandatory commitment, rely on the vaue of post-trial commitment as a necessary discovery device to ascertain whether the acquitted defendant is still dangerous, and on the extra social protection gained by institutionalizing insanity acquittees, "just in case." But if this is the reason *par excellence* for the continued intervention of the criminal law in the insanity acquittee's life, then, as we shall see, the criminal law's nonintervention in the automatism acquittee's life becomes difficult to explain indeed.

The Disposition of Automatism Acquittees

Automatism, or involutariness of behavior, is a defense that has gained recognition in the United States only recently. Nonetheless, the proposed Model Penal Code has seen fit to include such a defense. Sectin 2.01 (1) provides that: "A person is not guilty of an offense unless his liability is based on conduct which includes a voluntary act which it was physically possible not to perform." "Involuntary" is defined only by description of certain bodily movements that are *prima facie* not voluntary, such as:

1. a reflex or convulsion;
2. a bodily movement during unconsciousness or sleep;
3. conduct during hypnosis or resulting from hypnotic suggestion;
4. a bodily movement that otherwise is not a product of the effort or determination of the actor, either conscious or habitual.[24]

Anyone who can demonstrate that when he purportedly committed crime x he was behaving involuntarily, has established an automatism defense and is entitled to an outright acquittal. But whereas such an acquittal is of the no-strings-attached variety, as we noted in the case of the typical insanity acquittee, acquittal

strings assume the dimensions of thick ropes or straightjackets. This seems most problematic, however, from the vantage point of the public. The rage of a knife-wielding psychotic is not easily distinguished from the rage of a knife-wielding automaton plagued with an inoperable brain tumor. Why, then, shouldn't the criminal law protect the public from dangerous automatism acquittees as well as from dangerous insanity acquittees?

Interestingly, some theorists attempt to justify the differential disposition of automatism and insanity acquittees by contrasting the involuntary character of an automaton's acts with the voluntary, though certainly irrational, nature of a mentally ill person's acts. Herbert Fingarette notes that what we see in the random flailing or convulsive motions of the epileptic during a grand mal seizure is the absence of "purpose." Such bodily movements are purposeless because they are "not coordinated in terms of will, intent, or motive." If they are to be understood at all, it is "in terms of physico-chemically induced energies activating individual muscles to increase or decrease the physical tension of the muscle fibers." Where insanity is at issue, however, the person's comportment is typically "purposive." "The offending act manifests the characteristics of conduct initiated, coordinated, and carried out with some skill by the person to achieve some end," however bizarre.[25] In other words, when the epileptic has a fit, the matter is entirely out of his hands. Were he to sit down and decide to have a fit, he would be staging rather than undergoing a fit. In contrast, when a psychotically infanticidal mother determines to kill her newborn, she does so knowingly and willingly. To be sure, her conduct is utterly irrational, but the ability "to respond relevantly to what is essentially relevant"[26]—namely that the fate of a defenseless human being is in one's hands—is different from the ability to be conscious of one's bodily movements and/or to be in control of them. Borrowing Fingarette's distinction, others go on to suggest that since the criminal law cannot intervene in the life of every dangerous acquittee of the "can't-help-it" sort, it may as well draw the line at automatons whose conduct is totally involuntary. But why? One would think that of all acquittees, automatons would be the most dangerous because they are the least in control. Seemingly, there can be but two reasons for such a decision, both of them exceedingly poor.

In the first place it may be implied that whereas automatism is a physical condition easily cured, insanity results from a generally intractable mental condition; and that whereas automatism acquittees know enough to seek a medical cure, insanity acquittees do not have the presence of mind to seek psychiatric help. But, of course, these stereotypic assumptions are more myth than reality. Some forms of automatism (epilepsy) are very difficult to cure and others (rage reactions due to an inoperable brain tumor) are simply impossible to cure; in contrast some types of mental illness (depression) are relatively easy to cure. Similarly, although some automatons refuse medical treatment, some insanity acquittees eagerly seek psychiatric assistance. Given the weakness of this line of reasoning, it is secondarily suggested that whereas the criminal law can have no deterrent effect on those whose conduct is involuntary, it can have such an effect on those whose conduct is voluntary. To be sure, but can irrational people be deterred? Were a policeman standing at his elbow, the exhibitionist might refrain from his activities; but would the psychotic religious fanatic respond similarly?[27] Perhaps not. And even if the voluntary acts of all irrational persons were indeed deterrable, this would be at most an argument for eliminating the insanity defense, not for first acquitting and then detaining irrational defendants. In any event, even if these arguments were more convincing, the real reason why the criminal law currently interferes with insanity acquittees but not with automatism acquittees is that the former are perceived as much more dangerous than the latter. But, as we noted, this perception is misleading; automatism acquittees can be just as dangerous as insanity acquittees. Realizing this, some theorists have suggested that the automatism/insanity dis-symmetry be

resolved either by assimilating the automatism plea to that of insanity or by construing automatism as a plea, carrying with it conditions similar to those appended to the insanity plea. But neither of these courses seems satisfactory.

The assimilation approach is most dubious. If automatism is to be construed as an insanity defense, then at least some experts must be willing to concede that certain automatous conditions are mental rather than physical disorders (diseases). And there are such experts. According to Earl Rose, for example, organic diseases such as epilepsy, arteriosclerosis and senility, metabolic and endocrine disturbances, certain infections, neoplasis (cancer), genetic abnormalities, intoxication, delirium tremens, drug addiction, and brain disease should give rise to an insanity defense for they can, and often do, cause mental aberrations.[28] Nonetheless, equally respected authorities claim that these very same diseases, *because they are organic* (physical), should not be viewed in the same light as functional mental disorders, and should therefore continue to give rise to the unique defense of automatism.[29] Particularly instructive in this respect are the American epilepsy cases. In *Sprague v. State,* for example, the court ruled that a "psychomotor seizure" might produce an incapacity that would fit within the American Law Institute test for insanity. Said the court:

> . . . while medically, psychomotor epilepsy may be considered physical rather than mental in origin, the disease is one which, during the period of a seizure, affects the mental processes of the person afflicted. Thus it may be legally classified as a mental disease or defect for the purpose of determining criminal responsibility.[30]

In contrast, it was held in *People* v. *Freeman* that epilepsy does not constitute matter for an insanity defense:

> Epilepsy is only one of a number of causes for unconsciousness. It differs from insanity in that the latter generally means an unsoundness of

mental condition which modifies, or removes, individual responsibility because it "is such a deprivation of reason that the subject is incapable of understanding and acting with discretion in the ordinary affairs of life." . . . The epileptic displays no such loss of brain function although at the time of or immediately preceding a convulsion he may experience physical aurae such as a dreary state or one of terror.[31]

Viewing these two assertions in juxtaposition forces many to conclude that insofar as the analysis of the automatism defense is concerned, "whether a disorder directly impinging on brain tissue is to be classified as mental or physical can involve nothing more than a preference between labels or an unarticulated choice between unarticulated policies directed toward achieving some unarticulated end."[32]

In any event, although construing automatism as insanity would covertly secure for treatment another class of acquitted dangerous defendants who would otherwise be left to their own devices, it has been questioned whether broadening the definition of "disease of the mind" would not be "a cure worse than the ill it is intended to remedy."[33] It makes little sense, for example, to declare insane a person whose hypoglycemia is at the root of his crime, and then send him to the hospital for the criminally insane in order that a social worker or psychiatrist can treat him as if the roots of his problem were all social or psychological. For this reason those who wish to restrain acquitted automatons, but who also seek to avoid the mental gymnastics involved in assimilating cases of automatism to insanity, urge a more overt approach to the disposition of acquitted automatons. Such theorists suggest that all debate should cease about whether lack of consciousness and/or lack of control due to organic brain disease calls for a different legal result than irrational conduct due to functional mental illness; and that the criminal courts simply be authorized to detain acquitted automatons along with acquitted insanity defendants.

But although this overt approach would, like the covert approach, also ensnare automatons in the penal net, it justifies nothing. Moreover, it continues a worrisome trend. If today the criminal law protects the public from automatism as well as insanity acquittees, tomorrow it may protect normal citizens from all acquittees who cannot help being dangerous; and the day after next it may start protecting the public from those who will not help being dangerous by encouraging such offenders to redescribe themselves as persons who cannot help being dangerous; and finally, it may simply begin to protect society from all dangerous people—of either sort, acquitted or not.

This is, of course, the worst possible scenario; but it can be nipped in the bud if the criminal law is unable to provide an internally consistent, theoretical rationale for restraining insanity acquittees, let alone other acquittees. To date there have been attempts to provide such a rationale; but these attempts fail and with them fail the criminal law's expansionist policies.

Criminal Law Theory and the Disposition of Those Who Cannot Help Being Dangerous

Herbert Fingarette argues that there is a fundamental and rational legal basis for denying to those held not guilty by reason of insanity that immediate freedom granted to those held simply not guilty; namely, that though such a person may not have the "fault of blameworthiness," he or she does have the "fault of incapacity." He claims that this

. . . past adjudicated fault is the legitimate ground for giving the court authority, at its option, to investigate the circumstances and to impose, within limits and consistent with the aims of the law, a set of conditions. In short, where guilt or grave incapacity under law is at issue, the person who has proven to have offended should not go immediately free as a matter of right.[34]

Moreover, continues Fingarette, this past adjudicated fault is sufficiently unique to justify the criminal law in its quest to develop its own criteria for dealing with the criminally insane instead of referring solely to the criteria for civil commitment of dangerous persons.[35] It would also seem potent enough to permit the penal sanction to develop its own standards for holding acquitted automatons and perhaps all acquitted defendants who cannot help being dangerous.

But is this "fault" really sufficiently strong to bear the weight of all these incapacitative practices? I think not. Not only, as Fingarette himself admits, is the fault of incapacity not the fault of blameworthiness; it is not even a fault in the sense that blameworthiness is a fault. There are at least two different senses of the term "fault" as applied to persons. In its first usage—that which signals the state of being at fault—a person grants that due to certain of his voluntary decisions and accompanying actions, unfortunate events took place and/or unfortunate situations were created. In its second usage—that which refers to a fault in psychological or physiological makeup—a person is merely admitting that he is to some degree defective.

Seemingly, there is an equivocation upon the term "fault" here. Yet however unsatisfying are the details of Professor Fingarette's analysis, there is much to be said for its bold outlines. Although pristine criminal law theory justifies only the practice of punishing blameworthy criminal offenders, all along it has endorsed measures of security and care with respect to non-blameworthy criminal offenders. Realizing this, Helen Silving suggests that a clean breast be made of the whole affair, and that a dual system of penal law be devised in which the retributive-punitive demands of the criminal sanction are clearly separated from its protective exigencies. Professor Silving wants to restructure the criminal law in such a way that although only blameworthy offenders would be punished, society could still protect itself from whole classes of non-blameworthy but dangerous offenders. She proposes that the criminal law sanction

with non-punitive measures of security and care not only the insanity acquittee, but the automaton, the inadvertently negligent person, the intoxicated or otherwise addicted individual, the psychopath, and so forth—provided that such persons have actually manifested their dangerousness in some sort of criminal conduct that would have constituted a crime had they not been physically, psychologically, and/or environmentally disadvantaged (incapacitated).[36]

The distinction between "criminal conduct" and "crime" is essential in Silving's system. Rather than assuming crime to be the systematically initial construct of criminal law, Silving suggests that a more elementary basic concept be adopted—"criminal conduct." This concept signifies conduct which, but for the absence of guilt, would constitute a crime. That is, only when elements of guilt are added to criminal conduct is crime constituted, giving rise to punitive responsibility. When elements of guilt are not present, there is no crime; but if dangerousness is established, then measures of security and care may be in order.[37] In sum, Silving is pressing the following: once a person effects a legally prohibited public harm, he falls within the grasp of the criminal law. The law's grip upon said person shall not be released until it is established that he is blameless (not guilty) and that he does not pose a threat to society in the sense of being unable to forsake his dangerousness at will. If someone is blameless (not guilty) but poses a threat to society in the requisite sense, he may be subjected only to measures of security and care. If someone is blameworthy (guilty) but does not pose a threat to society in the requisite sense, he may be subjected only to punishment. Insofar as the class of those who cannot help being dangerous is concerned, there exists no individual who is blameworthy as well as a threat to society. Therefore, under no circumstances may such a person be first punished and then "secured," or vice versa. This point is what distinguishes Silving's *dual* system from German and Italian *dual track* systems that frequently heap punishment upon "care" or vice versa.[38] On the other hand, what differentiates her system from the Anglo-American system is that Silving enables the criminal law to sentence those who cannot help being dangerous in an entirely overt manner rather than in a largely covert fashion.

Professor Silving's proposal seems well-balanced and well-considered, especially since she later promises that no person may be punished or treated unless his rights as a citizen and as a person have been and are being safeguarded.[39] Nonetheless, I reject her proposal because it unncessarily expands the limits of the criminal sanction, the most fearsome of the state's arms, providing it with unnecessary powers.

Conclusion

The alternative to Silving's and, to a lesser extent, Fingarette's conception of criminal law seems to be this: the criminal law as it is now but further decentralized, further refined, and made to work for the public rather than against it. The machinery of the criminal law should process and secure ultimate control only over those who are truly responsible; it should hand over all other dangerous persons as soon as possible to the *relevant* civil authorities. Assuming that these civil authorities are indeed experts in their respective fields, they should be given ultimate treatment and release authority over those in their care, provided that their wider social responsibilities are clearly delineated, and provided that they do not abuse the rights of those under their care. Of course, this means that there will be continued tension between health professionals and the criminal justice system. But this tension may, after all, be healthy; and complaints about the ongoing battle between lawyers and psychiatrists may be misdirected. To be sure, lawyers are raiding the mental hospitals looking for rational or non-dangerous people; and psychiatrists are invading the prisons looking for sick or irrational inmates. Admittedly, such lawyers and psychiatrists are adversaries; but one wonders what would happen if they were all working for the same

arm of the law as they would be in Silving's system. One suspects that fewer wrongs would be righted, that even more purportedly dangerous individuals would be confined unnecessarily and/or for too long. As I see it, the distinctions between the psychiatric, medical, and social welfare functions of the state on the one hand, and its police and punishment powers on the other hand are not a matter of mere happenstance. History teaches that when these powers are confused, justice is frequently short-circuited. The religious and political nonconformist is just the type of person easily mistaken for a "madman," and therefore *real* madmen should not be left in the hands of the criminal law, since it is traditionally allied with state power and the political status quo. Seemingly, what keeps a society such as ours operative—what keeps it trying to maintain a balance between social order and individual freedom—is its reliance on a delicate system of checks and balances aimed at keeping authorities in their place and on their toes. To upset this finely tuned system is to risk abuses of power.

Given these observations, it would seem that the criminal law should divest itself of as much power as possible. It can begin by handing over acquitted dangerous persons to the responsible civil authorities. It can continue by exercising its discretion wisely and trying not to process such persons in the first instance. A weak criminal law is the sign of a healthy society. It is also the index of a government that does not have to keep any cards up its sleeves because it is not gambling against its citizens, but creating for and with them a society worth protecting.

Notes

1. Cited in John C. Coffee, Jr., "The Repressed Issues of Sentencing: Accountability, Predictability, and Equality in the Era of the Sentencing Commission," 66 *Georgetown Law Journal* 977 (1978).

2. See Willard Gaylin, *Partial Justice* (New York: Knopf, 1974). Gaylin shows how the social, economic, and racial biases of judges affect their sentencing policies.

3. Marvin Frankel, *Criminal Sentences: Law Without Order* (New York: Hill and Wang, 1973), 106–115; 86–102.

4. See Norval Morris, *The Future of Imprisonment* (Chicago: University of Chicago Press, 1974); Andrew von Hirsch, *Doing Justice: The Choice of Punishments* (New York: Hill and Wang, 1976); and Hyman Gross, *A Theory of Criminal Justice* (New York: Oxford University Press, 1979).

5. See Alexander Brooks, *Law, Psychiatry and the Mental Health System* (Boston: Little, Brown, 1974).

6. "Behavior Mod Behind the Walls," *Time,* 11 March 1974, p. 74.

7. *Knecht v. Gillman,* 488 F.2d 1136 (8th Cir. 1973).

8. Eldridge Cleaver, *Soul on Ice* (New York: McGraw-Hill, 1968).

9. Charles E. Silberman, *Criminal Justice, Criminal Violence* (New York: Random House, 1978).

10. See Herbert Packer, *The Limits of the Criminal Sanction* (Stanford, Calif.: Stanford University Press, 1968).

11. Ernest van den Haag, *Punishing Criminals* (New York: Basic Books, 1975), p. 243.

12. *Model Sentencing Act,* National Council on Crime and Delinquency (1972 Revision), Article I, Section I.

13. Gross, *A Theory of Criminal Justice,* pp. 36–37.

14. Cited in Gaylin, *Partial Justice,* p. 177.

15. For example, see "Comment: Criminal Responsibility and the Drug Dependency Defense—A Need for Judicial Clarification," 42 *Fordham Law Review* 361 (1973); *Robinson* v. *California,* 370 U.S. 660 (1962); and *Powell* v. *Texas,* 392 U.S. 514 (1968).

16. For example, see "Note: The Plight of the Sexual Psychopath: A Legislative Blunder and Political Acquiescence," 41 *Notre Dame Lawyer* 527 (1966).

17. For example, see *Sas* v. *Maryland,* 334 F.2d 506 (4th Cir. 1964).

18. See Mary Kay Harris, "Disquisition on the Need for a New Model for Criminal Sanctioning Systems," 77 *West Virginia Law Review* 277 (1975).

19. This is the policy in a few jurisdictions. See Brooks, *Law, Psychiatry and the Mental Health System,* pp. 321–474.

20. Ibid., p. 111.

21. See *Washington* v. *United States,* 390 F.2d 444 (D.C. Cir. 1967).

22. F. B. Koller, "The Insanity Defense: The Need for Articulate Goals at the Acquittal, Commitment, and Release Stages," 112 *University of Pennsylvania Law Review* 739 (1964).

23. See Brooks, *Law, Psychiatry and the Mental Health System,* pp. 109–110.

24. *Model Penal Code,* 2.01 (2), Proposed Official Draft at p. 24 (1962).

25. Herbert Fingarette, *The Meaning of Criminal Insanity* (Berkeley: University of California Press, 1972), p. 161.

26. Ibid., p. 203.

27. This is the traditional test for so-called irresistible impulses.

28. Earl Rose, "Criminal Responsibility and Competency as Influenced by Organic Disease," 35 *Missouri Law Review* 226–248 (1960).

29. Sanford J. Fox, "Physical Disorder, Consciousness, and Criminal Liability," 63 *Columbia Law Review* 645 (1963).

30. *Sprague* v. *State,* 52 Wis. 2d 89, 187 NW 2d 784 (1971).

31. *People* v. *Freeman,* 61 Cal. App. 2d 110, 115, 142 P.2d 435, 438 (Dist. Ct. App. 1943).

32. Fox, "Physical Disorder, Consciousness, and Criminal Liability," p. 658.

33. R. Cross, "Reflections on Brathy's Case," 78 *Law Quarterly Review* (1962).

34. Fingarette, *The Meaning of Criminal Insanity,* p. 135.

35. Ibid.

36. Helen Silving, *The Constituent Elements of Crime* (Springfield, Ill.: Charles C Thomas, 1967), pp. 3–35.

37. Ibid., p. 27.

38. Ibid.

39. Ibid.

Suggested Further Reading

Fingarette, Herbert, "Punishment and Suffering," Presidential Address, Fifty-first Annual Pacific Meeting of the A.P.A., Portland, Oregon, March 26, 1977.

Korn, Richard, "Of Crime, Criminal Justice and Corrections," *University of San Francisco Law Review,* 74 (1971).

Mackie, J. L., "Morality and the Retributive Emotions," *Criminal Justice Ethics,* 1, no. 1 (Winter/Spring 1982), 3–10.

Schoenfeld, C. G., "In Defense of Retribution in the Law," *Psychoanalysis Quarterly,* 35 (1966), 108–21.

Wertheimer, Alan, "Deterrence and Retribution," *Ethics,* 86 (1976), 181–99.

15. ISSUES IN LAW ENFORCEMENT

1. POLICE DISCRETION

Once the state decides which acts are criminal, it becomes the responsibility of the police to enforce those decisions. Strictly speaking, the police are mandated to enforce all the laws in every case. Because of the number of laws and lawbreakers relative to the small number of police, officers in practice exercise considerable *discretion* in carrying out the task of enforcement.

In addition to investigating crimes, police are expected to maintain order and to perform a variety of public duties, from directing traffic to escorting dignitaries and rescuing lost children. Given the broad scope and complexity of the police officer's job, the question of discretion becomes a critical one. Police agencies must decide how much time to allot to each function, which laws to enforce most vigorously, and what means to employ in performing their several tasks.

The issue of police discretion poses several ethical problems. Although discretion may be a practical necessity in law enforcement, it is difficult to justify on ethical grounds. A prime question involves the fairness of selective enforcement: unless everyone who commits a crime is pursued by police, is it fair for anyone to be arrested? One criterion for justice is that similar cases be treated similarly. Another standard requires that each case be decided on its individual justice-making merits. Which crimes should the police investigate and why? Who will be arrested, charged, and eventually tried?

Who should make the decisions, and what criteria ought to be used in making them?

A utilitarian approach to the issue of police discretion stresses the deterrent effect of enforcing some laws more strictly than others. In this view, since the goal of a criminal justice system is to deter crime, police are justified in concentrating their efforts on apprehending violators whose arrest is most likely to prevent other crimes from occurring. The question of fairness is secondary to that of effective crime prevention.

The deontological goal of criminal justice is retribution. On this view, all lawbreakers ought to be held accountable for their offenses and punished appropriately. Police discretion is justified deontologically by reference to the requirement that punishment be appropriate. Deontologists hold that punishment should be proportional to the amount of harm a crime causes. Thus, if police cannot arrest all violators, they are justified in pursuing offenders whose crimes are more harmful. This assessment does not, however, provide us with criteria for determining greater harm. Should we say, for example, that "street crimes" (mugging, rape, assault and the like) are more harmful or less harmful than "white-collar crimes" such as embezzlement, stock market manipulation, and tax fraud?

Discretion in policing is related to similar problems in other areas of criminal justice. Plea bargaining and the discretion allowed judges in sentencing raise similar ethical questions. The article by Elizabeth Beardsley in Chapter 17 of this unit addresses the issue of discretion in sentencing.

In the following essay Egon Bittner examines the effects of police discretion in the criminal justice system. Bittner holds that many statutes are drafted with loopholes which tacitly permit discretionary enforcement. Such laws have the effect of becoming "all purpose control devices" in the hands of police. The author believes that some discretionary enforcement is justified. He argues that making police officers licensed professionals will help to reduce undesirable discretionary practices.

EGON BITTNER

Arrest and Detention

No other aspects of police practice have received more scholarly attention in the recent past than the procedures and decisions connected with invoking the law. The principal result of these inquiries was the discovery that policemen have, in effect, a greater degree of discretionary freedom in proceeding against offenders than any other public official. This is so because an officer's decision not to make an arrest is not a matter of record, contrary to the decision of the prosecutor not to prosecute, and the decision of the judge to dismiss or to acquit. The condition creates something of a legal paradox because, according to the discovered facts, the policeman who is in terms of the official hierarchy of power, competence, and dignity, on the lowest rung of the administration of justice, actually determines the "outer perimeter of law enforcement," and thus actually determines what the business of his betters will be. The vexation increases when one realizes that this situation is not the result of simple misunderstandings or evasions, which could be remedied by direct corrective measures, but is deeply rooted in the nature of the law itself. For example, the penal codes of many states contain provisions that make gambling a culpable offense. Yet, according to prevailing interpretations, these statutes, though they were drafted in ways allowing no exception, were directed only against some forms of gambling. Since writing this interest into the law would have created loopholes permitting the activity the control of which was desired to elude prosecution, it becomes necessary to rely on the good judgment of the arresting policeman to put the legislative intent into effect. Thus, when a policeman comes upon a gathering of citizens engaged in a game of chance, it is his duty to consider first whether this is an instance of what the legislators had in mind before he makes an arrest. Accordingly, all the courts can consider in the realm of gambling offenses is what the police have found, according to their understanding, to be suitable for their concerns.

The problem does not end, however, with the duty of the police to discern tacit legislative intent implied in a large number of the provisions of the penal codes. Associated with it is another difficulty of at least equal seriousness. Since the reasons the officer has to invoke the law selectively are implied, rather than explicit, there is no way of ascertaining whether his reasons are in accord with legisla-

Reprinted with permission from *The Functions of the Police in Modern Society* by Egon Bittner (Rockville, Md.: U.S. Department of Health, Education and Welfare, National Institute of Mental Health, 1970). DHEW Publication No. (HSM) 72-9103. Footnotes have been edited and renumbered.

tive intent. For example, a group of youths tossing coins on the sidewalk can be arrested and charged with gambling even though the legislature supposedly did not intend to bar such games. In such cases the decision to invoke the law could be based on the officer's desire to get at these people because they are troublesome in some other ways. Perhaps they are known panderers, but evidence cannot be secured to charge them with pandering. The point is, laws, the enforcement of which is meant to be discretionary, do not impinge only on a specifically intended area of application. Instead, they become all-purpose control devices.[1] As long as even a moderately sizable inventory of such laws is available, any policeman worth his salt ought to be able to arrest almost anyone on formally defensible grounds, with relatively little effort. Naturally, this condition creates favorable conditions for the expression of personal prejudice and for the advancement of corrupt interest. But even if no policeman ever invoked the discretionary law outside the scope of its intended application with any but reputable purposes in mind, a condition in which most people appear to have a license to transgress that can be denied to some by no more than an officer's fiat must obviously trouble the legal mind. Panderers should be arrested for pandering. If they can be arrested for merely pitching pennies, then everybody who merely pitches pennies should be arrested. It is one thing to say that the legislature implicitly exempted friendly games from prosecution and quite another to say that they exempted only some friendly games and not others and it is for the policeman to decide which ones they meant.

The main reason why policemen do not follow a simple rule of impartiality in the enforcement of laws is that their conception of the import of law differs from that which lawyers entertain. To be sure, these two conceptions have an area of overlap encompassing all major crimes that are universally proscribed. Here, for policemen and lawyers alike the rule is that whosoever transgresses will be arrested for that reason and that reason

alone. Outside of this area policemen follow the explicit or implicit instructions of the law only occasionally. That is, people who are thought to have committed a robbery are arrested for that reason, but people who are arrested and charged with begging are rarely so treated because they were caught begging and virtually never for that reason alone. To put it bluntly, in discretionary law enforcement involving minor offenses, policemen use existing law largely as a pretext for making arrests. This makes it specious to inquire whether arrest practices conform with the law; in most cases they do, without, however, the law being the determining factor for making the arrest. Because persons who in the judgment of the police should be detained must be charged with something the law recognizes as valid grounds for detention, many arrests have the outward aspects of adhering to principles of legality. In point of fact, however, the real reasons for invoking the law are wholly independent of the law that is being invoked. The point to be emphasized is not that this procedure is illegal, though it often enough is, but that it has nothing to do with considerations of legality. The earlier mentioned panderers were really gambling, but the reason why they were arrested was that they were panderers, a fact that is not legally recognizable in the charge lodged against them. Is this procedure justifiable? It certainly cannot be easily impugned, for there is no question about the fact that the charged offense has taken place. But the practice has some remarkable consequences. For instance, the suspension of vagrancy statutes need not in any way affect the rates of persons who were earlier arrested under these provisions. They are simply charged with some other kind of offense. Similarly, it could not possibly matter less that the New York State "Stop and Frisk" law is surrounded by rules that are supposed to govern its application. It is impossible to imagine a situation in which a patrolman could not cite these rules to justify invoking the law, whatever the real reasons were that motivated him. This puts lawmakers in a curious position. They are not unlike the engineer who develops a screwdriver that is marvelously designed for a specific purpose only to find that people use it to open cans, to knock holes into walls, to chastise children, to spread mayonnaise, and to do all sorts of other things that need doing, occasionally even to tighten a screw.

While for the lawyer police detention is justifiable only as a first link in a chain of legal processes,[2] for the policeman it is, in the large majority of cases, merely a practical device, the legal aspects of which are a pure outward formality about which he has little if any care. He might wish that the people he arrests would receive harsher treatment in the courts than they do, but knowing that this will not come to pass, that, indeed, a large number of people whom he arrests will either not be prosecuted at all or discharged if prosecuted, does not stop him from making arrests. This is so because in all cases but those involving major crimes, arrests are remedies with an immediate import, they are attuned to situational exigencies, they are not preliminary to punishment but punishment in themselves. Thus, even when a trial follows such arrests it "becomes not the determiner of guilt or innocence but a procedure for release of the accused from punishment previously meted out."[3]

Throwing people into jail for periods of time ranging anywhere from a few hours to a few days, without any intention of prosecuting them, is probably the oldest police routine in existence. No one knows the true extent to which this practice exists today, whether it is on the increase or the decline. Some jurisdictions seem to have succeeded, or nearly succeeded, in abolishing it and in them all arrestees are presented to magistrates. But we also have data indicating that in some cities more than 95 percent of all persons detained because of allegation of prostitution or gambling are simply released from custody after a day or two. The larger picture of how many people are in police jails across the country on any particular night, who they are, and why they are there cannot be estimated in even terms of a rough guess.

What we do know, however, is that it has been argued for a long time that policemen need the power to place some persons in temporary detention. For example, the so-called "golden rule" directs the overnight detention of inebriates for their own protection.[4] It is very likely that the net cast to catch the drunk also takes in persons who are simply sick, feeble, disoriented, and without a place to stay. And there are some persons who are jailed for short periods on the request of their relatives who, however, do not wish to go so far as instituting prosecution.[5] Finally, large numbers of persons, such as known prostitutes, gamblers, and con-artists, are detained temporarily for the sole purpose of inducing them to be less brazen and to impede their illegal activities, i.e., as part of a harassment program.

Clearly the powers of the police to abridge the freedom of citizens temporarily is not simply a legal problem and, therefore, not solvable by increasing the volume and specificity of legal regulation. Only on the police blotter or in the court record does it appear that detained persons were detained because they engaged in some specific illegal activity. For some this reflects reality well enough. But from the vantage point of police interest and in consideration of the real reasons that determined the decision to take someone into custody, the vast majority of detained persons appear to have been perceived as diffusely troublesome, inappropriate in their manner, vaguely dangerous, dissolute, disruptive, or in various other ways a bane.[6] The presently prevailing opinion of most knowledgeable legal students of police practice is that discretionary law enforcement should be brought into closer accord with legal norms. But it is virtually certain that this approach, by itself, will produce no more than a specious kind of correctness. It is, after all, inconceivable that an officer could not find some label in any code to justify detention, and the more comprehensive the code, the more likely that he will be devious about it. In the last analysis, it will remain the officer's judgment that must be evaluated when he makes an arrest; and because judgment is inherently difficult to control we must see to it that we have officers whom we can trust not only because they are personally honest but also because they are expert.

Many of the practices encompassed by the discretionary freedom policemen enjoy are revolting, but the pressures to do something about it should not lead to fruitless efforts. Moreover, for the moment at least, it is certainly profoundly regrettable but not altogether repugnant that a man who is so lacking in self-control as to risk squandering his weekly earnings on drink, depriving his family of its livelihood, be kept in jail for a short period. Nor is it inhuman of an officer to arrest a skid-row derelict for no other reason than to spare him from the risks of exposure or assault. It is easy to say that other kinds of services should be made available to serve such needs. In fact, very little movement in this direction is discernible. And there are good reasons for saying that making other resources available will become a viable prospect only if and when the police will establish continuous cooperative relations with medicine, psychiatry, and social work. At present, these relations could scarcely be worse. Policemen are generally hostile and distrustful toward physicians and welfare workers, and the latter make no attempt to conceal their often less than well founded feelings of superiority. This condition will not change until the policeman achieves the status that is in a real sense coequal to that of other remedial agents, that is, until he actually becomes, and will be recognized as, a licensed professional. Though this will not answer the question whether panderers should be arrested because they violated gambling laws, nor whether prostitutes should be jailed for purposes of harassment, it will at least create conditions in which such questions can be addressed jointly by all concerned agents and discussed without aspersions and acrimony.

In sum, police recourse to temporarily abridging the freedom of citizens deserves recognition as a practical peace-keeping method that has only in its most outward aspects the character of a legal action. Though it is often resorted to for inadequate or deplorable reasons, it is not wholly without justification. In its seemingly justified form the procedure involves a good deal of knowledge and considerate judgment. Like the use of physical force, temporary detention is a measure of last resort, and no policeman who is methodical in his work uses it in any other way.

Notes

1. Herman Goldstein writes, "Broadly stated laws are, after all, one of the lesser concerns of the police. Most attention of law-enforcement officers in recent years has focused upon legal provisions which are too narrow. The average police official is not very concerned about having the authority to enforce adultery statutes and not having the manpower or the community support necessary to do so. He is much more concerned because of his inability to attack organized crime effectively. And there may be an occasion upon which he can use an obscure or otherwise unenforced law to launch an oblique attack against a situation or activity which he feels warrants action on his part. His attitude is often that the law should be left on the books; it may come in handy sometime. Why impose self-limitations on police authority beyond those established by the legislature?" at p. 40 of his "Dealing with Crime: Can All Laws Be Enforced?" *Current*, 46 (February 1964) 39–42.

2. The law appears to allow a genuine error. If it is learned that an arrest was a mistake, the suspect can be released without having been presented before a magistrate. This raises the question of how freely policemen may err.

3. C. D. Robinson, "Alternatives to Arrest of Lesser Offenders," *Crime and Delinquency*, (January 1965) 8–21, at p. 9.

4. The term "golden rule" refers to the practice of overnight detention of derelicts in city jails. The practice was once advocated as part of an urban reform movement. See R. H. Bremmer, "The Civic Revival in Ohio: Police, Penal and Parole Policies in Cleveland and Toledo," *American Journal of Economics and Sociology*, 14 (1955) 387–398.

5. In these cases arrests are ordinarily made only when the offending person also fails in being as obsequious towards the intervening officer as the latter expects. At other times, officers bring the quarreling parties to a "hearing" at the police station: see R. L. Parnas, "Police Response to Do-

mestic Disturbance," *Wisconsin Law Review* (1967) 914–960.

6. This problem has an obverse facet that deserves mention. Just as police often arrest persons on specious grounds, they often do not arrest others who should, according to principles of legality, be charged with crimes. When this policy, which exists everywhere, was once officially proclaimed (in England), it resulted in the dismissal of the candid police official: W. N. Osborough, "Immunity for the English Supermarket Shoplifter?" *American Journal of Comparative Law,* 13 (1964) 291–299. Osborough quotes Lord Morris of Borthy-y-Gest with reference to this way of exculpating offenders: "The fact that prosecutions have been, and doubtless will continue to be, infrequent demonstrates that the law is the handmaiden of reason." *ibid.,* p. 297.

Suggested Further Reading

American Friends Service Committee, "Discretion," *The Struggle for Justice.* New York: Hill and Wang, 1971, Chapter 8.

Cohen, Howard, "A Dilemma for Discretion," in *Police Ethics: Hard Choices in Law Enforcement,* ed. W. Heffernan and T. Stroup. New York: John Jay University Press, 1984.
——"Authority: The Limits of Discretion," in *Moral Issues in Police Work,* ed. F. Elliston and M. Feldberg. Totowa, N.J.: Rowman and Allanheld, 1984.
Dillon, Martin C., "What Are Police For?" in *The Police in Society,* ed. Emilio C. Viano and Jeffrey Reiman. Lexington, Mass.: Lexington Books, 1975, pp. 11–18.
Doyle, James F., "Police Discretion, Legality and Morality," in *Police Ethics: Hard Choices in Law Enforcement,* ed. W. Heffernan and T. Stroup. New York: John Jay University Press, 1984.
Goldstein, Joseph, "Police Discretion Not to Invoke the Criminal Process: Low Visibility Decisions in the Administration of Justice," *Yale Law Journal,* 69 (November–March 1959–60).
Hanewicz, Wayne, "Discretion and Order," in *Moral Issues in Police Work,* ed. F. Elliston and M. Feldberg. Totowa, N.J.: Rowman and Allanheld, 1984.

DECISION SCENARIO 1

Police Discretion

The Governor's office was leading a campaign against unethical behavior of elected officials. The Governor himself was pressing for a legislative package to enforce his views. The legislature was resistant by nature to his proposals. In particular, the legislators turned a deaf ear to this one, saying it was another stepping-stone the Governor was using in his quest for the White House.

On orders from the Governor himself, the Attorney General's office began a preliminary investigation into the actions of local officials. When the investigators ascertained some reason to believe misconduct prevailed, they informed the Attorney General that evidence was scarce and hard to find. Official misconduct at this level, they told him, used the "old boy" system. The local supervisor, for instance, would hire a crony for a municipal project and accept a bill two or three times higher than the actual work. A percentage of the padded account would be returned to him in the form of services in his nonofficial business.

To find good evidence would be difficult, an aide to the Attorney General reasoned, even with the presumption of guilt. It would take months for a single locale, and there were nearly five hundred throughout the state. And each town and village had many different officials. Why not, he asked, be methodical and efficient? He proposed to concentrate on one kind of official in thirty-five "politically sensitive" areas.

The office of the Attorney General accepted the scheme. Someone in the road construction machinery business was recruited. For months he plied the state, back and forth, holding meetings with the highway supervisors of the preselected towns. After gaining their confidence, he suggested that each could utilize a portion of their snow-removal budget in the following way: He would draw up a bill of sale of a moderately priced salter with a greatly inflated shipping charge. For delivery, he would send a bottom-of-the-line model, indistinguishable except for the engine and transmission. The net difference was $25,000, of which his cut was 25 percent.

The following summer the Attorney General's office announced indictments against all but two of the highway supervisors. The Governor was pleased with the timing, since his Ethics in Politics bill was being debated by the state assembly.

Questions

1. Did the Attorney General's office use ethically sound means for a just end? Unsound means? Was it fair to act on a presumption of wrongdoing?

2. How does the utilitarian justify the Attorney General's use of entrapment?

3. Was the privacy of the local highway superintendents wrongly invaded?

4. Critics of the Governor said that his policy of investigation would breed contempt for and disrespect of the moral force of the law. Is this libertarian rhetoric or does it have moral substance?

5. Only five of the thirty-three indictments were returned with a guilty verdict. Furthermore, more than half the officials won reelection to their position. What effect, if any, do these facts have regarding the deterrent effect of entrapment?

2. THE PROBLEM OF ENDS VERSUS MEANS

Police officers have direct power over the lives of citizens, a power greater and more immediate than that of all other public officials. Exercise of this power involves many ethical considerations. For example, inflicting harm on others is generally considered wrong, yet the police have the authority and opportunity to inflict intentional harm, even to kill. How can the harm be justified? In particular, can the use of lethal force be justified? In states that have abolished the death penalty, police are still licensed to kill through the use of deadly force. It is paradoxical that a suspect who could *not* be executed if tried and convicted might be lawfully killed by police before any trial takes place.

Another ethical issue in police work involves the use of deception by officers. Is it ethically permissible for police to lie or practice trickery to detect or deter crime? Does such deception constitute entrapment? Critics argue that the use of deceptive tactics by police is not justified. They claim that the practices breed mistrust and dishonesty and are counterproductive to the goals of a lawful society. Proponents of the use of deceptive tactics contend that one must "fight fire with fire." They insist that some criminals are so sophisticated and pose such a threat to society that extraordinary means are needed to deal with them. Ethical questions about deception by police are related to similar questions in the health care and legal professions. However, deception by physicians or attorneys is usually justified on grounds of benefit (paternalism) to the patient or client, while deception in law enforcement is justified on grounds of benefit to society as a whole. In each instance proponents argue that deception is justified if it produces important benefits unattainable by other means. [**See Health Care, Chapter 5, Section 4 and Criminal Justice, Chapter 16, Section 2.**]

While it is an important goal of criminal justice and especially of law enforcement officers to investigate and apprehend criminals, the goal of protecting the innocent is also of paramount importance. These goals often are incompatible. If a large amount of evidence is required for conviction, fewer people will be convicted and more guilty persons will escape punishment. On the other hand, if less evidence is required, fewer guilty people will be acquitted while more innocent persons will be mistakenly convicted. American law places considerable emphasis on the rights of the accused and stresses protection of the innocent. A suspect is considered innocent until proven guilty by the state, and so the accused does not have the burden of proof. Such an emphasis leads to restraints on the methods which police may use in obtaining evidence. Police officers and their supporters complain that their effectiveness is undermined by the restraints. Critics of their position insist that still more restraints are needed to ensure the protection of the innocent and guarantee due process of law to suspects.

In the following selection Carl B. Klockars discusses situations in which a police officer feels compelled to use "dirty" means to accomplish undeniably good ends. The author contends that the public demands such actions by police on occasion. His solution to the ethical dilemma involved is to make officers legally accountable for their acts. Klockars argues that police will be less likely to use their power inappropriately if they are liable to legal redress.

In the second article David Appelbaum examines deontological justifications for the police use of lethal force, with particular reference to the work of Charles Fried and Deborah Johnson. The justifications for such force are framed in the context of "special duties, rights, and responsibilities" which characterize professional roles, including that of the police. The author contends that these justifications are inadequate, in part because the police are an institution as well as a profession and, as an institution, they are more properly providers of aid and assistance and less the state's agents of self-defense against criminals. On his account, lethal force has little or no legitimate part in police work.

CARL B. KLOCKARS

The Dirty Harry Problem

When and to what extent does the morally good end warrant or justify an ethically, politically, or legally dangerous means for its achievement? This is a very old question for philosophers. Although it has received extensive consideration in policelike occupations and is at the dramatic core of police fiction and detective novels, I know of not a single contribution to the criminological or sociological literature on policing that raises it explicitly and examines its implications.[1] This is the case in spite of the fact that there is consider-

Carl B. Klockars, "The Dirty Harry Problem," ed. Frederick A. Elliston and Michael Feldberg, *Moral Issues in Police Work* (Totowa, N.J.: Rowan & Allanheld, 1985), pp. 55–71.

able evidence to suggest that it is not only an ineluctable part of police work, but a moral problem with which police themselves are quite familiar. There are, I believe, a number of good reasons why social scientists have avoided or neglected what I call the "Dirty Harry" problem in policing, not the least of which is that it is insoluble. Yet, a great deal can be learned about police work by examining some failed solutions, three of which I consider in the following pages. First it is necessary to explain what a Dirty Harry problem is and what makes it so problematic.

The Dirty Harry problem draws its name from the 1971 Warner Brothers film *Dirty Harry* and its chief protagonist, antihero Inspector "Dirty Harry" Callahan. In the film are a number of events which dramatize the problem in different ways, but the most explicit and most complete episode places Harry in the following situation. A 14-year-old girl has been kidnapped and is being held captive by a psychopathic killer. "Scorpio," who has already struck twice, demands $200,000 ransom to release the girl, whom he has buried with just enough oxygen to keep her alive for a few hours. Harry delivers the ransom and, after enomorus exertion, finally meets Scorpio, who decides to renege on his bargain, let the girl die, and kill Harry. Harry manages to stab Scorpio in the leg, but not before Scorpio seriously wounds Harry's partner, an inexperienced, idealistic, slightly ethnic, former sociology major.

Scorpio escapes, but Harry tracks him down through the clinic where he was treated for his wounded leg. Harry breaks into Scorpio's apartment, finds guns and other evidence of his guilt, and finally confronts Scorpio on the 50-yard line of a football stadium and shoots him in the leg. Standing over Scorpio, Harry demands to know where the girl is buried. Scorpio refuses to disclose her location, demanding his rights to a lawyer. As the camera draws back from the scene Harry stands on Scorpio's bullet-mangled leg to torture the information from him.

As it turns out, the girl is already dead and Scorpio must be set free. Neither the gun found in the illegal search, nor the confession Harry extorted, nor any of its fruits—including the girl's body—would be admissible in court.

The preceding scene, the heart of *Dirty Harry,* raises a number of issues of far-reaching significance for the sociology of the police.

The End of Innocence

As stated already, the Dirty Harry problem asks when and to what extent the morally good end warrants or justifies an ethically, politically, or legally dangerous means to its achievement. In itself, this question assumes the possibility of a genuine moral dilemma and posits its existence in a means–ends arrangement that may be expressed as shown in Table 1.

It is important to specify clearly the terms of the Dirty Harry problem not only to show that it must involve the juxtaposition of good ends and dirty means, but also to show what must be proven to demonstrate that a Dirty Harry problem exists. If one could show, for example, that Box B is always empirically empty or that in any given case the terms of the situation are better read in some other means–end arrangement, Dirty Harry problems vanish. At this first level, however, I suspect that no one could exclude the core scene of *Dirty Harry* from the class of Dirty Harry problems. There is no question that saving the life of an innocent kidnapping victim is a

Table 1

| | | MEANS | |
		Morally good (+)	Morally dirty (−)
E Morally good		A	B
N (+)		+ +	− +
D			The Dirty Harry Problem
		———	
S			
Morally dirty		C	D
(−)		+ −	− −

"good" thing, nor that grinding the bullet-mangled leg of Scorpio to extort a confession is "dirty."[2]

In addition, a second level of criteria of an empirical and epistemological nature must be met before a Dirty Harry problem actually comes into being. The criteria involve the connection between the dirty act and the good end. What must be known and, which is most important, known before the dirty act is committed, is that it will result in the achievement of a good end. In any absolute sense this is impossible to know, of course, in that no acts are ever completely certain in their consequences. Thus the question is always a matter of probabilities. But it is helpful to break those probabilities into classes that attach to various subcategories of the overall question. In the given case, this level of problem seems to require that three questions be satisfied, although not all with the same level of certainty.

The first question, is Scorpio able to provide the information Harry seeks, is an epistemological question about which, in *Dirty Harry*, we are absolutely certain. Harry met Scorpio at the time of the ransom exchange. Not only did Scorpio admit the kidnapping, but with the ransom demand he sent one of the girl's teeth and a description of her clothing, which positively identified his victim.

Second, we must know that dirty means and nothing other than dirty means are likely to achieve the good end. One can, of course, never be sure that one is aware of or has considered all possible alternatives, but in *Dirty Harry* there appears to be no reason for Scorpio to confess to the girl's location without being coerced to do so.

The third question to be satisfied at this empirical and epistemological level concedes that dirty means are the only possible effective method, but asks whether or not, in the end, they will be in vain. We know in *Dirty Harry* that they were, and Harry himself, at the time of the ransom demand, admits he believes that the girl is already dead. Does not this possibility or likelihood destroy the justification

for Harry's dirty act? Although it surely would if Harry knew positively that the girl was dead, it does not while even a small probability exists of her being saved. The good to be achieved is so unquestionably good that even a small possibility of its achievement demands that it be tried. For this reason, in philosophical circles the Dirty Harry problem has largely been restricted to questions of national security, revolutionary terrorism, and international war. Also for this reason, the Dirty Harry problem in detective fiction almost always involves murder.

Once we have satisfied ourselves that a Dirty Harry problem is conceptually possible and that, in fact, we can specify one set of concrete circumstances in which it exists, one might think that the most difficult question is what ought to be done. On the contrary, I suspect that most people would want Harry to do something dirty in the situation. I know I would want him to do what he did, and what is more, I would want anyone who policed for me to be prepared to do so. Put differently, I want to have men and women of moral courage and sensitivity as police officers.

For this reason, the Dirty Harry problem poses its most irksome predicament: that a police officer, at least in this specific case, cannot be both just and innocent. The troublesome issue in the Dirty Harry problem is not whether a right choice can be made, but that the choice must always be between at least two wrongs. And in choosing to do either wrong, the police officer inevitably taints or tarnishes himself.

Similar situations created by Dashiell Hammett, Raymond Chandler, Raoul Whitfield, Horace McCoy, James M. Cain, Lester Dent, and dozens of other authors of hard-boiled detective stories distinguished these writers from what has come to be called the "classical school" of detective fiction. What these men could not stomach about Sherlock Holmes (Arthur Conan Doyle), Inspector French (Freeman Wills Crofts), and Father Brown (G. K. Chesterton), to name a few of the best, was not that they were virtuous, but that their virtue was unsullied; that the classi-

cal detective's occupation, how he worked, and the jobs he was called upon to do left him morally immaculate. Even the most brilliant defender of the classical detective story, W. H. Auden, was forced to confess that that conclusion gave the stories "magical function," but rendered them impossible as art.[3]

If popular conceptions of police work have relevance for its actual practice—as Egon Bittner and a host of others have argued that they do[4]—the Dirty Harry problem, in one version or another in countless detective novels and in paler imitations on countless television screens (for example, labeled "Parental discretion is advised") is not a minor contribution to police work's "tainted" quality. But we must remember that the revolution of the tough-guy writers, so these writers said, was not predicated on some mere artificial, aesthetic conception. They claimed, with few exceptions, that their works were art. That is, at all meaningful levels the stories were true. I will next examine this claim in the real-life context of the Dirty Harry problem.

Dirty Men and Dirty Work

Dirty Harry problems arise often. For real, everyday policemen, Dirty Harry problems are part of their job and thus considerably more than rare or artificial dramatic exceptions. As an illustration, I will translate some familiar police practices, street stops and searches, and victim and witness interrogation, into Dirty Harry problems, using the three criteria mentioned earlier.

Good Ends and Dirty Means

The first question our analysis must satisfy is, do these activities present the cognitive opportunity for policemen to juxtapose good ends and dirty means to their achievement? It is sufficient to say here that police find crime prevention and the punishment of wrongful or criminal behavior a good thing to achieve. Likewise, they, perhaps more than any other group in society, are intimately aware of the varieties of dirty means available for the

achievement of those good ends. In the case of street stops and searches, these dirty alternatives range from falsifying probable cause for a stop, to manufacturing a false arrest to legitimate an illegal search, to simply searching without the fraudulent covering devices of either. In the case of victim or witness interrogations, dirty means range all from dramaturgically "chilling" (a *Miranda* warning by an edited or unemphatic rating) to Harry's grinding a bullet-shattered leg to extort a confession from him.

While all these practices may be "dirty" enough to satisfy certain people of especially refined sensitivities, does not a special case have to be made, not for the public's perception of the "dirtiness" of certain illegal, deceptive, or sub rosa acts, but for the police's perception of their dirtiness? Hard-boiled police are less sensitive to such things than most of us. How does this "tough-minded" attitude toward dirty means affect our argument? At least at this stage it seems to strengthen it. That is, the failure of police to regard dirty means with the same hesitation as do most citizens seems to suggest that the police use dirty means to achieve good ends more quickly and more readily than would most of us.

The Dirty Means Must Work

In phrasing this second standard for the Dirty Harry problem, we gloss over a whole range of qualifying conditions, some of which we have already considered. The most critical, implied in *Dirty Harry*, is that the person on whom dirty means are to be used must be guilty. It should be pointed out, however, that this standard is far higher than any student of the Dirty Hands problem in politics has ever admitted. In fact, the moral dilemma of Dirty Hands is often dramatized by the fact that dirty means must be visited on innocent victims. These are the innocents, for example, to whom the Communist leader Hoerderer (in Sartre's *Dirty Hands*) refers when he says, "I have dirty hands. Right up to the elbows. I've plunged them in filth and blood. But what do

you hope? Do you think you can govern innocently?"[5]

But even if cases in which innocent victims suffer dirty means commonly qualify as Dirty Harry problems, and by extension innocent victims would be allowable in Dirty Harry problems, a number of factors in the nature and context of policing suggest that police themselves are inclined toward the higher "guilty victim" standard. Although there may be others, the following are probably the most salient.

1. *The Operative Assumption of Guilt.* In street stops and searches as well as interrogations, it is in the nature of the police task that guilt is assumed as a working premise. That is, in order for a police officer to do his/her job, he/she must, unless clearly knowing otherwise, assume that the person seen is guilty and the behavior witnessed is evidence of some concealed or hidden offense. If a driver looks at him "too long" or not at all, or if a witness or suspect talks too little or too much, only the police officer's operative assumption of guilt makes those actions meaningful. Moreover, the police officer is often not in a position to suspend his working assumption until he has taken action, sometimes dirty action, to disconfirm it.

2. *The Worst of All Possible Guilt.* The matter of operative assumption of guilt is complicated further because the police officer is obliged to make a still higher-order assumption of guilt, namely, that the person is not only guilty, but dangerously so. In street stops and searches, for instance, although the probability of encountering a dangerous felon is extremely low, police quite reasonably take the possibility of doing so as a working assumption on the understandable premise that once is enough. Likewise, the premise that one who has the most to hide will try hardest to hide it is a reasonable assumption for interrogation.

3. *The Great Guilty Place Assumption.* The frequency with which police confront the worst of people, places, and occasions creates an epistemological problem of serious psychological proportions. As a consequence of his or her job, the police officer is constantly exposed to highly selective samples of his environment. That he comes to read a clump of bushes as a place to hide, a roadside rest as a homosexual "tearoom," a sweet old lady as a possible robbery victim, or a poor young black as someone about to accost her is not a question of a perverse, pessimistic, or racist personality, but of a person whose job requires that he/she strive to see race, age, sex, and even nature in an ecology of guilt, which can include him if he fails to see it so.[6]

4. *The Not Guilty (This Time) Assumption.* With considerable sociological research and conventional wisdom to support him, the police officer knows that most people in the great guilty city in which he works have committed numerous crimes for which they have never been caught. Thus when a stop proves unwarranted, a search comes up "dry," or an interrogation fails, despite the dirty means, the police officer is not obliged to conclude that the person is innocent, only that, and even this need not always be conceded, he or she is innocent *this time.*

Dirty Means as Ends in Themselves

How do these features of police work, all of which seem to incline police to accept a standard of a guilty victim for their dirty means, bear upon the Dirty Harry problem from which they derive? The most dangerous reading suggests that if police are inclined, and often quite rightly inclined, to believe they are dealing with factually (if not legally) guilty subjects, they become likely to see their dirty acts, not as means to the achievement of good ends, but as ends in themselves—as punishment of guilty people whom the police believe deserve to be punished.

If this line of argument is true, it has the effect, in terms of police perceptions, of moving Dirty Harry problems completely outside the fourfold table of means–ends combinations created to define it. Also important, in terms of our perceptions, Dirty Harry problems of this type can no longer be read as cases of dirty means employed to the

achievement of good ends. For unless we are willing to admit that in a democratic society a police arrogates to itself the task of punishing those whom they think guilty, we are forced to conclude that Dirty Harry problems represent cases of employing dirty means to dirty ends, in which case no one, not the police and certainly not us, is left with any kind of moral dilemma.

The possibility is quite real and quite fearsome, but it is mediated by certain features of police work, of which some inhere in the nature of the work itself and others, imposed from outside, have a quite explicit impact on it. The most important "naturalistic" feature of policing that belies the preceding argument is that the assumption of guilt and all the configurations in the police officer's world that serve to support it often turn out wrong. Precisely because the operative assumption of guilt can be forced on everything and everyone, the police officer who must use it constantly comes to find it leads him/her astray as often as it confirms his/her suspicions.

Similarly, a great many of the things police officers do, some of which we have already conceded appear to police less dirty than they appear to us (faked probable cause for a street stop, manipulated *Miranda* warnings, and so forth), are simply impossible to read as punishments. This is particularly so if we grant a hard-boiled character to our cops.

Of course, neither of these naturalistic restrictions on the obliteration of the means–ends schema is or should be terribly comforting. The extent to which the first is helpful assumes a certain skill and capacity of mind that we may not wish to award to all policemen. The willingness to engage in the constant refutation of one's working worldview presumes a certain intellectual integrity that can go awry. Likewise, the second merely admits that on occasion policemen may do some things that reveal they appreciate that the state's capacity to punish can be greater than theirs.

To both these "natural" restrictions on the obliteration of the means–ends character of Dirty Harry problems, we can add the exclusionary rule. Although the exclusionary rule is the manifest target of *Dirty Harry*, it, more than anything else, makes Dirty Harry problems a reality in everyday policing. It is the great virtue of exclusionary rules—applying in various forms to stops, searches, seizures, and interrogations—that they emphasize the intolerable (though often, I think, moral) desire of police to punish. These rules make the very simple point to police that the more they wish to see a felon punished, the more they are advised to be scrupulous in their treatment of him. Put differently, the best thing Harry could have done for Scorpio was to step on his leg, extort his confession, and break into his apartment, since these actions resulted in his ultimate nonconviction.

If certain natural features of policing and particularly exclusionary rules combine to maintain the possibility of Dirty Harry problems in a context in which a real danger appears to be their disappearance, it does not follow that police cannot or do not collapse the dirty means–good ends division on some occasions and become punishers. I only hold that on many other occasions, collapse does not occur and Dirty Harry problems, as defined, are still possible. What must be remembered, on the way to making their possibility real, is that polic know, or think they know, before they employ a dirty means, that a dirty means and only a dirty means will work.

Only a Dirty Means Will Work

The moral standard that the police know in advance that a dirty means and only a dirty means will work rests heavily on two technical dimensions: (a) the professional competence of the police officer and (b) the range of legitimate working options available to him. Both are intimately connected, although the distinction between them is that the first is a matter of the police officer's individual competence and the second, of the competence of the institutions for which (his department) and with which (the law) he works.

In any concrete case, the relations between these moral and technical dimensions of the Dirty Harry problem are extremely complicated. But it follows that the more competent a police officer is at the use of legal means, the less he or she will be obliged to resort to dirty alternatives. Likewise, the department that trains its policemen well and supplies them with the resources—knowledge and material—to do their work will find that its policemen will not resort to dirty means "unnecessarily," only on those occasions when an acceptable means will not work as well as a dirty one.

While these two premises follow *a priori* from raising the Dirty Harry problem, questions involving the moral and technical roles of laws governing police means invite a very dangerous type of *a priori* reasoning:

> Combating distrust [of the police] requires getting across the rather complicated message that granting the police specific forms of new authority may be the most effective means for reducing abuse of authority which is now theirs; that it is the absence of properly proscribed forms of authority that often impels the police to engage in questionable or outright illegal conduct. Before state legislatures enacted statutes giving limited authority to the police to stop and question persons suspected of criminal involvement, police nevertheless stopped and questioned people. It is inconceivable how any police agency could be expected to operate without doing so. But since the basis for their actions was unclear, the police—if they thought a challenge likely—would use the guise of arresting the individual on a minor charge (often without clear evidence) to provide a semblance of legality. Enactment of stopping and questioning statutes eliminated the need for this sham.[7]

Herman Goldstein's argument and observations are undoubtedly true, but the danger in them is that they can be extended to apply to any dirty means, not only illegal arrests to legitimate necessary street stops, but dirty means to accomplish subsequent searches and seizures all the way to beating confessions out of suspects when no other means will work. But, of course, Goldstein does not intend his argument be extended in these ways.

Nevertheless, his *a priori* argument, dangerous though it may be, points to the fact that Dirty Harry problems can arise wherever restrictions are placed on police methods, and are particularly likely to do so when police themselves perceive that those restrictions are undesirable, unreasonable, or unfair. His argument succeeds in doing what police who face Dirty Harry problems constantly do: rendering the law problematic. But while Goldstein, one of the most distinguished legal scholars in America, can urge change in books, articles, and lectures, it is left to the police officers to take upon themselves the moral responsibility of subverting it with dirty and hidden means.

Compelling and Unquestionable Ends

If Dirty Harry problems can be shown to exist in their technical dimensions—as genuine means—ends problems where only dirty means will work—the question of the magnitude and urgency of the ends that the dirty means may be employed to achieve must still be confronted. Specifically, it must be shown that the ends are so desirable that the failure to achieve them would cast the person who is in a position to do so in moral disrepute.

The two most widely acknowledged ends of policing are peace-keeping and law enforcement. If both these ends were held to be undesirable, Dirty Harry problems would disappear, and some arguments do challenge both ends. For instance, certain radical sectors attempt to reduce the peace-keeping and law-enforcing functions of the police in the United States to acts of capitalist oppression. From such a position flows not only the denial of the legitimacy of any talk of Dirty Harry problems, but also the denial of the legitimacy of the entire police function.[8]

Regardless of the merits of such critiques, it will suffice for the purpose of this analysis to maintain that there is a large "clientele," to use Albert Reiss's term, for both types of police function.[9] And it should be no surprise to anyone that the police themselves accept the legitimacy of their own peace-keeping and law-enforcing ends. Some comment is needed, however, on what the size of the clientele for those functions is and on how compelling and unquestionable are the ends of peace-keeping and law enforcement for them.

There is no more popular, compelling, urgent, or more broadly appealing idea than peace. In international relations, it is potent enough to legitimate the stockpiling of enough nuclear weapons to exterminate every living thing on earth a dozen times over. In domestic affairs, it gives legitimacy to the idea of the state, and the aspirations to it have succeeded in granting to the state an absolute monopoly on the right to legitimate the use of force and a near monopoly on its actual, legitimate use: the police. That peace has managed to legitimate these highly dangerous means to its achievement in virtually every advanced nation in the world is adequate testimony that it qualifies, if any end does, as a good end, so unquestionable and so compelling that it can legitimate risking the most dangerous and dirtiest of means.

The fact is, though, that most American police officers prefer to define their work as law enforcement rather than peace-keeping, even though they may in fact do more of the latter. It is a distinction that should not be allowed to slip away in assuming that the police officer's purpose in enforcing the law is to keep the peace. Likewise, to assume that police simply enforce the law as an end in itself, without meaning, purpose, or end, is contradicted by the widely discretionary behavior of working police and the enormous underenforcement of the law that characterizes most police agencies.

An interpretation of law enforcement that is compatible with empirical studies of police behavior—as peace-keeping is—and police talk in America—which peace-keeping generally is not—is an understanding of the ends of law enforcement as punishment. There are, of course, many theories of punishment, but the police seem inclined toward the simplest: that people who have committed certain acts deserve to be punished for them. What can be

said about the compelling and unquestionable character of this retributive ambition as an end of policing and police?

Both historical and sociological evidence proves that punishment is almost as unquestionable and compelling an end as peace. Historically, we have a long and painful history of punishment, a history longer in fact than the history of the end of peace. Sociologically, the application of what may well be the only culturally universal norm, reciprocity, implies the direct and natural relations between wrongful acts and their punishments.[10] Possibly the best evidence for the strength and urgency of the desire to punish in modern society is the extraordinary complex of rules and procedures democratic states have assembled that prevents legitimate punishment from being administered wrongfully or frivolously.

If we can conclude that peace and punishment are ends unquestionable and compelling enough to satisfy the demands of Dirty Harry problems, we are led to one final question on some sociological theories of the police. If the Dirty Harry problem is at the core of the police role, or at least near it, how can police reconcile their use of—or their failure to use—dirty means to achieve unquestionably good and compelling ends?

Public Policy and Police Morality: Three Defective Resolutions of the Dirty Harry Problem

The contemporary literature on policing appears to contain three quite different types of solution or resolution. But because the Dirty Harry problem is a genuine moral dilemma, that is, a situation that will admit no real solution or resolution, each is necessarily defective. Also, each solution or resolution presents itself as an answer to a somewhat different problem. In matters of public policy, such concealments are often necessary and probably wise, although they have a way of coming around to haunt their architects sooner or later. In discovering that each is flawed and in disclosing the concealments that allow the appearance of resolution, we do not urge that it be held against sociologists that they are not philosophers, nor do we argue that they should succeed where philosophers have failed. Rather, we only wish to make clear what is risked by each concealment and to face candidly their inevitably unfortunate ramifications.

Snappy Bureaucrats

In the works of August Vollmer, Bruce Smith, O. W. Wilson, and those progressive police administrators who follow their lead, a vision of the perfect police agency and the perfect police officer has gained considerable ground. Labeled "the professional model" in police circles—although entirely different from any classical sense of profession or professional—it envisions a highly trained, technologically sophisticated police department, operating free from political interference, with a corps of well-educated police responding obediently to the policies, orders, and directives of a central administrative command. It is a vision of police officers, to use Bittner's phrasing, as "snappy bureaucrats,"[11] cogs in a quasi-military machine who do what they are told out of a mix of fear, loyalty, routine, and detailed specification of duties.

The professional model, unlike other solutions to be considered, is based on the assumption that the police officer's working goals are located within his or her department. The officer will, if told, work vice or traffic, juvenile or homicide, patrol passively or aggressively, and produce one, two, four, or six arrests, pedestrian stops, or reports per hour, day, or week as his department sees fit. In this way the assumption and vision of the professional model in policing is little different from that of any bureaucracy that specifies tasks and sets expectations for levels of production—work quotas—to coordinate a regular, predictable, and efficient service for its clientele.

The problem with this vision of *sine ira et studio* service by obedient operatives is that when the product to be delivered is some form of human service—such as, education,

welfare, health, or police bureaucracies—the result always falls short of expectations. On the one hand the would-be bureaucratic operatives—teachers, social workers, nurses, or police—resent being treated as mere bureaucrats and resist the translation of their work into quotas, directives, rules, regulations, or other abstract specifications. On the other hand, to the extent that the vision of an efficient and obedient human service bureaucracy is realized, the clientele of such institutions typically receive the impression that no one in the institution truly cares about their problems, i.e., is an inhuman bureaucracy. In that the aim of bureaucratization is to locate employees' motives for work within the bureaucracy, the clientele are absolutely correct in their feelings.

To the extent that the professional model succeeds in making the ends of policing locate within the agency, as opposed to moral demands of the tasks the police are asked by their clients to do, it appears to solve the Dirty Harry problem. When it succeeds, it does so by replacing the morally compelling ends of punishment and peace with the less-human, though by no means uncompelling, ends of bureaucratic performance. This resolution does not imply that dirty means will disappear, however, only that the motives for their use will be career advancement and promotion. Likewise, on those occasions when a morally sensitive police officer is compelled by the demands of the situation to use a dirty means, the bureaucratic operative envisioned by the professional model will merely do his/her job. Ambitious bureaucrats and obedient timeservers fail at being the type of morally sensitive souls we want to be policemen. The professional model's bureaucratic resolution of the Dirty Harry problem fails in every other human service agency: it is quite simply an impossibility to create a bureaucrat who cares for anything but his bureaucracy.

The idealized image of the professional model, which has been responded to with an ideal critique, is probably unrealizable. Reality intervenes as the ideal type is approached. The bureaucracy seems to take on weight as

Notes

1. In the contemporary philosophical literature, particularly in relation to the vocation of politics, the question is commonly referred to as the Dirty Hands problem after J. P. Sartre's treatment in *Dirty Hands* (Les Maines Sales, 1948) and in *No Exit and Three Other Plays* (New York: Modern Library, 1950). Despite its modern name, the problem is very old and was taken up by Machiavelli in *The Prince* (1513) and *The Discourses* (1519) (New York: Modern Library, 1950); by Max Weber, "Politics as a Vocation" (1919) in *Max Weber: Essays in Sociology,* ed. and trans. H. Gerth and C. W. Wills (New York: Oxford University Press, 1946), and by Albert Camus, "The Just Assassins" (1949) in *Caligula and Three Other Plays* (New York: Alfred A. Knopf, 1958). See Michael Walzer's brilliant critique of these contributions, "Political Action: The Problem of Dirty Hands," *Philosophy and Public Affairs* 2:2 (Winter 1972). Likewise, the Dirty Hands/Dirty Harry problem is implicitly or explicitly raised in virtually every work of Raymond Chandler, Dashiell Hammett, James Cain, and other *Tough Guys of the Thirties,* ed. David Madden (Carbondale: Southern Illinois University Press, 1968), as they are in all the recent work of Joseph Wambaugh, particularly *The Blue Knight, The New Centurions,* and *The Choirboys* (Little, Brown).

2. "Dirty" here means both "repugnant," in that it offends widely shared standards of human decency and dignity, and "dangerous," in that it breaks commonly shared and supported norms, rules, or laws for conduct. To "dirty" acts there must be both a deontologically based face validity of immorality and a consequentialist threat to the prevailing rules for social order.

3. W. H. Auden, "The Guilty Vicarage," in *The Dyer's Hand and Other Essays* (New York: Alfred A. Knopf, 1956), pp. 146–58.

4. Egon Bittner, *The Functions of Police in Modern Society,* (Rockville, MD: National Institute of Mental Health, 1970), and "Florence Nightingale in Pursuit of Willie Sutton," in *The Potential for Reform of the Criminal Justice System,* vol. 3, ed. H. Jacob (Beverly Hills, CA: Sage Publications, 1974), pp. 11–44.

5. Sartre, *Dirty Hands,* p. 224.

6. One of Wambaugh's characters in *The Choirboys* makes this final point most dramatically when he fails to notice that a young boy's buttocks are flatter than they should be and reads the child's large stomach as a sign of adequate nutrition. When the child dies through his mother's neglect and abuse, the officer rightly includes himself in his ecology of guilt.

7. Herman Goldstein, *Policing a Free Society,* (Cambridge, MA: Ballinger, 1977), p. 72.

8. See, for example, John F. Galliher, "Explanations of Police Behavior: A Critical Review and Analysis," *The Sociological Quarterly* 12 (Summer 1971): 308–18; Richard Quinney, *Class, State, and Crime* (New York: David McKay, 1977).

9. Albert J. Reiss, Jr., *The Police and the Public* (New Haven: Yale University Press, 1971), p. 122.

10. These two assertions are drawn from Graeme Newman's *The Punishment Response* (Philadelphia: J. B. Lippincott Co., 1978).

11. Bittner, *The Functions of Police,* p. 53.

12. Ibid., p. 72.

13. Jerome Skolnick, *Justice Without Trial,* 2nd ed., (New York: Wiley, 1966), p. 182.

DAVID APPELBAUM

Looking Down the Wrong Side of the Gun: The Problems of the Police Use of Lethal Force

Why should one be allowed to kill when others are not? When others are liable for punishment for causing injury or death, why should some be given the right to inflict harm? Philosophers in recent years have turned increasing attention to the ethical issues which arise in the practice of various professions. The question of justifying the practices of the police—especially the use of force, sometimes lethal—has a critical importance. Police are allowed to harm persons in ways whch would be considered immoral in most other contexts. In the extreme case, a police professional is given license to kill a person. Furthermore, the present climate of abuse or misapplication of the entitlement to use deadly force has made the matter of justification all the more necessary.

Ethics of Professionals

The focus of this paper is on the police and their infliction of harm, sometimes lethal. But the issues I want to raise are issues set in the context of the ethics of professionals in general. While it is true that the policeman's job has its own duties, rights, and responsibilities, it shares with the jobs of other professions—in medicine, law, social work, civil service, education—the fact that individuals entering professional roles have special duties, rights, and responsibilities neither they nor others have as private citizens. A basic problem of the ethics of professionals is to make sense of these special moral considerations which characterize being a professional. I want to begin with a brief look at the ethical roles of professionals, as outlined in the works of Charles Fried and Deborah Johnson.[1] The importance of their work lies in the attempt to provide a justifica-tion of the duties, rights, and responsibilities of professionals from a non-consequentialist, or deontological, perspective.

Most frequently, the actions of professionals are justified and defended by pointing out the good that will result from undertaking them. For instance, when a fireman batters down a door to save a sleeping child, it is said that the wrongness of the act of destroying property is strongly overridden by the rightness of rescuing the child. Or, when a physician has a patient undergo a painful, unan-aesthetized examination procedure, we say that the pain suffered is greatly outweighed by the good of diagnosing the illness. Similarly, people frequently argue that the police use of lethal force in the end benefits society, i.e., keeps it strong and well-ordered. I do not plan to discuss the shortcomings of consequential-ist ethical theories. Instead, I want to examine the possibility of a deontological justification of lethal force—a justification based on ethics and moral obligation. Because deontological theories usually include a categorical impera-tive against all killing whatsoever, there will be special significance in this endeavor.

In particular, this paper will point up a ma-jor shortcoming of Fried's and Johnson's deontological analysis of the question of lethal force. I will use this occasion to examine the so-called right of police to inflict lethal harm within the context of recent contract theory, as elaborated by John Rawls.[2]

Fried's General Views

Let me begin by speaking about Fried's gen-eral views concerning the ethics of profession-als. For Fried, the overall structure of morality is one having a great deal of latitude in it. There is a primary moral duty "to do right and avoid wrong." Essentially, this involves rendering fair shares to others and avoiding harming them intentionally. Though these norms of actions are categorical—they cannot be overridden by any set of consequences— they define only the limits of a wide moral space within which a person is free to choose to do whatever he likes. When we examine the categorical norms more closely, the space widens.

The negative injunction against wrongdoing is an injunction against *intentional* harm. Not all harm is committed intentionally. Again, the firefighter who drags a person through rubble, or the physician who breaks the patient's arm to reset it, does not intentionally do harm. Fried acknowledges that, because the eventual outcomes of long causal chains resulting from our actions may produce harm, we would be paralyzed to act if our morality prescribed doing harm *simpliciter*.

Central to his view is the doctrine of double effect. The doctrine of *double effect* states that a person x does not intend the side-effects of his action, even when x knows or has reason to believe those side-effects will occur. For instance, the firefighter means to rescue the person caught in the burning building. He knows that dragging the victim is bound to cause him harm. Nonetheless, his causing the victim harm is not done intentionally. His causing harm is neither the means of, nor the end to, his action. Or, the physician means to perform an eye transplant on A, using B's eyes. He does not thereby blind B intentionally. Blinding B is neither an end nor a means to what he does, though he knows what he does will render B blind. The doctrine of double effect, together with its notion of intention, remains problematic, a fact which Fried acknowledges.

Given the breadth of free choice not constrained by moral considerations, an individual, on Fried's account, can choose various roles in life, professional and nonprofessional. The effect of being in a professional role is to create an umbrella of moral permissibility. Under this umbrella, a professional is to undertake actions which may, on the balance, bring harm to other persons, while serving the interests of his client. This is so because the harm is the unintended, though foreseen, side-effect of the action. That is, the doctrine of double effect guarantees the professional the immunity necessary to carry out the mission of his profession. Thus, the psychiatrist of a suspected burglar is free to withhold information that might lead to his client's conviction and to the recovery of stolen property. He is free to do so because his intention is to serve his client, the judicial harm and the injury to the burgled party being but the foreseen but unintended consequence.

Much more needs to be said about Fried's views, particularly with regard to how professional obligations do not conflict with the obligations of morality. But this much can serve as a basis of discussion of how the police professional's right to use lethal force can be justified.

Within the broad limits of action set by morality, one may choose a professional role, and benefit from the umbrella of permissibility the profession affords. Fried's views, however, do not create a free-for-all. A person, for instance, cannot choose to be a professional terrorist, since being a terrorist involves intentionally bringing harm and even death to other persons. Parallel considerations might seem to apply to the choice of a police professional, since causing injury, harm, and suffering is an integral part of the policeman's job. It would be difficult to conceive of police work without this particular element. Can Fried's account show the permissibility of police use of force, sometimes lethal?

Let us take a typical example from the newspapers.[3] An officer arrives at a supermarket and recognizes an escaped felon holding a gun to the manager's head. The robber lets the manager go, who darts out the front door. Believing it to be the felon, the officer opens fire and kills the manager. Now, it is certain that harm has been caused by the policeman; is it *intentional*? Suppose we try to apply the doctrine of double effect, which distinguishes what is done intentionally from what is merely foreseen. In either case, it can be neither our means nor our end to harm someone. Clearly, the officer did not have as his end to kill the suspect. His *end* was to uphold the law or to maintain the order of society or to stop a crime in progress. But as certainly, his means was to harm the person fleeing, even if it was not to cause his death. To harm the fleeing suspect was his means of stopping him. The policeman, therefore, *intentionally* harmed the person.

Innocent Aggressor Rule

If Fried's account is to justify this typical instance of police action, some principle other than that of the double effect must be brought to bear. It is here that Deborah Johnson amplifies Fried's views. Any such qualifying principle clearly must be consistent with the ethical foundation of the categorical form of action, of not inflicting harm intentionally. The principle which she seeks to establish is a version of the principle of self-defense, labeled the "innocent aggressor" (IA) rule. The moral defense of police force is cast into a more or less traditional mold, since self-defense is one of the legal defenses commonly given for a policeman's use of the gun.[4]

The innocent aggressor IA rule is more complex than simple self-defense, for reasons we can easily see by returning to our example. In the case of mistaking the identity of the fleeing suspect, the police officer is not under attack. The suspect runs. The officer shoots. There is no clear and manifest danger to his life or limb. It might be argued that the policeman is countering an attack on society. One theory of criminal action has it that the action of the criminal, if grave or violent enough, endangers the fabric of the social order. If this were true, one might regard the police, as Plato did the Guardians of his Republic, as the protectors of the state. This qualification fails, however, because at the time of the shooting, the man is only *suspected* of committing a

crime and thereby endangering the state. And, this assumption proves to be tragically mistaken.

Fried describes IA as follows:[5]

> A and B have a violent quarrel at the conclusion of which B rushes off threatening to get his gun, which is just downstairs, and to shoot B. Moments later, C, who has heard the noise and rushes to lend assistance to A, runs up the stairs and bursts into the room. A, believing this is B returning to kill him, knocks C unconscious as he enters. . . . A thought that the kind of argument I offered to justify self-defense covered him, but he was wrong. Should that matter? Not at all, if the issue is a moral condemnation of A for his original act. For he acted just as we would have him act, had the facts been as he believed them to be. And if there are no grounds for condemning the way he came to that conclusion—for instance, negligently—then how can we say to him that he chose wickedly? . . . If we judge the actor's choice, if we ask how he should choose in the situation that confronts him, then from that perspective we can urge no different action on him than in the paradigm case of self-defense. So, though his case is unfortunate, it is not difficult.

In this description, the role of the police profession is that of A. It is a case of mistaken identity. C is innocent, but the officer causes injury, believing C has attacked B.

Notice that, in order to make IA apply to a case of lethal force, we need to make several additional assumptions.

1. That committing a crime is attacking the state, so that being suspected of committing a crime is being suspected of attacking the state.
2. That the police are the legitimate agents of the state for returning the attack.
3. That the police, when countering the attack, believe the suspect had endangered the laws of the state.

There is also a fourth assumption, which Johnson calls the proportionality thesis, that the police, when countering the attack, undertake an act in severity no greater than the severity of the act of attack itself. Only if these four assumptions are reasonable would we be in a position to say the IA rule justifies police use of force, even lethal force. For, then, police would intend to injure only those persons who threaten to endanger the state. They would not intend to harm the innocent, though sometimes, as in my example, the innocent happen to be harmed.

But do these assumptions have plausibility? The first would appear not to. A person cannot be said to "attack" the state in the same way he might attack another person. An act of assault, or libel, for instance, involves tangible threat to a person's life, property, or livelihood. No such threat to the life of the state exists. If we accept the questionable view that the state is a kind of supra-individual personality, it is still as difficult to see how a civil rights violation, which threatens an individual with loss of opportunity, also threatens the state. Furthermore, when we include the breadth of criminal acts—not only ones of individual violence, but, e.g., ones of embezzlement, failure to report taxable revenues, neglect of alimony payments; mail fraud, conspiracy to withhold information, etc.—the concept becomes even less tenable.

The second assumption views police action as the state's self-defense response. This description cannot be fit to the bulk of police work, which consists of aiding persons in distress. But it is important in that it raises the question of legitimate authority via-à-vis the police. It is both the least questionable and the most questionable assumption, in that while popularly and historically, the claim is credible, how police action serves the interests of a just society remains problematic. I want to return to this problem in the next section.

The third assumption states that the police must have reason to believe suspects have committed an act endangering the state before they apply lethal force. In Fried's descriptions, this corresponds to A's harming innocent aggressor C because "he acted just as we would have him act, had the facts been as he

believes them to be." The police can use force only if they have plausible reasons for believing such an intervention is applicable. This claim breaks down into two parts: (a) the factual claim that the professional does in fact have such reasons at the time he acts, and (b) the normative claim that such reasons count as plausible. We cannot know, without empirical research, the soundness of (a). On the other hand, (b) constitutes the crux of the normative judgment which police professionals undertake in their daily work.

What the criteria are for plausibly believing a person's behavior indicates his having committted a crime involves indices like: his use of violent means, his negative response to preliminary investigation, his apparent attempt to evade capture, etc. The real difficulty with the third assumption, however, is that it posits an order of prudential reasoning which, in many cases of police use of lethal force, may not be present. If, in my example, the police officer responds to the fleeing suspect with a gut reaction to deliver "summary justice," then the third assumption does not pertain. If, that is, it is through negligence rather than plausible belief that the trigger is pulled, the IA view breaks down.

Finally, the proportionality thesis appears to have sufficient appeal for the IA view: use an amount of force consistent with the suspect's own attack. This entails, however, a normative decision as to how much force against what kind of person. There are overtones of a retributive view of punishment in this. The retributivist says that the severity of punishment must fit the crime, since the purpose of punishment is to have one quantum of suffering offset another. Retribution thereby raises the question of how the pain of one compensates for the pain of the other. Similarly, Johnson's idea that police use of lethal force must be commensurate with the suspected criminal action raises the problem of compensatry action. Does the severity of fleeing the scene of a marijuana bust or a petty larceny warrant the proportional response of the policeman's gun? It does, according to this account, if the social pain resulting from breaking the law is sufficiently great. The normative decision to shoot, furthermore, is favored by the fleeing felon laws of most states.

But this is a strange conclusion. Just as a retributive view of punishment overstresses the damage caused, so too Johnson's model places too much weight on the breach of law, without attending to circumstances which might excuse or extenuate the act. It places the burden of decision on the beliefs of the police professional, who in the heat of the moment, may judge that use of the strongest possible force is necessary to thwart the suspect's attack. No doubt, such a burden inclines the professional toward the delivery of summary justice, or toward committing an irrevocable error in judgment: the killing of an innocent person.

If this analysis is correct, the account of the innocent aggressor, which Johnson offers as a justification for police use of force, is incorrect. It is incorrect because it makes the means of violence too readily disposable to the police professional. It is also incorrect because it mistakes the institutional nature of the police. I want to take each of these points up in subsequent sections, in the last, returning to the problem of justification.

Further Considerations

Suppose there were a right, the abuse of which was fairly frequent, and which led to the harm or death of the victims of its abuse. What would the deontologist say? On first glance, one might believe the deontologist would say nothing, since a right is a right, and its abuse, after all, belongs to the consequences. But is the deontologist so callous on the subject of dangerous rights?

What if we agreed that physicians had the right to prescribe mercy-killings for those patients who wished it and who were in terminal stages of incurable diseases, suffered unceasingly from unbearable and untreatable pain, or had undergone irreversible brain damage that left them with only a vegetative function?

Suppose there were a right to administer voluntary euthanasia. Let us first look at the deontological framework, as conceived by Fried and Johnson, in which physicians would face their decisions to euthanize a particular person. That framework distinguishes, by means of the doctrine of the double effect, between what the physician intends to do, and what foreseen, but unintended, consequences follow on his action. For instance, a physician might intend to inject a lethal dosage of morphine into a terminal cancer patient, in order to bring an end to his unending misery. Though death follows, it does not, according to this doctrine, follow, that the physician has intentionally killed the patient. He has not. He has simply let the patient die.

Some philosophers have had doubts about this general line of analysis.[6] Suppose your nephew A was caretaking for his rich uncle B, who is frail, blind, and senile. B stands unknowingly at the top of a steep flight of stairs. Your nephew sees this, and recognizes the danger to A's life, should he fall. He decides that he will do nothing, neither cry out nor otherwise interfere with the plight of his uncle. He reasons to himself: I will intentionally be still, foreseeing the consequences that my uncle will fall, and possibly kill himself; but in this case, I will not intentionally kill him but merely let him die. Contrast this case with that where A intentionally gives B a shove down the stairs. The questions raised by those leery of the double effect is, what is the difference in moral terms between the two cases? Pushing or letting fall are morally equivalent in their failure to protect the life of B. That is to say, A's beliefs and intentions make no difference in determining the rightness of his act. They may affect our judgments about his character, but morally, as well as legally, it is what is done, rather than which is believed to be done, that counts.

We can now see some general difficulties with relying on the doctrine of double effect to justify police use of lethal force. A policeman shoots and kills A, believing A to be a hardened criminal who has escaped prison. A turns out to be the store manager. What difference do the officer's beliefs and intentions make vis-à-vis the rightness of the act of killing? The act is wrong. If it is defensible, that defense must be based on excusing or extenuating circumstances demonstrating the difficulties facing the officer making the normative decision to shoot. A plea of justifiable homicide or manslaughter does not annul the moral wrongness of the killing. It simply claims that under the circumstances, a mistake was made, and that this attenuates the judgment on the act. Attenuates, but does not annul.

It is difficult not to notice that as soon as we bring in the circumstances of the shooting, for its defense, we have escaped the deontological frame which Fried and Johnson provide.[7] How do these normative decisions operate? Return to the physician's right to active voluntary euthanasia. Physicians then inject lethal doses of morphine, upon the patient's request, and bring about the patient's death. There are several kinds of considerations that would influence the physician's decision to apply the dangerous right. He would want to know whether his beliefs about what was the case matched the medical facts. He would check consent forms and authorizations. He would want to reflect on similar decisions he and his colleagues faced in the past.

I think he would also calculate the effects of his action on the clear and present danger the right involves: that active voluntary euthanasia provides the opening wedge for active involuntary euthanasia. The physician who has to live with justifying his normative decisions would have to remain sensitive to the fact that overzealous exercise of his right could have immoral consequences. This consideration clearly is not deontological in nature. Nor can it be. A professional's right of life or death over another person must take cognizance of how the exercise of that right appears, not only how it is. This is so because of the overpresent danger in its misuse or abuse, and of the effects of mistaken professional judgment on the order of the state as a whole.

Similar reasoning applies to the dangerous

right of police professionals to use lethal force. So long as the potential effects of misuse do not enter the normative decision of police to shoot, their beliefs leading them to pull the trigger are not morally informed. Perhaps this is one meaning which can be applied to the charge of summary justice: that the full justice of applying the right to lethal force has not been considered. And, where the police professional undertakes this informed normative decision, and decides to shoot, at least part of his justification is not deontological. Thus, if this account is correct, when police professionals justifiably inflict harm or cause death, their not violating a categorical injunction is based in part on reference to consequences.

Another Way to Arrive at Justification

Johnson's amplification of Fried's account justifying the police professional's right to use lethal force fails to provide an adequate deontological framework for its analysis. It does not, for reasons which Johnson suggests at the end of her paper, because it presents the problem as one of justifying an individual's choice of professional roles, and the duties, rights, and responsibilities attaching to those roles. The police are not simply a profession. They are a social institution. Social institutions constitute the basic structure of the state. In this last section, I want to suggest another possible way of arriving at a justification of the right to lethal force within a deontological frame which is institutionally sensitive. Necessarily, I will be brief.

Justifying the police professional's action in this case is tantamount to arguing for its inclusion in practices chosen by a hypothetical group of indivdiuals contracting together to form a society. When the action belongs to a fair practice of an institution chosen by people contracting into a society, it serves the interests of justice. Modern social contract theory originated in the work of Locke, Kant, and Rousseau, and has recently been amplified by John Rawls.

What exactly does the institution comprised of police professionals do? Earlier, I discussed Johnson's view that the police are essentially the self-defense agency of the state. In them resides the special authority to counter any attack on society. This view is one-sided. It conceives the institutional role of the police professional from the vantage-point of the newsworthy: aggressive enforcement of criminal law. Where over 80 percent of all 911 calls in New York City are requests for aid and assistance by private citizens, or reports of minor infractions of housing or motor vehicle laws, the police are ill-conceived as an institution whose practices primarily concern a response to serious criminal threat. It is important to see the police professional maintaining and regulating the social order on all levels and to all degrees, not merely those established by criminal—and civil—laws. The young child lost on the street, the elderly requiring assistance in entering a premises, the foreigner asking after directions—each turns toward the police professional, who responds according to the accepted practice of the institution, and offers help. The policeman's helping hand is more than a PR slogan; it is the time-worn emblem of his service.

I say this because much of the appeal of Johnson's account derives from a narrow view of police action. If the primary action were countering suspects who threaten to inflict harm on others, or on the state, we would be more inclined to sanction the availability of lethal force to them. But it is not. Over 90 percent of all police never encounter a professional situation which requires them to draw their guns and fire. What Johnson's account fails to provide, moreover, is precisely a justification of the availability of lethal force, its easy potential for use.

To justify the practices of a social institution is, for the contractualist, to attempt to derive it from an initial situation in which people possessing a general equality of opportunity and a desire to join together, agree to undertake the cooperative venture of a society. This is how Locke conceived the problem. The set of practices is just if, on the whole, no social

group is more disadvantaged by them than without, and if the practices tend to maximize the distribution of goods and services throughout the society. Rawls labels this the maxi-min principle, and further stipulates that the choice of institutions in the initial situation is conducted in such a way that no individual knows ahead of time what social position he will occupy. For instance, in choosing the institutions of government, no one can say for sure whether he will end up belonging to the most or the least disadvantaged group, or anywhere between.

Given this all too brief sketch, what kinds of choices of institutions of mutual aid are individuals in the choice situation apt to make? Although no contractualist addresses this problem directly, it is likely that individuals in a position of initial equality would agree to a social institution which would provide assistance to those in difficulty or distress. They would do so because the agency would represent a non-threatening means of enhancing their own opportunities and those of the enterprise as a whole. Thus, the set of practices I have associated with the police professional are ones which a group of individuals would assent to, when contracting together to form a society.

In addition to mutual assistance, this group would have to decide on the matter of mutual defense against threats to the order they are enacting. What powers would they grant to the police? Here, I do not see that the easy availability of lethal force would be one such choice. The right thereby conferred upon the police would be too dangerous, in two ways: (a) it would be easily misapplied or abused, as in the delivery of summary justice, leading to the disadvantaging of some group or groups; and (b) it would lead to the escalation of the use of such force, decreasing the life-opportunities of all. What degree of force would be agreed upon is too complex a problem to take up here. It suffices to say it would be a non-lethal one.

What this account says is that the wide availability of lethal force to the police professional is not morally permissible. It says, on quite general grounds, that the type of situation Johnson envisages, where an innocent aggressor is mortally wounded by a police gun, is morally disallowed. It leaves open the question of a much more limited police use of lethal force, as in SWAT units, along the lines of the British model. Furthermore, it is deontological, in that it comes to these conclusions without reference to the consequences of police action.

Still, it might be objected, in the real world, the police professional *is* the legitimate agent for returning a criminal attack. If he can't return with lethal force, who can? Does this account have anything to say about the permissibility of force police professionals actually use? In their reluctance to accord the dangerous right to the police, individuals agreeing to the social contract indicate a general attitude about police rights. To protect itself against the mismanagement of such rights, the contracting individuals would agree to keep them minimal. It is true that police are part of a system of justice, and have special duties in apprehending, restraining, and arresting suspects; and it is true these practices are for the preservation of a system of rights. But if these practices permit means which are out of keeping with those rights, the system as a whole suffers. In a certain sense, according to this view, police are simply citizens who have undergone training to make them expert in what any citizen morally and legally can do: stop a suspected criminal act. If there is force, it should fall under the same considerations as any citizen's use of force, in self-defense, or where there is a clear and present danger to a third party. In that way, there may be no special police rights with respect to lethal force, except under certain specifiable conditions. The police gun would fall silent.

Conclusions

This paper has attempted to show certain deficiencies in the deontologist's attempt to justify police professionals' use of lethal force. The unique professional responsibilities of the police have been discussed with respect to the fact that they act in the name of society. I have said nothing about the issue of their enforcement of unjust laws, or laws that do not serve the interests of justice, though this issue is real. Against this account, it might be urged that the state owns, by definition, the means to violence, and police agency derives from this ownership.

This is wrong. The fact that police act in the name of the state does not give them immunity from morality. Their professional duties may at times conflict with morality. If they always conflict, they are not so much police as professional henchmen. So long as the state can be said to serve the interests of justice, one function of the philosopher is to minimize this conflict. The apparent impracticability of the policeman without this gun could as easily be a blindness to a more reasonable way of doing business.

Notes

1. Charles Fried, *Right and Wrong* (Cambridge: Harvard University Press, 1978); Deborah G. Johnson, "Morality and Police Harm" (unpublished manuscript).
2. *A Theory of Justice* (Cambridge: Harvard University Press, 1971).
3. *The New York Times,* August 27, 1980, p. 37.
4. Common law justification for police use of lethal force generally includes six situations: self-defense, prevention of a crime in progress, recapture of an escapee of an arrest or a penal institution, stopping a riot, and effecting a felony arrest.
5. Op. cit., p. 48.
6. E.g., James Rachels, "Action and Passive Euthanasia," *The New England Journal of Medicine,* vol. 292, no. 2 (Jan. 9, 1975), pp. 78–80.
7. Johnson seems to acknowledge this; see p. 13.

Suggested Further Reading

Audi, Robert, "Violence, Legal Sanctions, and Law Enforcement," in *Reason and Violence,* ed. Sherman N. Stanage. Totowa, N.J.: Littlefield, Adams, 1974, pp. 29–50.

Betz, Joseph, "Police Violence," in *Moral Issues in Police Work,* ed. F. Elliston and M. Feldberg. Totowa, N.J.: Rowman and Allanheld, 1984.

Bittner, Egon, "The Capacity to Use Force as the Core of the Police Role," in *The Functions of the Police in Modern Society.* Rockville, Md.: National Institute of Mental Health, 1970, pp. 36–47.

Cumming, Elaine, et al., "Policeman as Philosopher, Guide and Friend," *Social Problems,* 12 (Winter 1965), 276–86.

Elliston, Frederick A., "Deadly Force: An Ethical Analysis," in *New Perspectives in Urban Crime,* ed. Steven Lagoy. Cincinnati: Anderson/Pilgrimage, 1981, pp. 91–110.

Garver, Newton, "The Ambiguity of the Police Role," *Social Praxis,* 2 (1974), 310–23.

Reiman, Jeffrey, "Police Autonomy vs. Police Authority," in *The Police Community,* ed. Jack Goldsmith and Sharon Goldsmith. Pacific Palisades, Calif.: Palisades Publishers, 1974, pp. 225–33.

Sherman, Lawrence, "Execution Without Trial: Police Homicide and the Constitution," *Vanderbilt Law Review,* 33, no. 1 (1980), 71–100.

Skolnick, Jerome, "Deception by Police," in *Criminal Justice Ethics,* 2 (Summer/Fall 1982), 40–54.

DECISION SCENARIO 2

Police Use of Lethal Force

The police dispatcher received a 911 emergency call that a domestic dispute had erupted. The apartment was located in an urban renewal project in an inner-city neighborhood. It was past midnight when Officers Towson and McGregor, both veteran policemen, arrived at 432 East 138th Street.

A small crowd in front of the lobby moved aside as the two men entered. Headquarters had notified them that Mrs. Michaels, the head of the house of the given address, had a record of charges for child abuse and shoplifting. She had never been convicted. It was also learned that she was a violent personality with a history of outpatient treatment at the local hospital. According to the computer, there was no licensed firearm in the household.

The police officers took the back stairs up. "Might be a teenage son she has to deal with," Towson said.

"Or a lover. Or someone wanting something. We don't know," replied McGregor.

"Let's take it easy."

"Especially you, Gene, with four kids and two years to retirement."

When they arrived at the fourth floor apartment, there were shouts of a woman's voice and the impact of a heavy object against a wall. In accordance with department regulations, they drew their revolvers and waited for a response to Officer Towson's call to open the door. Nothing. He rapped with his knuckles. The altercation inside seemed to increase.

"We've got to get that door open, buddy," McGregor said. "Someone's getting hurt!"

He kicked once and was about to batter the door with his shoulder when it suddenly opened. A large black woman, weighing over 250 pounds, stood inside. Her eyes had a crazed appearance. In her right hand was a long kitchen knife.

"What do *you* want?" she screamed.

Before McGregor could answer, she raised the knife over her head and lunged for Towson, who was nearer. The next moment, McGregor simultaneously shouted "Watch it!" and fired two shots in rapid succession at the woman. She collapsed and rolled over. When the EMT team arrived, they pronounced her dead. It was Mrs. Michaels.

Questions

1. Did Officer McGregor do the right thing? Was there an error of judgment on his part?

2. What were some of the alternatives open to the officers as they arrived on the scene?

3. Both officers were white, and Mrs. Michaels, black. In the subsequent police investigation, they had to answer to charges of racial prejudice. Are these charges relevant to the use of lethal force?

4. Is it possible for the police to do their work without lethal force?

16. ISSUES IN CRIMINAL PROSECUTION

1. THE "IDEAL CRIMINAL"

The ideal criminal, from the standpoint of prosecution and sentencing, is a rational adult who freely and deliberately violates the rules of law for personal gain. Convicting and punishing the ideal criminal poses few ethical problems once the state defines acts of crime and sets penalties for them. Many criminals do not fit the mold, however. For example, a large number of crimes are committed by juveniles. Should they be treated in the same manner as adult offenders? Other crimes are committed by adults who did not make a rational decision to break the law but rather were influenced by passion, intoxication by drugs or alcohol, or mental instability or defect. Should the same process of criminal justice be applied to all, regardless of circumstances?

A variety of excuses, mitigations, and justifications are offered to temper the way an individual is handled by the criminal justice system. What these arguments have in common is that they begin with an admission that the individual committed the crime of which he or she stands accused. In contrast to what occurs in many trials, no effort is made to demonstrate that the person has been wrongly accused. Rather, defendants attempt to show that a strong reason exists for them to be not punished to the usual extent or not punished at all.

A well-known example of an *excuse* is the insanity defense. This argument holds that individuals should not be punished because they are not responsible for their actions by reason of a defective mental condition. A *mitigation* is an argument that a criminal act is less blameworthy than it might usually be and therefore less deserving of the usual punishment. An example is finding one's spouse in bed with a lover and killing them in a moment of jealous rage. A *justification* is an argument that, while a crime has occurred, it is not wrong in this particular instance. Self-defense is a good example of a justification. Is it right for the criminal justice system to take extenuating arguments into account when deciding guilt and punishment? Which excuses, mitigations, and justifications are legitimate?

By recognizing a wide array of extenuating circumstances, the law expresses the idea that punishment should be administered only when a guilty act (*actus reus*) is accompanied by a guilty mind (*mens rea*). Mere violation of the law is not in itself sufficient to justify punishment. Administering punishment presupposes certain conceptions of what a criminal must be like.

A different characterization of the nature of criminals is offered by advocates of the idea that lawbreakers are similar to sick persons and should be treated like patients rather than felons. Still others believe that social pressures such as poverty and racism cause people to commit crimes. On this liberal view, crime can be eliminated by eradicating unjust social conditions, not by punishing or even providing mental health services to those who break the law.

The utilitarian approach seeks primarily to deter crime through the criminal justice system. It assumes that the criminal makes a rational choice of behavior. Presumably, the threat of punishment deters persons from making that choice (crime, in other words, does not pay). If the criminal does *not* act rationally, however, if he or she has a mitigation or an excuse, should the person still be punished? "Perhaps," the utilitarian might say—if that punishment deters another from committing a crime. Such an analysis points to the conclusion that a "guilty mind" is not necessary to justify punishment. Justifications are more acceptable to the utilitarian since, with a justification, an act usually seen as a crime is not blameworthy in a particular instance. If a justification establishes that the committed act is more likely to have socially beneficial consequences than punishing its perpetrator, the act should not be treated as a crime. In a case of self-defense, for example, others might be deterred from attacking someone—a desirable outcome. On the other hand, punishing self-defense would not deter attacks but rather discourage people from defending themselves (for this reason, it might actually encourage attacks).

Advocates of a deontological, retributive approach believe that persons with excuses or mitigations should not receive the usual punishment, because all punishment must be deserved. If a criminal is not responsible (excuse) or not as responsible as usual (mitigation), the usual punishment is not deserved or appropriate. With a justification, such as self-defense, the perpetrator does not violate another's rights. An attacker killed by his or her intended victim has forfeited the right not to be harmed. Therefore, no crime has occurred because no rights are violated.

In the article that follows, Herbert Fingarette examines the insanity defense, which has come under increasing public scrutiny and criticism in recent years. Reform and even abolition of the insanity defense—and other mental disability defenses—have been demanded. Fingarette maintains that such defenses are fundamental to our idea of individual responsibility under law. Respect for individual responsibility must include the recognition that some persons are incapable of responsibility. The author attempts to analyze conceptual problems involved in the insanity defense and suggests ways in which it might be more clearly formulated.

HERBERT FINGARETTE

What Is Criminal Insanity?

The idea of madness or lunacy is not only ancient, but culturally very widespread. In our own legal history we find the idea in records that go back to earliest English law.

In A.D. 1203, the fifth year of King John's reign, in Shrewsbury, Robert of Herthale killed in self-defense Roger; for Roger, as the Pleas of the Crown record it, had "slain five men in a fit of madness—per insaniam."[1] There was already a relatively rich legal vocabulary for insanity—for example, "furore," "demenciam," "stultitiam," "lunaticus."[2]

In 1582, the English law recorder William Lombard wrote: "If a man or a natural fool or a lunatic in the time of his lunacy, or a child who apparently has no knowledge of good or

Reprinted with permission from *Ethics, Public Policy, and Criminal Justice*, ed. Frederick Elliston and Norman Bowie (Cambridge, Mass.: Oelgeschlager, Gunn & Hain, Inc., 1982), pp. 228–44.

evil do kill a man, there is no felonious act, for they cannot be said to have any understanding will."[3]

In 1724, in the case of *Arnold*, the court announced that the accused must be exculpated if "he doth not know what he is doing, no more than . . . a wild beast."[4]

And again in 1843, in their famous *M'Naghten* opinion, the Law Lords of England defined legal insanity and declared that the legally insane must be found not guilty of the crime they are charged with committing.[5]

The insanity defense still remains, in 1980, part of the basic law of this land and of England and the Commonwealth countries.[6] And it surely still embodies an idea that intuitively makes sense.

And yet the insanity defense to a criminal charge has generated great controversy in the criminal law. There is voluminous scholarly literature on it, and of course the popular press has again and again taken up the topic to debate it or to take righteous stands on it, both pro and con.[7]

Why should controversy be so endemic to this area of law? If a person is truly irrational, insane, and because of this insanity does something that is prohibited by the law, can we in fairness or justice view such a person as a criminal, to be criminally condemned and punished?

Of course the offenses of persons claiming insanity have at times had peculiarly bizarre or shocking features that tend to arouse almost instinctively a passion for retribution. Then, too, there is often fear that such persons, if declared legally insane, will be sent to hospitals only to be released and thus be free to offend again. In Michigan several years ago, two offenders who had been found not guilty because of insanity were eventually released from the hospital. Within a month one beat his wife to death and the other raped two women. We have all read such stories. In this case, the Michigan legislature, provoked by the public outcry, immediately went to work to change the laws to try to get around the insanity defense.[8]

From a political standpoint, there is little doubt that the criminal justice system would have a far more peaceful and prosperous time of it if the insanity defense and other forms of mental disability defenses, such as diminished mental capacity, were not available. Then too, many lawyers and scholars despair as they contemplate the internal complexity and confusion of the law in this area, and the unedifying spectacle of psychiatrists regularly contradicting each other on the witness stand. Why not, as some have suggested, abolish the insanity defense and related defenses such as diminished mental capacity?[9] After all, these defenses really aren't used that much, in a statistical sense, in any case.[10]

As I see it, the fundamental reason for resisting the move to abolish these defenses is that they reflect the very soul of our legal system. The insanity plea is a litmus test of our commitment to the idea of citizen responsibility under law. To hold an insane or mentally disabled person responsible to the law in the same way we hold citizens to it generally is to make a mockery of the idea of responsibility. It also would be a major step toward abandoning the idea of guilt as we know it in law. The law would then be merely a device for social *control*, lacking any moral content. The concept of guilt in our law is built on the twin foundation stones of the *actus reus* and *mens rea*—the guilty act *and* the guilty mind. To abolish mental disability defenses would be a major step toward abandoning the idea that there is no criminal guilt unless there is a guilty mind.

My main aim here, however, is not to justify the insanity defense but to trace a bit of its conceptual history, to analyze the conceptual problems internal to it, and to propose some clarifying reformulations.

First, then, let's trace briefly the modern development of the legal concept of insanity.

The modern common law concept of insanity has its inception in the famous *M'Naghten* case in 1843.[11] The historical context was one of many deep political tensions, combined with the advent of scientific knowledge and technology. Of special pertinence to the *M'Naghten* case, however, was the amazing new growth in knowledge about the body, about diseases, and particularly about the peculiar importance of the brain in relation to the human mind. In the nineteenth century, an inordinately optimistic scientific materialism was sweeping the sciences, the medical profession, and specifically medical psychology.

It was in this atmosphere that Daniel M'Naghten, an ex-soldier wounded in the head during the Napoleonic wars, became deluded into thinking that the Tory party was carrying forward a great conspiracy to pursue him, persecute him, and destroy him. The solution, as M'Naghten saw it, was to kill the Tory leader, the great Prime Minister Peel. M'Naghten carried out the assassination— though, one of life's losers to the end, he managed to shoot the wrong man, not Peel but Peel's secretary.

The medical evidence at the murder trial was so persuasive of madness that the judge practically directed the jury to find M'Naghten insane and thus not guilty. But the acquittal aroused a storm of public protest: Queen Victoria had already had three attempts made on her life; the Prince Consort had been the target of one attempt. The Queen demanded that the law members of the House of Lords review the law in such cases, and give formal answers on what the correct law was. The central feature of the response was the legal definition of insanity known as the M'Naghten test, which has ever since dominated English law, Commonwealth law, and American law.

The Lords said that a defendant is criminally insane if he was "labouring under such a defect of reason, from disease of the mind, as not to know the nature and quality of the act he was doing, or if he did know it, that he did not know he was doing what was wrong." This formulation, and the basic ideas in it, have remained central in our law.

There are four main elements in this definition. First, there must be a "defect of reason." This element has generally been silently dropped by courts and legislatures since then. As my later remarks about the centrality

of rationality will reveal, this notion, though lost from sight, is in my opinion closer to the essence of legal insanity than any of the other elements of the test. But let's leave it for now.

Second, there must be "disease of the mind." This element reflects the new medical optimism of the time of M'Naghten. Madness was no longer to be viewed as a visitation of God, or as possession by evil spirits, but as a *disease*, an objectively identifiable medical condition, whose true nature or real cause would no doubt soon be demonstrably explained in terms of bodily pathology, probably brain pathology.

But for *legal* insanity, "disease of the mind," though necessary, was not enough. The presence of one or both of the third and fourth elements of the M'Naghten test was required. The defendant, by reason of the mental disease, must have suffered a defect of knowledge—either he did not know the nature and quality of the act he was doing, or the defendant did not know that what he was doing was wrong.

In 1897, the U.S. Supreme Court added a third alternative effect of "mental disease"— an "irresistible impulse."[12] This alternative clause was never accepted in English law, but had already received some acceptance in state courts in the United States.

One may well ask why all these complicating clauses about lack of knowledge or lack of self-control are required. Why wouldn't it be sufficient merely to say that there was criminal insanity if the act was a product of a mental disease?

This much simpler alternative was in fact the test used in a famous English case that preceded M'Naghten's—the *Hadfield* case.[13] Moreover, it seems to have been the test actually used at M'Naghten's trial, though the Law Lords in their famous opinion ignored that. This simple test was formally adopted by one American state, New Hampshire, in the 1870 case of *State v. Pike*.[14] Except for New Hampshire, however, once all the Law Lords had given their more complex response to the Queen in 1843, the idea that an insane act is simply any act resulting from mental disease had no other takers for almost one hundred years. Then, in 1954, came the ground-breaking *Durham* case in the District of Columbia.[15] *Durham* reflected a century of widespread legal criticism of *M'Naghten*. It was hailed as a breakthrough. Yet *Durham* failed; after over a decade of struggle to make it work, the District of Columbia abandoned it. Why?

The *Durham* test in effect posed two apparently simple questions to the psychiatric expert witnesses. Did the defendant have a mental disease at the time of the offending act? If so, was the act a product of the disease? Presumably both of these questions are appropriately answered by an expert in the science of medical psychology.

The danger in this soon became evident. The psychiatrist witnesses might for practical purposes settle the question of legal insanity, and then the verdict of the jury would simply amount to a rubber stamp.

All well and good, you may say; better to settle the question scientifically than on the basis of archaic legal formulas or on the basis of the opinion of a psychiatrically untrained jury. But the experts didn't perform as hoped.

As a matter of fact, the courts soon began to realize that the experts were changing their classifications of "mental disease" in ways that had momentous legal results, and they were doing so not because of new scientific evidence, but on the basis of changing policy decisions by local hospital committees of psychiatrists. In one famous instance, a hospital staff reclassified the diagnosis "anti-social personality" from "not a mental disease" to "mental disease."[16] By this staff decision, they compelled the court to reverse one offender's conviction, and they potentially affected the legal status of a large class of offenders. Thus the psychiatrists were in effect manipulating the law as they saw fit, by changing their labels on the basis of their social views rather than because of new scientific evidence.

Individual psychiatric witnesses often disagreed among themselves in their testimony about whether the defendant had a mental disease—that is, they disagreed about whether to apply the *label*, even though they often agreed on the essential *facts*.

Also, it became evident that too often the individual physician, in testimony, would personally decide whether to apply the "mental disease" label or not on the basis of what the physician personally thought best for the defendant.[17] In short, the desired legal result, in the preference of the psychiatrist, would dictate the testimony, which could then indeed determine the legal result. This is very different, of course, from having the result determined by testimony based only on scientific fact.

All these developments rapidly made it apparent that in *Durham* the court had abdicated its responsibility, and had in effect handed over the power of law to members of a different profession who were not authorized to be judge or jury, and who were professionally unconcerned about legal guilt or the administration of criminal law and justice.

Against this background there was a reaction against the sole emphasis in *Durham* on "mental disease" as cause of the act, and a renewed interest in the more fully explicit *M'Naghten*. *M'Naghten* also requires "mental disease," of course, but it is differentiated from *Durham* by its also having the additional explicit qualifying clauses—the specification that as a result of the mental disease the defendant didn't know the nature of the act, or didn't know it was wrong, or (in later versions) suffered an irresistible impulse. These qualifications seemed to pinpoint more specifically how and why it is that the insane person is not held responsible: if I don't know what I'm doing, or that it's wrong, or if I can't help myself, how can you blame me?

Because of widespread dissatisfaction with the exact phraseology of *M'Naghten*, and because of a sense that it belonged to the nineteenth century and was somehow outdated, a new version of it was developed in the 1950s and 1960s by the American Law Institute and embodied in its Model Penal Code. In recent years this new version has increasingly come to dominate the field in U.S. law, though *M'Naghten* is still widely used. This new version is supposed to be in language that is much more scientifically up-to-date, and legally less narrow and rigid. It reads: "A person is not responsible for criminal conduct if at the time of such conduct as a result of mental disease or defect he lacks substantial capacity either to appreciate the criminality (or wrongfulness) of his conduct or to conform his conduct to the requirements of law."[18]

You will notice that the old *M'Naghten* phraseology, "does not know the nature and quality of the act," and "does not know that it's wrong" get verbally transmuted into "lacks substantial ability to appreciate the criminality of the act"; and the old "irresistible impulse" idea is recognizable behind the ALI language, "lacks substantial capacity to conform his conduct to the requirements of law." The *M'Naghten* requirement that these result from "mental disease" remains in the ALI formula. So in spite of all the applause for its scientific modernity, the ALI test is in its essentials the nineteenth century *M'Naghten* concept. The more English idiom of the old version is merely replaced by a more legalese American style. Improvements of nuance are claimed but are dubious.

Up to this point I've been reporting mainly on the history of the insanity test formula. We have seen that the attempt to rely mainly on the notion of "mental disease" was in fact a failure in the *Durham* experiment. But we have not said *why* the "disease" notion led to such poor results. Now let us analyze more directly the role of each main element of the currently used insanity tests—whether as found in the usual *M'Naghten*-plus-irresistible-impulse form, or as expressed in the more recent ALI version.

First let's examine carefully the notion of "mental disease." Since 1843 *every* version of the insanity test—M'Naghten, Durham, ALI—has retained this element. And with the recent rise in acceptance of the ALI test, the law is again locking this notion in, even though; as I remarked in connection with *Durham*, it was already becoming evident by the 1960s that the so-called medical model of insanity, based primarily on the notion of "mental disease," was bankrupt. The same may be said of any of the obvious varient forms such as "mental illness" or "mental disorder," insofar as their use in any criminal law defense is concerned.

The basic reason for the confusion these notions create is that they simply do not have any agreed or adequate definitions, nor do they have any systematic scientific use. In fact, "mental disease" and "mental illness" have either been dropped from the medical vocabulary, or they are used vaguely, allusively, and occasionally, where there is no need for or intent to imply any clear meaning or systematic scientific use. The distinguished judge and legal reformer who wrote the 1954 *Durham* opinion, Judge David Bazelon, had to acknowledge by 1967, in *U.S.* v. *Washington*, that "In fact, the medical profession has no clearly defined category" of mental illness.[19] He added with regard to the question of whether the act was a product of the mental disease, that: "the term *'product'* has *no* clinical significance for psychiatrists."[20] I might add, finally, that the most recent official Diagnostic Manual of the American Psychiatric Association—a voluminous tome based on years of vastly extensive consultation—contains no use in the text or in the index or glossaries of "mental disease" or "mental illness."[21] The phrase "mental disorder," which is used as the global rubric in the manual, is introduced with the explicit disclaimer that it has no clear or well-defined meaning, and is only to be incompletely explained in a few lines.[22]

The phrase "mental disease" is plainly a placeholder for unexpressed ideas that work surreptitiously. Retention of the phrase for a century and a half is no doubt in part a testimony to the law's conservatism and passion for precedent, even when the language used is known to be bankrupt. But there is more to it than that. The retention of the notion, in spite of the difficulties it creates, suggests that some idea is at work underneath the surface, probably some essential idea or ideas that have not yet been well formulated.

I must digress for a moment here to warn against a very possible misunderstanding of my thesis of the unscientific status of the notion of "mental disease." I am not here espousing the popular anti-psychiatry views of such people as Thomas Szasz, R. D. Laing, and others for whom medical psychiatry is a charade, a fundamentally phony enterprise, a process of labeling people who are nuisances and then invoking the social authority of medicine to keep those who are so labeled in institutions where they can no longer bother us. That kind of wholesale attack on psychiatry, whatever you may think of it, is not what's at issue here. I am reporting something that is authoritatively accepted by the psychiatric profession itself.

The point, briefly, is this. In physical medicine there are syndromes—objectively identifiable recurrent patterns of signs and symptoms—that are associated with labels such as "measles," "tuberculosis," "diabetes," "carcinoma," "arterial hypertension." And so, too, in medical psychology there are objectively identifiable patterns of signs and symptoms associated with such labels as "schizophrenia," and "manic-depression." A physician may know all there is to know about measles, may report and explain it all; and yet if you ask if measles is a "disease," the answer can only be, "People commonly call it a disease, and I surely don't dissent, but to say measles is a disease adds no specific or necessary scientific information to what I already have said, since the word "disease" has no systematic or agreed usage in medicine." Similarly, suppose we ask a psychiatrist: "What scientific information, over and above what you told us about the diagnosis, causes, prognosis, and therapy of schizophrenia, would you *add* by labeling schizophrenia as a mental disease?" Only one correct answer can possibly be given—"It would add no specific scientific information to what I have already told you—"mental disease" is just a label that many people, especially in the law, or in certain social agencies, like to use." Thus "measles" and "schizophrenia" do have a systematic and essential scientific role as authoritatively defined medical concepts. But the notion of "mental disease" has no such role in medicine. Yet it is *the* key term in the criminal insanity tests.

Could the law merely substitute for "mental disease" the list of specific mental disorders in the diagnostic manual, or simply require that some condition so listed be present?

Unfortunately, the diagnostic manual names and describes many conditions that are of psychiatric interest but that would not seem appropriate to serve in establishing criminal non-responsibility. For example, "compulsive personality disorder" is defined by three criteria. As I now list them, consider whether you would want the possession of these traits to be enough to excuse a person from any criminal offense associated with these traits. First, the compulsive personality is one that shows restricted ability to express warm and tender emotions. Second, the compulsive personality is perfectionist; and third, it is unaware of the feelings caused in others by insisting that things be done its own way.

Among the three hundred pages of items listed in the manual of mental disorders, there are other diagnostic categories of comparable innocuousness. So we can't simply adopt the manual as the criterion of mental disease for criminal insanity purposes. Nor can the law pick and choose only some of the disorders listed in the manual unless it has criteria for selection—that is, some understanding of the reasons why it uses the notion, and thus which disorders would be pertinent. What is it, specifically, that the law has in mind, then, when it says insanity must include "mental disease"?

In recent years a number of courts have, understandably, established their own *legal* definitions of mental disease, thus trying to come to grips with this question and spell out the legally pertinent sense of the phrase. These legal definitions of mental disease have followed a pattern. They are built on the following elements: (1) there is a "mental abnormality" or a "disorder of thought or mood": (2) this abnormality or disorder in turn substantially affects or impairs (3) either mental-emotional processes, capacity for judgment, or awareness of reality, or (4) behavioral capacities, ability to cope with practical life situations.

Such legal definitions obviously amount merely to vaguer and more generalized versions of *M'Naghten* and the ALI test. Instead of the phrase "mental disease," we now have "abnormality of mind" or "disorder of thought or mood"—words so vague as to convey almost no definite meaning. And instead of the remaining elements of M'Naghten and ALI—"knowing the nature of the act and that it's wrong," or "appreciating" its "criminality," and "being able to conform one's conduct to the requirements of law"—we now have such far vaguer notions as "impairs thought and mood," "impairs judgment," "affects behavior controls" or "impairs ability to cope," all now built right into the meaning of "mental disease"!

Plainly we are going around in circles. If it's so vague, undefined, troublesome, and misleading, maybe we should adopt the exact opposite strategy from *Durham*, which placed the entire weight on the notion of "mental disease"; maybe we should drop that notion entirely. If we now pursue *this* direction, we get some good insight into the job that the phrase "mental disease" really does, and why something is needed here.

We have already seen that in *M'Naghten* and in the ALI variant of it, there are indeed other key clauses besides the "mental disease" clause. There is, first, the impairment of understanding: "not knowing the nature of the act, or its wrongness," "not appreciating its criminality." Then there is the element of impairment of will: "irresistible impulse," or "lack of capacity to conform conduct to the requirements of law."

On the face of things it seems simple to explain the rationale for putting these in an exculpatory formula. It is basic law that I may have a complete defense to a criminal charge if I was mistaken or ignorant as to a fact about what I was doing, and if that fact was material to its being criminal.[23] So one goes on to think, *of course*—if a person is mentally ill in a way that produces ignorance or mistaken belief about a material fact, and if that in itself is a defense, what need is there to provide the special and very troublesome defense of insanity at all? Why not just say, if the defendant really doesn't know—for *whatever* reason— some fact material to the act's being a crime, then the *mens rea*, the guilty mind, is absent, and the act is *not* a crime. But this seems to carry us too far. We have not only got rid of

the "mental disease" element, but it seems we have also got rid of the insanity defense itself!

There is a response to this paradox. It lies in the fact that mere mistake or ignorance is not always a defense. It is usually held in U.S. and English law that to be a defense the mistake must be *reasonable*. Of course, ignorance or mistaken belief arising out of insanity is in the nature of the case *not* reasonable. Therefore the *standard* defense of mistake of fact—i.e., reasonable mistake—will not do the job if the mistake or ignorance arises out of insanity.

So we do need a special plea if a madman's mistaken belief, unreasonable though it be, is nevertheless to be a defense. But *why* should unreasonable mistake be an excuse? Because the person is mad? But we began this series of remarks by saying that madness should excuse because it produces mistaken belief! Now we're saying the mistaken belief should excuse if it's due to madness! So it's circular reasoning. The escape from this circularity provides the insight we seek.

If we look behind the "reasonableness" test, we see that it is designed to exclude defenses based on mistake or ignorance of fact when this is due to the defendant's own negligence or recklessness. To put it more generally, the reasonableness requirement is intended to exclude mistake or ignorance *culpably* (unreasonably) brought about by the defendant. Suppose, for example, the defendant voluntarily got drunk, and then, because of a mistake or confusion brought about by drunken gross negligence, caused someone's death without having meant to do so. Should the law allow that person to say, "I did not know what I was doing, and didn't mean to cause death, so I am not guilty of any crime"? One way to avoid such a use of voluntary intoxication as an excuse for committing a crime is to require that the mistake be a reasonable one. The drunken person's mistake is not a reasonable mistake, and the voluntary drinker is culpable for getting drunk.

In short, the reasonableness requirement is designed to assure the non-culpable origin of the mistake or ignorance. I propose that one non-explicit but crucial role played by the phrase "mental disease" has been to establish in certain cases the non-culpability of an unreasonable ignorance or false belief. If this is the logical role of the phrase, why not *say* so? The law should abandon the pseudo-medical conception of mental disease, with all its attendant obfuscations, and replace it by the pertinent *legal* concepts expressing the normative—not medical—idea that the defendant's mental confusion was "not culpable in origin." This proposal is the first element in the legal doctrine of disability of mind that Ann Hasse and I have developed as the basis for reform of the law on insanity and indeed for all mental disability criminal law defenses.

Analogous comments can be made about the idea of incapacity to conform one's conduct to the law, or, in the old phrase, "irresistible impulse." Insofar as a transgression of law is conceived as not voluntary, as beyond the person's control, this is generally recognized as a defense.[24] (I am putting aside the complications of strict liability law, which do not bear substantially on this issue.) If involuntariness *is* a defense, however, it would again seem that the special insanity plea would be unnecessary, except that, again, the involuntariness must not have been culpably brought about by the defendant (for example, by heavy drinking). This requirement of non-culpable origin is what the phrase "mental disease" has seemed to address. Again I say that if this is so, why shouldn't the law emphasize explicitly the legal norms of culpability here, and speak of a loss of self-control that is of non-culpable origin, rather than using the pseudo-medical phrase "mental disease"?

Finally, I come in this brief review of the main elements of the insanity tests to the element of "right and wrong"—the criminality of the conduct. Does unawareness of the criminality of the act explain why the insanity plea should exculpate? In general, it definitely is not a defense in law to say "I didn't know it was wrong," or "I didn't know it was against the law."[25] Putting aside legal complications irrelevant to our topic and purpose, we will do well enough here to recall the old legal maxim, "Ignorance of the law is no excuse." The retort will come back, "But this is *different*. It's not just that the defendant didn't understand that it was wrong or illegal; it's that the defendant was unable to understand this because of insanity, because the defendant was mentally diseased, mentally ill." Of course this retort, too, is viciously circular because it was the failure to know the act was wrong that was supposed to explain why insanity exculpates, and now we are saying that the lack of knowledge of the law, or of the wrongness of the act, exculpates in this case unlike all other cases because of the insanity, or the mental disease.

Non-culpability will not help us at this point, for even an innocent failure to know an act is criminal is generally no excuse in law for that crime. So if we seek to disentangle the rationale lying beneath our intuition that the moral blindness of an insane person *is* an excuse, we must put aside for the moment the question of culpable origin, and turn to another question—the question of mental capacity.

The responsible citizen has the mental capacity, generally speaking, to understand what it is for an act to be criminal or not; though in a particular instance such a person may not happen to know that a particular act is against some law. That is, a responsible citizen may lack information about a legal regulation or statute. That's no legal excuse. "Insanity," however, implies not merely a failure to have a piece of information, but a mental incapacity to appreciate the right-wrong distinction as it applies in the circumstances. It is this incapacity, if it in turn is non-culpable in origin, that renders a person incompetent with regard to criminal law standards, and hence not a responsible agent in that respect. Here, too, the phrase "mental disease" played a role. It embodied, tacitly, the notion that the person is mentally incapable of applying certain distinctions that are crucial to law-abiding conduct. Again my question is, if this is so, why not say so, and drop the obscure notion of "mental disease"? Why not speak of a non-culpably caused lack of mental capacity to understand and apply the relevant legal standards to the particular circumstances? Whatever the difficulties of interpretation, at least we say what we mean, and do not evade the issues by using pseudo-scientific concepts.

Until now I have been talking only about the insanity defense. But there has developed an increasing role in the law in recent decades for what is called the "diminished capacity" defense, and I must say at least a few words about this new and closely related development.[26] Diminished capacity is a defense option that allows the claim that even though the defendant's mental disability was not severe enough, or of the kind, to fit the legal definition of insanity, still there was a substantial enough mental disability at least to reduce the gravity of the crime for which the defendant can be convicted.

The diminished capacity defense has opened up a whole new range of criminal law defense argument and testimony. Not surprisingly, the kinds of conceptual confusion that I've been discussing in connection with insanity have rapidly cropped up in the doctrines of diminished capacity. It is already widely acknowledged that the diminished capacity concepts are not only incoherent in themselves, but—especially in California, which is leading the way—they are increasingly tending to merge with the elements of the insanity defense, thus producing a monumental blur.

And yet the general notion of diminished capacity is *intuitively* as plausible and forceful as is the insanity defense: it provides a halfway house between full guilt and complete insanity. It is a category that has forced itself into the arena in a society that is increasingly sensitive to making distinctions where human rights, human dignity, human welfare are concerned.

This idea can be easily handled within the disability of mind doctrine that I have mentioned. The legal issues are framed this way: in partial disability of mind, the defendant's mental capacities for rational conduct in regard to the criminality of the conduct are gravely impaired, but they are not so to the point of complete insanity, i.e., of full disabil-

ity of mind. This is enough to warrant a less severe punitive sentence, and therefore also enough to require a mental examination to determine whether some kind of future care for the person is needed. The principle of non-culpable origin that was previously enunciated should also apply here. If this partial mental disability was culpably brought about by the defendant, say by use of drink or drugs, mitigation should be less or even not at all; whereas if it was not culpably brought about—neither voluntarily and knowingly nor even recklessly brought about—then mitigation should be substantial. It may be difficult to find this halfway line, but juries and more enlightened courts have demanded the option.

Historically, however, the courts have tried to justify this move by arguing that they were simply applying basic law on *mens rea*, requiring no new basic concepts about mental disability. They have argued that the issue comes down to nothing more than saying that a mental disability may be evidence of the absence of some specific mental element, such as intent or knowledge, that is included in the definition of the crime. In the absence of a required mental element of the crime, elementary law requires that the defendant must be found not guilty. Then there will be some lesser crime, with a lesser penalty of which the defendant *can* be found guilty. So, by this indirect route, the desired result of mitigation is in effect achieved.

Now unfortunately the fact is that defendants who obviously are gravely mentally impaired enough to warrant a diminished capacity verdict very often *do* have the intent or other mental state required to constitute the offense—they *do* often mean to commit what they *know* is a crime. In fact, it is their mental disability that leads them to intentionally commit the crime. Therefore, if the defense is to work, the courts are forced to redefine the words referring to the mental elements (as has happened in California) in order to make them mean that an element is absent when in fact it is present! Thus, elements of *mens rea*— deliberation, premeditation, malice, intent, and even consciousness—have been provided special definitions for the diminished capacity context, so that what is deliberation or malice in most contexts is declared not to be so in this one. The defendant is then found not guilty of the alleged crime, since one of the required mental elements was missing. Having found legally absent a mental state that was obviously psychologically present, the court must hope that there remains some lesser crime in which the defendant could still technically be found guilty, thus receiving a lesser penalty and not escaping entirely as in the case of full-fledged insanity. Of course if there is no appropriate lesser crime, the logic calls for the defendant to go completely free. And since this *does* happen, the way has now been opened (in California) for such offenders, with only partial disability, even if culpably caused, to go completely free!

The dramatic effect of the diminished capacity defense is to be seen in the case of Dan White, who took his gun from his house, went to the San Francisco City Hall, sought out his two political enemies, shot each one dead, and was found not guilty of intentional killing with malice! Riot erupted, literally, in San Francisco. One hates to think of what would have happened had there not fortunately been a lesser crime, manslaughter, of which he still could be and subsequently was convicted.

All this confusion arises and continues because the courts have been unwilling to acknowledge the true, distinctive elements at issue in both insanity and diminished capacity defenses, and indeed in *all* criminal law mental disability defenses. They have refused to acknowledge that in all these cases there are two key questions, different from those asked in any other criminal defenses. First, was the defendant lacking the mental capacity to act rationally in regard to the criminality of the act? And second, if the defendant *was* lacking in such rational capacity, was this condition culpably brought about by the defendant, or was it non-culpable in origin? These two basic questions express, I believe, the basic intuitions underlying this entire area of law. These

are the basic disability of mind doctrine questions.[27]

These questions cannot be answered decisively on the basis of systematic medical knowledge. They are formulated in terms of legal norms of responsibility. Not only is the present state of scientific knowledge incomplete and uncertain as it pertains to most of these cases, but even when all the psychiatric and other data about the defendant's mentality are in, the judgment also involves a normative, decisional element. The trier of fact must confront the question of what sorts of disability, and how much of the specific disability in question, shall under the particular circumstances in question count as enough to warrant the legal label "disability of mind."

This is a judgment of responsibility that cannot be disentangled from the judgment as to rationality—rationality in the sense of having what it takes, mentally, to get along at least minimally and on your own in society. The judgment also expresses the limits of tolerance in this regard of the society making the judgment.

This is the sort of judgment that typically juries must make. They are the representatives of the community. They make factual findings in the legal sense of the "fact," that is, they select from a set of legally defined alternative findings of fact, on the basis of a legally orchestrated sequence of testimony about those facts. In selecting the legally available finding that best fits the testimony, they also have a marginal, but at times crucial, opportunity to apply community standards. They apply standards they are competent to apply, the standard of what it is to behave rationally.

The nearest parallel to the judgment of disability of mind is the judgment of what a "reasonable man" would do in the circumstances. The law has found the notion of the reasonable man to be a necessary and vital one. There is no doubt that the absence of an explicit definition of reasonable man raises troublesome questions. But this notion, and such other logically analogous basic notions as "due care," reflects the need to introduce at certain crucial points in the law the element of the lay person's practical judgment, without formal definition, but within a carefully orchestrated presentation of specific fact.

Having made the judgment as to whether there was disability of mind or partial disability of mind, the next judgment to be made (again a legal one, not a medical one) is whether the defendant culpably brought that condition of irrationality into being. Here the questions of intent, knowledge, recklessness, negligence, and capacity for rationality are pertinent. In the disability of mind doctrine this completes the inquiry as to culpability wherever any mental disability is at issue.

Sometimes as I contemplate this approach to the problem, I say to myself, "It's so simple, so obvious."

And yet one finds today in this area of law a proliferation of legal doctrines and concepts, casuistry, arbitrary redefinitions, controversy, confusion, and general frustration.

So the question arises, is the quest for clarity, coherence, and relative simplicity worth it? I think so. For, as I have said, this area of law is one in which the key ideas touch the very soul of the law as we conceive it. The law is an institution in which our methods of social control are fundamentally constrained by our commitment to the idea of individual responsibility—to respect for individual responsibility where it exists, and to concern for the dignity as well as the special status of those persons who are incapable of responsible conduct. I believe we cannot afford to abandon this distinction because of a narrow concern with social control alone, or on pragmatic grounds of cost and convenience. Working to make these concepts of law coherent and vital is worth the cost and the effort.

Notes

1. F. W. Maitland, ed., *Pleas of the Crown*, Vol. I. No. 70 (London, 1888).

2. See ibid., Nos. 70, 113, 187.

3. Quoted from William Lombard, *Office of the Justice of the Peace*, 1582, in John I. Morre, Jr., "M'Naghten Is Dead—Or Is It?" 3 *Houston Law Review* 58, 62 (1965).

4. *R. v. Arnold* (1724) 61 How. St. Tr. 695, 765.

5. *M'Naghten's Case*, 8 Eng. Rep. 718 (H.L. 1843).

6. See generally: Herbert Fingarette, *The Meaning of Criminal Insanity* (Berkeley: University of California Press, 1972); A. Goldstein, *The Insanity Defense* (New Haven: Yale University Press, 1967).

7. For a selected bibliography, see; A. Brooks, *Law, Psychiatry and the Mental Health System* (Boston: Little, Brown, 1974), pp. 113–114.

8. For an account, see Sharon M. Brown and Nicholas J. Wittner, "1978 Annual Survey of Michigan Law: Criminal Law," 25 *Wayne Law Review* 335, 356–367 (1979).

9. See: Joseph Goldstein and Jay Katz, "Abolish the 'Insanity Defense': Why Not?" 72 *Yale Law Journal* 853 (1963); Barbara Wootton, *Crime and the Criminal Law* (London: Stevens & Sons, 1963); H. L. A. Hart, "Changing Conceptions of Responsibility," in Hart, *Punishment and Responsibility* (New York: Oxford University Press, 1968), Ch. VIII.

10. See: Herbert Fingarette and A. F. Hasse, *Mental Disabilities and Criminal Responsibility* (Berkeley: University of California Press, 1979), p. 259, n. 9, and Fingarette, *The Meaning of Criminal Insanity*, p. 6, n. 14.

11. Cited fully in note 5.

12. *Davis* v. *U.S.*, 165 U.S. 373 (1897).

13. *Hadfield's Case* (1800) 27 Howell 1281.

14. *State* v. *Pike*, 49 N.H. 399 (1870).

15. *Durham* v. *U.S.*, 214 F.2d 862 (D.C. Cir. 1954).

16. See discussion in: *Blocker* v. *U.S.*, 288 F.2d 853, 860 (1961).

17. For the most explicit confession on the record, see Bernard Diamond, "Criminal Responsibility of the Mentally Ill," 14 *Stanford Law Review* 59, 61–62 (1961).

18. American Law Institute, *Model Penal Code*, proposed official draft, 1962, sec. 4.01.

19. *U.S.* v. *Washington*, 390 F.2d 444, 446 (D.C. Cir. 1967).

20. Ibid., p. 456 (emphasis added).

21. *Diagnostic and Statistical Manual of Mental Disorders*, 3rd ed. (DSM-III) (Washington, D.C.: American Psychiatric Association, 1980).

22. Ibid., 5–6.

23. For a full discussion of this and of the following remarks bearing on mistake and ignorance,

see: Fingarette and Hasse, *supra* note 10 *Mental Disabilities*, Ch. 3, sec. I.

24. For a full discussion of this and of the following remarks bearing on involuntariness, see Ibid., Ch. 4.

25. For a full discussion of this and of the following remarks bearing on ignorance of the law, or right and wrong, see Ibid., Ch. 3, secs. II and III.

26. For a full discussion of this and of the following remarks bearing on diminished capacity, see Ibid., Chaps. 6, 7, and especially 8.

27. This doctrine is elaborated fully in Ibid., especially in Part I, Part V, and Appendix I.

Goldstein, Joseph, and Jay Katz, ''Abolish the 'Insanity Defense'—Why Not?'' *Yale Law Journal*, 72 (1963), 353–76.

Hatch, Orrin, ''Insanity Defense Reform,'' *Criminal Justice Ethics*, 3, no. 2 (Summer/Fall 1984), 2, 85–88.

Roche, Philip Q., ''A Plea for the Abandonment of the Defense of Insanity,'' in *Crime, Law and Corrections*, ed. Ralph Slovenko. Springfield, Ill.: Charles C Thomas, 1966.

Ross, Neil W., ''Some Philosophical Considerations of the Legal-Psychiatric Debate of Criminal Responsibility,'' *Issues in Criminology*, Vol. 1, 1965.

Suggested Further Reading

Fletcher, George P., ''Rights and Excuses,'' *Criminal Justice Ethics*, 3, no. 2 (Summer/Fall 1984), 17–27.

DECISION SCENARIO 3

Extenuation: The Insanity Plea

Paul and Lou Pitchard were bachelor brothers, aged 55 and 52, who had lived together since their widowed mother had died, twenty-two years earlier. Their home, 134 Willow Street, was the showplace of the neighborhood. Both held responsible positions in the local carpenter's union. They were hard-working, taciturn, meticulous men who took pride in keeping a spotless house. In general, they did not enjoy socializing except for an occasional union function. They had few friends and in the evenings enjoyed watching television over a couple of beers.

Paul could joke about their compulsive cleaniness in the home. He told the minister how once when their cousin Lois came for an evening, Lou got out the vacuum as soon as she dropped a potato chip and cleaned right

then and there. Lou saw nothing humorous in his action.

Lou was called away unexpectedly for a week, when his Navy unit had a reunion in San Diego. On his return, when he walked through the door of 134 Willow, he had an anxiety attack. Chairs were overturned, dirty glasses cluttered the floor, and a cigarette burn charred the solid oak mantelpiece. Trembling, he went to his brother's study to confront him. There, Paul sat with a strange woman.

''Lou!'' Paul began, ''I want you to meet . . . .''

Lou never let him finish. He fled, shattered, to the back patio. The same nerve-shattering chaos met his eyes. The entire afternoon he did not respond to his brother's entreaties to join him and his new girlfriend. Revulsion made Lou's mind whirl. He felt exiled from his own home. There was nowhere to go, no one to turn to. He began not to know his own mind. Paul and that strange woman were sitting in *his* living room. Soon it would no longer be his.

Shortly before midnight, Lou could bear it no longer. He took his .38 service revolver from his sock drawer and shot Paul twice in the head as he lay asleep.

In court, his lawyer, Milton Jacobs, entered the plea of not guilty by virtue of temporary insanity.

Questions

1. Granting that Lou was not himself, was he "insane," even temporarily? What are some of the ways to draw the line between reason and insanity?

2. How is the insanity plea morally justified?

3. Is it better, from a moral point of view, that pleading insanity protects some people from conviction who are incapable of taking responsibility, while allowing others who are guilty to escape punishment?

4. Some moral and legal protections of individual liberty carry strong tendencies for abuse. Does this possibility make them morally dangerous or useless?

2. THE LAWYER'S ROLE

When someone is accused of committing a crime in the United States, he or she has the right to be represented throughout the proceedings by a person with professional expertise in the intricacies of legal process—in ordinary terms, a lawyer. If the accused cannot afford to secure legal representation, it is provided by the court. While on rare occasions a defendant chooses to waive the right, the importance of being represented by a professional legal advocate is underscored by the familiar adage that "A person who acts as his own attorney has a fool for a client."

Acting as legal counsel for a person accused of breaking the law is a serious responsibility. As Alan H. Goldman points out in *The Moral Foundations of Professional Ethics*, it is argued that:

> In a criminal trial the defense attorney is alone in protecting the accused against the vast powers of the state. Only zealous advocacy can put the state's evidence to a full test, affording maximum protection for those who are accused of crime but innocent.[1]

[1]Alan H. Goldman, *The Moral Foundations of Professional Ethics* (Totowa, N.J.: Rowman & Littlefield, 1980), p. 106.

Such "zealous advocacy" is recognized by the American Bar Association *Code of Professional Responsibility* as one of three specifically professional (or nonordinary) moral obligations of an attorney. The other professional obligations specified by the Code include the duty to exercise independent judgment for a client (in essence, to avoid conflicts of interest), and the duty to preserve a client's confidentiality.[2]

Under the rubric of zealous advocacy an attorney is permitted wide latitude in the use of tactics which might otherwise be viewed as morally unacceptable. The special license of professional obligation is also used to justify questionable conduct by corporate managers and by engineers. **[See Business, Chapter 11, Section 4 and Chapter 13, Section 1.]** A lawyer may use any legal means helpful to a client's cause and is absolved of moral or legal responsibility for the adverse effects the tactics have on the rights of persons other than the client.

[2]Michael J. Kelly, *Legal Ethics and Legal Education* (Hastings-on-Hudson, N.Y.: The Hastings Center, Institute of Society, Ethics and the Life Sciences, 1980), p. 32.

This degree of role differentiation, excusing the lawyer from all moral consequences of legal actions in behalf of his client, is extreme. He may do for his client what he could not morally do for himself, his friend, or even his wife or child (if the action involves violating rights of others for trivial interests of his family). He may do what is immoral for the client to even suggest for himself.[3]

The moral license implied by the duty of zealous advocacy has led to practices sharply criticized by observers of our legal system. For example, a common strategy of attorneys representing defendants accused of rape is to impugn the sexual morality of the victim. The practice is so widespread that rape victims sometimes refuse to press charges against their assailants rather than risk the humiliation of being accused of promiscuity or of having intimate details of their sex lives examined in open court.

Tactics like harassing or degrading witnesses, instituting delaying actions, not revealing facts or evidence adverse to the client, and taking advantage of "loopholes" or technicalities in the law are disturbing to critics. Yet under the *adversary system* practiced in American courts the use of such tactics is not only permissible but obligatory. "Ethical Consideration 7" of the ABA Code responds to those who criticize lawyers for using maneuvers that seem morally questionable:

> Persons who make this charge are unaware, or do not understand, that the lawyer is hired to win, and if he does not exercise every legitimate effort in his client's behalf, then he is betraying a sacred trust.[4]

The professional obligations of exercising independent judgment for a client and preserving client confidentiality are mandated by the adversary system. Exercising independent judgment means that a lawyer must not only use his or her legal expertise

strictly for the client's benefit (regardless of the interests of others), but must act without considering his or her personal moral beliefs. A lawyer who agrees to act as a criminal defense attorney may not withdraw on grounds of conscience when the withdrawal would seriously damage the client's cause. Further, a defense attorney may not refuse—either on conscience or in the belief that the client is guilty—to adopt customary trial procedures likely to aid the client's case. Proponents of these rules maintain that they are required by the ideal of respect for individual autonomy. On this view, lawyers should not attempt to substitute their own moral judgment for that of their clients, nor usurp the capacity of clients to make their own decisions.

Successful functioning of the adversary system requires that clients must be able to trust their lawyers. Mounting an effective defense necessitates knowing all facts relevant to the case. If clients are to deal openly and candidly with their attorneys, maintaining confidentiality is essential. This requirement is similar to the obligation on the part of health care professionals. **[See Health Care, Chapter 5, Section 2.]** While preserving client confidentiality is a strong ethical obligation for lawyers, there are exceptions. For example, although an attorney is forbidden (under the 1983 ABA *Model Rules of Professional Conduct*) to divulge client confidences "to prevent substantial financial loss to third parties, caused by the client's wrongful conduct," disclosure *is* permitted when it is necessary in order to collect the attorney's fee or to defend the attorney against allegations (not necessarily formal charges) of misconduct.

If the adversary system obliges lawyers as professionals to engage in ethically dubious behavior, some writers conclude that the system itself requires modification or reform. Proponents of the adversary system maintain that a strong presentation of opposing viewpoints is the best method of arriving at truth and justice, the objective of trial proceedings. Critics claim that a system

---

[3]Goldman, *Moral Foundations*, pp. 96–97.
[4]ABA Code, EC 7, n. 3.

in which opponents intentionally suppress relevant facts that might be damaging is not conducive to uncovering the truth. Even if one concedes the effectiveness of the adversary system, the question remains whether desirable ends are sufficient to justify morally suspect means. The question echoes similar concerns regarding deceptive practices in police work and the health care professions. **[See Health Care, Chapter 5, Section 4 and Criminal Justice, Chapter 15, Section 2.]**

The principle of full advocacy has its moral foundations in the safeguarding of innocent persons wrongly accused. The emphasis on the rights of accused persons and on protection for the innocent pervades our criminal justice system. One example is the restrictions placed upon police methods of obtaining evidence. It is not clear, however, that the use of any and all legal tactics by defense attorneys—in disregard of their personal moral judgment and the adverse effects on nonclients—can be defended on these grounds. If, for example, a lawyer who knows a client to be guilty is professionally obligated to overlook that knowledge and zealously pursue acquittal, how can such a duty be justified on grounds of protecting the innocent? The answer given is that even guilty persons are entitled to due process under the law; they "deserve to be treated as persons and do not forfeit all rights by their criminal activity."[5] However, under the adversary system, lawyers are expected to ignore moral constraint to respect the dignity or rights of nonclients. Just as deceptive tactics by police may foster dishonesty and mistrust, some believe that requiring lawyers to wear moral blinders to fulfill their professional obligations is out of keeping with the goals of a lawful society.

Another ethical problem in the legal profession is paternalistic authority.

[A] problem fundamental to law practice and shared with most other professions . . . [is]

the issue of professional dominance of lay people. The special expertise of the professional can be easily used to restrict, rather than enhance the autonomy and range of choice exercised by the lay client.[6]

Lay clients are often unfamiliar with the workings of the law and require an attorney's special knowledge and skills. At the same time, they are at a disadvantage in the lawyer–client relationship.. Lawyers are enjoined by the ABA Code to pursue a client's interests loyally and vigorously. Given the complexity of laws and legal processes, how can clients adequately judge whether their lawyer's advice and actions are competent and appropriate? The usual relation of client to attorney is reminiscent of that of patient–physician and entails a similar risk of abuse of paternalism. **[See Health Care, Chapter 5, Section 1.]** Would a different relationship be more morally acceptable?

The responsibility of the legal profession to provide the public with adequate access to legal services is another ethical concern. The availability of legal services depends upon the ability to pay. The result is an underrepresentation for impoverished clients and groups. Arguments in favor of the adversary system and zealous advocacy presuppose equal representation for all parties, but private legal services are prohibitively expensive for many people. A defendant in a criminal case is entitled to a court-appointed attorney if he or she cannot afford to retain private counsel; however, public defenders are notoriously overworked and generally have little time to devote to individual cases. The problem is one of distributive justice and is related to allocation questions in the area of health care. **[See Health Care, Chapter 9, Section 2.]**

While the ABA Code states the desirability of competent legal representation being available to all, no explicit obligation exists for law departments or law firms to extend services to unpopular clients or those who

[5]Goldman, *Moral Foundations*, p. 118.

[6]Kelly, *Legal Ethics*, p. 41.

cannot afford them. Individual practitioners retain the prerogative to accept or reject any prospective client. What changes in our system of distributing legal services are needed to remedy problems of underrepresentation? Critics argue that correcting the problems requires a major overhaul of our social and economic structure. Reformers advocate measures such as advertising by attorneys (to promote competition and thus lead to a reduction in fees), group-financed services, and legal clinics for the poor. Conservative supports like the Bar Association have at various times mounted campaigns against each of these proposals.

In the following selection Richard Wasserstrom discusses two moral criticisms directed at lawyers. The first concerns amoral or immoral behavior toward nonclients. The second involves the dominance and paternalism which may characterize attorneys' dealings with their clients. Both of the problems arise from—and are sometimes said to be justified by—the nature of a professional role. Wasserstrom argues that role-differentiated behavior on the part of professionals (lawyers and others) may not be justified except in special circumstances. The author suggests that one way to eliminate "morally objectionable features" of lawyer–client relationships would be to "deprofessionalize" the law.

RICHARD WASSERSTROM

Lawyers as Professionals: Some Moral Issues

In this paper I examine two moral criticisms of lawyers which, if well-founded, are fundamental. Neither is new but each appears to apply with particular force today. Both tend to be made by those not in the mainstream of the legal profession and to be rejected by those who are in it. Both in some sense concern the lawyer–client relationship.

The first criticism centers around the lawyer's stance toward the world at large. The accusation is that the lawyer–client relationship renders the lawyer at best systematically amoral and at worst more than occasionally immoral in his or her dealings with the rest of mankind.

The second criticism focuses upon the relationship between the lawyer and the client. Here the charge is that it is the lawyer–client relationship which is morally objectionable because it is a relationship in which the lawyer dominates and in which the lawyer typi-

cally, and perhaps inevitably, treats the client in both an impersonal and a paternalistic fashion.

To a considerable degree these two criticisms of lawyers derive, I believe, from the fact that the lawyer is a professional. And to the extent to which this is the case, the more generic problems I will be exploring are those of professionalism generally. But in some respects, the lawyer's situation is different from that of other professionals. The lawyer is vulnerable to some moral criticism that does not as readily or as easily attach to any other professional. And this, too, is an issue that I shall be examining. . . .

I

One central feature of the professions in general and of law in particular is that there is a special, complicated relationship between the professional and the client or patient. For each of the parties in this relationship, but especially for the professional, the behavior that is involved is to a very significant degree what I call role-differentiated behavior. And this is significant because it is the nature of role-differentiated behavior that it often makes it both appropriate and desirable for the person in a particular role to put to one side considerations of various sorts—and especially various moral considerations—that would otherwise be relevant if not decisive. Some illustrations will help to make clear what I mean both by role-differentiated behavior and by the way role-differentiated behavior often alters, if not eliminates, the significance of those moral considerations that would obtain, were it not for the presence of the role.

Being a parent is, in probably every human culture, to be involved in role-differentiated behavior. In our own culture, and once again in most, if not all, human cultures, as a parent one is entitled, if not obligated, to prefer the interests of one's own children over those of children generally. That is to say, it is regarded as appropriate for a parent to allocate excessive goods to his or her own children, even though other children may have substantially more pressing and genuine needs for these same items. If one were trying to decide what the right way was to distribute assets among a group of children all of whom were strangers to oneself, the relevant moral considerations would be very different from those that would be thought to obtain once one's own children were in the picture. In the role of a parent, the claims of other children vis-à-vis one's own are, if not rendered morally irrelevant, certainly rendered less morally significant. In short, the role-differentiated character of the situation alters the relevant moral point of view enormously.

A similar situation is presented by the case of the scientist. For a number of years there has been debate and controversy within the scientific community over the question of whether scientists should participate in the development and elaboration of atomic theory, especially as those theoretical advances could then be translated into development of atomic weapons that would become a part of the arsenal of existing nation states. The dominant view, although it was not the unanimous one, in the scientific community was that the role of the scientist was to expand the limits of human knowledge. Atomic power was a force which had previously not been utilizable by human beings. The job of the scientist was, among other things, to develop ways and means by which that could now be done. And it was simply no part of one's role as a scientist to forego inquiry, or divert one's scientific explorations because of the fact that the fruits of the investigation could be or would be put to improper, immoral, or even catastrophic uses. The moral issues concerning whether and when to develop and use nuclear weapons were to be decided by others; by citizens and statesmen; they were not the concern of the scientist *qua* scientist.

In both of these cases it is, of course, conceivable that plausible and even thoroughly convincing arguments exist for the desirability of the role-differentiated behavior and its attendant neglect of what would otherwise be morally relevant considerations. Nonetheless, it is, I believe, also the case that the burden of proof, so to speak, is always upon the proponent of the desirability of this kind of role-differentiated behavior. For in the absence of special reasons why parents ought to prefer the interests of their children over those of children in general, the moral point of view surely requires that the claims and needs of all children receive equal consideration. But we take the rightness of parental preference so for granted, that we often neglect, I think, the fact that it is anything but self-evidently morally appropriate. My own view, for example, is that careful reflection shows that the *degree* of parental preference systematically encouraged in our own culture is far too extensive to be morally justified.

All of this is significant just because to be a professional is to be enmeshed in role-differentiated behavior of precisely this sort. One's role as a doctor, psychiatrist, or lawyer alters one's moral universe in a fashion analogous to that described above. Of special significance here is the fact that the professional *qua* professional has a client or patient whose interests must be represented, attended to, or looked after by the professional. And that means that the role of the professional (like that of the parent) is to prefer in a variety of ways the interests of the client or patient over those of individuals generally.

Consider, more specifically, the role-differentiated behavior of the lawyer. Conventional wisdom has it that where the attorney–client relationship exists, the point of view of the attorney is properly different—and appreciably so—from that which would be appropriate in the absence of the attorney–client relationship. For where the attorney–client relationship exists, it is often appropriate and many times even obligatory for the attorney to do things that, all other things being equal, an ordinary person need not, and should not do. What is characteristic of this role of a lawyer is the lawyer's required indifference to a wide variety of ends and consequences that in other contexts would be of undeniable moral significance. Once a lawyer represents a client, the lawyer has a duty to make his or her expertise fully available in the realization of the end sought by the client, irrespective, for the most, of the moral worth to which the end will be put or the character of the client who seeks to utilize it. Provided that the end sought is not illegal, the lawyer is, in essence, an amoral technician whose peculiar skills and knowledge in respect to the law are available to those with whom the relationship of client is established. The question, as I have indicated, is whether this particular and pervasive feature of professionalism is itself justifiable. At a minimum, I do not think any of the typical, simple answers will suffice.

One such answer focuses upon and generalizes from the criminal defense lawyer. For what is probably the most familiar aspect of this role-differentiated character of the lawyer's activity is that of the defense of a client charged with a crime. The received view within the profession (and to a lesser degree within the society at large) is that having once

agreed to represent the client, the lawyer is under an obligation to do his or her best to defend that person at trial, irrespective, for instance, even of the lawyer's belief in the client's innocence. There are limits, of course, to what constitutes a defense: a lawyer cannot bribe or intimidate witnesses to increase the likelihood of securing an acquittal. And there are legitimate questions, in close cases, about how those limits are to be delineated. But, however these matters get resolved, it is at least clear that it is thought both appropriate and obligatory for the attorney to put on as vigorous and persuasive a defense of a client believed to be guilty as would have been mounted by the lawyer thoroughly convinced of the client's innocence. I suspect that many persons find this an attractive and admirable feature of the life of a legal professional. I know that often I do. The justifications are varied and, as I shall argue below, probably convincing.

But part of the difficulty is that the irrelevance of the guilt or innocence of an accused client by no means exhausts the altered perspective of the lawyer's conscience, even in criminal cases. For in the course of defending an accused, an attorney may have, as a part of his or her duty of representation, the obligation to invoke procedures and practices which are themselves morally objectionable and of which the lawyer in other contexts might thoroughly disapprove. And these situations, I think, are somewhat less comfortable to confront. For example, in California, the case law permits a defendant in a rape case to secure in some circumstances an order from the court requiring the complaining witness, that is, the rape victim, to submit to a psychiatric examination before trial.[1] For no other crime is such a pretrial remedy available. In no other case can the victim of a crime be required to undergo psychiatric examination at the request of the defendant on the ground that the results of the examination may help the defendant prove that the offense did not take place. I think such a rule is wrong and is reflective of the sexist bias of the law in respect to rape. I certainly do not think it right that rape victims should be singled out by the law for this kind of special pretrial treatment, and I am skeptical about the morality of any involuntary psychiatric examination of witnesses. Nonetheless, it appears to be part of the role-differentiated obligation of a lawyer for a defendant charged with rape to seek to take advantage of this particular rule of law—irrespective of the independent moral view he or she may have of the rightness or wrongness of such a rule.

Nor, it is important to point out, is this peculiar, strikingly amoral behavior limited to the lawyer involved with the workings of the criminal law. Most clients come to lawyers to get the lawyers to help them do things that they could not easily do without the assistance provided by the lawyer's special competence. They wish, for instance, to dispose of their property in a certain way at death. They wish to contract for the purchase or sale of a house or a business. They wish to set up a corporation which will manufacture and market a new product. They wish to minimize their income taxes. And so on. In each case, they need the assistance of the professional, the lawyer, for he or she alone has the special skill which will make it possible for the client to achieve the desired result.

And in each case, the role-differentiated character of the lawyer's way of being tends to render irrelevant what would otherwise be morally relevant considerations. Suppose that a client desires to make a will disinheriting her children because they opposed the war in Vietnam. Should the lawyer refuse to draft the will because the lawyer thinks this a bad reason to disinherit one's children? Suppose a client can avoid the payment of taxes through a loophole only available to a few wealthy taxpayers. Should the lawyer refuse to tell the client of a loophole because the lawyer thinks it an unfair advantage for the rich? Suppose a client wants to start a corporation that will manufacture, distribute and promote a harmful but not illegal substance, e.g., cigarettes. Should the lawyer refuse to prepare the articles of incorporation for the corporation? In each case, the accepted view within the pro-

fession is that these matters are just of no concern to the lawyer *qua* lawyer. The lawyer need not of course agree to represent the client (and that is equally true for the unpopular client accused of a heinous crime), but there is nothing wrong with representing a client whose aims and purposes are quite immoral. And having agreed to do so, the lawyer is required to provide the best possible assistance, without regard to his or her disapproval of the objective that is sought.

The lesson, on this view, is clear. The job of the lawyer, so the argument typically concludes, is not to approve or disapprove of the character of his or her client, the cause for which the client seeks the lawyer's assistance, or the avenues provided by the law to achieve that which the client wants to accomplish. The lawyer's task is, instead, to provide that competence which the client lacks and the lawyer, as professional, possesses. In this way, the lawyer as professional comes to inhabit a simplified universe which is strikingly amoral—which regards as morally irrelevant any number of factors which nonprofessional citizens might take to be important, if not decisive, in their everyday lives. And the difficulty I have with all of this is that the arguments for such a way of life seem to be not quite so convincing to me as they do to many lawyers. I am, that is, at best uncertain that it is a good thing for lawyers to be so professional—for them to embrace so completely this role-differentiated way of approaching matters.

More specifically, if it is correct that this is the perspective of lawyers in particular and professionals in general, is it right that this should be their perspective? Is it right that the lawyer should be able so easily to put to one side otherwise difficult problems with the answer: but these are not and cannot be my concern as a lawyer? What do we gain and what do we lose from having a social universe in which there are professionals such as lawyers, who, as such, inhabit a universe of the sort I have been trying to describe?

One difficulty in even thinking about all of this is that lawyers may not be very objective or detached in their attempts to work the problem through. For one feature of this simplified, intellectual world is that it is often a very comfortable one to inhabit.

To be sure, on occasion, a lawyer may find it uncomfortable to represent an extremely unpopular client. On occasion, too, a lawyer may feel ill at ease invoking a rule of law or practice which he or she thinks to be an unfair or undesirable one. Nonetheless, for most lawyers, most of the time, pursuing the interests of one's clients is an attractive and satisfying way to live, in part just because the moral world of the lawyer is a simpler, less complicated, and less ambiguous world than the moral world of ordinary life. There is, I think, something quite seductive about being able to turn aside so many ostensibly difficult moral dilemmas and decisions with the reply: but that is not my concern; my job as a lawyer is not to judge the rights and wrongs of the client or the cause; it is to defend as best I can my client's interests. For the ethical problems that can arise within this constricted point of view are, to say the least, typically neither momentous nor terribly vexing. Role-differentiated behavior is enticing and reassuring precisely because it does constrain and delimit an otherwise often intractable and confusing moral world.

But there is, of course, also an argument which seeks to demonstrate that it is good and not merely comfortable for lawyers to behave this way.

It is good, so the argument goes, that the lawyer's behavior and concomitant point of view are role-differentiated because the lawyer *qua* lawyer participates in a complex institution which functions well only if the individuals adhere to their institutional roles.

For example, when there is a conflict between individuals, or between the state and an individual, there is a well-established institutional mechanism by which to get that dispute resolved. That mechanism is the trial in which each side is represented by a lawyer whose job it is both to present his or her client's case in the most attractive, forceful light and to seek to expose the weaknesses and defects in the case of the opponent. . . .

. . . When the lawyer functions in his most usual role, he or she functions as a counselor, as a professional whose task it is to help people realize those objectives and ends that the law permits them to obtain and which cannot be obtained without the attorney's special competence in the law. The attorney may think it wrong to disinherit one's children because of their views about the Vietnam war, but here the attorney's complaint is really with the laws of inheritance and not with his or her client. The attorney may think the tax provision an unfair, unjustifiable loophole, but once more the complaint is really with the Internal Revenue Code and not with the client who seeks to take advantage of it. And these matters, too, lie beyond the ambit of the lawyer's moral point of view as institutional counselor and facilitator. If lawyers were to substitute their own private views of what ought to be legally permissible and impermissible for those of the legislature, this would constitute a surreptitious and undesirable shift from a democracy to an oligarchy of lawyers. For given the fact that lawyers are needed to effectuate the wishes of clients, the lawyer ought to make his or her skills available to those who seek them without regard for the particular objectives of the client. . . .

. . . I do believe that the amoral behavior of the *criminal* defense lawyer is justifiable. But I think that jurisdiction depends at least as much upon the special needs of an accused as upon any more general defense of a lawyer's role-differentiated behavior. As a matter of fact I think it likely that many persons such as myself have been misled by the special features of the criminal case. Because a deprivation of liberty is so serious, because the prosecutorial resources of the state are so vast, and because, perhaps, of a serious skepticism about the rightness of punishment even where wrongdoing has occurred, it is easy to accept the view that it makes sense to charge the defense counsel with the job of making the best possible case for the accused—without regard, so to speak, for the merits. This coupled with the fact that it is an adversarial proceeding succeeds, I think, in justifying the amorality of the criminal defense counsel. But this does not, however, justify a comparable perspective on the part of lawyers generally. Once we leave the peculiar situation of the criminal defense lawyer, I think it quite likely that the role-differentiated amorality of the lawyer is almost certainly excessive and at times inappropriate. That is to say, this special case to one side, I am inclined to think that we might all be better served if lawyers were to see themselves less as subject to role-differentiated behavior and more as subject to the demands of the moral point of view. In this sense it may be that we need a good deal less rather than more professionalism in our society generally and among lawyers in particular.

Moreover, even if I am wrong about all this, four things do seem to me to be true and important.

First, all of the arguments that support the role-differentiated amorality of the lawyer on institutional grounds can succeed only if the enormous degree of trust and confidence in the institutions themselves is itself justified. If the institutions work well and fairly, there may be good sense to deferring important moral concerns and criticisms to another time and place, to the level of institutional criticism and assessment. But the less certain we are entitled to be of either the rightness or the self-corrective nature of the larger institutions of which the professional is a part, the less apparent it is that we should encourage the professional to avoid direct engagement with the moral issues as they arise. And we are, today, I believe, certainly entitled to be quite skeptical of the fairness and of the capacity for self-correction of our larger institutional mechanisms, including the legal system. To the degree to which the institutional rules and practices are unjust, unwise or undesirable, to that same degree is the case for the role-differentiated behavior of the lawer weakened if not destroyed.

Second, it is clear that there are definite character traits that the professional such as the lawyer must take on if the system is to work. What is less clear is that they are admirable ones. Even if the role-differentiated amorality of the professional lawyer is justified by the virtues of the adversary system, this also means that the lawyer *qua* lawyer will be encouraged to be competitive rather than co-operative; aggressive rather than accommodating; ruthless rather than compassionate; and pragmatic rather than principled. This is, I think, part of the logic of the role-differentiated behavior of lawyers in particular, and to a lesser degree of professionals in general. It is surely neither accidental nor unimportant that these are the same character traits that are emphasized and valued by the capitalist ethic—and on precisely analogous grounds. Because the ideals of professionalism and capitalism are the dominant ones within our culture, it is harder than most of us suspect even to take seriously the suggestion that radically different styles of living, kinds of occupational outlooks, and types of social institutions might be possible, let alone preferable.

Third, there is a special feature of the role-differentiated behavior of the lawyer that distinguishes it from the comparable behavior of other professionals. What I have in mind can be brought out through the following question: Why is it that it seems far less plausible to talk critically about the amorality of the doctor, for instance, who treats all patients irrespective of their moral character than it does to talk critically about the comparable amorality of the lawyer? Why is it that it seems so obviously sensible, simple and right for the doctor's behavior to be narrowly and rigidly role-differentiated, i.e., just to try to cure those who are ill? And why is it that at the very least it seems so complicated, uncertain, and troublesome to decide whether it is right for the lawyer's behavior to be similarly role-differentiated?

The answer, I think, is twofold. To begin with (and this I think is the less interesting point) it is, so to speak, intrinsically good to try to cure disease, but in no comparable way is it intrinsically good to try to win every lawsuit or help every client realize his or her objective. In addition (and this I take to be the truly interesting point), the lawyer's behavior is different in kind from the doctor's. The lawyer—and especially the lawyer as advocate—directly says and affirms things. The lawyer makes the case for the client. He or she tries to explain, persuade and convince others that the client's cause should prevail. The lawyer lives with and within a dilemma that is not shared by other professionals. If the lawyer actually believes everything that he or she asserts on behalf of the client, then it appears to be proper to regard the lawyer as in fact embracing and endorsing the points of view that he or she articulates. If the lawyer does not in fact believe what is urged by way of argument, if the lawyer is only playing a role, then it appears to be proper to tax the lawyer with hypocrisy and insincerity. To be sure, actors in a play take on roles and say things that the characters, not the actors, believe. But we know it is a play and that they are actors. The law courts are not, however, theaters, and the lawyers both talk about justice and they genuinely seek to persuade. The fact that the lawyer's words, thoughts, and convictions are, apparently, for sale and at the service of the client helps us, I think, to understand the peculiar hostility which is more than occasionally uniquely directed by lay persons toward lawyers. The verbal, role-differentiated behavior of the lawyer *qua* advocate puts the lawyer's integrity into question in a way that distinguishes the lawyer from the other professionals.[2]

Fourth, and related closely to the three points just discussed, even if on balance the role-differentiated character of the lawyer's way of thinking and acting is ultimately deemed to be justifiable within the system on systemic instrumental grounds, it still remains the case that we do pay a social price for that way of thought and action. For to become and to be a professional, such as a lawyer, is to incorporate within oneself ways of behaving and ways of thinking that shape the whole person. It is especially hard, if not impossible, because of the nature of the professions, for one's professional way of thinking not to dominate one's entire adult life. Thus, even if the lawyers who were involved in Watergate were not, strictly speaking, then and there function-

ing as lawyers, their behavior was, I believe, the likely if not inevitable consequence of their legal acculturation. Having been taught to embrace and practice the lawyer's institutional role, it was natural, if not unavoidable, that they would continue to play that role even when they were somewhat removed from the specific institutional milieu in which that way of thinking and acting is arguably fitting and appropriate. The nature of the professions—the lengthy educational preparation, the prestige and economic rewards, and the concomitant enhanced sense of self—makes the role of professional a difficult one to shed even in those obvious situations in which that role is neither required nor appropriate. In important respects, one's professional role becomes and is one's dominant role, so that for many persons at least they become their professional being. This is at a minimum a heavy price to pay for the professions as we know them in our culture, and especially so for lawyers. Whether it is an inevitable price is, I think, an open question, largely because the problem has not begun to be fully perceived as such by the professionals in general, the legal profession in particular, or by the educational institutions that train professionals.

II

The role-differentiated behavior of the professional also lies at the heart of the second of the two moral issues I want to discuss, namely, the character of the interpersonal relationship that exists between the lawyer and the client. As I indicated at the outset, the charge that I want to examine here is that the relationship between the lawyer and the client is typically, if not inevitably, a morally defective one in which the client is not treated with the respect and dignity that he or she deserves.

There is the suggestion of paradox here. The discussion so far has concentrated upon defects that flow from what might be regarded as the lawyer's excessive preoccupation with and concern for the client. How then can it also be the case that the lawyer *qua* professional can at the same time be taxed with promoting and maintaining a relationship of dominance and indifference vis-à-vis his or her client? The paradox is apparent, not real. Not only are the two accusations compatible; the problem of the interpersonal relationship between the lawyer and the client is itself another feature or manifestation of the underlying issue just examined—the role-differentiated life of the professional. For the lawyer can both be overly concerned with the interest of the client and at the same time fail to view the client as a whole person, entitled to be treated in certain ways.

One way to begin to explore the problem is to see that one pervasive, and I think necessary, feature of the relationship between any professional and the client or patient is that it is in some sense a relationship of inequality. This relationship of inequality is intrinsic to the existence of professionalism. For the professional is, in some respects at least, always in a position of dominance vis-à-vis the client, and the client in a position of dependence vis-à-vis the professional. To be sure, the client can often decide whether or not to enter into a relationship with a professional. And often, too, the client has the power to decide whether to terminate the relationship. But the significant thing I want to focus upon is that while the relationship exists, there are important respects in which the relationship cannot be a relationship between equals and must be one in which it is the professional who is in control. As I have said, I believe this is a necessary and not merely a familiar characteristic of the relationship between professionals and those they serve. Its existence is brought about by the following features.

To begin with, there is the fact that one characteristic of professions is that the professional is the possessor of expert knowledge of a sort not readily or easily attainable by members of the community at large. Hence, in the most straightforward of all senses the client, typically, is dependent upon the professional's skill or knowledge because the client does not possess the same knowledge.

Moreover, virtually every profession has its own technical language, a private terminology which can only be fully understood by the members of the profession. The presence of such a language plays the dual role of creating and affirming the membership of the professionals within the profession and of preventing the client from fully discussing or understanding his or her concerns in the language of the profession.

These circumstances, together with others, produce the added consequence that the client is in a poor position effectively to evaluate how well or badly the professional performs. In the professions, the professional does not look primarily to the client to evaluate the professional's work. The assessment of ongoing professional competence is something that is largely a matter of self-assessment conducted by the practicing professional. Where external assessment does occur, it is carried out not by clients or patients but by other members of the profession, themselves. It is significant, and surely surprising to the outsider, to discover to what degree the professions are self-regulating. They control who shall be admitted to the professions and they determine (typically only if there has been a serious complaint) whether the members of the profession are performing in a minimally satisfactory way. This leads professionals to have a powerful motive to be far more concerned with the way they are viewed by their colleagues than with the way they are viewed by their clients. This means, too, that clients will necessarily lack the power to make effective evaluations and criticisms of the way the professional is responding to the client's needs.

In addition, because the matters for which professional assistance is sought usually involve things of great personal concern to the client, it is the received wisdom within the professions that the client lacks the perspective necessary to pursue in a satisfactory way his or her own best interests, and that the client requires a detached, disinterested representative to look after his or her interests. That is to say, even if the client had the same knowledge or competence that the professional had, the client would be thought to lack the objectivity required to utilize that competency effectively on his or her own behalf.

Finally, as I have indicated, to be a professional is to have been acculturated in a certain way. It is to have satisfactorily passed through a lengthy and allegedly difficult period of study and training. It is to have done something hard. Something that not everyone can do. Almost all professions encourage this way of viewing oneself; as having joined an elect group by virtue of hard work and mastery of the mysteries of the profession. In addition, the society at large treats members of a profession as members of an elite by paying them more than most people for the work they do with their heads rather than their hands, and by according them a substantial amount of social prestige and power by virtue of their membership in a profession. It is hard, I think, if not impossible, for a person to emerge from professional training and participate in a profession without the belief that he or she is a special kind of person, both different from and somewhat better than those nonprofessional members of the social order. It is equally hard for the other members of society not to hold an analogous view of the professionals. And these beliefs surely contribute, too, to the dominant role played by a professional in any professional–client relationship. . . .

. . . The lawyer *qua* professional is, of necessity, only centrally interested in that part of the client that lies within his or her special competency. And this leads any professional including the lawyer to respond to the client as an object—as a thing to be altered, corrected, or otherwise assisted by the professional rather than as a person. At best the client is viewed from the perspective of the professional not as a whole person but as a segment or aspect of a person—an interesting kidney problem, a routine marijuana possession case, or another adolescent with an identity crisis.[3]

Then, too, the fact already noted that the professions tend to have and to develop their own special languages has a lot to do with the depersonalization of the client. And this certainly holds for the lawyers. For the lawyer can and does talk to other lawyers but not to the client in the language of the profession. What is more, the lawyer goes out of his or her way to do so. It is satisfying. It is the exercise of power. Because the ability to communicate is one of the things that distinguishes persons from objects, the inability of the client to communicate with the lawyer in the lawyer's own tongue surely helps to make the client less than a person in the lawyer's eyes—and perhaps even in the eyes of the client.

The forces that operate to make the relationship a paternalistic one seem to me to be at least as powerful. If one is a member of a collection of individuals who have in common the fact that their intellects are highly trained, it is very easy to believe that one knows more than most people. If one is a member of a collection of individuals who are accorded high prestige by the society at large, it is equally easy to believe that one is better and knows better than most people. If there is, in fact, an area in which one does know things that the client doesn't know, it is extremely easy to believe that one knows generally what is best for the client. All this, too, surely holds for lawyers.

In addition there is the fact, also already noted, that the client often establishes a relationship with the lawyer because the client has a serious problem or concern which has rendered the client weak and vulnerable. This, too, surely increases the disposition to respond toward the client in a patronizing, paternalistic fashion. The client of necessity confers substantial power over his or her well-being upon the lawyer. Invested with all of this power both by the individual and the society, the lawyer *qua* professional responds to the client as though the client were an individual who needed to be looked after and controlled, and to have decisions made for him or her by the lawyer, with as little interference from the client as possible.

Now one can, I think, respond to the foregoing in a variety of ways. One could, to begin with, insist that the paternalistic and impersonal ways of behaving are the aberrant rather than the usual characteristics of the lawyer–client relationship. One could, therefore, argue that a minor adjustment in better legal education aimed at sensitizing prospective lawyers to the possibility of these abuses is all that is required to prevent them. Or, one could, to take the same tack described earlier, regard these features of the lawyer–client relationship as endemic but not as especially serious. One might have a view that, at least in moderation, relationships having these features are a very reasonable price to pay (if it is a price at all) for the very appreciable benefits of professionalism. The impersonality of a surgeon, for example, may make it easier rather than harder for him or for her to do a good job of operating successfully on a patient. The impersonality of a lawyer may make it easier rather than harder for him or for her to do a good job representing a client. The paternalism of lawyers may be justified by the fact that they do in fact know better—at least within many areas of common concern to the parties involved—what is best for the client. And, it might even be claimed, clients want to be treated in this way.

But if these answers do not satisfy, if one believes that these are typical, if not systemic, features of the professional character of the lawyer–client relationship, and if one believes, as well, that these are morally objectionable features of that or any other relationship among persons, it does look as though one way to proceed is to "deprofessionalize" the law—to weaken, if not excise, those features of legal professionalism that tend to produce these kinds of interpersonal relationships.

The issue seems to me difficult just because I do think that there are important and distinctive competencies that are at the heart of the legal profession. If there were not, the solution would be simple. If there were no such competencies—if, that is, lawyers didn't really help people any more than (so it is sometimes claimed) therapists do—then no significant social goods would be furthered by the mainte-

nance of the legal profession. But, as I have said, my own view is that there are special competencies and that they are valuable. This makes it harder to determine what to preserve and what to shed. The question, as I see it, is how to weaken the bad consequences of the role-differentiated lawyer–client relationship without destroying the good that lawyers do.

Without developing the claim at all adequately in terms of scope or detail, I want finally to suggest the direction this might take. Desirable change could be brought about in part by a sustained effort to simplify legal language and to make the legal processes less mysterious and more directly available to lay persons. The way the law works now, it is very hard for lay persons either to understand it or to evaluate or solve legal problems more on their own. But it is not at all clear that substantial revisions could not occur along these lines. Divorce, probate, and personal injury are only three fairly obvious areas where the lawyers' economic self-interest says a good deal more about resistance to change and simplification than does a consideration on the merits.

The more fundamental changes, though, would, I think, have to await an explicit effort to alter the ways in which lawyers are educated and acculturated to view themselves, their clients, and the relationships that ought to exist between them. It is, I believe, indicative of the state of legal education and of the profession that there has been to date extremely little self-conscious concern even with the possibility that these dimensions of the attorney–client relationship are worth examining—to say nothing of being capable of alteration. That awareness is, surely, the prerequisite to any serious assessment of the moral character of the attorney–client relationship as a relationship among adult human beings.

I do not know whether the typical lawyer–client relationship is as I have described it; nor do I know to what degree role-differentiation is the cause; nor do I even know very precisely what "deprofessionalization" would be like or whether it would on the whole be good

383

ɔnvinced, however, that this,
worth taking seriously and
to more systematically than
ᴄase to date.

Notes

1. *Ballard* v. *Superior Court*, 64 Cal. 2d 159, 410 P.2d 838, 49 Cal. Rptr. 302 (1966).
2. I owe this insight, which I think is an important and seldom appreciated one, to my colleague, Leon Letwin.
3. This and other features are delineated from a somewhat different perspective in an essay by Erving Goffman. See "The Medical Model and Mental Hospitalization: Some Notes on the Vicissitudes of the Tinkering Trades," in E. Goffman, *Asylums* (Garden City, N.Y.: Doubleday, 1961), especially Parts V and VI of the essay.

Suggested Further Reading

Curtis, Charles P., "The Ethics of Advocacy," *Stanford Law Review*, 4 (1951), 3–23.

Freedman, Monroe H., "Professional Responsibility of the Criminal Defense Lawyer: The Three Hardest Questions," *Michigan Law Review*, 64 (1966), 1469.

Fried, Charles, "The Lawyer as Friend: The Moral Foundations of the Lawyer-Client Relation," *Yale Law Journal*, 85 (1976), 1060.

Morgan, Thomas, "The Evolving Concept of Professional Responsibility," *Harvard Law Review*, 90 (1977), 702.

Noonan, John, "The Purposes of Advocacy and the Limits of Confidentiality," *Michigan Law Review*, 64 (1966), 1495.

Schnapper, Eric, "The Myth of Legal Ethics," *ABA Journal*, 64 (1978), 202.

DECISION SCENARIO 4

The Lawyer's Role

Mr. Gerhart found Bill to be an annoying client. Bill had come to Mr. Gerhart's office seeking counsel for a charge of company fraud. Bill had been a sales manager for a company which sold contracts for aluminum siding to single-family homeowners. A federal agency in charge of investigating fraudulent claims in the aluminum siding industry informed Bill two months before of his indictment.

Bill seemed confused to Mr. Gerhart. He didn't seem to want to win his case. Mr. Gerhart had no doubt that Bill was guilty. But then, all of Bill's friends and colleagues at the Swampland Siding Company were too—probably those in competing companies as well. Bill's conscience bothered him. He felt that he was guilty of doing wrong and that he needed to protect his buddies and take the rap.

Mr. Gerhart tried to talk some sense into his client. The idea was to put up a good defense. That meant names and addresses of possible co-conspirators. Show the prosecutor that there were standards in the industry and that Bill was simply following orders. Bill balked at the idea of turning stool pigeon.

When Mr. Gerhart saw there was no talking sense to Bill, he quietly began his own investigation. Finding the essential information about the Swampland Siding Company was not hard. Bill had already given him enough information to open doors. Mr. Gerhart was sure that Bill would be happier with a light rather than a heavy sentence. As long as Bill kept a tight lip in court, Mr. Gerhart knew he could get him off.

Questions

1. Was Mr. Gerhart right in using his professional judgment rather than his client's?

2. What moral limits do you believe are needed to Mr. Gerhart's aggressive legal action?

3. How should the matter of Bill's acknowledged fraudulent activity be weighed in with Mr. Gerhart's action?

4. Did Mr. Gerhart honor his obligations of confidentiality?

5. How does our legal system work if it permits lawyers to plead a case they know to be untrue?

17. THE ETHICS OF PUNISHMENT

1. NATURE AND GOALS OF PUNISHMENT

One important output of a criminal justice system is punishment. Can the concept of punishment be justified? As was mentioned earlier, some argue that lawbreakers suffer from something akin to illness and should therefore receive treatment instead of punishment. Others argue that persons who break the law are compelled to do so by unjust social conditions: hence they are not responsible agents and ought not to be punished. On this view, public resources should be used to eliminate social injustice rather than maintain a criminal justice system.

If the idea of punishing lawbreakers is accepted, the question then arises whether it is possible—or necessary—to punish in a humane way. American law prohibits the use of "cruel and unusual" punishment. Our criminal justice system relies on fines, probation, imprisonment, and, rarely, death, as punishments for crime. Imprisonment, the predominant form, is so commonplace that we forget that its widespread use is a relatively new development. Nineteenth-century reformers advocated imprisonment as a humane alternative to forced labor, corporal punishment, or death—the usual punishments in Western societies up to that time. The reformist movement had a strong influence on American criminal justice policies. The idea emerged that prisons should provide rehabilitation along with punishment and thereby produce greater long-term benefits for society and for criminals.

The brutal conditions prevailing in many prisons are widely known. Some critics argue that imprisonment can no longer be considered a humane form of punishment. In addition, underfunding and an enormous rise in the prison population have led some to pay no more than lip service to rehabilitation as a goal. Can imprisonment, given the violence and overcrowding of prison life, be justified as a form of punishment? Are there workable alternatives which ought to be considered? Suggestions in this vein include work-release programs, sentencing criminals to perform community service, and requiring them to make restitution to their victims. New York State recently began experimenting with a new form of confinement for criminals. The program relies on the use of small transmitters worn by "prisoners," who remain at home and are permitted to go out only to work. A computer monitors the transmitters and warns of any unauthorized movement by the convicts. The plan is aimed at easing overcrowding in prisons and reducing the high costs of maintaining prisoners. An additional benefit arises of preventing the suffering caused by harmful, if unintended, conditions of prison life.

Preferences among different types of punishment are influenced by one's views concerning its purpose. A utilitarian analysis stresses the deterrent effects of punishing criminals. Some utilitarians argue that imprisonment is not a cost-effective form of punishment because it has an inadequate deterrent effect compared with the burden it puts on a society's resources. Statistics showing a high rate of recidivism among prisoners are sometimes cited to support this argument. Similarly, utilitarians tend to favor a system of fines (or possibly corporal punishment) over imprisonment. Since on the utilitarian view all punishment is a necessary evil, the relative humaneness of any particular form is not a paramount consideration.

Deontologists stress the goal of retribution in regard to punishment. They view the goal of deterrence to be at odds with the Kantian ethic of not using persons merely as means to an end, no matter how desirable that end might be. For deontologists, the severity of punishment should be proportional to the harm caused to crime victims. On this view, if one were to determine that imprisonment is a more severe punishment than its original advocates envisioned, its use would have to be adjusted to make it more proportional to the harmfulness of specific crimes.

In the following article Hugo Adam Bedau examines current theories regarding the nature and justification of punishment. The author maintains that, while "a world without punishment is both unattainable and undesirable," it is possible and desirable to make a clear distinction between the intentional deprivation of rights involved in punishment and the unintended but actual harm which many prisoners suffer. Bedau argues that by defining the purpose and nature of punishment more precisely we can evaluate and respond to a number of familiar criticisms of the criminal justice system and move toward narrowing the "gap between theory and practice" in punishing criminals.

HUGO ADAM BEDAU

A World Without Punishment?

Today, in contrast to whatever may have been true in earlier, more complacent times, current modes of punishment and the criminal justice system which prevails in our society have become the object of various familiar objections.[1]

1. Too many classes of acts (e.g., gambling) and conditions (e.g., public nudity or drunkenness) are punishable offenses; we suffer from an acute case of "overcriminalization."
2. Too few of those who are guilty of dangerous and harmful acts are caught, too few convicted, and too few punished.
3. Too many people are behind prison bars mainly on account of their class or status rather than as a result of their acts, e.g., they are blacks, or long-hairs, or poor, or all three.
4. Too many people are sentenced to overly harsh punishments: harsh because severe, e.g., long term imprisonment for possession of marijuana; harsh because vague, e.g., indeterminate sentences for any offense.
5. Too many people are punished by imprisonment rather than being dealt with alternatively by the criminal justice system, e.g., conscientious draft resisters who during the 1960s were prosecuted and convicted as common criminals rather than treated non-punitively in light of their conscientious motives.
6. Too many punishments are imposed by statutes which rest on vague grounds of general deterrence and lack empirical evidence to

Reprinted with permission from *Punishment and Human Rights*, ed. Milton Goldinger (Cambridge, Mass.: Schenkman Books, Inc., 1974), pp. 141–62.

show that such threats are likely to influence the conduct of large numbers of potential offenders.

7. Too many people suffer from harms and hardships which are not properly part of their punishment but which they cannot escape once they are at the mercy of those charged with the administration of punishment, e.g., the bail-or-jail system, overcrowded pre-trial detention facilities, abuses by the custodial staff in prison, victimization at the hands of other inmates.

8. Too many people are simply the victims of official lawlessness inflicted upon them by the corrupt and the vindictive, e.g., police brutality, judicial venality.

9. Too many people are being made worse by the prevailing system of punishment.

While particular grievances inspire such criticisms, they have led some to mount a radical challenge against the whole system. These grievances have inspired the vision of a *world without punishment*, a utopia long admired by anarchists and socialists, in which not only the whip and the gallows have disappeared, but in which shackles and bars, and all other devices whereby the state enlists coercive force against its own citizens in the name of "law and order," are abandoned. The combined effect of piecemeal objections to punishment can be the dream of a non-punitive, non-repressive society, a true community. This vision is interesting to contemplate if only because it raises some hard questions. Could we in fact entirely abolish all our punitive institutions and practices without utter chaos? What would be the result of such an anti-penal orientation in practice if we left everything else in society the same, e.g., did not simultaneously become hermits or saints, did not pursue radically different social and economic policies, did not confront acute limitations on natural resources? Would the result be a reasonable bargain for everyone, worth paying the costs of no punishment in order to get the advantages of no punishments? If the bargain seems a bad one (as it must to most people), and yet if the particular complaints aired against the prevailing system

of punishment are nevertheless true, what modifications might we make either in our theory of punishment or in our penal practice so as to get a better system than we have at present?

The position I defend would answer some of these questions as follows. First, punishment necessarily has some features about it, viz., the deprivation of rights or the imposition of pain, which are bound to make it unattractive to decent persons and also to lend itself to abuses. Second, a fair assessment of current theory as to the nature and justification of punishment shows that the present system of punishment is unintelligible and indefensible. The resulting effects of this assessment upon the theory of punishment are as yet uncalculated. Third, except for fatal and mutilative punishments, whose direct effects are clear, we are not able to predict the total effect upon any given person of subjecting him to a given punishment for a given offense. This should make us extremely cautious about imposing some modes of punishment, e.g., long term detention, upon anyone who is expected subsequently to assume (or resume) a place in society as a normal individual. Fourth, the notorious harms imposed by the existing system of punishment justify immediate experimentation with radical alternatives wherever feasible. Even if abolition of the current penitentiary system of imprisonment is highly desirable, one should not suppose that this can be done without considerable costs and new incentives which may turn out to contradict essential features of our post-industrial society. Fifth, at the present time there is no general alternative available to us and acceptable by the public which is at once superior to punishment in avoiding its harms and abuses and not less effective in response to the genuine problem of criminal violence. Finally, whereas the grievances against the present system of punishment are genuine and legitimate, other considerations show that a world without punishment is both unattainable and undesirable.

It is not possible in brief compass to establish in detail the truth of all these claims, so far stated without even the semblance of argument. However, if we critically examine the current ideas among philosophers as to the nature and justification of punishment, we can see at least how the first three of the above half-dozen claims are correct, and, along the way, add some explanatory support for the other claims as well.

II

During the past twenty years, philosophers in the English-speaking world have reached general agreement as to the nature of punishment. The roots of this conception are at least as old as Hobbes's *Leviathan*,[2] but not until fairly recently has the task been undertaken of giving an exact and formal definition of punishment. The task may at first seem quite easy ("Everyone understands what punishment is," says conventional wisdom), but it is not. A formal definition of any concept poses certain constraints. In addition, there are many things which are like or concurrent with punishment and thus difficult to distinguish from it, and this will confuse all but the most alert and skillful. For instance, in order to understand the idea of *punishing a person*, it is necessary to distinguish it from such related but different notions as controlling a person's conduct, revenge, intentionally harming another, unintentionally harming another, treatment, blaming, and shaming. Similarly, one must distinguish a person's being punished from a person's being taxed, feeling guilty, being blamed, being hurt. And one must be prepared to say whether God (if there is or were a God) could punish a person, whether a person can punish himself, whether the innocent can be punished, whether a dog can be punished, and so forth. It is out of the attempt to make these distinctions and answer these questions that the current consensus on the nature of punishment has emerged.[3] It can be expressed in the following statement:

A person, P, is punished by something, x, if and only if

(i) x is some pain or other consequence normally considered unpleasant,
(ii) x is intentionally imposed upon P by someone else, Q,
(iii) Q has the authority under the rules of the (legal or other) system to impose x upon P,
(iv) x is imposed on P by Q on account of an offense as defined by the (legal or other) rules,
(v) because P is authoritatively found to be the offender.

For our purposes, the emphasis upon *legal* rules in the above definition is unobjectionable, because in the present discussion, the idea of punishment and its attendant institutions are those of punishment within legal systems (in contrast to the punishment parents visit upon their children, school authorities upon students, etc.). Punishment, of course, is not confined to acts of government under law. Yet it is such punishments which pose the gravest social problem and which are primarily at issue whenever one seriously contemplates the idea of a world without punishment.

Now, if what one wants to do is to attack or criticize the very idea of punishment in order to eliminate the practice or institution of punishment from public life, theoretically the easiest way to do this would be to argue, on some ground or other, that one or more of the five conditions used in this definition has *no* proper application in human affairs. Consider in this light the complaint, mentioned earlier, that we suffer from an acute case of "overcriminalization."[4] The point of this complaint amounts to an attack under clause (iv) in the above definition; "overcriminalization" is the complaint that consensual conduct should not be made a criminal offense, and that we should repeal or nullify all statutes in the penal code which do so. The result would be a vast increase in the amount of conduct which is no longer criminal and therefore no longer punishable as such. In order to attack punishment by the route of pressing the objection of "overcriminalization," a further step must be taken. One must argue either that the conduct in question is not really harmful, or that although it is harmful it must be permitted because it cannot be prevented, or that its harmfulness can be controlled and regulated in non-punitive ways. In a similiar manner, all the classic complaints against punishment can be understood and diagnosed by reference to this definition of punishment.

Before turning to a major objection to punishment as here defined, it is useful to consider first two relatively minor objections. Alternatives to punishment are almost invariably inspired by the feature of punishment identified in clause (i) of the above definition: the infliction of *pain*. Decent people are naturally repelled by the deliberate infliction of pain by one person upon another, except, perhaps, when the person has given his knowing consent to the suffering (as in earlier days, before the development of effective anesthesias, when a gangrenous limb had to be amputated to avoid death). It should be understood, however, that pain—the sensation or the feeling of physical or psychological pain—is neither a necessary nor a sufficient condition of punishment. That it is not a sufficient condition is shown, of course, by the presence of four other conditions in the standard definition of punishment. That it is not a necessary condition, however, is not so readily grasped. Yet consider the death penalty. It is hardly to be denied that killing persons is both a conceivable and an actual mode of punishment. But are we to suppose that it would cease to be a punishment if the sentence of death were carried out by administering (as, supposedly, happened to Socrates when he drank the hemlock) a lethal potion which is *entirely painless*? One might argue that such a painless execution is not as much of a punishment as an agonizingly painful execution; but this hardly matters. What does matter is that by executing a person, one has destroyed his capacity for any future experiences and conduct; one has *deprived* him of his life, something which, presumably, he values (most people do) and to which he has (absent his criminal conduct) a *right*. Accordingly, I would propose that the reference to pain in clause (i) of the standard definition of punish-

ment be revised so as to refer instead to the deprivation of a person's rights.[5] A punishment, especially a punishment under law, always deprives a person of something to which he normally has a right, e.g., his life (the death penalty), his liberty (prison), or his property (fines). Whether or not he minds this, whether or not it also hurts him in some ordinary sense, is incidental. He has lost something of value, whatever he thinks or feels about it; and to do that to a person, in conformity with the other features of the concept of punishment outlined above, is to have punished him. Incidentally, it is just this feature of the revision of clause (i) above which helps us to see what it is about "enforced treatment," such as the regimen of "behavior modification" displayed in Anthony Burgess's *A Clockwork Orange*, which explains why one feels that the society therein depicted has not really abandoned punishment for therapy, but merely exchanged one mode of punishment for another. What remains constant in both cases, as the novel (and movie) show, is the deprivation of offenders' rights by duly constituted authority in consequence of the violation of the criminal code. And that is punishment, whatever else we may choose to call it.

The second preliminary objection is concerned with what we are to infer from our definition of punishment as to the *point* of punishing people. Even though, under this definition, punishing a person is an *intentional* undertaking, it is not clear *what* the intention is with which, in general, we punish people at all. To clarify the problem, consider what a judge should say to a typical burglar when sentencing him to three years in the penitentiary. If the judge is persuaded by our definition of punishment, he might say, "By the authority vested in me, I hereby sentence you to three years in the penitentiary *because* of your conviction on the offense as charged and the statutes providing such punishment for burglary." But what should the judge say if he begins in this way: "By the authority, etc., three years in the penitentiary *in order* to . . . ?" In order to *what*? In order to prevent him from any further burglary during the next three years? In order to make the burglar less inclined to further burglary after the next three years? In order to discourage other would-be burglars? In order to make the convict worse off, as cynics and the recidivism statistics would indicate? The definition of punishment under consideration gives no single answer to this question, and the issue before us is whether this is a merit or defect in the definition, or neither.

Some theorists think it is a defect, because when they define punishment, they do not leave open this question of point in punishment. Thus, Herbert Packer defines (he says "describes") punishment as "all the ways of dealing with people that are marked by . . . a dominant purpose that is neither to compensate someone injured by the offense nor to better the offender's condition but to prevent further offenses or to inflict what is thought to be deserved pain on the offender."[6] Similarly, Joel Feinberg has said that the standard definition of punishment "seems to many to leave out . . . altogether the very element that makes punishment theoretically puzzling and morally disquieting."[7] What is that "element"? Feinberg answers that it is the point, or purpose, or aim of the institution of punishment itself: "the expression of attitudes of resentment and indignation, and of judgments of disapproval and reprobation [toward the offender], on the part either of the punishing authority himself or of those 'in whose name' the punishment is inflicted."[8] Notice that, although Packer and Feinberg agree in objecting to our definition of punishment, they disagree over the presumed intention with which society punishes. But is either of their criticisms correct?

Feinberg's is certainly the more plausible. What Packer calls "the dominate purpose" of punishment and would therefore incorporate *within* the nature and definition of punishment is what many theorists would, rightly, I think, regard as part of its *justification* and therefore as something *external* to the definition. To accept Packer's account of the purpose of punishment forecloses the justification of punishment by deterrence ("to prevent further offenses") and retribution ("to inflict what is thought to be deserved pain on the offender"). But once this is done, what is there left to appeal to as the justification of punishment? Furthermore, it would seem impossible, on Packer's view, to claim to have punished someone and yet not to have tried (and succeeded?) either to prevent further offenses or to cause deserved pain. Yet this does not seem self-contradictory or unintelligible at all; in fact, it often happens. The "expressive function" of punishment, however, does seem at least internal to the nature of punishment and thus a feature of every act of punishing someone. How could we punish a person and fail to express our condemnation of his unlawful conduct? If, therefore, it seems outrageous to suppose that there is no answer to our hypothetical question posed earlier ("An offender is punished 'in order to'—what?"), the proper way for the judge to speak to the guilty is to say in effect, "We sentence you to three years in the penitentiary *in order to* express society's condemnation of your felonious deed." All further purposes, particularly of deterrence and prevention, can be left to the justification of punishment. They need not be built into the very concept of punishment itself.

Yet, plausible as this is, it may still be in error. Why *must* there be any general intention with which society punishes its deviant and dangerous members? Why *must* there be some one thing (or, for that matter, some two or three things) which we do when we punish? A stray remark of Wittgenstein's anticipates these hesitations:

> 'Why do we punish criminals? Is it from a desire for revenge? Is it in order to prevent a repetition of the crime?' And so on. The truth is there is no one reason. There is the institution of punishing criminals. Different people support this for different reasons, and for different reasons in different cases and at different times . . . And so punishments are carried out.[9]

Wittgenstein has not given an argument for the view that there is no single "in order to" about punishment. All he has done is help us to see that, in believing there is some one "in order to," we are ourselves in the grip of a certain picture about the institution of punishment under law, a picture for which we lack adequate evidence, a picture *not necessary*. Even if he is in error and views such as Feinberg's (or even Packer's) are correct, it still remains true that the motives, intentions, purposes, aims or goals of punishment are to some extent hidden from view and to some extent simply fictions derived from imputing to society notions (such as intentions, etc.) which have exact and literal reference only to particular individuals. If the standard definition of punishment leaves the institution of punishment an ambiguously (or vacuously) purposive practice, that may be a mark in favor of the definition. Of course, it may also provoke challenges to the idea of an institution as pervasive and as painful as punishment which lacks any central purpose. In any case, since there is no way for society (or the legislature, or even the judiciary) to say what its intentions are in preserving the institution of punishment, it is extremely difficult to see how we can hope to resolve this dispute either way.

Notice, finally, how natural it is, if we follow the standard conception of punishment, to exclude from a person's punishment all those things which he finds unpleasant, harmful, degrading, or a rights deprivation and which are also distinguishable from the things of this sort to which he was *sentenced* by someone having the authority to impose such deprivations on him. The standard conception of punishment encourages us to identify as a person's punishment for burglary, say, only and exactly the three years in prison to which he was sentenced by a judge for that crime.

The reality of prison life, however, suggests that this conception is amiss. The quality of life which the typical prisoner experiences in the typical prison while serving his sentence is not adequately conveyed in the phrase, "three years in prison," even though in theory it is that phrase which denotes the entirety of his

punishment. There is a vast range of deprivations and harms, indiginities and inconveniences, injuries and terrors, which typically afflict the prisoner during his imprisonment. The *Attica* report and other recent prison documents amply establish this point in convincing detail.[10] No one can read this literature without a shudder at the thought of spending several years in such a place. But of such deprivations there is no allusion whatever in the prisoner's sentence itself. Are they, therefore, to be regarded as incidental aggravations, as theoretically irrelevant abuses of the penal system, and thus as defects of the system of actual punishment but not actually defects in penal theory and the concept of punishment?

We have here, I suggest, a glimpse of the most significant reason why there is practical relevance in a firm grasp of conceptual matters. It is only by relying on a fixed and trustworthy conception of what punishment is that we can proceed to understand the sort of criticism which it is appropriate to make of a given deprivation inflicted upon a person in the name of punishment. Some deprivations, as we have seen, are inseparable from the idea of punishment, but others are separable in theory and perhaps in practice as well. The problem is that many of the theoretically incidental aggravations of punishment in prison are widespread, long-standing, predictable, and beyond the power of most reformers to uproot. Moreover, as the *Attica* report and related documents show, it is often these seemingly incidental aggravations which the prisoner feels most acutely during his term of imprisonment, no matter what the sentencing authority, the general public, or philosophers fixed upon a narrower conception of punishment may think.

There are really only two ways to respond to this gap between theory and practice. One way is to accept it and to try to understand and remove aggravations endemic to actual prison life but ancillary to the necessary deprivations of punishment. The other way is to alter our definition of punishment so as to take these aggravations into account in a systematic, theoretical way as components of the true nature of punishment through imprisonment. At the present time, the pattern of arguments made by prison reform spokesmen is noticeably in favor of the former alternative.[11] According to most reformers, punishment does not require the miseries which imprisonment makes inevitable. Short of abandoning the idea of punishment itself as something unworthy of institutionalized practice, we must press for greater separation between unnecessary deprivation and punishment. We cannot even begin to think through this distinction without an adequate grasp of the idea of punishment itself. The standard conception of punishment, revised perhaps in the directions discussed earlier, goes a long way toward satisfying that need.[12]

III

Textbooks and treaties inform us that there are fundamentally three justifications of punishment: Retribution, Prevention (or Deterrence), and Reformation (or Rehabilitation).[13] Actually, the truly traditional justifications have been only the first two. Because I intend here to concentrate on them exclusively, it is best to say a brief word now about what is wrong with reformation or rehabilitation as the justification of punishment, which came into prominence only during the past century. Rarely has reformation or rehabilitation been held to be the *sole* or even the *primary* justification of punishment. Those who conceive of a world without punishment, and are thus ready to condemn all punishment for anyone no matter what the offender has done, do not have rehabilitation or reformation of offenders in mind when they do so. On the contrary, they often want to get rid of "punishment" in order to rehabilitate offenders. What they condemn is the abuse or neglect of the rehabilitative ideal. In other words, today, reformation or rehabilitation as the goal, aim, or justification of punishment has become progressively blurred with a *non-punitive alternative* to punishment, i.e., Treatment or Therapy.[14] This is but one result of viewing crime less as an example of individual wickedness

and more as an instance of social sickness (as is neatly conveyed in the quip from *West Side Story*, "He's depraved on account of he's deprived"). For these reasons we can afford to omit any further canvass of punishment as rehabilitative in this discussion.

Before we can come to grips with the traditional justifications, we need to make an important distinction as to what it is those justifications purport to justify. There are two possibilities. Is it to try to justify the punishment meted out to a given offender for a particular offense? Penal statutes and prison and parole regulations, actual judicial and administrative tribunals, are set up to deal precisely with this task. It is their responsibility not to set general policy but to apply it in individual cases. If that is so, then the justification of any given punishment in an individual case must be entirely a function of two things—the facts in the particular case on the one side and the general rules or policies on the other side. But if that is so, there is nothing more in general to be said about the justification of punishment in individual cases, except possibly to attack this whole approach by arguing for the abandonment of rules, systems, practices, and their institutional counterpart in boards, tribunals, and officers whose task is to administer justice under the rules. Sometimes it does appear as if such an approach were being repudiated by those who preach "individualized" punishment. Actually, however, what is under attack is more likely to be the prevailing system of rules, a system which leaves little room for discretion (and then most of it only to judges in sentencing). What is favored instead is a system which provides a great deal of discretion, most of it allotted to psychiatrists and social workers who deal with the offender after sentencing. The issue, therefore, is not between rules and no rules, but between two different systems of rules. Those on either side of this dispute tacitly agree that what justifies punishment (or treatment) in any given case are the facts of that case and the general policies which apply to it. The true alternative to a system of punishment based on rules is not "individualization" but impulsive and arbitrary responses to individual cases. It is a mistake to suppose that a defense of rules or general policies commits one to a defense of rigid, exceptionless, and unchangeable rules. It is equally a mistake to suppose that the way to improve on bad rules is by abandoning all rules. Consequently, I shall assume henceforth that the only issue before us is one of justifying the system, practice, or institution of punishment in general.

This is particularly important because of the objection often made against Utilitarianism, that it would justify punishing the innocent in some cases, indeed, in all cases where there would be greater social good than harm from such an undertaking. Any system of punishment will have to put up with (that is, excuse) occasional miscarriages of punitive justice. Human frailty guarantees judicial miscarriages, just as it guarantees deliberate occasional abuses of the penal (and all other) institutions of society. By a miscarriage of punitive justice, I mean a case where the person found guilty of a criminal offense and accordingly punished for it was, in fact, not guilty even though he was believed to be guilty by those with the authority to determine guilt and innocence. (I ignore here the problem of a person who is guilty but who, through a miscarriage of justice, is punished more severely than he deserves.) The objection to Utilitarianism is that it allows not only judicial miscarriages but systematic use of scapegoats. Scapegoating—a practice which would allow persons not even believed to be guilty to be processed by the courts as though they were—is not a specially outrageous system of punishment, possibly justifiable on Utilitarian grounds. It is not a form or a part of a system of punitive justice at all! It is, rather, a system of legally sanctioned injury administered in the name of the public whereby innocent victims are framed and the innocent public duped. Neither Utilitarianism nor any other social philosophy cold hope to justify or permit such a system.[15] We may fail to realize this so long as we do not distinguish between a system or practice of punishment as such and a particular instance or application of that

practice through which each punitive act acquires its own particular nature and character. Justifying a practice, parasitic on true punishment, of systematic scapegoating is one thing; excusing a particular miscarriage of justice within a genuine system of punishment is another. The former would never be justifiable, the latter is all but inevitable.

Let us turn now to the justificaton of punishment through appeal to retribution. Conceptually, punishment is retributive, as we have seen. There is general agreement that what we mean by punishment is the infliction of some deprivation on someone on account of his infraction of some rule. Retribution therefore enters into the very concept of punishment in a double sense. First, it is retribution which tells us *what* to do in order to punish: "Pay him back in the same coin." Punishment, unlike restitution and compensation to the victims of crime, leaves the person punished worse off than before because the coin in which he is paid back is a deprivation of his rights. Second, it is retribution which tells us *whom* to punish: "The guilty deserve to be punished" is a retributivist tautology. (This, by the way, shows us something peculiar about the very idea of punishing hostages in wartime. Punishment normally requires an identity between the person who is believed to be guilty of an offense and the person punished for it, whereas the practice of punishing hostages deliberately breaks this requirement. Perhaps the phrase, "punishing hostages" is a misnomer.) I see nothing wrong with these two retributivist features of punishment, and I cannot see anything in our institutions of punishment which would be improved by systematically abandoning either of these requirements. The fact that there may be more useful, non-retributive ways of handling criminals than punishing them is not an argument for a notion of non-retributive punishment.

Retribution is also often thought to give us possible, even if not necessary, answers to two other questions: Why in general ought we to punish anyone? What in general ought to be a person's punishment for a given offense? The familiar retributivist maxim, "Let the punishment fit the crime," is a partial answer to the second question, and (as is well known) is of little use to us except at the margins. Thus, this maxim assures us that a slap on the wrist for murder is an improper punishment, given the gravity of the offense and the triviality of the punishment. Likewise, death for over-parking suffers from the converse flaw. The problem is to go beyond these margins, and the difficulty for the retributivist lies in showing us *how* we are to assess the relative gravity of other crimes, e.g., rape, kiting checks, and *what* constitutes proportionate severity in punishment for the gravity of each type of offense. But that is not all. Pure retributivism also requires us to be persuaded that no non-retributive considerations should enter into fitting punishments to crimes and to criminals, and that no non-retributive theory has any rational basis for apportioning the severity of punishments to the gravity of offenses. These are strong claims, and, because no version of pure retributivism has made them good, retributivism has been held for some years in low esteem.[16] As to why in general we ought to punish anyone, retributivism seems to be capable of nothing more than the unhelpful circular answer "Because people who commit crimes deserve to be punished." If we ask the retributivist, "Why, in general, do criminals deserve punishment?" either he gives us no answer at all, or he abandons pure retributivism by telling us about the *good on balance* which a system of punishment produces. But this is an ill-disguised, quasi-Utilitarian account of the justification of punishment, and whereas it may be acceptable in its own right, it is not a type of justification open to the pure retributivist.

The only other alternative for the retributivist is to appeal to the idea that *justice* requires punishment of offenders, and that the good which punishment achieves is the good of justice. Sometimes it has even been claimed that punishment is in general a *good to those punished*, irrespective of the overall good to society of having offenders punished. If this is correct, and if this good cannot be obtained in any other way than by punishing offenders,

then we have a very strong argument from the moral point of view (the only point of view worth considering on this issue) against a world without punishment. The position has been argued mainly by philosophers influenced by Kant; its most important defense in recent years has been by Herbert Morris.[17] Essential to Morris's restatement of the Kantian theme is the idea that in the typical case it is only by punishing a guilty person that we treat him as a person. "We treat a human being as a person," according to Morris, "provided: first, we permit the person to make the choices that will determine punishment happens to him and, second, when our responses to the person are responses respecting the person's choices."[18] Crucial in the application of these unexceptionable principles to the idea that punishment is a good to persons punished is the belief that in committing a crime a person acts on his deliberate choices and knows that in committing a crime he makes himself liable to some punishment or other.

The chief objection which one might make to this view is quite simple. It would be absurd to imply (as Morris does not) that it follows from the above argument that offenders have a right to be punished by *existing* systems of imprisonment, or that to punish a person in an Attica or a Folsom is to do him some good. Even if a person has the right to be punished, and if deserved punishment does a person good, the offender still has the right to be free of the kind of abuse which existing systems of imprisonment typically impose on him.[19] What makes the very ideas of a right to be punished and of the good of being punished so difficult to accept is their apparent incompatibility with the rights not to be punished in certain ways and not to be abused in the name of punishment, and with the harm which actual imprisonment does. These Kantian themes in punishment are somewhat more palatable, I believe, if it is realized that they are advanced (as in Morris's case) in order to offset the undeserved influence of the therapeutic alternative to punishment, which requires us to regard persons who commit crime not as free agents but as sick and help-less. A world without punishment, unless it is also a world without crime, a world without the unjustified violation of the rights of indi-viduals, is certain to be a world with coercion and restraint just the same, with "hospitals" substituted for prisons, "therapists" replacing prison guards, and so on. The net result may be a greater loss of human dignity, as many have argued.[20] The solution here is not (pace Austin) any frying pan in a fire; it is to avoid both the freedom-restrictive and rights-viola-tive character of mental and penal institutions as we currently know them.

Is it, then, the retributivist features of pun-ishment which in particular deserve the ob-jections of reformers and visionary critics? I think not, or not mainly, if by this term we mean only the doctrines endorsed so far. We have seen how: (a) punishment involves de-priving a person of some of his normal rights; (b) such a deprivation may be visited only upon the guilty (or those authoritatively found to be guilty); (c) the gravity of the offense must to some degree be reflected in the severity of the punishment; and (d) it is not proper to treat a person who deliberately chose to com-mit a crime as though he were a helpless in-fant, imbecile, or non-person. It is difficult to see how the institution of punishment could be improved (either in our understanding of it or in its function) by contradicting any of these four principles. Rather, the very reverse of humanization and liberation would result. To abandon these principles is either to make punishment more savage than it already is or to abandon punishment altogether in favor of some more savage alternative. To concede this much in no way requires endorsing any further retributivist principles, whatever they may be. Retributivism no doubt encompasses a variety of principles and notions, but there is no reason why we shouldn't pick and choose among them, retaining only those which fit to-gether rationally with each other and with non-retributive considerations. To the degree to which this is done, the attack upon punish-ment because of its retributive features should diminish.

Let us turn now to deterrence. There is some confusion as to the nature of deter-rence, and since deterrence is the aim or justi-fication of punishment which has become most prominent in our civilization, it is impor-tant to clarify this concept at the start. Punish-ment is generally favored as a systematic way of dealing with offenders because it is be-lieved that punishment prevents crime. But crime prevention as such and prevention by deterrence are two different things. Deter-rence, as its etymology suggests, consists in control or influence over the behavior of someone by a *threat*, including the threat of penal sanction. Prevention, however, can be accomplished by any number of methods. For instance, crime can be prevented by manipu-lating the offender's external environment, e.g., through placing him in prison or stocks, or by banishment. It can be accomplished by alteration of his bodily capacities, through in-capacitative and irreversible acts (death, muti-lation), or by more subtle and temporary methods (drugs, chemotherapy). Theoreti-cally, all of these are ways of preventing per-sons from behaving in certain ways and thus from committing criminal acts. *None involves deterrence at all.*

The idea of punishment as a deterrent is complex. Even if prevention is kept distinct from the narrower issue of deterrence, there still remains the further distinction between what is called *special* and what is called *gen-eral* deterrence. Special deterrence is usually defined as deterring person A from commit-ting a crime by punishing him for some prior offense; general deterrence is usually defined as deterring persons, B, C, D . . . from com-mitting a crime by punishing person A for some offense. Yet both of these definitions are ambiguous because they cut across a further distinction. Consider the situation of special deterrence. Theoretically, we could inflict on any given offender, A, who has committed a crime, x, a punishment, P, and obtain either or both of two deterrent effects: one could be the deterrence from another offense of the same sort, x^1, and another could be the deter-rence from an altogether different offense, y (as when, after his ten years imprisonment for burglary, Smith is deterred not only from further burglary but also from assault). Let us call the former *primary* deterrence and the latter *secondary* deterrence. The same distinction applies within general deterrence. We have, then, four possible combinations of kinds of deterrence: special and general, primary and secondary. One would conjecture that the imposition of any given penalty would be most effective as a special, primary deterrent, and least effective as a general, secondary deterrent (that is, we would be far more likely to deter Smith from further burglary by punishing him for a prior act of burglary than we would be likely to deter Brown and Jones from assault by punishing Smith for burglary).

Since the time of Beccaria and Bentham, the deterrence efficacy of any given punishment has been understood to be a function of at least five presumably independent variables: severity, certainty, celerity, frequency, and publicity (degree of public perception of the liability to and imposition of the sanction). Subsequent analysis has shown that personality differences among potential offenders are also a relevant variable, and that each of the classic five variables is itself a complex of several factors. Crimes, too, vary in their nature, from the "expressive"—those which evince an inner drive or compulsion and in which prudential self-interest of the offender enters little or not at all—to the "instrumental."[21] It is easy to say, as one of the leading theoreticians of punitive deterrence has written, that "It is . . . a fundamental fact of social life that the risk of unpleasant consequences is a very strong motivational factor for most people in most situations."[22] It is another thing to verify quantitatively its many corollaries. What is the *degree of risk* that persons are willing to run of incurring the legally designated sanction? How *strong a motivational factor* is apprehension of this risk, and on what does its strength depend? How *large a role* does the legal sanction in the narrowest sense—the punishment meted out to an offender by a judge under a statute—play in these "unpleasant consequences"? The truth

is, we have almost no reliable answers to these questions, for any given class of offenders, offenses, and sanctions.

Consider, as an example, the ongoing controversy over the relative effect of *severity* and *certainty* of sanctions in deterrence. Classic doctrine would maintain that these two factors are additive, but like much other conventional wisdom this assertion has been attacked. Some have argued that, at least where severe penalties are involved, the two are inversely related (the greater the severity of a sentence, the less certain its application, and conversely). Part of the problem is to determine which statistical model is the best to use in testing these hypotheses. Another part is conceptual: what is the best way to define "certainty" and "severity" in a punishment? Much of the problem lies in the available data on offenses, arrests, prison admissions, and release records. The most recent review of the whole set of issues leaves all of these questions essentially unanswered.[23] This ignorance should make us cautious in the face of the popular maxim, "The greater the severity of a punishment, the greater its deterrent efficacy." In the present state of our knowledge, we have little or no reason to believe that by increasing the severity of a punishment we can achieve a downturn in the crime index, or that by decreasing the severity we should expect an upsurge in crime. The folly of such ideas lies in the notion that we can leave everything else in society the same and control the rate of crime merely by alterations in sanction severity. It is difficult to think of a more naive approach to crime control.

I have stressed these conceptual complexities and empirical difficulties in our knowledge about deterrence because they affect the role it is reasonable to assign to deterrence in the theory of punishment and its justification. Philosophers of a Utilitarian persuasion, such as Bentham and Mill in the last century, tend to stress the importance of deterrence as the sole or the dominant justification of punishment. It is to be found also in the influential views of H. L. A. Hart, who defends the institution of punishment by appealing to its "beneficial consequences" when compared with alternative systematic ways of dealing with crimes and criminals.[24] The chief beneficial consequence of a system of punishment is in "preventing harmful crime."[25] Since incapacitation of convicted offenders plays only a small part in crime prevention, it is deterrence which emerges as the "General Justifying Aim" of punishment (in Hart's phrase).

We have seen how, in anything we could properly call an act or a system of punishment, several undeniably retributive features must be present. Can the same be said for deterrence? We have seen earlier how the very nature of punishment would be shaped by some who would build into it a preventative function, and we have also seen the difficulty in giving a retributive account of why anyone ought to be punished at all (i.e., why have a system of punishment?). In addition, we have seen how small a part in justifying punishment is played by appeal to the reform or rehabilitation of convicted offenders. What, then, is left, except an appeal to deterrence and prevention, "social defense" as some now fashionably call it? A dilemma, however, looms precisely at this point, and it is one perhaps better appreciated by the opponents of punishment (or, at any rate, the opponents of a purely deterrence justification of punishment) than by its advocates. The dilemma is that it is difficult to see how deterrence can justify punishment, when (a) we know so little about the deterrent effects, whether special or general, primary or secondary, and when (b) deterrence requires punishing (that is, inflicting a rights-deprivation upon) a person *now* for something he did in the *past* in order to control someone's *future* conduct. Either we must justify both (a) and (b) or we cannot justify deterrence. But if one maintains that deterrence is a necessary justification of punishment, and if deterrence is unavailable to us in theory, then punishment cannot be justified as a system at all!

The idea that it is a moral outrage to inflict pain on a person now in order to influence his or anyone else's conduct in the future we owe to Kant. Recent attempts to get by Johannes

Andenaes[26] and Zimring and Hawkins[27] around Kant's objections are not adequate. Andenaes does not even face the dilemma formulated above, much less resolve it. Instead, he appeals to wholly independent moral considerations of proportionality in severity of sentence to gravity of offense and of equality for all offenders before the law. But these two principles neither support nor flow from the idea of deterrence; the fact that they are not incompatible with it, and indeed may limit its abuses, is hardly to the point. Zimring and Hawkins can only fall back on the argument that, in a society which recognizes the rights and interests of offenders as well as citizens generally, convicted offenders forfeit their right not to be deprived of their rights for the good of others on the assumption that they were initially free to conform their behavior to the requirements of the law.[28] But this argument, instead of justifying the forfeiture of rights for the sake of others, merely shows that such forfeiture is required if we are going to punish persons on grounds of deterrence. Those who favor punishment, and especially punishment as justified by its deterrent effects, confront an embarrassment to their views in this unresolved dilemma over deterrence.

IV

Some years ago John Rawls observed that most people regard punishment as "an acceptable institution. Only a few have rejected punishment entirely," he remarked, and as an afterthought added, "which is rather surprising when one considers all that can be said against it."[29] I have tried to show that the concept of punishment is something against which men naturally rebel, for punishment essentially involves a loss of freedom, of rights, and typically is painful and unpleasant for those who must suffer it. I have also tried to show how it is impossible to encompass under the concept of punishment many of the actual indignities and harms inflicted upon the persons who are punished by imprisonment. There is a considerable gap between what its theory of punishment (its conception and justification) can explain and what our practice reveals is in need of explanation.

Meanwhile, crime—not mere law-breaking, but dangerous and harmful conduct inflicted on persons without their consent—continues to be a prominent feature of our lives. There is no immediate prospect of its disappearance from our midst. So long as crime cannot be abolished, or at least diminished to a tolerable level (whatever that might be), there is no likelihood that the practice of punishment will disappear. To say this is not to defend the existing system of imprisonment. The prison system (jails, penitentiaries, prison farms, half-way houses, juvenile detention centers) touches the lives of more than a million offenders every year in this country. It was not built in a day, and it will not be dismantled in a day, not by administrative directive from above, nor by scholarly critique from outside, and not even by riot or rebellion from within. As a human institution, punishment has a disgraceful past; it probably does not have a glorious future. Still, punishment under law as a systematic way of dealing with dangerous and harmful conduct may be the least ugly, the least destructive institution available to us. Bad as it is, the alternatives are worse.

Notes

1. See, e.g., *Struggle for Justice*, A Report on Crime and Punishment Prepared for the American Friends Service Committee, New York, Hill and Wang, 1971.

2. Thomas Hobbes, *Leviathan* (1960), Chapter xxviii, reprinted in part in Gertrude Ezorsky, ed., *Philosophical Perspectives on Punishment*, Albany, State University of New York Press, 1972, pp. 3–5.

3. Writers who have contributed to this consensus include A. G. N. Flew, Stanley I. Benn, and H. L. A. Hart. See especially Hart, "Prolegomena to the Principles of Punishment," *Proceedings of the Aristotelian Society* (1959–60), reprinted in his *Punishment and Responsibility*, New York, Oxford University Press, 1968, pp. 1–27, especially pp. 4–5. My definition is adapted from Hart's with only minor changes.

4. For discussion, see Norval Morris and Gordon Hawkins, *The Honest Politician's Guide to Crime Control*, University of Chicago Press, 1970, Chapter i; and the forthcoming book by Godwin Schurs and myself on crimes without victims.

5. This revision is not original with me. It may be found already in John Rawls, "Two Concepts of Rules," *The Philosophical Review* (1955), reprinted in H. B. Acton, ed., *The Philosophy of Punishment*, London, Macmillan, 1969, at p. 111, where Rawls says that he proposes to "define" punishment in terms of a person's being "deprived of some of his normal rights."

6. Herbert L. Packer, *The Limits of the Criminal Sanction*, Stanford University Press, 1968, pp. 33–34.

7. Joel Feinberg, "The Expressive Function of Punishment," *The Monist* (1965), reprinted in his *Doing and Deserving*, Princeton University Press, 1970, pp. 95–118, at p. 98.

8. Feinberg, loc. cit.

9. Ludwig Wittgenstein, *Lectures and Conversations on Aesthetics, Psychology and Religious Belief* (ed. Cyril Barrett), Oxford, Basil Blackwell, 1966, p. 50.

10. See *Attica*, The Official Report of the New York State Special Commission on Attica, New York, Bantam Books, 1972; and *Prison*, Interviews by Leonard J. Berry, New York, Grossman Publishers, 1972.

11. See, e.g., *A Program for Prison Reform*, The Final Report of the Annual Chief Justice Earl Warren Conference on Advocacy in the United States, June 9–10, 1972, Cambridge, Mass. This report includes three essays: Caleb Foote, "The Sentencing Function"; Gerhard O. W. Mueller, "Imprisonment and Its Alternatives"; and Herman Schwartz, "Prisoners' Rights: Some Hopes and Realities."

12. See H. A. Bedau, "Penal Theory and Prison Reality Today," *Juris Doctor*, 2 (December 1972), pp. 40–43, where this point is elaborated.

13. See, e.g., Ted Honderich, *Punishment: The Supposed Justifications,* London, Hutchinson, 1969; Rudolph J. Gerber and Patrick D. McAnany, eds., *Contemporary Punishment*, University of Notre Dame Press, 1972; Stanley E. Grupp, ed., *Theories of Punishment*, Indiana University Press, 1971; Acton, ed., op. cit.; Packer, op. cit.; and Ezorsky, ed., *op*, cit.

14. See e.g., Karl Menninger, *The Crime of Punishment*, New York, Viking Press, 1969; and Giles Playfair and Derrick Sington, *Crime, Punishment and Cure*, London, Secker & Warburg, 1965. Perhaps the classic modern source for this idea is the

essay by George Bernard Shaw, *The Crime Imprisonment*, New York, Philosophical Library, 1946.

15. This is a brief and quite incomplete paraphrase of an argument originating with Kurt Baier, "Is Punishment Retributive" and John Rawls, op. cit., both reprinted in Acton, ed., op. cit.

16. See H. L. A. Hart, *Punishment and Responsibility*," Oxford University Press, 1968, pp. 230 ff.

17. Herbert Morris, "Persons and Punishments," *The Monist*, (1968), reprinted in Grupp, ed., op. cit., pp. 76–101.

18. Op. cit. p. 92.

19. See, e.g., Herman Schwartz, op. cit.; and Philip J. Hirschkop, "The Rights of Prisoners," in Norman Dorsen, ed., *The Rights of Americans*, New York, Pantheon Books, 1971, pp. 451–468.

20. See, e.g., Francis A. Allen, "Criminal Justice, Legal Values and the Rehabilitative Ideal," reprinted in Grupp, ed., op cit., pp. 317–330.

21. Franklin E. Zimring and Gordon J. Hawkins, *Deterrence: The Legal Threat to Crime Control*, University of Chicago Press, 1973, provides by far the best general discussion of all these issues.

22. Johannes Andenaes, "The Morality of Deterrence," *University of Chicago Law Review*, 37 (1970), pp. 649–664, at p. 664.

23. William C. Bailey and Ronald W. Smith, "Punishment: Its Severity and Certainty," *Journal of Criminal Law, Criminology and Police Science*, 63 (1972), pp. 530–539.

24. Hart, op. cit., pp. 8–9.

25. Hart, op. cit., pp. 235–236.

26. Andenaes, op. cit.

27. Zimring and Hawkins, op. cit.

28. Op. cit., quoting Hart, op. cit., p. 244.

29. Rawls, op. cit., p. 106.

Suggested Further Reading

Barnes, Harry Elmer, "The Contemporary Prison: A Menace to Inmate Rehabilitation and the Repression of Crime," *Key Issues*, 2 (1965), 11–23.

Bittner, Egon, and A. M. Platt, "The Meaning of Punishment," *Issues in Criminology*, 2 (1979), 79–99.

Lesnoff, M., "Two Justifications of Punishment," *Philosophical Quarterly*, 21 (1971).

Morris, Herbert, "Persons and Punishment," *The Monist*, 52, no. 4 (October 1968), 475–501.

Rubin, Sol, "The Model Sentencing Act," *NYU Law Review*, 39 (April 1964), 251–62.

DECISION SCENARIO 5

Punishment

Cheryl M. was a 17-year-old high school student on trial for contracting someone to kill her father. The person she hired was a classmate, who had already been given a twenty-year sentence for second-degree murder.

Cheryl had turned herself in after her father was fatally wounded by a shotgun blast upon leaving the house one morning. She never denied plotting to kill him. Her plea was that ever since her mother had died six years before, she had been a victim of her father's sexual abuse. At first she thought it was only his affection, but as she came to understand, she felt repulsion and fear. Furthermore, she said, there were repeated threats of bodily harm and of institutionalization in a state asylum.

Cheryl said she had decided to have her father killed when she noticed his attraction to Denise, her sister, six years younger. She also said she regretted nothing.

Acute nervousness made it almost impossible for her to testify in court on her own behalf. Her lawyer brought forward numerous expert witnesses to verify the psychological and social aspects of her case. Her classmates and teachers described her as always anxious and fearful. The judge received a flood of sympathetic letters from female victims of sexual abuse.

Her mother's sister gave testimony to Cheryl's "vile imagination" and disclaimed any sexual relation between Cheryl and her father. Other relatives also doubted the story, but, as one psychiatrist put it, "the family had a history of dismissing such improprieties."

The judge had the option of charging Cheryl with conspiracy to commit murder, a major felony carrying a sentence of twenty years to life. Instead he sentenced her to six months in jail and five years' probation.

Questions

1. What position would a retributivist take regarding Cheryl's punishment?
2. What kinds of evidence could be cited by a rehabilitationist or reformist that Cheryl lacked a "criminal psychology"?
3. Could any punishment have deterred future victims of sexual abuse from undertaking punitive action on their own behalf?
4. Could Cheryl have entered a self-defense plea?
5. What are the legal dangers of victims' taking the law into their own hands? Is it ever morally correct for a victim to take the path of summary justice?

2. THE JUSTICE OF PUNISHMENT

How can it be determined whether a punishment is just? As we have seen, utilitarians view punishment as a necessary evil that is justified when its use (or threatened use) prevents the occurrence of even greater evils to society. They claim that punishment is not just in and of itself, rather that it serves a just end. Retributionists, on the other hand, are concerned with redressing evil that has already occurred.

> By breaking laws, offenders use wrongful ways to advance their interests, or to gratify their desires. . . . Punishment thus restores the balance (retributes, pays back) the offender had tried to tip in his favor. This metaphor often is visually represented by statues of justice holding a balance (as well as a sword, for retribution).[1]

Statues representing justice are, as a rule, blindfolded figures, indicating that the law ideally treats everyone alike, without regard

for individual status, class, race, or gender. Using this criterion, one feature of a just punishment is equal application to all persons convicted of similar crimes. An important ethical problem in punishing criminals concerns the amount of *discretion* permitted to judges in imposing sentences. Some people argue that giving judges leeway in sentencing promotes justice because a judge can tailor punishment more exactly to fit an individual crime or set of circumstances. They maintain that judicial discretion allows for flexibility in an overly rigid system. Opponents of the view argue that it is more equitable to impose mandatory sentences (determined legislatively) that treat like offenses alike and eliminate judicial discretion.

In the first of the following articles Elizabeth Beardsley examines the ethics of mandatory sentencing. She analyzes sentences with a view to their determinateness, proportionality, and uniformity, and considers how each feature is connected with mandatory sentencing. The author argues that mandatory determinate sentences are morally superior to nonmandatory ones because

[1]Ernest van den Haag, "Punishment as a Device for Controlling the Crime Rate," in *Ethics, Public Policy, and Criminal Justice*, ed., Frederick Elliston and Norman Bowie (Cambridge, Mass.: Oelgeschlager, Gunn & Hain, Inc., 1982), pp. 208–9.

they are more humane, have greater deterrent effect, and preserve individual rights. Beardsley further argues that mandatory sentences are better suited to preserving the ethically desirable features of proportionality and uniformity in punishment.

Another area of ethical concern in the punishment of criminals is the widespread practice of *plea bargaining*. Plea bargaining is a form of negotiation between prosecutors and defendants in which an accused person agrees to plead guilty (without a trial) to a lesser offense in return for the promise of lighter punishment associated with that offense. The criminal thus convicted receives a punishment different from the one mandated for the crime of which he or she was originally accused. Can plea bargaining be justified? Some claim that it can because it helps unclog crowded court calendars, promotes speedier trials, and results in punishing guilty persons who might otherwise escape conviction. Opponents argue that plea bargaining is wrong because it results in the punishment of persons who would not have been convicted on the evidence and thus interferes with due process of law as guaranteed by the Constitution. In addition, they argue that innocent persons may be manipulated into making confessions out of fear or ignorance. Utilitarians support plea bargaining because it produces a greater deterrent effect (since it increases the number of criminals convicted) and reduces the costs of court procedures. Deontologists oppose plea bargaining because it results in less appropriate punishments, both for the guilty (who receive lighter sentences than they deserve) and for the innocent (who ought not to be punished at all).

The use of capital punishment has long been a subject of intense debate, and in recent years the controversy has grown even more heated. A number of states have modified old laws concerning capital punishment to conform with U.S. Supreme Court rulings. Under the new statutes the number of state executions has increased at a rate that critics find alarming. Opponents of capital punishment hold that it is fundamentally wrong for the state deliberately to take a human life, even to punish the most atrocious crimes. Supporters respond that some crimes are so horrible that nothing less than the death penalty can be considered just punishment.

In a case recently decided by the Supreme Court, lawyers for a black defendant argued that the death penalty was applied in a prejudiced manner against blacks. They cited statistics which they held would show that a much higher proportion of black persons received the death sentence than white persons convicted of similar crimes. The Court ruled against the appeal in a landmark decision handed down in April 1987, and the defendant, Alvin Moore, Jr., was executed in Louisiana on June 9 of the same year. If capital punishment is administered more often to some groups of people than to others, does that mean that its use is unjustified?

In the second article that follows, Robert Johnson presents a detailed description of the experience of prisoners on death row in Alabama. Johnson argues that the helplessness and despair induced by the death row environment results in prisoners' total dehumanization and causes them to suffer a kind of "living death" before their execution. Their confinement, Johnson maintains, must be viewed as a form of brutality tantamount to torture. He concludes that "for all intents and purposes, a death sentence amounts to death with torture in a society that has explicitly renounced torture as a remnant of barbarism."

ELIZABETH L. BEARDSLEY

The Ethics of Mandatory Sentencing

Is mandatory sentencing for criminal offenses (fixing criminal penalties by law) justified on ethical grounds. This question often elicits a response that is emotional rather than reasoned. Certain features of sentences are regarded with approval and are taken as somehow connected with the practice of mandatory sentencing. I shall discuss three features of sentences: their *determinateness*, their *proportionality*, and their *uniformity*. With respect to each feature, I shall ask first, whether it is indeed one that we should approve of, and second, just how it is connected with mandatory sentencing.

Determinateness

Determinate sentences are sentences in which the term of incarceration is fixed, in contrast to indeterminate or open-ended sentences, in which the date of an offender's release remains to be decided at a later time. I shall argue that determinate sentences are morally preferable to indeterminate sentences, on three grounds. First, they can plausibly be held to have a greater deterrent power, second, they are more humane, and third, they preserve an essential right held by every citizen, whether he or she is a potential offender or a law-abiding citizen.

Empirical studies of deterrence are said to have been extremely limited in their focus.[1] If this is the case, it cannot be claimed with assurance that determinate sentences have more deterrent force than do indeterminate ones. It is plausible, however, to suppose that they do. Perceived certainty of punishment is a variable whose relation to crime rates may not yet have been sufficiently examined by social scientists. But if, as seems probable on common sense grounds, this variable is found

to be correlated with deterrence, a case for determinate sentences can be made. Determinate sentences are naturally perceived as more certain than indeterminate ones. Logically, the question whether a sentence will be imposed at all is not the same as the question whether it will have a specified duration. But psychologically a general aura of certainty attaches to determinate sentences.

It should be noted that the fact that a *sentence* is perceived as certain can have its deterrent power eliminated or reduced if *conviction* is perceived as uncertain. If a determinate sentence is regarded as unacceptably harsh, either in itself (like the death penalty) or in relation to the gravity of the offense (like some prison terms for drug offenses), juries and judges are demonstrably reluctant to convict. This consideration does not mean that determinate sentences as a class do not have a greater deterrent power than indeterminate ones. It should serve as a reminder, however, that there are other significant variables to be studied.

The first argument must await empirical support before it can bear a great deal of weight. It is offered here as a small part of an ethical case for determinate sentences. The other two arguments are stronger.

In his book *Criminal Sentences*, Judge Marvin Frankel provides a powerful indictment of indeterminate sentences.[2] He charges that they have "produced . . . cruelty and injustice" and a "hated regime of uncertainty and helplessness."[3] Tracing the adoption of indeterminate sentences to the influence of the "rehabilitative ideal," Frankel proceeds to argue that the latter is confused and unworkable. An assessment of rehabilitation as a goal of sentencing lies largely beyond the scope of the present chapter. But that indeterminate

Reprinted with permission from *Ethics, Public Policy, and Criminal Justice,* ed. Frederick Elliston and Norman Bowie (Cambridge, Mass.: Oelgeschlager, Gunn, & Hain, Inc., 1982), pp. 219–27.

sentences inflict more suffering and indignity on offenders than determinate sentences do is difficult to deny. Some may argue that the additional pain can simply be regarded as part of an offender's punishment. This argument can be rebutted, however, by showing that indeterminacy adds cost in pain to the offender without adding benefit in well-being to the public. It can also be rebutted, even more successfully, by showing that indeterminate sentences manifest a lack of respect for the offender's humanity.[4]

The third ground for claiming that determinate sentences are morally preferable to indeterminate ones is the strongest of all. This is the thesis that determinate sentences preserve the right of every individual citizen to predict the legal consequences of his or her acts. Frankel articulates this claim clearly when he writes that "In a just legal order, the law shall be knowable and intelligible, so that . . . a person meaning to obey the law may know his obligations and predict, within decent limits, the legal consequences of his conduct."[5] Frankel evidently believes that "decent limits" have been overstepped when the legal consequences of an act can be predicted only to the extent that one who commits it knows that he or she will be liable to incarceration of some duration or other.[6]

Another writer who has emphasized individuals' rights to be able to plan their lives free from unpredictable official intrusions is the distinguished legal philosopher H. L. A. Hart.[7] Hart does not apply this principle explicitly to the issue of determinate or indeterminate sentences, but the application can easily be made.

I have argued that, on all three grounds discussed, determinate sentences are morally preferable to indeterminate sentences. But this conclusion does not provide an automatic argument for mandatory sentencing; the connection between the two must therefore be examined next.

First, it is clear that both indeterminate and determinate sentences can be legally mandated. As Frankel points out, "A number of state legislatures . . . have opted for indeter-

minacy in recent revisions of their laws."[8] But we must also inquire whether mandatory sentencing is a necessary condition for obtaining determinate sentences—in other words, can determinate sentences be obtained by discretionary sentencing?

Here the answer is certainly that they can. A given sentencer, say Judge Doe, can consistently exercise his discretion to impose determinate sentences rather than open-ended ones. But determinate sentences imposed in this way rather than through the practice of mandatory sentencing will retain only one of the three ethical advantages noted above—namely, the more humane treatment of an offender. The advantages of more effective deterrence, if the suggestion is correct that this is a function of greater perceived certainty of punishment, would be jeopardized. An offender contemplating a certain act could say to himself only, "If I perform A, and *if* I am caught and convicted, and *if* I come before Judge Doe, I shall receive such-and-such a sentence." The second if-clause cannot be eliminated by mandatory rather than discretionary sentencing, but the third one can. Its presence can only detract from the "perceived certainty of punishment," and thus weaken the deterrent power of the sentencing structure.

Similar difficulties arise in connection with the remaining argument for determinate sentences—the claim that they preserve the right to be able to predict the legal consequences of our acts. If all that can be predicted is what the consequences will be if a certain individual judge does the sentencing, we do not have the condition for a "just legal order" set forth by Frankel and Hart. For the magnitude of the issue whether the potential offender comes before Judge Doe or Judge Roe can hardly be exaggerated. A study cited by Willard Gaylin showed that, of two judges in Iowa, "One judge gave ten times as many suspended sentences as his colleague."[9] Thus, for the aspect of sentencing that Judge Lois Forer vividly shows to be uppermost in an offender's mind (and undoubtedly also in the mind of a potential offender)—the "'In or Out' question"—predictability that is contingent on coming before Doe or Roe can do very little to safeguard a citizen's rights.[10]

Mandatory sentencing is a necessary condition for determinate sentences that possess all three of the ethical advantages discussed above. I conclude that the case for the determinateness of sentences does indeed generate a good ethical argument for mandatory sentencing.

Proportionality

The second feature of sentences that I shall discuss is their appropriateness for the offenses for which they are imposed. It is convenient to refer to this as their "proportionality." What von Hirsch terms the "principle of commensurate deserts" captures this feature of sentences.[11]

As an ethical thesis, the claim that a sentence should be proportional to the gravity of the offense is not likely to be contested. Questions should be raised about it, however: first, about the concept of the "gravity" of an offense, and second, about who should decide how grave various offenses are.

Two recent accounts of the gravity of an offense are helpful.[12] The simpler one will suffice for my present purposes. In analyzing what he calls the "seriousness of crimes," von Hirsch asserts that "seriousness has two major components: *harm* and *culpability*." By "degree of harm," he explains, is meant "degree of injury caused or risked."[13] By "culpability" is meant essentially the moral blameworthiness of an offender for his or her offense.

When the decision is made to criminalize conduct of a certain kind, it is made on the basis of a judgment regarding the degree of harm typically caused or risked by conduct of that kind. This judgment, of course, is based on a more fundamental judgment regarding the value of the interest or interests that would be harmed by the conduct in question. Judgments concerning harm and interests underlie not only a decision to criminalize conduct, but also the definition of the crime thus brought into being. Those charged with making these decisions are our legislators. That their decisions for the most part accord with the views of the communities for which they legislate may be inferred from the relative infrequency of protests against them.

Those objections that *are* raised are chiefly directed against offenses regarded as "crimes without victims." Contemporary movements to decriminalize these have been to a large extent, perhaps to a surprising extent, successful. In any case, offenses regarded as "crimes with victims" have generated relatively little controversy about their criminality. There are also acts whose status as "crimes with victims" or "crimes without victims" is currently a matter of dispute. Here one thinks of offenses against the environment, against unborn humans, against animals, possibly against works of art. The multiplicity of these new offenses, and the questions of both theory and practice that they raise, constitute one of the most striking phenomena of contemporary moral life.[14]

Empirical studies are said to "suggest that people from widely different walks of life can make common sense judgments on the comparative gravity of offenses and come to fairly similar conclusions.[15]

Culpability as a dimension of the gravity of offenses has received less attention from the general public than has harm. But the influence on legislators of the treatment of culpability in the Model Penal Code has been considerable. Noteworthy in this connection is the following statement from a current textbook on criminal law: "The Model Penal Code sets forth four distinct states of mind that may give rise to culpability, depending on how the crime in question is defined: (1) "purposely"; (2) "knowingly"; (3) "recklessly"; and (4) "negligently.". . . This Model Penal Code scheme has had a substantial impact upon the drafting of criminal statutes."[16]

To sever the decision on how severely to punish a criminal offense from the decision to criminalize it and the decision on how to define it seems arbitrary and irrational. Proportionality of sentences is best achieved and preserved if penalties are attached to crimes by those who draft and enact criminal statutes—that is, through mandatory sentencing. Given that culpability as well as harmfulness can be dealt with by criminal statutes, there is no argument based on proportionality that supports discretionary rather than mandatory sentencing. It is important, moreover, not to allow harm or culpability to count twice against an offender. These factors rightly determine what offense he should be charged with. But if he has been duly convicted of that offense, harm and culpability should not be taken into account again at the stage of sentencing. The proportionality of a sentence is preserved when a sentence fits the crime for which an offender stands convicted. Considerations of culpability that mitigate or aggravate an offense should be set forth in criminal statutes, not permitted to affect sentencing through the bias of individual judges. A vivid account of the latter process is provided by Willard Gaylin.[17]

On the position I am here defending, the distinction between "mitigation of sentence" and "mitigation of offense" cannot be maintained.[18] The only reasons with power to mitigate are those that mitigate an offense itself. These should be included in statutes. Conceivably there might be reasons for leniency in sentencing an individual offender, but these could not count as "mitigating," unless they were also factors that mitigated his offense. If a sentence is reduced because of considerations other than what the offender deserves by virtue of the gravity of his crime, it is lessened, but it is not mitigated.

The proportionality of sentences is their most significant ethical feature. It is most effectively preserved in a principled form if it is determined by mandatory sentencing.

Uniformity

The third feature of sentences to be considered here is their uniformity. This is a feature that sentences have only in relation to other sentences. It belongs to what has been termed by Feinberg "comparative justice," which, he says, "involves, in one way or another, equality in the treatment accorded to all the members of a class."[19] Again, as we saw to be the case for proportionality, the thesis that sentences ought to be uniform will be regarded by many as self-evident. Just as the punishment should fit the crime, the same crime should receive the same punishment.

Writers dealing with this thesis have not disputed it, but have pointed out that it is less simple than it first appears. Some of the questions it raises center around the expression "the same crime." As Judge Lois Forer has said, "The nomenclature of crimes frequently does not distinguish between greater and lesser offenses."[20] She goes on to illustrate this point by describing two offenses, both classified as "burglary." In one case the offender was frightened off before anything could be taken; in the other, valuable jewelry and a coin collection were taken.

There is, however, no reason why criminal statutes cannot be made as precise as one wishes, and, as argued in the previous section, those who draw up definitions of crimes can specify either their harmfulness or the state of mind of those who commit them, or both. This process has evidently been carried out more fully with respect to crimes against the person than with respect to crimes against property. As criminal statutes are revised and improved, puzzles about how to tell when offenders have committed the "same crime" can be expected to disappear.

The expression "the same punishment" has evidently seemed less troublesome. The amount of unpleasantness *characteristically* associated with a certain prison sentence or a certain fine can be calculated with fair reliability, and this has seemed enough to validate the concept of "sameness of punishment."

It is clearly something of an oversimplification to assume that incarceration varies only in length of time to be served. Conditions in American prisons, and even between prisons within states systems, differ strikingly in their impact on the physical and mental health of inmates, on the job-training and other educational programs they provide, in their measures of surveillance, and so forth. Still, as proponents of the "new retributism" have emphasized, deprivations of liberty are all experienced as severely unpleasant in *some* of the same ways, so that prison sentences are to a certain extent commensurable.

Some philosophers would argue that what members of a class are entitled to is equality of *treatment*, not equality in the distribution of benefits or burdens. In moral contexts we tend to speak here, following Frankena, of "equal consideration."[21] In legal contexts we tend (especially if we are Americans) to speak of "due process" and "equal protection." It would be a mistake, however, to place too much weight, in connection with the uniformity of sentences, on the distinction between procedural and substantive equality.

What offenders are equally entitled to is not sentences that are uniform but sentences that are proportional. Nonuniformity among sentences (usually called "disparity") is presumptive evidence that some offenders have not received proportional sentences.

The ethical thesis that sentences should be proportional is thus fundamental to the thesis that sentences should be uniform. If proportionality is always present, the requirements of uniformity will have been met. Accordingly, if the argument in the previous section that proportionality requires mandatory sentencing is sound, and if proportionality insures uniformity, it follows that mandatory sentencing will yield sentences that are uniform.

I have argued that an examination of three ethically valuable features of sentences yields a strong ethical case for mandatory sentencing. A case against discretionary sentencing would require an examination of rehabilitation and reform. I believe that such examination would show that as goals for sentencing, these are ethically flawed.[22] But the arguments that seem to me most strongly to support this claim must be set forth on another occasion.[23]

Notes

1. See Jack P. Gibbs, *Crime, Punishment and Deterrence* (New York and Amsterdam, 1975), p. 237.
2. Marvin E. Frankel, *Criminal Sentences* (New York, 1973), ch. 8.
3. Ibid., p. 86–87.
4. The general theses defended by Herbert Morris in his influential "Persons and Punishment" could be used for this purpose. See *On Guilt and Innocence* (Berkeley, Calif., 1976), pp. 31–63.
5. Frankel, *Criminal Sentences*, p. 3.
6. Ibid., p. 96.
7. H. L. A. Hart, *Punishment and Responsibility* (Oxford, 1968), p. 206.
8. Frankel, *Criminal Sentences*, p. 88.
9. Willard Gaylin, *Partial Justice* (New York, 1974), p. 10.
10. Lois Forer, *Criminals and Victims* (New York, 1980), p. 2.
11. See A. von Hirsch, *Doing Justice* (New York, 1976), ch. 8.
12. One is that of von Hirsch, in *Doing Justice*, ch. 9. The other is that of Hyman Gross, in *A Theory of Criminal Justice* (New York, 1979), pp. 77–82.
13. von Hirsch, *Doing Justice*, p. 79.
14. In this connection, see Peter Singer, *Practical Ethics* (Cambridge, 1979).
15. von Hirsch, *Doing Justice*, p. 79.
16. Steven Emmanuel, *Criminal Law* (New Rochelle, N.Y., 1970), p. 14. See also E. L. Beardsley, "Blaming," *Philosophia* 8 (1979), pp. 573–583.
17. In Gaylin, *Partial Justice*, ch. 3.
18. The distinction is made by Gross in *Theory of Criminal Justice*, pp. 449–450.
19. Joel Feinberg, "Noncomparative Justice," in Feinberg and Gross, eds., *Justice* (Encino, Calif., 1977), p. 56.
20. Forer, *Criminals and Victims*, p. 57.
21. William K. Frankena, "Some Beliefs about Justice," in Feinberg and Gross, eds., *Justice*, pp. 46–54.
22. For a good discussion of some of the flaws, see Sidney Gendin, "A Critique of the Theory of Criminal Rehabilitation," in Milton Goldinger, ed., *Punishment and Human Rights* (Cambridge, Mass.: 1974), pp. 17–37.
23. I attempt to do this in "The Ethics of Discretionary Sentencing," in progress.

ROBERT JOHNSON

Capital Punishment: The View from Death Row

My topic is capital punishment, and my aim is to convey the view from death row. The subject is timely, since many Americans express strong views on capital punishment but few realize that lengthy and painful human warehousing is the fate of condemned prisoners. In fact, some nine-hundred persons are warehoused for death in our prisons, a sizable number of them awaiting electrocution in Alabama. I've spoken at length with many of Alabama's condemned prisoners, and shall describe how death row confinement and the death penalty affect these prisoners and others like them.

To cover this subject I shall consider, first, the custodial regime of death row and the feelings of powerlessness it produces; second, the nature of death work and the fear it produces; and third, the total human environment of death row, which produces emotional emptiness and a kind of "living death." Finally, I shall conclude with a discussion of the human costs of death row confinement and the justice of the death penalty.

The Death Row Environment

The physical environment of death row is imposing, stark, and austere. Alabama's death row, the setting for my research, is no exception to the general rule. Under the auspices of the Southern Poverty Law Center and with

For a more detailed discussion of this subject, see *Condemned to Die: Life Under Sentence of Death* (Elsevier, 1981), by Robert Johnson, portions of which are reprinted in this article with permission. My appreciation is extended to Bradford Morse, Jeffrey Reiman, F.A. Elliston, Richard Burgh, and Hugo Bedau for their helpful comments concerning the presentation upon which this essay is based.

active support from its director, John Carroll, I conducted in-depth interviews in September 1978 with thirty-five of the thirty-seven men then confined in Holman Prison on Alabama's death row. The nature of the death row experience emerged from these conversations with disturbing clarity.

Death row is a prison within a prison, physically and socially isolated from the prison community and the outside world. Condemned prisoners live in virtual solitary confinement. Twenty-three and one-half hours alone in their cells is punctuated by thirty minutes devoted to private exercise in a closely guarded outdoor cage. Passive recreation—principally reading—comprises the program services available to the condemned. Boredom is necessarily the death row prisoner's intimate companion, his routine the grinding, dull redundancy of life lived in sterile, cloistered quarters.

The theme of custody permeates and circumscribes death row. Control is the leitmotif of the death row environment; the setting is run with disciplinary precision. The men are considered dangerous, both to themselves and to others, and they are classified as escape risks. Watched closely and frisked often, death row prisoners are handcuffed behind their backs and heavily guarded during rare excursions from their cells. Only one prisoner is moved at a time. Death row inmates even exercise alone: they are afforded free run, if you will, of a modest recreation cage. Though prisoners are also free to pace unhandcuffed in their recreation cage, the experience proves unrewarding because it is so obviously an extension of the close confinement in which they live.

Custodial procedures are extended to in-

Reprinted with permission from *Ethics, Public Policy, and Criminal Justice*, ed. Frederick Elliston and Norman Bowie (Cambridge, Mass.: Oelgeschlager, Gunn & Hain, Inc., 1982), pp. 305–20.

clude restrictions on mail, visits, and other contacts with the outside world. Packages are limited in weight and number, and are carefully searched for contraband. Purchases from the prison store are similarly limited and carefully monitored by staff. Men are restricted to one hour per month of what is prosaically called "contact visitation." That is, for one hour per month, each man can sit in a guarded room and his loved ones can touch and embrace him. Noncontact visits—during which the inmate sits in a submarine-like structure and shouts through paint-clogged apertures in a metal grid separating him from his intimates—are more frequently available. They are easier to monitor and pose fewer security risks than do contact visits. But noncontact visits are considered by inmates to be sufficiently inferior to contact visits as to be abnormal and less than real.

The sterile prison setting and its pervasive custodial measures are not experienced by inmates as neutral facts of life, or as routine responses by the prison administration to its task of holding condemned and arguably dangerous men. Instead, inmates experience the environment as a series of needless assaults on their sensibilities. The physical setting is seen as punitively barren; surveillance and security are viewed as ways to inflict pain. The inmates feel that the guards want them to suffer on the prison's terms, in addition to those imposed by the sentence.

Custody, through constriction, harassment, and neglect, serves to isolate prisoners from the larger world and from each other. Isolation is a theme uniting prison policy in the seemingly disparate provinces of cell time, exercise, mail, and visits. Whether intended or not, the experience of isolation is a central feature of life on death row. The prisoners thus isolated feel powerless, vulnerable, and alone, defenseless against the might of their keepers and unable to alter their fate.

Death Work and the Crucible of Fear

On death row, custody is the vehicle through which men are kept safe and alive for even-

tual execution. Guards are thus simultaneously agents of custody (who seek to maintain life) and agents of execution (who oversee and inflict death). Inmates are exquisitely sensitive to the duality of the death row guard's role, and draw the bottom line around the electric chair and the fact of execution. A deep and perhaps unbridgeable chasm separates inmates from staff. The inmates know the guards must take part in their executions, and they sense that men who seek out such work are ready and willing to engage in violence to control their prospective victims.

Such perceptions reveal an aura of violence that hangs like a shroud over death row. As the inmates see it, harassment is the norm. An underlying theme of abusive encounters is one of basic disrespect for the inmate as a person. Inmates who are obviously unable to command respect—those who are disturbed, shy, weak, or otherwise unimpressive persons—may come in for special abuse. Prisoner accounts suggest that vulnerable men provide fodder for staff games of diversion and amusement. Such persons appear as common targets of ridicule because they are highly susceptible (and hence highly entertaining) quarry.

The picture of the environment communicated by death row prisoners features a powerful custodial regime that is unwilling to brook opposition from its captives. Under such conditions, virtually any activity may provoke violence. Inmates buttress this view by arguing that even expressions of opinion contrary to those of the staff have produced beatings. "These people are something else," stated one prisoner, "it's just whatever you get, you just be satisfied with that, because if you voice your opinion about it, you're going to get a whipping." Inmates see themselves as helpless victims of tyrannical control. "If you retaliate," one inmate despondently observed, "you know you're going to die."

Psychological survival on death row can be equated with walking a long tightrope, where even slight deviations from expected behavior can produce disaster. Safety becomes a matter of nonaction, and action a matter of risk. A person feels safest in his cell. Outside the cell he is handcuffed and vulnerable; guards can secrete him in private areas of the prison and subject him to beatings with impunity. Nonessential excursions from the cell are therefore to be avoided at all costs, and essential excursions are undertaken in a state of apprehension and fear.

A few men become paralyzed with fear under such conditions. They strive to maintain a low profile on death row, to disappear as it were, from the sight of malevolent guards. Adaptation entails efforts to sleep away the day and to hide in the corner of one's cell, seeking sanctuary from the danger that lurks just beyond the cell door. These men feel completely defenseless and overpowered by the dangerous world that surrounds and threatens to engulf them. Their view of guards as tyrants administering their own brand of brutal justice leaves them fearful that their executions could occur at literally any time, at the whim of their captors.

Adaptation in this unstable world is possible, but everyone knows (or fears) that violence may ultimately touch and consume them. They know that there is nothing they can do to avoid it, or to defend themselves, or to retaliate. On death row the logic of despair reigns supreme, and the prisoners feel trapped and helpless, "pinned to the wall," as one man poignantly stated, "waiting to be shot."

Contemplating Execution

The death sentence dramatically affects the social environment of death row, defining and polarizing executioners and victims and otherwise contributing to an atmosphere of violence and fear. The sentence itself also is an independent source of stress and suffering for condemned prisoners.

The prospect of execution, for example, gives rise to intense preoccupation. The future is necessarily uncertain, and men feel vulnerable and afraid. "I'm scared twenty-four hours a day" related one man, "because I don't know what's going to happen." Uncertainty and insecurity are aggravated by a "domino theory" of sentencing espoused or endorsed by many inmates. Given the presence of at least one of their peers who has volunteered to get his punishment over with, men fear that a series of executions may be set in motion. Recent executions in other states feed these fears.

Death anxieties are also fed by staff harassment about execution. Men have been given tours of the death room, for example, where they view the electric chair as though it were an exhibit in a museum. The implication, as the inmates see it, is that guards are anxious to carry out the inmates' sentences. This message is also conveyed in interactions where guards are seen as making light of an inmate's situation, or when a guard asks an inmate if he's "ready" for his punishment.

Death work, no matter how it is carried out, is intrinsically demeaning. Electrocution may seem a particularly ugly mode of execution. "This is the way you do a beast when you are killing him," stated one man, "like a hog at slaughter." The process is unavoidably gruesome. Men speculate about the mechanics of electrocution and its likely impact on the body, which they visualize in vivid detail. The spectre of electrocution brings to mind the frying and melting of organs, and the general disfigurement of the body. It also represents a test or trial by ordeal, since the inmate should complete his "last walk" under his own power, and with some poise and composure. Dwelling on the details of the sentence naturally breeds tension, anxiety, and fear. Of greater concern, however, may be the human legacy of execution, the image left behind for loved ones to contemplate and remember the prisoner by—the ugly memory of the seared and burned body; the humiliating image of the man who breaks down under pressure, providing enjoyment for his keepers and for the official witnesses to the spectacle.

The death sentence is a major concern of many condemned prisoners, a source of worry, anxiety, fear, even dread of the unknown and of a despoiled death. For some of the men, the sentence is a constant concern. "There is not a day that passes," stated one such inmate, "that I don't think about the electric chair and the death sentence." For others, the sentence seems less tangible and immediate; they appear free of the burden carried by men who personally shoulder the weight of the death sentence. But their reprieve may prove short-lived and self-defeating, and illusion supported by the need to hide from reality behind a facade of gallows humor. "When things get hard and everybody stops joking," observed one prisoner in reference to impending executions in Alabama and elsewhere, "that's when you are going to see about ten people just go crazy from the jump. All of us are going to bug out sooner or later."

Human Environment of Death Row

Thus far we have surveyed the death row environment in terms of its physical and social characteristics, its custodial fixations, its loneliness, violence, danger, and fear. But in focusing on specific pressures of death row confinement, we have highlighted significant trees but bypassed the experiential forest in which they are rooted. Death row confinement, in other words, is experienced as a totality, and it is to this totality of human suffering that we now turn.

A range of insoluble problems emerge *ad seriatim* on death row to torment the condemned prisoner. In general, the experience is one of being frustrated and unable to rectify problems, and depressed about one's future prospects in such a situation. Persistent feelings of powerlessness and despair in turn breed anger that remains suppressed, directionless, and without targets. There is also an overwhelming sense of depression and defeat. The men feel trapped, entombed, suffocated—helpless in the face of indictments of their human worth that emanate from the death row environment, from the death sentence, and from lives characterized by chronic failure and inadequacy.

The pressures of death row confinement

are enormous. Deterioration under this massive environmental assault is therefore a contingency that must be reckoned with. For some men, deterioration is felt as a chillingly impersonal and inexorable process, much like the gradual but persistent wearing down of sandstone when it is exposed to a harsh desert milieu. Prisoners speak of slowing down mentally, of feeling confused, lethargic, listless, and drowsy. They diagnose themselves as increasingly weak, susceptible, and drained, beaten by an overwhelming environment against whose onslaughts their resistance proves futile, and finally falters and disappears. The haunting prospect of deterioration is brought home to prisoners in the unnerving presence of a man who has been transformed on death row from a healthy prisoner into a psychiatric casualty. The moral of this person's life is transparent to the men of death row. "We all know we can do just like him," affirmed one prisoner, "go crazy." Such fears possess plausibility on death row, where deterioration has a visceral reality and manifests itself in a sequence of slow death that is steeped in the imagery of sleep and gradual disengagement from sanity and life.

A Living Death

Some death row inmates characterize their existence as a living death and themselves as the living dead. They speak in symbolic terms, providing an imagery appropriate to the human experience in a world where life is overshadowed by death. "Living death" is the death row prisoners' metaphor for their loss of personal autonomy and loss of command over resources critical to psychological survival, for their enforced isolation from the living, and for their barren existence on death row.

Emotional death appears to lie at the core of the experience of living death. Men feel abandoned by the living—in the world and on death row—and sink into a deathlike existence. "You need love and it just ain't there," stated one prisoner who mournfully counted himself among the living dead, "it leaves you empty inside, dead inside. Really, you just stop caring." Emotional death spawns a psychic numbness that appears comparable to "ontological insecurity." This condition was labeled by R. D. Laing to describe the experience of people who fear they are petrifying and becoming frozen in place as lifeless objects or things, alive as organisms but dead as persons.[1] But Laing, it is wise to remember, studied psychotics; we speak here, for the most part, of normal persons succumbing to abnormal conditions.

The death row environment reinforces the image of living death by its macabre priorities. Medical and emotional needs of inmates, for example, routinely take a back seat to the impersonal requirements of custody. In fact, such needs are often discounted entirely.

The priorities on death row seem perverse where visits are concerned. A man whose teeth are rotting for want of dental care may be forced to shave before being permitted a visit. While the public image of the prison is no doubt at issue, and stubbled chins connote slovenly conditions more readily than do hidden cavities, the visiting ritual under such circumstances seems reminiscent of the viewing at a wake. "He's never looked better," hypothetical visitors might exclaim, acknowledging the clean-shaven and perhaps fattened countenace of the condemned prisoner, who sits quiet and erect, hands cuffed across his lap. To be sure, surreal scenarios apply elsewhere in the prison. Prison is a setting that is, after all, "impersonal enough to help a man suspect that others want him dead."[2] Such morbid suspicions, culled from subtle environmental cues, take on the cast of ironclad and self-evident truth on death row. Here, prison policy, in the word of one inmate, uniformly "reflects that (we) prisoners are already doomed and forgotten."

A living death is what death row has to offer its inhabitants. It is a world purposely denuded of normal social functions and rewards. Condemned men are offered an existence, not a life. They are invited to sustain the physical organism while its emotional and spiritual counterparts wither and die.

"The living dead is actually what it adds up to," concluded one man. Continuing, he posed and answered a question that captured the essence of his despair: "I mean, what does a maggot do? A maggot eats and defecates. That's all we do: eat and defecate. Nothing else. They don't allow us to do anything else."

Capital Punishment: The View from Death Row

I have tried to describe the enormous suffering caused by death row confinement. This suffering must be recognized as a major human cost of capital punishment as it is administered today. My research suggests that the cost is too high. The fact that prisoners are capital offenders does not invalidate their claim to humane confinement. Humane confinement, however, may be impossible to achieve on death row. To be sure, reforms can reduce the harm occasioned by death row confinement. (In fact, the court case for which this research was conducted did result in some modest reforms.) But no reform can alter the basic reality of death row confinement—a regime of confinement that qualifies as torture.

What does it mean to call death row confinement torture? Torture is normally thought to comprise extreme physical or psychological brutality, the object of which is to produce a range of harmful effects: suffering for its own sake; conversion to an ideology, religion, or cause; confession of guilt or inadequacy; the betrayal of trust. To inflict torture is therefore conceived as an intended event; torture also implies active harm rather than passive indifference or neglect. Yet torture need not be restricted to situations in which physical or psychological brutality is consciously employed to achieve an end. Standard instances of torture and death row confinement have in common an assault on the person that causes him intense suffering and violates his integrity as a human being by treating him as if he were a mere animal or object. That either or both of these conditions is not intended as torture is irrelevant.[3] The palpable deterioration and decay of death row prisoners stand as proof that they have suffered real harm far in excess of that required by sentence, and that they have been victims of real brutality. Thus, for all intents and purposes, a death sentence amounts to death with torture in a society that has explicitly renounced torture as a remnant of barbarism.

Moreover, death row prisoners are exposed to conditions that will typically, if not inevitably, produce a torturous regime. Explanations of massacres and other occasions of institutionalized violence suggest that moral restraints against brutality are removed or seriously weakened when three conditions apply: first, when officials are authorized to harm; second, when procedures are made routine; and third, when prospective victims are dehumanized.[4] These conditions apply with particular salience and impact on death row. Correctional personnel responsible for death row are explicitly and unambiguously *authorized* to warehouse prisoners who are awaiting execution. Guards and their superiors can readily view themselves as impersonal instruments of authority; as such, they bear no individual moral responsibility for the actions necessary to maintain an orderly death row, or for the executions that may take place under their auspices. And since *routine* is almost blindly relied upon to structure each day, and especially each execution day, correctional personnel are further removed from the human consequences of the policies they implement. Finally, death row inmates are effectively isolated from one another and from the larger world, and hence they are denied the personal and group support necessary to retain their autonomy. Thus, their *dehumanization* emerges as the end product of instruments of authority acting within stipulated routines on condemned prisoners rendered as objects to be stored and ultimately dispatched in the execution chamber. Given the structure and psychology of the death row situation, torturous confinement and killing occurs, but nowhere is there found a person who takes full moral responsibility for these acts.

Reforms of death row can and must be undertaken on humanitarian grounds. That we minister to persons in stress, however, does not mean that we relieve their hurt. Nor do such ministrations, however valuable in themselves, absolve us of the responsibility to judge public policy in terms of its human consequences. In a democratic society, public policy is assessed from the standpoint of the consumer. As Edmund Cahn observed:

> Only when we . . . adopt a consumer perspective are we able to perceive the practical significance of our institutions, law, and public transactions in terms of their impacts on the lives and homely experiences of human beings. It is their personal impacts that constitute the criteria for any appraisal we may make. How, we ask, does the particular institution affect personal rights and personal concerns, the interests and aspirations of the individual, group, and community? We judge it according to its concussions on human lives.[5]

The experience of condemned prisoners is relevant to any assessment of the practical significance of death row and the death penalty. The deterioration and living death the prisoners suffer underscore the "concussions on human lives" produced by confinement under sentence of death. Albert Camus may have been correct when he maintained that capital punishment killed the offender twice: once on death row while awaiting execution and once again in the death chamber. This punishment is excessive, seen by the hard reckoning of the person who demands the life of the murderer in return for the life of the victim. The justice of capital punishment thus remains very much in doubt. As Camus said:

> As a general rule, a man is undone by waiting for capital punishment well before he dies. Two deaths are inflicted on him, the first being worse than the second, whereas he killed but once. Compared to such torture, the penalty of retaliation seems like a civilized law. It never claimed that the man who gouged out one of his brother's eyes should be totally blinded.[6]

It could be argued, of course, that some murderers cold-bloodedly claim multiple victims or torture their victims, and thus deserve the additional suffering inflicted by death row confinement. Experience with capital punishment laws indicates that it would be impossible to reliably identify such persons; terms like "heinous" or "atrocious" are liberally construed by judges and juries, and hardened offenders are frequently wise enough to plea bargain and thus obtain prison terms instead of death sentences.[7] Moreover, the closer one gets to identifying murderers who replicate the unemotional calculation of state-sanctioned killing, the more likely it is that serious mental health problems are indicated. Capital punishment is then inapplicable, since the subject of punishment must freely choose his crime and hence deserve his punishment, and the mentally impaired offender cannot rightly be said to exercise free choice. It is doubtful, in any event, that the state should seek to imitate the cruelty of some criminals in order to achieve justice.

It is not only the suffering of condemned prisoners—their experience under sentence of death—that has implications for the justice of the death penalty. The condemned prisoners' perspective on the justice of their punishment is also germaine. Condemned prisoners are possessed of a sense of simple justice that is shaped by the experience of death row confinement and the tragic sense of life it confers. The frailty of man and his judgments seem painfully apparent to them. Absolute judgments, they know, terminate lives that might be rehabilitated and allowed to make partial reparations for the harms they have caused. Though none of the prisoners spoke of having read Camus on the right to life and the crucial link between the moral status of the judge and the morality of his judgments, the intuitive validity of Camus's arguments would be apparent to them. They stand squarely on the moral terrain of which he writes. Quoting Camus once again:

> There are no just people—merely hearts more or less lacking in justice. Living at least allows

us to discover this and to add to the sum of our actions a little of the good that will make up in part for the evil we have added to the world. Such a right to live, which allows a chance to make amends, is the natural right of every man, even the worst man. The lowest of criminals and the most upright of judges meet side by side, equally wretched in their solidarity. Without that right, moral life is utterly impossible. None among us is authorized to despair of a single man, except after his death, which transforms his life into destiny and then permits a definitive judgment. But pronouncing the definitive judgment before his death, decreeing the closing of accounts when the creditor is still alive, is no man's right. On this limit, at least, whoever judges absolutely condemns himself absolutely.[8]

Two important issues are raised here, and will be discussed in turn. The first is the assertion of a natural right to life; the second is the presumed impropriety of absolute judgments rendered by imperfect judges operating in an imperfect world.

A natural, universal, and inalienable right to life, according to Murphy, is premised on the assumption that

> the most important thing in a human life (something stressed by philosophers from Socrates through Kant and by such other admirable and insightful individuals as Jesus and Tolstoy) is the *development of one's own moral character*, the development of oneself in such a way that one's life can honestly be said to be coherent, meaningful, and perhaps even admirable. . . . The development of a morally coherent personality is the most crucial task or project of any human life. . . . To block or interrupt this project (or to preclude one's ever having an opportunity to have a change of heart, reflect on one's life, and *start* such a project) is . . . the gravest harm that one can do to a person.[9] (Italics in original.)

Some scholars, such as Locke and, more recently, van den Haag, have argued that the murderer, in violating the right to life of his victim, himself forfeits the right to live. Yet, as Hugo Bedau has observed, "(T)here is no intrinsic feature of any right, including the natural right to life, that makes it subject to loss through forfeiture. The only basis for supposing that any right is forfeited rather than grossly violated by society when it punishes an offender with death is that just retribution and social defense together require the death penalty."[10] This case, Bedau goes on to demonstrate, cannot be convincingly made. Just retribution requires only that the scale of crimes and punishments be commensurate, such that the most serious crimes receive the most serious punishments; social defense, according to available evidence, is served equally by life imprisonment and the death penalty.[11] Moreover, "(E)ven if it is concluded that a murderer or other felon does forfeit the natural right to life, it does not follow that a murderer *must* be put to death. . . . Forfeiting one's *right* to life is not identical with forfeiting one's life. Also, forfeiting one's right to life does not confer upon anyone else the *duty* to take the forfeited life."[12] Indeed, the sparing of life in this context may constitute both a recognition of the awesome violence in which the death penalty implicates us all, and a modest refusal to inflict godlike punishments in a human world.

> The death penalty, more than any other kind of killing, is done in the name of society and on its behalf. Each of us has a hand in such a killing, and unless such killings are absolutely necessary they cannot really be justified. Thus, abolishing the death penalty represents extending the hand of life even to those who by their crimes have "forfeited" any right to live. It is a tacit admission that we must abandon the folly and pretense of attempting to secure perfect justice in an imperfect world.[13]

Camus, of course, finds no judges of sufficient innocence to render even the "absolutely necessary" death sentences alluded to by Bedau. The lineage of Camus's argument is old and venerable. A connection between innocence and judgment has roots in Christ's injuction against persons who would condemn their neighbors, judging others as if they themselves were righteous and without fault or responsibility for the failings of their fellow men. For a system of justice to comply with this moral imperative against false judgment, judgments rendered under color of law must be commensurate with the human frailty we are born with, and with the responsibility for one another each of us carries as members of the human community. Richard Korn conveyed the essence of this proposition when he called for "the transformation of a criminal justice system based on retaliation and disablement to a system based on reconciliation through mutual restitution."[14] The transformation, according to Korn, "must be conducted by Each Man in his role of Everyman."[15] Each of us, then, must see ourselves in others and take seriously the mandate to be our brother's keeper. This identification with one's fellow man reduces the legitimacy of retributive justice.[16] Ideally, crime and its correction are seen as a joint responsibility of the offender and the community. Crime is taken as a critique of the community; both the criminal and the community have failed one another and owe each other reparations. "Crime as a form of social criticism: mutual restitution and service as instruments of reconciliation—these are the ways in which offenses are dealt with among those with the kind of conscience which demand that they treat others as they themselves wish to be treated."[17]

The collective wisdom of the condemned in the matter of the morality of capital punishment might be summarized as follows. Absolute judgments require absolute certainty on the part of the judge and absolute guilt on the part of the offender. To render a sentence of death—a cool, calculated, and irrevocable social judgment—demands no less than this. The implication of a death sentence is that the offender deserves to be put to death because he is irredeemably corrupt and unsalvageable, and that society has the right to reach this verdict because it bears no responsibility for the offender's actions.[18] Society, playing God, takes on His mantle of innocence; the capital offender, personifying evil, forfeits his humanity. Executions proceed with impunity. When would such conditions be met? Probably never, and surely not with today's capital offenders, who are invariably drawn from the ranks of the underprivileged and inadequate. Each and every one of these persons can point to mitigating circumstances that relieve them of full culpability for their crimes and implicate society as partly to blame for their actions.

To be sure, serious crime cannot be excused. To speak of mitigating circumstances is not to imply absence of guilt, and to strive for a justice system based on mutal restitution and service is not to rule out punishment as a response to crime. While law can be thought of as an undertaking in which both correct behavior and the resources required to behave correctly must go hand-in-hand, existing laws are essentially one-directional exercises of power in which defiant wills are punished.[19] As a practical matter, then, justice systems must dispense punishment, even though they may do so imperfectly and in the context of unjust societies. The defense for these anomalies may lie in balancing matters of equity, redress, and obligation. Fair procedures must be sought to minimize the likelihood of arbitrary harm at the hands of the law. Final judgments must be withheld to leave room for correction of errors or compensation for losses. Some effort must be made to balance obligations incurred as a consequence of societal benefits received, with obligations incurred as a consequence of law violations. The condemned prisoners' experiences with the justice system, however, highlight its inadequacies and weak points: easily accepted guilt when standard street crime and criminals are involved in adjudication; responsiveness to differences of class and color; susceptibility to pressure for convictions in order to allay community fears. The indebtedness of capital offenders to the society is simply stipulated, even though the case can be made that many of these men have received little guidance, support, or even sustenance from the society that now stands in absolute judgment over them.[20]

Most condemned prisoners conclude from their experiences with the justice system that they have been railroaded into their death sentences. For many of them, the death sentence figures as the culmination of past and current abandonments by the very justice system that is presently demanding their lives. A number of men contemplate suicide as their final naked rebuke to this system and the society it serves. Tragically, suicide may well be a rational rejoinder to a society that subjects men to lengthy regimes of state-sanctioned violence—today on death row, tomorrow in the death chamber.

Notes

1. R. D. Laing, *The Divided Self* (London: Penguin Books, 1965).

2. Hans Toch, *Men in Crisis* (Chicago: Aldine, 1975), p. 101.

3. J. Murphy, *Retribution, Justice, and Therapy* (Hingham, Mass.: Kluwer Boston, 1979), p. 233.

4. The concepts of authorization, routinization, and dehumanization are borrowed from the research of Kelman and Milgram and applied to the death row situation. See Kelman, "Violence Without Moral Restraint: Reflections on the Dehumanization of Victims and Victimizers," 29 (4) *Journal of Social Issues* 25 (1973), and S. Milgram, *Obedience to Authority* (New York: Harper & Row, 1975).

5. Edmund Cahn, *The Predicament of Democratic Man* (New York: Dell, 1962), p. 30.

6. Albert Camus, "Reflections on the Guillotine," in Camus, ed., *Resistance, Rebellion and Death* (New York: Knopf, 1969), pp. 174 and 205.

7. Stephen Gettinger, *Sentenced to Die* (New York: Macmillan, 1979).

8. Camus, "Reflections," p. 221.

9. Murphy, *Retribution, Justice, and Therapy*, pp. 242 and 243.

10. Hugo Bedau, "Capital Punishment," in T. Regan, ed., *Matters of Life and Death* (New York: Random House, 1980), Chap. 5.

11. Speaking in a broader context, Fingarette observed that "(T)he famous retributivist principle of *lex talionis*—the idea of retaliation in kind—[can be given] a completely general meaning:—The reason for punishment is an act manifesting a will that would frustrate the power of law. What is the response in kind? It is for the law, in turn, to frustrate the power of that will. . . . Interpreting these principles in this way leaves room for an indefinite variety of specific forms of punish-

ment—which we do in fact find in different times and places." Fingarette, "Punishment and Suffering," Presidential Address, Fifty-first Annual Pacific Meeting of the American Philosophical Association in Portland, Oregon, March 26, 1977. Quotation on p. 511.

12. Bedau, "Capital Punishment."

13. Ibid., pp. 179 and 180.

14. Richard Korn, "Of Crime, Criminal Justice and Corrections," 6 (1) *University of San Francisco Law Review* 74 (1971).

15. Ibid.

16. Included under the term retributive justice are not only revenge and just deserts, but also the "humbling of the defiant—or at least disrespectful—will" (Fingarette, "Punishment and Suffering," p. 510). The conception of law and its application here is one of a *mutual* humbling of wills, not the one-directional relationship normally characteristic of the exercise of the power of law. Law can be conceived as a statement of mutual goals and obligations, with violations of law seen as shared failures.

17. Korn, "Of Crime," pp. 44 and 45.

18. Camus, "Reflections," p. 221. The human basis of social institutions is intentionally distorted by some, who argue that the very imperfections of these institutions must be shielded by a cloak of false majesty. Perversely, the death penalty is advanced as a means to secure popular support for the fiction that law and government are grounded in an immutable moral order. For example:

> Capital punishment . . . serves to remind us of the majesty of the moral order that is embodied in our law and of the terrible consequences of its breach. The law must not be understood to be merely a statute that we enact or repeal at our will and obey or disobey at our convenience, especially not the criminal law. Wherever law is regarded as merely statutory, men will soon enough disobey it, and they will learn how to do so without any inconvenience to themselves. The criminal law must possess a dignity far beyond that possessed by mere statutory enactment or utilitarian and self-interested calculations; the most

powerful means we have to give it that dignity is to authorize it to impose the ultimate penalty (W. Berns, *For Capital Punishment*, New York: Basic Books, 1979, pp. 172–173). Thankfully, "only a relatively few executions are required to enhance the dignity of the criminal law . . ." (p. 183).

19. Fingarette, "Punishment and Suffering." As Fingarette has observed, "some of the great teachers of civilizations have seen that punishment is dominion over the will, that it flows necessarily from law as dominion over the will, and they have *for these very reasons* rejected government by law in their ideal visions." It is unclear to me, however, whether outright rejection of law or the attempt to forge laws along transactional lines—as a statement of mutual goals and obligations framed in the context of the distribution of resources and benefits—is more utopian.

20. See, particularly, Chapter 2 of Robert Johnson, *Condemned to Die: Life Under Sentence of Death* (New York: Elsevier, 1981).

Suggested Further Reading

Allen, Francis A., "Criminal Justice, Legal Values, and the Rehabilitative Ideal," *Journal of Criminal Law, Criminology, and Political Science*, 50 (1959), 226–32.

Card, Claudia, "Retributive Penal Liability," *American Philosophical Monographs*, No. 7 (1973), pp. 17–35.

Goldinger, Milton, "Punishment, Justice and the Separation of Issues," *The Monist*, 49 (1965).

Newman, Donald J., "Pleading Guilty for Considerations: A Study of Bargain Justice," *Journal of Criminal Law, Criminology and Police Science*, 46 (156), 780–90.

Zeisel, Hans, "The Deterrent Effect of the Death Penalty: Facts vs. Faith," in *The Supreme Court Review*, ed. P. B. Kurland. Chicago: University of Chicago Press, 1977, pp. 317–43.

GLOSSARY FOR UNIT IV

CRIMINAL JUSTICE

adversary system. The system of trial by law in which attorneys for the contending parties take on the role of adversaries in the arena of the court, each representing the interests of his or her client, with the judge and jury as impartial arbiters.

advocacy. Pleading the cause of a client before a tribunal of the law.

capital punishment. The death penalty; sentencing of the felon convicted of a major crime to legal execution.

"dirty means." The use of techniques by law enforcement officials which tend to violate a person's right to privacy, confidentiality, or respect; examples are wiretapping and entrapment.

discretion. The power of free decision or latitude of choice within certain legal bounds, ascribed to law enforcement officers and judges.

excuse. A circumstance or condition of action which is offered as grounds for removing blame.

harm principle. The rule by which acts whose consequences inflict injury (intentional or otherwise) on other persons are judged to be morally unacceptable.

incapacitation. The confinement of criminals in order to remove them from society and thereby protect law-abiding citizens.

insanity plea. A legal excuse which holds that a person should not be punished for acts that the person was not responsible for by reason of a defective mental condition.

lethal force. The capacity of certain weapons to cause death.

mitigation. A circumstance or condition of action which makes the legal judgment of blame less harsh or severe.

plea bargaining. Negotiation between prosecutors and defendants in which an accused person agrees to plead guilty without a trial to a lesser offense in return for the promise of the lighter punishment which accompanies that offense.

proportionality. The doctrine that the punishment must be proportional in severity or gentleness to the crime.

rehabilitation. The goal of criminal punishment whose objective is the reeducation of offenders for the purpose of reintegrating them into society.

retribution. The idea that punishment is a payment exacted from the offender for the committed crime.

victimless crime. A criminal act that lacks an identifiable person or group that is harmed or injured.

SELECTED
SUPPLEMENTARY READING

HEALTH CARE

Bayles, Michael D., *Reproductive Ethics*. Englewood Cliffs, N.J.: Prentice-Hall, 1984.

Benjamin, Martin, and Joy Curtis, *Ethics in Nursing*. New York: Oxford University Press, 1981.

Bok, Sissela, *Lying: Moral Choice in Public and Private Life*. New York: Pantheon Books, 1978.

Corea, Gena, *The Hidden Malpractice: How American Medicine Treats Women as Patients and Health Care Professionals*. New York: Morrow, 1977.

Goffman, Erving, *Asylums*. New York: Doubleday Anchor, 1961.

Hastings Center Report. Hastings-on-Hudson, N.Y.: Institute of Society, Ethics and the Life Sciences.

Holmes, Helen B., et al., eds., *The Custom-Made Child? Woman-Centered Perspectives*. Clifton, N.J.: Humana, 1981.

Illich, Ivan, *Medical Nemesis*. New York: Pantheon Books, 1976.

Kübler-Ross, Elizabeth, *On Death and Dying*. New York: Macmillan, 1969.

Ramsey, Paul, *The Patient as Person*. New Haven, Conn: Yale University Press, 1970.

Reich, Warren T., ed., *Encyclopedia of Bioethics*. New York: Macmillan, 1978.

Steinbock, Bonnie, ed., *Killing and Letting Die*. Englewood Cliffs, N.J.: Prentice-Hall, 1980.

Szasz, Thomas, S., *Ideology and Insanity: Essays on the Psychiatric Dehumanization of Man*. New York: Doubleday, 1970.

BUSINESS

Blackstone, William T., and Robert D. Heslep, eds., *Social Justice and Preferential Treatment*. Athens, Ga.: University of Georgia Press, 1977.

Coleman, James, *Power and the Structure of Society*. New York: Norton, 1974.

Eisenberg, Melvin Aron, *The Structure of the Corporation*. Boston: Little, Brown & Co., 1976.

Ewing, David, *Freedom Inside the Organization*. New York: Dutton, 1977.

Friedman, Milton, *Capitalism and Freedom*. Chicago: University of Chicago Press, 1962.

Galbraith, John Kenneth, *Economics and the Public Purpose*. Boston: Houghton Mifflin, 1973.

419

Harrington, Michael, *Socialism*. New York: Saturday Review Press, 1974.

Nader, Ralph, Mark Green, and Joel Seligman, *Taming the Giant Corporation*. New York: W. W. Norton & Co., 1976.

Packard, Vance, *The Hidden Persuaders*. New York: McKay, 1957.

Rand, Ayn, *Capitalism: The Unknown Ideal*. New York: Signet Books, 1967.

Rescher, Nicholas, *Distributive Justice*. New York: Bobbs-Merrill, 1966.

Sethi, S. Prakash, *Up Against the Corporate Wall*, 4th ed. Englewood Cliffs, N.J.: Prentice-Hall, 1982.

Singer, Peter, *Animal Liberation*. New York: New York Review of Books, 1975.

Terkel, Studs, *Working*. New York: Pantheon Books, 1974.

TECHNOLOGY

Dahlberg, Kenneth, *Beyond the Green Revolution: The Ecology and Politics of Global Agricultural Development*. New York: Plenum Press, 1979.

Ellul, Jacques, *The Technological Society*. New York: Continuum, 1980.

Florman, Samuel C., *The Existential Pleasures of Engineering*. New York: St. Martin's Press, 1976.

Glover, Jonathan, *What Sort of People Should There Be?* New York: Penguin Books, 1984.

Illich, Ivan, *Tools for Conviviality*. New York: Harper & Row, 1973.

Johnson, Deborah G., *Computer Ethics*. Englewood Cliffs, N.J.: Prentice-Hall, 1985.

——and John W. Snapper, eds., *Ethical Issues in the Use of Computers*. Belmont, Calif.: Wadsworth, 1985.

Kahn, Herman, and B. Bruce-Briggs, *Things to Come: Thinking About the Seventies and Eighties*. New York: Macmillan, 1972.

Meadows, Donella, et al., *The Limits to Growth*. New York: Signet Books, 1972.

Morison, Elting E., *From Knowledge to Nowhere: The Development of American Technology*. New York: Basic Books, 1974.

Nader, Ralph, and John Abbotts, *The Menace of Atomic Energy*. New York: W. W. Norton, 1977.

Press, Frank, Leon T. Silver, et al., *New Pathways in Science and Technology*, New York: Vintage, 1985.

Rescher, Nicholas, *Unpopular Essays on Technological Progress*. Pittsburgh: University of Pittsburgh Press, 1980.

Rifkin, Jeremy, with Nicanor Perlas, *Algeny*. New York: Viking, 1983.

Schumacher, E. F., *Good Work*, New York: Harper & Row, 1979.

Thurow, Lester, *The Zero-Sum Society*. New York: Penguin Books, 1980.

Toffler, Alvin, *Future Shock*. New York: Random House, 1970.

——, *The Third Wave*, New York: William Morrow & Co., 1980.

CRIMINAL JUSTICE

Abbott, Jack Henry, *In the Belly of the Beast: Letters from Prison*, New York: Random House, 1981.

American Friends Service Committee, *The Struggle for Justice*. New York: Hill & Wang, 1971.

Arendt, Hannah, *Eichman in Jerusalem*. New York: Viking Press, 1963.

Atkins, Burton, and Mark Pogrebin, eds., *The Invisible Justice System: Discretion and the Law*, Cincinnati, Ohio: Anderson Publishing Co., 1978.

Capote, Truman, *In Cold Blood*. New York: Random House, 1965.

Feinberg, Joel, *Doing and Deserving*. Princeton, N.J.: Princeton University Press, 1970.

Foucault, Michel, *Discipline and Punish*. New York: Pantheon Books, 1977.

Haley, Alex, *The Autobiography of Malcolm X*. New York: Grove Press, 1964.

Hart, H. L. A., *Punishment and Responsibility*. New York: Oxford University Press, 1968.

Kittrie, Nicholas N., *The Right to Be Different*. Baltimore, Md.: Johns Hopkins Press, 1971.

Luban, David, ed., *The Good Lawyer: Lawyers' Roles and Lawyers' Ethics*. Totowa, N.J.: Rowman and Allanheld, 1984.

Mailer, Norman, *The Executioner's Song*. Boston: Little, Brown, 1979.

Menninger, Karl, *The Crime of Punishment*. New York: Viking Press, 1968.

Millet, Kate, et al., *The Prostitution Papers*. New York: Avon Books, 1973.

Reiss, Albert, J., Jr., *The Police and the Public*. New Haven, Conn.: Yale University Press, 1971.

Sartre, Jean Paul, *Saint Genet: Actor and Martyr*,

trans. Bernard Frechtman. New York: Braziller, 1968.

Schur, Edwin, *Crimes Without Victims*. Englewood Cliffs, N.J.: Prentice-Hall, 1965.

Shaw, George Bernard, *The Crime Imprisonment*. New York: Philosophical Library, 1946.

Wasserstrom, Richard A., *Morality and the Law*. Belmont, Calif.: Wadsworth, 1971.

SAMPLE CODES OF PROFESSIONAL ETHICS

AMERICAN MEDICAL ASSOCIATION

Principles of Medical Ethics

I. A physician shall be dedicated to providing competent medical service with compassion and respect for human dignity.

II. A physician shall deal honestly with patients and colleagues, and strive to expose those physicians deficient in character or competence, or who engage in fraud or deception.

III. A. physician shall respect the law and also recognize a responsibility to seek changes in these requirements which are contrary to the best interests of the patient.

IV. A physician shall respect the rights of patients, of colleagues, and of other health professionals, and shall safeguard patient confidences within the constraints of the law.

V. A physician shall continue to study, apply and advance scientific knowledge, make relevant information available to patients, colleagues, and the public, obtain consultation, and use the talents of other health professionals when indicated.

VI. A physician shall, in the provision of appropriate patient care, except in emergencies, be free to choose whom to serve, with whom to associate, and the environment in which to provide medical services.

VII. A physician shall recognize a responsibility to participate in activities contributing to an improved community.

AMERICAN NURSES' ASSOCIATION

Code for Nurses

1. The nurse provides services with respect for human dignity and the uniqueness of the client unrestricted by considerations of social or economic status, personal attributes, or the nature of health problems.
2. The nurse safeguards the client's right to privacy by judiciously protecting information of a confidential nature.
3. The nurse acts to safeguard the client and the public when health care and safety are affected by the incompetent, unethical, or illegal practice of any person.
4. The nurse assumes responsibility and accountability for individual nursing judgments and actions.
5. The nurse maintains competence in nursing.
6. The nurse exercises informed judgment and uses individual competence and qualifications as criteria in seeking consultation, accepting responsibilities, and delegating nursing activities to others.
7. The nurse participates in activities that contribute to the ongoing development of the profession's body of knowledge.
8. The nurse participates in the profession's efforts to implement and improve standards of nursing.
9. The nurse participates in the profession's efforts to establish and maintain conditions of employment conducive to high-quality nursing care.
10. The nurse participates in the profession's effort to protect the public from misinformation and misrepresentation and to maintain the integrity of nursing.
11. The nurse collaborates with members of the health professions and other citizens in promoting community and national efforts to meet the health needs of the public.

AMERICAN HOSPITAL ASSOCIATION

Statement on a Patient's Bill of Rights

The American Hospital Association presents a Patient's Bill of Rights with the expectation that observance of these rights will contribute to more effective patient care and greater satisfaction for the patient, his physician, and the hospital organization. Further, the Association presents these rights in the expectation that they will be supported by the hospital on be-

half of its patients, as an integral part of the healing process. It is recognized that a personal relationship between the physician and the patient is essential for the provision of proper medical care. The traditional physician–patient relationship takes on a new dimension when care is rendered within an organizational structure. Legal precedent has

---

established that the institution itself also has a responsibility to the patient. It is in recognition of these factors that these rights are affirmed.

1. The patient has the right to considerate and respectful care.
2. The patient has the right to obtain from his physician complete current information concerning his diagnosis, treatment, and prognosis in terms the patient can be reasonably expected to understand. When it is not medically advisable to give such information to the patient, the information should be made available to an appropriate person in his behalf. He has the right to know, by name, the physician responsible for coordinating his care.
3. The patient has the right to receive from his physician information necessary to give informed consent prior to the start of any procedure and/or treatment. Except in emergencies, such information for informed consent should include but not necessarily be limited to the specific procedure and/or treatment, the medically significant risks involved, and the probable duration of incapacitation. Where medically significant alternatives for care or treatment exist, or when the patient requests information concerning medical alternatives, the patient has the right to such information. The patient also has the right to know the name of the person responsible for the procedures and/or treatment.
4. The patient has the right to refuse treatment to the extent permitted by law and to be informed of the medical consequences of his action.
5. The patient has the right to every consideration of his privacy concerning his own medical care program. Case discussion, consultation, examination, and treatment are confidential and should be conducted discreetly. Those not directly involved in his care must have the permission of the patient to be present.
6. The patient has the right to expect that all communications and records pertaining to his care should be treated as confidential.
7. The patient has the right to expect that within its capacity a hospital must make reasonable response to the request of a patient for services. The hospital must provide evaluation, service, and/or referral as indicated by the urgency of the case. When medically permissible, a patient may be transferred to another facility only after he has received complete information and explanation concerning the needs for and alternatives to such a transfer. The institution to which the patient is to be transferred must first have accepted the patient for transfer.
8. The patient has the right to obtain information as to any relationship of his hospital to other health care and educational institutions insofar as his care is concerned. The patient has the right to obtain information as to the existence of any professional relationship among individuals, by name, who are treating him.
9. The patient has the right to be advised if the hospital proposes to engage in or perform human experimentation affecting his care or treatment. The patient has the right to refuse to participate in such research projects.
10. The patient has the right to expect reasonable continuity of care. He has the right to know in advance what appointment times and physicians are available and where. The patient has the right to expect that the hospital will provide a mechanism whereby he is informed by his physician or a delegate of the physician of the patient's continuing health care requirements following discharge.
11. The patient has the right to examine and receive an explanation of his bill regardless of source of payment.
12. The patient has the right to know what hospital rules and regulations apply to his conduct as a patient.

No catalog of rights can guarantee for the patient the kind of treatment he has a right to expect. A hospital has many functions to perform, including the prevention and treatment of disease, the education of both health professionals and patients, and the conduct of clinical research. All these activities must be conducted with an overriding concern for the patient, and, above all, the recognition of his dignity as a human being. Success in achieving this recognition assures success in the defense of the rights of the patient.

BYLAW 19, ACM CODE OF PROFESSIONAL CONDUCT

Association for Computing Machinery

Preamble

Recognition of professional status by the public depends not only on skill and dedication but also on adherence to a recognized code of Professional Conduct. The following Code sets forth the general principles (Canons), professional ideals (Ethical Considerations), and mandatory rules (Disciplinary Rules) applicable to each ACM Member.

The verbs "shall" (imperative) and "should" (encouragement) are used purposefully in the Code. The Canons and Ethical Considerations are not, however, binding rules. Each Disciplinary Rule is binding on each individual Member of ACM. Failure to observe the Disciplinary Rules subjects the Member to admonition, suspension or expulsion from the Association as provided by the Procedures for the Enforcement of the ACM Code of Professional Conduct, which are specified in the ACM Policy and Procedures Guidelines. The term "member(s)" is used in the Code. The Disciplinary Rules of the Code apply, however, only to the classes of membership specified in Article 3, Section 5, of the Constitution of the ACM.

Canon 1

An ACM member shall act at all times with integrity.

Ethical Considerations

EC1.1. An ACM member shall properly qualify himself when expressing an opinion outside his areas of competence. A member is encouraged to express his opinion on subjects within his area of competence.

EC1.2. An ACM member shall preface any partisan statements about information processing by indicating clearly on whose behalf they are made.

EC1.3. An ACM member shall act faithfully on behalf of his employers or clients.

Disciplinary Rules

DR1.1.1. An ACM member shall not intentionally misrepresent his qualifications or credentials to present or prospective employers or clients.

DR1.1.2. An ACM member shall not make deliberately false or deceptive statements as to the present or expected state of affairs in any aspect of the capability, delivery, or use of information processing systems.

DR1.2.1. An ACM member shall not intentionally conceal or misrepresent on whose behalf any partisan statements are made.

DR1.3.1. An ACM member acting or employed as a consultant shall, prior to accepting information from a prospective client, inform the client of all factors of which the

---

From the Constitution of the Association for Computing Machinery, Inc. Reprinted courtesy of ACM.

member is aware which may affect the proper performance of the task.

DR1.3.2. An ACM member shall disclose any interest of which he is aware which does or may conflict with his duty to a present or prospective employer or client.

DR1.3.3. An ACM member shall not use any confidential information from any employer or client, past or present, without prior permission.

Canon 2

An ACM member should strive to increase his competence and the competence and prestige of the profession.

Ethical Consideration

EC2.1. An ACM member is encouraged to extend public knowledge, understanding, and appreciation of information processing, and to oppose any false or deceptive statements relating to information processing of which he is aware.

EC2.2. An ACM member shall not use his professional credentials to misrepresent his competence.

EC2.3. An ACM member shall undertake only those professional assignments and commitments for which he is qualified.

EC2.4. An ACM member shall strive to design and develop systems that adequately perform the intended functions and that satisfy his employer's or client's operational needs.

EC2.5. An ACM member should maintain and increase his competence through a program of continuing education encompassing the techniques, technical standards, and practices in his fields of professional activity.

EC2.6. An ACM member should provide opportunity and encouragement for professional development and advancement of both professionals and those aspiring to become professionals.

Disciplinary Rules

DR2.2.1. An ACM member shall not use his professional credentials to misrepresent his competence.

DR2.3.1. An ACM member shall not undertake professional assignments without adequate preparation in the circumstances.

DR2.3.2. An ACM member shall not undertake professional assignments for which he knows or should know he is not competent or cannot become adequately competent without acquiring the assistance of a professional who is competent to perform the assignment.

DR2.4.1. An ACM member shall not represent that a product of his work will perform its function adequately and will meet the receiver's operational needs when he knows or should know that the product is deficient.

Canon 3

An ACM member shall accept responsibility for his work.

Ethical Considerations

EC3.1. An ACM member shall accept only those assignments for which there is reasonable expectancy of meeting requirements or specifications, and shall perform his assignments in a professional manner.

Disciplinary Rules

DR3.1.1. An ACM member shall not neglect any professional assignment which has been accepted.

DR3.1.2. An ACM member shall keep his employer or client properly informed on the progress of his assignments.

DR3.1.3. An ACM member shall not attempt to exonerate himself from, or to limit his liability to clients for his personal malpractice.

DR3.1.4. An ACM member shall indicate to his employer or client the consequences to be expected if his professional judgment is overruled.

Canon 4

An ACM member shall act with professional responsibility.

Ethical Considerations

EC4.1. An ACM member shall not use his membership in ACM improperly for professional advantage or to misrepresent the authority of his statements.

EC4.2. An ACM member shall conduct professional activities on a high plane.

EC4.3. An ACM member is encouraged to uphold and improve the professional standards of the Association through participation in their formulation, establishment, and enforcement.

Disciplinary Rules

DR4.1.1. An ACM member shall not speak on behalf of the Association or any of its subgroups without proper authority.

DR4.1.2. An ACM member shall not knowingly misrepresent the policies and views of the Association or any of its subgroups.

DR4.1.3. An ACM member shall preface partisan statements about information processing by indicating clearly on whose behalf they are made.

DR4.2.1. An ACM member shall not maliciously injure the professional reputation of any other person.

DR4.2.2. An ACM member shall not use the services of or his membership in the Association to gain unfair advantage.

DR4.2.3. An ACM member shall take care that credit for work is given to whom credit is properly due.

Canon 5

An ACM member should use his special knowledge and skills for the advancement of human welfare.

Ethical Considerations

EC5.1. An ACM member should consider the health, privacy, and general welfare of the public in the performance of his work.

EC5.2. An ACM member, whenever dealing with data concerning individuals, shall always consider the principle of the individual's privacy and seek the following:

- To minimize the data collected.
- To limit authorized access to the data.
- To provide proper security for the data.
- To determine the required retention period of the data.
- To ensure proper disposal of the data.

Disciplinary Rules

DR5.2.1. An ACM member shall express his professional opinion to his employers or clients regarding any adverse consequences to the public which might result from work proposed to him.

ACCREDITATION BOARD FOR ENGINEERING AND TECHNOLOGY

Code of Ethics for Engineers

The Fundamental Principles

Engineers uphold and advance the integrity, honor and dignity of the engineering profession by:

  I. using their knowledge and skill for the enhancement of human welfare;

 II. being honest and impartial, and serving with fidelity the public, their employers and clients;

III. striving to increase the competence and prestige of the engineering profession; and

IV. supporting the professional and technical societies of their disciplines.

The Fundamental Canons

1. Engineers shall hold paramount the safety, health and welfare of the public in the performance of their professional duties.

2. Engineers shall perform services only in the areas of their competence.

3. Engineers shall issue public statements only in an objective and truthful manner.

4. Engineers shall act in professional matters for each employer or client as faithful agents or trustees, and shall avoid conflicts of interest.

5. Engineers shall build their professional reputation on the merit of their services and shall not compete unfairly with others.

6. Engineers shall act in such a manner as to uphold and enhance the honor, integrity and dignity of the profession.

7. Engineers shall continue their professional development throughout their careers and shall provide opportunities for the professional development of those engineers under their supervision.

INSTITUTE OF ELECTRICAL AND ELECTRONICS ENGINEERS

Code of Ethics for Engineers

Preamble

Engineers, scientists and technologists affect the quality of life for all people in our complex technological society. In the pursuit of their profession, therefore, it is vital that IEEE members conduct their work in an ethical manner so that they merit the confidence of colleagues, employers, clients and the public. This IEEE Code of Ethics represents such a standard of professional conduct for IEEE members in the discharge of their responsibilities to employers, to clients, to the community and to their colleagues in this Institute and other professional societies.

Article I

Members shall maintain high standards of diligence, creativity and productivity, and shall:

1. Accept responsibility for their actions;
2. Be honest and realistic in stating claims or estimates from available data;
3. Undertake technological tasks and accept responsibility only if qualified by training or experience, or after full disclosure to their employers or clients of pertinent qualifications;
4. Maintain their professional skills at the level of the state of the art, and recognize the importance of current events in their work;
5. Advance the integrity and prestige of the profession by practicing in a dignified manner and for adequate compensation.

Article II

Members shall, in their work:

1. Treat fairly all colleagues and co-workers, regardless of race, religion, sex, age or national origin;
2. Report, publish and disseminate freely information to others, subject to legal and proprietary restraints;
3. Encourage colleagues and co-workers to act in accord with this Code and support them when they do so;
4. Seek, accept and offer honest criticism of work, and properly credit the contributions of others;
5. Support and participate in the activities of their professional societies;
6. Assist colleagues and co-workers in their professional development.

Article III

Members shall, in their relations with employers and clients:

1. Act as faithful agents or trustees for their employers or clients in professional and business matters, provided such actions conform with other parts of this Code;
2. Keep information on the business affairs or technical processes of an employer or client in confidence while employed, and later, until such information is properly released, provided such actions conform with other parts of this Code;
3. Inform their employers, clients, professional societies or public agencies or private agencies of which they are members or to which they may make presentations, of any circumstances that could lead to a conflict of interest;
4. Neither give nor accept, directly or indirectly, any gift, payment or service of more than nominal value to or from those having business relationships with their employers or clients;
5. Assist and advise their employers or clients in anticipating the possible consequences, direct and indirect, immediate or remote, of the projects, work or plans of which they have knowledge.

Article IV

Members shall, in fulfilling their responsibilities to the community:

1. Protect the safety, health and welfare of the public and speak out against abuses in these areas affecting the public interest;
2. Contribute professional advice, as appropriate, to civic, charitable or other nonprofit organizations;
3. Seek to extend public knowledge and appreciation of the profession and its achievements.